The Supreme Court in the American Legal System

JEFFREY A. SEGAL
State University of New York at Stony Brook

HAROLD J. SPAETH
Michigan State University

SARA C. BENESH
University of Wisconsin–Milwaukee

CAMBRIDGE
UNIVERSITY PRESS

CAMBRIDGE UNIVERSITY PRESS
Cambridge, New York, Melbourne, Madrid, Cape Town, Singapore, São Paulo

Cambridge University Press
40 West 20th Street, New York, NY 10011-4211, USA

www.cambridge.org
Information on this title: www.cambridge.org/9780521780384

First published 2005

Printed in the United States of America

A catalog record for this publication is available from the British Library.

Library of Congress Cataloging in Publication Data

Segal, Jeffrey Allan.
The Supreme Court in the American legal system / Jeffrey A. Segal,
Harold J. Spaeth, Sara C. Benesh.
   p. cm.
ISBN 0-521-78038-1 (hardback) – ISBN 0-521-78508-1 (pbk.)
1. United States. Supreme Court. 2. Courts – United States. 3. Judicial process –
United States. I. Spaeth, Harold J. II. Benesh, Sara Catherine. III. Title.
KF8742.S433   2005
347.73'26–dc22   2004019022

ISBN-13   978-0-521-78038-4 hardback
ISBN-10   0-521-78038-1 hardback

ISBN-13   978-0-521-78508-2 paperback
ISBN-10   0-521-78508-1 paperback

The Supreme Court in the American Legal System

This book examines the American legal system, including a comprehensive treatment of the U.S. Supreme Court. Despite this treatment, the *in* of the title deserves emphasis, for the authors extensively examine lower courts, providing separate chapters on state courts, the U.S. District Courts, and the U.S. Courts of Appeals. The book analyzes these courts from a legal/extralegal framework, drawing different conclusions about the relative influence of each based on institutional structures and empirical evidence. The book is also tied together through its attention to the relationship between lower courts and the Supreme Court. Additionally, Election 2000 litigation provides a common substantive topic linking many of the chapters. Finally, it provides extended coverage of the legal process, with separate chapters on civil procedure, evidence, and criminal procedure.

Although this volume contains original research, such research is presented at a level that does not require methodological sophistication. Furthermore, all data used for the authors' original research, and all commands to run the analyses, are provided on the book's Web site.

Jeffrey A. Segal is Distinguished Professor of Political Science at the State University of New York at Stony Brook. He received his Ph.D. in 1983 from Michigan State University. He is the coauthor of six books, including, most recently, *The Supreme Court and the Attitudinal Model Revisited* (Cambridge University Press, 2002), with Harold J. Spaeth. He is also the author of *Majority Rule or Minority Will* (Cambridge University Press, 1999), with Harold J. Spaeth, which won the C. Herman Pritchett Award for best book in law and courts. Segal has also published dozens of scholarly articles, including "Predicting Supreme Court Cases Probabilistically: The Search and Seizure Cases, 1962–1981," which won the Wadsworth Award for a book or article ten or more years old that has made a lasting impression on the field of law and courts.

Harold J. Spaeth is Research Professor of Law and Emeritus Professor of Political Science at Michigan State University. He received his Ph.D. from the University of Cincinnati and his J.D. from the University of Michigan. He is the author or coauthor of sixteen books, including *Stare Indecisis: The Alteration of Precedent on the Supreme Court, 1946–1992* (Cambridge University Press, 1995), with Saul Brenner; *The Supreme Court and the Attitudinal Model Revisited* (Cambridge University Press, 2002), with Jeffrey A. Segal; and *Majority Rule or Minority Will* (Cambridge University Press, 1999), with Jeffrey A. Segal. He is the recipient of a Lifetime Achievement Award from the Law and Courts section of the American Political Science Association and serves as Principal Investigator of the United States Supreme Court Judicial Databases.

Sara C. Benesh is an assistant professor of political science at the University of Wisconsin–Milwaukee. She previously taught in the Department of Political Science at the University of New Orleans and was awarded a grant for research from the National Science Foundation. She is the author of *The U.S. Courts of Appeals and the Law of Confessions: Perspectives on the Hierarchy of Justice* (2002).

To my coauthor, mentor, and friend, Harold J. Spaeth

–SB

To Lois Kass Kleinberg and the ever-loving memory of Cindy Kass April   *–JS*

For my grandchildren, Sean Thomas and Samantha Rose Kelly

–HS

Contents

List of Illustrations	*page* viii
List of Tables	x
Preface	xiii

I. INTRODUCTION

1	Judicial Policy Making	3
	Policy Making	4
	The Mythology of Judging	16
	Summary and Conclusions	17
2	Approaches to Judicial Decision Making	19
	Models	20
	The Legal Approach	22
	Extralegal or Policy-Based Approaches	34
	Summary and Conclusions	39
3	The Supreme Court in American Legal History	41
	Before the Constitution	41
	The New Constitution	43
	The Marshall Court	44
	The Civil War Era	47
	Economic Regulation	51
	Changes in the State Courts	53
	The New Deal	54
	Supreme Court Supervision of State Courts	55
	First Amendment Freedoms	57
	Criminal Procedure	59
	Equal Protection	60
	The Right to Privacy	62
	The Supreme Court and the Distribution of Power	64
	Summary and Conclusions	70

II. JUDICIAL PROCESS

4 Civil Procedure   75
   The Adversary System   76
   Jurisdiction   80
   Pleadings   85
   Discovery   88
   Trial Procedure   89
   Multiparty and Multiclaim Litigation   94
   Summary and Conclusions   96

5 Evidence   97
   The Genesis of Evidence Law   97
   Relevance   98
   Hearsay   103
   Circumstantial Evidence   105
   *Constitutional Provisions Impacting the Production
   of Evidence*   106
   Privileges   108
   Expert Testimony   112
   Eyewitness Testimony   115
   Summary and Conclusions   117

6 Criminal Procedure   119
   Crime   121
   Prearrest Investigations   124
   From Arrest to Trial   128
   Trial   133
   Appeals   140
   Conclusions   141

III. LOWER COURTS IN THE AMERICAN LEGAL SYSTEM

7 State Courts   147
   The State Courts   148
   The Selection of State Court Judges   149
   Accessing State Courts   160
   Caseload   171
   State Court Decision Making   172
   Summary and Conclusions   185

8 The U.S. District Courts   187
   Origins   190
   Growth   190
   Appointment Process   191
   Jurisdiction   194
   Caseload   196
   Procedures   199
   Decision Making   200
   Conclusion   211

9 The U.S. Courts of Appeals   213
   The U.S. Courts of Appeals   215
   Origins   216
   Growth   217
   Appointment Process   218
   Jurisdiction   220
   Caseload   221
   Procedures   226
   Decision Making   230
   Conclusion   241

IV. THE SUPREME COURT

10 Staffing the Court   245
   Presidential Selection   248
   Senate Confirmation   252
   Summary and Conclusions   273

11 Getting into Court   275
   Case Selection   275
   The Supreme Court's Caseload   281
   Which Cases for Decision?   285
   Future Changes?   296
   Summary and Conclusions   297

12 Supreme Court Decision Making   299
   Process   301
   The (Final) Vote on the Merits: Legal Approaches   305
   The Decision on the Merits: Extralegal Approaches   318
   Conclusions   329

13 Opinions and Assignments   332
   Voting and Opinion Options   332
   Opinion Assignment   337
   Opinion Assignments and Opinion Coalitions   348
   The Politics of Coalition Formation   349
   Who Influences Whom?   354
   Summary and Conclusions   358

V. IMPACT

14 The Impact of Judicial Decisions   363
   The Impact of Courts in America   364
   A Framework for Understanding Impact   365
   Compliance   370
   Impact   380
   The Courts and Public Opinion   388
   Summary and Conclusions   389

Case Index   393

General Index   398

Illustrations

6.1	Criminal Case Processing in the United States	*page* 142
7.1	Grant Rate for Petitioners in Texas Supreme Court, 1994–1998, by Petitioner Campaign Donations	156
7.2	Three Examples of State Court Organization	162
8.1	Types of Civil Cases and Their Resolution in the U.S. District Courts, 2002	195
8.2	Caseload of the U.S. District Courts	196
8.3	Percentage Liberal Decisions by Party Identification, U.S. District Courts, 1933–1987	202
8.4	Percentage Liberal Decisions by Region, U.S. District Courts, 1933–1987	203
9.1	Sources of Appeals in the Circuit Courts, September 2002	221
9.2	Caseload of the Circuit Courts of Appeals (Cases Filed)	222
9.3	Types of Cases Terminated in the Courts of Appeals, September 2001–September 2002	223
9.4a	Types of Opinions or Orders Filed, September 2001–September 2002	224
9.4b	Percentage Unpublished Decisions by Circuit, September 2001–September 2002	225
9.5	Total Case Participations on the Circuit Courts by Judge Type	227
9.6	Dissensus in the Appeals Courts: Percentage of Cases with Dissenting Votes	236
9.7	Percentage Liberal Decisions in Criminal Procedure Cases	237
9.8	Percentage Liberal Decisions in Civil Liberties Cases	237
10.1	Dilbert: Dogbert's Supreme Court Nomination Hearings	253
10.2	Proportion Liberal in Civil Liberties during Presidential Regimes	272
10.3	Liberalism of Outgoing and Incoming Justices, by Presidential Regime	273
11.1	Cases Filed, 1880–2000	282

12.1   Scatterplot of Justices' Ideology and Voting Liberalism in
       Criminal Cases   321
12.2   Scatterplot of Justices' Ideology and Voting Liberalism
       in All Cases   322
12.3   A Conceptual Model of the Influence of Public Opinion on
       Supreme Court Decisions   327
13.1   Dyadic Influence Matrix, Rehnquist Court, 1986–2001 Terms   357
14.1   Pretest–Post-test Possibilities   382
14.2   Number of Abortions by Year   387

Tables

2.1	Hypothetical Choices of Three Legislators among Three Alternatives	*page* 29
6.1	The Selective Incorporation of Criminal Rights Provisions in the Bill of Rights	121
6.2	Role of Deliberations in Verdicts	136
6.3	Judge/Jury Verdict Concordance	136
6.4	Regression Analysis of Sentencing Decisions in Pennsylvania	138
7.1	Selection and Retention in the States	150
7.2	Voting on Confessions by Method of Retention, 1970–1991	159
7.3	Voting on Confessions by Docket Control, 1970–1991	166
7.4	Caseload of State Courts, 2001 (in millions)	172
7.5	Voting on Confessions by Ideology	172
8.1	Authorized Judgeships in the District Courts	192
8.2	Types of Criminal Cases and Court Action in the U.S. District Courts, 2002	198
8.3	U.S. Sentencing Commission Sentencing Table	208
8.4	Determinants of Sentencing in U.S. District Courts, 2001 (in months)	209
9.1	Circuit Judgeships	215
9.2	Circuit Assignments of the Supreme Court Justices Effective September 30, 1994	218
9.3	Voting in Criminal Cases Sample, 1960–1996	238
9.4	Voting in Civil Rights Cases Sample, 1960–1996	238
9.5	Voting in Criminal Cases Accompanied by Dissent Sample, 1960–1996	238
9.6	Voting in Civil Rights Cases Accompanied by Dissent Sample, 1960–1996	239
9.7	Voting in Criminal Cases by Gender and Party Sample, 1960–1996	239

9.8 Voting in Civil Rights Cases by Gender and Party Sample,
1960–1996   240

9.9 Voting in Criminal Cases by Race and Party Sample,
1960–1996   241

9.10 Voting in Civil Rights Cases by Race and Party Sample,
1960–1996   242

10.1 Rejected Supreme Court Nominees   254

10.2 Nominee Margin, Vote Status, Ideology, and Qualifications   264

10.3 Confirmation Voting by Nominee Qualifications   266

10.4 Confirmation Voting by Ideological Distance   266

10.5 Confirmation Voting by Qualifications and Distance:
Percentage Pro   267

10.6 Confirmation Voting by Presidential Status   267

10.7 Confirmation Voting by Presidential Partisanship   268

10.8 Confirmation Voting by Presidential Approval   268

10.9 Confirmation Voting by Interest Group Opposition   269

11.1 Nonmeritorious Resolution of Orally Argued Cases,
1953–2003 Terms   279

11.2 Case Selection by Issue Area Controlled for Court   284

11.3 Grant Rate Percentage by Desire to Affirm or Reverse in the
Burger Court, 1969–1986   286

11.4 Grant Rate Percentage by Winning or Losing on the Merits in
the Burger Court, 1969–1986   288

11.5 Effect of Predicted Success on the Merits on Granting
Certiorari (gamma coefficients) Contingent on Affirming or
Reversing in the Burger Court, 1969–1986   289

11.6 Affirmation and Reversal by Court   290

11.7 Reversal Rate Percentage by Term   291

12.1 The Impact of Precedent versus Preferences on the O'Connor,
Kennedy, and Souter Opinion in *Casey*   312

12.2 Justices' Precedential Behavior by Case Type   314

12.3 Justices' Votes on Overturning Precedents   317

12.4 Justices' Ideology, Liberalism in Criminal Cases, and
Liberalism in All Cases, 1953–2003 Terms   320

13.1 Behavioral Options Exercised by the Rehnquist Court Justices,
1986–2003 Terms   336

13.2 Opinion Assignment in the Vinson Court   339

13.3 Opinion Assignment in the Warren Court   339

13.4 Opinion Assignment in the Burger Court   340

13.5 Opinion Assignment in the Rehnquist Court,
1986–1990 Terms   340

13.6 Deviation of Assignments per Assignment Day from
Distributional Equality by Term   344

13.7   Cumulative Number of Deviations from the Most Equal
       Distribution of Assignments per Assignment Day per Justice
       per Term   347
13.8   Interagreement in Special Opinions, 1986–2001 Terms   352
13.9   Frequency of Special Opinions as a Proportion of Votes Cast   353
13.10 Dyadic Influence Matrix, 1986–2001 Terms   355
14.1   Confessions Upheld in the Courts of Appeals before and
       after *Miranda*   372
14.2   Confessions Upheld in the Courts of Appeals during and after
       the Warren Court   372
14.3   Confessions Upheld in the Courts of Appeals by Partisanship
       of Panel Majority   373
14.4   Confessions Upheld in the Courts of Appeals by Lower
       Court Disposition   373

Preface

In planning work subsequent to *The Supreme Court and the Attitudinal Model* (1993), we determined that the best course would be to update it initially with a focus on game theory and multivariate analyses appropriate for a professional and graduate student readership. The result was *The Supreme Court and the Attitudinal Model Revisited*, which Cambridge University Press published in 2002. The next step, we decided, was to write a separate (but related) volume, less methodologically oriented, more broadly focused, and thus more suitable for undergraduate classes and a more general, less professional audience. Thus, *The Supreme Court in the American Legal System.*

The spotlight of *The Supreme Court and the Attitudinal Model Revisited* obviously remained on the Supreme Court, to the nearly complete exclusion of other courts. Moreover, as those familiar with the book well know, the book focused extensively on the Supreme Court's decision on the merits, carefully comparing, theoretically and empirically, legal, attitudinal, and rational choice models. Alternatively, although *The Supreme Court in the American Legal System* also centers on the Supreme Court, the *in* of the title deserves emphasis. In this volume, we extensively examine the lower courts, providing separate chapters on state courts, the U.S. District Courts, and the U.S. Courts of Appeals. Needless to say, we pay special attention to the relationship between these courts and the Supreme Court. We also pay extended attention to the legal process, with separate chapters on civil procedure, evidence, and criminal procedure.

Although we continue to provide original research, we present such research at a level that does not require methodological sophistication. Usually we present our results without multivariate analyses, but only when alternative analyses demonstrate the reliability of the bivariate results. In one instance, that is impossible: We require multivariate regression analysis to test hypotheses about judges' sentencing decisions, but the results are presented in a readily understandable manner. Furthermore, we provide all data used for our original research, and all commands to run the analyses, on the book's Web site: http://www.cambridge.org/9780521780384.

The data for this book were gathered from a series of grants separately provided to each of us by the National Science Foundation (NSF). Without the NSF's support neither this book nor its two predecessors could have been written. Needless to say, we are deeply grateful and indebted to the NSF for its support.

State University of New York at Stony Brook provided Segal with sabbatical leave toward the end of this project, during which time he was a visiting scholar at the Hauser Global Law School program at New York University School of Law. He thanks both institutions for their support.

We thank Professor Bradley Canon for comments on Chapter 14. We also thank Scott Graves and Chad Westerland for expert research assistance and Armin Gharagozlou for superb editorial assistance. Susan Thornton expertly imbued the manuscript with the grammatical, syntactical, and stylistic niceties that our prose so often lacks. Helen Wheeler, our production editor, efficiently shepherded the transformation of the manuscript from typescript to book.

PART I

INTRODUCTION

1

Judicial Policy Making

December 12, 2000, 10:00 P.M.

Without any fanfare at all, the Supreme Court's public information officer released the decision. The case, one of dozens filed regarding the events of November 4, began when the Gore campaign filed suit in a Florida circuit (trial) court, contesting the officially certified results of Florida's presidential election tally.

That official certification, made by Secretary of State Katherine Harris on November 26, had itself been the subject of innumerable suits, including one over Palm Beach County's infamous "butterfly" ballot, which led thousands of Gore supporters to vote mistakenly for the right-wing third-party candidate Pat Buchanan; a few other suits contesting the thousands of undercounted votes resulting from dimpled, pregnant, and hanging chads on the antiquated IBM punch cards; and, most notably, Harris's decision to use her seemingly discretionary authority not to accept recounted votes past Florida's one-week statutory deadline.[1] That decision had been overturned by the Florida Supreme Court, which extended the recount deadline to November 26. Eventually, the U.S. Supreme Court remanded (sent back) that decision to the Florida Supreme Court for further clarification, but before the recount could be completed even the Florida Supreme Court's deadline had passed, and Harris, who cochaired Bush's Florida campaign, certified Bush the winner.

The Gore campaign contested the results of the certification under the provision of Florida law that allowed judicial review of the certification if the election results include "receipt of a number of illegal votes or rejection of a number of legal votes sufficient to change or place in doubt the result of the election."[2]

---

[1] Harris's competence to supervise and apply Florida election law was further exemplified by her failure to comply with the requirement that she resign before becoming a congressional candidate. Media publication belatedly forced her to quit as secretary of state so that she might make her run for Congress.

[2] §102.168 of the Florida Code.

The circuit court judge, N. Sanders Saul, ruled against Gore on December 4, incredibly claiming that Gore had not demonstrated a "reasonable probability" that the results of this closest of all national elections would be different with a recount. Four days later, the Florida Supreme Court reversed by a 4–3 vote, claiming that the recount must go forward under the "intent of the voter" standard that had been well established under Florida law.

The very next day, the U.S. Supreme Court issued an injunction preventing further recounts while it reviewed the issues. On December 12, as we will discuss in greater detail later, the Court majority ruled (1) that the intent of the voter standard, which was to be implemented by a different canvassing board in each county, violated the equal protection clause of the Fourteenth Amendment; (2) that the deadline for recounting votes was midnight on December 12; and (3) that therefore no recount would be afforded Vice President Gore.[3] George W. Bush would become the forty-third president of the United States.

We live in a democracy, but within that democracy we give judges broad discretion to determine, for instance, whether abortions should be allowed, death penalties inflicted, homosexuality criminally punished, and, every century or so, who should be president.[4] All judges make policy; at the top of the judicial policy-making pyramid rests the United States Supreme Court.

POLICY MAKING

We begin by defining judicial policy making as simply a choice among alternative courses of action, which choice binds those subject to the policymaker's authority. Phrased more succinctly: A policymaker authoritatively allocates resources. So, if you find yourself suing someone in a court of law over a contested piece of property and the court rules in your favor, you win and the opposing party loses. Short of an appeal to a higher court, the court's decision ends the matter. This, then, becomes a final judgment and thus a policy.

But why should a court's decision end the matter? Why not some other governmental or private authority? Before we answer, let us back up a bit. All nations have their set of cherished beliefs that serve to guide and justify the actions of its citizenry. The fact that some or all of these beliefs do not correspond with reality tends not to affect the public's adherence to them. Among the most ancient of these from Americans' standpoint is the belief that judges decide their cases dispassionately, impartially, and objectively.

Admittedly, politically aware persons realize the inaccuracy of the preceding statement, citing reports of judicial misconduct both on and off the bench, the

---

[3] *Bush v. Gore*, 531 U.S. 98 (2000).

[4] In 1876, five justices of the Supreme Court served on a congressional commission to resolve twenty-one disputed electoral votes. The two Democratic justices on the commission voted to give each disputed vote to the Democrat Tilden, and the three Republican justices voted to give each disputed vote to the Republican Hayes. The congressional members of the commission, split evenly between Democrats and Republicans, similarly voted a straight party line. Thus did the justices of the Supreme Court legitimize the most fraudulent presidential election in U.S. history.

corrupting influence of money, and the partisanship manifest in many judicial decisions, for example, *Bush v. Gore*. Nonetheless, we tend to accept courts' decisions unquestioningly; again, *Bush v. Gore* provides an excellent example. Rare are the situations in which a judicial decision produces organized opposition: Same-sex marriage and proabortion decisions come to mind, as do those in the 1950s, 1960s, and 1970s dealing with Southern public school desegregation.

Now it is indisputable that public acceptance of judges' decisions does not result from the courts' coercive capabilities. They have none. Government has two coercive resources: the power of the purse (taxation) and the power of the sword (fines, imprisonment, and the death penalty). Courts exercise neither. When a court addresses any matter that pertains to either purse or sword, it depends on nonjudicial officials to apply and enforce its decision. Legislative bodies possess the former; the executive branch the latter. This being the case, why do Congress or state legislatures and presidents or governors not simply ignore a court decision with which they disagree?

Complicating the answer is the fact that though our courts lack coercive capability, they are nonetheless the most authoritative of our governmental decision-making bodies, not Congress and not the president. Their word, literally, is law – no ifs, ands, or buts about it. On the surface, this appears to be a contradiction in terms: How can a governmental body, incapable of forcing anybody to do anything, be more authoritative than the president or Congress?

Adding to the implausibility of the foregoing statement is a further fact: American courts possess a range of decision-making authority far broader than that provided the courts of other nations. What other countries regard as decisions that only the legislature or the executive may make, we vest in the courts.

Five interrelated factors provide the answer to this very strange scenario: fundamental law, distrust of governmental action and those who engage in it (politicians), federalism, separation of powers, and judicial review. We cannot say that any one of these is more or less important than the others. Rather, they appear to form one rather seamless web.

Fundamental Law

Fundamental U.S. law dates from the arrival of the English colonists at the beginning of the seventeenth century. Those settling in New England were refugees from religious persecution. Though we now view them as heroic, stalwart individuals, their religious beliefs were extreme, bordering on fanaticism. They viewed themselves as righteous God-fearing people; all others were sinful reprobates, egregious sinners, beyond the pale of God's redemption. They introduced with them the notion that all human and governmental action should conform to the word of God or the strictures of nature as their leaders decreed.[5]

---

[5] See Kermit L. Hall, *The Magic Mirror: Law in American History* (New York: Oxford University Press, 1989), pp. 12–17, 24–27.

Just as they were unable to get along with their neighbors in England, so also did they lack the ability to accommodate religious disagreements among their brethren. Dissenters were expelled from Plymouth and Massachusetts Bay. Moving west, like-minded refugees founded their own settlements in Rhode Island and Connecticut.

The overtly religious motivations that inspired the founding of new settlements were reflected in charters, constitutions, and the statutes that the settlers wrote. And although the theocratic parochialism – manifested by an established church in various colonies or, alternatively, a single nonconformist church serving all residents in the local village or town – of the early colonies and individual towns and villages within them had lost much of its steam by the beginning of the Revolutionary War, the notion of a fundamental law had not.

The persistence of the notion of a fundamental law stems from the circumstances of life during the colonial period, circumstances that continue to be manifest, though in altered form, today. Not only did the original English colonists find themselves in a highly dynamic environment; so also did the millions of immigrants who arrived later. The stabilizing influences of the Old World did not exist: No longer was there a common religion, or culture, or stratified social system, or static economic system. In their place, dynamic diversity flourished. The religiously disaffected merely had to pull up stakes and move a few miles west to establish a community of like-minded believers. New sects and denominations have continued to arise. Today, the United States has more religious denominations than the countries of the rest of the world combined.

The movement of the frontier ever westward produced marked social and economic turbulence that persisted into the twentieth century. And though we no longer have a geographic frontier, social and economic change continues apace led by science and the technological applications that flow from it. Consider only the recent changes in communication, transportation, medicine, industrial and agricultural production, and chemical and biological warfare.

Cultural uniformity did not last long either. Waves of immigrants began to arrive even before the Revolutionary War, to say nothing of the forcible importation of thousands upon thousands of African slaves. Cultural diversity continues apace, so much so that black, Hispanic, and Asian peoples outnumber those of European ancestry in much of the country.

We like to think of our nation as either socially middle class or striving to achieve that status. This perception, however, overlooks the fact of changes in lifestyle that constantly occur and affect – for better or for worse – the economic well-being and the social and cultural status of millions of people. To mention but a few: single-sex civil unions/marriages (first legalized in Vermont), divorce almost as commonplace as marriage, the steadily increasing number of women in occupations and professions that a generation ago were virtually the exclusive province of men, the ever-increasing life expectancy of both men and women, and a two-way communications revolution that makes information on any given subject as obtainable as the manipulation of a mouse and, conversely, puts us in touch with millions of people around the world with a few strokes on a keyboard.

The upshot is an environment in which social, cultural, economic, and religious change is the order of the day. And indeed, we view marked – even drastic – change in these areas of life as desirable, associating them with progress and freedom. Where, then, do we look for stability? Individuals cannot function effectively in a world of constant change. Life becomes frightening if events are beyond individual or human control. The answer: the political order, governed and established by fundamental law.[6]

Consciously or otherwise, the objective of the Constitution's Framers when they met in Philadelphia in the summer of 1787 was to transform the religious notion of fundamental law into a secular context. How so? By enshrining the Constitution that they intended to create as a secular substitute for Holy Writ.

They succeeded beyond their wildest dreams. Our Constitution is the world's oldest and shows no signs of suffering from old age. If a Framer rose from the dead, he would recognize his handiwork, appalled perhaps by its size, but not otherwise. The Constitution's longevity has established political stability as a distinctive feature of American life. With but few exceptions, other societies do not share this characteristic. For most of the world, politics is the vehicle of major societal change. Radical regime changes, bloody or otherwise, are the order of the day. What is dynamic in American life is fixed and stable elsewhere: an established religion to which virtually all pay at least lip service; a relatively rigid class or caste system, determined by birth, not achievements; an economic system in which individuals tend to be locked – willy-nilly – into a hereditary occupation (e.g., Daddy is a peasant; you will be one also); and a cultural environment in which all speak the same language and share a common ethnic or tribal background.

Distrust of Governmental Power

In a society wedded to a fundamental law somebody has to interpret its provisions authoritatively. Language, at least English, is woefully imprecise. What is *reasonable* in, for example, *reasonable cause*? It and its opposite, *unreasonable*, are lawyers' and judges' favorite words. What constitutes *due* process? *Ordered* liberty? Consider further that the Constitution's Framers, for political reasons, deliberately left its provisions undefined; the only exception is treason.[7] For

---

[6] For a treatment of fundamental law, see Edward A. Corwin, "The 'Higher Law' Background of American Constitutional Law," 42 *Harvard Law Review* 149, 290 (1928).

[7] According to James Wilson, a delegate to both the Constitutional Convention and the convention in Pennsylvania convened to ratify the Constitution, definitions of treason varied from one government to another. And he asserted "that a very great part of their tyranny over the people has arisen from the extension of the definition of treason." Hence, we have a specific constitutional definition that could not be easily altered. Max Farrand, ed., III *The Records of the Federal Convention of 1787* (New Haven, CT: Yale University Press, 1966), p. 163.

reasons that follow, American society bestowed the task of interpreting the fundamental law on the courts.

As colonists subject to imperial British mandates, Americans did not take kindly to many of the motherland's edicts, especially after the French and Indian War that ended in 1763. British efforts to tax the colonists for the cost of the war were viewed as inimical to their rights and liberties. Colonial opposition grew over the next decade and led to the onset of the Revolutionary War. Concomitantly with the outbreak of hostilities occurred a domestic struggle within each of the colonies for control of the newly formed state governments. This struggle broadly pitted the socioeconomic elite – such as it was – against small farmers, backwoods dwellers, and urban artisans.

This internal struggle persisted after the end of hostilities in 1783. Unsettled economic conditions severely strained the governmental capabilities of both the state governments and the Continental Congress that the Articles of Confederation of 1781 established. The latter made no provision for a chief executive or a judiciary; it had no power to levy taxes; nor did its limited power extend to individual conduct; and it was amendable only by unanimous consent of all states. Governmentally, it was akin to an international organization, such as the United Nations, rather than a sovereign state.

Governmental power, as a result, rested with the individual states, which were largely free to do their own thing – whatever it might be. To protect their own interests, some states imposed taxes and other trade barriers on incoming goods from other states. A number yielded to the demands of debtors and printed large amounts of paper money that they decreed to be legal tender. Stay laws extended the period of time debtors could pay their creditors. States refused to pay their proportionate share of the costs of the Continental Congress and the Revolutionary War, with the result that not even interest payments on the national debt could be made.

Efforts to strengthen the governmental system arose from a number of sources: political figures who argued that the ability of a single state to block change endangered all the states, merchants and other commercial interests concerned about state-imposed trade restrictions, pioneers along the frontier fearful of Indian attacks, and veterans and members of the Continental Congress whose loyalties extended beyond a single state's boundaries.

The fifty-five delegates who gathered for the Constitutional Convention quickly concluded that the Articles of Confederation were beyond salvaging, and, instead of constructing proposals for reform, they decided to create an entirely new governmental system. They astutely realized that though their personal interests were those of the social and economic elite, a new government had to be one that no special interest or "faction" could control. Neither the haves nor the have nots should be capable of domination. Although the national level needed strengthening, and the power of the states reduction, the Framers envisioned a system in which neither level would do much governing.

Accordingly, the national government would assume responsibility for military affairs – foreign and domestic; it would coin money, establish a postal system, regulate interstate commerce, and impose taxes, within specified limits, of course. The states were forbidden to interfere with the tasks accorded the federal government. Article I, Section 10, of the proposed Constitution prohibits states from engaging in economic activities preferably left to the federal government or those that only a single national level could effectively perform, such as, making treaties, coining money, enacting bills of attainder or ex post facto laws, abridging contracts, taxing goods imported into or exported from a state, and maintaining an army or a navy.

Correspondingly, the federal government may not suspend the writ of habeas corpus except for national emergencies; no direct taxes can be imposed except in proportion to the census;[8] bills of attainder and ex post facto laws are banned; no taxes can be levied on exports, nor preference given to ports of one state over another; and all expenditures have to be legally appropriated and authorized.

In short, the Framers cleverly limited the power of the federal government in two distinct ways: (1) They placed certain activities off limits. These were the matters that government could not consider. Constitutionally speaking, they were actions that the Framers deemed beyond the sphere of governmental competence, for instance, determining what is religiously true or false. (2) The powers bestowed on the federal government could only be exercised in accordance with certain prespecified procedures; for example, a person accused of crime could only be convicted by the unanimous vote of a jury of twelve persons drawn from the area where the trial was held; for a bill to become a law, it had to be passed word for word by both houses of Congress and submitted to the president for his approval. If he vetoed it, it could become law only if each of the houses favored it by a two-thirds vote. The sum of these substantive and procedural limitations on the exercise of federal governmental power is known as *constitutionalism*.[9]

We parenthetically note that though the Framers meant for the Constitution to apply primarily to the federal government and not to those of the states and their subdivisions, the drafters of the various state constitutions also imposed limits on the substantive activity and procedures of government, thus ensuring that the popular notion "that that government is best that governs least" was realized in fact.

Why did the politically active portion of the population accept the severe limits that the Constitution imposed on the exercise of governmental power? (Note that women, blacks, Native Americans, and landless males had no vote and, hence, could not participate in the political process.) Although the supporters of the Constitution had to wage a hard-fought struggle to obtain its ratification, they eventually won out because both supporters and opponents realized that half a loaf was better than none. Opponents primarily composed

---

[8] Constitutional limits on direct (income) taxes were overturned by the Sixteenth Amendment.

[9] Jeffrey A. Segal and Harold J. Spaeth, *The Supreme Court and the Attitudinal Model Revisited* (Cambridge: Cambridge University Press, 2002), pp. 18–21. Charles H. McIlwain, *Constitutionalism: Ancient and Modern*, rev. ed. (Ithaca, NY: Cornell University Press, 1947).

the lower socioeconomic segments of society: debtors, small yeomen farmers, urban artisans, and those residing along the frontier. They lacked experience in affairs of state and were deeply suspicious of strong centralized government. If not for them personally, certainly for their ancestors, government had been a tool of oppression. Those along the frontier had little need of government except for an occasional military foray to pacify unruly natives.

Arrayed against them were the landed gentry, merchants, other commercial interests, and the better educated. Far better organized and politically astute, they were concerned with retaining their position atop the socioeconomic ladder. As long as the power of government was not used against them, they sensibly realized that they could maintain their position in society, given their wealth, education, and social status.

Consequently, a rigorously limited system of government was not antithetical to the self-interest of either of these factions. Subsequent developments perpetuated attachment to limited government: The influence of the frontier throughout the nineteenth century, the millions of immigrants for whom government represented tyranny and oppression, notions of the survival of the fittest, the gospel of wealth, and rugged individualism blended to support distrust of governmental action and the Jeffersonian concept of limited government.[10]

Federalism

Federalism is simply and straightforwardly defined as the geographical division of governmental power between the central and local units. The fundamental law specifies this division by indicating which actions are the province of the central government and which belong to the states. In our system, federalism also enumerates the actions that neither the federal government nor the states may perform. On the other hand, both levels may engage in certain common activities, such as taxation.

The pertinent constitutional language, however, as is the case throughout the Constitution, does not specify who may do what with any precision. The only guidance is the supremacy clause of Article VI:

This Constitution, and the laws of the United States which shall be made in pursuance thereof; and all treaties made, or which shall be made, under the authority of the United States, shall be the supreme law of the land; and the judges in every State shall be bound thereby, anything in the Constitution or laws of any State to the contrary notwithstanding.

Though this language may appear to give the upper hand to the federal government, such is not the case. The Constitution does not say who should resolve federal–state conflicts, and though, as we shall see, the Supreme Court took it upon itself to resolve these controversies, that course has not always resulted

---

[10] Segal and Spaeth, *The Supreme Court*, pp. 14–20. Max Lerner, *America as a Civilization* (New York: Simon & Schuster, 1957), pp. 353–464.

in the expansion of federal power, and decidedly not since the inception of the Rehnquist Court in 1987.

As a consequence, the Supreme Court has confronted a steady stream of litigation throughout its history that has required the justices to draw an ever shifting line between federal and state power.

Separation of Powers

Whereas federalism divides governmental power geographically, separation of powers does so functionally. Congress legislates, the president performs the executive function, and the courts adjudicate resulting conflicts. This tripartite division ensures the independence of each from the others. Each branch has its own personnel who serve terms of office different in length from those of the others and who – in the case of Congress and the president – are chosen by different constituencies.

The effect of this division prevents any branch from compelling action by either of the other two. Consequently, conflict is institutionalized, most especially between Congress and president. To ensure that separation persists, and that no branch dominates the others, the Framers gave each a few powers that functionally belong to one of the others. Thus, the president possesses the legislative power to veto congressional legislation, and the upper house of the legislature (the Senate) participates in the selection of officials who help the president "take Care that the Laws be faithfully executed." Both branches check the federal courts, the president by nominating judges and the Senate by consenting to their selection. The courts in turn check Congress and the president by their power of judicial review, the final distinguishing feature of our constitutional system.

But before we consider judicial review, we should note that the Framers were most concerned that Congress might overwhelm the other two branches. At the time the Constitution was written and adopted, public participation in government was largely untried and the Framers, representative of the economic and social elite, were concerned that those at the lower end economically and socially might gain too much political power, given their numerical superiority. The Framers and those they represented were much more comfortable with and experienced in conducting governmental affairs without involvement by the bulk of the population. Indeed, the fact that a number of the state governments were in the hands of the lower strata of society gave them real reason for concern. Actions benefiting the average person at the expense of the well-to-do had been enacted by several of the states. The suffrage was broadened to include property-poor males; cheap paper money was issued to enable debts to be paid relatively painlessly; and stay laws lengthened the time in which debts could legally be paid.

To lessen their fear of legislative dominance, and to effect a compromise between large and small states, the Framers divided Congress into two houses: the Senate and the House of Representatives. Senators served six-year terms, with one-third chosen every two years, and representatives served but two. Every state was allocated the same number of senators, and numbers of representatives would vary with a state's population, with slaves counted by a 5:3 ratio. For Congress to act, each house had to enact precisely the same law, identical down to the last comma. Failure to do so? No law.

Judicial Review

The federal courts escaped the Framers' application of separation of powers because their fears ran in the opposite direction: that the courts might become the tool of either the legislative or the executive branch. Hence, they gave to the courts lifetime tenure, no salary reduction, and a selection process that neither the president nor the Senate could entirely control.

The doctrine of judicial review – the power of a court to void actions of the legislative and executive branches of government – best demonstrates that the insulation from the conflicts between Congress and president the Framers provided the federal courts was effectively realized. Note that nowhere does the Constitution make provision for judicial review. However, it fits exceptionally well into the constitutional fabric that the Framers otherwise wove.

1. If the Constitution is to be the fundamental law of the land, some body must have the capacity to determine whether the actions of government conform to its provisions. Theoretically, any one of the three branches could do so. All of their officials take the same oath of office as federal judges. But given Americans' distrust of government, perceptions of bias would likely confront any actions either Congress or the president took that enhanced its own power. Better to leave such decisions to judges. Their independence from the other branches and their lifetime tenure insulate them from partisan and electoral strife.

2. Inasmuch as separation of powers guarantees conflict between legislature and executive, allowing the insulated judiciary to function as the balance of power between them, resolving the squabbles that perpetually characterize their behavior, perceived as it is as partisan and self-serving, makes sense.

3. Given the fact of federalism, an umpire is also needed to resolve conflicts between the two levels of government. To allow either level to resolve such conflicts guarantees perceptions of bias. And though the federal judiciary is a branch of the federal government, its insulation from partisan strife and the perception of judges as principled decision makers warrant their functioning as the umpires of the federal system. We discuss this mythological aspect of judicial behavior later.

The Enunciation of the Doctrine of Judicial Review. The story of how judicial review formally became part of our constitutional system warrants detailed presentation. Not only is the story fascinating in its own right, it also exemplifies exceptionally well the shenanigans of which judges, especially those who sit on the U.S. Supreme Court, are capable.

As are federalism and separation of powers, judicial review is definable simply as the authority of a court to pass upon the compatibility of actions of the other branches with the fundamental law (the Constitution), with which, as we have seen, all governmental action must comport. It is noteworthy that all American courts, state and federal, not just the Supreme Court, have the power to pass upon the constitutionality of the actions of legislative and executive officials. Those that in a court's estimation fail to do so are unconstitutional: that is, null and void.

The Saga of **Marbury v. Madison.** John Adams and the Federalist political party, decimated by the Jeffersonians in the election of 1800, licked their wounds and sought to fight another day from the bastion of the federal judiciary. This they accomplished by the enactment of the Judges' Bill of 1801, which created a host of new federal judgeships, to which faithful, but soon to be unemployed, Federalists were appointed. How, you ask, was this possible? Were not the Federalists clobbered in the November 1800 election? Indeed they were. But the Framers, in their wisdom, had specified that Congress shall meet annually on the first Monday in December (Article I, Section 4).[11] This meant that *defeated* congresspersons remained in office until the following March, when the newly elected members took office. These so-called lame-duck sessions presented manifold opportunities for mischief whenever a switch in partisan control occurred, as happened in November 1800.

Oliver Ellsworth, chief justice since 1796, retired on December 15, 1800. The defeated president, John Adams, nominated John Marshall, his secretary of state, as Ellsworth's successor. The lame-duck Senate duly confirmed him. Marshall, however, decided to remain as secretary of state until Adams's administration went out of business on March 4, 1801, on which date Thomas Jefferson would be sworn in as president.

As secretary of state, Marshall had the responsibility of delivering the commissions of each of the new judges that the Act of 1801 had created. These commissions entitled the recipient to occupy the office to which he had been appointed. For an unknown reason Marshall failed to deliver the commission of one William Marbury as justice of the peace for the District of Columbia. March 4 came and went without Marbury receiving his commission. James Madison, the new secretary of state, refused to hand over the commission. Marbury did what any red-blooded American does: He sued. But rather than waste time in the lower federal court, he went right to the top and sought a writ of mandamus from the Supreme Court that would compel Madison to deliver to him his commission. He did so on the authority of the Judiciary Act of

---

[11] The Twentieth Amendment, adopted in 1933, changed this arrangement so that members of Congress elected in November took office the following January, thus doing away with the December session.

1789, which purportedly gave the Supreme Court authority to issue writs of mandamus as an original matter, and not as a case on appeal. Thus began the case of *Marbury v. Madison.*

Marshall, speaking for a unanimous Court, ruled that though Marbury had a right to receive his commission, the Court had no authority to issue its delivery. The reason? The relevant provision of the Judiciary Act of 1789, which authorized the Court to issue writs of mandamus without the matter having been heard in any lower federal court, was unconstitutional. Why? Because the act expanded the Court's original jurisdiction, the subjects of which are specified in the Constitution itself. Because the Constitution, said Marshall, specifies exactly what subjects the Supreme Court may hear as an original matter, Congress may neither contract nor expand them. Mandamus does not appear among these subjects. Hence, the provision at issue is unconstitutional.

An eminently logical decision, no? Definitely not. Its logic overlooks Marshall's own conduct and the unstated assumptions that underlie his opinion:

1. Elementary canons of judicial ethics unequivocally require judges who have a personal interest or connection with a matter presented to them for resolution to disqualify, that is, recuse, themselves. Marshall's own actions (or nonaction), as we have seen, occasioned Marbury's lawsuit. Marshall, however, realized he would have no better opportunity to place the Court in a position to superintend the actions of the other branches of government.
2. As Marshall's opinion makes clear, Marbury was in the wrong court. He should have commenced legal action in the federal trial (district) court. Again, elementary legal canons decree that litigants bringing an action in the wrong court should simply be directed to the proper one, without the wrong court considering the merits of the controversy.

Marshall chose to address the merits of Marbury's case, realizing correctly that an opportunity to elevate the Supreme Court to a position above that of Congress and president would not likely come his way again. In this, he was absolutely correct. Not until the case of *Scott v. Sandford* in 1857, some fifty-four years later, did the justices declare another act of Congress unconstitutional.

In his opinion, Marshall struck a posture that resonated very well with the American public: He ruled against his own political party. Marbury lost his case.[12] What better evidence of judicial objectivity and impartiality! But the reality was just the opposite. Though he lost this battle with the Jeffersonians, Marshall won the war because the battle gave him the opportunity to enunciate the doctrine of judicial review.

---

[12] Another noteworthy aspect of Marshall's opinion was that enforcing it required no action by anybody in Jefferson's administration. It automatically enforced itself. The Supreme Court merely shut its doors to Marbury's case.

The unstated assumptions on which Marshall based his opinion are the following:

(1) In ruling that the Supreme Court could not decide as an original matter any issue not specifically listed in the Constitution, Marshall disregarded the fact that the Judiciary Act of 1789 probably did no such thing, as the clause on writs of mandamus follows a discussion of the Court's *appellate* authority, not the earlier listing of its original jurisdiction.[13] Marshall simply formulated the doctrine of judicial review without applying it to any specific language. As best we can determine, this may be the only instance in the Court's *Reports* that does not identify the offending statutory language.

(2) The act was enacted by the First Congress, the membership of which disproportionately contained members of the Constitutional Convention. Marshall, not incidentally, was *not* among them. If any individuals knew the meaning and intention of the Constitution's provisions, they had to be those who authored the document.

(3) Furthermore, the provision declared unconstitutional was written by Oliver Ellsworth, Marshall's predecessor as chief justice! The irony that a chief justice, a member of the first Congress, and a delegate to the Constitutional Convention would violate his oath of office by writing a provision into law that contravened the fundamental law boggles the imagination. Yet Marshall apparently thought Ellsworth perfectly capable of such behavior, notwithstanding that he, like Marshall, was a dyed-in-the-wool Federalist Party member.

(4) Marshall's opinion tenders a view of judicial competence and integrity that rests only on unsubstantiated arguments and assertions that demean and debase the personnel and activities of the other branches. For better or for worse, Americans have come to accept them in large part because of the mind-set underlying the other features of our constitutional system discussed previously. Thus, "it is a proposition too plain to be contested, that the constitution controls any legislative act repugnant to it; or, that the legislature may alter the constitution by an ordinary act."[14]

Typically of judicial opinions, the logic is impeccable. But consider the unwritten assumption: Congress, aided if not abetted by the president, is fully capable of acting unconstitutionally. Query: Why not assume the same of judges?

Marshall develops his argument further by arguing that those who controvert the rule that the Constitution is the fundamental law of the land "must close their eyes on the constitution, and see only the law. This doctrine would subvert the very foundation of all written constitutions.... It would declare that if the legislature shall do that which is expressly forbidden, such act, notwithstanding

---

[13] Charles Warren, *The Supreme Court in United States History* (Boston: Little, Brown, 1922), I, 242; William Van Alstyne, "A Critical Guide to *Marbury v. Madison*," 1969 *Duke Law Journal* 1, at 15.

[14] *Marbury v. Madison*, 1 Cranch 137 (1803), at 177.

the express prohibition, is effectual."[15] Again, consider the implication: Congress may consciously and deliberately behave unconstitutionally – even though it did nothing of the sort here. Contrast the congressional behavior with Marshall's devious conduct and dubious ethics. Might it not be more appropriate to view the Court as being a source of unconstitutional action or as being capable of intruding into matters that the Constitution clearly authorizes the other branches to resolve?

(5) Marshall concludes his opinion by dispensing with logic and self-righteously posing rhetorically an ethical question:

> Why otherwise does [the Constitution] direct the judges to take an oath to support it? This oath certainly applies in an especial manner, to their conduct in their official character. How immoral to impose it on them, if they were to be used as the instruments, and the knowing instruments, for violating what they swear to support.
>
> Why does a judge swear to discharge his duties agreeably to the constitution of the United States, if that constitution forms no rule for his government?[16]

As evidence of the fatuousness of Marshall's argument consider the fact that all federal officials take the same oath. This, however, gave him no more pause than it gives us today. Clearly, what is sauce for the goose is emphatically not sauce for the gander. Only politicians betray their oath of office, certainly not judges, especially those sitting on the U.S. Supreme Court.

THE MYTHOLOGY OF JUDGING

Given (1) that different courts and judges do not reach a common decision about a given case, (2) that appellate court decisions – especially those of the Supreme Court – commonly contain dissents, and (3) that a change in a court's membership not atypically produces a different result, why do so many persist in believing that judicial decisions are objective, dispassionate, and impartial? Judges are said not to have discretion; they do not decide their cases; rather it is the law or the Constitution speaking through them that determines the outcome. Judges, in short, are mere mouthpieces of the law. To deny the falsity of the foregoing, we adopt an ostrich posture. As Justice Roberts famously said for himself and four colleagues in a major anti–New Deal decision: "When an act of Congress is appropriately challenged in the courts as not conforming to the constitutional mandate the judicial branch of the government has only one duty – to lay the article of the Constitution which is invoked beside the statute which is challenged and to decide whether the latter squares with the former."[17]

We do so because we have given judges the authority to play God with regard to the life, liberty, and property of those who appear before them. Whether trivial or earthshaking, the final decision typically rests with a court. Such

---

[15] *Id.* at 178.
[16] *Id.* at 179.
[17] *United States v. Butler*, 297 U.S. 1 (1936), 62.

autotheistic power ought not be vested in mere mortals. But because American society has chosen to allow it to be, we have devised myths to sustain and rationalize such an awesome exercise of power.

Reverence and respect are basic ingredients of mythology. Secrecy and mystery shroud the decision-making process. Hence, we distinctively clothe judges in black robes. And though some other governmental officials also wear distinctive garb – the military, police, some postal workers – none wears black, the most solemn and mysterious of colors. Courthouses and courtrooms replicate temples and churches. Instead of from altars, judges preside from elevated benches to which all participants must look up. Proceedings are ritualized, accompanied by pomp and ceremony, and conducted (at least before the onset of plain meaning laws and the decline of legal jargon) in language largely unintelligible to laypersons. Chief Justice Taft effectively stated the utility of the judicial robe:

> It is well that judges should be clothed in robes, not only, that those who witness the administration of justice should be properly advised that the function performed is one different from, and higher than, that which a man discharges as a citizen in the ordinary walks of life; but also, in order to impress the judge himself with the constant consciousness that he is a high priest of the temple of justice and is surrounded with obligations of a sacred character that he cannot escape.[18]

Judicial mythology blunts criticism and insulates judges from the hue and cry that permeates governmental action (and nonaction), thereby enabling judges to do as they wish, obligated to none but themselves. As enigmatic technicians, as so many Delphic oracles, they objectively dispense revealed truth and wisdom. One astute commentator got it exactly right, albeit irreverently:

> Like oysters in our cloisters we avoid the storm and strife. Some President appoints us, and we're put away for life. When Congress passes laws that lack historical foundation, We hasten from a huddle and reverse the legislation. The sainted Constitution, that great document for students, provides an airtight alibi for all our jurisprudence. So don't blame us if now and then we seem to act like bounders; Blame Hamilton and Franklin and the patriotic founders.[19]

SUMMARY AND CONCLUSIONS

We began by defining policy making as a choice among alternative courses of action, which action binds those subject to the policymaker's authority. Given that American courts possess a broader and more authoritative range of such power, what explains it? We identified five interrelated factors that do so: fundamental

---

[18] William Howard Taft, *Present Day Problems* (New York: Dodd, Mead, 1908), pp. 63–64. Judge Jerome Frank, in his classic work *Courts on Trial* (New York: Atheneum, 1963), pp. 254–261, candidly and incisively critiqued the symbolism surrounding judicial decision making as "the cult of the robe."

[19] Arthur Lippmann, "Song of the Supreme Court," *Life*, August 1935, p. 7.

law, distrust of government and politicians, federalism, separation of powers, and judicial review.

Given the awesome power that we vest in our courts, which, as we pointed out, extends even to determining the outcome of presidential elections, we explored the mythology of judging, noting that it flows directly into the legal approach to judicial decision making. Indeed, where the mythology stops and the legal approach starts is by no means clear because they overlap so substantially, as we show in our discussion of the legal model in the next chapter.

2

Approaches to Judicial Decision Making

Although judicial voting depends on variables more deeply rooted than political party affiliation, that does not gainsay that such affiliation is totally irrelevant or uncorrelated with the justices' values and attitudes. In a predecessor volume, two of us wrote – presciently, as it turned out – that "if a case on the outcome of a presidential election should reach the Supreme Court . . . the decision might well turn on the personal preferences of the justices."[1] *Bush v. Gore*, of course, admirably and accurately illustrates.[2]

Given that judges make policy when they decide cases, attempting to provide explanations of how judges decide their cases becomes incumbent upon us.

In this chapter, we present and assess two broad approaches that are used to help us understand judicial decision making: a legal approach and an extralegal, policy-based approach. Beneath these broad approaches lie more specific models that animate or give life to these approaches.

At the most fundamental level, we can think of judges as pursuing two different types of goals when deciding cases.[3] One goal might be to try to find the legally best answer to the case. That is, by weighing precedents, constitutional and statutory texts, the intent of the Framers, and other legally relevant criteria, the judge tries to come up with a "correct" answer to legal controversies.[4] Alternatively, because judges themselves make public policy, they might wish those policies to reflect, as nearly as practicable, their personal policy preferences.

From these approaches flow more specific models. For example, one class of legal models suggests that there is a single, deterministically correct answer to legal questions; another more modestly argues that legal criteria have instead

---

[1] Jeffrey A. Segal and Harold J. Spaeth, *The Supreme Court and the Attitudinal Model* (Cambridge: Cambridge University Press, 1993), p. 70.

[2] 531 U.S. 98 (2000).

[3] See Lawrence Baum, *The Puzzle of Judicial Behavior* (Ann Arbor: University of Michigan Press, 1997).

[4] See, e.g., Ronald Dworkin, *Taking Rights Seriously* (Cambridge, MA: Harvard University Press, 1978).

a gravitational pull on the decisions of justices; a third, giving up entirely any hope for objectively determined influence, argues only that judges believe – that is, convince themselves – that they are attempting to follow legal principles. Before considering these legal models, plus two policy-based models, we pause to discuss what models are and why we use them.

MODELS

The world, obviously, is highly complex, especially the portion that involves human beings and their behavior. Unlike nature and its phenomena, whose behavior sometimes reduces to precise mathematical formulations, such as $E = mc^2$, human activities are highly complex and interwoven. Thus, an explanation of a single court decision can – and frequently does – easily produce a book, as in the case of the Supreme Court decision of *Gomillion v. Lightfoot*,[5] to cite but one example. Although such "case studies" enable the reader to learn as much as possible about singular events, shortcomings also result. (1) Even the most intense study may leave the causes of a single event poorly understood. (2) Retention of the innumerable facts surrounding even a single decision, much less a number of them, is difficult, as students cramming for examinations well know. (3) The causes of one particular action or case may not be applicable to others. Consequently, the study of a single event may be descriptively useful but cannot explain action independent of that event with any degree of confidence.

As an alternative to the singular case study, the modeling approach recognizes the world's complexity and simultaneously realizes that attempting to learn all there is about one thing may not be the best tactic to increase knowledge. Instead, we might attempt to focus on the explanatory aspects of a wide range of similar behavior. Learning the factors that affect thousands of decisions may prove more beneficial than knowing those of only one.

This, then, is where models enter the picture. They are only a simplified representation of reality. They do not constitute reality itself. By ignoring certain aspects of reality in order to concentrate on those that allegedly explain the behavior in question, models provide a useful handle for understanding that more exhaustive and descriptive approaches do not. Thus, for example, suppose that identified changes in three or four variables explain the outcome in 95 percent of presidential elections. The resulting model is obviously of major utility in understanding and predicting the likely outcome of a future election. From the standpoint of social science, a good model serves two contradictory purposes: It accurately explains the behavior in question and it does so parsimoniously, that is, sparingly or frugally. The contradiction results because the more complex the model the more behavior one can explain. But increasing a model's complexity also increases the number of idiosyncratic

[5] 364 U.S. 339 (1960). The book, by the same name, was written by Bernard Taper (New York: McGraw-Hill, 1962).

variables, lessens its coherence, and – most importantly – destroys its parsimony. Inasmuch as no model can, by definition, explain everything, the objective is to discover the most economic explanation that can account for the largest portion of the behavior in question. The model that best accomplishes this result provides us with the most useful handle on an admittedly complex reality.

A necessary feature of any model is that testing of its explanatory capability demands that it be falsifiable. The model must identify, a priori, the conditions that, if observed, would refute the model's accuracy. For example, we will discuss later a specific policy-based model that holds that the Supreme Court defers to Congress in its statutory decision making out of fear of being overruled. After noting that the Supreme Court often does not defer, such models have been extended by arguing that when the Court does not defer, it is trying to provide Congress information to persuade it that the Court took the correct tack. Thus, if the Court follows Congress's preferences, the model is correct under the deference tack; if the Court does not follow Congress's preferences, the model is correct under the information tack. Either result – deferring to Congress or not deferring to Congress – is consistent with the model. As such, no amount of empirical evidence can refute the model. Hence, it is not falsifiable and thus has no scientific value.

In short, a model that excludes no potentially observable outcomes necessarily explains nothing, for explanation requires an account of why one path was taken and another was not. If all paths may be taken, then nothing is explained. Alternatively, consider an extralegal model, what we will later describe as the attitudinal model, which holds that Supreme Court justices, and to a lesser extent other judges, base decisions on their sincere policy preferences. If liberal justices typically voted no differently than conservative justices, or actually voted more conservatively than conservative justices, such evidence would be counter to the predictions of the model.

Three final points: (1) A model's validity does not depend on the breadth of action encompassed. Other factors being equal, the more global the model the better, assuming of course that it has been scientifically validated through empirical testing. But a narrowly focused model does not lack value, especially if it validly explains an important aspect of human behavior. (2) Models exist to explain behavior, rather than to predict behavior. But, and this is an important *but*, prediction is often the best test of how well a model explains. And though prediction without explanation has definite value – for instance, pre-Newtonian predictions of the height of tides, modern attempts to predict the swings of a stock market – it lacks the utility, the understanding, that explanation provides. (3) The usefulness of a model might vary with the institutional context in which the decision maker operates. Lower court judges follow precedents set by higher courts (vertical *stare decisis*) in a way that is simply inapplicable to U.S. Supreme Court justices. Similarly, elected state court judges must be much more mindful of public opinion than life-tenured federal judges.

THE LEGAL APPROACH

Models formulated by legalists rest in whole or in part on the mythology described in the two final sections of Chapter 1. Legalists have formulated a number of models over the years. One may fairly state that they differ but incidentally from one another: (1) None of them has been successfully tested – least of all by those who formulate them. They are nothing more than verbal formulations – unsubstantiated assertions – that judges decide cases in this way rather than in that. Empirically, their differences amount to six of one, half a dozen of another. (2) Without empirical substantiation, words displace actions as the measure of reality.

Over the last century, dominant legal models include mechanical jurisprudence, which posited that legal questions had a single correct answer that judges were to discover. The most apparent legacy of this model is the assertion that judges in deciding their cases "find" the law, as though it were a bedbug in a mattress. More recent legalists have similarly alleged that law is determinate, that it contains "internally-correct answers to all legal questions."[6] If these scholars provide an explanation of how scholars could determine, in advance, what the correct answers to legal questions are, then perhaps the mechanical model could be tested. Without such a priori answers, the model is unfalsifiable, and from a scientific point of view, worthless. If this view were actually true, we would not need judges – just programmed computers.

A more modest account of legal decision making holds that although factors such as text, intent, and precedent do not absolutely determine legal decisions, they have a significant and substantial gravitational effect on such decisions.[7] This gravitational model, as we call it, has in recent years been subject to systematic tests, as we will discuss later.[8]

Currently, the vogue is "post-positivism," for whose adherents the only required influence of law is a subjective influence that resides within the judge's own mind. That is, all that is expected under this model is that judges believe they are trying to find the best legal answers to the cases before them. No actual influence of legal principles is required. Although this model is in a sense falsifiable, in that one could conceivably recover documentary evidence, perhaps from private diaries that indicate whether judges believe they are trying to rule on the basis of the best legal criteria, the model cannot explain, and does not try to explain, which decisions judges actually make.

---

[6] Richard S. Markovits, *Matters of Principle: Legitimate Legal Argument and Constitutional Interpretation* (New York: New York University Press, 1998), p. 1. Also see Kent Greenawalt, *Law and Objectivity* (New York: Oxford University Press, 1992), who argues that "any extreme thesis that law is always or usually indeterminate is untenable" (p. 11).

[7] See, e.g., Ronald Dworkin, *Taking Rights Seriously* (Cambridge, MA: Harvard University Press, 1978), chap. 4.

[8] See, e.g., Harold J. Spaeth and Jeffrey A. Segal, *Majority Rule or Minority Will* (Cambridge: Cambridge University Press, 1999), and Robert M. Howard and Jeffrey A. Segal, "An Original Look at Originalism," 36 *Law and Society Review* 113 (2002).

But at least these and other legalistic approaches are not completely disconnected from one another. They contain a common core, pieces of which may be differentially emphasized from one school to another. All of them, however, maintain the relevance, whether subjectively or objectively, of the material facts of the case in light of the plain meaning of the statutes and constitutional provisions that relate to the matter, the intent of their Framers, and/or precedent.

Facts

Facts – case stimuli – are central to all models of decision making. They are obviously central to all judicial decision making, whether as part of a model or not. At the trial court level, if a jury is used, it has responsibility to determine the facts of the case. Otherwise, the judge decides what the facts are. But even with a jury, the judge does not become irrelevant. The determination of whether a specific matter is a material fact – that is, one that the fact finder may consider in reaching a decision – is the province of the judge acting compatibly with the rules of evidence. Rules of evidence, however, are by no means self-evident prescriptions. Even facts that go directly to guilt or innocence, or to considerations of liability, may not be admissible because they run counter to values on which society places a higher premium than determining who did what to whom; examples are exclusionary rules that deny admission of evidence that establishes guilt because of privacy interests or a property owner who by repairing a defective staircase immediately after someone is injured conceals her liability because society does not want to discourage safety precautions. Although appellate courts have no authority to ascertain the facts of a matter, they have responsibility to determine, on the basis of the case facts, whether the trial court's decision properly applied the relevant statutory or constitutional provision.

Insofar as the legal model, as its name indicates, focuses on the law, we need not further consider case facts. Instead, we move on to plain meaning, intent, and precedent as the considerations on which the legal model focuses. Clearly, judges and justices use these factors to justify their decisions in the legal opinions they hand down, but whether these factors actually *influence* their decisions or, instead, are merely *justifications* for them, remains to be seen.

Plain Meaning

Plain meaning applies not only to the language of laws and constitutions, but also to the words of judicially formulated rules. It simply says that judges base their decisions on the plain meaning of pertinent language. Their decisions should give force and effect only to what the legal language provides: nothing more, nothing less. Note that this formulation says nothing about intelligibility or the possibility that the language makes no sense. Courts not uncommonly note this to be the situation: "It may be well to acknowledge at the outset that it is quite impossible to make complete sense of the [legal] provision at issue here."[9]

For several reasons, plain meaning explains little if anything about a judicial decision, only that the court said it based its ruling on this approach. Dissenters commonly say the same thing. Both may well be right for the following reasons:

(1) The English language lacks precision. Words have a multiplicity of meanings, not all of which are congruent. Indeed, some conflict. Consider the common legal word *sanction*. It means to reward as well as punish. When a given word is combined with others, meaning loses even more clarity. The combination will likely be meaningful, but plainly so? Hardly.

(2) Legislators and framers of constitutional language typically fail to define their terms, legislators because passage of laws typically requires compromise. The easiest way to achieve compromise is to leave key provisions undefined. Framers of constitutions fail to define terms because they intend the document to have a long life. It will therefore confront situations unforeseen by the framers. Undefined language enables the document to be adapted to changing conditions and circumstances.

(3) Legal language does not form a seamless web: One statutory or constitutional provision may conflict with another. Though more recent language should take precedence over earlier words, conflict may inhere in the words of a single provision. And nothing requires a court to favor more recent conflicting language. The conservative wing of the Rehnquist Court, for example, gives precedence to the Eleventh over the Fourteenth Amendment.

(4) Identical words or phrases in different provisions need not have the same meaning. Thus, the Supreme Court defined *child support* differently in two provisions of the same law.[10] They accomplished this by use of two different dictionaries: *Webster's* and *Black's Law Dictionary*. Different meanings typically result because the court switches gears and applies a variant of the legal model: intention of the lawmakers. Problems also emerge when no dictionary contains the relevant word or phrase, for example, *non-curriculum-related student group*. The prevailing opinion admitted that the law failed to define the phrase and that even the law's sponsors did not know what it meant. In dissent, Justice Stevens accurately observed that

the Court relies heavily on the dictionary's definition of "curriculum." ... That word, of course, is not the Act's; moreover the word "noncurriculum" is not in the dictionary. Neither Webster nor Congress has authorized us to assume that "noncurriculum" is a precise antonym of the word "curriculum." "Nonplus," for example, does not mean "minus" and it would be incorrect to assume that a "nonentity" is not an "entity" at all.[11]

Judges, of course, deny that their constitutional opinions deviate from a fair-minded interpretation of the text. Elementary common sense clearly establishes

---

[9] *Asgrow Seed Co. v. Winterboer*, 513 U.S. 179 (1995), at 185–186.
[10] *Sullivan v. Stroop*, 496 U.S. 478 (1990), at 489–490.
[11] *Westside Community Schools v. Mergens*, 496 U.S. 226 (1990), at 291.

the opposite. In 1905, the Supreme Court prohibited New York from limiting the hours bakers could work on the basis of "freedom of contract," language nowhere found in the Constitution and since overruled.[12] In 1965, the Court prohibited Connecticut from criminalizing the use of contraceptives regardless of whether the user was married or not. A right to privacy protected such conduct. Again, no such language. But the Court said "penumbras and emanations" from six separate constitutional amendments made the law unconstitutional.[13] Relatedly, the right to marry and to breed also escaped the authors of the Constitution, but like privacy it is constitutionally protected.[14] In the economic sphere, the Supreme Court, concerned about the well-being of American business, ruled that corporations are citizens for purposes of accessing the federal courts.[15] And if corporations are citizens, then they logically must be persons, and as such they may not be deprived of their property without due process of law.[16] We do not say that the justices behaved inappropriately when they created these rights. We only note that if the Court can read unlisted rights into or explicit rights out of the Constitution, then the plain meaning approach fails as an explanation of what the Court has done.

In short, plain meaning does not explain any court's decisions because judges plainly do not necessarily mean what they say. Nor do they provide criteria that inform analysts when they intend to act as snollygosters and pseudologists. Indeed, they go further still and tell us that sometimes plain meaning ought not be used at all.

Legislative and Framers' Intent

The legislative and framers' intent aspect of the legal model refers to construing laws and constitutions according to the preferences of those who originally drafted and supported them. Unfortunately, as a guide to legal meaning neither improves on plain meaning. Indeed, quite often these two versions buttress opposite results in a given case. Needless to say, courts provide no empirically supportable basis for choosing one over the other. Hence, a judge's choice necessarily rests on considerations other than the model itself. These considerations, as we shall see, are the judge's preferred outcome of the case. Plain meaning, intent, and precedent merely provide the means – the rationale – to support the judge's preselected outcome.

We make one qualification to what we have just written. Judges typically begin their decision-making process by using plain meaning. But nothing prevents them from moving to intent if they find that plain meaning does not serve their desired case outcome. No criterion governs when such a shift may or should be made.

---

[12] *Lochner v. New York*, 198 U.S. 45; *West Coast Hotel v. Parrish*, 300 U.S. 379 (1937).
[13] *Griswold v. Connecticut*, 381 U.S. 479.
[14] *Zablocki v. Redhail*, 434 U.S. 374 (1978).
[15] *LC&C R. Co. v. Letson*, 2 Howard 497 (1845).
[16] *Santa Clara County v. Southern Pacific R. Co.*, 118 U.S. 394 (1886).

At the constitutional level, intent goes by the label of *interpretivism* or *originalism*. One addicted to it would support the death penalty because the Fifth Amendment makes three explicit references to it. Such person would also insist that only a unanimous jury of twelve persons could convict a person of a federal crime because that is what the Sixth Amendment meant in 1791. We may assume, however, that such person would deviate from his rule and allow women to serve as jurors even though they were prohibited from doing so in 1791, and no supporter of the Fourteenth Amendment's equal protection clause claimed it would apply to females.

Although conservative politicians and legal scholars find interpretivism their cup of tea, it is not necessarily a right-wing doctrine. Justice Hugo Black, for example, a forceful advocate for freedom of communication and the applicability of all the provisions in the Bill of Rights as binding on the states, fairly consistently argued for interpretation tied to the text and history of the Constitution.

Whatever the merits of interpretivist/originalist allegations about intent, empirical reality is another ballgame. The first question that requires an answer is whether the concept of legislators' or framers' intent is at all meaningful. Obviously, the Constitution's Framers never conceived of most issues confronting a twenty-first- (or even a twentieth-) century Court, from abortion to workers' comp. But even if they were prescient enough to do so, how do we determine who the Framers were? Though this may seem to be a rhetorical question, rest assured that it is not. Were they all of the fifty-five persons who showed up at one time or another? Some came and went. Only thirty-nine signed the final document. Some probably had not even read it. Assuredly, they were not all of a single mind. Apart from the nonsigners, what about the delegates to the various state conventions called to ratify the Constitution? Should they not be considered Framers? Devotees of intent exclude these persons from consideration.

The intent of constitutional amendments is no less problematic. For example, two of the leading participants in the drafting of the Fourteenth Amendment concluded oppositely about what the equal protection clause guaranteed. One asserted that it precluded racially separate public schools; another, that it covered only the right to travel, to enforce contracts, and to buy and sell property.[17]

So, if group intent is problematic, whose do we consider? Some argue for the person(s) who drafted the document; others, for the pivotal participant – the one whose vote made or could have broken the deal.[18] Even if we assume that the latter person can be empirically identified and his or her intentions known (most improbable under any set of circumstances), the words of Justice

[17] See Judith Baer, *Equality under the Constitution* (Ithaca, NY: Cornell University Press, 1983), pp. 96–97.

[18] McNollgast, "Legislative Intent: The Use of Positive Political Theory in Statutory Interpretation," 57 *Law and Contemporary Problems* 3 (1994).

Antonin Scalia writing an opinion in a landmark decision that considered the constitutionality of a state statute warrant weighty consideration:

The number of possible motivations, to begin with, is not binary, or indeed even finite. In the present case, for example, a particular legislator need not have voted for the Act either because he wanted to foster religion or because he wanted to improve education. He may have thought the bill would provide jobs for his district, or may have wanted to make amends with a faction of his party he had alienated on another vote, or he may have been a close friend of the bill's sponsor, or he may have been repaying a favor he owed the Majority Leader, or he may have hoped the Governor would appreciate his vote and make a fundraising appearance for him, or he may have been pressured to vote for a bill he disliked by a wealthy contributor or a flood of constituent mail, or he may have been seeking favorable publicity, or he may have been reluctant to hurt the feelings of a loyal staff member who worked on the bill, or he may have been mad at his wife who opposed the bill, or he may have been intoxicated and entirely unmotivated when the vote was called, or he may have accidentally voted "yes" instead of "no," or, of course, he may have had (and very likely did have) a combination of some of the above and many other motivations. To look for the sole purpose of even a single legislator is probably to look for something that does not exist.

Putting that problem aside, however, where ought we to look for the individual legislator's purpose? We cannot...assume that every member present...agreed with the motivation expressed in a particular legislator's pre-enactment floor or committee statement....Can we assume...that they all agree with the motivation expressed in the staff-prepared committee reports...[or] post-enactment floor statements? Or post-enactment testimony from legislators, obtained expressly for the lawsuit?...Media reports on...legislative bargaining? All these sources, of course, are eminently manipulable.

...If a state senate approves a bill by a vote of 26 to 25, and only one intended solely to advance religion, is the law unconstitutional? What if 13 of 26 had that intent? What if 3 of the 26 had the impermissible intent, but 3 of the 25 voting against the bill were motivated by religious hostility or were simply attempting to "balance" the votes of their impermissibly motivated colleagues? Or is it possible that the intent of the bill's sponsor is alone enough to invalidate it – on a theory, perhaps, that even though everyone else's intent was pure, what they produced was the fruit of a forbidden tree.[19]

Despite Scalia's demolition of the meaningfulness of intent, let us unrealistically assume for the sake of argument that legislative intent does exist. This presents us with the question, Where might we find it?

For starters, we might assess the record that the authors of the language left. Sometimes we find reasonably substantial records, other times little or nothing. State legislatures in particular leave no footprints in the sand. As for the original Constitution, we have only a "carelessly kept" journal, plus James Madison's notes, which he did not get around to editing until 1819, thirty-two

---

[19] *Edwards v. Aguillard*, 482 U.S. 578 (1987), at 636–638. Also see equivalent language by Justice Stevens in *Rogers v. Lodge*, 458 U.S. 613 (1982), 642–648. The other justices essentially disagree with Scalia's antiintent position because "common sense suggests that inquiry benefits from reviewing additional information rather than ignoring it." *Wisconsin Public Intervenor v. Mortier*, 501 U.S. 597 (1991), at 611, n. 4.

years after the events he reports! They were not published until 1840, four years after Madison's death. Supplementing Madison are scattered notes from eight of the delegates. None of these documents, however, for both obvious and nonobvious reasons, fathoms the Framers' intent in even the most rudimentary fashion.[20]

Apart from fragmentary records, even official records that conceivably may convey intent falsify, obfuscate, and mislead. Consider the *Congressional Record*, which judges and others peruse to ascertain legislative meaning as well as intent. Until 1978, members were free to add, subtract, edit, and delete remarks never uttered on the floor of either the House or the Senate. Thus, 112 pages of material appeared on a day when the Senate met for eight seconds and the House not at all.[21]

The upshot? Partisans on both sides of any legal or constitutional issue have no trouble finding language supporting their version of intent. Grist for this enterprise not only includes the official records, but also majority and minority committee and subcommittee reports, off-the-record statements by sponsors and opponents, testimony and comments of nonlegislative officials and private persons, to say nothing of other court decisions construing the language at issue.

Given the foregoing, is it any wonder that a respected federal judge, Alex Kozinski of the Ninth Circuit Court of Appeals, could say that "legislative history can be cited to support most any proposition, and frequently is."[22] Speaking of constitutional interpretation, a noted legal scholar has said, "The case for [its being] bound to text and history is only slightly stronger than the case for the proposition that we inhabit a flat earth."[23]

Although we do not wish to engage in overkill, completeness demands that we document the fact that intent is commonly spun to conflict with plain meaning, with the result that plain meaning loses. A truly classic example concerns a racial quota that was challenged as violating the Civil Rights Act of 1964, which makes it unlawful for an employer "to discriminate...because of...race." Over the objections of Burger and Rehnquist, who said the quota system was plainly illegal, the majority ruled the system legal because, citing an 1892 decision, "It is a familiar rule that a thing may be within the letter of the statute and yet not within the statute, because not within its spirit, nor within the intention of its makers."[24] Within its spirit? We leave such matters to

---

[20] Max Farrand, ed., *The Records of the Federal Convention of 1789*, rev. ed. (New Haven, CT: Yale University Press, 1966), I, pp. xi–xiv, xv–xix.

[21] Marjorie Hunter, "Case of the Missing Bullets," *New York Times*, 15 May 1985, p. 24. See Harold J. Spaeth, *Supreme Court Policy Making* (San Francisco: W. H. Freeman, 1979), p. 72, and the references cited for other examples of how Congress doctors its official records.

[22] Robert Pear, "With Rights Act Comes Fight to Clarify Congress's Intent," *New York Times*, 18 November 1991, p. A1.

[23] Lief Carter, *Contemporary Constitutional Lawmaking* (New York: Pergamon Press, 1985), p. 41.

[24] *Steelworkers v. Weber*, 443 U.S. 193 (1979), at 199–200, 201.

Table 2.1. *Hypothetical Choices of Three Legislators among Three Alternatives*

	Legislator		
	1	2	3
First choice	A	C	B
Second choice	B	A	C
Third choice	C	B	A

mystagogues, charlatans, and others of similar ilk – including, of course, robed originalists and interpretivists.

The message is clear. Simply dust off this language to evade any linguistic clarity, as well as any expression of intent. But a court need not clothe itself even in this tattered garment. It can stand stark naked and bare-facedly state its druthers, the language and any discernible intent to the contrary notwithstanding: Consider *Maryland v. Craig*, in which the majority said that the confrontation clause of the Sixth Amendment does not mean what it says because the provision's purpose is to ensure that evidence against the accused is reliable and subject to "rigorous adversarial testing." The four dissenters focused on the obvious: "the defendant's constitutional right 'to be confronted with witnesses against him' means, always and everywhere, at least what it explicitly says: the 'right to meet face to face all those who appear and give evidence at trial.'"[25]

The Meaninglessness of Group Intent. Finally, circumstances abound in which fathoming group intent becomes meaningless. Mathematical proof demonstrates that every method of social or collective choice – that is, every arrangement whereby individual choices are pooled to arrive at a collective decision – violates at least one principle of fair and reasonable democratic decision making. In American society, this means (1) There is either majority rule or at least plurality rule, in which the winner receives more votes than any other option. (2) Each vote is of equal value: one person, one vote. (3) Among a range of choices, each decision maker is free to rank them as he or she sees fit. (4) In exercising such choice, an option no one prefers may not be imposed. (5) Conversely, if everyone prefers a to b, b may not become the winner.

These principles – as obvious and fair-minded as possible – can produce a cyclical outcome such that unless one of the principles is violated, no choice wins. Consider for example a three-member panel with the preferences shown in Table 2.1. Legislator (or Framer) 1 prefers A to B, and B to C. Legislator 2 prefers C to A, and A to B. Legislator 3 prefers B to C, and C to A.

Using majority rule, option A loses because 2 and 3 prefer C. B loses because 1 and 2 prefer A. And to complete the cycle, C loses because 1 and 3 prefer B.

[25] 497 U.S. 836 (1990), at 857, 862.

Although the validity of legislative intent remains in dispute,[26] legislators, Framers, and, for that matter, appellate court judges (who always sit in panels of no fewer than three members) are a "they," not an "it."[27] Thus, preferences alone may produce no winner and group intent simply makes no sense.

Given this litany of reasons why intent may not exist and, if it does, the problems inherent in finding it, a rational course would discard completely judicial and legalistic efforts to fathom intent.

Precedent

The last of the legal approaches to decision making is precedent, which is definable simply as adherence to what has been decided before. The Latin equivalent is *stare decisis*: to stand on what has been decided. Today's decisions become linked with those of yesteryear. The law thus develops a quality of connectedness, an appearance of stability.

At the most basic level, precedent certainly matters to lower court judges, as no such judge worthy of the name is likely to uphold prohibitions on previability abortions, require the segregation of students on racial grounds, or allow public school officials to lead students in prayer service, regardless of the judge's predilections on these issues.

Furthermore, on matters of little policy import, a judge might find that the consistency of following precedent results in fairer outcomes than deciding each case on a clean slate. A judge may not care whether a slip on a driveway is the responsibility of the owner who did not shovel or the visitor who was not careful, but once such rules are established, justice generally requires that they consistently be followed. At the Supreme Court, however, precedent no more restricts judicial discretion than plain meaning or intent; nor does it explain why judges decide their cases in favor of one party rather than the other.

Unlike plain meaning and intent, precedent is used by judges as a verbalized explanation for almost every decision they make. Although it sometimes appears in isolation from the other approaches, it is used more commonly in association with one or the other of them. That is, judges will assert that plain meaning or intent means this rather than that by citing a number of previously decided cases.

As are plain meaning and intent, precedent is used in cases interpreting constitutional provisions as well as statutory matters. Judges, however, admit that precedent has putatively more binding force in statutory construction because the legislature can always change the law and with it a court's interpretation. But in the case of a constitutional provision, the only means of changing a court's decision is via an amendment, unless the Court itself chooses to alter or abandon its precedent. Justice Scalia, citing Justice Douglas, has voiced

---

[26] McNollgast, "Legislative Intent."

[27] Kenneth Shepsle, "Congress Is a 'They,' Not an 'It.': Legislative Intent as Oxymoron," 12 *International Review of Law and Economics* 239 (1992).

an additional justification for judicial alteration of constitutional precedent: "A judge looking at a constitutional provision may have compulsions to revere past history and accept what was once written. But he remembers above all else that it is the Constitution which he swore to defend and support, not the gloss which his predecessors have put on it."[28] Though precedent, as plain meaning and intent do, looks backward, that viewpoint does not severely restrict judges' discretion for several reasons.

(1) Most basically, precedents lie on both sides of all appellate controversies. If parties losing at trial have no basis for an appeal – which means, at a minimum, that no precedents support their contentions – none is taken. As a well-known judge of the Court of Appeals, Frank M. Coffin, said, "If precedent clearly governed, a case would never get as far as the Court of Appeals, the parties would settle."[29] Another well-known Court of Appeals judge, Frank H. Easterbrook, added: "Given that litigation is so expensive, why are parties willing to take their cases up? It's because precedent doesn't govern. Precedent covers the major premise. But the mind-set of the judge governs the minor premise."[30]

(2) Further evidencing the existence of precedent to support the contentions of the parties on both sides of a controversy, simply consult a case containing a dissenting opinion. Both will likely cite numerous precedents. If one checks them, one finds that those cited by the majority support its decision; those cited by the dissent support its position. The same may be said for cases without a dissent, as a reading of the litigants' briefs will demonstrate.

(3) Judges use precedent, not only to overrule other precedents, but also to create new law. The Supreme Court's decision that created a new right to privacy cited twelve cases to support its new rule, which cases then became precedent for the right that the decision created.[31] A more recent example concerns the right to die. In establishing the right of a competent person to refuse unwanted medical treatment, Chief Justice Rehnquist cited five cases as precedent: one pertaining to compulsory vaccination, another to search and seizure, a third to forcible medication of prisoners, and the final pair to mandatory behavior modification and the confinement of children.[32]

(4) Precedent consists of two components: the court's decision and the material facts that the court took into account in making its decision. The facts in two appellate cases, however, invariably differ to some degree. How similar the facts in two cases need be to constitute a precedent involves an intensely personal and subjective judgment. Hence, judges pick and choose among these facts and the precedents they support in order to produce a decision most compatible

---

[28] *South Carolina v. Gathers*, 490 U.S. 805 (1989), at 835.

[29] Linda Greenhouse, "Precedent for Lower Courts, Tyrant or Teacher," *New York Times*, 29 January 1988, p. 12.

[30] *Id.*

[31] *Griswold v. Connecticut*, 381 U.S. 479 (1965), at 482–486.

[32] *Cruzon v. Director, Missouri Dept. of Health*, 497 U.S. 261 (1990), at 278–280.

with their policy preferences, while asserting – of course – that the chosen ones most accord with the facts of the case for decision.

(5) Jurists disagree over what constitutes a precedent. Is it a court's decision, plus the facts on which it was based, as previously mentioned? Or is it the *ratio decidendi*, the underlying principle on which the decision rests? The latter lacks a meaningful definition, other than to say that it turns on a fairly basic consideration and thus is more global than the rule of law a court cites as authority for its decision.

Two incompatible decisions illustrate the latter approach. Both involve the inheritance rights of illegitimates in Louisiana. The U.S. Supreme Court ruled in the first case that such children could sue because of their mother's wrongful death and that the law prohibiting such suits was unconstitutional because the asserted rights "involve the intimate, familial relationship between a child and his own mother."[33] Three years later, the three *Levy* dissenters were joined by Nixon's first two appointees, Burger and Blackmun, to uphold the constitutionality of a law that prohibited unacknowledged offspring from sharing in their father's estate equally with their legitimate siblings. The law has a rational basis: of "promoting family life and of directing the disposition of property left within the State."[34] Thus, if the justices wish to support illegitimates financially, they cite *Levy*; if not, *Labine*.

Legal Limitations on Precedent. Clearly, then, precedent provides no more of a guide to a justice's decisions than the other elements of the legal model. All one can accurately say about it is that good legal form warrants citation of precedents. It certainly does not limit a justice's policy preferences. And in the rare situation in which the Court confronts only a single line of precedents, it has acceptable legalistic devices that enable it to deviate from what has been decided. These are four in number.

(1) *Obiter dicta* allows a court to view portions of a previous opinion as surplus language that does not limit the court's discretion in the case before it. The classic example concerns the president's removal power. The first case said a president could remove any and all executive officials at will. The second case qualified the first by holding that the original language applied only to persons performing purely executive office functions.[35] Those exercising quasi-legislative or quasi-judicial functions (i.e., members of various regulatory agencies) did not serve at the president's will and could be removed only for congressionally specified reasons.

(2) Precedents may be distinguished. This merely involves an assertion that the facts of the case for decision differ from those of a presumably relevant precedent. As we have pointed out, facts of cases on appeal always differ one from another.

[33] *Levy v. Louisiana*, 391 U.S. 68 (1968), at 70–71.
[34] *Labine v. Vincent*, 401 U.S. 532 (1971), at 536.
[35] *Myers v. United States*, 272 U.S. 52 (1926), and *Humphrey's Executor v. United States*, 295 U.S. 602 (1935).

(3) Precedents may be limited in principle. Unlike the two previous alterations, this one formally alters the scope of a precedent. Note that the reverse may also be true: A precedent's scope may be formally extended. *Roe v. Wade*, the abortion decision, illustrates. The Court held that during the first three months of pregnancy a woman had an untrammeled right to an abortion. Subsequent decisions qualified this holding to read that government could restrict a woman's right to an abortion during the first six months so long as it did so without undue interference; for example, by refusing to pay for poor women's abortions, or by establishing a no-abortion policy in government hospitals.[36]

(4) Precedents may be formally overruled. Because of the alternate means of manipulating precedent, none of which shatters the appearance of consistency, overruling rarely occurs. Since the beginning of the Warren Court in 1953, the justices have overruled precedents in an average of only 2.7 cases per term.

We may conclude our treatment of the legal model with a comment from Richard Posner, the highly regarded federal appeals court judge and author. "There is a tremendous amount of sheer hypocrisy in judicial opinion writing. Judges have a terrible anxiety about being thought to base their opinions on guesses, on their personal views. To allay that anxiety, they rely on the apparatus of precedent, much of it extremely phony."[37]

The Post-Positive Retreat

Because of the failures of the legal approach to explain the decisions that judges make, post-positive legalists now argue that all that can be expected of judges is that they believe that they follow legal principles. Howard Gillman well states this position:

In the version of the argument that might be called "post-positivist," legalists make claims, not about the predictable behavior of judges, but about their state of mind – whether they are basing their decisions on honest judgments about the meaning of law. What is post-positivist about this version is the assumption that a legal state of mind does not necessarily mean obedience to conspicuous rules; instead, it means a sense of obligation to make the best decision possible in light of one's general training and sense of professional obligation. On this view, decisions are considered legally motivated if they represent a judge's sincere belief that their decision represents their best understanding of what the law requires. Burton [Steven J., *Judging in Good Faith*, Cambridge: Cambridge University Press] (1992:xi–xii, 44) has persuasively argued that this notion of "judging in good faith" is all we can expect of judges.[38]

Thus, under the post-positivist approach, virtually any decision can be consistent with the legal model. And any decision is consistent with the model

---

[36] *Maher v. Roe*, 432 U.S. 464 (1977), and *Webster v. Reproductive Health Service*, 492 U.S. 490 (1989).

[37] Linda Greenhouse, "In His Opinion," *New York Times*, 26 September 1999, p. A13.

[38] Howard Gillman, "What's Law Got to Do with It? Judicial Behavioralists Test the 'Legal Model' of Judicial Decision Making," 26 *Law and Social Inquiry* 465 (2001), at 486.

as long as the judge has sincerely convinced herself – that is, subjectively rationalized – that the decision is legally appropriate.

The problems with this approach are clear. First, the model is not falsifiable in terms of which decisions judges actually make.[39] Thus, by accepted standards of scientific research, the model cannot provide a valid explanation of what judges actually do.[40]

Second, the post-positivist model fails to appreciate the fundamental influence of motivated reasoning in human decision making. As classic social psychological findings demonstrate, the ability to convince oneself of the propriety of what one prefers to believe psychologically approximates the human reflex.[41] This is particularly true when plausible arguments support one's position, as is invariably the case for the types of cases that come to court. Ultimately, because a priori expectations cannot be made and, indeed, are not desired under the post-positivist position, it cannot provide us with what we seek – an explanation for what the justices actually do. Thus, regardless of whether judges are capable of convincing themselves that Congress cannot block slavery in the territories,[42] that the due process clause implies a right to contract,[43] that the Civil Rights Act allows race to be a factor in hiring and promotions,[44] that the Eleventh Amendment applies to suits by a citizen of the state being sued,[45] and that, as implausible as it might seem, the Florida recount violated the Fourteenth Amendment,[46] this model cannot, and does not even try to, provide an explanation for what judges actually do.

EXTRALEGAL OR POLICY-BASED APPROACHES

We next consider extralegal or policy-based approaches to judicial decision making. These approaches move beyond legally relevant factors and view judges as policymakers who try to make decisions that most closely approximate

---

[39] *Id.*, p. 485: "Behavioralists want to force legalists into offering testable hypotheses so that beliefs about law's influence can be verified by a kind of scientific knowledge that behavioralists consider more authoritative; however, legalists believe that doing such tests has the effect of changing the concept of 'legal influence' so that it no longer represents what they believe."

[40] See the discussion in *Daubert v. Merrell Dow*, 509 U.S. 579 (1993), at 593.

[41] E.g., Roy Baumeister and Leonard Newman, "Self-Regulation of Cognitive Inference and Decision Processes," 20 *Personality and Social Psychology Bulletin* 3 (1994); and Ziva Kunda, "The Case for Motivated Reasoning," 108 *Psychological Bulletin* 480 (1990). Of course, humans are also motivated to find correct answers. Baumeister and Newman refer to this as the "intuitive scientist" model. They refer to the search for preferred answers as the "intuitive lawyer" model (p. 4). We have little doubt that Supreme Court justices are better represented as lawyers than as scientists.

[42] *Scott v. Sanford*, 19 Howard 393 (1857).

[43] *Lochner v. New York*, 198 U.S. 45 (1905).

[44] *Steelworkers v. Weber*, 443 U.S. 193 (1979).

[45] *Board of Trustees v. Garrett*.

[46] *Bush v. Gore*, 531 U.S. 98 (2000).

their personal policy preferences.[47] How might they best achieve their goals? Sometimes judges can most closely achieve their policy desires by voting their sincere preferences, with the *Bush v. Gore* justices a rather obvious example. But judges might need, to some extent, strategically to balance their own preferences against legislators' or other judges' desires, so as to prevent a reversal that leaves the case even further from their most preferred position.

These two different means to the same end characterize two policy-based models: the attitudinal model and the rational choice model. The attitudinal model emphasizes, not surprisingly, the attitudes of judges and justices. The institutional protections (e.g., life tenure, docket control, and the lack of a supervisory authority) surrounding the Supreme Court arguably allow the justices to reach decisions almost completely based on their sincere policy preferences. Attitudes also play a significant role for lower court judges, even if the possibility of appellate review and lack of docket control means that such judges do not have the unbridled discretion of Supreme Court justices.

Rational choice models emphasize the interdependence of judicial choice: that judges and justices, whether policy-minded or in search of other goals, must take into account the preferences of other political actors when making their decisions if they wish to win. According to one set of proponents, rational choice perspectives argue

that because justices take into account the preferences of the ruling regime (even if they do not necessarily share those preferences) and . . . the actions they expect the regime to take, the Court's decisions typically will never be far removed from what contemporary institutions desire. . . .

This does not mean, however, that the Court will never . . . strike down federal laws.[48]

Despite these differences in emphasis, overlap exists. Beyond the fundamental notion of policy-based goals, rational choice judicial models recognize, though often quietly, that the "rational" response may be one's sincere preferences. Similarly, attitudinal studies have long recognized the interdependence inherent in certiorari decisions in which four votes are needed to decide the merits of the case,[49] to say nothing of hierarchical limits on lower courts.[50]

---

[47] Extralegal approaches need not be limited to policy goals, as judges might be motivated by alternative extralegal goals, such as maximizing leisure time. Nevertheless, we focus our attention on policy making.

[48] Lee Epstein and Thomas Walker, "The Role of the Supreme Court in American Society: Playing the Reconstruction Game," in Lee Epstein (ed.), *Contemplating Courts* (Washington, DC: Congressional Quarterly Press, 1995), pp. 323–324.

[49] Glendon Schubert, "The Certiorari Game," in *Quantitative Analysis of Judicial Behavior* (Glencoe, IL: Free Press, 1959), pp. 210–254; and Robert L. Boucher, Jr., and Jeffrey A. Segal, "Supreme Court Justices as Strategic Decision Makers," 57 *Journal of Politics* 824 (1995).

[50] Jeffrey A. Segal, Donald R. Songer, and Charles M. Cameron, "Decision Making on the U.S. Courts of Appeals," in Lee Epstein (ed.), *Contemplating Courts* (Washington, DC: Congressional Quarterly Press, 1995).

Rational Choice

Rational choice models attempt to apply and adapt the theories of economics to political and social interactions generally. Though some may quibble, the core of rational choice stipulates that actors must be able to rank their choice of goals, values, tastes, and strategies, and that their choices maximize their satisfaction. These choices must be "transitive," so that if one prefers reversing a decision to refusing to decide the matter and refusing to decide to affirming, a fortiori the actor must prefer reversing to affirming. No restrictions are placed on what produces satisfaction. Thus although judicial rational choice models typically assume policy goals, this is not a necessary choice. Generally speaking, no goal is ruled out. Consequently, where a model states the goals of the participants, the model may be falsified, but not the theory of rational choice because if all goals are allowed, some goal must exist that explains the behavior in question.

When an actor assesses available options and their consequences, orders them preferentially, and acts accordingly, said actor behaves strategically. This may take two forms: sincere adherence to preferences or sophisticated adherence to preferences where the actor settles for half a loaf, so to speak, because he or she judges that that outcome is the best that can be attained given the institutional situation, that is, his colleagues' incompatible preferences or the likelihood of future litigation that might exacerbate the situation, forcing the actor to settle for even less than half a loaf.

Judicial rational choice models are themselves divisible into three types: those that focus on internal court strategies, those that treat constraints imposed on lower courts by higher courts, and those that treat constraints imposed on the courts by other political actors, primarily Congress (the so-called separation of powers [SOP] model).

Judges on collegial courts have many opportunities to use internal strategies to help achieve their policy goals. When judges have control over which cases they hear, most notably at the U.S. Supreme Court, they must consider not only whether they would prefer to hear the case, but what the likely outcome on the merits would be; it does a justice little good to vote to hear a case when she dislikes the lower court decision only to have the Supreme Court affirm that decision on the merits. So, too, judges who vote with the majority must negotiate over the contents of the majority opinion. Mere threats to dissent might lead to desired changes in the Court's opinion. Moreover, withholding a dissent in one case might lead to a colleague's withholding her dissent in another.

All courts lower than the Supreme Court, with the potential exception of state supreme courts acting solely on issues pertinent only to their particular state, must be concerned about being overturned by higher courts. This arrangement typically leaves lower court judges with a fair amount of leeway, but again, not nearly enough to prohibit abortions, allow school prayers, or otherwise ignore the fundamental policies established by the Supreme Court. Therefore, the judges on these courts likely make decisions with at least some consideration of higher court precedent.

Judges may also be concerned with external actors in their political environment: public opinion, executives, and, most prominently, legislatures. Here, judges might choose policies that are not as close to their preferences as they would like in order to prevent attacks on their independence and overrides of their decisions. The extent to which judges must account for external preferences undoubtedly depends on the institutional environment in which the court operates. When judges may readily be removed from office (as in many state courts), when the political environment is highly centralized (as in various states), or when the public can directly overrule courts through referenda and initiatives, we expect relatively more judicial deference to the political environment. But when judges have life tenure (as do federal judges), when they face a decentralized political environment that creates innumerable opportunities to block override legislation (think: congressional committees), and when the courts have a reservoir of public support that makes attacking their independence politically difficult, we expect no such deference. Any court that can effectively elect the president in a reputedly representative system of government hardly needs to worry about Congress, probably the least efficient and ineffective legislature of any modern nation, one that arguably personifies the concept of kakistocracy (government by the worst).

If Congress does laboriously override a Court decision, chances are it is one that the Court has invited Congress to overrule because the Court found it impossible to determine either the meaning of congressional language or what the law was supposed to accomplish. But the Court did not hesitate to tell Congress that determining the meaning of constitutional provisions was none of its business when Congress virtually unanimously attempted to undo the Court's religious freedom decision in *Boerne v. Flores*. Determinations of congressional power and authority, said the majority, are the Court's province, not that of legislative kakistocrats.[51] Thirty years earlier, Congress had howled and threatened the Court when it handed down a series of reapportionment decisions that effectively terminated the careers of legislators from grossly overrepresented rural areas in both Congress and the state legislatures.[52] Typically, such congressional blustering amounts to naught but sound and fury signifying nothing. Thus, this same result – nothing – occurred after the Court's two flag-burning decisions, although again an incensed Congress fulminated against the five-member Court majority.[53]

Though SOP models bear only the most incidental relationship to reality (and even that statement arguably grossly overstates their connection), other game theoretic case studies can cast light on past events. Thus, recent analyses

---

[51] 521 U.S. 507 (1997).

[52] *Baker v. Carr*, 369 U.S. 186 (1962); *Gray v. Sanders*, 372 U.S. 368 (1963); *Reynolds v. Sims*, 377 U.S. 533 (1964); *WMCA v. Lomenzo*, 377 U.S. 633 (1964); *Lucas v. Forty-Fourth Colorado Assembly*, 377 U.S. 713 (1964).

[53] *Texas v. Johnson*, 491 U.S. 397 (1989), and *Eichman v. United States*, 496 U.S. 310 (1990). The former declared it unconstitutional for a state to punish flag burners; the latter, a congressional law that sought to do the same.

of *Marbury v. Madison* arguably clarify the strategic choices facing President Jefferson and Chief Justice Marshall.[54] Unfortunately, the validity of generalizing from one particular case remains highly dubious.

The Attitudinal Model

We turn now to the remaining model that scholars use to explain judicial decision making: the attitudinal. It asserts that judges base their decisions on the facts of a case juxtaposed against their personal policy preferences. Theoretically, nothing precludes the application of the attitudinal model to all judges, state and federal, trial and appellate. Nevertheless, the fit of the attitudinal model will be better in situations in which the institutional environment favors unfettered choice, as we will discuss later.

The attitudinal model requires one to evaluate the influence of case facts (i.e., case stimuli), which are central to both the legal and attitudinal models, along with attitudes, which are key only to the attitudinal.

The centrality of case facts hardly needs substantiation. Trial courts and juries must determine whether an accused committed the deeds alleged by the prosecution, or in a civil matter whether the plaintiff has been negligently injured by actions (or nonactions that should have been taken) of the respondent. Self-defense against an attacker is not the same as gratuitous killing of another; residential use of a sound truck at 2:00 A.M. differs from use at a Fourth of July parade; misrepresentation of the quality of purchased goods contrasts with misrepresentation of the character of an elected official.

From the standpoint of attitude theory, behavior may be said to be a function of the interaction between an actor's attitude toward an "object" (i.e., persons, places, institutions, and things) and the actor's attitude toward the situation in which the object is encountered.[55] Insofar as judicial decision making is concerned, attitude objects are the litigants to the lawsuit, and the situations consist of the "facts": that is, what the attitude object was doing, the legal and constitutional context in which the object acted. Research shows that situations explain behavior much better than objects. Indeed, the matter could hardly be otherwise. Responses to questions about the president or students lack meaning unless a context is provided. Students doing what? Rioting in the streets or studying in the library? To a greater extent than attitude objects, situations are subjectively perceived. Judges, as well as others, commonly dispute the facts of a matter.

Notwithstanding, facts matter. Analysis has shown that in the context of a specific situation – for instance, persons allegedly subject to an unreasonable search and seizure – case facts predict more than 75 percent of the Court's

---

[54] Robert Lowry Clinton, "Game Theory, Legal History, and the Origins of Judicial Review," 38 *American Journal of Political Science* 285 (1994), and Jack Knight and Lee Epstein, "On the Struggle for Judicial Supremacy," 30 *Law and Society Review* 87 (1996).

[55] Milton Rokeach, *Beliefs, Attitudes, and Values* (San Francisco: Jossey-Bass, 1968), pp. 112–122.

decisions.[56] Such purely fact-based models suffer from one major deficiency: They do not consider how changing membership changes the Court's decisions. When such a variable is added, explanation improves substantially. Hence, we need to consider the attitudes and values of the participating justices in any analysis of judicial behavior.

We made mention that nothing inherently precludes the attitudinal model from operating across the judicial system. But several characteristics facilitate the model's operation at the Supreme Court level, as mentioned briefly earlier.

(1) The justices are free agents in the sense that they are beholden to none but themselves. They serve for life; therefore, they lack electoral or political accountability. Only one justice was impeached, very early in our history, but the Senate failed to convict him. They are, therefore, essentially untouchable.

(2) They have no ambition for higher office. As Justice Sandra O'Connor said when asked after her confirmation about future positions, "This is it, the end of the line."[57] During the entirety of the twentieth century, only three justices resigned to take other positions. One, Charles Evans Hughes, returned as chief justice fourteen years after his defeat in the 1916 election. A second, James Byrnes, resigned at the behest of President Roosevelt during the darkest days of World War II to assume responsibility for the domestic side of the war effort. The third, Arthur Goldberg, resigned after three years on the Court under the blandishments of President Johnson that he wanted him to help end the Vietnam War as United Nations (UN) ambassador. These people are at the pinnacle of their legal career. Ambition cannot be seen as a plausible influence on their behavior.

(3) The Supreme Court constitutes a court of last resort that determines and controls its own caseload. As a court of last resort, it cannot be judicially overruled. It need not concern itself with a higher authority. And, as we have seen, although Congress has some tools it could use to overturn Court decisions, it rarely does so – especially without a Court invitation. And although docket control does not guarantee that the justices will vote their policy preferences, its absence guarantees they will not. Many meritless cases exist that no self-respecting judge would decide on the basis of personal policy preferences, and so the ability to choose cases allows increased opportunity to make policy by deciding only the most important/controversial/difficult cases. The presence of these three factors minimizes, if not eliminates, the need for the justices to engage in strategic behavior on the merits and, instead, allows them to behave sincerely.

SUMMARY AND CONCLUSIONS

We precede the two major approaches to judicial decision making – the legal and policy-based – with an explanation of what a model is and what its utility is.

---

[56] Jeffrey A. Segal, "Predicting Supreme Court Decisions Probabilistically: The Search and Seizure Cases, 1962, 1981," 78 *American Political Science Review* 891 (1984).

[57] Lawrence Bodine, "Sandra Day O'Connor," 69 *American Bar Association Journal* 1394 (1983), at 1398.

We examine three legal models: mechanical, gravitational, and post-positive. Mechanical jurisprudence requires far more than words and doctrine could ever supply: a correct answer to legal decisions that judges rummage around to find. Alternatively, the post-positive model requires far too little, providing no guidance as to what judges actually do. The gravitational model, which requires a substantial impact of text, intent, precedent, and the like, will be examined throughout the book, but we note for now that precedent is far more likely to be an influence on lower courts than on higher courts.

Two policy-based models – the attitudinal and the rational choice – have been formulated. The judicial rational choice model focuses on the constraints placed on judges by other actors in the judges' environment, whether within the same court, on other courts, or external to the judiciary. Alternatively, the attitudinal model focuses on the impact of the judges' own attitudes and values. As we will see throughout the book, these models will have differential impacts in different situations, with attitudinal considerations dominating where institutional constraints are minimal, as is the situation on the Supreme Court.

3

The Supreme Court in American Legal History

We explained in Chapter 1 why courts in our constitutional system – especially the Supreme Court – have such authoritative policy-making capability and how the powerful Supreme Court makes decisions. In this chapter, we will illustrate manifestations of this capability that have occurred over the course of our history.

BEFORE THE CONSTITUTION

When colonists arrived to settle the New World, they carried from England their heritage, their customs, and their law. English law was predominantly judge-made law. This judge-made law evolved out of local customs that helped local judges decide local disputes. As royal authority grew, Henry II (1154–1189) established royal courts that could issue decisions in the king's name. This structure ultimately required consistent rules throughout the land. Some local customs were dropped, and others spread. Those that survived became the customs common to all England and formally became known as the *common law*.

As in England, statutory authority grew in the New World. The Massachusetts Body of Liberties, adopted in 1641, was New England's first legal code.[1] While establishing a Christian state, the code also guarded against the deprivation of life, liberty, and property "unlesse it be by vertue or equitie of some expresse law;" protected the citizens' "Immunities and priveledges;" and guaranteed to all residents, "whether Inhabitant or forreiner," "the same justice and law." Torture was prohibited for the purpose of obtaining confessions but could nevertheless be used after conviction in order to obtain the names of co-conspirators, but only if the torture was not "Barbarous and inhumane." Note that although protections against involuntary confessions and rules against the

---

[1] The text of the document can be found at a variety of sites on the Web, including http://history. hanover.edu/texts/masslib.htm.

deprivation of life, liberty, and property found their way into the nation's Bill of Rights, protections of our privileges and immunities and guarantees of equal protection of the law did not appear until the passage of the Fourteenth Amendment in 1868.

Statutory authority in colonial times of necessity dealt with slavery, which in the earliest years infected both northern and southern colonies. Africans originally entered the colonies as servants, largely indistinct from indentured servants of other races. But slavery soon established itself and spread. By 1662, Virginia law declared that the children of female slaves would themselves be slaves, codifying the inheritability of this most noxious of institutions.[2] Note should be made that inheritance under the common law passed through the father. If the colonies did not change this rule, the offspring of liaisons between slave owners and slaves, a common occurrence, would be free – a development intolerable to the plantation-dominated South.

Statutory authority was accompanied by judicial review from the mother country via the King's Privy Council. The council struck about 5 percent of the laws challenged before it.[3]

Civil rules dealt with the usual suspects – property, estates, and other economic questions – and criminal laws dealt not just with murder, burglary, and the like, but with blasphemy, witchcraft, and sexual misconduct.[4] Among the most common crimes was drunkenness, but a staggering 38 percent of all prosecutions in seven Massachusetts counties were for fornication: that is, sex between unmarried persons.[5]

Independence

The Declaration of Independence listed the colonists' grievances against the king. Among the charges were that the king limited the right to trial by jury, and "He has made Judges dependent on his Will alone, for the tenure of their offices, and the amount and payment of their salaries."[6]

The newly independent states, loosely bound through the Articles of Confederation (1777), began to replace their colonial charters with written constitutions, documents that laid out the structures of government, the limits

---

[2] Lawrence M. Friedman, *A History of American Law*, 2nd ed. (New York: Simon & Schuster, 1985), pp. 85–86.

[3] Richard Morris, *Studies in the History of American Law*, 2nd ed. (Philadelphia: J. M. Mitchell Co., 1959), p. 62.

[4] Before 1660, Massachusetts executed four Quakers, two adulterers, two people for "buggery," and two witches. The Salem witch trials led to the execution of nineteen more witches. On the former, see Bradley Chapin, *Criminal Justice in Colonial America, 1606–1660* (Athens: University of Georgia Press, 1983), p. 58.

[5] William E. Nelson, *The Americanization of the Common Law* (Cambridge, MA: Harvard University Press, 1975), p. 39.

[6] The Declaration can be found at many sites on the Web, including http://www.archives.gov/exhibit_hall.

on that government, and the rights retained by the people. They did not, however, replace the common law, which continued to govern in the wide areas where legislation was silent.

The Articles themselves said little about judicial power, which was largely decided by the states. Congress would decide boundary disputes between states and had the authority to establish admiralty courts, but that was about it.[7]

Although the critical weaknesses of the Articles (lack of an executive branch, lack of direct taxing power, and others) soon became apparent to all but the most obtuse observer, Shay's Rebellion (1786) forced the issue. Daniel Shay and his armed supporters shut down a variety of Massachusetts state courts to prevent making of debtor judgments against poor farmers. Fearful of mob rule and cognizant of the inability under the Articles to remedy instability's causes or effects, Congress called for a constitutional convention to amend the Articles.

THE NEW CONSTITUTION

The constitutional convention that met in Philadelphia during the sultry summer of 1787 did not produce amendments to the Articles that the states could ratify, but a new constitution that it submitted to the people of the various states for ratification. The proposed constitution remedied many of the problems of the Articles by granting broad (but limited) powers to Congress and by creating both an executive and a judicial branch of government. The judicial branch, the least dangerous branch in Alexander Hamilton's famous phrase, consisted of a Supreme Court plus such other courts as Congress might choose to establish.

The Constitution was soon ratified, and among the first acts of the first Congress was the submission to the states of a proposed Bill of Rights, a condition of several states' ratification. The Bill of Rights set a variety of limitations on the national, but not the state, government. Thus whereas Congress was prohibited, under the First Amendment, from establishing a national religion, states were free, if they chose, to establish a state religion. Indeed, when the Constitution was adopted, only Virginia and Rhode Island guaranteed unqualified religious freedom, whereas nearly half the states had a formally established religion.[8]

That first Congress also passed the Judiciary Act of 1789. Consistently with the federal (part national, part state) nature of the Constitution, the act established thirteen district (trial) courts, essentially one within each state,[9] each court consisting of a judge who resided in that state and held court only within

---

[7] http://www.archives.gov/exhibit_hall.

[8] Note. "Rethinking the Incorporation of the Establishment Clause: A Federalist View," 105 *Harvard Law Review* 1700 (1992).

[9] The thirteen districts included two for territories that were not yet states: the Maine District (carved out of Massachusetts) and the Kentucky District (carved out of Virginia). North Carolina and Rhode Island had not yet ratified the Constitution.

that state. The act also created three regional circuit courts, which had both trial and appellate responsibilities. These circuit courts sat in three-judge panels that consisted of two district court judges and one Supreme Court justice. Finally, the act set membership of the constitutionally created Supreme Court at five associate justices and one chief justice.[10]

Notwithstanding the eminence of the first chief justice, John Jay, the earliest Supreme Court lacked the power and prestige attached to it today. Jay resigned from the Court to become governor of New York and, on renomination to the Court in 1800, declined. Jay and his successor, Oliver Ellsworth, admittedly had very few cases to decide: by our count a grand total of 61, an average of but 5.5 per year. These courts did, however, decide at least two cases of major consequence, one of which boomeranged: *Chisholm v. Georgia.*[11]

The ruling that nonresidents of a state could sue that state in federal court produced a vehement reaction, namely, the adoption of the Eleventh Amendment, which prohibited such suits. This was the first of the very few occasions when the federal courts have had their power curbed. The effect of the amendment necessarily expanded the decision-making capacity of the state courts because nonresidents could now only sue in the courts of the state whose action was the source of complaint. And though this amendment generated little litigation and less controversy over most of its life, that state of affairs changed with the onset of the Rehnquist Court, as we shall see in due course. The other major action of these early Courts was the definitive interpretation of the ex post facto clause, one of the few provisions that expressly limit both the state and the federal government.[12]

THE MARSHALL COURT

Not only did Marshall dominate his Court as no justice since, he also has had a greater effect on the operation of our constitutional system than any other person. It is no stretch to go further and assert that he has had a greater effect on the course of American life – political and otherwise – than anyone else. Under his aegis, the Court established three enduring legacies: (1) judicial supremacy, (2) national supremacy, and (3) a broad interpretation of the scope of national power.

(1) *Marbury v. Madison*, which we discussed in Chapter 1, positioned the federal courts in general, and the Supreme Court in particular, as the authoritative governmental policy makers.

(2) Although Article VI of the Constitution specifically states that federal law is supreme over that of the states, Marshall's insistence that the provision be

---

[10] The Judiciary Act can be found at http://usinfo.state.gov/usa/infousa/facts/democrac/8.htm.
[11] 2 Dallas 419 (1793).
[12] *Calder v. Bull*, 3 Dallas 386 (1798). Laws retroactively criminalizing actions that were innocent when done, as well as laws that heightened punishment after the fact of a crime's omission, are unconstitutional.

given literal force and effect was not taken kindly. The state courts especially objected, arguing basically that though Article VI did make federal law supreme, nothing in the Constitution stated that conflicts between state and federal authority were to be resolved by U.S. Supreme Court, rather than state court, decisions. Construing language of the Judiciary Act of 1789 that authorized the Supreme Court to review decisions of state supreme courts in which they had interpreted and applied provisions of the U.S. Constitution, the Marshall Court ruled that if a state court were free to determine the compatibility of its own laws with federal action, any given constitutional provision, act of Congress, or treaty would likely mean something different in every state. The uniformity of federal law would cease to exist along with the unity of the several states. In reality, if states authoritatively construed federal law, each state would be as fully sovereign as the individual member nations of the United Nations (UN).

In a last-ditch effort, Virginia – which had led the opposition to national supremacy – convicted two persons who sold lottery tickets authorized by the District of Columbia (DC). Virginia forbade lotteries. The convicts appealed to the U.S. Supreme Court. Virginia objected, arguing that the Supreme Court has only original, not appellate, jurisdiction when a state is party to a lawsuit. Marshall, displaying the political astuteness that served him in such good stead when he decided *Marbury v. Madison*, ruled that his Court did have appellate jurisdiction, adding that Congress did not intend lottery sales to occur outside DC. Those who sold lottery tickets acted at their peril. As in *Marbury*, Marshall won the war by losing the battle. Virginia had no court order to disobey.

(3) Three distinct lines of cases illustrate Marshall's strengthening of federal power vis-à-vis the states: (a) a set of decisions that broadly interpreted the interstate commerce clause, (b) a concomitantly broad definition of the necessary and proper clause, and (c) a set of decisions that construed state powers narrowly.

(a) Taking another page from *Marbury v. Madison*, Marshall used the first interstate commerce case, *Gibbons v. Ogden*,[13] to decide much more than necessary to resolve the controversy: the rival licensing of steamboats by New York and Congress. He observed that the Constitution used the word *among* the states in reference to commerce, which he interpreted as "intermingled with them."[14] The intermingling, he said, was a matter of intercourse, rather than simply traffic. Hence, commerce did not stop at a state's boundaries and certainly was not limited to business activities. And though Marshall's language did not preclude state regulation, the supremacy clause would resolve any conflict between that of a state and Congress.

(b) Unlike in the creation of national supremacy, but as in judicial review, Marshall needed only one decision to settle the scope of federal

---

[13] 9 Wheaton 1 (1824).
[14] *Id.* at 194.

power: *M'Culloch v. Maryland.*[15] Two questions required an answer: Did Congress have the power to establish a national bank? If so, could a state tax it? Marshall answered the first question yes, the second no.

Although the Constitution nowhere makes reference to a bank, it does provide for coining and borrowing money, paying government debts, levying taxes, regulating commerce, waging war, and raising and maintaining an army and navy, and all laws that are "necessary and proper" to the foregoing powers. The expressly delegated powers, combined with the necessary and proper clause, said Marshall, imply a power to establish a national bank as an appropriate means whereby the national government may effectively exercise these stated powers. "Let the end be legitimate, let it be within the scope of the constitution, and all means which are appropriate, which are plainly adapted to that end, which are not prohibited, but consist with the letter and spirit of the constitution, are constitutional."[16]

As for state taxation of the bank, Marshall based his response on the supremacy clause, observing that the power to tax involves the power to destroy. A half-century later, the Court evened the playing field, holding that just as the state governments could not tax federal instrumentalities, neither could the federal government tax state employees, property, or activities. This scheme of intergovernmental tax immunity lived on until the eve of World War II. Its only major remnant exempts income from state and municipal bonds from federal taxation.

(c) Marshall's final contribution to American constitutional development also reflected Federalist ideology, which is commonly known as *Hamiltonianism*, after Alexander Hamilton, the major theorist of strong central government. Primarily relying on the constitutional prohibition that the states do nothing to impair "the obligation of contracts," Marshall broadly defined a contract to extend to land grants by asserting that a grant implies a contract, and that the constitutional language does not distinguish among types of contracts. Hence, the state effort to repeal the grant was unconstitutional.

We note in passing that this decision was the first to declare a state law unconstitutional, that its primary beneficiaries were land speculators who had bought virtually all of present-day Alabama and Mississippi for $500,000 by bribing Georgia's kakistocratic[17] legislators, and that the case was not a bona fide "case or controversy," which the Constitution requires a litigant to have before accessing the federal court for redress.[18]

---

[15] 4 Wheaton 316 (1819).

[16] *Id.* at 421.

[17] The opposite of aristocratic: government by the worst.

[18] The case was *Fletcher v. Peck*, 6 Cranch 87 (1810). Both Fletcher and Peck had a nonadversarial interest; both wished the Court to void the repeal of the original land grant. Marshall, true to character, did not allow procedural irregularities to prevent him from deciding the case and thereby writing a major canon of Hamiltonianism into the Constitution. Justice Johnson, in his separate opinion, alludes to the friendly character of the litigation. *Id.* at 147–148. Also see C. Peter McGrath, *Yazoo: Law and Politics in the New Republic* (New York: Norton, 1966).

Marshall subsequently extended the applicability of the contract clause further still, ruling that corporate charters were also protected from state abridgment. These decisions effectively positioned existing (i.e., vested) property rights alongside those that the Constitution specifically prohibited government from abrogating. As we shall see, the Court vastly expanded the protection accorded private property rights after the Civil War – especially those of a corporate and commercial character – through a creative and wholly novel interpretation of the due process clauses.

The State Court Systems

Though Marshall turned federalism into nationalism, his rulings did not deprive the state courts of their business. Since the inception of the Republic state courts have decided the vast majority of cases. Compared with the federal courts, whose subject matter jurisdiction the Constitution strictly specifies, state courts have a much broader range.

But as did the federal system, states divided theirs into trial and appellate courts. An intermediate court of appeals, to which losing litigants could take their case, was not available. If trial court losers sought to appeal, they typically went directly to the state supreme court. In this regard, as in virtually all other structural respects, the state governments largely acted as miniature federal governments. In only one major respect did they tend to differ: As a result of the democratizing trends popularized by President Andrew Jackson and his supporters, newly admitted states elected, rather than appointed, their judges. With the demise of property qualifications for voting and for holding public office, universal white male suffrage became the rule and with it the notion that any male was competent to hold almost any political office. Judgeships, as were other public offices, became subject to partisan election. The only holdouts were the original thirteen states, which retained executive or legislative appointment as their selection method.

States' rights sentiments, a logical outgrowth of the Jeffersonian focus on autonomous local self-government that the democratizing impetus produced by Jackson and his supporters further enhanced, made state courts jealous of their prerogatives and a bulwark against efforts to expand the sphere of federal authority and control.

THE CIVIL WAR ERA

The Marshall Court ended with the death of its chief justice in 1835. Andrew Jackson nominated Roger Taney as his successor and filled five other vacancies on the Supreme Court. No other president since Washington had had an opportunity to appoint a majority of the justices. And though Jackson and his nominees did not share the Hamiltonian orientation of Marshall and the Federalists, by no means did they undo what the Marshall Court had wrought.

The Taney Court

Expectations of Jackson and his supporters that democratization would curtail vested property and commercial interests and expand the sphere of states' rights were largely unrealized. The nominees of Jackson and his successors did not appreciably forgo the use of the policies established by the Marshall Court.

Utilizing the attitudinal model presented in Chapter 2, analysis of the voting behavior of the Taney Court justices from the mid-1840s to the eve of the Civil War in the late 1850s indicates that what divided the justices were various aspects of federalism and various issues relating to property rights, a continuation of the concerns that explain the decisions of the Marshall Court. Interestingly, the justices did not address slavery until the infamous case of *Scott v. Sandford* in 1857.[19] The majority of the cases producing division in the Court concerned the jurisdiction of the federal courts vis-à-vis those of the states, whether Congress or the states should have power to regulate various types of business activity, the scope of the contract clause, the adjudication of title to land in the public domain, patent claims, the scope of the Supreme Court's decisional authority, compensation claims of federal employees, and the finality of juries' verdicts.

Further analysis shows these issues to be interrelated and to reveal a consistent pattern of voting of the Taney Court justices: nationalistic tendencies, coupled with support for business, and vested property rights. Opposed to them were a states' rights, antibusiness, and anti–special privilege orientation. The former comports well with Hamiltonianism, the latter with Jeffersonianism. Hamiltonian justices – a decided majority of those who sat from the mid-1840s to the late 1850s – supported increased power for the federal courts, while opposing those of the states. They also backed federal regulation of business along with strict construction of the contract clause lest the states meddle with vested property rights. Hamiltonians regarded land titles as sacred. These primarily involved Spanish and Mexican land grants in Texas, California, and southern portions of the Louisiana Purchase. Justices inclined toward Jeffersonianism wanted to void these grants and place the land in the public domain. Pioneer farmers – God's chosen people, according to Jefferson – would thereby benefit; speculators would not. With regard to patents, Hamilton himself founded the Society for Establishing Useful Manufactures. And the legacy of *Marbury v. Madison* continued to be a live issue, as the Hamiltonians supported Supreme Court judicial review, and Jeffersonians opposed it.

Although issues of federal employee compensation and the finality of jury verdicts less obviously pertain to a Hamiltonian–Jeffersonian division, the justices' voting indicates that they do. Elitist Hamiltonians viewed public office as the province of the "natural aristocracy" of persons of proven competence. By contrast, the Jeffersonians and their Jacksonian descendants based appointments to federal office on their fatuous belief in the competence of the

---

[19] 60 Howard 393.

"common man," notwithstanding manifest nescience and blatant bigotry. As for jury verdicts, one should not expect a Hamiltonian justice to be particularly respectful of a verdict rendered by a group of locally empaneled jurors selected more or less by lot.

Significant here is not the proportion of the justices who adhered to either of these value systems (i.e., ideologies), but rather the likely fact that they shared alternative ideologies subscribed to by the vast majority of politically active Americans. These value systems, moreover, were ingrained in the culture, traditions, and life experiences of Americans generally.

The Case of *Scott v. Sandford*

The *Scott v. Sandford* decision totally colors the reputation of the Taney Court. Its other actions pale by comparison. The decision precipitated the Civil War and lowered the Court's reputation to its lowest point in history.

Scott, a slave, sought to obtain his freedom on his return to Missouri, a slave state, after several years' sojourn with his master in Wisconsin. He brought suit in a federal trial court alleging that because he and his owner were citizens (residents) of different states, federal jurisdiction existed. When the case reached the Supreme Court, each justice wrote an opinion, with Taney's being dispositive.

We quote key passages from his opinion not only to reveal its blatant racist bigotry, but also to indicate that it voiced the views of a majority of the justices, along with those of millions of Americans. Because no black – slave or free – could be an American citizen, none could sue in a federal court. The reason? At the time of the Constitution's adoption, blacks were considered as a subordinate and inferior class of beings, "who had been subjugated by the dominant race, and whether emancipated or not, yet remained subject to their authority, and had no rights or privileges but such as those who held the power and the government might choose to grant them."[20] Did no constitutional provisions protect them? The same answer – no:

"for more than a century" blacks had been regarded as beings of an inferior order; and altogether unfit to associate with the white race ... and so far inferior, that they had no rights which the white man was bound to respect; and that the negro might justly and lawfully be reduced to slavery for his benefit. He was bought and sold, and treated as an ordinary article of merchandise and traffic, whenever a profit could be made by it. This opinion was at that time fixed and universal in the civilized portion of the white race.[21]

No ifs, ands, or buts here, only pure racist gospel. But might not language in the Declaration of Independence refute the "universal" perception of black

---

[20] *Id.* at 404–405.

[21] *Id.* at 407. If the chief justice's statement applied only to "the civilized portion of the white race," what must have been the attitude of the *uncivilized* portions, segments that certainly applied to Southerners generally, as well as to Irish immigrants in northern states?

inferiority? Specifically, references to "all men" being "created equal" and "endowed by their Creator with certain inalienable rights"? Certainly not, Taney derisively replied. "The language in the Declaration of Independence is equally conclusive."

[I]t is too clear for dispute, that the enslaved African race were not intended to be included, and formed no part of the people who framed and adopted this Declaration; for if the language, as understood in that day, would embrace them, the conduct of the distinguished men who framed the Declaration of Independence would have been utterly and flagrantly inconsistent with the principles they asserted; and instead of the sympathy of mankind, to which they so confidently appealed, they would have deserved and received universal rebuke and reprobation.[22]

Thus, by a vote of 7–2, the justices made it crystal clear that the Constitution formed a government of, by, and for white males alone. The die was cast. It took a civil war to undue the damage. Hostilities began four years later, and three years after they ended, the Fourteenth Amendment was ratified, permanently interring the most shamelessly disgusting decision in the Court's history. Not that its burial ended American racism: far from it. It obviously lives today. Neither the legal nor the ideological mind takes no for an answer. As legalists on both sides of any controversy know, there are many ways to skin a cat. By reformulating a legal issue, losers may live to fight another day. For example, freedom of speech includes freedom not to speak; due process of law also applies to the substance of legislation and governmental action; the right "to be confronted with the witnesses against" the accused does not apply to those accused of molesting young children.

The revulsion felt by large segments of the North occasioned a bottoming out of the Court's power and influence. Congress displayed its contempt by altering its size three times within a decade, all for partisan political purposes. But the Court soon regained some luster. Lincoln appointed five justices whom history highly regards. The American bar, newly organized and increasingly influential, paid it homage. And the justices themselves rarely strayed from the middle of the ideological road, ratifying policies of the other branches rather than initiating its own.

By the 1880s the Court had regained much of its lost prestige and had begun anew to make authoritative policy, in the areas of civil rights and economic regulation in particular.

Civil Rights

After gutting congressional legislation in the mid-1870s designed to protect Southern blacks who exercised the right to vote,[23] the justices addressed the scope of protection the Fourteenth Amendment afforded blacks. Over the

---

[22] *Id.* at 409, 410.
[23] *United States v. Reese*, 92 U.S. 214 (1876), and *United States v. Cruikshank*, 92 U.S. 542 (1876).

dissent of Justice John Marshall Harlan, a former slave owner, the Court voided congressional legislation designed to outlaw discrimination in places of public accommodation. The amendment, wrote the majority, does not extend to private discrimination, only that resulting from deliberate state governmental action.[24]

The decision in the Civil Rights cases did not end the Court's racist focus, of course, notwithstanding the bloodiest war in American history and three constitutional amendments. Instead white supremacy was legitimated and strict segregation under a mass of Jim Crow legislation institutionalized. Both were rationalized and justified under the constitutional doctrine of separate but equal.[25] Application of the doctrine belied its two-dimensional focus. As long as the facilities in question were separate, no attention was paid to whether or not they were equal. No two were.

ECONOMIC REGULATION

With the transition of the economy from agriculture to industry, powerful forces sought to immunize this development from government regulation. In this effort, the Supreme Court proved to be a major proponent. Economic theories justifying the rise and desirability of industrial development, most notably what was known as laissez-faire economics, became wildly popular among capitalists, financiers, businessmen, and others who identified themselves with the gospel of wealth. The Reverend Russell Conwell, THE Billy Graham of the last half of the nineteenth century and past president of Temple University, candidly stated this view:

The number of poor to be sympathized with is very small. To sympathize with a man whom God has punished for his sins, thus to help him when God would still continue a just punishment, is to do wrong, no doubt about it, and we do that more than we help those who are deserving.... Let us remember there is not a poor person in the United States who was not made poor by his own shortcomings, or by the shortcomings of someone else. It is all wrong to be poor, anyhow.[26]

The doctrines the Court formulated to immunize business regulation from adverse governmental action were basically two: (1) substantive due process and (2) the exclusion of mining, manufacturing, and agriculture from the realm of interstate commerce. The former is oxymoronic: a pointedly foolish contradiction in terms. That which for the better portion of a millennium had pertained exclusively to the *procedures* whereby laws were enforced now became applicable to the *substance* of legislation.

---

[24] *The Civil Rights Cases*, 109 U.S. 3 (1883).
[25] *Plessy v. Ferguson*, 163 U.S. 537 (1896).
[26] Quoted in A. T. Mason, *Free Government in the Making*, 2d ed. (New York: Oxford University Press, 1956), p. 565.

Substantive Due Process

Despite the fact that economic regulation of prices and wages and, indeed, social welfare legislation itself, predate the Constitution by more than a century, and despite the fact that no one had heretofore suggested that such legislation, unlike debtor relief laws, was among the abuses that led to replacing the Articles with the Constitution, the New York Court of Appeals became the first to suggest that the due process clause (in this case, the state's) could be used to protect economic liberties. The case, *Wynehamer v. People*,[27] struck down New York's prohibition statute on the ground that it deprived saloon keepers of their property without due process of law. The state supreme court found nothing objectionable in the way the legislature enacted the law, nor in the procedure whereby it was enforced. It simply did not like the fact that the law put saloon keepers out of business.

At the federal level, separate clauses prohibit the states (Fourteenth Amendment) and the federal government (Fifth Amendment) from depriving persons of life, liberty, or property without due process of law. Although the Supreme Court eventually adopted the *Wynehamer* doctrine to void state (and occasionally federal) economic regulations,[28] it focused primarily on "liberty," secondarily on "property." "Life" did not enter the equation. Given our penchant for violence and gun ownership and the highest homicide rate year in and year out in the supposedly civilized world, ranking life as important as liberty or property would have been completely alien to the American way of life.

The justices construed liberty to include the right to contract freely with others. To make this new freedom of contract an even more effective protector of wealth, the Court of its own volition, without any argument whatsoever, decreed corporations to be "persons" entitled to due process.[29] With doctrine now established – notwithstanding its utter novelty and divergence from precedent – the Court plunged full speed ahead, striking down maximum hour and minimum wage laws, statutes barring employers from prohibiting employees from joining unions, and price regulations. Occasionally, the justices would uphold such social and economic legislation, particularly when it concerned the conditions of women's work or activities of which the justices disapproved, such as gambling.

The Constriction of Interstate Commerce

The exclusion of major economic activity from the scope of the commerce clause did not mean that the states could regulate it. As we have just seen, the treatment of due process as a substantive limit on government regulation, coupled with

[27] 13 New York 378 (1856).
[28] *Allgeyer v. Louisiana*, 165 U.S. 1 (1897).
[29] *Santa Clara County v. Southern Pacific R. Co.*, 118 U.S. 394 (1886).

freedom of contract, immunized business from hostile policy making by either the states or the federal government.

An 1895 decision nicely illustrates.[30] It pertained to the enforcement of the Sherman Antitrust Act of 1890, which made "every contract, combination . . . or conspiracy in restraint of trade or commerce among the several states, or with foreign nations . . . illegal."[31] The Department of Justice brought the case to break up the sugar trust, one company that through acquisitions had acquired control of 98 percent of the nation's sugar refining. Conceding that the sugar trust was an illegal monopoly, the majority, with only one justice in dissent, nonetheless ruled that Congress had no power to suppress monopolies. These were a matter for state regulation. How states could regulate them, given substantive due process and freedom of contract, was another matter, of course. But Congress could regulate interstate commerce. Nevertheless, as pointed out earlier, manufacturing precedes commerce and is not a part of it. Such monopolies affect commerce only indirectly.

Occasionally, the Court upheld an antibusiness regulation. In 1905, it ruled that price fixing at a stockyard did violate the Sherman Act even though the fixing occurred within a single state. Why? Because, said the justices, it was part of "a current of commerce among the States."[32] Other businesses did not benefit from the Court's laissez-fairism because their activity did not comport with the Puritan ethic (e.g., interstate sale of lottery tickets). But such rulings were exceptions to the rule; much more typical were the child labor cases. In 1916, Congress prohibited the interstate shipment of goods made by children younger than age fourteen or those younger than sixteen years old who worked more than forty-eight hours per week. Uh, uh, said the Court: Production of goods antecedes commerce. The justices distinguished child labor from lotteries for the nonsensical and mind-boggling reason that the former was not harmful; lotteries were. In reaction, Congress imposed a 10 percent tax on the profits of firms using child labor. The passage of the income tax amendment appeared to support Congress's action. Not so, said the Court: The tax was not a tax, but rather a "penalty."[33] Hence, where child labor was concerned, heads the employer won; tails the kids lost.

CHANGES IN THE STATE COURTS

Progressive era reforms occurred between the 1890s and World War I. Along with the rise of the Populist Political Party and the split in the Republican Party between the Old Guard and the Teddy Roosevelt–led Bull Moosers, these and other reformist elements sought to lessen, if not remove, the causes of government corruption, especially at the state and local levels. The income

[30] *United States v. E. C. Knight Co.*, 156 U.S. 1.
[31] *Id.* at 6.
[32] *Swift and Co. v. United States*, 196 U.S. 375, at 398–399.
[33] *Hammer v. Dagenhart*, 247 U.S. 251(1918); *Bailey v. Drexel Furniture Co.* 259 U.S. 20 (1922).

tax amendment, the direct election of U.S. senators, prohibition, and women's suffrage were all manifestations of this reformist impulse. States adopted the initiative, referendum, and recall, which allowed the public to vote directly on policies of major concern and to remove unresponsive officials before the expiration of their term of office. States, particularly those most subject to Progressive era reforms (the Midwest and the Great Plains), abolished partisan election of their judges and replaced that system with nonpartisan elections.

Formally, this change merely removed party identification from the judicial ballot. Though this lessened the impact of partisan political behavior in judicial elections, it did not prove to be an unmixed blessing. "Name" candidates (i.e., candidates who bore at least the surname of famous political figures) began to surface. Qualifications became a secondary consideration, if they had any effect at all, for such candidates. They rather hoped that the electorate would confuse them with their highly regarded namesake. Not infrequently this occurred, except in elections in which an incumbent was running and was identified as such. Typically, no name proved more popular than *incumbent judge*, assuming, of course, that no scandal had besmirched the incumbent's reputation.

This behavior provided a further manifestation of the unintended counter-productive consequences that frequently follow the adoption of governmental reforms. An additional factor also minimized the effectiveness of nonpartisan judicial elections. Many states allowed the governor, with or without the approval of the state senate, to fill judicial vacancies that occurred between elections. Such appointees were then permitted to appear as *incumbent judge* on the ballot at the next election.

Not all states adopted nonpartisan elections. Where powerful political machines held sway – as in New York, Pennsylvania, and Illinois – and in one-party areas – such as the South – the dominant political party opposed the change because it would open the door for candidates of the minor party to gain election, because the public would not be able to determine without a party label which candidates were in which political party.

THE NEW DEAL

Laissez-faire remained in the saddle, riding herd on human beings until the latter years of the Great Depression, notwithstanding New Deal legislation proposed by President Franklin Roosevelt and enacted by Democratic Congresses that established codes of fair competition, farm subsidies, and maximum and minimum prices and hour and wage standards in the coal industry. The four conservative justices – James McReynolds, Willis Van Devanter, George Sutherland, and Pierce Butler – along with the moderate Owen Roberts and sometimes Chief Justice Hughes as well voted to void efforts to alleviate the effects of the Depression. The objections of the liberals – Benjamin Cardozo, Louis Brandeis, and Harlan Stone – proved unavailing.

After his landslide reelection in 1936, Roosevelt proposed a so-called Court-packing plan that would have allowed him to appoint a new justice for every judge older than seventy who did not resign. This would have increased the Court's size to fifteen. The plan received little support from either the public or Congress as both continued to adhere to the insipidly childish myth of a neutral judiciary. However, in the spring of 1937, the three liberals garnered the votes of the two moderates in a case challenging a state minimum wage law for women and thereby undid forty years of freedom of contract policy making.

The Constitution does not speak of freedom of contract. It speaks of liberty and prohibits the deprivation of liberty without due process of law. In prohibiting that deprivation the Constitution does not recognize an absolute and uncontrollable liberty. . . . Liberty under the Constitution is thus necessarily subject to the restraints of due process, and regulation which is reasonable in relation to its subject and is adopted in the interests of the community is due process.[34]

Two weeks later, by the same vote the Court upheld the National Labor Relations Act, which outlawed unfair labor practices and recognized the right of labor to bargain collectively. The Court ruled that a steel company headquartered in Pennsylvania, with mines, warehouses, and factories in eight other states – mirabile dictu – actually affected interstate commerce. Near the end of May, a third identical 5–4 vote declared the Social Security Act to be within Congress's tax powers. A final nail was driven into the coffin of laissez-faire when, at the end of the term, Justice Van Devanter resigned. Roosevelt would have his first appointee, and the shaky 5–4 margin would increase to 6–3. Before he died eight years later, Roosevelt would seat seven new justices on the Court, excluding the promotion of Stone to the chief justiceship and the abbreviated service of James Byrnes (1941–1942), who resigned to direct the domestic war effort of World War II.

With this string of appointments, the Court shifted its policy-making focus from economic matters to the issues of criminal procedure and civil liberties. The Court effectively washed its hands of constitutional supervision of the economy by systematically upholding such activity and instead involved itself only in the interpretation of statutory language and administrative regulations.

SUPREME COURT SUPERVISION OF STATE COURTS

Notwithstanding the supremacy clause and the willingness of the Supreme Court to overturn state court decisions upholding antibusiness economic regulation, the state courts basically functioned without meaningful federal supervision for most of their history, except when their decisions infringed on vested economic rights. The primary link – and for much of our history the only link – between the state courts and the federal courts connected the state and U.S. Supreme Courts. A decision of the Marshall Court had held, compatibly with

---

[34] *West Coast Hotel Co. v. Parrish*, 300 U.S. 379, at 391.

the language of the Constitution, that the Bill of Rights bound only the federal government, not the state governments. Hence, civil liberties and criminal
procedure were areas in which the state courts could – and did – do as they
pleased without Supreme Court oversight.

Comity and the Abstention Doctrine

Adding to the lack of oversight is a system of comity limiting federal court involvement in state affairs, the origins of which antedate the nineteenth century.
The effect of comity has been the development of practices that further ensure
state court autonomy, the chief element today of which is the abstention doctrine. It states that the Supreme Court will not intrude itself into ongoing state
court proceedings, notwithstanding the presence of a federal question. Historically, the Court implemented the abstention doctrine with a rule that assumed
that a state court decision intermixed with questions of federal law rested "on
an adequate and independent state ground" and, as such, raised no question
within the Supreme Court's jurisdiction. We will see later in this chapter that the
Burger Court changed this rule to admit of Supreme Court review of state court
decisions with which it disagreed, thus giving the lie to its asserted principled
deference to considerations of federalism.

The Nationalization of the Bill of Rights

Paving the way for closer scrutiny of state court decisions was the Court's
broadened definition of due process to include various provisions of the Bill
of Rights. Starting shortly after the end of World War I, the justices began to
incorporate the various guarantees of the First Amendment – for example, those
related to freedom of speech, press, and assembly – as integral components of
the "liberty" persons could not be deprived of without due process of law.
Note that the contents of the First Amendment pertain to the substance of
government action, not to the procedures used to enforce and apply the law.
Hence, the justices had created a new variety of substantive due process that by
the eve of World War II had replaced the economic one. During the 1960s, in
the heyday of the liberal Warren Court, the justices applied most of the other
provisions of the Bill of Rights to the states. These other provisions, however,
do pertain to process rather than substance (e.g., self-incrimination, search and
seizure, double jeopardy, right to counsel, trial by jury).

   This incorporation of the Bill of Rights into the due process clause meant
that the phrase *due process* included virtually all the words of the Bill of Rights.
The effect tremendously broadened the range of cases subject to Supreme Court
review. And inasmuch as the states generally gave short shrift to freedom of communication (the First Amendment) and to the various procedural guarantees
of the Bill of Rights, a very substantial number of state court decisions were
overturned, though not without vociferous objection from the states and their
anti–civil libertarian supporters. But the Warren Court paid such complaints

no more heed than its predecessors did to negative reaction to their economic decisions or its successors did to the outrage attending *Bush v. Gore*.

Doctrinally, the Court adopted a presumption opposite of that governing economic legislation that applied to federal as well as state action affecting civil liberty and criminal procedure. Action that facially abridges a provision of the Bill of Rights, restricts access to normal political processes (e.g., the right to vote), or unreasonably discriminates against "insular minorities" (e.g., blacks, women,[35] juveniles, aliens, illegitimates) does not receive the presumption of constitutionality. Instead, such action is considered unconstitutional unless the governmental unit in question can demonstrate to the Court's satisfaction that the action is "narrowly tailored" to sustain "a compelling governmental interest." Where women, juveniles, and illegitimates are concerned, the action need only be "substantially" related to an "important governmental interest." Obviously, important governmental interests outnumber those that are compelling, and more activities can be substantially related to an objective than those that are narrowly tailored. But beyond this, these words and phrases lack content, as is par for the course of legal language. The presumption of unconstitutionality and the tests discussed apply to federal as well as state and local governmental action.

FIRST AMENDMENT FREEDOMS

The Court did not have particular occasion to decide cases involving freedom of communication before World War I. Other than in relation to the infamous Alien and Sedition Acts, which expired when Jefferson became president, Congress did not particularly legislate on First Amendment freedoms earlier, and state legislation did not become subject to Supreme Court review until the 1920s, as mentioned. Early federal legislation concerned subversive activities, in response to which the Court formulated the clear and present danger doctrine, which in its current guise prohibits government to "forbid or proscribe advocacy of the use of force or of law violation except where such advocacy is directed to inciting or producing imminent lawless action and is likely to incite or produce such action."[36] This is a high standard for prosecutors to meet – at least verbally. But not all communication is protected. Obscenity, fighting words, and libel are not protected because the Court considers them to lack "redeeming social value." At the other extreme, the justices generally accord political speech more protection than that dealing with other subjects. Decisions of the Warren, Burger, and Rehnquist Courts have extended the First Amendment to cover symbolic speech (e.g., demonstrations, flag burning), the right to silence (e.g., nondisclosure of membership lists, not saluting the flag), and commercial communication (e.g., advertising).

---

[35] One may question the inclusion of women as an "insular minority," but as we pointed out in Chapter 1, the Court creates its own dictionary when it finds it convenient to do so.

[36] *Brandenburg v. Ohio*, 395 U.S. 444 (1969), at 447.

Religious Freedom

Historically, among First Amendment freedoms, the free exercise of religion has been least subject to government restriction. Indeed, individuals acting under religious auspices may engage in certain otherwise illegal activities. Hence, door-to-door religious solicitations trump homeowner privacy rights; nor may communities require a license for those so engaged. Courts may not ascertain the truth or falsity of religious beliefs, bizarre and unconventional though they may be. Thus, televangelists who guarantee a cure for most every ailment known – including those medically incurable – may not be prosecuted for false advertising, fraud, or violation of broadcasting regulations unless government can prove them insincere. The Amish need not send their children to high school. No one may be compelled to salute the flag or display a state-mandated ideological message inimical to his or her religious beliefs (e.g., license plate slogans). Individuals may not be denied unemployment compensation because they are fired for refusing to work on their sabbath. Congress may constitutionally permit religious institutions to discriminate purposefully against women, ethnic minorities, or nonbelievers (e.g., a male-only priesthood, no black members). Of course, not all religious action is protected. Bigamy is a crime whether or not one is Mormon; Indians can be prosecuted for using peyote in their religious ceremonies.

As a result of a decision by the conservative Rehnquist Court that held that laws of general applicability (e.g., no use of peyote) could be applied to religious activities even though such laws were not narrowly tailored to a compelling governmental interest, Congress enacted the Religious Freedom Restoration Act in 1993, which reimposed the strict scrutiny standard: no governmental restriction of religion unless it furthered a compelling governmental interest and did so in the least restrictive fashion. For a Republican Congress to take umbrage at a conservative Supreme Court decision is virtually unprecedented. Moreover, not a single member of the House of Representatives and only three senators voted against the bill. Notwithstanding, when the challenged law reached the Court, six justices disdainfully declared it unconstitutional – not because of anything particularly related to religion – but because Congress, said the majority, wantonly trampled on the Court's prerogatives and thereby violated the separation of powers. Brandishing *Marbury v. Madison*, the majority imperiously asserted that it alone possessed the authority to construe the Constitution.[37] As we explain in a later section of this chapter, we view the Rehnquist Court's action as a function of its hostility to Congress as a branch of government rather than as animus toward religion or drug use.

The other First Amendment guarantee pertaining to religion is the establishment clause. Echoing Thomas Jefferson's view that it created a "wall of separation" between church and state, the Warren Court voided organized classroom prayer and devotional Bible readings. Fundamentalists in the Bible Belt expressed outrage. A Georgia congressman declared that the Court first

---

[37] *City of Boerne v. Flores*, 521 U.S. 507 (1997).

"put the n__ in the schools – now they put God out."[38] The Court, however, has persistently condemned sectarian influences in public schools (e.g., school-sponsored prayers at graduation ceremonies and football games), while permitting government aid to the secular programs of religious schools (e.g., bus transportation, lunches, loans, tuition tax credits, and, most recently, vouchers). But the Court does not require the provision of such aid (e.g., the exclusion of devotional theology from a roster of subsidized courses of study).[39]

CRIMINAL PROCEDURE

Provisions in the Fourth, Fifth, Sixth, and Eighth Amendments contain the heart of the protections afforded persons against arbitrary police and law enforcement tactics. We limit our discussion to the most important provisions of each of these amendments, as we discuss them in greater detail in Chapter 6 (Criminal Procedure).

The Fourth Amendment prohibits unreasonable searches and seizures. A Court-created exclusionary rule prevents such evidence from being used against the accused. Warrants issued by a judicial officer are generally required to conduct a search. The police must show probable cause that a crime has been committed, and the warrant must describe the place to be searched or the persons to be seized. Exceptions to the warrant requirement exist, for example, searches incident to an arrest or where seized items are in plain view.

The Fifth Amendment's protection against self-incrimination prevents coerced, or otherwise involuntarily made, confessions. Physical, as well as psychological, coercion is prohibited. Difficulty in determining the facts leading up to confessions caused the liberal Warren Court to formulate the *Miranda* warnings, from a case of the same name. Police must inform suspects before to any custodial interrogation that (1) they have the right to remain silent; (2) that anything they say may be used against them; and (3) that they have the right to an attorney, free if they cannot afford one.

The Sixth Amendment's guarantee of the right to an attorney's counsel antedated the application of the Fourth and Fifth Amendments to the states. In 1932, the justices required that indigent defendants be provided with an attorney under certain circumstances, for instance, if they were minors or were accused of a capital offense. Subsequently, the Court ruled that indigents must be provided counsel in all felony cases. The conservative Burger Court went further still and banned jailing any unrepresented indigent for any offense.[40] This decision was one-upped by the Rehnquist Court, which ruled that counsel is required in any case in which a jail sentence is merely possible.

Synonymous with the Eighth Amendment is the death penalty. Although capital punishment is specifically referenced in several constitutional provisions, the

---

[38] Quoted in Fred Friendly and Martha Elliott, *The Constitution: That Delicate Balance* (New York: Random House, 1984), p. 109.
[39] *Locke v. Davey*, U.S. (2004).
[40] *Argersinger v. Hamlin*, 407 U.S. 25 (1972).

Burger Court ruled it unconstitutional in 1972, objecting to the standardless discretion allowed jurors at the time. In response to the Court's decision, thirty-five
states reimposed the death penalty, some mandating it for first-degree murder,
others imposing guidelines. In reaction, in 1976, the Court ruled mandatory
sentences unconstitutional, but otherwise had no further objections per se.

EQUAL PROTECTION

With the formulation of the separate but equal doctrine, discussed previously,
the equal protection clause became a dead letter for black Americans. Not until
1954 did the Court temper its and America's racist hypocrisy by overruling
the separate but equal doctrine, replacing it with a mandate to desegregate
public facilities – especially schools – "with all deliberate speed."[41] Mindful
that its decision almost occasioned a second civil war, evidenced by a vogue
in hooded sheets and burning crosses, the Court gave full responsibility to
the local federal district courts to apply the all-deliberate-speed mandate. The
"Fifty-Eight Lonely Men" charged with doing so tried, sometimes to the best
of their ability, sometimes not, to follow the Supreme Court's mandate,[42] in
each case with little impact. For the next fifteen years, the Court effectively
ducked school desegregation before it ruled that schools were to be immediately
desegregated.

Note that the Court required desegregation, not integration. The two terms
are by no means synonymous, the media's usage to the contrary notwithstanding. The constitutional wording, as are virtually all constitutional guarantees, is
negatively phrased: no state may "deny to any person . . . the equal protection of
the laws." Accordingly, racially distinct public institutions and programs were
to be dismantled. The Constitution does not require that they microcosmically
reflect the racial and ethnic composition of the community or area in which
they operate (i.e., quotas). That would be integration. The only exception occurs when a court orders quotas to remedy past unconstitutional discrimination.
Once racial exclusiveness is ended, so also are quotas.

Desegregation in the South did not produce desegregation in the North.
Violations of equal protection require purposeful governmental action. Thus,
private discrimination is beyond equal protection, but Congress may constitutionally outlaw it on such bases as the interstate commerce clause – for example, places of public accommodation (hotels, restaurants, etc.) – or spending for
the general welfare – for example, educational institutions, business subsidies,
and government contracts. The states may similarly exceed the requirements
of equal protection through their police powers: that is, action to promote the
public health, welfare, morals, safety, and/or convenience. Accordingly, discrimination that is only the unintended effect of governmental action or that occurs

---

[41] *Brown v. Board of Education*, 347 U.S. 484 (1954); 349 U.S. 294 (1955).
[42] J. W. Peltason, *58 Lonely Men* (Urbana: University of Illinois Press, 1961). Also see Gerald
Rosenberg, *The Hollow Hope: Can Courts Bring About Social Change* (Chicago: University of
Chicago Press, 1991).

without any governmental action is de facto only (i.e., a civil service exam that minorities pass at lower rates than whites, or preferential hiring of veterans for civil service positions, thus discriminating against women), unlike that which is de jure (i.e., a result of purposeful or deliberate government action that is intended to discriminate, such as mandated racially separate public schools).

Affirmative Action

In the absence of purposeful discrimination, government may, however, take voluntary (i.e., affirmative) action to alleviate the presence of de facto discrimination. As described in the Supreme Court's *Bakke* decision, such action (1) may only set goals, not quotas; (2) race (or later sex) may be only one among a number of factors that determine eligibility for the relevant program; (3) the program must serve a compelling governmental interest; and (4) it must be narrowly tailored to remedy past evidence of discrimination.[43] Some lower courts, state as well as federal, have nevertheless construed precedent to forbid affirmative action. Thus, the Fifth Circuit ruled that race could not be used as a factor in university decisions, a decision that the 2003 University of Michigan cases overturned.[44]

Given the racism ingrained in the American way of life, sauce for the black goose is not sauce for the white gander. Affirmative action programs – with or without quotas – that benefit whites do not violate the equal protection clause. Thus, public educational institutions typically give preference to the offspring of alumni. The fact that the vast majority are white makes no difference. Seniority systems may constitutionally contain a last-hired, first-fired provision. The fact that this disadvantages blacks and other minorities – and quite possibly women – is just too bad. States may subsidize suburban school students much more than those who live in urban ghettos or rural slums.

Apart from affirmative action, American racism has lost much of its zing since the days of white supremacy and Jim Crow policies. Congress has enacted a number of civil rights laws outlawing discrimination (sex as well as race) in places of public accommodation, in voting, and in some types of housing. Although the Court delayed termination of the most pathological aspect of racism – interracial marriage (miscegenation) – for thirteen years after it overturned the separate but equal doctrine, when it did so it ruled emphatically, declaring such laws a violation of both equal protection and due process in a most felicitously titled case: *Loving v. Virginia*.[45]

Sex and Other Discrimination

Notwithstanding what the Framers of the Fourteenth Amendment may have intended, the Burger and Rehnquist Courts have ruled that women, aliens,

[43] *Bakke v. California*, 438 U.S. 265 (1978).
[44] *Grutter v. Bollinger*, 156 L. Ed. 2d 304 (2003), and *Gratz v. Bollinger*, 156 L. Ed. 2d 257 (2003).
[45] 388 U.S. 1 (1967), at 527, 480.

illegitimates, the mentally ill, the physically handicapped, and the elderly also may not be subject to unreasonably discriminatory governmental action. The Warren Court had added indigents and malapportioned state legislatures to this list in the 1960s. Though cases involving these groups, except aliens, do not receive the scrutiny accorded instances of purposeful racial discrimination, all receive judicial inspection of instances of alleged discrimination. The Warren Court, for example, viewed women "as the center of home and family life" and, as such, properly subject to protective disabling legislation (e.g., exemption from jury duty, notwithstanding the right to an impartial jury). Not until 1975 – over the dissent of Justice Rehnquist – did the Court admit that "no longer is the female destined solely for the home and the rearing of family, and only the male for the marketplace and the world of ideas."[46]

Since the mid-1970s the Court has decided a steady stream of gender-related cases. It voided the male-only admission policies of a public southern college, construed the congressional prohibition against sex discrimination to apply to same-sex workplace harassment, and made employers vicariously liable for their employees' conduct. But by no means have all recent decisions favored women. The same Rehnquist five who decided *Bush v. Gore* declared the Violence against Women Act unconstitutional. The act authorized victims of rape, domestic violence, and other sexually motivated crimes to sue their attacker in federal court. Nothing in the Constitution gives Congress the power to so legislate, said the majority, although thirty-six states joined the brief supporting the law, and only one (Alabama) opposed it.[47]

THE RIGHT TO PRIVACY

Though a number of constitutional provisions bear on privacy, such as search and seizure, self-incrimination, and First Amendment freedoms, none does so explicitly. Nonetheless, the Warren Court saw fit to establish such a self-standing right in its landmark decision in *Griswold v. Connecticut*, in which the justices voided "an uncommonly silly law" (according to Justice Stewart) that made it a crime for any person – including a married couple – to use, assist, or counsel others to use "any drug, medicinal article or instrument for the purpose of preventing conception."[48] Recognizing the unprecedented character of its decision, the majority stated that "specific guarantees in the Bill of Rights have penumbras, formed by emanations from those guarantees that help give them life and substance," from which they concluded:

We deal with a right of privacy older than the Bill of Rights – older than our political parties, older than our school system. Marriage is a coming together for better or for worse, hopefully enduring, and intimate to the degree of being sacred. It is an association

---

[46] *Hoyt v. Florida*, 368 U.S. 57 (1961), at 62, and *Stanton v. Stanton*, 421 U.S. 7, at 14–15.
[47] *United States v. Morrison*, 146 L. Ed. 2d 658 (2000).
[48] 381 U.S. 479 (1965).

that promotes a way of life, not causes; a harmony in living, not political faiths; a bilateral loyalty, not commercial or social projects. Yet it is an association for as noble a purpose as any involved in our prior decisions.[49]

The Court has positioned associational privacy above human equality where truly private organizations are concerned. "Members only" policies are thereby constitutional so long as they are not hung on the doors of places of public accommodations or large-membership all-male service clubs. Consequently, the B'nai B'rith need not accept *goyim* (gentiles) or the Knights of Columbus non-Catholics. The Society of Mayflower Descendants may deny membership to members of the Mafia, and the Daughters of the American Revolution may exclude the significant others of those who invaded Iraq in 1991 or 2003. For those engaged in truly private affairs – those characterized by social, sexual, racial, and religious exclusiveness – snobbery, if you will, is constitutionally protected.

Abortion

The conservative Burger Court established the right to abortion in 1973 in *Roe v. Wade*.[50] Though its original scope has been somewhat narrowed, the right of a woman to an abortion was explicitly reaffirmed in *Planned Parenthood v. Casey*.[51] Decisions since have focused on abortion procedures and the efforts of opponents to disrupt abortion clinics. The right itself, a classic example not only of substantive due process, but also of judicial legislation, is located among the liberties protected by due process. The right, atypical of most, exemplifies a rarity among court-made rules: Its application is absolutely clear. Relying on the common law and the plain meaning of the operative constitutional word *persons*, the *Roe* Court ruled that the right to life protects only persons, and that personhood begins at birth. When life begins – whether at conception, implantation, or some later point – is simply irrelevant constitutionally.

Though one may correctly argue that an all but delivered fetus is better endowed with potential life than a person born acephalously, a raving maniac, or a senescent victim of Alzheimer's disease, and that the Court's equation of personhood with birth is arbitrary, indisputably the latter have been born and fetuses, by definition, have not.

Homosexuality

Not all activities labeled private have had constitutional protection, however. In one of its last decisions, *Bowers v. Hardwick*, the Burger Court distinguished conventional sexual activities from those engaged in by consenting adult homosexuals. Only choices fundamental to heterosexual conduct warranted constitutional protection: marriage, procreation, child rearing, and

---

[49] *Id.* at 484, 486.
[50] 410 U.S. 113.
[51] 505 U.S. 833 (1992).

family relationships. Although the law at issue flatly banned oral and anal sex regardless of marital status or sexual orientation, the majority rewrote the statute to apply only to homosexuals and, as so construed, justified its ruling because "proscriptions against that conduct have ancient roots" and at the time of the adoption of the Fourteenth Amendment, "all but five of the 37 States in the union had criminal sodomy laws."[52] Of course, laws prohibiting interracial marriage have equally "ancient roots." Yet the Court unconstitutionalized them, as mentioned previously.

More recently, the Court, over the dissent of the three most conservative justices (Scalia, Thomas, and Rehnquist), voided a Colorado amendment that (1) repealed laws protective of gays and (2) prohibited their future reenactment. The resulting disqualification, said the majority, is jurisprudentially unprecedented. The amendment does not deprive gays of special rights; it "imposes a special disability on those persons alone." The "disadvantage is born of animosity" that the Constitution prohibits.[53]

And most recently, the Court – by the same alignment as in the Colorado case – overruled its decision in *Bowers v. Hardwick*. The prevailing majority opinion held that the private sexual activities of consenting adults were no business of government and that all antisodomy laws unconstitutionally violate the liberty of gays and lesbians – to say nothing of the laws of states such as Alabama, Florida, Idaho, Michigan, Utah, and Virginia that criminalize the liberty of heterosexuals who engage in oral or anal sex.[54]

The Right to Die

As in the examples of abortion, marriage, and family rights, no constitutional language specifies a right to die. Nonetheless, the Court held that persons who make their wishes clearly known have a constitutional right to terminate life-sustaining care: "The principle that competent persons have a constitutionally protected liberty interest in refusing unwanted medical treatment may be inferred from our prior decisions."[55] However, the right to die does not extend to assisted suicide[56]; the distinction is the tacit removal of support versus the active seeking of death.

THE SUPREME COURT AND THE DISTRIBUTION OF POWER

The Court's focus on civil liberties, criminal procedure, and civil rights during the last half of the twentieth century has not precluded it from addressing other

---

[52] *Bowers v. Hardwick*, 478 U.S. 186 (1986), at 192, 193.

[53] *Romer v. Evans*, 517 U.S. 620 (1996), at 631, 632, 633. But the Rehnquist five did rule successfully that freedom of association allowed the Boy Scouts to deny membership to gays. *Boy Scouts of America v. Dale*, 147 L. Ed. 2d 554 (2000).

[54] *Lawrence v. Texas*, 156 L. Ed. 2d 208 (2003).

[55] *Cruzan v. Missouri Health Dept.*, 497 U.S. 261 (1990), at 278.

[56] *Washington v. Glucksberg*, 521 U.S. 702 (1997), and *Vacco v. Quill*, 521 U.S. 793 (1997).

issue areas, such as economic regulation, the supervision of the lower federal courts, and federal–state relations. But lest those matters overshadow others, we discuss five major decisions that pertain to the Court's role as arbiter among the three branches of the federal government and with the states.

The Japanese Internment Cases

Two months after the Japanese attack on Pearl Harbor, President Roosevelt – at the urging of West Coast military authorities and the California governor, Earl Warren (soon to become chief justice) – issued an executive order for the removal of all 110,000 persons of Japanese ancestry who resided west of the Rocky Mountains, whether citizen (most of them) or alien, and their relocation to hastily constructed isolated camps. Congress ratified the president's order. The action did not apply to Japanese Americans in Hawaii, notwithstanding that a greater proportion of those residing in Hawaii were aliens and that the Japanese had attacked Hawaii itself at Pearl Harbor. Whereas the Hawaiian Japanese performed the "stoop" and unskilled labor on which Hawaii's economy depended, those on the West Coast – particularly in California – provided unwelcome competition for the native-born poor whites who fled to California from Oklahoma, Kansas, Texas, and other Dust Bowl states adversely affected by the Great Depression of the 1930s.

The program remained in effect through the war years notwithstanding that no charges of disloyalty or subversion were filed against any person of Japanese ancestry. In what typifies much military intelligence, the army asserted that the absence of subversive activity was evidence that such would soon occur. It is also noteworthy that many Japanese Americans served their country in segregated units, garnering disproportionate awards for combat bravery.

In the key decision, *Korematsu v. United States*, the Supreme Court upheld Japanese detention. The majority declared itself "unable to conclude that it was beyond the war power of Congress and the Executive to exclude those of Japanese ancestry from the West Coast area at the time they did."[57] Rationalizing its decision, the majority further stated that though "all legal restrictions which curtail the civil rights of a single racial group are immediately suspect, that is not to say that [they] . . . are unconstitutional." Denying that racism had any influence on the removal order, the majority further rationalized, "Pressing public necessity may sometimes justify the existence of such restrictions; racial antagonism never can."[58]

The decision remains good law. A mere allegation of military necessity suffices to warrant the summary incarceration of any individual or group without any judicial determination of wrongdoing whatsoever. Indeed, during the Persian Gulf War, Arab Americans expressed fear that hysteria could subject them to a similar relocation. But officials denied that any such plans were afoot.

[57] 323 U.S. 214 (1944), at 217–218.
[58] *Id.* at 216.

Significantly, said officials did not suggest that any such plans would be unconstitutional. After the September 11 attacks President Bush ordered any noncitizen suspected of terrorist activity to be tried by a special military tribunal. Military officers, dependent on their superiors for promotion, act as judge and jury. Only a two-thirds vote of the tribunal members suffices to convict and to impose any sentence they please, except death, which requires a unanimous decision, as dictated by Department of Defense regulations. The accused has no right to confront his or her accusers or see the evidence against; he or she cannot appeal a conviction to any other state or federal court; and the proceedings can be held in secret.[59]

In three decisions in June 2004, the Supreme Court rebuffed the Bush administration's actions that those captured while fighting with the Taliban in Afghanistan may be indefinitely jailed incommunicado without being charged with any crime and denied the right to consult an attorney. Bush's position was that he alone has the power to determine who is an "enemy combatant" (including native-born citizens), and that no court may release such persons or allow them to consult an attorney. The Supreme Court ruled that war does not give the president a blank check. As a result, those alleged to be enemy combatants must be allowed to challenge their detention before an impartial decision maker.[60]

The Steel Seizure Case

Unlike the deference paid president and Congress in relocating Japanese Americans, the Court refused to support President Truman's order that the steel mills be seized to thwart a strike that would imperil the war effort in Korea. The main difference between the two situations was that the president's action not only was unilateral, but contradicted congressional policy. After mediation failed to deter strike plans announced by the United Steelworkers Union, Truman issued an executive order on the eve of the strike deadline directing the secretary of commerce to seize the steel mills because of the indispensability of steel production to the Korean War effort. The workers returned to work; the steel companies filed suit.

The majority opinion noted that the Constitution grants "all legislative powers" to Congress. As Congress had enacted no law authorizing such a seizure, and indeed, had explicitly refused to give the president such power, the president could not be acting under his constitutional authority to take "care that the laws be faithfully executed." Nor did his role as commander in chief of the armed forces authorize the action as the steel mills were not part of the theater of war.

As a result, the Court placed limits on the president's conduct of foreign affairs. If it had not, what limits, if any, would exist on unilateral presidential

---

[59] Anthony Lewis, "Right and Wrong," *New York Times*, 24 November 2001, p. A25.
[60] *Rumsfeld v. Padilla*, 159 L. Ed. 2d 513 (2004); *Rasul v. Bush*, 159 L. Ed. 2d 548 (2004); and *Hamdi v. Rumsfeld*, 159 L. Ed. 2d 578 (2004).

action in foreign affairs would be unknown. On the other hand, as in the Japanese relocation case, this decision, though unused, remains good law.

The Watergate Tapes Case

Though presidential conflicts with Congress occur regularly, presidential–judicial conflicts are rare. But when they do occur, the judiciary itself decides the outcome.

In March 1974, a grand jury indicted seven top aides of President Nixon for breaking into and then covering up their after-hours entry into Democratic Party headquarters in the Watergate Hotel. Nixon himself was named an unindicted coconspirator. The Watergate special prosecutor, Leon Jaworski, subsequently obtained a subpoena ordering Nixon to provide tape recordings and other evidence relevant to the break-in. Nixon refused to comply. The matter quickly reached the Supreme Court. Nixon's lawyer argued that presidential privilege protected the conversations from disclosure and that the president might not comply with a decision less than definitive. The threat of noncompliance proved a tactical mistake, as it all but guaranteed a "definitive" decision.

Although other presidents, such as Jackson and Lincoln, had stood up to the Supreme Court, Nixon in the summer of 1974 certainly was in no position to do so. In a unanimous opinion, the Court reasserted Marshall's famous *Marbury v. Madison* stance: "[It] is emphatically the province and duty of the judicial department to say what the law is."[61] Though the Court did support the existence of executive privilege, it also held that such privilege cannot outweigh an even more ancient rule, dating from medieval times, that a court has the right to everyone's evidence, most especially that relevant to criminal proceedings.

Nixon complied. The tapes showed that he had directed the cover-up. In the face of imminent impeachment, Nixon resigned.

The Line Item Veto Case

Notwithstanding endemic conflict between Congress and president, a Republican Congress enacted legislation in 1996 that gave Bill Clinton, a Democratic president, authority to veto specific provisions of tax and spending legislation. Until then, presidents had only the option of accepting or vetoing an entire bill, not just portions of it. The bill attempted to limit "pork barrel" appropriations and tax legislation whereby congresspersons scratched one another's back by inserting unrelated provisions (riders) benefiting special interests partial to the sponsoring congressperson. These actions tied the president's hands because the bills invariably contained appropriations crucial to the conduct and operation of the federal government (e.g., salaries of government workers, the functioning of the Defense Department).

[61] *United States v. Nixon*, 418 U.S. 683 (1974), at 703, 705.

Notwithstanding this action of a self-effacing Congress renouncing one of its major perquisites – costly and inefficient though it was – the Rehnquist Court, true to form, brusquely intruded itself into the matter and by a 6–3 vote declared the Line Item Veto Act unconstitutional. Although the majority recognized the Constitution's silence "on the subject of unilateral Presidential action that either repeals or amends parts of duly enacted statutes," they nonetheless asserted that "there are powerful reasons for construing constitutional silence . . . as equivalent to express prohibition." And what might these "powerful" reasons be? (1) "The 'finely wrought' procedure" of the Presentment Clause, which is all of sixty-three words in length, and (2) the words of George Washington – acclaimed for many accomplishments, none even remotely related to constitutional scholarship, however – that the Presentment Clause required him either to "approve all the parts of a Bill, or reject it in toto."[62]

In a related decision, the Court, before the line item veto case, had considered the Independent Counsel Act, enacted in 1974 in the aftermath of Watergate and reenacted in 1994. With only Justice Scalia dissenting, and Kennedy not participating, the Court upheld the law against a variety of challenges based on the structure of the federal government as created by the Founders of the Constitution and ratified by the original thirteen states.[63]

Scalia's dissent pointed out the obvious, which the Monica Lewinsky affair and Clinton's impeachment made perfectly clear: that independent counsels are "principal" officers of the executive branch for whom the Constitution requires presidential nomination and senatorial confirmation and not "inferior" officers named in this case by a panel of three lower court judges. Scalia, writing as though he were addressing clueless colleagues, pointed out the obvious: "Inferior" officers require a superior, who manifestly does not exist. Hence, independent counsels lack accountability and accordingly are superior to everybody – the Supreme Court alone excepted, of course.

As we explain in Chapter 1, ours is a government of limited powers characterized by checks and balances. Because the Independent Counsel Act mandates the investigation of persons and not crimes (standard criminal procedure), it can grow as a mushrooming cancer. Answering to no one, independent counsels operate with unlimited budgets and without deadlines.

In 1995, belatedly realizing how far they had drifted from constitutional moorings, the justices united behind Scalia in an opinion that distinguishes *Morrison v. Olson* and requires inferior officers, including independent counsels, to be supervised by presidential nominees whom the Senate has

---

[62] *Clinton v. New York City*, 141 L. Ed. 2d 343 (1998), at 414, 415. The presentment clause reads as follows: "Every Bill which shall have passed the House of Representatives and the Senate, shall, before it becomes a law, be presented to the President of the United States; If he approve he shall sign it, but if not he shall return it, with his Objections, to that House in which it shall have originated, who shall enter the Objections at large on their Journal, and proceed to reconsider it."

[63] *Morrison v. Olson*, 487 U.S. 654 (1988).

confirmed.[64] The status of *Morrison v. Olson* became a moot point when Congress in 1999, breathing an apparent sigh of relief, unremorsefully allowed the Independent Counsel Act to die a natural death.

Bush v. Gore

Beyond dispute, the most telling decision in the nation's history concerning the distribution of government power was the midnight decision in *Bush v. Gore*.[65] Although ideologically partisan decisions have typified the Court since the days of John Marshall, as we have documented in this chapter and as we shall show more specifically in subsequent chapters, the partisanship of *Bush v. Gore* manifested itself politically. Indeed, one may accurately say that never in history has a majority of the Court behaved in such a blatantly politically partisan fashion.

(1) The Court's five most conservative members, Republicans all (Rehnquist, O'Connor, Scalia, Kennedy, and Thomas), ruled that disparate standards for recounting Florida's ballots, varying from county to county, violated the equal protection clause. The majority's position was totally unprecedented because, heretofore, government action – as pointed out in the discussion of equal protection – could violate the provision only on a showing of purposeful intent to discriminate.

More basically, if counties may not count their own ballots, as the majority asserted, how can it be constitutional for judges and juries to apply totally different subjective standards to deprive persons of life, liberty, and property? As Justice Stevens observed in dissent, the standard that the Florida Supreme Court prescribed – intent of the voter – can hardly "lead to results any less uniform than ... the 'beyond a reasonable doubt' standard employed every day by ordinary citizens in courtrooms across the country." Note further that this intent of the voter standard mandated by the Supreme Court as a key element of due process cannot be defined in any meaningful sense.[66]

(2) The Rehnquist five ruled that the time needed to carry out a recount under a single uniform standard had expired. But the Court itself had stopped the recount in advance of its decision, thus aiding and abetting Bush's effort to run out the clock. It was as though, in the waning minutes of a crucial football game, the referees called time out to review a previous play but allowed the clock to continue running while they argued over their decision. The majority indicated in its initial judgment that a recount of the Florida votes before its final decision would do Bush irreparable harm (perhaps by informing the world

---

[64] *Edmond v. United States*, 520 U.S. 651 (1997).

[65] 531 U.S. 98 (2000). The decision was actually handed down at 10:15 P.M. EST. For a Court whose formal decisions invariably antedate noon, midnight is only a slight exaggeration.

[66] *Id.* at 125. Walter F. Murphy and C. Herman Pritchett, *Courts, Judges, and Politics*, 4th ed. (New York: Random House, 1986), pp. 358–359. Also see Jerome Frank, *Courts on Trial* (New York: Athenaeum, 1963), pp. 108–145.

of how Florida's voters intended to vote?). Of course, the real irreparable harm was done to Gore, who faced an impossible deadline of the majority's making. We discuss these aspects of the Court's decision more fully later.

The intrusion of the Rehnquist five stands the Constitution on its head. Presidents have always had the power to nominate the justices. But now the worm has turned: The justices may select the president.

SUMMARY AND CONCLUSIONS

This chapter has outlined the ideological considerations that have largely produced the Court's decisions since its inception. But what is most significant in this regard is not the ideologies that have reigned supreme, but rather the fact that in deciding its cases, the justices have not marched to the beat of alien or enigmatic drums, even though those drums have typically beaten a stridently ideological cadence. In doing so, the justices have found that the elements of the legal model – plain meaning, legislators' and Framers' intent, and precedent – enable them to have their cake and eat it also. Thus, the atavistic judicial activism that the Rehnquist five displayed in *Bush v. Gore* to produce an arrogantly anti–states' rights decision did not preclude the same five justices from producing an unprecedented series of eight states' rights decisions in four and a half years that would delight John C. Calhoun or any other traitorous Civil War secessionist. These decisions formalistically redefined federal–state relationships by construing the immunity accorded the states in the Eleventh Amendment to nullify various other constitutional provisions.[67]

As Supreme Court decision making in the first half of the nineteenth century fell along a Hamiltonian–Jeffersonian dimension, the votes of today's justices largely fall along what is commonly understood as the basic liberal–conservative (or Left–Right) dimension.[68] Although the fit of this dimension varies across issue areas, no other dimension (e.g., populism, libertarianism) explains significant variance in the justices' decisions. Relative to conservatives, liberal justices generally favor the rights of individuals against governmental authority in criminal, First Amendment, and privacy cases. They typically favor national

---

[67] *United States v. Lopez*, 514 U.S. 549 (1995); *Seminole Tribe v. Florida*, 517 U.S. 44 (1996); *Idaho v. Coeur d'Alene Tribe*, 521 U.S. 261 (1997); *Printz v. United States*, 521 U.S. 898 (1997); *Florida Board v. College Bank*, 527 U.S. 627 (1999); *College Savings v. Florida Board*, 527 U.S. 666 (1999); *Alden v. Maine*, 527 U.S. 706 (1999); and *Kimel v. Florida Board of Regents*, 528 U.S. 62 (2000).

[68] See Keith Poole, "The Unidimensional Supreme Court," at http://voteview.uh.edu/the_unidimensional_supreme_court.htm. Poole reports 93.1% classification accuracy from the single dimension. For similar results, see Andrew D. Martin and Kevin M. Quinn, "Dynamic Ideal Point Estimation via Markov Chain Monte Carlo for the U.S. Supreme Court, 1953–1999," 10 *Political Analysis* 134 (2002); and Bernard Grofman and Timothy Brazill, "Identifying the Median Justice on the Supreme Court through Multidimensional Scaling: Analysis of 'Natural Courts' 1953–1991," 112 *Public Choice* 55 (2002). But see also Timothy M. Hagle and Harold J. Spaeth, "Ideological Patterns in the Justices' Voting in the Burger Court's Business Cases," 55 *Journal of Politics* 492 (1993).

authority over states' rights in national supremacy cases, national and state authority over individual autonomy in economic cases, and the claims of racial and other minorities in civil rights cases.

As for *Bush v. Gore*, we doubt that this decision will preclude the Court from perpetuating its position as the authoritative policymaker on any subject that it decides to address. We find no evidence that the *Bush v. Gore* fallout has diminished the Court's stature. We also doubt (and the majority so state) that the decision will form a precedent for future decisions in the area of equal protection as long as the conservative legacy of the Rehnquist Court remains operative. On the other hand, nothing prevents a future Court from disregarding or overturning this holding, any more than any Court is precluded from deviating from a predecessor's decision.

Whether the public views the justices as motivated by ideological or political partisanship or by what passes as legal reasoning, it will not likely alter its view of the Court as other than supreme. If a choice had to be made among president, Congress, and Court as to which should rule, we continue to put our money on the justices. And we doubt that even if the public's faith in the rule of law dissipates as completely as the effervescence in an opened bottle of champagne, such an altered perception will not affect the popular conviction that the emanations from the justices' marble palace alone, and not the pestiferous effluent generated by the kakistocratic lowlifes perceived by the public to occupy the political branches of government, safeguard the American way of life.

PART II

JUDICIAL PROCESS

4

Civil Procedure

Determinative of the outcome of many cases are the procedures – the rules of the judicial game – that govern trial court processes. Rules of procedure also apply at the appellate court level, but these are largely limited to the amount of time losing litigants have to file their written appeals and the form and structure of their supporting brief. Unlike the verbal focus of most of the trial court process, that of the appellate courts is written. Though time for oral argument is commonly available at the first appeal – which is typically the only one that the losing litigant has a right to have – these arguments largely rehash material in the written brief and are supplemented by questions put to the litigants' attorneys by members of the panel of appellate court judges.

In this chapter we emphasize those aspects of noncriminal court procedures that touch on constitutional law, which, of course, is the special province of the Supreme Court. But because of the interrelationship between the constitutional and nonconstitutional aspects of civil procedure, we also provide a succinct overview of civil procedure's nonconstitutional features so that the reader may readily grasp its scope and importance. But we do not concern ourselves with criminal procedure here, but rather in Chapter 6. Criminal procedure is fundamentally charted by the provisions of Amendments Four, Five, Six, and Eight of the Bill of Rights, not by statutes or court rules.

We begin with a description of our adversary system of justice, followed by a more complete discussion of jurisdiction, a subject that we peripherally addressed in Chapter 1. We note that jurisdiction has two components: that governing the parties to a lawsuit and that pertaining to the subject matter of the parties' lawsuit. We then address the plaintiff's complaint and the answer filed by the person being sued. Complaint and answer are collectively known as

---

We apologize if this chapter strikes the reader as unduly technical. Informal surveys of law school students commonly specify civil procedure as the most difficult and boring of their courses. We try to enliven our presentation without truncating the scope or minimizing the importance of civil procedure.

the *pleadings*. In order to isolate and narrow the issues for trial, and to reduce unfair surprise, the parties engage in discovery. Discovery precedes trial and allows both parties – the plaintiff and the respondent – to obtain information from the other about any nonprivileged matter relevant to the subject matter of the pending litigation. Trial follows the completion of discovery, unless the parties reach a settlement. The Seventh Amendment to the Constitution applies to civil trials and their procedures, such as the burden of proof and verdict.

We conclude the chapter with a major feature of modern litigation: the presence of multiple parties and multiple claims in a single lawsuit.

THE ADVERSARY SYSTEM

Our adversary system of dispute resolution originated in trial by ordeal and trial by battle. Various ordeals existed. Among the more popular – perhaps because of its entertainment value – was the tossing of the alleged wrongdoer into the village pond; sinking evidenced her lack of culpability. Alternatively, he might be required to grasp a white-hot iron. His smoldering hand was then bandaged, and if, after a specified number of days, no infection had set in, innocence was decreed. Note that the less probable result evidenced innocence. The rationale – if such it may be called – behind such tests was the gullibly pious (or perhaps sanctimonious) belief that God protects the innocent.

Trial by battle saw the litigants combat one another either personally or by hired champions. Only the wealthier could afford the latter option. Death rarely resulted because armor protected the torso and the permitted weapon was a stave about the length of a baseball bat. Fighting began at sunrise and could continue until darkness with no recesses. Death, surrender, or a draw terminated the contest. A draw resulted in victory for the defendant because the burden of "proof" lay with the person claiming to have been wronged.

Early in the thirteenth century, the Roman Catholic Church forbade further use of trial by ordeal or battle (perhaps because it only accidentally produced a "just" result). It thus became necessary to develop alternative means of dispute resolution. After an extended period of experimentation, the rudiments of our trial by jury took hold by the end of the thirteenth century. This method of dispute resolution, however, remained adversarial. Verbal warfare replaced bloodshed, with the jury rendering a verdict based on the parties' self-serving assertions of what happened and discredited rendition of the other litigant's explanations. The parties or their counsel present what they perceive to be the facts of the matter, each doing so in a completely partisan fashion. The fact finder – jury or judge – acts as an umpire rather than as one charged with uncovering evidence of who did what to whom.

The adversary process rationalizes this procedure by alleging that this battle of wits coincides with the truth. To some slight extent it may. Partisan lawyers may bring to a court's attention evidence that a dispassionate inquiry might overlook. Much more likely is the suppression of relevant evidence harmful to the client of a well-paid lawyer – a common allegation of indigents who appeal their convictions. The lawyers might also introduce niceties of the legal rules with which the judge is unacquainted. But judges are certainly not known for admitting ignorance. However slight either of these eventualities, no more can be said about the validity or reliability of the adversary process as a vehicle for discerning the truth.

If truth were the objective, why would jurors not take notes? The answer, further evidencing the hidebound and truth-disconnected features of jury trials, dates to a time of widespread illiteracy and the fear that a literate juror could exercise disproportionate influence. The upshot, in lengthy trials, requires jurors to "weigh the equivalent of thousands of pages of testimony and instructions without benefit of notes, transcripts, or the right to ask clarifying questions."[1]

Actually, the basic strength of the adversary process is its ability to reach a decision, not whether the decision corresponds with the "truth" or whether it is "fair," "reasonable," or "just." In what remains a classic statement of the adversary process more than a half-century after original publication, the federal court of appeals judge Jerome Frank pointed out that if a trial fundamentally sought the truth, it would recognize the inherent fallibility of witnesses and do everything possible to remove real and apparent errors in their testimony. Instead, we do just the opposite. Recognizing the "importance of witnesses' demeanor as clues to their reliability, we would do our best to make sure that they testify in circumstances most conducive to a revealing observation of that demeanor,"[2] that is, a calm, comforting, familiar, and nonthreatening environment.

The name of the game, however, is winning. Truth takes a back seat – assuming it is present at all. False impressions become paramount, very much the order of the day. One's witnesses are paragons of virtue and incapable of shading the truth. Those of the opponent, however, consciously prevaricate or suffer from delusions of adequacy. To demonstrate this, lawyers create false impressions. Thus, with a timid witness, frightened by the courtroom, the lawyer plays on that timidity in order to sow confusion and make the witness appear to be concealing significant facts, if not appearing to be a blithering imbecile. Truthful, cautious witnesses may be subject to rapid cross-fire examination or otherwise intimidated and disconcerted so that truthful testimony appears false. Questions deliberately intended to cause embarrassment, shame, or anger are posited to lessen the witness's credibility.

Lest it appear we exaggerate, consider the following excerpt from a quarter-page ad of an attorney and licensed psychologist that appeared in the official

---

[1] Franklin Strier, "What Can the American Adversary System Learn from an Inquisitorial System of Justice?" 76 *Judicature* 109 (1992), at 110.

[2] *Courts on Trial: Myth and Reality in American Justice* (New York: Athenaeum, 1963), p. 81.

journal of the Michigan Bar Association. The ad offered services "utilizing forensic psychological techniques to promote *maximal chaos, confusion & demoralization* to opposing parties during trial" (emphasis added).[3]

Witnesses are coached to respond favorably to the attorney's client. They are taught to cloak mannerisms and demeanor that might discredit them. In short, stage-manage the witness however necessary to advantage the client. On cross-examination, do not allow an adverse witness to explain an inconsistent statement that benefits your client. And by all means ask no question whose answer you, the attorney, do not know. Instead, employ "disruptive objections and emotional appeals to distract the factfinder and dilute the effect of adverse testimony."[4] As Frank points out:

These, and other like techniques, you will find unashamedly described in many manuals on trial tactics written by and for eminently reputable trial lawyers. The purpose of these tactics . . . is to prevent the trial judge or jury from correctly evaluating the trustworthiness of witnesses and to shut out evidence the trial court ought to receive in order to approximate the truth.[5]

Criticism of the adversary system emanates from conservatives, as well as liberals. For example:

The notion that a body of inoperative knowledge can be presented to a jury, with an "expert" advocate on one side and an "expert" advocate on the contrary side, in the expectation that the jury can adjudicate between the antagonistic positions is quite simply voodoo law.

If say, Einstein and Fermi could not agree on the way in which to weigh matter in space, the idea that a jury could, listening to both men, come up with the "right" answer, is . . . a superstition.[6]

Discovery

Recognition of the foregoing shortcomings has produced mild reform to lessen the high probability that luck, skill, and resources will determine adversarial outcome. The most significant of these is pretrial discovery – the most important and time-consuming aspect of civil procedure, and one that we address more systematically later. No longer do surprise witnesses and unanticipated testimony affect trial outcomes – much to the undoubted chagrin of movie and television screenwriters and others who thrive on the dramatic outcome. The Federal Rules of Civil Procedure, adopted in 1938, authorize both sides in a lawsuit to scrutinize the others' evidence. Hence, witness lists are exchanged

---

[3] Advertisement for Luria Neuropsychology & Forensic Laboratory, Traverse City, MI. *Michigan Bar Journal*, November 1995, p. 1201.

[4] Strier, "American Adversary System," fn. 1.

[5] Frank, *Courts on Trial*, fn. 2, at 85.

[6] William F. Buckley, "Voodoo Law and a Jeer for the Jury," *Detroit Free Press*, 29 June 1982, p. 15.

and relevant evidence made known. Issues are clarified and the scope of controversy narrowed.

Unfortunately, these benefits incur costs, which enable the adversary process to retain its sporting characteristics.

Opposing parties can now try to "outdiscover" each other, and as a result, the party unwilling or unable to pay for the most extensive pretrial discovery may be at a disadvantage.... [T]he party willing to invest most heavily in...discovery...can significantly increase the cost of litigation and wear his or her adversary down.[7]

This results because the Federal Rules, plus those of many of the states, allow parties to seek information relevant to the pending action even when whether the evidence discovered admits of admissibility at trial cannot be shown. It suffices if the information sought "appears reasonably calculated to lead to the discovery of admissible evidence."[8]

A more sensible solution to the deficiencies of the adversary process – but one that only a masochist would advocate because of our universal conviction that our trial system is at least as fundamental to our way of life as the Constitution itself – would require judges to be trained investigators with authority to ferret out witnesses and evidence themselves. And if a jury is to be involved – a feature of the trial process of all non–common law democracies[9] – it would be composed of a small number of lay and professional judges. The latter would bring their experience to bear in discovering and evaluating the evidence, and the lay members would preclude professionals from acting on the basis of prejudice or politics. Hair-splitting battles over the admissibility of evidence (see Chapter 5) would not occur. The investigation would proceed calmly and decorously under the direction of a public prosecutor and examining judges.

Such a procedure would preclude such tactics as playing the race card, as in the O. J. Simpson trial for the murder of his wife. His attorney, Johnnie Cochran, could not have asked the jury to send a message to the Los Angeles police if the jury had consisted of the trial court judge, several magistrates, and a few professionally reputable laypersons. But, of course, playing the race card was completely acceptable for several hundred years when the shoe was on the other foot. For a black then to testify against a white – much less to accuse one of wrongdoing – was legally impermissible, and extralegally such testimony could make the black a prime candidate for castration and lynching.

[7] Malcolm Feeley, "The Adversary System," in Robert J. Janoski (ed.), *Encyclopedia of the American Judicial System*, vol. 2 (New York: Scribners, 1987), p. 759. The two major methods are the deposition of witnesses and written interrogatories that parties, but not witnesses, are required to answer. Both lend themselves to fishing expeditions, even though they beneficially simplify trial issues, lessen the number of needed witnesses, preclude surprise witnesses and testimony, and ensure that what is said or written in response to pretrial inquiries accords with that presented at trial.

[8] Federal Rules of Civil Procedure 26(b)1.

[9] Michael Lind, "Jury Dismissed," *The New Republic*, 23 October 1995, p. 10.

JURISDICTION

Jurisdiction is of three types: *in personam, in rem,* and *quasi in rem.* A court may have authority to decide cases in which the parties are physically present in the state (*in personam*). It may also decide cases in which the thing at issue (the *rem*) is located within the state. As a result of the Supreme Court's decision in *Shaffer v. Heitner*[10] – the facts of which we detail later – the celebrated legal fiction of *quasi in rem* jurisdiction was subsumed into *in personam* jurisdiction. No longer could in-state property be used as a means to reach a nonresident defendant in order to adjudicate rights pertaining to the out-of-state defendant that were unrelated to the in-state property. The fiction viewed the in-state property as the personification of the defendant.

In personam Jurisdiction

Until the middle of the twentieth century courts ruled that state judicial authority did not extend beyond the state's boundaries.[11] But with the growth of interstate commerce and industry, the Court found this doctrine wanting and so overruled it, stating that due process requires only that if the defendant not be within the state, he or she need only have "minimum contacts" with the forum state, such that the maintenance of the lawsuit does not offend "traditional notions of fair play and substantial justice."[12]

Though the concept of "minimum contacts" has implicit meaning, that cannot be said for "traditional notions of fair play and substantial justice." The phrase reads mellifluously, but its meaning is as gossamer as a spider web. How does one operationalize "traditional notions" or "substantial justice"? How does one distinguish them from plain, unadulterated "justice"? Be that as it may, the minimum-contacts test is warp and woof of constitutional law, even though the resulting lawsuit need not necessarily be limited to the subject of the contacts. If individuals have substantial contacts with the forum state (e.g., visitors who travel there several times a year to visit relatives or friends, truckers who regularly cross the state to reach destinations in other states, businesses that buy and sell goods or render services to their counterparts in other states), they subject themselves to "general" personal jurisdiction: A binding judgment may be entered against them on any claim. "Limited" personal jurisdiction, on the other hand, permits judgments only on claims arising out of the specific minimum contacts had with the forum state. For example, a nonresident real property owner whose property the state seizes for nonpayment of taxes can appear and contest the seizure without subjecting himself or herself to unlimited *in personam* jurisdiction. The same applies to a person who enters a state to contest the provisions of a will being probated therein. The line between "limited"

[10] 433 U.S. 186 (1977).
[11] *Pennoyer v. Neff,* 95 U.S. 714 (1877).
[12] *International Shoe Co. v. Washington,* 326 U.S. 310 (1945), at 316.

and "general" personal jurisdiction is not sharply etched. Nonetheless, it serves a useful purpose.

The utility of the minimum-contacts test is that it allows for balancing the various interests involved: the interest of the state, the character of the contacts, fairness to the defendants, and available alternative action. Though these considerations have the utility of allowing the test to be adapted and tailored to meet specific situations, they do not, of course, ensure either an objective or a consensual decision. Consider the case of *Burnham v. Superior Court*, in which an out-of-state husband made a brief visit to the home of his estranged wife to return one of their children who had been visiting him, whereupon she surprised him by serving him with divorce papers. He objected, stating that he visited the wife's state (California) only on infrequent business trips and for the purpose of visiting their children while there. Although the justices unanimously agreed that minimum contacts existed, they required four opinions to justify their decision, none of which commanded majority support.[13]

Other factors being equal, minimum contacts is more easily sustained when the controversy concerns a tort – an injury to person or property – rather than a contract. In the former situation, state interests come into play – typically public health, safety, or welfare – plus the fact that the defendant likely entered the forum state voluntarily, thus tipping the scales in favor of the courts of the state where the injury occurred. Moreover, witnesses and evidence may not be movable to the defendant's state. Contracts, however, present a different scenario. The defendant may have had no choice but to enter the forum state to perform the contract, or the plaintiff may be a major player in the contractual game – a nationwide corporation, say – for whom a distant forum provides convenient access, whereas the defendant would be unfairly burdened by traveling to the forum state.

From a policy standpoint, the main concern about minimum contacts is its use to sustain jurisdiction on a single out-of-state tort with in-state consequences, even though the consequences were foreseeable. If, for example, a retailer or other small business can be required to defend in a distant state's courts for injuries resulting from its products therein, availability to suit would travel with every item the retailer sold or the small business manufactured. As a result, sellers might refuse to do business with out-of-state customers, thereby deterring interstate commercial activity. The Supreme Court allayed such fears in *Worldwide Volkswagen Corp. v. Woodson*.[14]

New York residents who had purchased a vehicle from a New York dealer brought a product liability action in an Oklahoma court against the seller and distributor for injuries suffered in an Oklahoma accident. The Court ruled that the defendants' only contact with Oklahoma was that a single vehicle sold in New York to New York residents happened to suffer an accident while passing through Oklahoma. The defendants closed no sales, performed no services,

---

[13] 495 U.S. 604 (1990).
[14] 444 U.S. 286 (1980).

and solicited no Oklahoma business through either salespersons or media. The record displayed none of the affiliating circumstances that necessarily predicate the assertion of a court's jurisdiction. As for the likelihood that the seller and distributor could plausibly foresee the possibility that one of its vehicles might have an accident in Oklahoma, such foreseeability is not totally irrelevant. But for purposes of due process, the relevant foreseeability is that the defendants' conduct and connection with Oklahoma are such that they could reasonably anticipate being hauled into court there.

In rem Jurisdiction

If the "thing" (*res*) in controversy is located within the state, such as a piece of real estate, the local courts may, for example, determine the owner thereof. Or if the state has granted a person a certain "status," such as a license or custody of another person, the state in question has jurisdiction over its dissolution or alteration. The rationale for *in rem* jurisdiction is that the state's sovereignty gives it authority to adjudicate all matters located within its confines.

In rem litigation rarely raises minimum-contacts questions for the simple reason that the property is located within the physical confines of the state, or the status in controversy was voluntarily entered into within the state or the state provides it with protection. The federal courts are similarly governed: Federal law allows the district courts to reach defendants nationwide "to enforce any lien upon or claim to, or to remove any encumbrance or lien or cloud upon the title to, real or personal property within the district."[15]

Quasi in rem Jurisdiction

Quasi in rem jurisdiction posed few problems as long as it addressed only real property. But with its twentieth-century extension to movable property, intangibles, and contingent obligations, difficulties surfaced. Legal fictions determined the location of bank deposits (in the bank where they were made), stock (where the certificates were held), and debts (wherever the debtor happened to be).

The facts of *Shaffer v. Heitner*,[16] which subjected *quasi in rem* jurisdiction to the requirement of minimum contacts, illustrate well the deficiency of *quasi in rem* jurisdiction: A stockholder sued a corporation's nonresident officers and directors in Delaware, the corporation's place of incorporation. None of the action complained of occurred in Delaware; neither did any of the defendants have contact with the state. The corporation was headquartered in Arizona, in which state it conducted most of its business. The plaintiff gained jurisdiction because Delaware law allowed stockholders to attach the stock of a Delaware corporation because all the stock of such entities was irrebuttably presumed

---

[15] 28 U.S. Code 1655.
[16] 433 U.S. 186 (1977).

to be located in Delaware.[17] The million dollars' worth of attached stock confronted the defendants with a Hobson's choice: Fail to defend and forfeit their stock, or defend and thereby subject themselves to unlimited liability. The no-win situation resulted because Delaware, as well as other states, does not allow defendants to make a limited appearance.

With only Justice Brennan dissenting, the Court ruled that all assertions of state jurisdiction, including *in rem* and *quasi in rem* actions, must be evaluated compatibly with the minimum-contacts standard. Neither the presence of the nonresidents' stock in Delaware nor the fact that the nonresident defendants were officers of a Delaware chartered corporation provided sufficient contacts to establish jurisdiction in Delaware courts.

Limited and Special Appearances

As suggested, some states allow out-of-state defendants to make a limited appearance to contest an *in rem* or *quasi in rem* suit. The policy's utility lies in the fact that defendants limit their liability to the property in question. Their presence within the state to defend does not open them to other *in rem* proceedings or to unlimited personal liability. Thus, for example, a custodial divorced parent garnishes the out-of-state father's wages to pay overdue child support. The garnished wages, however, do not equal the overdue amount. A limited appearance permits the father to appear to contest the garnished amount without opening him to liability for the balance of the owed amount.

A special appearance, by contrast, pertains to personal jurisdiction. It allows a defendant to challenge the legality of the asserted personal jurisdiction. Such an appearance does not subject the defendant to the court's jurisdiction other than to decide the merits of the defendant's claim that sufficient contacts do not exist to enable the court to exercise personal jurisdiction over him.

The federal courts and many state courts have abolished the special appearance. In its stead, the defendant may motion the court to dismiss for want of personal jurisdiction. Such motion does not subject the mover to other judicial action. Because the Federal Rules of Civil Procedure make no reference to limited and special appearances, most federal courts follow the rule of the state in which they sit.

Notice

In order to exercise jurisdiction over persons or things, due process requires that the person being sued be given notice of the pending lawsuit. The leading case on the subject is *Mullane v. Central Hanover Trust Co.*, in which the Supreme Court ruled, "An elementary and fundamental requirement of due process . . . is notice reasonably calculated, under all the circumstances, to apprise interested

---

[17] An irrebuttable presumption is the classic legal rule that guarantees that a court will not be confused by contrary facts.

parties of the pendency of the action and afford them an opportunity to present their objections."[18] Notice takes various forms: a legal notice in a newspaper serving the area where the property is located or the owner domiciled, first-class mail, registered letter, or personally delivered summons. The extent to which new forms of communication – e-mail and fax – constitutionally meet notice requirements remains unresolved. Given the absence of complaints of inadequacy, traditional means remain dominant.

The Court subsequently supplemented the *Mullane* ruling with *Memphis Light, Gas and Water Division v. Craft*,[19] in which it held that notice must also inform recipients of avenues of redress open to them should they wish to contest the matter. In this case, the municipally owned and operated utility failed to inform a ratepayer threatened with termination of service of a procedure for contesting the proposed termination.

Long-Arm Statutes

In addition to notice, out-of-state defendants must be within the jurisdiction of the court in which the action has been filed. For a state's courts to establish such jurisdiction, the state must authorize its exercise, as they all do by means of a long-arm statute. Absent such authorization, personal jurisdiction out of state does not exist.

Although they vary in detail, long-arm statutes take two general forms. One type authorizes jurisdiction of any controversy in which the defendant has minimum contacts with the state sufficient to meet the Supreme Court's test. The other type specifies the activities in which a defendant must engage in order to trigger the state's courts' jurisdiction. The most common example are nonresident motorist statutes. These provide for the assertion of jurisdiction over out-of-state drivers who cause accidents in the forum state. Also common are the conduct of business in the state, out-of-state action that causes an in-state injury, and the use or possession of real property in the forum state.

Venue and *forum non conveniens*

Defendants served with judicial process may object to the forum in which the proceedings are scheduled. State and federal statutes specify the court where a given lawsuit must be brought. Venue does not become a consideration until jurisdiction over the parties has been established.

Venue typically allows the plaintiff to bring an action based on his or her place of residence, the residence of the defendant, or the place where the events giving rise to the lawsuit occurred. If one of the parties is a business, the action may be brought in the state of incorporation, of the headquarters of the

---

[18] 339 U.S. 306 (1950), at 314.
[19] 436 U.S. 1 (1978).

business, or of the location where most of its activity occurs. If government is a party, action may be brought where the seat of government is located. If one of the parties is represented by an agent, that person's place of residence may be the chosen forum.

Although the initial choice of forum vests in the plaintiff, the defendant may object on the basis that the chosen forum is inconvenient and works a hardship: that is, is a *forum non conveniens*. Defendants may so move even though the court in which the action is brought has jurisdiction both statutorily and constitutionally. The court uses its discretion in ruling on the motion and should be guided by two independent policy considerations: the convenience of – and in criminal matters fairness to – the defendant and the burden on a state's courts in deciding litigation unconnected with the state. The convenience to the plaintiff does not enter into the equation inasmuch as the plaintiff, in making the initial choice of forum, has already exercised choice.

The factors courts consider are whether the plaintiff is a resident of the state or district where action is brought. Such residence should entitle one to access the local courts. Other considerations look to the forum in which witnesses and evidence are most available, and the forum best acquainted with the law that will govern resolution of the dispute. In criminal cases, a change of venue most often occurs because pretrial publicity makes empaneling a jury uninfluenced by media reportage difficult, if not impossible. And, perhaps needless to say, the publicity given to sensational pretrial events will likely be such that only a jury of hermits will have been uninfluenced, in which case, a venue change amounts to six of one, a half-dozen of the other.

PLEADINGS

The purpose of pleading has varied over time. The rigidity of the common law, which focused on the specification of the issues for trial, gave way in the last half of the nineteenth century to code pleading, initiated by New York in 1848. The codes were designed to disclose the underlying facts on which the plaintiff's claim rested. This focus avoided the highly technical hazards with which the common law abounded – any one of which could shipwreck the plaintiff's case – and that made the discovery of "truth" or the rendering of "justice" an incidental outcome at best. Pleading, therefore, no longer remains a game in which one misstep dooms the plaintiff. The Federal Rules of Civil Procedure, dating from 1938, which the states have largely adopted in whole or in part, shifted the focus of pleading to the provision of notice so that all parties would know the nature of the lawsuit and be able to make preparations for trial. The rules of evidence – the subject of the next chapter – specify the facts and the manner in which they may be presented at trial.

In limiting the focus of pleading to providing the sued person with information sufficient to enable her to understand why she is being sued and to formulate a response, the other historic functions of pleading have been relegated to separate procedures: fact revelation to discovery, and issue formulation to discovery and the pretrial conference.[20] We discuss each in turn in subsequent portions of this chapter.

Pleadings take two required and one supplementary form: the plaintiff's complaint and the respondent's (i.e., defendant's) answer to the complaint. At the discretion of the judge or when the respondent's answer contains a counterclaim, the plaintiff is allowed to reply. The reply thus constitutes an answer to the answer. If the respondent's response does produce a counterclaim, the plaintiff's reply must be limited to the counterclaim lest the scope of the lawsuit expand as the pretensions of a bombastic politician's policy utterances do.

The Complaint

Complaints typically contain three features: a brief assertion of the basis for the court's jurisdiction over the matter, a concise statement of the claim that entitles the plaintiff to relief, and a demand for a ruling that provides the requested relief. The jurisdictional statement is especially important for the federal courts because of their limited subject matter jurisdiction. The statement of the claim requires little in the way of factual or technical detail. Discovery and other pretrial procedures can eliminate any gaps that occur here. As a result, dismissals of complaints for failure to state a claim for which relief can be granted rarely occur. The defense would have to show that no set of facts could support the claim.

This, however, does not mean that plaintiffs' attorneys may file claims with impunity. Even though a claim does not meet the criterion for summary dismissal, subsequent proceedings before and during trial may reveal the claim to be frivolous or insubstantial. To guard against such, plaintiff's attorney must aver that she brings the claim in good faith and that it has a legitimate basis. Nonetheless, very few cases actually sanction offending attorneys. Either the definitions of *frivolous* and *insubstantial* have a very low threshold, or attorneys behave with an integrity far surpassing that of other professionals, such as accountants and stockbrokers. Take your pick.

The relief the complaint seeks includes one or more of the following items: money damages; injunctive or other equitable relief, such as a court order prohibiting the defendant from engaging in certain specified activity or, alternatively, requiring the defendant to do certain specified things; or a declaratory judgment in which the court spells out the parties' rights and obligations. Money damages, of course, are most common, declaratory judgments least.

Inconsistent with the requirement that the complaint be short and to the point is the duty to plead certain "special matters" with particularity. The reason is that these are matters that the opposing party will not deem relevant to her client's defense unless they are called to her attention. These include incapacity to sue or be sued, circumstances that give rise to allegations of fraud

---

[20] A fourth function, access controls on the flow of litigation, is discussed in Chapter 7 in the section on standing to sue.

or mistake, material facts of time and place, and special damages. The last are costs incurred that are not part of the natural consequences of the defendant's tort; examples are injuries suffered in an automobile accident that caused the injured party to miss the deadline for completing performance of a contract or a lessee's violation of the terms of a lease that resulted in foreclosure of the lessor's (owner's) mortgage. Failure to plead a special matter precludes recovery for it.

The Answer

As must the complaint, the defendant's answer must be short and to the point and should rebut each claim asserted. Also as with the complaint, the respondent may assert defenses that are incompatible with one another. Thus, to an allegation that the defendant damaged the plaintiff's property, the respondent may allege that the complainant did not own the property, and even if he did, he caused the damage himself.

Denials, not surprisingly, characterize the answer. Because denials must be truthful and cannot mislead, they tend to be specific and qualified. Assertions not objected to become admissible. One type of answer – lack of firsthand knowledge – pertains to large organizations with many employees, the officers of which may be ignorant of what transpires outside the corporate board-room (or even within it, as Enron's, WorldCom's, and K-Mart's fall from grace demonstrate).

Apart from the answer, the defendant has two other replies available: the affirmative defense and the counterclaim. The former admits some or all of the plaintiff's allegations but does so only as a defense. Thus, the respondent may claim that the matters alleged are *res judicata* – previously adjudicated matters that may not be reopened to further litigation, on the basis that litigants only get one bite of the apple – and once they have had their day in court and the controversy resolved by a final and binding judgment on the merits, finality of decision prevails and the matter may not be opened to further scrutiny. (For example, for an automobile accident in which two bystanders were injured, in a lawsuit brought by one of the bystanders, a court authoritatively decides the driver of the car was at fault. When the second bystander sues, the driver may not defend on the ground that he was not at fault.) Or the respondent may allege fraud or allege that the complaint was filed after the expiration of the statute of limitations.

The counterclaim essentially positions the defendant as a plaintiff. The same considerations that govern pleading a complaint apply when the answer takes the form of a counterclaim.

Challenges to the Pleadings

Apart from the answer, defendants may challenge the complaint in a variety of ways. They may claim that the court lacks jurisdiction or that the plaintiff has failed to state a claim for relief or an appropriate cause of action. Because of today's liberal pleading rules, such action by the respondent tends only to delay the onset of litigation; it does not terminate it. Other tactics include demurrer, whereby the defendant can challenge ambiguous or indefinite allegations. If the court judges that the plaintiff cannot respond adequately, the motion will be granted. If not, the defendant must await discovery to obtain clarification.

Unlike in common law, in which the pleadings dominated and controlled judicial proceedings, today's liberal rules allow easy amendment of the pleadings, as well as considerable variance between the pleadings and the proof offered at trial. These options obtain in order that decisions will be made on the merits and not on procedural technicalities that preclude rendering "substantial justice."

DISCOVERY

As independent court systems, the state and federal courts are free to formulate separate rules of civil procedure. And though this has happened, discovery is one aspect in which state and federal procedures closely converge, as the states have adopted most of the relevant Federal Rules of Civil Procedure.

Discovery permits the pretrial disclosure of any relevant unprivileged material.[21] It primarily requires the parties to disclose – on request – information that would otherwise not be forthcoming. As such, it largely precludes the production of surprise witnesses or testimony. The trial, accordingly, becomes much less a battle of wits between opposing counsel than the presentation and evaluation of facts that gave rise to the dispute. Discovery also obtains and preserves evidence that if not obtained now might be unavailable at the time of trial, such as the testimony of a terminally ill or elderly witness. It also helps narrow the issues that require trial resolution. New leads may be uncovered that may, in turn, lead to still others, thus helping to provide a "fair" outcome. It may also produce a summary judgment as the only issues in dispute are questions of law, not of fact. Finally – and arguably most importantly – discovery serves to check perjury by displaying any incompatibility between what a witness or party said before trial and what he or she states at trial. But, of course, if the witness prevaricates compatibly at pretrial and trial, discovery will not reveal a discrepancy.

The rules of evidence (see Chapter 5) do not determine the scope of discovery. It suffices for discovery if the material be relevant to the subject matter of the lawsuit, although not to the precise issues raised at the trial. If the information sought is not privileged and may reasonably relate to the discovery of evidence admissible at trial, objections to its detection will not be sustained. Hearsay evidence provides an apt example. Deponents (persons subject to discovery) may not object to information elicited from a secondhand source because the

---

[21] "Relevance" is a key consideration of the law of evidence. We discuss it in the next chapter.

hearsay obtained from such a person may well lead to the individual who has firsthand knowledge of the matter of inquiry. We will discuss the use of hearsay at trial in the chapter on evidence.

Discovery Devices

Depositions may be taken from both witnesses and parties. The deposed person appears before a court officer and testifies under oath in response to questions posed by attorneys on both sides of the case. The rules of evidence do not apply here except for the important exceptions of relevance and privileged information. A signed, hard copy of the transcribed testimony is made.

An alternative, less costly type of deposition consists of written questions. A proposed list is prepared by one side, who sends it to the other, who in turn submits her own questions. A form of cross-examination thereby results. The deponent responds to the questions, and a court reporter records the responses. This arrangement tends to be employed to obtain the testimony of distant witnesses and to save money. Attorneys need not be present as the questions are submitted to each side in advance of their being answered.

Interrogatories differ from depositions in that they comprise written responses to questions, not oral answers. Second, only parties to the lawsuit are subject to them. Answers are made under oath, and typically with the assistance of counsel. Although the scope of the interrogatory is the same as that of the deposition, queries are not limited to matters within the party's personal knowledge. The individual may be required to search relevant records for the answer. Hence, interrogatories are most useful in an organizational setting. And though costs to the questioner are minimal, that may not be the case for the responder, depending on the scope of the search and the complexity of the questions. Because of the hearsay and best evidence rules, evidence secured from interrogatories tends to be inadmissible at trial. Hence, they serve as a start-up device – a fishing expedition, if you will – whereby leads are uncovered and trial issues best framed. Obviously, interrogatories may heavily burden the questioned party and admit of substantial abuse, harassment, and delayed litigation. In an effort to shift some of the burden to the requesting party, a number of jurisdictions allow the responder merely to designate the records in which answers can be found. Curiosity here kills no cat. It rather rewards the beast that assiduously digs deepest.

TRIAL PROCEDURE

The Pretrial Conference

Trial procedure actually begins with the pretrial conference, which takes place after discovery and is presided over by the trial court judge. Though a few jurisdictions mandate such conferences, judges utilize them when they deem them useful as an aid to simplifying the issues for trial and, ideally, to reaching an out-of-court settlement, thereby obviating the need for any further judicial action.

The success – the effectiveness – of the pretrial conference depends on the judge. Familiarity with the facts and issues as revealed by discovery may produce undue pressure on the parties to settle. But if the same judge does not preside at both the pretrial and the trial, the incentive of the pretrial judge to familiarize herself with all facets of the controversy, with expertise thereby obtained, diminishes. On the other hand, use of different judges lessens the likelihood of undue pressure to settle. The parties need not fear that their failure to agree on an issue insisted upon by the pretrial judge will prejudice the client's case at trial.

Summary Judgment

It sometimes becomes apparent, as a result of the pretrial conference or at an early stage in the trial itself, that the controversy lacks a genuine dispute about the material facts on which the outcome of the trial will necessarily hinge. A motion for summary judgment requires the opposite party to present evidence that the key fact(s) differs from the mover's version. The burden of proof on whether to grant summary judgment requires that the pertinent evidence be viewed as more favorable to the opposing party.

Trial Procedure

Once discovery is completed and pretrial motions are resolved, the case is placed on the court's trial docket and a date assigned. Absent any postponements or continuances, the trial will commence. If the trial is by jury, one must be chosen before any evidence is presented. Otherwise, jury and judge (bench) trials proceed similarly.

Counsel begin with opening statements, with plaintiff's attorney speaking first. These statements emphasize what each side intends to prove. Plaintiff's evidence and witnesses are examined and cross-examined, followed by those of the respondent. Rebuttal evidence may then be admitted, but surrebuttal (a rebuttal of a rebuttal) is rare. Closing arguments summarize the evidence. Again, plaintiff begins first and has the right to rebut after the defendant's closing remarks.

If a jury rather than the judge finds the facts, the judge instructs the jury about the law they are to apply to the facts as revealed by the testimony and witnesses. The judge may also summarize the evidence, and in federal and some state courts judges may evaluate and comment on the quality of the evidence. If the judge sits without a jury, she evaluates the evidence and renders a judgment. The distinction between law and facts is by no means clear, and even where it is reasonably so, juries not uncommonly disregard the law if they perceive it as incompatible with their sense of justice, warped though it may be. The all-time classic example is the Southern criminal trial pitting whites against black defendants in which perjured testimony and nonexistent evidence result in a guilty verdict, commonly coupled with a lengthy sentence and capital punishment. A horrendous example from the twenty-first century – not from the age of Jim Crow – concerns the wholesale conviction of more than three dozen blacks in a drug sting in a small West Texas town, far from the Mexican border, on the unquestioned, unsubstantiated, and prevaricated testimony of a "nefarious narc bent on making arrests and a name for himself."[22]

On the other hand, judges sometimes remove a case from further jury consideration if they believe the jury is likely to nullify the relevant law in reaching its decision – for instance, a jury that effectively disregards a civil rights statute to reach an antiequality decision or one that disregards the jurisdiction's negligence law in order to find for the injured party, or one that acquits a medical marijuana provider who has violated federal law.

The Jury

The Seventh Amendment permits a jury trial as it existed under the common law in all federal cases in which the amount in controversy exceeds a mere twenty dollars. This means that the plaintiff has a right to a jury in virtually all noncriminal cases that do not pertain to the law of equity. The Supreme Court, however, has held that the language of the Seventh Amendment does not apply to the states. Hence, the states are free to leave the resolution of civil controversies to judges alone or to administrative tribunals. Not so, however, in criminal matters: These are governed by the Sixth Amendment. Choice vests in the plaintiff in a criminal case.

Because the states need not provide a jury trial in civil controversies, differences exist between federal and state court trial procedures. States commonly use fewer than twelve jurors and frequently allow less than unanimous verdicts. Federal courts may also use as few as six jurors.[23] The Supreme Court has not decided whether to permit nonunanimous verdicts in civil controversies. The fact that they allow criminal defendants to be convicted nonunanimously (ten of twelve votes) strongly harbingers that they will.[24]

Jury Selection

Voir dire is the method whereby jurors are selected. Either the judge or, in more important litigation, the parties' attorneys orally question potential jurors to determine any biases that could cloud their judgment of the case they might have.

---

[22] Editorial, "Tulia a Textbook Case of What's Wrong with Texas Justice System," *Austin American-Statesman*, 14 June 2003; Monica Davey, "Texas Frees 12 on Bond after Drug Sweep Inquiry," *New York Times*, 17 June 2003, p. A16. The print and electronic media heavily covered this story during the first three weeks of June 2003.

[23] *Colgrove v. Battin*, 413 U.S. 149 (1976).

[24] *Apodaca v. Oregon*, 406 U.S. 404 (1972).

If such are discovered, the potential juror is dismissed for cause. Potential jurors may also be dismissed peremptorily, that is, without cause. Unlike dismissals for cause, peremptory dismissals are limited. Federal practice allows each party three. Moreover, the Supreme Court interprets the Fourteenth Amendment to preclude peremptory dismissals based on race in criminal and civil cases.[25]

Posttrial Proceedings

Juror misconduct or prejudicial errors by the judge may warrant a new trail. Harmless errors, however, do not. Any error or defect that does not adversely affect the substantial rights of a party amounts to a harmless error, for example, if the party sued received notice of the lawsuit, which he acted upon, by first-class mail rather than by personal summons.

Short of a new trial, either party may move for a directed verdict. The defense may make such a request at the close of the plaintiff's case. Either party may do so when both have rested their case. A directed verdict takes the case from the jury, and the resulting judge-made decision becomes the court's final judgment, subject to reversal on appeal but not otherwise. Somewhat variant from the directed verdict is a judgment notwithstanding the verdict, abbreviated from the Latin as *JNOV*: a judgment *non obstante veredicto*. Whereas the directed verdict precedes the fact finder's decision, JNOV occurs afterward as a result of a motion by the losing party. But, at least in the federal courts, a motion for a directed verdict is prerequisite to a JNOV.

In lieu of an outright reversal of a verdict, a judge may conditionally order a retrial unless the plaintiff agrees to a lessening of the dollar amount of the damages awarded by the jury (*remittitur*), or the defendant agrees to increasing them (*additur*). Judges do so when they agree with a jury's finding of liability but believe the jury has miscalculated the damages. Federal practice allows for the former, but not the latter, considering *additur* to impinge on the Seventh Amendment because it impermissibly limits the jury's determinations. The Supreme Court ruled that at the time the amendment was adopted, *additur* was not part of the common law, and, second, *remittitur* merely trims the awarded amount whereas *additur* adds dollars not part of the original verdict.[26]

Punitive Damages

The modern manifestation of constitutional limits on jury awards concerns punitive damages. In an early decision, the Supreme Court rejected a constitutional attack on punitive damages while admitting that some might be sufficiently extreme as to violate due process. The justices, however, did not define the constitutional limit, stating instead that so long as discretion is exercised

---

[25] *Edmonson v. Leesville Concrete Co.*, 500 U.S. 614 (1991).
[26] *Dimick v. Schiedt*, 293 U.S. 474 (1935).

within reasonable constraints, there is no problem.[27] Of course, what is reasonable in this regard may be anything but to a losing litigant.

Five years later, however, the Court for the first time overturned a punitive damage award as grossly excessive. A customer who paid forty-one thousand dollars for a partially repainted "new" car received $2 million in damages. In ruling for the distributor, the majority provided three "guideposts": the degree of reprehensibility, the mathematical ratio between the punitive award and the actual damages, and the availability of civil fines or criminal punishment for the offending conduct. The four dissenters objected to the majority's intrusion into an area traditionally the province of state courts.[28] The Court subsequently applied and elaborated its guidelines, holding that juries generally should not consider the defendant's wealth when determining punitive damages, nor whether the individual or business is unsavory. In general, punitive damage awards should not exceed nine times the compensatory – the actual – damages the plaintiff suffered.[29]

As further indication of hostility toward punitive damages, the Court ruled that all appellate courts must employ a de novo standard of review rather than the more lenient abuse of discretion standard. This de novo standard requires searching scrutiny of whether a jury's award is grossly excessive. Such thorough review is expected to curb costly awards and impose a degree of consistency on a matter of high and unpredictable variation.[30] On the other hand, it will effectively pooh-pooh instances of unconsciously callous respondent behavior.

Burden of Proof

Burden of proof has two aspects: the burden of production and the burden of persuasion. The former requires the party to provide some evidence with regard to a particular fact or issue; failing that, the fact finder (judge or jury) must find for the other party. Determination of whether the burden of production has been met is reached if the evidence supports sending the matter to the fact finder.

To some extent, the burdens coincide. The party bearing the burden of persuasion has to produce evidence. Production of evidence is obviously prerequisite to persuasion. The burden of production can and does shift between the parties. If the plaintiff produces persuasive evidence, the production burden then shifts to the respondent in order to rebut. Failure to do so results in victory for the plaintiff.

The scope and character of the burdens vary with the cause of action. In a contract action, for example, the plaintiff needs to establish that an agreement exists; that it is supported by a consideration (i.e., the nonobligatory inducement – typically money – to enter into a contract); that she performed

---

[27] *Pacific Mutual Life Insurance Co. v. Haslip*, 499 U.S. 1 (1991).
[28] *BMW of North America v. Gore*, 517 U.S. 559 (1996).
[29] *State Farm Mutual Automobile Insurance Co. v. Campbell*, 538 U.S. 408 (2003).
[30] *Cooper Industries v. Leatherman Tool Group*, 532 U.S. 424 (2001).

the contract, which the respondent then breached, resulting in damages. Evidence supporting each element of the parties' claims, charges, and defenses must be produced.

The burden of persuasion requires the fact finder, at the end of the trial when all the evidence has been presented, to rule that the relevant party has established the truth of his claim. If not, the verdict upholds the other party. This occurs if the relevant evidence more likely supports one party's contentions than the other's. This criterion is known as the preponderance of the evidence. Unlike the determination of guilt or innocence in a criminal proceeding, which constitutionally requires a finding of guilt "beyond a reasonable doubt," in civil proceedings the standard at least lends itself to theoretical definition. As in all other respects in which the law employs "reasonableness" or "reasonable" to guide its decisions, what is beyond a reasonable doubt is wholly subjective: It locates in the mind of the faithful and is impervious to empirically established counterarguments.

Preponderance of the evidence, however, does admit to verbal quantification: more likely than not. The standard does not require any specific measure of "likelihood." An iota or a trifle more suffices. Of course, disagreement will characterize the weight to be assigned any particular bit of evidence, but at least the ascribed weights – though arbitrary – can be added up and a presumably rational decision meaningfully justified. Of course, injustice and miscarriages of justice can and do occur under either standard. But at least *preponderance* admits of definition, unlike *reasonable*.

A third, more recently established, standard exists: "clear and convincing evidence." It applies primarily in cases governed by equitable, rather than strictly legal, procedures: that is, those not governed by the common law, such as wills and trusts, injunctions, termination of parental rights, and custody. It requires less "proof" than beyond a reasonable doubt, but more than a preponderance of the evidence. As such, it may be viewed as a halfway house. Consider *Stenberg v. Carhart*,[31] in which the Supreme Court upheld the findings of the lower federal court that the so-called partial-birth procedure used by the physician defendant was superior to and safer than dilation and extraction and other procedures used for abortions performed during the second trimester of pregnancy. In this case, clear and convincing medical evidence, which admitted of quantification empirically, substantiated the finding that the physician's procedure threatened health less than the alternatives.[32]

MULTIPARTY AND MULTICLAIM LITIGATION

Common law did not allow for more than a single plaintiff and a single respondent in a lawsuit. Equity courts, however, which were established to overcome

---

[31] 539 U.S. 914 (2000).

[32] We parenthetically note that the double-jeopardy clause of the Constitution does not prohibit a defendant from being civilly tried after a criminal verdict.

the inflexibility and limitations of the common law, permitted all aspects of a case to be considered simultaneously. State and federal rules, developed over the past 150 years, merged law and equity, a result of which is multiparty and multiclaim litigation. The most common form is the counterclaim.

Counterclaim

If the defendant believes she has a valid claim against the plaintiff, she may file a counterclaim. Joinder of such claims lessens the number of separate law-suits and enables all of the parties' claims against one another to be resolved in one judicial proceeding. Two types exist: permissive and compulsory counter-claims. The federal courts and most states use both. The former encompasses any defendant's claim that does not arise out of the claims of the opposing party. Hence, the respondent may introduce any matter concerning the plain-tiff as a counterclaim. The only requisite, effectively, is that the plaintiff be the sued party. A compulsory counterclaim, by contrast, must be filed or forever be barred, with a couple of minor exceptions. Such a claim arises out of the transaction or occurrence that is the subject matter of the plaintiff's claim.

Whether a counterclaim arises out of the subject matter of the plaintiff's action, and thus is compulsory, may rest on its logical connection with the plaintiff's claim. But no more than the concept of reasonableness does logic lend itself to a fair or just result. Any conclusion, no matter how ludicrous or absurd, may be encased in a logical framework. Much to be preferred, though still lacking empirical definition, is a rule that substantial evidence bear on both the claim and the counterclaim.

Joinder of Claims and Parties

Either additional claims or additional parties may be joined to the action brought by the original plaintiff against the original respondent. Joinder of claims need not detain us. If a party has made a claim against another party, she may attach to her initial claim all others she has against the same party. Although the claimant need not join all her claims in the lawsuit, prudence and rules against splitting of a cause of action dictate joinder as a general rule.

Though much joinder of parties is permissive, the joinder of some is com-pulsory as the later section, Necessary and Indispensable Parties, will show. The test for the permissive joinder of additional plaintiffs or respondents is the same: A single transaction, or occurrence, or series of such must have occurred and, second, at least one question of law or fact common to all must be present. The same test for determining the existence of these considerations applies here as in permissive counterclaims: a logical connection or common evidence.

Joinder requires the court to have personal jurisdiction over each joined defendant as determined by the minimum-contacts test. Each of them must be personally served with notice of the pending proceedings. And though the court may have *in personam* jurisdiction over the defendants, they must also be within the reach of the state's long-arm statute. Federal courts adhere to the long-arm statute of the state in which they sit. If the case arises under diversity jurisdiction in federal court,[33] complete diversity must exist among the parties: That is, each party on one side must be a resident of a state different from all of those on the other side.

Necessary and Indispensable Parties

Rules compel the joinder of necessary and indispensable parties to protect persons who might be harmed by a judgment entered in their absence, as well as those who might not obtain complete relief without the participation of such parties. The distinction between them lacks clarity when applied to concrete situations. A necessary party is one who has an interest in the litigation and whose interest might be adversely affected if not joined. An indispensable party is one whose interest would definitely be affected by any final judgment of the court.

SUMMARY AND CONCLUSIONS

In this chapter, we have focused on our adversary system of justice and the five major components of civil procedure: a court's jurisdiction over persons and things, the plaintiff's complaint and the respondent's answer, discovery, trial procedures, and multiparty and multiclaim litigation. Our overall treatment, of course, only highlights the essentials of civil procedure. Not only is much detail omitted, so also are many of its ramifications. And though these subjects do not excite the legally inclined, it is not inaccurate to posit that a practitioner's possession of the skills attendant to their mastery – along with mastery of the rules of evidence – determines the outcome of most litigation.

Even a cursory appraisal of this chapter should make the reader aware of the interrelationships among these components of civil procedure. Especially important is an awareness that the rules governing civil procedure – as with those applicable to legal fields generally – not only do not admit of mathematical precision, but do not even bear a modicum of objectivity. As noted, the eye of the beholder determines their applicability. The fact that many of the law's rules and tests are labeled *objective* no more evinces their truth, or their correspondence with reality, than it does the figments of one's imagination. As they do for Humpty Dumpty in *Through the Looking Glass*, words mean what courts, judges, and attorneys choose them to mean. As Alice said, "The question is whether you *can* make words mean so many different things." That is not the question, said Humpty Dumpty. "The question is ... which is to be master, that's all."[34]

---

[33] Diversity jurisdiction is discussed in Chapter 8.

[34] Lewis Carroll, *Alice's Adventures in Wonderland and Through the Looking Glass* (New York: Oxford University Press, 1971), p. 190.

5

Evidence

Trial court decisions, as well as those of administrative agency tribunals, depend on the facts of the matter at issue. The admissibility and inadmissibility of facts depend, in turn, on the rules of evidence. Perhaps more than in any other field of law, evidence embodies features that distort "truth" and debase "justice," however defined. Each state has its own rules of evidence, as do the federal courts. State rules substantially copy the federal rules, although except for rules that impact constitutional provisions – such as, the privilege against self-incrimination – the states are free to devise their own.

The federal rules, however, are not exclusive to the federal courts. They do not govern the actions of the Supreme Court, and Congress has authorized various agencies, such as the Departments of Agriculture and Interior, to formulate their own rules for certain of their administrative proceedings. Congress has also specified distinctive rules for the exclusion of some imported goods, requests by convicted criminals for habeas corpus relief, and certain admiralty matters.

The original source of the rules of evidence is the common law. Codification did not occur until the middle of the twentieth century. In 1953, a national conference of judges, law professors, and lawyers approved the Uniform Rules of Evidence, which were meant for state adoption. In 1972, the Federal Rules of Evidence (FRE), drafted by another distinguished group of law-related professionals, were approved by the Supreme Court. Congress revised them somewhat, and they became effective in 1975. Almost forty states have since modeled their rules on the FRE.

THE GENESIS OF EVIDENCE LAW

Evidence law began to develop more than five hundred years ago, when trial by jury began to assume its modern form. Juries today are depicted on stage and screen, in books and articles. Incessant popularization has made the jury the bedrock of our judicial system. Alteration elsewhere has become feasible, but only a monomaniacal masochist would attempt meaningful reform of our jury system. Evidence law also manifests continuity, but unlike the jury system it has been subject to emendation and alteration. Its one constant feature has been its *mistrust* of juries. Given this focus, the rules of evidence have little application to bench trials – those that judges decide without a jury.

This mistrust was rooted in apprehension that jurors were – or at least could readily be – misled by certain information. Testimony about a person's character or previous behavior could incline the jury to find an accused innocent or guilty, regardless of other considerations. Second- or thirdhand statements – he said or she said that *x* said that *y* did such and such – could in itself damn or exonerate. Disclosure of confidential matters could subvert relationships of far greater import than what the trial was all about: that of husband and wife or priest and penitent, to say nothing of that of the attorney and client. As a result, the law of evidence largely turns on what juries may see and hear, and what they may not.

That is not to say, however, that evidence law has no other functions than to allay mistrust of juries. It does, but at root they may be viewed as offshoots of this historic suspicion. In what follows, we will focus on manifestations of suspectness: relevance, the hearsay rule, circumstantial evidence, constitutional provisions impacting the production of evidence, privileges, expert witnesses, and eyewitness testimony.

These foci do not exhaust the scope of the law of evidence, of course, but at least they enable us to cast some much needed light into the Stygian ooze of evidence law and perhaps unravel the Labyrinthian maze in which it thrives.

Recognize that evidence rules, no more than other aspects of the legal and judicial process, do not treat everyone equally. The playing field tilts to certain litigants' advantage. An unrepresented party, for example, will almost certainly lose in a conflict with a represented opponent because of ignorance of the rules of evidence. An attorney's mastery of cross-examination may effectively enable her to destroy the credibility of those who take the stand in opposition to her client – regardless of the truthfulness of their testimony.

RELEVANCE

Although major trials, civil as well as criminal, not uncommonly run on for what appears to be an inordinate length of time, if relevance were no consideration, their duration would prodigiously lengthen until the less persistent party threw in the towel. The cost of litigation – certainly not cheap – would balloon exponentially, and, coupled with resources, stamina would become the mark of the successful litigant. "Justice," as conventionally understood, would be an ineffective – indeed a meaningless – aspect of courtroom proceedings. The scales would tilt even more than they do now in favor of wealthy defendants.

In other words, without the rule of relevance, a trial would run on interminably and, as in a Senate filibuster, range as far afield from the facts of the dispute as an enterprising attorney cared to carry them. Relevance, therefore, restricts and confines the lawsuit to material that closely pertains to the heart of the dispute. The FRE defines *relevant evidence* as "evidence having any tendency to make the existence of any fact that is of consequence to the determination of the action more probable or less probable than it would be without the evidence." The language *any tendency* to make the action more or less probable clearly sets a very low threshold of admissibility.

"Sufficiency of evidence," a major consideration in federal workers' compensation cases, is not its equivalent. Commentators have analogized "any tendency" to a brick in a wall; "sufficiency" to the wall itself.

A second rule circularly says that "all relevant evidence is admissible" and that "evidence which is not relevant is not admissible." The rule, however, goes on to exclude from the definition of *relevant evidence* anything decreed to be irrelevant by the Constitution, acts of Congress, the FRE itself, plus rules and decisions of the Supreme Court.

A final rule authorizes trial court judges to exclude – at their discretion – relevant material that they believe will be outweighed by its prejudicial effect, juror confusion, and/or unnecessary delay in the conduct of the trial. Do note, however, that all evidence is intended to be prejudicial to the party against whom it is introduced. What the rule prohibits is *unfair* prejudice. And of course this raises the specter of subjectivity. As it does in the criterion of reasonableness, what is fair or unfair largely locates in the eye of the beholder: the trial court judge. If the proffered evidence is on all fours with that in a previous case, precedent will likely control. But precedent covers very little of the waterfront except in mundane matters. And even then the judge may find that existing precedents support admissibility and others equally authoritatively support inadmissibility. As we have noted elsewhere, precedents exist on both sides of all but the most commonplace controversies.[1]

The upshot: Juries often do not hear relevant evidence because of possible misunderstandings of one sort or another, yet those same juries are expected to digest and evaluate hundreds or thousands of pages of testimony – usually without notes or a copy of the transcript, as we mentioned in our discussion of the adversary system at the beginning of Chapter 4. A more mind-boggling oxymoronic arrangement is hard to imagine.

Admissibility

As the discussion of relevance indicates, the underlying issue at trial becomes a matter of admissibility. This concept also dates to the common law because no other criterion could provide any assurance that the secret and unsupervised

---

[1] Jeffrey A. Segal and Harold J. Spaeth, *The Supreme Court and the Attitudinal Model Revisited* (Cambridge: Cambridge University Press, 2002), pp. 77–80. Also see Harold J. Spaeth and Jeffrey A. Segal, *Majority Rule or Minority Rights: Adherence to Precedent on the U.S. Supreme Court* (Cambridge: Cambridge University Press, 1999).

deliberations of the jury would not become sidetracked. "So to control the quality and ensure the legitimacy of jury verdicts the common law did the next best thing – screen the evidence that juries got to hear and evaluate."[2] Thereby bias toward or against a party, deviation from the law, or the rendering of a "bad" verdict might be lessened.

Obviously, concern about admissibility has no place in bench trials. Judges make such determinations, and if only the judge hears and decides the merits of the case, what is the point of his or her admitting evidence or not admitting it? Indeed, administrative tribunals, small claims, and other nonjury courts have few limitations on admissibility. Relevance remains requisite, along with privileged matters (to be discussed later), such as attorney–client, husband–wife, or priest–penitent relationships. These warrant exclusion, along with unconstitutionally obtained evidence, not because they are irrelevant to the case, but because trials are a matter of public record (except proceedings arising from the acerebral paranoia unleashed by the 9/11 attacks), disclosure of private and confidential communications would become public knowledge.

So, why have antiadmissibility rules not been trashed in bench trials? There must be a point to their retention, notwithstanding the seeming witlessness of requesting a judge to blind herself to relevant evidence. Sheldon and Murray suggest three reasons.[3] The first is the increasing incidence of litigation in which one of the parties appears unrepresented by an attorney (*pro se*). Said person likely lacks knowledge of evidence law. If an attorney represents the other party and the judge (as is likely) gives effect to the antiadmissibility rules when the attorney objects, the outcome of the proceeding is likely preordained: The unrepresented party loses, notwithstanding an abundance of relevant and probative evidence found wanting only because it runs afoul of the hearsay rule, concerns character, lacks authentication, or constitutes opinion.

A second reason for retention is the organized bar. Evidence law in general and its exclusionary rules in particular make trial attorneys' services more valuable than they would otherwise be. Any lessening of their applicability would concomitantly lessen the scope of their services, to say nothing of their fees.

Finally, change produces discomfort, particularly change of a long-standing cherished tradition, here trial by jury and the adversary process of dispute resolution. And though it certainly is not a cherished tradition, we nonetheless, for example, composed this book on computer keyboards designed not for typists' convenience, but rather for the arrangement of their keys, which atavistically lessens the incidence of manual typewriter jamming.

One saving feature of the antiadmissibility rules in bench trials is that an appellate court is unlikely to reverse or remand to the trial court because it admitted the inadmissible, on the sensible assumption that the judge was not

---

[2] John Sheldon and Peter Murray, "Rethinking the Rules of Evidentiary Admissibility in Non-Jury Trials," 86 *Judicature* 227 (2003).
[3] *Id.* at 231.

improperly influenced by its admission. This is notwithstanding the fact that the FRE applies to bench as well as jury trials.

Mandated Exclusions of Relevant Material

A string of rules excludes from consideration evidence that – but for the exclusions – is clearly relevant both legally and logically. These are matters meant to restrict jury discretion either because unfair prejudice may result or because desirable social policies would be blunted if the material were admitted. Recognize that these exclusions result from legalistic mistrust of jurors. And further note that judges – lawyers all – have little discretion, even if they are so minded, about whether to exclude them when a proper objection is made. Although exclusion can be justified in jury trials, as noted in the preceding section, no such justification would apply in a rationally focused judicial system in which the judge alone hears and decides the case.

Remedial Measures. Injured plaintiffs commonly attempt to establish culpability by attempting to introduce evidence that the respondent (the sued party or tortfeasor) attempted to conceal his responsibility for the plaintiff's injury by making repairs or otherwise remedying the condition that gave rise to the plaintiff's injury. Thus the property owner repairs the step on which the plaintiff slipped or replaces a porch railing from which the injured person fell. Or a manufacturer quickly adds a safety feature to a product alleged to be subject to defective design.

The relevant rule states that such measures may not be introduced as evidence of fault, negligence, culpability, defective product, or failure to warn. In short, any effort to remedy or repair the offending item or condition after the occurrence of an injury may not be used as evidence of the respondent's liability. But the rule does not require exclusion if such evidence is introduced for some other purpose, such as ownership, control, or the feasibility of precautionary measures.

We have here an excellent example of the irreconcilability of conflicting legal principles: public safety versus individual responsibility.

Compromise or Settlement Offer. Assume a fender bender in which Driver rear-ends Victim. Realizing she was at fault, Driver offers to pay Victim one thousand dollars for the damage she has caused, plus any medical expense that Victim may incur. Victim declines Driver's offer and instead files a lawsuit assuming his case will become a slam dunk when the settlement offer is called to the court's attention. Wrong: Evidence rules strictly prohibit such. Apart from unduly influencing jurors, social policy encourages out-of-court settlements, as does the judicial system itself. Trial courts have enough to keep them busy. Hence, there is no desire to discourage extracourt settlement of disputes. But, as with matters of evidence generally, there are exceptions to most rules. In the preceding situation, for example, if the offer was made to preclude a traffic citation because Driver exceeded the speed limit or if she would lose her driver's license because of multiple offenses, the exception does not apply.

Insurance. Closely related to the preceding exclusion is the matter of insurance that covers the persons or property involved in the claimed injury. This rule results from the view that jurors are more likely to decree liability if the injuring party has insurance, on the assumption that assessment of damages will not harm the tortfeasor financially. This again further evidences juror distrust.

Character Evidence. Ambivalence about character evidence typifies evidence law. More often than not, it may not be admitted, but numerous circumstances allow its consideration.

Basically, a person's characteristics or traits may not be admitted if their purpose is to cause the jury to infer or conclude that because of the defendant's or the tortfeasor's trait, she behaved the same way in the context of the litigation currently before the court. In other words, a person's propensity for behaving in a certain fashion in the past is not admissible as evidence that he or she behaved the same way in the current case. This rule rests on two premises: It may simply be false, or it may unduly incline the jury to conclude that yesterday's trait explains today's conduct.

Three major exceptions warrant notice: First, if a defendant (this applies only to criminal, not civil, cases) introduces evidence of his or her *own* character, then the prosecution may introduce character evidence in rebuttal. Second, if such a defendant introduces evidence that the *victim* – rather than he – has the pertinent characteristic, again the prosecution may rebut, for instance, if a defendant claims self-defense and purports to show that the victim had a violent temper. The prosecution may rebut with evidence to the contrary.

The third major exception is a set of rules applicable to both criminal and civil sexual offenses that Congress added to the FRE in 1994. In pertinent part they read that an accusation of "sexual assault" or "child molestation" allows the prosecution or the victim in a civil case to introduce evidence of previous such offenses by the alleged perpetrator. Because such previous evidence is highly prejudicial, defendants are entitled to prior warning that it will be introduced.

As with the other rules we have considered, exceptions also exist here. Hence, character evidence is admissible in criminal cases, for example, to establish motive, opportunity, intent, plan, skill, or knowledge. But unlike in the other rules, here the jury is expected to segregate these alternative purposes from the determination of guilt or innocence. This expectation reeks of asininity. It has as much grounding in reality as a judge's instruction to a jury that it disregard all information to which a party's attorney has successfully objected.

The FRE and many state rules distinguish habit from a person's character, as evidence of habit is admissible usually on the testimony of witnesses. The distinction between them is their level of generality. Traits, or character, are general; habit specific. For the latter to exist, three factors are requisite: (1) specific behavior: for example, a driver who never runs a caution light as compared with one who always drives carefully; (2) regularity: for example, a daily activity that an individual engages in 95 percent of the time, as compared with one done only half the time; and (3) semiautomatic: such as the unreflective fastening of one's seat belt before starting the motor.

It may be noted that, by contrast, the routine activities of businesses and other organizations tend to be admissible without much question. The rationale – surprisingly sensible – is the importance of routine for successful organizational activity.

Criticism of the use of habit to sustain or refute relevant action has several bases. An individual can deviate from his or her habit in order to establish an alibi or other nonculpable behavior. Moreover, as noted, a habit need not be invariant. Perhaps on the crucial day, deviation occurred. Evidence of habit may be falsely alleged and difficult to refute. A mother may testify that on the days she drove her son to school, he always looked both ways before crossing the street in front of the school.

HEARSAY

Hearsay is an out-of-court statement – a verbal or written statement or assertive conduct – made by someone other than the person testifying that is offered to prove the truth of the matter asserted, which matter pertains to a disputed trial issue. The typical example is an assertion by the witness that "she said to me that . . . " or "he told his friend, who told me that. . . . " In other words, the person testifying did not witness the relevant event, and only witnessed a report of the event.

Courts exclude hearsay because the jury cannot determine whether the out-of-court communicator knew what he was talking about; whether she intended to tell the truth or remembered enough of the matter to relate it accurately; or even whether he had a vocabulary sufficient for meaningful communication. These conditions, of course, do not apply if the declarant is available for cross-examination, thus obviating the dangers of hearsay: that the declarant's statement was ambiguous, insincere, the product of erroneous memory or inaccurate perception.

The declarant's presence as a witness lessens such dangers because the witness testifies under oath (and presumably those so testifying do so more truthfully). In-court testimony allows the fact finder (judge or jury) to ascertain the witness's demeanor. But this does not necessarily lead to a correct verdict. Examples abound of judges – to say nothing of juries – who give credence to a witness's manner of presentation rather than to the veracity of what is said. A nervous, halting witness or one who testily, smugly, or condescendingly responds to questions may well be viewed as less believable than one on the other side who graciously and respectfully testifies in a dignified manner and in a mellifluous voice.[4]

---

[4] For an extreme, though not uncommon, example, see the editorial "Federal Judges vs. Science," *New York Times*, 27 December 1986, p. 14.

Better reasons for requiring in-court testimony are context and cross-examination. Providing the framework or milieu of the events about which a witness testifies allows the accuracy of the testimony to be assessed more accurately. Cross-examination is a favored practice of skilled litigators. "No technique known to jurisprudence is a better instrument for ascertaining the truth."[5] Though this sort of assertion may accurately apply to some lawsuits, that no better device exists for falsifying the truth is equally true. Not only is the law rife with such contradictory judgments, rules, and principles, it also readily employs devices that, as does water, readily sustain or destroy well-being.

Merely employing an attorney skillful in terrorizing opposing witnesses not uncommonly causes the other party to settle. The demeanor and behavior of the witness who is crucified on the stand thus become determinative, facts of the matter to the contrary notwithstanding.

Hearsay is only evidence that is presented to support the truth of what was spoken or written; if its purpose is something else, no problem. Thus, warnings do not legally amount to hearsay because they are not meant to state the truth, but rather to establish relevance to alleged negligence. A matter that does amount to hearsay, but that the FRE defines otherwise, is relevant out-of-court admissions made by a party to a lawsuit. The noncommunicating party – the opponent – may use these to her advantage.

The FRE contains more than two dozen such exceptions, all of which lessen the scope and applicability of the hearsay rule. Some of them apply only if the declarant is unavailable; thus testimony previously given under oath and subject to cross-examination is admissible, as are dying declarations, declarants' statements against their financial or property interests, as well as those inculpating the declarant in criminal or civil liability. The likelihood that they are true rationalizes these exclusions.

Hearsay exceptions admissible whether or not the declarant is available to testify include excited utterances made close in time to a startling or shocking event. The rationale here is that the event overcomes any tendency to lie. Other exceptions, regardless of the declarant's availability to testify, include statements of medical diagnosis and treatment, recorded past recollections, and organizational records of regularly conducted activity.

Medical diagnoses can be problematic if they occur independently of treatment. Persons who provide ongoing medical treatment are considered much less likely to speak untruthfully than a physician engaged solely in diagnosis, who may see an injured party only for the purpose of serving as an expert witness at trial. Less problematic are recorded past recollections, assuming, as the FRE specifies, that they were made proximate to the event in question. Adding to their evidentiary value are requirements of insurance adjustors and police that the declarant attest that the document she signed accurately and truthfully specifies what the witness saw or knew.

[5] Steven L. Emanuel, *Evidence*, 3d ed. (Larchmont, NY: Emanuel Law Outlines, 1996), p. 176.

CIRCUMSTANTIAL EVIDENCE

Circumstantial evidence contrasts with direct evidence. The latter asserts the existence of a fact requiring proof or, if the evidence in question is tangible rather than verbal, embodies or represents the contested fact. Direct evidence is always relevant, assuming, of course, that it pertains to a matter consequential to the lawsuit. Not so circumstantial evidence.

Circumstantial evidence implies proof. The proof neither asserts nor represents the fact to be proved, but rather allows the fact finder to infer the probability that the fact occurred. Thus, a suspect's deoxyribonucleic acid (DNA) that does not match that taken from the victim's body allows the fact finder to infer that it is extremely improbable (almost infinitesimally) that the suspect is guilty. Although public perception again deviates from reality, courts view circumstantial evidence as at least as trustworthy as direct evidence. Indeed, given what we know of the fallibility of eyewitness testimony, it is markedly more probative, so much so that criminal convictions may rest entirely on circumstantial evidence. A classic example is the conviction of a Manhattan plastic surgeon on the basis of opinions of a medical examiner, police pilot, and other experts that he murdered his five-foot three-inch, 110-pound wife; dismembered her body in ten minutes so that it fit into a thirty-six-inch package; transported it to New Jersey, loaded the package into a small airplane; and while flying alone tossed it into the Atlantic Ocean.[6]

In a capital case before the Supreme Court, Justice Kennedy reacted to a Texas attorney general's assertion that the prosecutor's use of race to exclude black jurors in cases other than the one before the Court, although not completely irrelevant, was little better than circumstantial. To which Justice Kennedy responded: "Why isn't this very significant evidence, to which we must give great weight? The best evidence is often circumstantial."[7] When the case was decided, Kennedy wrote the Court's opinion, agreed to by all but Justice Thomas, that the evidence in question was relevant and probative and that the convict was entitled to a hearing.[8]

Litigation lends itself well to circumstantial evidence – especially when coupled with expert testimony – in product liability cases; health claims, such as, tobacco litigation; immigration matters; sex discrimination; and intellectual property controversies.[9] Not uncommonly these sorts of cases wend their way

---

[6] *People v. Bierenbaum*, 301 A.D. 2d 119; 748 N.Y.S. 2d 563 (2002). Also see Tom Perrotta, "Conviction of Surgeon for Murdering Wife Upheld," *New York Law Journal*, 23 October 2002, p. 1.

[7] Linda Greenhouse, "Court Revisits Question of Jury Selection Bias," *New York Times*, 17 October 2002, p. A26.

[8] *Miller-El v. Cockrell*, 537 U.S. 322 (2003).

[9] *Lekkas v. Mitsubishi Motors Corp.*, No. 97 C 6070 (N.D. Ill. 2002); *Longden v. Philip Morris USA*, No. 00-C-442 (N.H. Super. Ct., Hillsborough County 2003); *United States v. Yoshida*, 303 F. 3d 1145 (9th Cir. 2002); *Costa v. Desert Palace*, 539 U.S. 90 (2003); *Moseley v. V Secret Catalogue Inc.*, 537 U.S. 418 (2003).

to the Supreme Court, as the citation of the last two of the preceding controversies attests.

Certain matters can only be proved by circumstantial evidence; the best example is spoliation – that is, a party's destruction, mutilation, alteration, or concealment of relevant evidence. Given the behavior of such major corporations as Enron, Arthur Anderson, and WorldCom caught up in the stockholding and financial-reporting shenanigans of the early years of the younger Bush administration, this is not an idle matter of mere speculation. Unfortunately, no uniform national standard has emerged either from Congress or from authoritative court decisions.[10] Granted that the nonspoliating party must provide evidence of the contents of the spoliated evidence, a matter that usually cannot be precisely defined. Thus, for example, must circumstantial evidence establish that the missing evidence would have been adverse to the spoliating party? And how culpable must the spoliating party have been for guilt to result?

Other matters that can only be proved circumstantially include the intent to deceive or defraud. Such matters, however, require more circumstantial evidence than mere suspicion.

CONSTITUTIONAL PROVISIONS IMPACTING THE PRODUCTION OF EVIDENCE

We preliminarily note that underlying all constitutional provisions pertaining to judicial resolution of disputes is the notion that persons are innocent until proven guilty. Although this rule most forcefully applies to persons accused of crime, it has its counterpart in civil proceedings in rules governing the burden of proof – a matter that we discussed in Chapter 4 in the section on burden of proof. It most especially applies where government institutes action – criminal or civil – against individuals. And though we assert that we value innocence highly, we silently discard it in times of perceived peril. The aftermath of 9/11 illustrates. A report by the Justice Department's inspector general – an official who functions as a quasi-ombudsman in many governmental agencies – said that the usual presumptions of the legal system were turned upside down in the aftermath of the 9/11 terrorist attacks. With the express approval of the attorney general, John Ashcroft, hundreds of persons were detained for inordinate lengths of time by the Federal Bureau of Investigation (FBI) on immigration charges, denied access to lawyers, denied bond, and denied release notwithstanding federal court orders to the contrary. "The department needed to disrupt such persons from carrying out further attacks by turning its focus to prevention, rather than investigation and prosecution."[11] Not

---

[10] See Drew D. Dropkin, "Note: Linking the Culpability and Circumstantial Evidence Requirements for the Spoliation Inference," 51 *Duke Law Journal* 1803 (2002).

[11] Adam Liptak, "For Jailed Immigrants, a Presumption of Guilt," *New York Times*, 9 June 2003, p. A14.

surprisingly, given our history,[12] federal courts of appeals have upheld similar action by federal authorities: refusing to disclose the names of persons arrested for immigration violations because their names might "help Al Qaeda figure out how law enforcement officials were conducting the nation's antiterrorist campaign."[13]

Although any number of constitutional provisions may, in specific situations, impact the rules of evidence, two apply directly and as such: the confrontation and compulsory process clauses of the Sixth Amendment.[14]

The confrontation clause simply states that "in all criminal prosecutions, the accused shall enjoy the right ... to be confronted with the witnesses against him." The clause clearly evidences the preference of the Framers of the Constitution for live, in-court, testimony. It also means that hearsay testimony, unless it contains substantial reliability or falls within an accepted exception, is inadmissible.

Nevertheless, it definitely does not mean what it flatly says: that persons accused of crime always and everywhere have the right to confront their accusers. *Maryland v. Craig*[15] nicely illustrates the matter: Maryland, along with more than half the states, permits juveniles to testify via one-way closed-circuit television in child abuse cases. This allows the demeanor of the child to be observed, but the child cannot see the defendant. The purpose obviously aids the prosecution of such cases. Direct confrontation might cause victims and witnesses to refuse to testify or to curb or qualify their testimony. As a result, a child might suffer emotional distress precluding effective communication. Nonetheless, in a 5–4 vote, the Court, speaking through Justice O'Connor, ruled that the clause did not amount to a command, but only a "preference" for direct confrontation. A showing that the witness would be traumatized overruled the constitutional language. Justice Scalia, joined by the Court's three most liberal members – Marshall, Brennan, and Stevens – dissented. "Seldom," he said, "has this Court failed so conspicuously to sustain a categorical guarantee of the Constitution against the tide of prevailing current opinion." "For good or

---

[12] Kirk A. Randazzo, "Defenders of Civil Liberties or Champions of National Security? The Federal Courts and U.S. Foreign Policy (unpublished Ph.D. diss., Michigan State University, 2003).

[13] Neil A. Lewis, "Secrecy Is Backed on 9/11 Detainees," *New York Times*, 18 June 2003, p. A1. Short of lengthy incommunicado detention, unsubstantiated terrorism tips – proved false after cursory investigation – have nonetheless led the named persons to be detained and suffer obloquy, loss of business, and inclusion on lists of potential suspects. See Michael Moss, "False Terrorism Tips to F.B.I. Uproot the Lives of Suspects," *New York Times*, 19 June 2003, p. A1, and the examples cited therein.

[14] Among others applicable in particular circumstances are the search and seizure clause of the Fourth Amendment, which prohibits the use of unconstitutionally obtained evidence, even though it is perfectly valid and reliable; the Fifth Amendment, which prohibits individuals from incriminating themselves for criminal offenses; and due process, which prohibits involuntary confessions and biased judicial decision makers, whether judge or jury, as well as other actions that run afoul of the nebulous notion of a fair trial.

[15] 497 U.S. 836 (1990).

bad, the Sixth Amendment requires confrontation, and we are not at liberty to ignore it."[16]

Notwithstanding *Maryland v. Craig*, the confrontation clause authorizes criminal defendants to exclude damaging evidence and serves, where necessary, to buttress rules against out-of-court and hearsay evidence, especially when cross-examination is not available to the accused. The compulsory process clause, on the other hand, is an inclusionary device that enables the accused to demand the presence of witnesses and evidence of an exculpatory sort. An exclusionary rule may thus run afoul of the clause if it prevents the defendant from presenting material and relevant evidence.

Thus, for example, a rule that allows the prosecution to present evidence against a coparticipant in a crime while denying that option to the codefendant violates the clause.[17] In a somewhat more complicated situation, the Court, over the solitary dissent of Justice Rehnquist, ruled that due process – to which both the confrontation and compulsory process clauses are closely related – barred a pair of state rules of evidence based on the common law. The defendant called a witness to introduce the witness's own confession to the crime. On cross-examination, the witness repudiated the confession and presented an alibi. The defendant then sought to cross-examine the witness but was denied the rights to do so on the basis that one may not impeach his own witness. The defendant then attempted to present the testimony of three witnesses to whom the first witness had confessed the crime. This action the judge rejected as hearsay. The Supreme Court reversed the conviction as a violation of due process because the rights to confront and cross-examine adverse witnesses and to present witnesses in one's own behalf were violated.

We may safely conclude, therefore, that rules that advantage the prosecution to the detriment of the accused's compulsory process or confrontation rights are typically unconstitutional, the common law or statutory rules of evidence to the contrary notwithstanding.

PRIVILEGES

Privileges are the right of individuals not to disclose information about a particular event. The FRE does not specify what privileges should be recognized in federal court. This decision is left to the individual district court, subject to review by higher courts, and should be based on such concepts as fairness, equal treatment, and the equitable notion "to do justice." In diversity actions involving residents of different states and that entail no federal question, the law of the state in which the federal court sits determines what constitutes a privilege. The states vary greatly in the privileges they recognize.

Privileges obviously exclude information relevant and probative to the outcome of judicial proceedings. As such, they run counter to the ostensible

---

[16] *Id.* at 860, 870.
[17] *Washington v. Texas*, 388 U.S. 14 (1967).

truth-seeking function of courtroom proceedings. Privileged information cannot be introduced into a trial; nor may it be subject to discovery. Its scope is actual statements made in the context of a confidential relationship. We will discuss the most common of them: attorney–client, husband–wife, priest–penitent, and physician–patient.[18]

Attorney–Client

The essence of the attorney–client privilege is the right of clients not to disclose confidential communications with their attorneys and to prevent their attorneys from doing so. Conditioning the privilege are several justifications: a genuine client–lawyer relationship, a reasonable expectation of privacy, communication pertinent to a legal matter, and no connection with planned criminal action.

A client need not be a human being; it may be a business, a public organization, or any for-profit or nonprofit organization or association. The privilege extends to paralegals or other employees of a lawyer who participate in the rendering of legal services. Communications may be verbal or written, personally, electronically, or otherwise transmitted. It is confidential if not disclosed to third persons other than those engaged in the furtherance of the services rendered by the attorney. Client identity and the source of payment for services rendered generally exceed confidential bounds unless such disclosure may incriminate the named person.

The privilege does not apply to business or other nonlegal advice that an attorney renders, but it does apply to all stages of the legal process, including pretrial discovery. It also outlives the client if claimed by the decedent's executor or other representative.

Spousal Communications

Two distinct privileges govern spousal relationships. The extent to which either of them governs single-sex marriages or other nontraditional relationships that function as marital substitutes depends on the laws and policies of individual states. As of the end of 2004, at the federal level neither the FRE nor the Supreme Court had addressed this matter.

---

[18] The privilege against self-incrimination differs from the foregoing list. Unlike the others, it is constitutionally provided. It applies to criminal defendants and to witnesses in any case who fear that what they say might subsequently be used against them in a criminal proceeding. Embarrassment and humiliation are not bases for refusal to testify. The privilege protects only persons, not nonhuman legal persons, such as corporations. The privilege extends to testimonial evidence (words and documents), but not to physical evidence. It applies only to compelled statements. If the testifier is granted immunity from subsequent prosecution, she must testify under pain of contempt. The immunity extended prohibits governmental (either state or federal) use of what was communicated, not the general subject of the communication (known as *transactional immunity*).

One of the privileges gives the spouse immunity from the adverse testimony of the other partner; the other one prohibits disclosure of confidential communications made by one partner to the other during the marital relationship or its equivalent. All states recognize confidential communications, but only about half accept immunity from adverse testimony. The federal courts recognize both. Their rationale is marital harmony, and, as a result of criticism of this explanation for adverse testimony in cases in which disharmony runs rampant, an alternate rationale has surfaced: the human dignity embedded in an especially confidential relationship that the state strongly protects and fosters.

The adverse testimony privilege prevents, for example, a wife from testifying about her husband's crime. Historically, this prevented prosecution of intrafamilial crimes, most especially spousal and child abuse. Currently, the privilege does not protect such wrongdoing. Punishment of this sort of violent behavior outweighs privacy. A couple must be married at the time of the trial to preclude adverse testimony. And if they are, their premarital communications, if intended to be confidential, may not be disclosed. Traditionally, only a party to the lawsuit may invoke it, and then only in a criminal proceeding. But in 1980, the Supreme Court put the federal courts in line with a majority of the states and vested the privilege in the testifying spouse, whether she was a witness or a party.[19] The privilege extends to spousal actions, as well as communications. Thus a wife who observed her husband stealing his neighbor's property can refuse to testify about his actions.

The confidential communications privilege applies as long as the parties were spousally associated at the time of the communication, even if the relationship has since ended through either death or dissolution. Unlike adverse testimony, it applies to both criminal and civil proceedings. And also unlike in adverse testimony, either partner may invoke it, as may a witness to the communication so long as it was shown to be confidential. But the matter at issue must be a communication rather than an action, although some jurisdictions include noncommunicative acts performed in privacy with the other partner present, such as, concealing stolen property. The presence of a third party, even a couple's child, voids the confidentiality of the communication.

Priest–Penitent

All states recognize the confidentiality of confessional statements made by penitents to Roman Catholic priests. Jurisdictions generally extend this privilege to ministers, rabbis, and other clergy whose religion recognizes the import of confession. Whether the privilege reaches counseling varies from state to state. In general, it does not. Neither would it apply to self-anointed clergy, nor to those in less highly regarded cults.

---

[19] *Trammel v. United States*, 445 U.S. 40 (1980).

Physician–Patient

The common law recognized the physician–patient privilege to a markedly greater extent than do most jurisdictions today. Sick persons have strong motivation to disclose an ailment to their physicians, regardless of any confidentiality that the privilege may bestow on them. This undoubtedly accounts for many of its exceptions, as does the fact that whereas persons consult attorneys for purposes that may lead to litigation, they rarely do so with physicians. Hence, the likelihood that the patient will fail to disclose relevant information because of fear of disclosure is largely absent.

However, if a patient includes her condition into the issues of a lawsuit, the privilege does not apply. Accordingly, statements made to a physician by a patient–litigator are not protected. In most jurisdictions, the privilege does not apply to criminal proceedings.

All states' and the Supreme Court's interpretation of the relevant FRE rule have extended the privilege to therapists.[20] Indeed, this aspect of the physician–patient privilege has attained separate status and is broader in scope, covering statements made to professionals who are not physicians. Hence, jurisdictions commonly extend this privilege to nonphysician therapists, such as clinical psychologists and psychiatrically trained social workers.

The Supreme Court itself resolved a dispute among the federal courts of appeals and ruled that confidential communications between a licensed psychotherapist and her patient in the course of diagnosis or treatment or between a licensed social worker and client in the course of psychotherapy are immune from compelled disclosure. The privileged communications include conversations and notes taken during counseling sessions. Justices Scalia and Rehnquist dissented.[21]

The case arose from an effort to protect the records of a licensed clinical social worker and her patient, a police officer, who had killed a man in the line of duty. The man's family brought a civil rights suit against the officer in federal court. In his dissent, Justice Scalia – presumably with a straight face – complained that the ruling derogated the "traditional judicial preference for the truth."[22]

But what of situations in which the patient informs the therapist that he intends to kill someone? In what was originally the leading case, the California Supreme Court ruled that the therapist has a duty to warn third parties of a patient's threats.[23] A psychologist's patient killed a person two months after he had told the psychologist he intended to do so. He alerted the police, who briefly detained the patient. The psychologist's physician supervisor directed

---

[20] Rule 501: "Except as otherwise required . . . the privilege of a witness, person, government, State, or political subdivision thereof shall be governed by the principles of the common law . . . *in the light of reason and experience*" (emphasis added).

[21] *Jaffee v. Redmond*, 518 U.S. 1 (1996).

[22] *Id.* at 19.

[23] *Tarasoff v. Regents of the University of California*, 17 Cal. 3d 425; 551 P. 2d 334 (1976).

that no further action be taken. The patient was released. And no one warned the victim of her peril. The Court ruled that therapists cannot escape liability simply because the victim is not their patient. When a therapist determines or should determine that his patient presents a serious danger to another, he incurs an obligation to use reasonable care to protect that person, for example, by warning the victim or others entrusted to her care or the police.

A unanimous decision of the Texas Supreme Court reached – not surprisingly – an opposite conclusion: that a psychiatrist's duty to preserve confidentiality overrides the risk of a patient's harming someone.[24] On facts similar to those in *Tarasoff*, a psychiatrist treated his patient for three years with a combination of psychotherapy and drug therapy for his paranoid and delusional beliefs about his stepfather. After the psychiatrist's notes revealed that the patient "feels like killing" his stepfather, but that he "has decided not to do it but that is how he feels," the patient was hospitalized and treated for seven days. Within a month of discharge he shot and killed his stepfather. The psychiatrist warned neither family member nor law enforcement agency of his patient's homicidal tendencies.

Distinguishing between a patient's threats and *treatment* that may endanger third parties, the court "declined to adopt a duty to warn" because the relevant Texas statute "makes it unwise to recognize such common-law duty."[25] A dilemma would otherwise result: Disclose idle threats and incur liability to the patient or fail to disclose a truthful threat and incur liability to the victim. The plaintiff's attorney described the result as one in which Texas psychiatrists need not acquire malpractice insurance because the state supreme court would take care of them. The psychiatrist's lawyer judged that the decision enabled therapists to avert disaster because the confidentiality rule would help doctors get to the root of the problem.[26]

EXPERT TESTIMONY

Courts prefer the best available evidence on all matters in dispute. This generally means firsthand knowledge and the prohibition of opinions. The former excludes hearsay, which we have previously discussed. Courts dislike opinions because the matter of making inferences belongs to the fact finder, not the witness. But today's courts tolerate opinions if they rationally relate to the witness's testimony and help to clarify it.

Courts admit the testimony of expert witnesses, whom they view as those whose specialized knowledge will help the court decide correctly. Of course, when both sides present witnesses who not only are equally expert, but also disagree, the resulting battle between them may do little to clarify matters. Such

---

[24] *Thapar v. Zezulka*, 994 S.W. 2d 635 (1999).

[25] *Id.* at 638.

[26] Nathan Koppel, "No Shrink Duty to Rat on Patients," *National Law Journal*, 19 July 1999, p. A4.

battles between experts commonly occur for the simple reason that a party's experts, like his attorneys, are hired guns paid to do whatever it takes, short of perjury, to enable the hiring party to win the lawsuit. Typically, an expert will not only have expertise in her professional subfield (e.g., civil engineering, internal medicine, organic chemistry), but also appear only on the side of an injured plaintiff or on the side of the alleged tortfeasor. Indeed, a considerable number of professional persons earn their living only as expert witnesses – and then only as either a plaintiff's or a respondent's expert.

The FRE employs a broad definition of who is an *expert*: one qualified "by knowledge, skill, experience, training, or education." This means, according to a federal appeals court, that the crucial issue of whether a particular sample of marijuana was domestically or foreign grown turned on the testimony of an "expert" who qualified as such because he frequently smoked Colombian marijuana and sold that and other types of grass.[27] Thus, his "experience" qualified him as an expert.

In addition to being qualified, the expert must testify about a suitable subject: one that is essential or helpful to the fact finder in reaching a correct decision. Thus the language of FRE 702: "If scientific, technical, or other specialized knowledge will assist the trier of fact to understand the evidence or to determine a fact in issue, a witness qualified as an expert by knowledge, skill, experience, training, or education, may testify thereto in the form of an opinion or otherwise."

In its definitive decision in *Daubert v. Merrill Dow Pharmaceuticals*, in which it construed the relevant provisions of the FRE, the Supreme Court identified five criteria to determine whether a theory or technique is scientific: (1) whether it can be tested (i.e., falsifiability); (2) whether it has been subject to peer review and publication (thus excluding findings in law reviews, which are not subject to peer review); (3) the rate of error its application has produced; (4) the existence and maintenance of standards controlling the technique's operation; and (5) the acceptance of the technique within the relevant scientific community.[28] These criteria, of course, preclude acceptance of astrologers, dowsers, and creation scientists as experts.

Experts base their opinions on personal knowledge, the evaluation of the testimony of other witnesses, and their response to hypothetical questions posed by a party's attorney. To the extent that such sources in specific cases rest on impermissible evidence, the modern trend admits such if it is "of a type reasonably relied upon by experts."[29] This may include hearsay.

Courts formerly admitted testimony based on scientific evidence or procedures generally accepted by the relevant field. But with the growth and popularization of "junk science" in recent years, the Supreme Court, interpreting the FRE, markedly strengthened and expanded the authority of federal trial

---

[27] *United States v. Johnson*, 575 F. 2d 1347 (1979).
[28] 509 U.S. 579 (1993), at 593–594.
[29] FRE 702.

court judges by requiring them to scrutinize the reliability of the proffered evidence.[30] General acceptance may be one element of acceptance, but it is not controlling without more (i.e., the criteria specified in connection with note 28).

Admissibility of scientific evidence must depend on its validity as well as its reliability. Validity turns on the method employed. It must rest on a principle that supports what the testimony purports to demonstrate. Reliability requires that repeated applications or tests of the principle must produce consistent results. Such results typically must produce a confidence level of 95 percent if the matter pertains to social and medical science. This means that the probability of the obtained results did not likely result from chance because 95 of every 100 trials produce the same general outcome or result.

Note that the *Daubert* rule did not discard the general requirement that all evidence must be relevant, sufficiently connected with the facts of the case that it can help the fact finder arrive at a decision. Other aspects of *Daubert* involve peer review and publication, on the assumption that if the theory or technique passes muster within the scientific community, flaws will more likely be uncovered. If well-maintained professional standards have been applied properly to the relevant scientific matter, that also increases its acceptability under the FRE. Also pertinent is whether the testifying expert has used the technique or approach independently of litigation. The latter is considered much more acceptable because the likelihood that a technique or testifying expert is biased is sensibly minimized.

Before *Daubert*, whether the technique or test had become generally accepted controlled its admissibility. Hence, testimony based on theories or processes on the cutting edge of science were likely to be rejected. Now, "generally accepted" is only an acceptable, but not the dispositive, consideration.

As to the scope of *Daubert*, it clearly applies to so-called hard scientific evidence. But it also applies to the social sciences. The Court's specification of scientific knowledge employs language applicable to them: "Scientific methodology ... is based on generating hypotheses and testing them to see if they can be falsified; indeed, this methodology is what distinguishes science from other fields of human inquiry." "Statements constituting a scientific explanation must be capable of empirical test." The "criterion of the scientific status of a theory is its falsifiability, or refutability, or testability."[31]

Nonetheless, the lower federal courts remained considerably confused about *Daubert's* scope; confusion was not resolved until the Court's decision in *Kumho Tire Company v. Carmichael*.[32] In an opinion by Justice Breyer, the Court increased the authority of the federal trial courts by extending *Daubert's* scope to include technical and other specialized knowledge and in the process made it more difficult for "expert" testimony to be

---

[30] *Daubert v. Merrell Dow Pharmaceuticals, Inc.*, 509 U.S. 579 (1993).
[31] *Id.* at 593.
[32] 526 U.S. 137 (1999).

admitted.[33] Thus, before *Kumho*, judges regularly admitted expert economic testimony in antitrust cases about the relevant market, analyzed the ways the defendant monopolized the market, and determined the damages plaintiffs suffered.[34] But the worm turned after *Kumho*.

Thus, an eminent Stanford University economist found his model of a hypothetical market not based on economic reality inadmissible, because it ignored inconvenient evidence. The court said that though a theory may meet some admissible factors, one that does not apply to the specific facts of the case should not be admitted. An Illinois court went one better, expertwise, and ruled the testimony of a Nobel Laureate inadmissible because he was ignorant of material testimony and other evidence, and because his opinions were inconsistent with the evidence and without scientific basis.[35]

The upshot: Judges should take a flexible, case-by-case approach tailored to the expert's experience and expertise. Life and the legal cases it generates are too complex for sharp dividing lines between different kinds of expertise. "It would prove difficult, if not impossible, for judges to administer evidentiary rules under which a gatekeeping obligation depended upon a distinction between 'scientific' knowledge and 'technical' or 'other specialized' knowledge."[36]

EYEWITNESS TESTIMONY

Probably the public's most deeply rooted evidentiary belief – inside the courtroom as well as out – is the accuracy of what one has seen. The fact is that innumerable experimental studies – most often using college students as subjects – have demonstrated beyond peradventure that witnesses' reports of what they have seen bear only the slightest connection with what actually happened. And do recognize that these experiments are staged in such a fashion as to elicit accurate information. Thus, they occur in the classroom, in which students are told that a film of an automobile accident will be shown and they will be asked the color and type of the vehicles; how fast they were going; and the presence or absence of conditions that made the accident unavoidable or not. Also note the artificiality of the scenario: In real-world situations, accidents occur without forewarning; they startle and frighten witnesses, whose sight and other senses were preoccupied with other matters. So, if alerted students vary widely in what they report they have seen, how much accuracy should one ascribe to a surprised and unsuspecting eyewitness? Yet, judges and juries constantly base their

---

[33] David Hechler, "Courts Toss Out Expert Testimony," *National Law Journal*, 7 January 2002, pp. A20, A26. Mike Rappeport, "Applying 'Daubert,'" *National Law Journal*, 21 January 2002, p. A17.

[34] *Concord Boat v. Brunswick*, 207 F. 3d 1039 (2000).

[35] *In re Brand Name Prescription Drugs Antitrust Litigation*, 248 F. 3d 668 (2001). Not only have economists been held to high standards in recent cases, so also have geological engineers and accountants. Hechler, "Courts Toss."

[36] 526 U.S. at 148.

decisions on such testimony, especially in criminal cases, in which the stakes – loss of life, liberty, and/or property – are much higher than in civil litigation.[37]

Perhaps the most graphic evidence was the admission of a woman, Jennifer Thompson, who was not only an eyewitness to but also the victim of a horrendous crime: When she was a twenty-two-year-old student, who had a 4.0 grade point average (GPA), a person broke into her apartment and raped her. During her ordeal, she "studied every single detail on the rapist's face. I looked at his hairline; I looked for scars, for tattoos, for anything that would help me identify him." Several days later she identified the man, Ronald Cotton, from police photos and then identified him in a lineup. "I was sure. I knew it. I had picked the right guy.... If there was the possibility of a death sentence ... I wanted to flip the switch."

On retrial a year later because an appellate court had overturned the conviction, the victim learned that a Bobby Poole in the same prison wing where Cotton was held bragged about being her attacker. Taken into court, Ms. Thompson was asked whether she had even seen Poole. She replied that she "had never seen him in my life. I have no idea who he is." Cotton was resentenced to two life terms.

Nine years later, Thompson provided a blood sample so that DNA tests could be run on evidence from her rape. The result according to the district attorney: "Ronald Coleman didn't rape you. It was Bobby Poole."

According to Ms. Thompson: "If anything good can come out of what Ronald Cotton suffered because of my limitations as a human being, let it be an awareness of the fact that eyewitnesses can and do make mistakes ... eyewitness error has been recognized as the leading cause of wrongful convictions."[38]

Efforts to introduce expert testimony to refute that of eyewitnesses have proved to be a mixed bag – sometimes admitted, other times rejected. A federal circuit court decision illustrates:[39]

In a robbery of a bank, the assistant manager by her own testimony allegedly saw the robber's face for three seconds from a distance of four feet. At a *Daubert* hearing (used to determine the admissibility of expert testimony), a university psychologist testified that several factors could potentially have affected the eyewitness's identification: the fourteen-month delay between robbery and trial, the distraction caused by the robber's gun, stress during the robbery, and viewing of the suspect on television. The expert offered "transference theory" to support misidentification from the television viewing. The trial court refused to allow the expert to testify on the ground that his testimony would not have assisted the jury's determination because it would have been within the jury's own understanding.

---

[37] For plenty of examples of wrongful convictions based on faulty eyewitness testimony, see Barry Scheck, Peter Neufeld, and Jim Dwyer, *Actual Innocence* (New York: Signet, 2001).

[38] Jennifer Thompson, "I Was Certain, but I Was Wrong," *New York Times*, 18 June 2000, section 4, p. 15.

[39] *United States v. Langan*, 263 F. 3d 613 (2001).

Although such a reason is a boilerplate explanation, a more likely reason for the trial judge's decision, which was affirmed by the court of appeals, was the unreliability of the expert's "transference theory." It was the subject of only a single scholarly publication, in which the expert himself stated that further research was needed to support it. Three years had passed since the article's publication, and as yet no further testing had been done. Lurking in the background was the fact that the robber headed a neo-Nazi group, the Aryan Republican Army – an irrelevant consideration, to be sure, but arguably one that won the robber no sympathy from the judge.

To counter eyewitness testimony, experts are commonly employed to testify that scientific studies demonstrate that cross-racial identification (i.e., the witness is of one race and the accused of another) is unreliable; that a witness's subjective degree of certainty bears no relationship to reality; that in-court identification may actually result from photo, lineup, or television viewing (all of which the Thompson rape case – discussed previously – exemplify); that a long gap between perception and identification lessens the likelihood of accuracy and increases the provision of apparently probative, but actually false, details.[40]

It is, of course, an empirical question whether the aftermath of *Daubert* has made it easier for litigants to use expert witnesses to rebut eyewitness testimony. The trial judge's discretion determines whether an expert's testimony will be admitted.[41] Only in extreme circumstances do appellate courts rule that trial judges abused their discretion. For example, five eyewitnesses viewed a fatal auto accident from five different vantage points. Each contradicted the others as to the speed of both vehicles before and at impact. The appellate court ruled that an expert should have been allowed to testify because the eyewitness testimony was manifestly confusing.[42]

SUMMARY AND CONCLUSIONS

We have described major aspects of evidence law, including the concept of relevance, circumstantial evidence, the hearsay rule, constitutional provisions impacting the production of evidence, expert witnesses, and eyewitness testimony. Evidence has its roots in the common law and exists because of a pessimistic – but realistic – view of human nature, particularly its intellectually deficient aspects.

But there would be no need for evidence law were it not for trial by jury, which in return resulted from our adversary system, which had its origins in trial by battle and ordeal. These activities slowly became transformed into a

[40] Emanuel, *Evidence*, p. 540. Also see David F. Ross et al., *Adult Eyewitness Testimony: Current Trends and Developments* (Cambridge: Cambridge University Press, 1994).

[41] *People v. Lee*, 96 N.Y. 2d 157; 750 N.E. 2d 63 (2001). Also see James C. McKinley, Jr., "Court Opens Door to Data on Eyewitness Fallibility," *New York Times*, 9 May 2001, p. A27.

[42] *Turner v. Williams*, 326 Ill. App. 3d 541; 762 N.E. 2d 70 (2001). At the time of this decision Illinois adhered to *Daubert*'s predecessor, *Frye v. United States*, 293 F. 1013 (1923), which held that scientific evidence need only be "generally accepted."

battle of wits: two attorneys fighting for their respective clients in a zero-sum-game setting presided over by a fact finder – judge or jury – who decides who wins and who loses. Parenthetically, note that a more wide ranging and socially significant example of the law of unintended consequences probably does not exist.

If our system of "justice" utilized the method employed by the reputedly civilized world other than those portions subject to the British common law scheme, we would employ the "inquisitorial" system in which judges – trained in investigation, as well as law – ascertained the facts on their own authority, with law enforcement and the parties' attorneys providing informational assistance. But in such an arrangement, the law of evidence itself has no relevance because professional fact finders' mistrusting themselves and their decisions – so long as they adhered to the rule of law and not the rules of evidence – would make no more sense than the Texas law that requires trains meeting at a railroad crossing to come to a full stop and not proceed until the other has departed.[43]

But, needless to say, we as a society are not about to discard trial by jury – even though it is used only in a very small percentage of lawsuits. It exists at the core of popular entertainment, and significant alteration – to say nothing of obliteration – would have far-ranging societal effects. In addition, it supports the economic well-being of trial lawyers, especially those whose income depends on tort – personal injury – litigation, in which use of juries is most commonplace. And so, although evidence would be a prime candidate for natural deselection in a rational world, such a change is no more likely than that sound economics will emanate from a presidential proclamation or an act of Congress.

---

[43] Marcia Chambers, "Bonehead Legislation," *National Law Journal*, 25 September 1989, p. 13.

6

Criminal Procedure

The Constitution set few limits on federal criminal procedure, and fewer still on that of the states. Thus, Congress could not suspend the privilege of the writ of habeas corpus – the right of individuals under detention to have a judge determine the legality of their imprisonment – except in cases of rebellion or invasion, and federal criminal trials had to be by jury. The crime of treason was defined, with evidence needed to convict (two witnesses to an overt act) and restrictions on inflicted punishment (limited to the life of the traitor) specified. Neither Congress nor the states could pass bills of attainder – legislative acts that single out individuals for punishment – or ex post facto laws (i.e., laws that make behavior criminal after the act was committed or increase punishment after sentencing). States were required to extradite alleged criminals and return fugitive slaves.

Passage of the Bill of Rights sharply increased these meager limitations. The Fourth Amendment prohibits unreasonable searches and seizures. The Fifth guarantees the general right to due process and the specific right to indictment by grand jury. It also prohibits double jeopardy and compulsory self-incrimination. The Sixth Amendment provides for the right to trial by jury in criminal cases and the right to compel testimony, confront witnesses, and have assistance of counsel. Finally, the Eighth Amendment prohibits excessive bail, excessive fines, and cruel and unusual punishments.

These constitutional protections, however, originally limited only the national government. Thus, short of bills of attainder or ex post facto laws, states, through the nineteenth century and much of the twentieth century, could run their criminal justice system as they saw fit. Because the Bill of Rights so clearly applied only to the federal government, few cases arose. In one of them, *Permoli v. New Orleans*,[1] decided in 1845, Justice Catron ruled for a unanimous Court that nothing prevented a state or local government from denying individuals

---

[1] 44 U.S. 589.

the right to exercise their religion freely. New Orleans had enacted an ordinance that required all funerals to be held in the city's "obituary chapel" on Rampart Street; clergy who held funeral services elsewhere were subject to a fifty-dollar fine. Though *Permoli* did not pertain to an amendment dealing with criminal procedure, a fine for exercising a First Amendment freedom arguably amounts to the same thing.

Opportunity for limiting state discretion over criminal procedure arose with the passage of the Fourteenth Amendment in 1868, which, among other provisions, prohibited states from denying to any person under its jurisdiction due process of law. As noted in Chapter 3, the Supreme Court belatedly – between the 1920s and the 1960s – used the due process clause to incorporate against the states those provisions of the Bill of Rights that were "implicit in the concept of ordered liberty."[2] Many early criminal incorporation cases either rejected the theory of incorporation or accepted the theory but rejected the result (i.e., refusing to find the particular provisions at issue "implicit in the concept of ordered liberty"); the Warren Court reversed this trend, holding virtually every criminal provision of the Bill of Rights binding on the states. We list criminal rights provisions that have been incorporated in Table 6.1.

The Constitution, or more aptly, the Supreme Court's interpretation of the Constitution, serves to create a level of uniformity in states' criminal procedures. Police investigations across the land, for example, are subject to the same minimal levels of search-and-seizure protections and coerced interrogation safeguards. The fact that every state but Louisiana derives its criminal laws from the English common law (e.g., assault, battery, the various classes and degrees of homicide) adds to national uniformity. Additionally, many states rely on model criminal codes prepared by offshoots of the American Bar Association.

Against these centripetal forces of uniformity lay many centrifugal forces of divergence. Many matters of criminal procedure – what to declare criminal, what the punishments for certain crimes shall be, which crimes police and prosecutors choose to enforce, and which crimes juries and judges choose to sanction – fall almost completely under local control. Political culture influences criminal laws in a variety of ways. For example, all but the most liberal states allow capital punishment. And whereas Texas has 454 inmates on death row, New York, with approximately the same population, has only 4.[3] In 1990, the conservative Louisiana House, in reaction to Supreme Court decisions providing First Amendment protections to flag burning, passed a bill making battery against a flag burner punishable by a mere twenty-five-dollar fine.[4] Alternatively, we do not venture guesses on the factors that lead the states'

[2] *Palko v. Connecticut*, 302 U.S. 319 (1937), at 325.

[3] Information from http://www.deathpenaltyinfo.org. As of June 24, 2004, New York's death penalty was declared unconstitutional.

[4] A Senate committee approved the bill as well, but in the session's final hours an amendment replaced the flag-burning bill with an antiabortion bill.

Table 6.1. *The Selective Incorporation of Criminal Rights Provisions in the Bill of Rights*

Amendment	Provision	Rejected	Accepted
Fourth	Search and seizure		*Wolf v. Colorado* (1949)
Fourth	Exclusionary rule	*Wolf v. Colorado* (1949)	*Mapp v. Ohio* (1961)
Fifth	Self-incrimination		*Malloy v. Hogan* (1964)
Fifth	Indictment by grand jury	*Hurtado v. California* (1884)	
Fifth	Double jeopardy	*Palko v. Connecticut* (1937)	*Benton v. Maryland* (1969)
Fifth	Self-incrimination	*Twining v. New Jersey* (1908)	*Malloy v. Hogan* (1964)
Sixth	Public trial		*In re Oliver* (1948)
Sixth	Right to counsel	*Betts v. Brady* (1942)	*Gideon v. Wainwright* (1963)
Sixth	Confrontation		*Pointer v. Texas* (1965)
Sixth	Jury trial	*Maxwell v. Dow* (1900)	*Duncan v. Louisiana* (1968)
Sixth	Compulsory process to obtain witnesses		*Washington v. Texas* (1967)
Eighth	Cruel and unusual punishment		*Louisiana ex rel. Francis v. Resweber* (1947)
Eighth	Excessive bail Excessive fines (criminal)		

age-of-consent laws to vary from a low of fourteen (Iowa, Missouri, and South Carolina) to a high of eighteen (Arizona and California, among others).[5]

CRIME

The criminal process does not begin with the commission of a crime, but with the creation by the state of a criminal offense. The legal principle *nullum crimen sine lege* – without law there is no crime – prohibits people from being prosecuted for events declared illegal *after* their commission. Moreover, fair notice of what is criminal has meant that criminal offenses be construed narrowly and that unduly vague criminal laws violate the Constitution.

Because the prohibition of ex post facto laws is so clear, government rarely prosecutes for a crime that was not illegal when committed. But changes in punishment are not unusual. Certainly, if the maximum punishment for a crime is ten years when it is committed, a state cannot retroactively increase that

[5] Information from http://www.ageofconsent.htm, as of November 7, 2004.

maximum for those previously indicted or convicted. But a variety of retrospective "punishments" have been allowed: for example, requiring released sex offenders to notify police of their residence for the rest of their life,[6] and civilly committing sex offenders to psychiatric prisons after completion of their terms of sentence.[7] More generally, states may reduce the frequency of parole hearings without running afoul of the clause.[8] But the Court has voided retroactive changes in statutes of limitations,[9] sentencing guidelines,[10] and "good time" provisions.[11] The recency of most of these decisions suggests the increased desire of state legislatures to get tough on crime, even if after the fact.

When criminal statutes are amenable to different interpretations, judges are supposed to construe them narrowly. Consider, for example, the National Motor Vehicle Theft Act of 1919, which defined the term *motor vehicle* to include "an automobile, automobile truck, automobile wagon, motor cycle, or any other self-propelled vehicle not designed for running on rails." An individual stole an airplane but contended on appeal that an airplane was not covered by the act. Justice Holmes, for the majority, noted that the types of motor vehicles enumerated in the statute indicate that "a vehicle running on land, is the theme.... Although it is not likely that a criminal will carefully consider the text of the law before he murders or steals, it is reasonable that fair warning should be given ... of what the law intends to do if a certain line is passed."[12]

The same logic holds in sentencing. In *Bell v. United States*, the Supreme Court narrowly construed the Mann Act, which declared that "whoever knowingly transports in interstate or foreign commerce ... any woman or girl for the purpose of prostitution or debauchery, or for any other immoral purpose ... shall be fined not more than $5,000 or imprisoned not more than five years, or both." Bell simultaneously transported two women across state lines in violation of the act. But was this one offense (one transport) or two (two women)? The trial court thought two and gave Bell consecutive sentences: one for each woman. The Supreme Court reversed.

When Congress leaves to the Judiciary the task of imputing to Congress an undeclared will, the ambiguity should be resolved in favor of lenity. And this not out of any sentimental consideration, or for want of sympathy with the purpose of Congress in proscribing evil or antisocial conduct. It may fairly be said to be a presupposition of our law to resolve doubts in the enforcement of a penal code against the imposition of a harsher punishment.[13]

---

[6] *Smith v. Doe* (2002).
[7] *Kansas v. Hendricks*, 521 U.S. 346 (1997).
[8] *California Department of Corrections v. Morales*, 514 U.S. 499 (1995).
[9] *Stogner v. California* (2003).
[10] *Miller v. Florida*, 482 U.S. 423 (1987).
[11] *Weaver v. Graham*, 450 U.S. 24 (1981).
[12] *McBoyle v. United States*, 283 U.S. 25 (1931), at 26–27.
[13] 349 U.S. 81 (1955), at 83.

Defendants do not always win these battles. Although the Mann Act was clearly aimed at prostitution and associated vices, that did not prevent the United States from prosecuting a group of Mormons for taking their multiple wives across state lines.[14]

Narrow construction of criminal statutes is a Court-created rule, not a constitutional requirement. It thus does not bind the states, though most states do in fact follow such a rule. Alternatively, the vice of vagueness does have constitutional consequences: It violates due process. Loitering and vagrancy are common examples. Thus, the Supreme Court struck down a California loitering law aimed at any person "who loiters or wanders upon the streets or from place to place with no apparent reason."[15] A Jacksonville, Florida, statute declared:

Rogues and vagabonds, or dissolute persons who go about begging, common gamblers, persons who use juggling or unlawful games or plays, common drunkards, common night walkers, thieves, pilferers or pickpockets, traders in stolen property, lewd, wanton and lascivious persons, keepers of gambling places, common railers and brawlers, persons wandering or strolling around from place to place without any lawful purpose or object, habitual loafers, disorderly persons, persons neglecting all lawful business and habitually spending their time by frequenting houses of ill fame, gaming houses, or places where alcoholic beverages are sold or served, persons able to work but habitually living upon the earnings of their wives or minor children shall be deemed vagrants and, upon conviction in the Municipal Court shall be punished as provided for Class D offenses.[16]

We bow to no one in our support for criminal crackdowns on jugglers, and the like; the Supreme Court, however, ruled the ordinance unconstitutionally vague.

Requirements that illegal activity be declared as such by statute in advance of the activity, that such laws clearly delineate legal and illegal activity, and that such laws be construed narrowly say nothing about the *substantive* domain of criminal laws. Generally, the only limits on the states' powers to declare activity illegal are those in the Constitution itself. For example, the right to privacy, inherent in the due process clause, prohibits states from criminalizing birth control,[17] partial-birth abortion,[18] and, only recently, homosexual behavior.[19] The equal protection clause prohibits states from criminalizing interracial marriage,[20] as the vast majority of states once did. Note, however, that the free exercise clause does not prohibit states from criminalizing conduct that religious sects might sanction, such as marijuana smoking by Rastafarians, so long as the law has a valid secular purpose.

---

[14] *Cleveland v. United States,* 329 U.S. 14 (1946).
[15] *Kolender v. Lawson,* 461 U.S. 352 (1983).
[16] *Papachristou et al. v. City of Jacksonville,* 405 U.S. 156 (1972).
[17] *Griswold v. Connecticut,* 381 U.S. 479 (1965).
[18] *Stenberg v. Carhart,* 530 U.S. 914 (2000).
[19] *Lawrence v. Texas* (2003).
[20] *Loving v. Virginia,* 388 U.S. 1 (1967).

These constitutional restrictions also bind Congress with an additional caveat, other than the constitutionally specified crimes (e.g., treason, crimes on the high seas), congressionally enacted criminal laws must be "necessary and proper" to one or more of the Court's enumerated powers. The Rehnquist Court thus asserted that the Gun Free School Zone Act, which criminalized weapons possession near schools, exceeded any legitimate congressional power.[21] Congress responded, however, by limiting school aid to states that do not pass state-level gun-free-school laws. Similarly, Congress can financially punish states that do not set speed limits or a drinking age that Congress commands. Nevertheless, Congress's role in directly defining criminal behavior is sufficiently limited that only 3 percent of felonies and 1 percent of lesser offenses are federally prosecuted.[22]

With crimes defined by national, state, or local government, the next step in criminal procedure requires a miscreant to break the law. This happens with alarming regularity in the United States. Despite the historic drop in crime rates in the United States through the 1990s, the homicide rate, which can be meaningfully compared across nations, is more than three times higher in the United States (5.9 per 100,000) than in the European Union (1.7 per 100,000).[23] Crimes other than homicide usually require that someone report them; that occurs in only about half of all committed crimes.[24]

PREARREST INVESTIGATIONS

With a crime reported, the police initially investigate. The Constitution places a significant limit on police investigations: the Fourth Amendment's prohibition on unreasonable searches and seizures. This prohibition applies after arrests as well. Alternatively, the *Miranda* requirements, based on the Fifth Amendment's prohibition of compelled testimony, apply only after the suspect has been arrested or otherwise taken into custody. Thus, nothing prevents police officers from questioning suspects. Nor is the state required to provide counsel to suspects who have not yet been arrested.

The Exclusionary Rule

The fundamental Fourth Amendment question concerns the use of evidence obtained by an unreasonable search and seizure. In 1914, the Supreme Court ruled that such evidence could not be admitted in federal trials. It declared that without such a rule, Fourth Amendment protections would be "of no value,

---

[21] *United States v. Lopez*, 514 U.S. 549 (1995).

[22] Yale Kamisar, Wayne R. LaFave, Jerold H. Israel, and Nancy J. King, *Basic Criminal Procedure*, 10th ed. (St. Paul, MN: West, 2002), p. 2. These figures exclude prosecutions in the District of Columbia.

[23] See http://www.homeoffice.gov.uk/rds/pdfs2/hosb502.pdf, visited August 8, 2003.

[24] George F. Cole and Christopher E. Smith, *The American System of Criminal Justice*, 10th ed. (Belmont, CA: Wadsworth, 2004), p. 73.

and, so far as those thus placed are concerned, might as well be stricken from the Constitution."[25]

Because most crimes are state offenses, this federal exclusionary rule was of minor significance. In 1949, however, the Supreme Court made the Fourth Amendment binding on the states.[26] The Court specifically ruled that Colorado had violated the Fourth Amendment rights of Wolf, a physician, by illegally seizing his appointment book, which was then used to convict him of conspiracy to commit an abortion. Nevertheless, the majority opinion refused to extend the exclusionary rule to the states, thus upholding Wolf's conviction and a one-to-five-year prison term.

The Court overruled its 1949 decision twelve years later in the first of the Warren Court's many landmark criminal rights decisions. The case in question, *Mapp v. Ohio*,[27] involved the warrantless search of the home of a woman who was believed to be harboring a man wanted for bombing the house of an alleged numbers racketeer, the future boxing promoter Don King. The police found no fugitive but did seize some pornographic pictures. Mapp was arrested and convicted for violating Ohio's obscenity statute. Speaking for a five-person majority, Justice Clark declared that the Constitution requires states to abide by the *Weeks* exclusionary rule, which precludes admission of illegally seized evidence at trial.

This controversial decision was under attack in the 1970s and 1980s by the more conservative Burger Court, four of whose members were chosen by President Nixon precisely because they did not support expansion of the rights of persons accused of crime. The rallying cry against the exclusionary rule originated with a dissenting statement by Judge (later Justice) Benjamin Cardozo: "The criminal is to go free because the constable has blundered."[28] The Burger Court refused to extend the rule to grand jury hearings,[29] civil cases,[30] habeas corpus relief,[31] or deportation hearings.[32] In 1984 the Court created a good-faith exception to the exclusionary rule, whereby illegally obtained evidence would not be suppressed if the police acted in objective good faith.[33] Given the conservatism of the Rehnquist Court, the exclusionary rule rests on extremely shaky ground.

Unreasonable Searches and Seizures

The decision to require exclusion of illegally obtained evidence does not answer the question of whether the evidence was illegally obtained in the first place. The

[25] *Weeks v. United States*, 232 U.S. 383 (1914), at 393.
[26] *Wolf v. Colorado*, 338 U.S. 25 (1949).
[27] 367 U.S. 643 (1961).
[28] *People v. Defore*, 242 N.Y. 13 (1926), at 21.
[29] *United States v. Calandra*, 414 U.S. 338 (1974).
[30] *United States v. Janis*, 428 U.S. 433 (1976).
[31] *Stone v. Powell*, 428 U.S. 465 (1976).
[32] *Immigration and Naturalization Service v. Lopez-Mendoza*, 468 U.S. 1032 (1984).
[33] *United States v. Leon*, 468 U.S. 897 (1984).

answer that the Court provides is that a search violates the Constitution if, as the Constitution says, it is "unreasonable." Although this wording seemingly begs the question of what makes a search illegal, the standard suggests the lack of hard-and-fast rules, and instead a case-by-case approach that balances the extent of the intrusion (where the search took place, how extensive the intrusion was) against the prior justification for the search (warrants and probable cause), with additional room for ad hoc exceptions that the Court creates from time to time.

The most common components of a reasonable search are a warrant and probable cause. The Fourth Amendment, though not requiring a warrant for all searches, explicitly lays out the criteria for a valid warrant for those (unspecified) situations in which one is necessary: "No warrant shall issue, but upon probable cause, supported by oath or affirmation, and particularly describing the place to be searched, and the person or things to be seized."

The most subjective aspect of the warrant requirement is the probable cause requirement. Probable cause constitutes evidence that would lead a prudent person to believe that a crime has been committed or that evidence is at hand. It is, as its name indicates, a question of probability, not certainty. As is the reasonableness of a search, it is usually judged by the totality of circumstances, rather than hard-and-fast rules.

The liberal Warren Court created an important exception to this totality-of-circumstances approach in relation to anonymous tips. Under the *Aguilar-Spinelli* rule,[34] an anonymous tip could be used to establish probable cause only if the tip

1. revealed the informant's basis of knowledge (i.e., how the informant came upon this information) *and*
2. provided facts establishing
   a. the veracity of the informant *or*
   b. the reliability of the report.

Needless to say, anonymous tipsters do not peruse Supreme Court decisions frequently and thus rarely know that they need to report the way they find information. They may say X is selling drugs out of his apartment, but few are well enough versed on Fourth Amendment doctrine to note specifically how they learned this information. Nor do they often provide details of their own veracity (Boy Scout merit badges, and the like).

The most likely explanation for these requirements is that the Warren Court did not trust police officer claims that they received confidential tips. Because the tipster is anonymous, corroboration of the tip is all but impossible.

Consider the case of *Illinois v. Gates*.[35] The anonymous tipster reported that Mrs. Gates frequently drove the family car to Florida and flew back the same day. Mr. Gates flew down to Florida, filled the car with drugs, and drove it back to Illinois. The tipster specified the times of one of their upcoming trips and

[34] *Aguilar v. Texas*, 378 U.S. 108 (1964); *Spinelli v. United States*, 393 U.S. 410 (1969).
[35] 462 U.S. 213 (1983).

noted statements by the Gates that they made their living selling drugs. But the tipster never revealed *how s/he came upon this information*, as required by the *Aguilar-Spinelli* rule.

Who, given this information, would believe that the car returning from Florida did not contain drugs? Although it may not have, it *probably* did. More trusting of police than the Warren Court, the Burger Court used this case to revert to the totality-of-circumstances approach started for anonymous tips.

An example of the mischief the Warren Court was trying to prevent occurred in 1991, when the town supervisor of Brookhaven, New York, Felix Grucci, just happened to receive an anonymous tip that a local fireworks company illegally stored fireworks at a Long Island farm. He notified the police, who conducted a raid that found nothing illegal but nevertheless resulted in the cancellation of one of the company's prime July 4 shows. One more thing: Mr. Grucci, later elected to Congress, owned his own fireworks company, whose only local rival was the company about which he allegedly received the anonymous tip.[36]

Probable cause is generally required whether or not a warrant is obtained, although evidence from warrants found lacking in probable cause can be used in court if the police officers acted in good faith.

Although the Fourth Amendment explicitly protects one's "person, houses, papers, and effects," the Court declared in a 1967 wiretap case that the "Fourth Amendment protects people, not places. What a person knowingly exposes to the public, even in his own home, is not a subject of Fourth Amendment protection. But what he seeks to preserve as private, even in an area accessible to the public, may be constitutionally protected."[37]

Thus, for a search to be unreasonable it generally must occur at a place where the accused has an expectation of privacy. The greatest expectation of privacy is that in one's home. "At the very core [of the Fourth Amendment] stands the right of a man to retreat into his own home and there be free from unreasonable governmental intrusion."[38] Commercial premises are likewise given great protection. "The businessman, like the occupant of a residence, has a constitutional right to go about his business free from unreasonable official entries."[39] Yet, commercial premises do not command the same expectation of privacy as a person's residence. Receiving protection, but to a still lesser degree, are one's person and one's car (or other motorized vehicle), but the protection afforded them is nevertheless great compared to that of places where one has no property interest, such as the home of a third party.

The type of search can be as determinative of reasonableness as the place of the search. Limited intrusions such as stops-and-frisks or detentive questioning require less prior justification than do full searches.

---

[36] Brian Donovan and Amanda Harris, "Grucci's Private, Public Roles Blur in Brookhaven," *Newsday*, 16 June 1998, p. A3.

[37] *Katz v. United States*, 389 U.S. 347 (1967), at 351.

[38] *Silverman v. United States*, 365 U.S. 505 (1961), at 511.

[39] *See v. Seattle*, 387 U.S. 541 (1967), at 543.

Finally, there are well-established exceptions to the warrant requirements. The most important of these is the right to search incident to a lawful arrest. This right generally extends to immediate searches of the arrestee and the area under his or her control. Lesser authority exists for searches that follow upon but are not incident to lawful arrests. Other exceptions include searches of evidence in plain view, searches with the permission of those having a property interest in the area being searched, searches after hot pursuit, and searches at fixed or functional borders, such as international airports.

FROM ARREST TO TRIAL

In about 20 percent of reported crimes, the police acquire enough information, that is, probable cause, to make an arrest.[40] Although arrest warrants are sometimes issued, arrests are usually made without warrants. Arrest rates are the highest for murder (64 percent), aggravated assault (56.5 percent), and rape (44.5 percent) and substantially lower for larceny (8 percent) and burglary (12 percent).[41]

After arrest, suspects are almost universally searched for weapons, contraband, and other evidence. As noted, such searches incident to a lawful arrest do not themselves require probable cause. Suspects are then taken to the police station, where they are booked.

Self-Incrimination

Only when a suspect is taken into custody or otherwise deprived of his or her freedom do the *Miranda* warnings against self-incrimination apply. Under *Miranda*, police must inform suspects before any custodial interrogation that (1) they have the right to remain silent; (2) if they choose to speak, anything they say may be used against them; (3) they have the right to an attorney; and (4) if they cannot afford an attorney, one will be provided to them.[42]

The Fifth Amendment's protection against self-incrimination was an understandable reaction to British attempts to coerce confessions, as in Star Chamber proceedings. Before the 1960s, the Supreme Court decided on a case-by-case basis whether the accused's will was overborne by physical or psychological duress. Such determinations were not easily made, especially when "facts" about the interrogation itself were often in dispute. Despair over the case-by-case system led the Court to seek a prophylactic rule that it hoped would put an end to involuntary confessions.

Not surprisingly, the *Miranda* rule was attacked by the Burger Court, which ruled in two cases that although incriminating statements made without *Miranda* warnings could not be used in the prosecution's case-in-chief, they

---

[40] Cole and Smith, *American System*, p. 73.

[41] Data are for 2001. See http://www.fbi.gov/ucr/cius01/01crime3.pdf, visited November 7, 2004.

[42] 384 U.S. 436 (1966).

could be used to impeach the credibility of witnesses if they took the stand and contradicted anything they had said before receiving *Miranda* warnings.[43] In 1984 the Court created a public safety exception to *Miranda*, holding that the accused's response to a question about the whereabouts of a gun hidden in a grocery store could be used in evidence even though no warnings had been given.[44] Despite these exceptions, the *Miranda* rule itself remains in place. At the end of its 1999 term, not only did the Court flatly reaffirm *Miranda*, stating that it has "become part of our national culture," but it also voided an act of Congress that had attempted to overrule it.[45]

The Right to Counsel

As the right against self-incrimination does, the right to counsel now accrues from the time of arrest. The right received strong support from the Court as early as 1932. In *Powell v. Alabama*,[46] the Court required the states to provide indigent criminal defendants with counsel under certain conditions. The case involved seven illiterate black youths who, after a fight with several white youths on a freight train, were falsely accused of raping two young white women. In a lynch-mob atmosphere, the youths were convicted in a series of one-day trials. The presiding judge had appointed all members of the local bar to defend them at their arraignment, but no one stepped forward to do so until the day of the trial. In reversing their convictions, the Supreme Court noted that

during perhaps the most critical period of the proceedings against these defendants, that is to say, from the time of their arraignment until the beginning of their trial, when consultation, thorough-going investigation and preparation were vitally important, the defendants did not have the aid of counsel in any real sense, although they were as much entitled to such aid during that period as at the trial itself.[47]

The Court not only declared that the right to counsel begins at arraignment, but also ruled that given the capital nature of the offense and the status of the defendants, a constitutional right to appointed counsel existed.

Evidencing the U.S. Supreme Court's incomplete control of state courts, Alabama subsequently retried four of the defendants, all of whom were again found guilty. Charlie Weems received a 75-year sentence in 1937 and was paroled in 1943; Andrew Wright, a 99-year sentence in 1937 and parole in 1944; Haywood Patterson, a 75-year sentence in 1936 (he escaped prison in 1948 and was later arrested and convicted for manslaughter); and Clarence Norris was convicted on retrial, sentenced to death, and his sentence commuted to life. He was paroled in 1944.

---

[43] *Harris v. New York*, 401 U.S. 222 (1971); *Oregon v. Hass*, 420 U.S. 714 (1975).

[44] *New York v. Quarles*, 467 U.S. 649.

[45] *Dickerson v. United States* (2000), at 419.

[46] 287 U.S. 45 (1932).

[47] *Id.* at 57.

Although the *Powell* ruling limited itself to capital cases in which the defendants were unable to defend themselves because of illiteracy or other extenuating circumstances, it further suggested that all indigent defendants should be afforded counsel. Nevertheless, in 1942 the Court ruled that the Constitution provided no unequivocal right to appointed counsel, only a right conditioned on the facts of each case.[48]

The Warren Court overruled the 1942 decision in 1963. The case, *Gideon v. Wainright*,[49] involved the trial and conviction of an individual for breaking and entering a pool hall with intent to commit a crime. Gideon had requested an attorney at his trial but was refused because Alabama only provided appointed counsel in capital cases. The justices ruled unanimously that states must afford indigent defendants appointed counsel in all felony cases.

The *Gideon* decision has fared reasonably well under the Burger and Rehnquist Courts. In 1972 the justices ruled that no indigent person could be jailed without court-appointed counsel or an intelligent waiver thereof.[50] On the other hand, whereas the Warren Court had pushed the entitlement to counsel back from the time of indictment to the time of arrest[51] and had extended the right to include the presence of an attorney at lineups,[52] the Burger Court declined to combine the two rules and extend the right to counsel to preindictment lineups.[53] The majority in the 5–4 decision included all four Nixon appointees.

Pretrial Procedures

After arrest, the accused goes through a series of pretrial procedures, most of which do not have the elaborate constitutional and doctrinal underpinnings that search and seizure and self-incrimination have.

The Decision to Charge. Both the police and the prosecutors screen the decision to charge after arrest. In less than 10 percent of arrests the police decide not to proceed. Prosecutors drop a substantially higher percentage of cases, often for reasons of insufficient evidence or witness difficulties.[54] On rare occasions, readily apparent search and seizure problems are the cause.[55] Agreements by the accused to make restitution or enter a drug rehabilitation program may also lead to dropped charges. Even after charges are filed, prosecutors retain the discretion to drop charges.

---

[48] *Betts v. Brady*, 316 U.S. 455.
[49] 372 U.S. 335.
[50] *Argersinger v. Hamlin*, 407 U.S. 25.
[51] *Escobedo v. Illinois*, 378 U.S. 478 (1964).
[52] *United States v. Wade*, 388 U.S. 218 (1967).
[53] *Kirby v. Illinois*, 406 U.S. 682 (1972).
[54] Cole and Smith, *American System*, p. 73.
[55] Tom Wicker, "Exploding a Myth," *New York Times*, 10 May 1983, A25.

Filing the Complaint. The decision to charge is followed in misdemeanor cases by filing of a complaint before a magistrate by the victim or the investigating officer. The complaint sets forth the charges, declaring that a particular person at a particular time and place engaged in specified illegal activity.

Probable Cause Hearing. When arrests precede an arrest warrant, judicial determination of probable cause has already been made, thus satisfying the Fourth Amendment's prohibition of unreasonable seizures. Most arrests, however, are made without warrants after police determinations of probable cause and are followed by prosecutorial decisions to file charges. Although an unjustly charged person can often have his or her rights vindicated at trial, by that point much harm may already have occurred. Because of the need to prevent persons from being held over for trial on the basis of insufficient evidence, the Supreme Court requires a preliminary hearing to determine probable cause before a neutral magistrate for those arrested without a warrant.[56] Such hearings, however, are not adversarial – the accused does not have the right to attend, to cross-examine witnesses, or to provide evidence in his or her own behalf.

First Appearance. The setting of bail is made at the first appearance, alternatively known as the *preliminary appearance, preliminary arraignment, initial presentment*, and so on. This hearing usually occurs within forty-eight hours of arrest. The defendant is represented by counsel, and when she or he cannot afford counsel, the court appoints an attorney.

The Eighth Amendment to the Constitution prohibits excessive bail, but as Chief Justice Rehnquist wryly noted, the clause "says nothing about whether bail shall be available at all."[57] Traditionally, the sole purpose of bail was to ensure that the accused would appear for trial. "The right to release before trial is conditioned upon the accused's giving adequate assurance that he will stand trial and submit to sentence if found guilty."[58] If the accused is a flight risk, bail need not be offered. If not, the seriousness of the charge, the quality of the evidence, the accused's ties to the community, and his or her financial resources may all be considered in setting the amount of bail.

In *United States v. Salerno* (1987), the Supreme Court upheld the preventive detention of Tony Salerno on the grounds that Salerno would commit future crimes while out on bail. The Court ruled that preventive detention did not violate the Eighth Amendment, for, as noted, the Eighth Amendment does not require bail, only bail that is not excessive. Nor was this a deprivation of Mr. Salerno's liberty without due process of law, for the Bail Reform Act on which the detention was based assertedly served the purpose of administrative "regulation," not criminal punishment.[59]

[56] *Gerstein v. Pugh*, 420 U.S. 103 (1975).
[57] *United States v. Salerno*, 481 U.S. 739 (1987), at 752.
[58] *Stack v. Boyle*, 342 U.S. 1 (1951), at 4.
[59] *United States v. Salerno*, 481 U.S. 739 (1987).

Preliminary Hearing. Preliminary hearings redundantly require the prosecutor to demonstrate probable cause before a magistrate. Unlike in the probable cause hearing noted previously, the prosecution's case must be made by live witnesses, not mere affidavits, and the defense can cross-examine the witnesses.

Defendants who intend to plead guilty, through a plea bargain or for other reasons, can waive the preliminary hearing.

Grand Jury. The Fifth Amendment commands that "no person shall be held to answer for a capital, or otherwise infamous crime, unless on a presentment or indictment of a Grand Jury." For the reasons noted, the mere ability to charge people with crimes can wreak havoc on their life, even if they are later found not guilty. Requiring grand juries to find sufficient evidence to indict people before they may be tried was intended to serve as a bulwark against prosecutorial abuse.

Nevertheless, the Supreme Court has not incorporated the grand jury provision into the Fourteenth Amendment's due process clause, thus relieving states of this obligation. But even in states that choose to use grand juries for indictment, this requirement is rather ineffective. Grand juries work in secret, and the accused may not even know she is under investigation. The defense is not allowed to present evidence, allowing prosecutors to give a one-sided view of events. And unlike in an actual trial, the prosecutor is not required to disclose exculpatory information.[60] Additionally, a simple majority is sufficient to issue an indictment. New York Chief Judge Sol Wachtler's aphorism certainly holds: A prosecutor could get a grand jury to indict a ham sandwich if she were so inclined.[61] Indeed, grand juries refuse to indict less than 5 percent of the time.[62]

In the absence of grand jury requirements, most states allow indictment by information, a formal process whereby the prosecutor simply presents information to a judge sufficient to establish that indictment is warranted.

Arraignment. After indictment, the accused is arraigned. At the arraignment the accused is informed of the charges and asked to enter a plea of guilty or not guilty; "not guilty" is the typical response at this point.

About three-quarters of suspects eventually plead guilty before trial, most through a plea bargain. Because of the large percentage of criminal defendants who plead guilty and the extensive discretion typically granted prosecutors to reduce the charge as part of the deal, prosecutors are often far more important in the disposition of criminal cases than are judges.

The Supreme Court had endorsed plea bargains, labeling them "an essential component of the administration of justice," enforcing a prosecutor's original

---

[60] *United States v. Williams*, 504 U.S. 36 (1992).

[61] David Margolick, "Law Professor to Administer Courts in State," *New York Times*, 1 February 1985, p. B2. Wachtler himself later was arrested, was indicted, and served time on harassment and extortion charges stemming from a soured love affair.

[62] Kamisar et al., *Basic Criminal Procedure*, p. 25.

bargain after a subsequent prosecutor unwittingly ignored his predecessor's sentencing recommendation.[63] The latitude enjoyed by prosecutors under this "essential component" of justice creates incentives to plead that otherwise might be labeled coercive. In 1970, the Court upheld, against the challenge of an involuntary confession, the guilty plea of an African American minor in North Carolina who did so in order to avoid the risk of execution. The particular crime punishable by death here for those who pleaded not guilty and obstinately availed themselves of their constitutional right to a trial: first-degree burglary.[64]

Prosecutors can not only lessen charges for those who plead guilty, but add charges for those who refuse to do so. In one case, the prosecutor successfully reindicted a defendant, the second time under a repeat-offender statute that carries mandatory life imprisonment, after the defendant refused to plead guilty to a simple forgery charge.[65]

Needless to say, the failures of the plea-bargain system also include criminals who are sentenced to far less time than they might otherwise deserve because overburdened prosecutors and judges need to clear cases quickly. This means, however, that even though judges must approve plea bargains, much of the output of the criminal justice system is the result of private bargaining between prosecution and defense attorneys.

Pretrial Motions. As the prosecutor and the defense prepare for trial, the defense can present a variety of motions to the judge, including requests to dismiss charges, exclude evidence, and change venue (the location of the trial). The defense automatically obtains access to the prosecutor's case file through the process known as *discovery*. Indeed, prosecutors have a positive responsibility to inform the defense about exculpatory evidence. Discovery is not a symmetrical obligation, however. Defense attorneys are under no obligation to provide prosecutors with damning evidence about their client and indeed, short of suborning perjury, would be prevented from providing such evidence to prosecutors.

TRIAL

In the rare criminal case that continues to trial, the defendant has a right to a jury trial as guaranteed by the Sixth Amendment. The right to a jury trial, made applicable to the states in *Duncan v. Louisiana* (1968),[66] applies to all cases that include the possibility of a six-month jail sentence. The defendant can waive the right to a jury trial, and about 30 percent of defendants do so.

---

[63] *Santobello v. New York*, 404 U.S. 257 (1971), at 260.
[64] *Parker v. North Carolina*, 397 U.S. 790 (1970).
[65] *Bordenkircher v. Hayes*, 434 U.S. 357 (1978).
[66] 391 U.S. 145.

Unsympathetic defendants who have committed bad acts, but not necessarily illegal ones, might so choose.

Jury Selection

The defense attorney and the prosecutor select the jury through the process known as *voir dire*. Jurors are interviewed to determine whether they have any personal connections to the participants in the case or the crime being prosecuted. Jurors who have potential conflicts of interest can be dismissed for cause, provided the judge agrees. The attorneys also have a limited number of peremptory challenges, challenges that can be made for nearly any reason, which do not require approval of the judge. In 1986, however, the Supreme Court ruled that prosecutors may not use peremptory challenges to eliminate jurors on the basis of race.[67]

Such practices evolved after the Supreme Court initially ruled that blacks could not be excluded from jury service. Thus a 1963 Dallas training manual for prosecutors warned them not to "take Jews, Negroes, Dagos, Mexicans, or a member of any minority race on a jury, no matter how rich or well educated."[68] It is not clear when this policy was officially abolished, but as recently as 2003 the Supreme Court overturned a Texas capital punishment conviction, finding that Texas had used peremptory challenges on more than 90 percent of African American jurors, but only 13 percent of nonblacks. In this case, prosecutors had used peremptory challenges to strike ten of eleven potential African American jurors. Justice Clarence Thomas dissented, finding the pattern of racial discrimination purely circumstantial.[69]

As far back as 1898 the Supreme Court declared that the jury guaranteed by the Sixth Amendment consisted "of twelve persons, neither more or less."[70] In 1970, however, the Supreme Court decided that the purpose of a jury, to prevent oppression by the government through "the interposition between the accused and his accuser of the commonsense judgment of a group of laymen," could be adequately served by juries as small as six.[71]

Trial Procedure

The trial begins with an opening statement by the prosecutor, which lays out the state's case. The defense, if it so chooses – and it usually does – may make its own opening statement. The state then produces witnesses, who may be cross-examined by the defense. This right of the defendant to be confronted with the witnesses against him or her is explicitly guaranteed by the Sixth

[67] *Batson v. Kentucky*, 476 U.S. 79.
[68] "Race and Juries," *Washington Post*, 11 March 2003, p. A22.
[69] *Miller-El v. Cockrell*, 537 U.S. 322 (2003).
[70] *Thompson v. Utah*, 170 U.S. 343 (1898), at 349.
[71] *Williams v. Florida*, 399 U.S. 78 (1970), at 100.

Amendment but is not always applied literally. Child witnesses in sex abuse cases, for example, may be allowed to testify via closed-circuit television without the defendant present.[72]

After the prosecution rests its case, the defense may present its side. As the burden of proof is on the state to prove its case, there is no obligation on the defense to do so. Indeed, if the prosecution's case is weak enough, the defense can ask the judge for a directed verdict of acquittal.

Assuming the defense presents its case, the Sixth Amendment guarantees the defendant the "compulsory process for obtaining witnesses in his favor." This right applies to the state as well (except for testimony by the defendant) and formed the basis of the challenge to President Nixon's refusal to hand over the Watergate tapes. "To ensure that justice is done, it is imperative to the function of courts that compulsory process be available for the production of evidence needed either by the prosecution or by the defense."[73]

The right against self-incrimination usually is reviewed in terms of pretrial interrogations but certainly applies to trials as well. The right not only means that the defendant cannot be forced to testify, but also that the prosecution cannot comment on the defendant's choice not to testify.

After the defense rests its case, the prosecutor (and then the defense) can call rebuttal witnesses. After testimony is complete, the defense issues a closing statement, followed by the prosecution's. The judge then instructs the jury as to what the charges mean, what elements of the case they must find proven in order to convict, and the burden of proof, which in criminal cases is "beyond a reasonable doubt."[74]

Verdicts. Juries are required to render verdicts unanimously in federal cases, but not in state cases.[75] This peculiar rule exists despite the fact that eight of the nine justices ruling in the cited case thought that the same standard should apply to both federal and state cases. Four justices, White, Burger, Blackmun, and Rehnquist, thought that unanimity was not required at either level of government. Four other justices, Stewart, Marshall, Brennan, and Douglas, thought that unanimity was required at both levels of government. Justice Powell split the difference, creating the fifth vote for unanimity at the federal level and the necessary fifth vote against unanimity at the state level.

Whereas it is now extraordinarily difficult to gather information on jury deliberations, one study from the 1950s was granted access to deliberation records in more than three thousand trials. Not surprisingly, the mythical role of the holdout juror who convinces her comrades of the correctness of her views, as in the movie *Twelve Angry Men*, does not withstand scrutiny. When a nonunanimous majority votes to convict on the first ballot, the jury eventually

---

[72] *Maryland v. Craig*, 497 U.S. 836 (1990).
[73] *United States v. Nixon*, 418 U.S. 683 (1972), at 709.
[74] *In re Winship*, 397 U.S. 358 (1970).
[75] *Apodaca v. Oregon*, 406 U.S. 404 (1972).

Table 6.2. *Role of Deliberations in Verdicts*

		Guilty Votes on First Ballot			
Final verdict	0	1–5	6	7–11	12
Not guilty	100	91	50	5	–
Hung	–	7	0	9	–
Guilty	–	2	50	86	100

Source: Harry Kalven and Hans Zeisel, *The American Jury* (Chicago: University of Chicago Press, 1971), p. 488.

Table 6.3. *Judge/Jury Verdict Concordance*

		Jury			
		Acquit	Convict	Hung	Total
Judge	Acquit	13.4	2.2	1.1	16.7
	Convict	16.9	62.0	4.4	83.3
	Total	30.3	64.2	5.5	100.0

Source: Harry Kalven and Hans Zeisel, *The American Jury* (Chicago: University of Chicago Press, 1971), p. 56.

votes to acquit only 5 percent of the time. And when a nonunanimous majority votes to acquit on the first ballot, the jury eventually votes to convict only 2 percent of the time[76] (see Table 6.2).

The cited study also questioned the judges in these cases as to what their verdict would have been. More than 75 percent of the time the judge and jury agreed, 19 percent of the time they disagreed, and in the remaining cases the jury was hung (i.e., could not reach a unanimous verdict). When the judge and jury disagreed, overwhelmingly the jury acquitted when the judge would have convicted. Only rarely did the jury convict when the judge would have acquitted (see Table 6.3).

If the jury finds the defendant not guilty, the Fifth Amendment's double jeopardy clause, which commands that no person "twice be put in jeopardy of life or limb," prohibits retrial. But the protection does not apply to hung juries, that is, juries that cannot find a person innocent or guilty unanimously or by lesser supermajorities (e.g., 11–1) that might be required by the particular state. The protection also does not apply to persons whose conviction is overturned on appeal. Defendants in either situation may readily be recharged. Double jeopardy also does not prohibit civil suits against the alleged perpetrator, as when O. J. Simpson was sued and found civilly negligent in the homicides of Nicole Simpson and Ronald Goldman after his acquittal on criminal charges. And if different evidence is required for conviction, the "same offense" requirement

[76] Harry Kalven and Hans Zeisel, *The American Jury* (Chicago: University of Chicago Press, 1971).

is not violated even though it is the same state (or alternatively) the federal government that is retrying the accused.

Finally, and most controversially, the double jeopardy clause does not prohibit different levels of government (i.e., state and federal) from retrying the defendant for the same acts. Thus after four police officers were acquitted in the infamous videotaped beating of Rodney King, touching off riots in Los Angeles that left fifty-four people dead, the officers were retried and two were convicted on the federal criminal charge of depriving King of his civil rights. So, too, Lemrick Nelson, acquitted of murder in the stabbing death of Yankel Rosenbaum after a night of anti-Semitic rioting in Brooklyn, was convicted on federal charges of depriving Rosenbaum of his civil rights.

Sentencing

A defendant who is found guilty of a noncapital offense is sentenced by the judge. Because of the large disparities frequently found in sentencing, both the federal government and many state governments have adopted sentencing guidelines that limit judicial discretion. Judges plug the crime characteristics (the offense, use of weapons, etc.) and the defendant characteristics (e.g., prior convictions) into a grid and derive a narrow range of lawful sentencing. The judge may be allowed to increase or decrease the sentence indicated by the guidelines, but written justification is usually required. Any factor that increases the penalty for a crime, beyond the prescribed statutory maximum, such as the use of a firearm, must be proved beyond a reasonable doubt by the jury.

Sentences can range from community service (e.g., Winona Ryder's shoplifting conviction) to probation, prison terms, and even the death penalty. We will examine federal sentencing in Chapter 8, but for now we provide an example of sentencing behavior by trial courts in Pennsylvania (see Table 6.4).

The data consist of thousands of sentencing decisions by hundreds of Pennsylvania trial court judges in 1998. We employ multiple regression analysis to examine how changes in our independent variables influence our dependent variable, the sentence handed down, in months, by the judge. We examine three types of variables: legally relevant variables (the offense gravity score set by the Pennsylvania Sentencing Commission and the number of prior convictions), extralegal variables (defendant characteristics such as race and sex), and trial characteristics (e.g., guilty plea, bench trial, jury trial).

The regression analysis provides us with three relevant statistics for each variable: the slope coefficient (listed in the table under the letter B), the standard error of the slope coefficient (S.E.), and the significance level of the variable (Sig.) The slope coefficient tells us, for each variable, the change in sentencing (in months) that occurs with a one-unit change in that independent variable. Because a new sample would not give us precisely the same results as this sample, here the standard error tells us how much that slope coefficient might typically change given repeated sampling. Finally, the significance level tells us how likely it is that the slope coefficients we observe could have differed from

Table 6.4. *Regression Analysis of Sentencing Decisions in Pennsylvania*

Category	Variable	B	S.E.	Sig.
Legal	Offense gravity score (1–14)	4.53	0.04	.001
	Prior record (0–8)	1.23	0.04	.001
Extralegal	Age	0.06	0.01	.001
(defendant	Female	−0.95	0.20	.001
characteristics)[a]	Black	−1.23	0.13	.001
	Hispanic	−2.49	0.37	.001
	Asian	1.18	1.40	.40
	Native American	−5.90	2.27	.01
	Other	−0.59	1.91	.76
Trial[b]	Nonnegotiated guilty plea	0.65	0.20	.001
	Nolo contendre	0.48	0.84	.57
	Bench trial	4.78	0.45	.001
	Jury trial	17.26	0.55	.001
	Other disposition	1.29	0.86	.13
	Constant	−13.08	0.34	.001

Notes: $R^2 = 0.509$; standard error of regression = 11.91; $N = 20584$.
[a] Race variables compared to a baseline of a white defendant.
[b] Trial variables compared to a baseline of a plea bargain.
Source: http://www.icpsr.umich.edu:8080/NACJD-STUDY/03450.xml.

zero (i.e., no effect) only as a result of chance. Conventionally, we look for significance below the .05 level.

Beginning with the legal variables, we see that the offense gravity score variable has an enormous impact on the sentence given. This means that judges take very seriously the severity of the crime prescribed by the state of Pennsylvania, as well they should and, indeed, as well they must. Each jump in the offense gravity score, which ranges from 1–14, corresponds to nearly a five-month increase in sentencing, a hefty increase given that the average sentence is less than eight months. Less significantly, the number of prior convictions adds to one's sentence: an extra one and a quarter months for each prior conviction.

The effects of the extralegal variables are not large, but many are statistically significant. Controlling for the type of crime and prior record, the sentences females receive are nearly one month shorter than those of men. As for race, note first that all the racial categories in the table are compared against a baseline of whites. Thus, controlling for other factors, blacks and Hispanics serve slightly less time in prison (1.24 and 2.49 months, respectively) per conviction when compared to comparably situated whites. Asians and Native Americans, though, do not serve statistically different sentences than comparable white convicts.

Finally, we consider the manner in which the convicts in this study were found guilty (e.g., a bench trial, trial by jury). Note that each category is compared to a plea bargain. First, pleading guilty without a bargain barely increases one's sentence over what a sentence with a bargain produces – by .65 month.

Being found guilty by a judge increases one's sentence by 4.78 months, whereas a guilty verdict by a jury increases one's sentence by more than 17 months. Overall, the effect of exercising one's right to a trial by jury *typically* can be quite severe.

One factor examined by other scholars with an extended version of the Pennsylvania sentencing data is the effect of periodic elections on sentencing. Pennsylvania trial judges serve staggered ten-year terms; thus it is possible to examine the effect of elections on sentencing behavior. Because Americans overwhelmingly believe that courts in their area are too lenient on crime, it should not be surprising that elected judges ratchet up sentencing as elections approach. Indeed, judges facing imminent reelection sentence 24–37 percent more harshly than judges just elected or reelected, even after controlling for offense seriousness, prior convictions, the judges' ideology, and a host of other factors.[77]

Nevertheless, the picture of sentencing presented here is overwhelmingly driven by legal factors, most notably, the maximum allowable sentence for the committed crime, and, to a lesser extent, one's prior record. *Any* systematic influence of race on sentencing is troubling, but nevertheless, it is hard to conclude from these data that the differences are large.

Whereas states can severely constrict the sentencing discretion by trial judges, the Constitution imposes few such limits. Thus, although the Eighth Amendment prohibits "cruel and unusual punishments," this is not an effective limit on the length of sentences states might set. Consider William James Rummel, whose convictions included (1) fraudulent use of a credit card ($80.00) in 1964, (2) passing a forged check ($28.36) in 1968, and finally (3) obtaining money under false pretenses ($120.75) in 1973.

The third conviction triggered Texas's recidivist (repeat offender) statute. We invite readers to ask themselves at what length of sentence would punishment begin to be "cruel and unusual" for a recidivist such as Mr. Rummel? The Supreme Court's answer was that not even Texas's sentence of life imprisonment constituted cruel and unusual punishment for people such as Rummel, who "are simply incapable of conforming to the norms of society as established by its criminal law."[78] In 2003, the Court upheld the *Rummel* precedent, affirming the sentence given a repeat nonviolent felon whose final offenses were stealing $153.54 worth of videos from two different K-Mart stores, with each theft triggering a separate twenty-five-year-to-life term.[79]

Capital Punishment. The Supreme Court has set greater restrictions on states when the punishment is death. In *Furman v. Georgia* (1972),[80] a highly

---

[77] Gregory A. Huber and Sanford C. Gordon, "Accountability and Coercion: Is Justice Blind When It Runs for Office?" 48 *American Journal of Political Science* 247 (2004).

[78] *Rummel v. Estelle*, 445 U.S. 263 (1980), at 275.

[79] *Lockyer v. Andrade*, 538 U.S. 63 (2003).

[80] 408 U.S. 238.

fractured Court declared unconstitutional capital punishment imposed at the untrammeled discretion of jurors. Justices Marshall and Brennan thought the death penalty always unconstitutional: Marshall because it is "morally unacceptable to the people of the United States at this time in their history";[81] Brennan not only because "its rejection by contemporary society is total," but because it is "severe," is "degrading," and fails to respect murderers for "their intrinsic worth as human beings."[82] Douglas thought the death penalty as applied discriminated against minorities and the poor, a contention that the Court rejected in 1987. Stewart and White, without emphasizing race or class, also believed the death penalty to be cruel and unusual because it was arbitrarily and capriciously imposed on some and not on others. Along with Douglas, they reserved judgment on the constitutionality of mandatory death sentences. The four Nixon appointees dissented, claiming no constitutional violation in the death penalty in general or as imposed.

In response to *Furman*, thirty-five states and Congress reimposed the death penalty, some making it mandatory, others imposing guidelines for juries. In July 1976 the Court responded by declaring mandatory capital punishment to be just as arbitrary as the totally discretionary death penalties struck in *Furman*,[83] but upholding the death penalty if juries are provided guidelines.[84] Brennan and Marshall dissented, again arguing that death is always cruel and unusual. Given overwhelming legislative support and massive public approval,[85] Marshall nevertheless argued that if only others knew as much about capital punishment as he did, they would find it "shocking, unjust, and unacceptable."[86]

The major blow to death penalty abolitionists since 1976 occurred when the Rehnquist Court rejected a claim that the death penalty was imposed in a racially discriminatory manner.[87] The abolitionists based their major claim not on the race of the convict, but on the race of the victim. A Georgia study of two thousand murders found that killing a white person made one 4.3 times more likely to receive the death penalty than killing a black person, even after controlling statistically for dozens of other factors. The Court nevertheless ruled that even if the death penalty were discriminatorily imposed, petitioners would have to prove intentional bias in their case. Short of a confession from jurors that they had done so, obtaining such proof would seemingly be impossible.

APPEALS

As the Supreme Court decisions we have discussed in this chapter make clear, conviction at trial does not necessarily produce the final word. Although no

---

[81] *Id.* at 360.

[82] *Id.* at 305.

[83] *Woodson v. North Carolina*, 428 U.S. 280 (1976).

[84] *Gregg v. Georgia*, 428 U.S. 153 (1976).

[85] Thomas R. Marshall, *Public Opinion and the Supreme Court* (Boston: Unwin Hyman, 1989).

[86] *Gregg v. Georgia*, 428 U.S. 153 (1976), at 232.

[87] *McCleskey v. Kemp*, 481 U.S. 279 (1987).

constitutional right to appeal exists,[88] each state statutorily allows appeals of criminal convictions to either intermediate appellate courts or state supreme courts. When appeal is allowed, the state must provide counsel to indigent defendants on their first appeal.[89] Although plea bargain agreements usually preclude appeal, about 90 percent of those convicted at trial and sentenced to prison file an appeal.[90] These appeals can be made on evidentiary grounds (a lack of evidence to sustain a conviction), statutory grounds (the criminal statute does not cover the activities committed), or constitutional grounds (one or more of the defendant's constitutional rights were violated).

If the appeal from a state conviction is made on statutory grounds, there is no federal question, and the state has the last word. A rare exception to this occurred when the Warren Court rejected a South Carolina Supreme Court interpretation of state law that had disingenuously applied it to civil rights protesters.[91] Similarly, appeals based on state constitutional rights that provide more protection for individual rights than federal constitutional rights do not involve federal questions (see Chapter 7).

Criminal appeals that have their federal claims rejected at the state court of last resort may be appealed to the U.S. Supreme Court, though the success rate for such appeals is currently about 1 percent. An alternative mechanism exists, however: a habeas corpus petition to the local federal district court. Once again, relief is rather rare: Only about 3 percent of such petitions involve any sort of remedy at all, and most such remedies are orders for further hearings.[92] Even within the state system, the vast majority of appeals are denied.

CONCLUSIONS

As Figure 6.1 shows, for every one thousand crimes committed, five hundred are reported to the police. Of the five hundred reported crimes, one hundred result in arrest. The one hundred arrests include thirty-five juveniles, who are typically dealt with by a separate system. Of the sixty-five adults arrested, thirty see their case dropped by police or prosecutors. Thirty-five cases remain for prosecution, but in five of those the defendant jumps bail, leaving only thirty cases for trial. In the thirty cases that go to trial, twenty-three plead guilty, most through a plea bargain; four are found guilty at trial, and three are acquitted. Of the twenty-seven who are found or plead guilty, eighteen are incarcerated, and the remaining nine are placed on probation.

The control of the Supreme Court over this process varies enormously from step to step. The Court has quite a bit to say about the manner in which police conduct investigations, that is, searching for evidence and questioning suspects.

---

[88] *Abney v. United States*, 431 U.S. 651 (1977).

[89] *Douglas v. California*, 372 U.S. 353 (1963).

[90] Kamisar et al., *Basic Criminal Procedure*, p. 29.

[91] *Bouie v. City of Columbia*, 378 U.S. 347 (1964).

[92] Kamisar et al., *Basic Criminal Procedure*, p. 29.

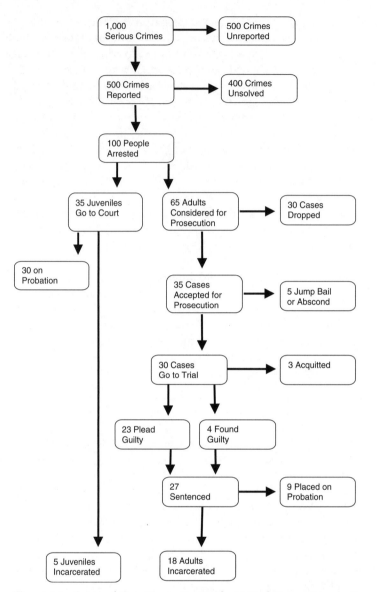

Figure 6.1. Criminal Case Processing in the United States. *Source:* George F. Cole and Christopher E. Smith, *The American System of Criminal Justice*, 10th ed. (Belmont, CA: Wadsworth, 2004), p. 73.

The Court's role in defining crimes, choosing cases for prosecution, plea bargains, sentencing, and – despite claims by Warren Court critics – encouraging crime, is rather limited.

Also recognize that although Supreme Court decisions speak authoritatively, their authority only extends to the floor below which constitutional rights may not descend. Nothing prevents state courts from bestowing on individuals greater rights than the Court construes the Constitution to require. Thus, in negative reaction to the Supreme Court decision in a *Miranda* warnings case and to two decisions upholding three-strikes-and-you're-out statutes that impose sentences as long as life for persons convicted of three relatively minor nonviolent crimes,[93] state courts in California and Delaware reopened the issues in these cases and mitigated their restrictive effects, thereby shaping the future of constitutional protection for the residents of these two states.

[93] *Chavez v. Martinez*, 538. U.S. 760 (2003); *Ewing v. California*, 538 U.S. 11 (2003); *Lockyer v. Andrade*, 538 U.S. 63 (2003). Also see Laurie L. Levinson, "Picking Up the Slack," *National Law Journal*, 18–25 August 2003, p. 33.

PART III

LOWER COURTS IN THE AMERICAN LEGAL SYSTEM

7

State Courts

Although Election 2000 was surely a federal matter, as evidenced by the federal court involvement therein, the problems started in the state of Florida. The legal battles began there, too, as the following analysis indicates.

On November 8, the day after the election, with every Florida county reporting, Bush held a 1,784-vote lead over Gore. Because of the closeness of the vote, Florida law called for an automatic machine recount, which cut Bush's margin to 229 votes of nearly 6,000,000 cast.

Florida law next allows unsuccessful candidates a chance (1) to "protest" the election before the state's certifying the winner and then a chance (2) to "contest" the election after certification. Thus, although certifying the winner was not the ultimate step in Florida's presidential campaign, the Gore campaign determined that certification of a Bush victory would be a mortal blow to their effort to win the state, and thus the election.

In the protest period, canvassing boards may, at the request of any candidate, authorize 1 percent manual recounts. If those recounts demonstrate an error in the vote tabulation that could affect the outcome, the boards shall correct the tabulation error, verify the tabulation software, or conduct a manual recount.

The problem for Gore was that any such recounts during the protest stage, which mainly envisaged mechanical and tabulation problems, had to be completed within one week of the election, and they were not getting done or likely to be completed in time. If any county's returns are incomplete at that point, Florida law is unclear what happens next. Under § 102.112(1) of the Florida election code, late returns "*may* be ignored" by the secretary of state. Under § 102.111 (1), however, such late returns "*shall* be ignored" (emphasis added) by the secretary of state.

Although this difference seems a stupid mistake for the Florida legislature to have made, given that the quoted provisions are adjacent to one another, this sort of human error along with modern statutory complexity make conflict of laws to say nothing of endemic legislative incompetence – inevitable. Under the guise of statutory interpretation, courts routinely smooth out statutory inconsistencies. But how they smooth out these inconsistencies is another question. In the trial court ruling, Judge Terry Lewis ruled that Secretary of State Katherine Harris could reject late ballots, as long as she did not do so arbitrarily.

The Florida Supreme Court, however, reversed. In a 9–0 decision, the completely Democratic court solipsistically transformed the "may ignore" and "shall ignore" requirements into *may not ignore* late ballots. In a ruling that hindsight demonstrates, for Gore at least, the validity of being careful for what you wish, the state supreme court gave local canvassing boards the period until November 26 to complete their recount.[1] Unfortunately for Gore, by November 26 Bush still led and Secretary of State Harris eventually certified him the winner. But more importantly, by extending the protest period, the contest period, which is open to an extended range of errors and remedies, had been significantly narrowed. In fact, by the time the Florida circuit court rejected a contest-period recount, the Florida Supreme Court reversed,[2] and the case had made its way to the U.S. Supreme Court,[3] insufficient time remained to recount the votes, not only under the U.S. Supreme Court's artificially created deadline of December 12, but probably also under a more legitimate deadline of December 18 – the date the Electoral College was required to vote. Indeed, the Florida Supreme Court's partisan decision in the protest case may have contributed to the U.S. Supreme Court's decision in *Bush v. Gore* not to entrust the Florida court with a December 12 remand to allow a counting of all the votes under consistent guidelines.[4]

THE STATE COURTS

Although state trial courts receive public attention when athletes and actresses have their inevitable legal problems, the 2000 election alerted the public to a range of state courts that it very rarely sees. Indeed, in most respects, the structure of state governments mirrors that of the federal government. The major exceptions are the features of the state judicial systems. Whereas federal judges are appointed by the president with the consent of the Senate and serve for life, state court judges serve terms of limited tenure except in the major trial courts and the supreme court of Rhode Island.[5]

Furthermore, the federal courts have a simple three-tiered structure of trial, intermediate appellate, and supreme courts. The states generally have a similar structure, but at the trial court level, it is anything but simple. Instead, myriad local trial courts extend across the typical state, with highly complex geographical and subject matter jurisdiction. Because state courts vary so much

---

[1] *Palm Beach County Canvassing Board v. Harris,* 770 So. 2d 1273 (2000).

[2] *Gore v. Harris,* 773 So. 2d 524 (2000).

[3] *Bush v. Gore,* 531 U.S. 98 (2000).

[4] The U.S. Supreme Court actually did remand the case, but the arbitrary December 12 deadline rendered any recount impossible.

[5] Bureau of Justice Statistics, *State Court Organization 1998* (Williamsburg, VA: National Center for State Courts, 2000), pp. 28, 45.

from one state to another, we will avoid specificity and instead focus on the few commonalities they possess.

THE SELECTION OF STATE COURT JUDGES

The one signal respect in which the form and structure of the state and federal courts differ is the selection of judges. Whereas federal judges serve lifetime appointments, those of the states, with the exception (at the moment) of Rhode Island, do not.[6] Indeed, the great majority of the states do not give their governor unencumbered appointment power, requiring either the participation of a nominating commission or a combination of initial appointment and some other form of retention.[7] The states, rather, prefer to elect their judges or, alternatively, to use a cleverly devised method of retention known, among other names, as the *Missouri Plan*. Table 7.1 shows the resulting variety.

Methods of Selection

Although the states use a finite number of methods to select their judges, generalizations about them are dangerous because of state tendencies to oscillate from one to another in whole or in part, depending on whether a judge is selected for a full term, is chosen to fill an unexpired vacancy, or seeks another term, with the result that part of a state's judiciary may be selected by one method, the remainder by another.

These methods may be divided between two types of appointment – executive and legislative – and two of election – partisan and nonpartisan. The fifth method is a modified hybrid, the Missouri Plan.

The original thirteen states and their immediate successors appointed their judges either by gubernatorial action or by that of the legislature. As a result, the voting public had no direct choice in the selection of judges. Many states continue to employ appointment in whole or in part. However, when state selection systems change, switching to judicial elections tends to be the most popular choice.

Elections

The election of judges was a major contribution of Jacksonian democracy. Andrew Jackson and his minions firmly believed in the equicompetence of most men for most tasks – especially with regard to the holding of public office. This

---

[6] All of Rhode Island's judges except those serving on probate, municipal, and administrative adjudication courts serve for life. All judges of Massachusetts's and New Hampshire's courts serve until age seventy. *Id.* at 27–28, 39, 41, 45.

[7] Some 91 percent of Minnesota's judges were so selected as of mid-2003, including six of seven on the state supreme court. An appointed judge enjoys the advantage of being labeled an incumbent on the next ballot. The Brennan Center Court Pester, Brennan.Center@nyu.edu, August 5, 2003, p. 2.

Table 7.1. *Selection and Retention in the States*

	Gubernatorial Appointment	Legislative Appointment	Partisan Election	Nonpartisan Election	Retention Election
Unexpired terms	AL HI MO ND UT AK ID MT OH VT AZ IN NE OK WA AR IA NV OR WI CA ME NH PA WV CO MD NJ RI DE MI NM SD FL MN NY TN GA MS NC TX	CT SC[a] VA	None	KY	None
Full terms	AK FL KS MO NY AZ HI ME NE UT CO IN MD NH VT DE OK MA NJ WY	CT SC[a] VA	AL NC AR PA IL TX NM WV	GA LA MS ND WA ID MI MT OH WI KY MN NV OR	CA OK SD TN
Retention	DE ME NH NJ NY	CT SC[a] VT[a] VA	AL AR NC TX WV	GA LA MT ND TN ID MI NV OH WA KY MN NM OR WI	AK FL KS NE SD AZ IL MD OK UT CA IN MO PA WY CO IA

Note: A couple of oddities were unable to be presented in the table. First, Illinois and Louisiana have their state court of last resort appoint justices when an unexpired term needs to be filled. Rhode Island appears only under unexpired terms because its justices are appointed for life. Hawaii uses a judicial nomination committee for its retention elections, and Massachusetts does not have a retention system because it appoints its justices for good behavior until age 70.

[a] Legislature elects a judge.

Source: Bureau of Justice Statistics, *State Court Organization, 1998* (Washington, DC: U.S. Government Printing Office, 2000).

belief, however, did not mean the total irrelevance of any and all qualifications. The test for holding public office did not differ from that required of Jackson's predecessors – party loyalty. The party may have differed, but evidence of partisan affiliation remained a sine qua non for selection. Jackson's supporters were located a couple of rungs on the socioeconomic ladder below those of earlier presidents. Universal suffrage (limited, of course, to those who were white and male) had become the order of the day, and with it the notion of popular sovereignty: that the man behind the plow or tending his still in the backwoods had as much of a stake in society as the banker, the merchant, or the ship owner; and that all adults (except women, Indians, and blacks, of course) were fully capable of governing themselves. This idea extended to choosing judges.

Today, although elections are used widely, they have been relatively low-information elections.[8] Judges have not campaigned as much as other office-holders have, and their campaigns typically received little media coverage. Lack of information, then, has been a real issue in these elections. But because of the 2002 Supreme Court decision in *Republican Party of Minnesota v. White*, which we discuss and evaluate in the next two sections of this chapter, state judicial candidates now have effectively unlimited freedom to communicate, including communicating how they intend to vote on highly partisan and controversial *issues* – but not on a specific *case* – that they will undoubtedly be asked to decide, such as abortion, capital punishment, criminal procedure. Granted, judicial elections were becoming more openly political before *White*; however, the Supreme Court's imprimatur certainly promoted the politicization of the contests.

Election of judges takes two forms – partisan and nonpartisan – with the former informing voters of a candidate's party affiliation. The more ancient form (and the one that began with Jacksonian democracy), partisan election, tends to be used in states in which a single party has historically been dominant (e.g., the South) and in states where political bosses have tended to hold sway (e.g., New York and Illinois). The party label that distinguished each candidate thereby enabled the dominant party to identify its candidates and ensured that the party faithful did not mistakenly vote for members of the opposition.

In reaction to the machine politics of the late nineteenth and early twentieth centuries, however, a number of states switched from partisan to nonpartisan elections, with the objective of removing partisan politics from the selection of judges. (Of course, in some states, such as Wisconsin, the election remains essentially partisan as a partisan primary precedes the nonpartisan election.) But as with many reforms, the remedy produced its own ill effects: name candidates and incumbency designations. Without a specification of party identification, voters had little information other than their familiarity with the candidates' names. Candidates quickly recognized the advantage of a recognizable name

[8] See, e.g., Lawrence Baum, "Electing Judges," in Lee Epstein (ed.), *Contemplating Courts* (Washington, DC: Congressional Quarterly Press, 1995).

and began to trade on the value of name recognition to the exclusion of other qualifications.

An example from Michigan illustrates: In the mid-1950s, there appeared on Detroit television a live (and lively) evening program titled *Juvenile Court*. The star of the show, complete with bona fide delinquents, was one Nathan Kaufman, an incumbent probate court judge. The popularity of the program caused other Kaufmans to seek judicial office: whether spelled with a *K* or a *C*, a single *f* or two, or one *n* or two made no difference. Only the pronunciation needed to remain constant. Finally, his five fellow probate court judges persuaded him to preside sans television cameras. Nathan Kaufman subsequently moved up the judicial ladder (having been replaced – not surprisingly – on the probate court with an Ira Kaufman) and ended his judicial career as a judge on the court of appeals.

In 1957, one Thomas M. Kavanagh, then state attorney general, was elected to the state supreme court after he was nominated for that position at the State Democratic Convention. He was handily reelected in 1966. Meantime, a Thomas G. Kavanagh was among eight persons elected to the newly created court of appeals in 1964, leading the other candidates by a comfortable margin in both the primary and general elections. In 1968, the Democrats, casting about for a nominee to the supreme court, reached an indisputably logical conclusion: If one Thomas Kavanagh could be elected to the state supreme court, why not two? The voters agreed and Thomas G. joined Thomas M. among the court's seven members.

But that is not the end of the story. Regardless of spelling, so long as the pronunciation does not vary, the name remains potent. When one of the Kavanaghs departed the bench, his replacement was a Michael Cavanagh.

Overriding the effect of a "good judicial name" was the allowance given judges seeking reelection (in some states) to designate themselves as an incumbent judge on the ballot. Incumbency designation is typically accorded not only to judges seeking reelection, but also to those who received a gubernatorial appointment because their predecessor resigned, retired, or died before the end of his or her term of office. The effect has been that once elected, a judge is virtually assured of reelection for life or until the mandatory retirement age (typically seventy) that bars a judge or a judicial candidate from appearing on a ballot.

Other factors being equal, incumbency designation beats a good judicial name. And do note that qualifications are electorally irrelevant, notwithstanding the ratings that state and local bar associations typically give to judicial candidates. But name recognition does not always benefit the incumbent. Incumbent judges who have riled their constituents by voting against intensely held views on controversial litigation are as easily identified for negative as for positive reasons. Thus, a trial judge who acquits a person viewed by the community as guilty as sin, or an appellate judge who regularly votes to void death sentences runs serious risk of voter wrath, as happened to California Chief Judge Rose Bird, who was removed from office in 1986. Off-the-bench behavior may also redound to the detriment of the incumbent. Again, an example from Michigan illustrates: A local judge, while on vacation, foolishly had an argument with a cab driver about the fare charged to take him to one of Nevada's establishments euphemistically known as "houses" that are not homes. A local reporter on the night beat wrote the story and put it on the Associated Press wire. When the Michigan press got wind of the story, the judge's fate was sealed. The upcoming uncontested primary suddenly spawned eight additional candidates, and the misbehaving incumbent finished ninth. Indeed, it seems the ideal judge is one who literally disappears from view when court is not in session.

As for name candidates, where a judicial vacancy exists, more than one name candidate may compete for the position, thus neutralizing name effects. In recent years, a candidate's sex may lessen and even displace the benefits of a good name. Evidence exists that the coattails of a popular woman at the head of a ticket may produce a win for others farther down on the ballot. (Candidates for judicial office typically locate at the end of the ballot, followed only by various propositions and constitutional amendments that are to be voted on.) And in recent years, depending on state or local circumstances, a female candidate – simply because she is female – may outpoll male opponents. So, too, with race; uninformed voters will use any potential cue to race or nationality on the ballot in order to cast their vote.

A former colleague tells his students the story of his first encounter with the nonpartisan judicial ballot. As a political science major, he conscientiously applied himself to learning all he could about all candidates. At the polls, he had no trouble casting votes for candidates for major offices, but by the time he reached the judicial ballot, complete blankness of mind had set in. Carefully memorized names escaped recall. What to do? He could have written a list, but he prided himself on his memory. To leave the rest of the ballot blank would be a dereliction of civic duty. Suddenly, a stroke of genius: As an individual who carried his Irish ancestry proudly, he would vote for Irish surnamed candidates. Scrutinizing the next day's newspaper for the results of the judicial elections, he found the list of winners complete with names and faces. A majority of his "Irish" candidates were unmistakably of African ancestry!

On a more embarrassing note, one of the authors of this book, having heard nothing about a supreme court election, looked over the choices on the ballot and proceeded to vote for all the women, only subsequently to discover that they were the most ideologically distant from the author's policy orientation.

The Politicization of Judicial Elections. Since the 2002 decision in *Republican Party of Minnesota v. White*[9] opening judicial elections to the partisanship, infighting, and rancor of campaigns for legislative and executive offices – to say nothing of their expense – the public is getting more "information" out of its judicial candidates. The polite behavior and lack of public and media attention

[9] 536 U.S. 765.

that accompanied judicial elections died a rather sudden death. Until the twenty-first century, judicial elections tended to be sedate affairs, with little campaigning by the candidates and even less expenditure of money. Judicial candidates might attend civic and social functions, shaking a few hands and uttering a few glittering generalities about the law and the importance of judicial impartiality and platitudinous assertions of objectivity. The high point of judicial campaigns was the release by the relevant bar association of its evaluations of the candidates. Frequently, all candidates received the same ranking: either qualified or well qualified.

Such limited activity did not mean a lack of interest on all fronts. Law firms and interests dependent on judicial favor involved themselves, but behind the scenes. Refinement and gentility characterized public appearances. As the perception of ideological and partisan behavior drew public and media attention to state courts, involving such issues as abortion, the death penalty, street and drug crime, substantial damages awarded to persons killed or injured by defective products, medical and other professional malpractice, and environmental hazards, affected interests perked up and began to realize that the attitudes of their judges could directly affect their economic and social interest and well-being. Stacking the bench with cronies and like-minded jurists became as important as controlling the legislative or executive branch.

In the twenty-first century, then, judicial campaigns in many states have become as plagued by partisanship and negative campaigning as those for legislative and executive offices, with an attendant increase in financial cost.

Judicial candidates, of course, except with incessant barrages of television advertising and candid statements of their positions on the burning issues of the day, acted as if nothing had changed. They obviously distance themselves from their campaign expenditures, facetiously alleging that they have no control of what other groups and organizations spend on their behalf and asserting that they personally fund their campaign with their own money, plus that from individual lawyers and their political action committees (PACs).

Such assertions are unmitigated balderdash. Judicial candidates may assert that they accept neither contributions nor endorsements from special interests, such as Right-to-Life, a labor union, or the chamber of commerce, but that they have no control if certain groups and organizations choose to support them. Granted that judicial candidates historically accepted contributions from fellow lawyers, but obviously that does not mean that a legal PAC may not be a front for special interests – political, ideological, or otherwise. To believe differently evidences meaningful quantitative difference between being blind in one eye and being unable to see with the other.

The states in which judges were elected in the fall of 2002 undoubtedly illustrated the wave of the future: very expensive and uninhibited campaigning. As in legislative and executive campaigns, anything goes – especially negative ads. The fact that successful candidates may spend many times their annual salary obviously means nothing. Neither does the fact that litigants appearing before a judge may have disproportionately contributed to the judge's selection.

Indeed, in Michigan between 1994 and 2000, campaign spending for major party supreme court candidates increased 250 percent, from $322,000 to $1.14 million. In one case, a losing motor company employee contesting a denial of unemployment compensation confronted the four justices of seven who had received almost $100,000 for their most recent campaign from the motor company. The four supreme court justices were among the five who voted against the employee.[10]

Spending on all state supreme court elections in 2000 totaled $45.6 million, up 61 percent from 1998 and double the amount spent in 1994. In addition, interest groups, such as the Chamber of Commerce and trial lawyers, spent millions of dollars on judicial campaigns, most of them for attack ads blasting candidates deemed insufficiently friendly to plaintiffs, to the death penalty, or to the unborn fetus.[11]

And so judges sit in judgment of their benefactors. But what else is new? In the good old days, those of the late nineteenth and early twentieth centuries, former railroad attorneys dominated the U.S. Supreme Court. Think railroads did not benefit? Guess again.

So much for a low-key, frugal campaign. Successful ones commonly require expenditures ten or more times the judge's annual salary. An additional effect of skyrocketing costs is that judges commonly decide cases involving their major campaign contributors. It is hard, say, for trial court judges to present the appearance of propriety when their major supporters are the same law firms and attorneys who regularly appear in their courtroom.

The same holds for appellate courts. A report by Texans for Public Justice assessed the effects of campaign contributions on the Texas Supreme Court.[12] The court has discretionary jurisdiction, meaning it may choose whether or not it will hear each of the hundreds of cases appealed to it each year. Between the years 1994 and 1998, the court granted review from noncontributors in 5.6 percent of those cases. Against that baseline, it granted review to 20 percent of campaign contributors, and the more you paid, the better you did (see Figure 7.1). Small contributors (less than one thousand dollars) won review 11 percent of the time, double the rate of noncontributors. Large contributors, more than $100,000, won review 36 percent of the time, and the largest contributors, who gave more than $250,000, won review 56 percent of the time!

Judicial Candidates' Freedom of Speech. Whatever restraint state court judges might have shown is now a historical artifact given the politicization of judicial elections, aided and abetted by the U.S. Supreme Court's 2002 decision in *Republican Party of Minnesota v. White*.[13]

---

[10] Brian Dickerson, "What Money Can – and Can't – Buy," *Detroit Free Press*, 3 May 2002, p. 1B.

[11] Derek Bok, "Too Many Beholden Judges," *National Law Journal*, 25 November 2002, p. A8.

[12] http://www.tpj.org/reports/paytoplay/index.htm.

[13] 536 U.S. 765.

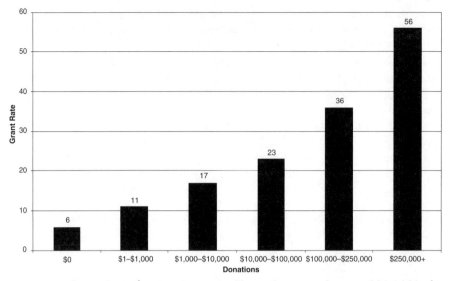

Figure 7.1. Grant Rate for Petitioners in Texas Supreme Court, 1994–1998, by Petitioner Campaign Donations. *Source:* Texans for Public Justice: http://www.tpj. org/reports/paytoplay/index.htm.

Minnesota, as the other states do, has laws and rules governing the conduct of judicial elections, the gist of which prohibits judicial candidates from announcing their views and taking sides in disputed legal and political issues, most particularly matters that the candidate will likely rule on if he or she becomes a judge.

As in *Bush v. Gore*, the vote was 5–4, with the same five justices who voted for Bush now voting that state laws restricting judicial campaigns unconstitutionally violated the First Amendment. Ironically, the five who declared these laws and regulations unconstitutional are the five who least frequently rule other laws and governmental action to be violations of the First Amendment, and the four dissenters are those who most frequently do.

The majority, strictly on free speech grounds, had the much better of the argument. The state prohibited communication on the basis of its content – very much a constitutional taboo – and exacerbated this factor by applying it to political activity, which, with only a few exceptions, is more protected from governmental abridgment or restriction than communication about nonpolitical matters.

Contrasted with the majority, the minority made disingenuous arguments demeaning the intelligence of even the most vapid citizen. Reverting to the myth of an objective, dispassionate, and impartial judiciary, the dissent averred that judicial campaigns fundamentally differ from those for policy-making offices; that judges occupy a special position of trust not possessed by other officials; and that if they do not adhere to what they said once in office, judicial independence and impartiality would be compromised and undermined.

Be the foregoing as it may – and we may certainly expect steady increases in the financial cost and in the negative tenor of campaign advertising – incumbency followed by a good judicial name are the roads to electoral success. Indeed, even dead incumbents can beat the opposition. Thus, an Oklahoma judge who died three months before his 1990 election nevertheless beat his opponent more than 9–1. And once the living attain judicial office, judges must deviate rather substantially from the righteous path that the electorate expects its judges to tread to lose their exalted position playing God with the life, liberty, and property of those who appear before them.

The Missouri Plan

The newest method of judicial selection, dating from the eve of World War II, is the Missouri Plan, named for the state of its origin. It has received more felicitous labels in the years since – the Lawyers' or the Judges' Plan, and egregiously euphemistically as the Merit Plan. Although variations exist, the method works as follows: The governor appoints to a vacancy one of three names received from a commission on judicial selection. The commission has seven members: three appointed by the governor, three elected or appointed by the state or local bar association, and the chief judge of the state or district. The nominee chosen by the governor serves as judge for a year or until the next general election, at which time his name appears on the ballot in the following form: "Shall John Goodfellow be retained as Judge? Yes or no?" Note that Judge Goodfellow does not run against anybody. If the yes votes outnumber the no votes, the judge serves for a specified term of years.

The strongest support for this selection method is that of bar associations and law-based organizations such as the American Judicature Society. They argue that the plan eliminates politics from the selection of judges. This is patently false. The plan only replaces conventional sorts of politics with the closed-door or smoke-filled-room variety in which only lawyers, judges, and the governor participate. Individuals and special interest groups still maneuver to influence the selection of judges, but the maneuvering does not involve public scrutiny or the assessment of responsibility for the persons chosen. The ballot question in which the public is asked whether a previously selected judge shall be retained in office is a sham, mere window dressing. The election label is a misnomer. It is nothing more than a plebiscite. Dictators of all stripes do not hesitate to employ it for the very simple reason that the first law of politics is that you cannot beat somebody with nobody, just as the outcome of a horse race is assured as long as only one horse is entered. And though unopposed judges may occasionally lose, they are typically retained in their office at a proportion approximating the alleged purity of Ivory soap: 99.44 percent. Furthermore, they tend to win overwhelmingly – with upward of 80 percent of the vote.[14]

---

[14] Melinda Gann Hall, "State Supreme Courts in American Democracy: Probing the Myths of Judicial Reform," 95 *American Political Science Review* 315 (2001).

Choosing a Selection System

One ought not be surprised that lawyers and bar associations support the Missouri Plan. Indeed, the American Bar Association reports, in typically understated style, that there exists "a pervasive public perception that campaign contributions influence judicial decision making"[15] and that because of that perception, judges ought not be selected via competitive elections.

As in other licensed occupations and regulated industries, it is in lawyers' economic self-interest to select those who directly affect their pocketbook. Telecommunications industries and the local gas and electric company find it advantageous to place their friends on state public utilities commissions, the Federal Communications Commission, and the Federal Energy Regulatory Commission. Defense contractors find it remunerative to decorate their executive suites with retired Pentagon brass. Brokers, investment bankers, and stock exchanges concern themselves mightily with the membership of the Securities and Exchange Commission, as the machinations that followed the collapse of the stock market early in the administration of George W. Bush illustrate. Thus do the regulated become the regulators. So also with lawyers.

But regardless of the interests involved, it is ultimately the states' duty to determine a method of selection and retention to fill their benches. Focusing on the state courts of last resort, Table 7.1 specifies which states use which method to fill what kind of vacancy: filling of an unexpired term, filling of a new term, and retention.[16]

As the table indicates, most states give the governor the power to make midterm appointments; for full terms, more states also choose gubernatorial appointment than any other system. However, most of those states employing this appointment system include the participation of a nominating committee, and so the power of selection is not wholly in the governor's hands. Nonpartisan elections provide the next most populous category of full-term selection. Those nonpartisan elections are also used frequently for retention decisions, although many states use regular retention elections (as defined previously) for that stage of selection.

The Missouri Plan has been growing in popularity at the expense of election and appointment, with little evidence of a difference in the quality of judging, evidenced in our table by the large number of states that use gubernatorial appointments. The low opinion with which the public views campaigns and elections has provided an opening for the Missouri Plan and the beguiling label that it is the "merit" plan. As in so many other respects, the public's limited interest and minimal knowledge of the realities of political behavior make them an easy mark for sophisticated peddlers of political snake oil.

---

[15] http://www.abanet.org/judind/report072001.pdf, p. 20.

[16] As mentioned, states are less than stable in their selection processes; hence this table applies only to 1998.

Table 7.2. *Voting on Confessions by Method of Retention, 1970–1991*

Ruling on Confession	Method of Retention			
	Competitive Election	Appointment	Retention Election	Life Tenure
Allow	264 (79.28%)	33 (78.57%)	211 (80.84%)	18 (72%)
Disallow	69 (20.72%)	9 (21.43%)	50 (19.16%)	7 (28%)
Total	333 (100%)	42 (100%)	261 (100%)	25 (100%)

Notes: $N = 661$; chi-square $= 1.1848$, not significant.
Source: Sara C. Benesh and Wendy L. Martinek, "State Supreme Court Decision Making in Confession Cases," 23 *Justice System Journal* 109 (2002).

As does the public, so, too, do state policymakers lack information about the effects of judicial selection on outcomes, and so their choices are often more popularity based than empirically based. Indeed, a recent analysis of the differences between partisan and nonpartisan elections argues that it is simply not the case that partisan-elected judges are more accountable per se or that nonpartisan-elected judges are per se more independent, and therefore, reformers who attempt to move states from partisan elections to nonpartisan elections or the Missouri Plan are not guided by a careful analysis of real differences in outputs of the various selection systems.[17] Much research on the point concludes similarly: that decision making is not necessarily affected by the means by which judges attain their seat.[18] "Despite the heated debate about how to select judges, it is not clear that formal systems make an enormous difference . . . studies have not found dramatic differences among the various formal systems in the characteristics of the state supreme court justices they produce."[19] Nor do they seem necessarily to affect the policy outputs of the courts. Indeed, as seen in Table 7.2, no relationship exists between a state supreme court's decision whether to exclude a confession and the method of retention to which that court is subject, although such differences may surface if other issue areas are analyzed.[20]

Given the foregoing, which is the most preferable method of judicial selection? About all one can say theoretically is that two criteria should govern evaluation of any selection system: the quality of the resulting decision making and the accountability of the judges to the public.

[17] Hall, "State Supreme Courts."

[18] See, e.g., Sara C. Benesh and Wendy L. Martinek, "State Supreme Court Decision Making in Confession Cases," 23 *Justice System Journal* 109 (2002). But see Paul Brace and Melinda Gann Hall, "Neo-Institutionalism and Dissent in State Supreme Courts," 52 *Journal of Politics* 54 (1990), and other studies of death penalty cases.

[19] Henry R. Glick and Craig Emmert, "Selection Systems and Judicial Characteristics: The Recruitment of State Supreme Court Justices," 70 *Judicature* 228 (1987).

[20] We use *retention* rather than *selection* because judges ought to be more concerned with those responsible for keeping them in office than those who merely put them there in the first place. Of course, in many states, the same actors select and retain.

Least accountable, of course, are lifetime appointees, which federal judges are mandated by the Constitution to be. But all knowledgeable persons consider these judges better than those of the states. Even federal trial court judges are viewed by many as superior to state supreme court justices. As for accountability, those most accountable are those about whom the voters have the most information: those elected on a partisan ballot. But they are commonly viewed as the least competent and the most partial to the special interests to whom they owe their position. So normative theory is of little help.

ACCESSING STATE COURTS

Litigants must meet two requirements to take their cases to a state (or a federal) court: The court must have jurisdiction over the controversy, and the party bringing the lawsuit must have standing to sue. Although all judges are cognizant of the limits on the cases they may decide, state courts (no less than federal) treat the requirements of standing rather cavalierly – as so many technicalities that sometimes get in the way of "doing justice."

Jurisdiction

We begin with jurisdiction. Its most basic definition is the authority by which a court accepts and decides matters called to its attention. It is manifested in three ways: geographically, hierarchically, and on the basis of subject matter.

State courts organize themselves along county lines, whereas the organizational unit of the federal courts is the individual state. The subject matter jurisdiction of state trial courts typically does not extend beyond the county line except in lightly populated parts of a state where more than one county may be combined to form a geographical judicial district. In more populated counties, municipalities may have their own courts, the jurisdiction of which lies within the city's boundaries. Appellate courts have jurisdiction over more than a single county and conceivably may be statewide. State supreme courts, of course, have jurisdiction over the entire state.

Hierarchically, states, as in the federal system, have trial and appellate courts. Whereas the federal system has an intermediate and a supreme court, some of the less populated states have no intermediate appellate court. Litigants who lose in the trial court appeal their case directly to the state supreme court.

The major difference between state and federal courts is jurisdictional. The federal courts are courts of general jurisdiction in the sense that they may decide almost any matter that lies within the federal courts' grant of constitutional decision-making authority.[21] The exceptions are the specialized federal

---

[21] Labeling federal courts as courts of general jurisdiction is misleading from this standpoint. Although they may decide most cases that the Constitution authorizes the federal courts to decide, they are courts of specialized jurisdiction inasmuch as the Constitution's subject matter jurisdiction does not begin to cover the waterfront of litigable controversies. As we have seen,

courts, which decide only limited types of federal questions (e.g., tax, intellectual property, military discipline). State courts, by contrast, are courts of limited jurisdiction except the appellate courts, which, with some exceptions,[22] may decide most matters that they wish to decide except those of peculiarly federal concern, such as the recognition of a foreign government or taxation of imported goods.

States have limited the jurisdiction of their trial courts not because they cannot have general jurisdiction trial courts, but rather because they consider it preferable that their trial court judges not spread themselves too thinly and instead focus on a limited set of controversies, especially given the variety and huge number of cases heard each year in the states. States vary widely in the extent of specialization confining their trial courts. As with methods of selection, generalization about subject matter jurisdiction necessarily ignores marked differences. We exemplify the extremes of specialization (New York) and simplicity (Nevada, California) in Figure 7.2.

With this caveat in mind, we can note a few patterns, however, which apply to the trial court level. States divide subject matter jurisdiction along major and minor lines. Criminal jurisdiction divides between felonies and misdemeanors. And it must be said that states have their own distinctive definition of which crimes fall into each of the two categories. On the civil side, a dollar amount in controversy divides the cases; and those of a specified lesser amount fall under the purview of common pleas. Neither fish nor fowl are probate courts, of which a state may have one or several. If several, they divide between or among juvenile, domestic relations, and wills and estates.

States are free to divide these aspects of subject matter jurisdiction among their courts as they see fit. Because Michigan has a rather simple set of courts that accommodates subject matter jurisdiction, we will start there, noting variations as we proceed. We parenthetically note that reasons for the jurisdictional divisions among a state's courts frequently appear to be arbitrary. We do not attempt to fathom the reasons therefore.

Structural and jurisdictional complexity abounds at the trial court level. The names of courts have little rhyme or reason. In Michigan, for example, the major trial courts are known as *circuit courts*. In the federal system, circuit courts are the intermediate courts of appeal. New York terms its supreme court the *court of appeals*, and its supreme court is its major trial court.

Michigan's major trial court – the circuit court – has subject matter jurisdiction over the county in which it sits. One such court has jurisdiction over more than one contiguous county in rural areas. This arrangement is about as standard as anything gets in the state court systems. In Michigan this court has jurisdiction over any matter not bestowed by state law on another court. All

---

federal courts substantially decide only federal questions and those arising under diversity of citizenship.

[22] The most notable exceptions are Oklahoma and Texas, which have two supreme courts with jurisdiction divided between civil and criminal matters.

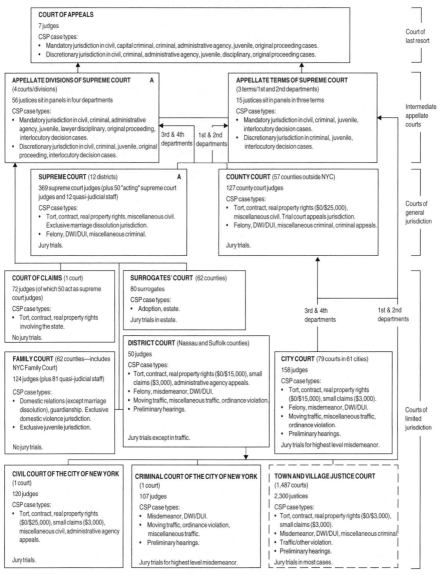

NEW YORK COURT STRUCTURE, 1998*

COURT OF APPEALS

7 judges

CSP case types:
- Mandatory jurisdiction in civil, capital criminal, criminal, administrative agency, juvenile, original proceeding cases.
- Discretionary jurisdiction in civil, criminal, administrative agency, juvenile, disciplinary, original proceeding cases.

Court of last resort

APPELLATE DIVISIONS OF SUPREME COURT   A
(4 courts/divisions)

56 justices sit in panels in four departments

CSP case types:
- Mandatory jurisdiction in civil, criminal, administrative agency, juvenile, lawyer disciplinary, original proceeding, interlocutory decision cases.
- Discretionary jurisdiction in civil, criminal, juvenile, original proceeding, interlocutory decision cases.

3rd & 4th departments   1st & 2nd departments

APPELLATE TERMS OF SUPREME COURT
(3 terms/1st and 2nd departments)

15 justices sit in panels in three terms

CSP case types:
- Mandatory jurisdiction in civil, criminal, juvenile, interlocutory decision cases.
- Discretionary jurisdiction in criminal, juvenile, interlocutory decision cases.

Intermediate appellate courts

SUPREME COURT (12 districts)   A

369 supreme court judges (plus 50 "acting" supreme court judges and 12 quasi-judicial staff)

CSP case types:
- Tort, contract, real property rights, miscellaneous civil. Exclusive marriage dissolution jurisdiction.
- Felony, DWI/DUI, miscellaneous criminal.

Jury trials.

COUNTY COURT (57 counties outside NYC)

127 county court judges

CSP case types:
- Tort, contract, real property rights ($0/$25,000), miscellaneous civil. Trial court appeals jurisdiction.
- Felony, DWI/DUI, miscellaneous criminal, criminal appeals.

Jury trials.

Courts of general jurisdiction

COURT OF CLAIMS (1 court)

72 judges (of which 50 act as supreme court judges)

CSP case types:
- Tort, contract, real property rights involving the state.

No jury trials.

SURROGATES' COURT (62 counties)

80 surrogates

CSP case types:
- Adoption, estate.

Jury trials in estate.

3rd & 4th departments   1st & 2nd departments

DISTRICT COURT (Nassau and Suffolk counties)

50 judges

CSP case types:
- Tort, contract, real property rights ($0/$15,000), small claims ($3,000), administrative agency appeals.
- Felony, misdemeanor, DWI/DUI.
- Moving traffic, miscellaneous traffic, ordinance violation.
- Preliminary hearings.

Jury trials except in traffic.

FAMILY COURT (62 counties—includes NYC Family Court)

124 judges (plus 81 quasi-judicial staff)

CSP case types:
- Domestic relations (except marriage dissolution), guardianship. Exclusive domestic violence jurisdiction.
- Exclusive juvenile jurisdiction.

No jury trials.

CITY COURT (79 courts in 61 cities)

158 judges

CSP case types:
- Tort, contract, real property rights ($0/$15,000), small claims ($3,000).
- Felony, misdemeanor, DWI/DUI.
- Moving traffic, miscellaneous traffic, ordinance violation.
- Preliminary hearings.

Jury trials for highest level misdemeanor.

Courts of limited jurisdiction

CIVIL COURT OF THE CITY OF NEW YORK
(1 court)

120 judges

CSP case types:
- Tort, contract, real property rights ($0/$25,000), small claims ($3,000), miscellaneous civil, administrative agency appeals.

Jury trials.

CRIMINAL COURT OF THE CITY OF NEW YORK
(1 court)

107 judges

CSP case types:
- Misdemeanor, DWI/DUI.
- Moving traffic, ordinance violation, miscellaneous traffic.
- Preliminary hearings.

Jury trials for highest level misdemeanor.

TOWN AND VILLAGE JUSTICE COURT
(1,487 courts)

2,300 justices

CSP case types:
- Tort, contract, real property rights ($0/$3,000), small claims ($3,000).
- Misdemeanor, DWI/DUI, miscellaneous criminal.
- Traffic/other violation.
- Preliminary hearings.

Jury trials in most cases.

*Unless otherwise noted, numbers reflect statutory authorization. Many judges sit in more than one court so the number of judgeships indicated in this chart does not reflect the actual number of judges in the system.

Figure 7.2. Three Examples of State Court Organization. *Source:* Court Statistics Project, *State Court Caseload Statistics, 2002* (Williamsburg, VA: National Center for State Courts, 2003), pp. 12, 36, 40.

NEVADA COURT STRUCTURE, 1998

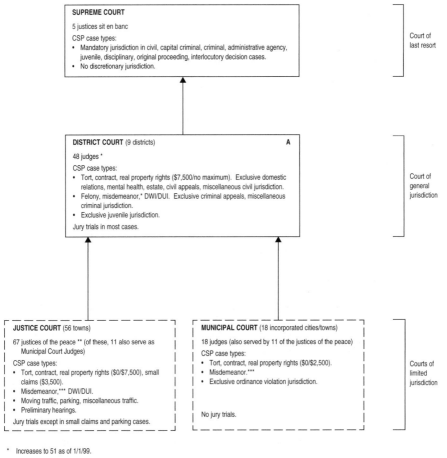

SUPREME COURT

5 justices sit en banc

CSP case types:
- Mandatory jurisdiction in civil, capital criminal, criminal, administrative agency, juvenile, disciplinary, original proceeding, interlocutory decision cases.
- No discretionary jurisdiction.

Court of last resort

DISTRICT COURT (9 districts)　　　　　　　　　　　　　　　　　A

48 judges *

CSP case types:
- Tort, contract, real property rights ($7,500/no maximum). Exclusive domestic relations, mental health, estate, civil appeals, miscellaneous civil jurisdiction.
- Felony, misdemeanor,* DWI/DUI. Exclusive criminal appeals, miscellaneous criminal jurisdiction.
- Exclusive juvenile jurisdiction.

Jury trials in most cases.

Court of general jurisdiction

JUSTICE COURT (56 towns)

67 justices of the peace ** (of these, 11 also serve as Municipal Court Judges)

CSP case types:
- Tort, contract, real property rights ($0/$7,500), small claims ($3,500).
- Misdemeanor,*** DWI/DUI.
- Moving traffic, parking, miscellaneous traffic.
- Preliminary hearings.

Jury trials except in small claims and parking cases.

MUNICIPAL COURT (18 incorporated cities/towns)

18 judges (also served by 11 of the justices of the peace)

CSP case types:
- Tort, contract, real property rights ($0/$2,500).
- Misdemeanor.***
- Exclusive ordinance violation jurisdiction.

No jury trials.

Courts of limited jurisdiction

* Increases to 51 as of 1/1/99.

** Increases to 69 as of 1/1/99.

*** District Court hears gross misdemeanor cases; Justice & Municipal Courts hear misdemeanors with fines under $1,000 and/or sentence of less than six months.

Figure 7.2. *(continued)*

civil cases when the amount in controversy is – or is valued at – more than ten thousand dollars begin here, as do all felonies plus a few of the more serious misdemeanors.[23]

Below a state's major trial court are so-called courts of limited jurisdiction. These typically have geographical jurisdiction over a city or a portion of a county. They hear civil cases in which the amount in controversy is less than

[23] The distinction between felonies and misdemeanors varies from state to state. Generally, a felony is any criminal offense for which the sentence may be a year or more. Misdemeanors are those whose maximum sentence is less than a year.

CALIFORNIA COURT STRUCTURE, 1998

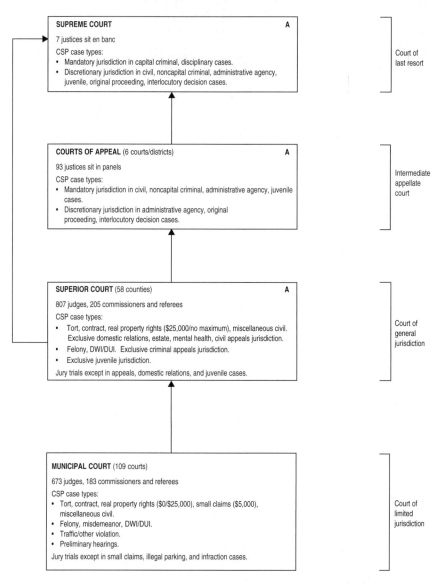

SUPREME COURT A

7 justices sit en banc

CSP case types:
- Mandatory jurisdiction in capital criminal, disciplinary cases.
- Discretionary jurisdiction in civil, noncapital criminal, administrative agency, juvenile, original proceeding, interlocutory decision cases.

Court of last resort

COURTS OF APPEAL (6 courts/districts) A

93 justices sit in panels

CSP case types:
- Mandatory jurisdiction in civil, noncapital criminal, administrative agency, juvenile cases.
- Discretionary jurisdiction in administrative agency, original proceeding, interlocutory decision cases.

Intermediate appellate court

SUPERIOR COURT (58 counties) A

807 judges, 205 commissioners and referees

CSP case types:
- Tort, contract, real property rights ($25,000/no maximum), miscellaneous civil. Exclusive domestic relations, estate, mental health, civil appeals jurisdiction.
- Felony, DWI/DUI. Exclusive criminal appeals jurisdiction.
- Exclusive juvenile jurisdiction.

Jury trials except in appeals, domestic relations, and juvenile cases.

Court of general jurisdiction

MUNICIPAL COURT (109 courts)

673 judges, 183 commissioners and referees

CSP case types:
- Tort, contract, real property rights ($0/$25,000), small claims ($5,000), miscellaneous civil.
- Felony, misdemeanor, DWI/DUI.
- Traffic/other violation.
- Preliminary hearings.

Jury trials except in small claims, illegal parking, and infraction cases.

Court of limited jurisdiction

Note: In 1998 Proposition 220 amended the state Constitution by providing for the voluntary unification of the superior (courts of general jurisdiction) and municipal (courts of limited jurisdiction) courts of a county into one countywide superior court. Originating as Senate Constitutional Amendment 4, the measure was passed by the Legislature in June, 1996, appeared as Proposition 220 on a statewide ballot during a primary election on June 2, 1998, and was approved by 64% of the voters. Proposition 220 became effective June 3, 1998.

Figure 7.2. *(continued)*

that of the major trial court, hence the fairly common name *court of common pleas*. In Michigan, they are known as *district courts* and also have jurisdiction over misdemeanors.

Because of the raft of business, these minor courts may also be subdivided into a small claims court, in which the parties waive their right to a jury trial, rules of evidence, attorney representation, and the right of appeal. Traffic offenses, landlord–tenant disputes, and nonpayment of consumer indebtedness may locate here. Although the regular minor court judge presides in these informal, quickly resolved cases, in some places magistrates are appointed to decide these matters. They may also set bail and accept bond, issue search warrants, accept guilty pleas, and impose sentence on traffic and other license violations.

Complicating the trial structure are the probate courts: those that resolve will contests, the division of estates, divorce, alimony, child custody, and juvenile proceedings. Probate matters may be divided among three separate courts: wills and estates, marital relationships, and juveniles. Michigan has a probate court with exclusive jurisdiction over juvenile proceedings, along with the settling of wills and estates. In the more populous counties, the probate court may have two separate divisions presided over by different judges to hear these two matters. Peculiarly enough (although peculiarity is the hallmark of at least some features of almost every state's judicial system), domestic relations – including divorce and paternity actions – are not a matter for the probate courts in Michigan. Their resolution vests in the major trial court.

Superficially strange is the fact that appeals from minor trial courts and the probate courts are heard in the major trial court of most states, notwithstanding that the latter is viewed as a trial court. In many states, appeals from decisions of many administrative agencies go to the trial court before heading off to the court of appeals. In some states, however, the appellate procedure of the major trial courts is less full blown than the procedure of the appeals court.

The clutter of trial courts disappears at the appellate level. The majority of states have an inferior or intermediate court of appeals. This court has jurisdiction over either the entire state or a defined region thereof, with subject matter jurisdiction over all matters entrusted to state law. This court may sit in rotating panels of three judges, as Michigan's does, or its entire membership may sit in all cases (*en banc*).

The state supreme court has authority to review all actions of lower courts, except in Oklahoma and Texas, which have two supreme courts, one for criminal matters, the other for civil cases. Most states have a blend of mandatory and discretionary jurisdiction; they must hear the former, whereas the latter gives judges discretion to choose among the cases they are petitioned to review. At the beginning of the twenty-first century, five states effectively have no mandatory jurisdiction: Michigan, New Hampshire, Tennessee, West Virginia, and Wisconsin. Six have no discretion and therefore must accept all

Table 7.3. *Voting on Confessions by Docket Control,*
1970–1991

Ruling on Confession	Jurisdiction over Criminal Appeals		
	Mandatory	Mixed	Discretionary
Allow	18 (100%)	117 (79.05%)	391 (78.99%)
Disallow	0 (0%)	31 (20.95%)	104 (21.01%)
Total	18 (100%)	148 (100%)	495 (100%)

Notes: $N = 661$; chi-squared $= 4.7494$, not significant.
Source: Sara C. Benesh and Wendy L. Martinek, "State Supreme
Court Decision Making in Confession Cases," 23 *Justice System Jour-*
nal 109 (2002).

appeals: Mississippi, Nevada, North Dakota, Utah, Vermont, and Wyoming.
Oklahoma accepts criminal appeals only.[24]

This institutional difference (control over docket) has ramifications for the
ability of the state courts of last resort to make policy. Table 7.3 shows that level
of docket control has some influence on judicial decision making, again using
allowance of a confession into evidence as the decisional variable. Supreme
courts with mixed and discretionary jurisdiction do not differ, whereas the
six mandatory jurisdictions, along with Oklahoma, admitted all eighteen of
the confessions they considered. This suggests that the more control a state
supreme court has over the cases they hear, the more carefully may they focus
on meritorious claims.

Like all appellate courts – state and federal – these are multimember courts
with five, seven, or nine judges (Louisiana uses eight). In most states, as in
Michigan, they sit *en banc*, although a number use a panel arrangement. And
Massachusetts also has a single-judge system for some cases.[25]

Standing to Sue

The other requirement that a party seeking access to the courts must meet is being a proper party. Courts do not resolve disputes simply on request. Whether a
plaintiff is a proper party depends on a number of constitutional and prudential
considerations. State courts do not insist that plaintiffs meet the requirements
of standing to sue with anything like the rigor of the federal courts. This dispar-
ity results because the federal courts may only exercise the limited jurisdiction
the Constitution specifies; states, by contrast, are free to resolve almost any
matter they desire. We address each of standing's elements separately, noting
deviations in state practice.

[24] Court Statistics Project, *State Court Caseload Statistics, 2002* (Williamsburg, VA: National
Center for State Courts, 2003), pp. 8–59.
[25] *Id.* at 29.

Case or Controversy. Article III of the Constitution limits the federal court to deciding "cases" or "controversies." No practical distinction between them exists. Compatibly with legal terms generally, their definition lacks precision: a legal dispute between two or more persons whose interest conflicts. The key word here, interestingly, is *between*. Litigation is a zero-sum game in which one party necessarily wins, and the other loses. Winners need not get everything they want, however, nor losers totally lose. And though a judicial decision may theoretically divide the spoils equally between the parties, as when the contest involves title to two identical cars or the liquidated assets of an estate, the dispute must be bifurcated between plaintiff and defendant. By contrast, the other elements in the definition have no empirically fixed meaning: what is *legal*, along with the *interest* and the kind of *conflict* involved.

The federal definition thus excludes hypothetical questions, advisory opinions, and "friendly" or feigned disputes. Some state judiciaries tolerate hypothetical questions and advisory opinions, but not cases in which both parties have the same objective.

Hypothetical questions typically result where a bona fide dispute becomes "moot" because of an out-of-court settlement, or when a retroactive change in the law eliminates the basis for a complaint, for example, a change in the statute of limitations that requires criminal prosecution within six months, rather than a year, of its alleged commission. However, short-lived disputes that end through no fault of the petitioner that are "capable of repetition, yet evading review,"[26] do not become hypothetical. If that were the case, a person denied the right to vote or a woman seeking an abortion would have no redress because the election ended or the baby was born before a court could address the matter.[27]

Advisory opinions result when someone, typically a governmental official, requests a court's opinion, usually the state supreme court, to assess the constitutionality of recently enacted legislation or proposed administrative regulations. Such requests lack a live dispute, but in their absence a bona fide dispute occurs as soon as the law or regulation is enforced. This being so, states commonly authorize the governor or attorney general to request them.

Collusive disputes most often occur in the guise of stockholder's suits, in which the investor enjoins the corporation from complying with a tax or other economically harmful regulation. Both parties obviously desire the same objective: voiding the law or regulation. Unlike hypothetical questions and advisory opinions, collusion is not always apparent. Decisions voiding the federal income tax and the application of the contract clause to state legislatures were

---

[26] *Southern Pacific Terminal Co. v. Interstate Commerce Commission*, 219 U.S. 498 (1911), at 515.

[27] Even federal courts can avoid mootness when they so desire. Consider the case in which one Michael Hardwick challenged Georgia's sodomy statute even though the state refused to prosecute him. The plaintiff then changed his tune and fallaciously alleged that he was in imminent danger of arrest. The Court bought the assertion and decided the case, ruling against Hardwick's allegation that the statute was unconstitutional. *Bowers v. Hardwick*, 478 U.S. 186 (1986). Cf. *Lawrence v. Texas*, 539 U.S. 558 (2003).

reputedly instituted as friendly suits.[28] Hence, both state and federal courts refuse them.

Legal Injury. A mere conflict of interest does not guarantee access to a court. The conflict must pertain to a statutorily or constitutionally protected right, or some personal or property interest that the law recognizes. Business competition ordinarily impacts no legal right. Traditionally, only injuries reducible to a dollar value could be litigated. But today, especially in the states, aesthetic, conservational, recreational, cultural, and religious injuries may be legally redressable. Note that the gravity of an injury does not determine a legal injury. Under the common law, a footstep on another's property, unwanted touching, or a threatening gesture constituted trespass, battery, and assault, respectively, even though no discernible damage resulted. The states define legal injury much more broadly than the federal government because the scope of their subject matter jurisdiction is so much broader than that which the Constitution provides the federal courts.

Personal Injury. Persons seeking to access the courts must establish that they have suffered or are threatened with personal injury. Individuals may not sue on behalf of others except when the litigant is incompetent or is a minor. However, an injured individual may associate others in the lawsuit along with himself. These so-called class actions save courts huge amounts of time and effort when a group of persons have all sustained the same injury. Much consumer protective and environmental litigation occurs as class actions, as does litigation involving such disasters as plane crashes and other events that kill or injure numerous persons. Of course, many argue that these mass torts are litigated by hungry attorneys seeking to prey on mistakes of doctors and businesses. But many others argue that without the class action predatory doctors and businesses would avoid responsibility for the negligent and deliberate injuries their actions cause because courts would be burdened with rehearing the same case – with only a plaintiff name change – as many as tens or hundreds of thousands of times.

The most graphic difference between the state and federal courts manifests itself in taxpayer's suits: cases in which an individual federal taxpayer sues to prevent the collection of a federal tax. Federal courts prohibit them on the ground that a person subject to a federal tax suffers no more than all other taxpayers.[29] Obviously, if one refuses to pay a tax and the government initiates an action for nonpayment, the individual may enter a defense that the tax is

---

[28] C. Peter Magrath, *Yazoo: The Case of Fletcher v. Peck* (New York: Norton, 1966); James B. Stoneking, *Collusive Suits*, in Kermit L. Hall (ed.), *The Oxford Companion to the Supreme Court* (New York: Oxford University Press, 1992).

[29] The Supreme Court allows taxpayers' suits when the challenge asserts that the tax exceeds some specific limitation on Congress's power to tax or spend money, usually on the basis of the First Amendment. For further detail, see Nancy C. Staudt, "Taxpayers in Court: A Systematic Study of a (Misunderstood) Standing Doctrine," 52 *Emory Law Journal* 771 (2003).

unconstitutional or otherwise illegal. The limitation on taxpayer's suits does not extend to state or local taxpayers who allege that the tax in question runs afoul of some federal constitutional provision, such as the interstate commerce or supremacy clauses, or the Twenty-First Amendment. States, however, are quite receptive to such lawsuits.

Pertinent to personal injury are implied or private causes of action. Not infrequently, legislation does not clearly indicate who is entitled to initiate litigation under a particular law. Thus, for example, does the Parental Kidnapping Prevention Act allow parents to challenge in federal court the validity of state child custody orders? Or does the 1978 Civil Service Reform Act authorize federal employees to sue their union for breach of the duty of fair representation? Federal courts, under the direction of the Supreme Court, insist that federal laws clearly specify who may sue to vindicate the provided rights. States, again, approach the matter much less technically, allowing common sense to operate freely.

Political Questions. The only meaningful definition of a political question is that it is whatever a court says it is. The purpose of labeling a controversy a political question is to enable the court to avoid deciding the matter because it views the dispute as inappropriate for judicial resolution. History records relatively few such matters. Among them: the ratification of a constitutional amendment, the legitimacy of two competing state governments, the adequacy of national guard training, and the elements of an impeachment trial. The U.S. Supreme Court considered legislative districting and apportionment such until the early 1960s.

State courts are even less inclined to consider controversies to be political questions. Allegations that a matter is such typically concern ballot proposals, the expenditure of duly authorized public funds, conflicts between a state legislature and the governor or between a county or other subdivision of the state and the state itself, and the use of initiative and referendum petitions to undo otherwise legitimate governmental action.[30]

Finality of Decision. To prevent the embarrassment of having a decision overruled by one of the other branches of government, and thereby undermine their authority, courts avoid controversies that may leave them open to such action. In giving courts their jurisdiction, legislatures do not necessarily grant them all that is available. They typically retain some for other decision makers, most especially various administrative or executive branch agencies, for example, vesting the termination of temporary non–civil service employees in an agency personnel department, leaving the apportionment of an agency's tasks to the discretion of the agency head, and giving the governor discretion to spend or withhold duly authorized and appropriated funds.

---

[30] See, for example, *AFL-CIO v. Eu*, 36 Cal. 3d 687 (1984), and *California Legislature v. Deukmejian*, 34 Cal. 3d 658 (1983).

A classic example, which, though applicable to the federal courts could also apply to the state courts, well illustrates this element of standing. Congressional Republicans inserted a provision into a domestic security bill that President Bush signed into law on November 25, 2002, protecting Eli Lilly, the manufacturer of a drug, thimerosal, from suit in the federal courts by requiring that all suits alleging that the drug caused autism and other neurological disorders in children be heard by a special master appointed for that purpose. Families are thereby forced to seek compensation for their children's injuries from this source rather than the regular federal courts.[31] State legislatures, needless to say, have similar capacity to remove personal injury lawsuits – a major staple of state court jurisdiction – from their courts to administrative bodies of one sort or another.

A court's ability to render the final and binding decision is not overcome because a higher court may overturn it. Nor does a change in a law by a later legislature or the passage of a constitutional amendment that conflicts with an earlier court's interpretation falsify this element of standing. It only requires that at the time of decision the court's ruling bind the parties and not be susceptible to alteration by legislative or administrative action.

Estoppel. Courts, both state and federal, rather rigorously limit litigants to one bite of the apple, in the sense that once they have had their day in court they may not relitigate the same matter a second time. Although estoppel has many aspects, its two main components are res judicata and collateral estoppel.

Res judicata prevents a party from relitigating the same cause of action against the same party or parties if it has been resolved on the merits by a final judgment. Thus, if a personal injury case ended because the jury was improperly empaneled, that would be a final judgment, but the decision would not have addressed the controversy's merits. Hence, the injured party could refile the lawsuit.

Although the common law historically defined a cause of action narrowly, courts today require the merger and joinder of claims. This prevents a plaintiff from suing joint wrongdoers separately or for only some of the injuries the wrongdoers inflicted on the victim.

Collateral estoppel, or claim preclusion, applies to subsequent litigation in which an earlier lawsuit actually decided the identical issue and this issue had to be decided to resolve the earlier case. A party, therefore, may be collaterally stopped from revisiting an issue if the original proceeding fully and fairly resolved it. The modifier *fairly* refers to relitigation that was or should have been reasonably foreseeable at the time of the original lawsuit. Thus, the second of two passengers injured in an automobile accident may not relitigate the driver's negligence if the driver was exonerated in the action brought by the first passenger. The doctrine also applies to defendants. If the first passenger had won,

---

[31] Sheryl Gay Stolberg, "Justice Dept. Seeks to Seal Vaccine Papers," *New York Times*, 27 November 2002, p. A15.

the driver could not argue that he was not negligent in a proceeding brought by the second passenger.

Estoppel's preclusion of multiple lawsuits serves several purposes: It increases the efficiency of judicial time and energy. It enables litigants to rely on a court's final judgment and thereby plan for the future. And it prevents the judicial system from being used to harass defendants.

Exhaustion of Administrative Remedies. Also enabling courts to save time and proceed more efficiently is the requirement that litigants exhaust any and all administrative remedies that the law provides before taking their case to court. This element bears similarity to comity and the abstention doctrine, except that exhaustion applies whether or not administrative proceedings have commenced. Abstention, by contrast, precludes the commencement of federal proceedings once state court action has begun. Exceptions to the exhaustion requirement are agency remedies unable to resolve the dispute, action of agencies beyond the scope of their authority, the onset of irreparable injury, or unconscionably dilatory agency action.

Summary

Standing has several utilities. It enables courts to determine whether litigants are proper parties who are filing lawsuits appropriately. Thus, hypothetical and redundant decisions may be circumvented, and unnecessary conflicts with other decision makers prevented. Standing also enables judges to duck issues they prefer to avoid and to cite good legal form in doing so.

As do other legal considerations, the elements of standing also effectively serve substantive judicial concerns of either a liberal or a conservative variety. If the nonjudicial decision maker serving as the judges' surrogate renders a conservative decision, and if the judges themselves are conservative on the issue, closing access advances the judges' policy preferences. Conversely, if the surrogate's decision is liberal, conservative jurists may open access so that the liberal decision may be altered.

CASELOAD

The caseload of the state courts is staggering in its girth; most judicial decision making occurs in state courts. Indeed, in 2001, nearly 93 million cases were filed![32] And although traffic matters constituted the majority (nearly 58 million), the courts also experienced an increase in nontraffic filings (see Table 7.4). As in the federal courts, civil cases outnumber criminal cases, but the states are unique in their attention to traffic, juvenile, and domestic cases.

---

[32] Brian J. Ostrom, Neal B. Kauder, and Robert C. LaFountain, eds., *Examining the Work of State Courts, 2002* (Williamsburg, VA: National Center for State Courts, 2003), pp. 10, 13.

Table 7.4. *Caseload of State Courts, 2001 (in millions)*

Case Type	Total	Jurisdiction		Change from 2000
		General	Limited	
Traffic	55.7	14.1	41.6	−0.1%
Civil	15.8	7.4	8.4	+5.6%
Criminal	14.0	4.8	9.2	−0.1%
Domestic	5.3	3.8	1.5	+2.2%
Juvenile	2.0	1.3	0.7	−0.4%
Total	92.8	31.4	61.4	+0.9%

Source: Brian J. Ostrom, Neal B. Kauder, and Robert C. LaFountain, eds., *Examining the Work of State Courts, 2002* (Williamsburg, VA: National Center for State Courts, 2003), pp. 10, 13.

Table 7.5. *Voting on Confessions by Ideology*

Ruling on Confession	Ideology (Mean of Majority)	
	Conservative	Liberal
Allow	474 (80.48%)	52 (72.22%)
Disallow	115 (19.52%)	20 (27.78%)
Total	589 (100%)	72 (100%)

Notes: $N = 661$; chi-squared $= 2.6889$, not significant. *Source:* Sara C. Benesh and Wendy L. Martinek, "State Supreme Court Decision Making in Confession Cases," 23 *Justice System Journal* 109 (2002).

STATE COURT DECISION MAKING

Most research on state court decision making has concluded that state courts are subject to myriad influences on their decision making and that institutional factors affect the policies they make. Scholars have found that judges' ideology matters; that selection system may matter; that docket control matters; that facts of the case matter; that precedent matters; that the policy preferences of those responsible for selecting judges matters; and that state constitutional provisions matter. However, many conclusions depend on the issue area analyzed.

So far, we have shown that selection system does not influence the decision whether to exclude a confession and that level of docket control does have some limited effect. But what about ideology? Table 7.5 shows its impact to be statistically insignificant in our set of confession cases, as liberal courts disallowed 8 percent more confessions than conservative ones. Nor does the ideology of other political actors influence confession decisions. According to one study, what seems to drive this decision making are the state courts' ideology (marginally, as noted), relevant U.S. Supreme Court's precedents, and the characteristics of the individual case.[33]

Federal–State Court Relations

As noted, the Constitution's Framers feared a strong, centralized government. Believing for various reasons that that government was best that governed least, they wrote a document that severely limited the power the federal government could exercise and further prescribed the procedures that the federal government had to follow to exercise those limited powers.

But the Framers' fear of government did not extend to that which governed only a particular locality. Except for a handful of prohibitions, the subnational units of government – states and their subdivisions – were free to do their thing. One of these "things," of course, was the creation of a judicial system independent of that of the federal government. And so, as a result of federalism – the geographic division of power between the central government and its constituent units – we have two autonomous court systems.

Jurisdictionally – and here we mean the subject matter of the cases that a court hears and decides, such as criminal cases, personal injury litigation, landlord–tenant disputes – the federal courts have authority to decide so-called federal questions: cases whose resolution depends on a provision of the Constitution, an act of Congress, or a treaty of the United States. Because of concern that state courts might bias their decisions in favor of local residents in conflicts with out-of-staters, the Constitution's Framers also authorized federal courts to resolve such disputes – labeled *diversity* cases – even though they contain no federal question.[34]

As a result, other disputes were the province of the states. Thus, state jurisdiction covered the remainder of the legal waterfront. But the two systems nonetheless overlapped. Many controversies containing a federal question also raised questions of purely state law. Thus, a routine criminal case might also produce a federal question because the state court denied the accused the right to a trial by jury or representation by an attorney or forced her to incriminate herself. As a result, many controversies produce concurrent jurisdiction. But concurrent jurisdiction could only exist if the state's action injected a federal question into its proceedings. Absent a federal question (or a matter of diversity), no concurrent jurisdiction exists.[35]

The upshot is that much federal jurisdiction is concurrent, with the exception of such purely federal matters as maritime and admiralty cases, whereas the vast majority of state litigation is exclusive to the state courts.

---

[33] Benesh and Martinek, "Confession Cases." p. 109.

[34] The Constitution also authorizes federal courts to decide other types of cases. These, however, are few in number and rarely concern anyone other than the parties.

[35] Again, minor exceptions exist.

Unfortunately, the distinction between state and federal court jurisdictions is less clear in operation than we have outlined. The Supreme Court uses four constitutional provisions – national supremacy, habeas corpus, sovereign immunity, and full faith and credit – plus three policies of its own design – comity, adequate and independent state grounds, and choice of law – to apportion jurisdictional responsibility between it and the state courts.

National Supremacy. Concurrent jurisdiction obviously occasions conflict. The Framers recognized this and made provision for its resolution by including a supremacy clause in the Constitution, the language of which reads as follows:

This Constitution, and the Laws of the United States which shall be made in Pursuance thereof; and all Treaties made, or which shall be made, under the Authority of the United States, shall be the supreme Law of the Land; and the Judges in every State shall be bound thereby, any Thing in the Constitution or Laws of any State to the Contrary notwithstanding.

The conflicts that this language is meant to resolve are those between the highest state court with authority to resolve the conflict and the U.S. Supreme Court. And though the language of the supremacy clause is clear, it does not specify which court, if any, is to resolve such conflicts. The First Congress eliminated this omission in Section 25 of the Judiciary Act of 1789, which authorized the U.S. Supreme Court to review and decide any state court decision that contained a federal question.

In allowing the Supreme Court to resolve federal questions authoritatively, Congress required losing litigants to exhaust all remedies under the law of the relevant state before seeking access to the Supreme Court; typically this meant either a final decision by the state supreme court or the refusal of that court to review the decision of the state court that last heard the matter.

State court judges did not take kindly to U.S. Supreme Court review of their decisions on federal questions, however. They did have a point, arguing that they took an oath to uphold and support the Constitution just as federal judges did. This, of course, included the supremacy clause. But, they continued, although we are bound by the language of the supremacy clause, we are not bound by the Supreme Court's interpretation of it. To be so bound would infringe on state sovereignty and the independence of state courts.

In what may well be the most important decision ever handed down by the Supreme Court, the justices, in the case of *Martin v. Hunter's Lessee*,[36] unequivocally rejected the argument of the Virginia supreme court:

Judges of equal learning and integrity, in different states, might differently interpret a statute, or a treaty of the United States, or even the constitution itself. If there were no revising authority to control these jarring and discordant judgments, and harmonize them into uniformity, the laws, the treaties, the constitution of the United States would be different in different states, and might, perhaps, never have . . . the same construction,

[36] 1 Wheaton 304 (1816).

obligation, or efficacy, in any two states. The public mischiefs that would attend such a state of things would be truly deplorable . . . the appellate jurisdiction must continue to be the only adequate remedy for such evils.

The justices' language is logically and empirically unimpeachable. Without the national uniformity that a Supreme Court decision produces, constitutional provisions, laws, and treaties would undoubtedly mean something different in each of the states, dependent on the vagaries of state court interpretations. A more glaring misnomer than *"United" States* would be hard to imagine. Each state would effectively become a sovereign nation unto itself, à la those of Latin America and the developing nations of Africa and Asia. Religious freedom, sex discrimination, freedom of speech, trial by jury, and the provisions of the Internal Revenue Code would all mean something different from one state to another as the individual state courts decreed.

Also note that this bit of glue that makes the United States a single nation rather than a collection of petty principalities is provided by Congress. And what Congress bestows, Congress may also withhold. Indeed, until well after the Civil War, legislation was regularly introduced into Congress to deny the Supreme Court jurisdiction to review state court decisions containing a federal question. None, however, succeeded.

Habeas Corpus. Habeas corpus, the "great writ," provides incarcerated individuals the right to challenge the legality of their confinement. So inherent is the writ to our liberties that the Framers of the Constitution did not provide for its provision; they only provided for the exceptional circumstances under which it could be suspended.

Because most provisions of the Bill of Rights, through the process of selective incorporation (see Chapter 3), have been made binding on the states, state criminal justice procedures are now subject to federal constitutional strictures. A state inmate whose federal constitutional rights have been violated and who has exhausted statewide remedies, usually through an adverse ruling by the state supreme court, may go to federal district court to seek appropriate remedies. Overwhelmingly, this is the main point of habeas corpus contact between the federal courts and the state courts, and it helps keep state courts in line with federal constitutional mandates, at least in the area of criminal justice.

In a decision of substantial impact to the American criminal justice system, however, the Supreme Court ruled in *Stone v. Powell* (1976)[37] that state prisoners who had been afforded the opportunity to raise Fourth Amendment considerations at their state trials and appeals could not also invoke the claim on federal habeas corpus review. Thus, short of the exceptionally rare willingness of the justices to review such a case, the final determination as to whether federal Fourth Amendment guarantees were met in state trials would be made by state courts.

[37] 428 U.S. 465.

One implication of *Stone* was that state judges would have much greater discretion in their implementation of the Supreme Court's Fourth Amendment doctrine. Before *Stone*, an errant state court decision could automatically be reviewed in federal district court. With mandatory review, such decisions could readily be overturned, limiting the incentives of state judges to skirt federal constitutional commands. Since *Stone*, the only safeguard is the Supreme Court's infrequently granted writ of certiorari.

Mincey v. Arizona (1978),[38] "a run-of-the-mill search and seizure case that raised no new, unusual, or even interesting constitutional questions,"[39] nicely illustrates the consequences of the *Stone* decision. Justice Marshall's concurrence describes the situation. In 1971, the Arizona Supreme Court created a "murder-scene" exception to the Fourth Amendment. On habeas review the Ninth Circuit found no constitutional basis for the exception and reversed. Subsequent to the Ninth Circuit decision, but prior to *Stone*, the Arizona Supreme Court appeared to follow the circuit's command. But after *Stone*, when reversal could only be obtained through an unlikely writ of certiorari, the Arizona court returned to its original stance, merely noting a conflict between its view of federal law and the Ninth Circuit's, which no longer had the ability to review the decision. According to Marshall:

Prior to Stone v. Powell, there would have been no need to grant certiorari in a case such as this, since the federal habeas remedy would have been available to the defendant. Indeed, prior to Stone petitioner here probably would not even have had to utilize federal habeas, since the Arizona courts were at that earlier time more inclined to follow the federal constitutional pronouncements of the Ninth Circuit. . . .

At the time of Stone my Brother BRENNAN wrote that "institutional constraints totally preclude any possibility that this Court can adequately oversee whether state courts have properly applied federal law." Because of these constraints, we will often be faced with a Hobson's choice in cases of less than national significance that could formerly have been left to the lower federal courts: either to deny certiorari and thereby let stand divergent state and federal decisions with regard to Fourth Amendment rights; or to grant certiorari and thereby add to our calendar, which many believe is already overcrowded, cases that might better have been resolved elsewhere. (internal citations omitted)[40]

These cases illustrate the ties that habeas corpus can provide between the federal and state systems. When the Ninth Circuit held the Arizona Supreme Court in check, it abided by the circuit's ruling on the "murder-scene" exception. Then when *Stone* eliminated habeas review, making the probability of federal review remote, the court reversed itself and reverted to its original position on the issue. But the state court lost after all, as its homemade exception in *Mincey* was too egregious for even the conservative Burger Court to accept.

---

[38] 437 U.S. 385.
[39] Craig R. Ducat, *Constitutional Interpretation*, 6th ed. (St. Paul, MN: West, 1996), p. 733.
[40] 437 U.S. at 307–308.

Sovereign Immunity. What does sovereign immunity have to do with federal–state relations? Actually, it should have little, if any, relevance to it. The doctrine originated as an aspect of the notion of the divine right of kings, a political and religious view of the later Middle Ages that asserted that rulers could do no wrong; hence, lawsuits seeking to hold them accountable for their actions – for injuries inflicted on others – could not be entertained. In England, the common law slightly altered the rationale, postulating that no writ could run against the king or queen because no court had power to enforce any judgment against him or her.

Whatever the rationale, sovereign immunity arguably has no place in a governmental system such as ours in which all persons from the president on down are considered subject to the law. But not uncommonly, when basic principles such as the rule of law bump up against other, less principled considerations, the basic principle becomes inoperative. Such is the situation when sovereign immunity in the United States is concerned.

We begin by noting that the Constitution, not surprisingly, says nothing about sovereign immunity.[41] Statutes, both state and federal, do, however, immunize specified governmental officials from the consequences of their official actions. Hence, one cannot sue a governor or a legislator for actions taken in the course of official duties, such as the declaration of a locality as a disaster area or statements made in the course of debate over proposed legislation. Such statutes and policies, however, do not rise to the level of sovereign immunity because they may be altered or expunged at will by legislative or executive action.

As a result of a Supreme Court decision in 1793[42] that allowed nonresidents to sue a state in federal court, Congress proposed and the states quickly ratified the Eleventh Amendment, which denies federal court jurisdiction to suits commenced by residents of one state or aliens seeking to sue another state. No language in the amendment prohibits a state's own residents from bringing suit against it, however.

But if a nonresident sues a state in that state's courts, and those courts hear the matter, the state implicitly assents to Supreme Court review of any federal issues raised in the litigation. And if a state intruded itself into a matter of federal concern, such as interstate commerce or the deprivation of persons' federally protected civil rights, they of course subjected themselves to federal liability, including money damages.

Enter the Rehnquist Court. Beginning in 1996, it rendered a series of decisions that declared several federal laws unconstitutional and others that

---

[41] One finds the closest constitutional language in Article I, Section 6, which, in reference to senators and representatives, says, "They shall in all Cases, except Treason, Felony, and Breach of the Peace, be privileged from arrest during their Attendance at the Session of their respective Houses, and in going to and returning from the same; and for any Speech or Debate in either House, they shall not be questioned in any other Place."

[42] *Chisholm v. Georgia*, 2 Dallas 419 (1792).

overruled precedents of various vintage. The upshot: If a state wrongs some-one, whether or not said person is a resident, no remedy may right that wrong, according to Chief Justice Rehnquist and Justices O'Connor, Scalia, Kennedy, and Thomas, unless the state willingly submits to suit. Not only may the erring state not be sued in federal court, it may not even be sued in its own courts. And the fact that the matter complained of is one that the Constitution vests exclusively in the federal government makes no difference. Suppose, for exam-ple, that a state college or university finds itself in poor financial condition and in order to lessen budget woes decides to sell patented Microsoft Windows® and other software not only to its students, but also to anyone off the street. Unless the five change their tune, the state university wins. Indeed, the five have gone further still. In declaring unconstitutional portions of the Americans with Disabilities Act that allowed state and local government employees to sue their employer for noncompliance with the act's provisions, they constricted federal authority by requiring Congress to prove convincingly that states themselves deliberately engaged in unconstitutional discrimination. Rehnquist dismissively derided congressional findings based on a dozen hearings and thirty-nine pages of official state acts discriminating against the disabled as "unexamined, anec-dotal accounts."[43]

According to the Rehnquist five, sovereign immunity reigns supreme over the principle of federalism, notwithstanding that federalism is embodied in the very structure of the Constitution and sovereign immunity is not. Apparently the ghost of John C. Calhoun, the high priest of nineteenth-century states' rights, haunts the chambers of Rehnquist and company, though only one of the five, Justice Thomas, is himself a Southern native.

The Full Faith and Credit Clause. The remaining constitutional provision gov-erning federal–state judicial relations is the full faith and credit clause, a pro-vision whose twenty-two words rarely generate public awareness: "Full Faith and Credit shall be given in each State to the public Acts, Records, and judicial Proceedings of every other State." The clause does not apply to state criminal proceedings, but only to final state court judgments in civil cases. These have the same force and effect in other states that they have in the courts of the rendering state, provided of course that the decision does not contravene the Constitution or controlling federal law.

Most full faith and credit cases concern commercial transactions. With very rare exceptions, these are automatically enforced. Not so those dealing with child custody, support, and spousal alimony because they lack a final judgment. Courts retain jurisdiction of such matters because of shifting circumstances and conditions that affect the interests of the benefited party, such as a minor child. Lacking a final judgment from the court in the rendering state, courts in other states are free to intrude themselves, with the result that the original decision

---

[43] *Board of Trustees v. Garrett*, 531 U.S. 356 (2001), at 370.

is modified, as occurs when the second state alters custody arrangements for minor children or substantially reduces initially ordered support payments.

The Supreme Court, of course, could remedy this situation by altering its precedents and subjecting all states to the decision of the initial court. Because they have failed to do so, deadbeat parents can evade responsibility by the simple expedient of taking up residence on the other side of the state line.

Lurking on the horizon is the matter of same-sex marriages. Vermont has legitimated them as "civil unions," and the Massachusetts Supreme Court has declared unconstitutional the state's law restricting marriage to persons of the opposite sex. The issue has thus become whether other states need to recognize such action. In response, Congress passed the Defense of Marriage Act, which grants states the right to refuse to recognize gay marriages. Although the Rehnquist Court might normally use the Tenth Amendment, to say nothing of the full faith and credit clause itself, to challenge the authority of Congress to pass such regulations, probably the staunchly conservative Court will carve out a public policy exception to full faith and credit that will uphold the statute.

Twentieth-century opposition to interracial marriage, which the Court declared unconstitutional as violating *both* equal protection and due process,[44] provoked much more vehement hostility than today's opposition to gay marriage, but for basically the same reasons: the use of biblical passages to justify racism and bigotry. None of the three dozen states that expressly forbid gay marriage makes it a criminal offense, unlike interracial marriage.[45]

The System of Comity. On its face, the Supreme Court's decision in *Martin v. Hunter's Lessee* appears to make state court decisions on federal questions superfluous because the ultimate decision in such cases rests with the U.S. Supreme Court. For two reasons, however, the facial appearance belies reality. First, the Supreme Court accepts and decides only a very small percentage of the cases it is asked to review – between 1 and 1.5 percent. Those the Court refuses to decide, as well as those that it affirms, become the law in the state making the decision. Second, mindful of the tender sensibilities of the states and their judges (which are much less tender than they were, say, during the 1950s and 1960s, when the South mounted massive resistance to desegregation and the outlawing of white supremacy in public places and facilities), the Court has further lessened the impact of *Martin v. Hunter's Lessee* by creating a system of comity – that is, deference to state court decisions – the effect of which minimizes conflict between the two judicial systems.

The means for minimizing federal–state conflict is the abstention doctrine, "whereby the federal courts 'exercising a wise discretion,' restrain their authority because of 'scrupulous regard for the rightful independence of the

---

[44] *Loving v. Virginia*, 388 U.S. 1 (1967).

[45] Adam Liptak, "Bans on Interracial Unions Offer Perspective on Gay Ones," *New York Times*, 17 March 2004, p. A16.

state governments' and for the smooth working of the federal judiciary."[46] As applied, the abstention doctrine requires federal courts to avoid intruding themselves into ongoing state lawsuits or otherwise duplicating litigation already begun in a state court. As with virtually every legal rule, doctrine, or principle, however, exceptions exist. In the case of the abstention doctrine, they have been narrowly drawn. A "great and immediate" showing of "irreparable injury" allows a federal court to enjoin state proceedings, a situation that obtains only when a person is prosecuted in bad faith, is subjected to official harassment, or is denied redress as a result of deliberately dilatory state procedures. If, in lieu of an injunction, litigants seek to have their cases removed to a federal court, equivalently stringent criteria apply.

Abstention requires litigants, once state court proceedings have commenced, to exhaust their administrative and judicial remedies before seeking access to the federal courts, excepting only in the situations mentioned. If a state court resolves any federal questions a case contains compatibly with federal law, the basis for Supreme Court review disappears.

Note that the federal question or questions that a state case holds is entwined with matters of state law. If the Supreme Court agrees to hear and decide the case, it may resolve only the federal question(s) in the case. The other issues are left to the state courts for decision. However, the law that the Supreme Court confronts in the cases it chooses to decide is indeterminate. And it matters not whether the case concerns the Constitution, federal statutes, the common law, or administrative actions of one sort or another. The language of law may occasionally be clear and definite, as in the case of a posted speed limit or the fee that one must pay to obtain a license permitting the holder to do what is otherwise forbidden, for instance, drive a car, practice law, or sell alcoholic beverages. But whatever law the Supreme Court confronts must be construed, interpreted, and applied to the facts of the case before it. Hence, whether an aspect of a case is, or is not, a federal question falls within the justices' discretion.

But we also live in a federal system in which governmental power is divided between Washington and the individual states. And the system of comity, which the Court established on its own authority, decrees a degree of deference toward the states and their courts. How much deference and the occasions of its application are, of course, again a matter for the justices to decide. Nonetheless, if the Supreme Court overturns a state court's decision it typically returns the case to the state court for further proceedings. The Court does so because, notwithstanding resolution of the federal issue, the justices may – compatibly with the system of comity (and their own policy preferences) – allow the state court and state law to control the outcome of the case.

To illustrate by way of an extreme example:

On March 10, 1953, Aubrey Williams, an African-American, was tried for the murder of a white man in the State of Georgia. The defense neither called witnesses in his behalf

---

[46] *Railroad Commission of Texas v. Pullman Co.*, 312 U.S. 496 (1941), at 501.

nor provided sworn testimony.[47] An all-white jury convicted Williams, who was then sentenced to death.

Subsequent to the Williams trial, the Supreme Court ruled in another case, *Avery v. Georgia*,[48] that Georgia's method of selecting jurors, whereby the names of whites were placed on white tickets and the names of blacks were placed on yellow tickets, violated the equal-protection clause of the Fourteenth Amendment. Though the same process had been used in Williams's trial, his court-appointed attorney failed at first to make a timely motion for appeal on those grounds. The Supreme Court of Georgia affirmed the conviction.[49] The following year, the state supreme court rejected Williams's extraordinary motion for a new trial.[50] The U.S. Supreme Court granted certiorari. In oral arguments, the state conceded that Williams's conviction failed to meet constitutional standards but nevertheless argued that because his attorney had failed to object properly to the procedure – a commonplace requirement in all courts that a party must object to anything adversely done at the time the event occurs – he had forfeited his right to a retrial.

The Supreme Court rejected Georgia's arguments, claiming that because the Georgia court had the discretion, under state law, to order a new trial, it could not refuse to do so when a federal constitutional right had been violated:

We conclude that the trial court and the State Supreme Court declined to grant Williams' motion though possessed of power to do so under state law. Since his motion was based upon a constitutional objection, and one the validity of which has in principle been sustained here, the discretionary decision to deny the motion does not deprive this Court of jurisdiction to find that the substantive issue [i.e., the unconstitutionality of the racial method of jury selection] is properly before us.[51]

However, Justice Frankfurter, who wrote the majority opinion, declined to take the bull by the horns and simply reverse the Georgia court's decision. Instead, he said, "The fact that we have jurisdiction does not compel us to exercise it."[52] And rather than reverse, he merely remanded it (the weakest action short of affirming the Georgia court), in the name of "orderly judicial procedure."[53] Given Georgia's admission that Williams's conviction was constitutionally infirm, Frankfurter assumed that "[f]air regard for the principles which the Georgia courts have enforced in numerous cases and for the constitutional

---

[47] His only defense was a short *unsworn* statement declaring that he had not committed the crime and that he had been "afraid" when he signed the written confession introduced against him. *Williams v. Georgia*, 349 U.S. 375, 377 (1955).

[48] 345 U.S. 559 (1953).

[49] *Williams v. State*, 78 S.E. 2d 251 (1953).

[50] *Williams v. State*, 82 S.E. 2d 217 (1954).

[51] 349 U.S. at 389.

[52] *Id.*

[53] *Id.* at 391.

commands binding on all courts" would preclude Georgia from "allow[ing] this man to go to his death as the result of a conviction secured from a jury which the State admits was unconstitutionally impaneled."[54]

A naïve expectation given the massive resistance accorded the ruling one year previously that Southern schools were to desegregate with all deliberate speed. And the Georgia court did not let the opportunity to vent its spleen pass. The sidebar contains the entirety of its unanimous opinion rejecting a new trial.

Sidebar 7.1. Georgia Supreme Court Decision in *Williams v. State*

"The powers not delegated to the United States by the Constitution, nor prohibited by it to the States, are reserved to the States, respectively, or to the people." Constitution of the United States, 10th Amendment.... Even though executives and legislatures, not being constitutional lawyers, might often overstep the foregoing, unambiguous constitutional prohibition of Federal invasion of State jurisdiction, there can never be an acceptable excuse for judicial failure to strictly observe it. This court bows to the Supreme Court on all Federal questions of law but we will not supinely surrender sovereign powers of this State. In this case, the opinion of the majority of that court recognizes that this court decided the case according to the established rules of law and that no Federal jurisdiction existed which would authorize that court to render a judgment either affirming or reversing the judgment of this court, which are the only judgments that court can constitutionally recognize.

The Supreme Court undertakes to remand the case for further consideration, and in their opinion has pointed to Georgia law vesting in the trial judge discretion in ruling on an extraordinary motion for a new trial and apparently concluded therefrom that this court should reverse the trial court because that discretion was not exercised in the way the Supreme Court would have exercised it. We know and respect the universally recognized rule that the exercise of discretion never authorizes a violation or defiance of law. In this case, as pointed out to us, that law is that the question sought to be raised must be raised before trial and not otherwise.

Not in recognition of any jurisdiction of the Supreme Court to influence or in any manner to interfere with the functioning of this court on strictly State questions, but solely for the purpose of completing the record in a case that was first decided by us in 1953, and to avoid further delay, we state that our opinion in *Williams v. State* is supported by sound and unchallenged law, conforms with the State and Federal Constitutions, and stands as the judgment of all seven of the Justices of this Court.

Judgment of affirmance rendered May 10, 1954 adhered to. All the Justices concur.[55]

Williams subsequently applied for another writ of certiorari, followed by a request for rehearing, but both were unanimously denied. Williams died in Georgia's electric chair on March 30, 1956.

---

[54] *Id.*
[55] 82 S.E. 2d 217 (1954).

In defense of Frankfurter's position, he did have a case. The contemporaneous objection rule provided a convenient rationale for avoiding a direct conflict with Georgia. The Supreme Court's jurisdiction in Williams's case extended only to the federal question: the method of jury selection. A contemporaneous objection rule, so long as it serves a legitimate state purpose – and this one admittedly did – is exclusively a question of state law, over which the federal courts have no jurisdiction.[56]

Comity and the abstention doctrine also produce an effect other than deference to the states and their courts: delay in federal court resolution of federal questions. The former justice Douglas put the matter well: "We do a great disservice when we send . . . tired and exhausted litigants [in the state judicial systems] into the desert in search of this Holy Grail [vindication of federal constitutional rights] that is already in the keeping of the federal courts."[57]

Adequate and Independent State Grounds for Decision. The second of the three nonconstitutional considerations governing federal–state relationships is adequate and independent state grounds for decision. Unlike comity, it can cut in either a federal or a pro-state direction. The Court may view state judges as devious decision makers who employ their law and constitutions to concoct policies at variance with those created by them. Or it may permit the states to avoid Supreme Court scrutiny of their decisions when doing so suits the policy preferences of a majority of the justices.

Historically, the Supreme Court had supplemented the abstention doctrine with the self-formulated assumption that if a state court decision contained a federal question along with state law question(s),[58] the decision rested on adequate and independent state grounds. Absent a statement that the state court based its decision on federal law, the justices assumed that the state court decided on the basis of its own law.

But in 1983 in a run-of-the-mill search and seizure case, the Burger Court rejected the historic policy and ruled that when

a state court decision fairly appears to rest primarily on federal law, or to be interwoven with the federal law, and when the independence and adequacy of any possible state law ground is not clear from the face of the opinion, we will accept . . . that the state court decided the case the way it did because it believed that federal law required it to do so.[59]

---

[56] See Richard A. Matasar and Gregory S. Burch, "Procedural Common Law, Federal Jurisdictional Policy, and the Abandonment of the Adequate and Independent State Grounds Doctrine," 86 *Columbia Law Review* 1291 (1986), and Catherine T. Struve, "Direct and Collateral Federal Court Review of the Adequacy of State Procedural Rules," 103 *Columbia Law Review* 243 (2003). Illuminating excerpts from the justices' conference discussion will be found in Del Dickson, ed., *The Supreme Court in Conference (1940–1985)* (New York: Oxford University Press, 2001), pp. 240–243.

[57] *Harris County Commissioners Court v. Moore*, 420 U.S. 77 (1975), at 91.

[58] A good example is *Williams v. Georgia*, the death penalty case discussed previously.

[59] *Michigan v. Long*, 463 U.S. 1032, at 1040–1041.

This contradictory presumption requires the state court to demonstrate that the cited federal decisions did not compel the decision reached, but were used only for guidance. If the state court "indicates clearly and expressly" that its decision rests "on bona fide separate, adequate, and independent grounds, we, of course, will not ... review the decision."[60] The addition of the words *bona fide* and *separate* enable the justices to review almost any state court decision they wish.

The question arises: Why did the conservative Burger Court, with its pro-state proclivities, suddenly reverse course? First, the reversal, though unequivocally phrased, has taken only a half-turn. Second, this half-turn applies only to *liberal* state court decisions, particularly those bearing on civil liberties and criminal procedure. The reason for this is that the federal Constitution provides a floor, not a ceiling, for state constitutional rights. State courts can construe their own constitutions to provide more rights than are guaranteed under the federal charter, but they cannot interpret their own constitutions so as to provide fewer rights. Thus, the adequate and independent state grounds doctrine can be used only to create more rights, and limiting the doctrine, as in *Long*, serves only to limit the ability of state courts to do so.

Indeed, Justice Powell's docket sheets for the *Long* case quote Justice Rehnquist as saying in the Court's conference, "We should not invite state courts to avoid Supreme Court review by basing decisions on state grounds. We could end up with fifty state courts being final on many issues."[61]

A more candidly antistate assertion is hard to imagine, emanating as it does from the Court's preeminent mouthpiece for state sovereignty. It clearly presaged the action of the Rehnquist five in *Bush v. Gore*. But do note that Rehnquist's assertion of national supremacy does not impede the states' freedom to do as they choose, so long as their choice accords with the preferences of the conservative majority.

Choice of Law. When conflict occurs between state and federal law, the supremacy clause, as we have seen, controls. But what about situations in which no controlling federal law exists? These effectively do not concern federal questions, but rather those arising under "diversity of citizenship," that is, those between residents of different states to which we previously made reference. Congress has supplemented the constitutional provision authorizing the federal courts to resolve such controversies by stipulating that the federal courts apply the law of the state in which the federal court sits. This diversity litigation primarily concerns property, commercial transactions, contracts, and torts (injury to persons and property).

In an 1842 decision the Supreme Court defined the state law relevant to the resolution of diversity disputes to be state constitutions and statutes, not the

---

[60] *Id.* at 1041.
[61] Powell's papers are on file at the Washington and Lee University Law School library.

states' judge-made law (common law).[62] Inasmuch as legislatures enacted few statutes before the twentieth century, and state constitutions emphasized what government could not do, rather than what it could, the range of common law was broadly based. Consequently, federal courts, sitting in diversity, had the freedom to make their own law to resolve these disputes. As a further consequence, plaintiffs planning to file a lawsuit against a nonresident were free to "forum shop": to select the court whose precedents best supported the plaintiffs' claims. Thus, the initiating party could choose the relevant court in his own state; that of his opponent; the federal district court in which he resided; that of his opponent; and if the cause of action arose in still another state, the state or federal courts thereof.

In 1938, however, the Supreme Court overruled its 1842 precedent, stating that the federal common law created by this decision derogated states' rights.[63] The failure of the federal courts to adhere to *all* the law of the state in which they sat constituted an unconstitutional assumption of decisional authority. Thus ended many of the excesses of forum shopping.

Summary. Use of these seven factors that govern the relationship between the state and federal court systems not only affects their relationship with each other, but enables justices to adapt their policy making to their personal policy preferences.[64] Indeed, as discussed in Chapter 14, these jurists are as faithful to the Supreme Court's precedent as their federal counterparts. Note also that a pro- or antistate orientation toward one of these factors does not control the justices' behavior toward the others. Thus, the conservative bloc on the Rehnquist Court can use the criteria for determining the existence of adequate and independent state grounds for decision in antistate fashion to overturn liberal state court criminal decisions, and simultaneously use the notion of sovereign immunity to expand the scope of state autonomy at the expense of federal regulation.

SUMMARY AND CONCLUSIONS

We have specified the constitutional provisions that govern relationships between the state and federal courts. Under the direction of the Supreme Court, relevant decisions have expanded and contracted the scope of state court policy making from one era to another. The Court, under Chief Justice Rehnquist, has especially supported states' rights at the expense of federal legislation.

---

[62] *Swift v. Tyson*, 41 U.S. 1 (1842).

[63] *Erie Railroad v. Tompkins*, 304 U.S. 64 (1938). The facts well illustrate forum shopping. Tompkins, a Pennsylvania resident, was injured by an object protruding from a passing train as he walked along Erie's tracks. He chose to sue in a federal court in New York, where the railroad was incorporated, because Pennsylvania common law viewed persons who walk a railroad right of way as trespassers. The New York federal court adhered to the 1838 Supreme Court precedent authorizing it to exercise its own independent judgment. It did so and held the railroad liable for Tompkins's injuries.

[64] See Benesh and Martinek, *Confession Cases*, p. 109.

States markedly differ from the federal government in their methods of judicial selection: "Many more judges (almost 25,000) stand for election than do all state governors, legislators, and executive officials combined."[65] As a result of increased awareness among various interests and favorable U.S. Supreme Court decisions, the financial cost of state judicial selection is increasing prodigiously, as is the bare-knuckled tenor of the resulting competition. As the emeritus president of Harvard University and its former law school dean reported: Spending in state supreme elections doubled between 1994 and 2000 and as a result of court decisions constitutionalizing their speech making, "candidates will be hard-pressed not to commit themselves to particular positions," especially on the most salient issues.[66] Although judges sitting in judgment of their benefactors is nothing new, the openness and the resultant opportunity for public awareness with which it is done definitely is.

Our overall specification of state court jurisdiction and the criteria governing litigant access to the courts only skims the surface, particularly our presentation of state court jurisdiction, because of great variations from state to state. One may note that the slightly most popular method of *initial* selection of judges is the Missouri Plan. Costs and overt competition are markedly less here than in other methods of selection because of the absence of meaningful voter participation. But lessened cost that results from minimal public involvement says nothing about the partisan impact and special interest involvement in the selection of judges. Given the closed-door manner of selection here, theoretically almost anything can go.

[65] Bok, "Beholden Judges," p. A8.
[66] *Id.*

8

The U.S. District Courts

The legal battle over Election 2000 eventually found its way into the federal courts. Hard to believe that an issue so closely associated with state autonomy – elections – would find entry to the federal court system. The lower federal courts, however, were not particularly sympathetic to the claims being made.

On November 11, 2000, Bush and Cheney, along with some Florida voters, filed an emergency motion for a temporary restraining order to halt the recounts that were progressing in Broward, Miami-Dade, Palm Beach, and Volusia counties, alleging that said recounts would compromise accuracy (because of the discretion entailed in manual recounts) and skew the results (because the counties being recounted might be more favorable to one candidate than the other), thereby violating the First and Fourteenth Amendments to the Constitution. Judge Donald M. Middlebrooks, district court judge for the Southern District of Florida, decided that the claimants had no cause of action and that intervention by a federal court at this point would be inappropriate. Citing the Florida statutory provisions over elections and recounts (as mentioned in Chapter 7), Judge Middlebrooks argued that all procedures were followed in accordance with the law of the state of Florida: An automatic recount was triggered by the close margin of victory (less than 0.5 percent); candidates or parties were able to (and the Democratic Party of Florida did) submit written requests for hand counts within seventy-two hours of the election and, if granted, the hand count would encompass at least three precincts or 1 percent of the vote, whichever is greater; if the initial recount indicates a difference that could affect the outcome of the election, a manual recount of all precincts is triggered. However, Bush and Cheney argued that the Florida state laws, especially the statute allowing for the manual recount, violated the U.S. Constitution.

Using the text of the Constitution and Supreme Court precedent as a guide, Judge Middlebrooks concluded, after reviewing the statute in question: "This state election scheme is reasonable and non-discriminatory on its face.... Florida's manual recount provision is a 'generally-applicable and evenhanded' electoral scheme designed to 'protect the integrity and reliability of the electoral process itself' – the type of state electoral law often upheld in federal legal challenges."[1] Although Judge Middlebrooks admitted that manually counting ballots might introduce discretion,

the provision is not wholly standardless. Rather, the central purpose of the scheme, as evidenced by its plain language, is to remedy "an error in the vote tabulation which could affect the outcome of the election." In this pursuit, the provision strives to strengthen rather than dilute the right to vote by securing, as near as humanly possible, an accurate and true reflection of the will of the electorate.[2]

He concluded, then, that the manual recount procedure served an important governmental interest.

He emphasized the strong state control over elections provided for by the Constitution, citing both Eleventh Circuit and Supreme Court precedent on point. In particular, he considered the following excerpt from the Supreme Court's decision in *Roudebush v. Hartke*,[3] a case about a state manual recount in a Senate election, which compels that:

unless Congress acts, Art. I, s 4, empowers the States to regulate the conduct of senatorial elections. This Court has recognized the breadth of those powers: "It cannot be doubted that these comprehensive words embrace authority to provide a complete code for congressional elections, not only as to times and places, but in relation to notices, registration, supervision of voting, protection of voters, prevention of fraud and corrupt practices, counting of votes, duties of inspectors and canvassers, and making and publication of election returns; in short, to enact the numerous requirements as to procedure and safeguards which experience shows are necessary in order to enforce the fundamental right involved." Indiana has found, along with many other States, that one procedure necessary to guard against irregularity and error in the tabulation of votes is the availability of a recount. Despite the fact that a certification of election may be issued to the leading candidate within 30 days after the election, the results are not final if a candidate's option to compel a recount is exercised. A recount is an integral part of the Indiana electoral process and is within the ambit of the broad powers delegated to the States by Art. I, s 4.

As does the broad authority granted to states to elect senators, so also Article II, Section 1, of the Constitution gives states the authority to select electors to elect the president. Indeed, the relevant language reads, "Each State shall appoint, in such Manner as the Legislature thereof may direct, a Number of Electors." That federal courts should not interfere with this process, except in the most egregious of cases, is "basic to federalism."[4] The plaintiffs did not demonstrate bias in the counties chosen for recounts, for they could have asked for manual recounts in counties favorable to their party as well but chose not to. Nor did they demonstrate "that manual recounts are so unreliable that their use

---

[1] 120 F. Supp. 2d 1041 (2000), at 1050.
[2] *Id.* Internal citations omitted.
[3] 405 U.S. 15, at 24, 1972.
[4] *Roe v. Alabama* 43 F. 3d 574 (1995), at 585.

rises to the level of a constitutional inquiry."[5] According to Middlebrooks, the state was attempting to count the ballots more accurately, and such an attempt could not possibly be seen as a dilution of voting rights. The plaintiff's injuries were speculative and not irreparable, leading Middlebrooks to conclude that injunctive relief was not necessary. Finally, the plaintiffs had adequate state remedies should the manual recounts go awry: They could contest the resulting certification in a Florida circuit court.

In short, I simply do not find Plaintiffs' claims to have demonstrated a clear deprivation of a constitutional inquiry or a fundamental unfairness in Florida's manual recount provision. . . . I agree with the Curry Court that "a federal court should not be 'the arbiter of disputes' which arise in elections" because it is not "the federal court's role to 'oversee the administrative details of a local election . . . '" Finally, I conclude that the public interest is best served by denying preliminary injunctive relief in this instance.[6]

"A federal court has a very limited role and should not interfere except where there is an immediate need to correct a constitutional violation."[7] Yet the U.S. Supreme Court, as we discuss in Chapter 12, did just that.

This case evidences the position of the U.S. District Courts in the federal judicial hierarchy: the courts of first instance or trial courts. Given their mandatory jurisdiction (which we discuss later), they are the busiest in the federal system, hearing hundreds of thousands of cases each year (compared with fewer than one hundred heard by the U.S. Supreme Court). It is no wonder many scholars call them the "workhorses of the federal judiciary."[8]

Judges on the U.S. District Court sit alone (except in rare instances[9]) and make many different types of decisions, including pretrial decisions on motions, procedural decisions during trial, some decisions over guilt or innocence (unless a jury is empanelled), and decisions about sentencing. This scope makes them quite different from the other federal courts in the system, as both the U.S. Courts of Appeals and the U.S. Supreme Court are collegial courts. Both are also appellate courts. So these district courts are different: They are busy, and they are arranged geographically so that no district appreciably crosses state boundaries.

---

[5] Case No. 00-9009, at 19. Id. at 1052.

[6] *Id.* at 1054. Internal citation omitted.

[7] *Id.*

[8] Robert A. Carp and Ronald Stidham, *Judicial Process in America* (Washington, DC: Congressional Quarterly Press, 1998), p. 45.

[9] In certain types of cases, Congress specifies that the matter be heard by a three-judge district court composed of two district court judges and one court of appeals judge. These three-judge panels were first used in the early 1900s to deal with alleged violations of the Sherman Antitrust Act. For a time, they also heard challenges to the constitutionality of state and federal statutes. Whenever a three-judge panel hears a case, an appeal of that ruling proceeds directly to the U.S. Supreme Court. However, because of the burden this system placed on both the lower federal courts and the Supreme Court, Congress reconsidered use of this option in 1976 and limited the use of three-judge panels to cases concerning reapportionment and some civil rights claims. Today, only about twenty cases per year are decided by three-judge panels.

ORIGINS

As mentioned, the Constitution does not explicitly call for the creation of any federal court but the Supreme Court and even then is not very specific about its composition or its role. Indeed, Article III, Section 1, merely reads, "The judicial Power of the United States, shall be vested in one supreme Court, and in such inferior Courts as the Congress may from time to time ordain and establish." Further, the Constitution specifies, again in Article III, Section 1, that "the Judges, both of the supreme and inferior Courts, shall hold their Offices during good Behaviour."

In its very first act, the Judiciary Act of 1789, Congress set up a federal court system that contained a Supreme Court composed of a chief and five associates, three circuit courts composed of two Supreme Court justices and one district court judge, and thirteen district courts (one for each state) plus one each for the territory that would become Maine and Kentucky, each having one district court judge. The 1789 act established the system that remains in existence, with some revision, updating, and expansion.

GROWTH

As new states were admitted into the Union, new judicial districts were created, always continuing the practice of having districts fully contained within state boundaries. In addition, district courts were added to serve the District of Columbia and the U.S. territories of Guam, Puerto Rico, the Virgin Islands, and the Northern Mariana Islands. Over time, some states became too large to have only one district court, so Congress began splitting some states into multiple districts. California, for example, has four districts (Central, Eastern, Northern, and Southern). (See Table 8.1 for a listing of every district, its number of authorized judgeships, and the circuit in which it sits.) There are now ninety-four districts.[10]

Increases in judgeships have also occurred, ostensibly in order to allow the district courts to deal with their dockets more effectively. Currently, every district except Guam and the Northern Mariana Islands has more than one judge. Indeed, the number of judgeships has exploded over time. In 1801, there were 20 on the entire lower federal bench; today, there are 665 on the district courts alone.[11]

Increases in judgeships and numbers of districts per state do not follow a totally rational plan; wide variation exists in the number of citizens served per court across the districts and states. For example, the Tenth Circuit contains Colorado and Oklahoma. Colorado's population, as of the 2000 census, was

---

[10] One of Oklahoma's authorized judgeships is shared among the state's districts, depending on the location of the case.

[11] See Deborah J. Barrow, Gary Zuk, and Gerard S. Gryski, *The Federal Judiciary and Institutional Change* (Ann Arbor: University of Michigan Press, 1996), and Administrative Office of the U.S. Courts, http://www.uscourts.gov.

4,301,261. Oklahoma's was 3,450,654.[12] So, we would assume that Colorado has more districts than Oklahoma, right? Not so. Oklahoma has three districts and Colorado one. Oklahoma even has more judges (see Table 8.1). Why does this happen?

Congressional action creating districts is intensely political. According to one set of scholars, the two most important factors are (1) an increase in business (both in the number of cases and in their complexity) and (2) political factors, such as whether the Congress and the presidency are controlled by the same party.[13]

APPOINTMENT PROCESS

Judges of the U.S. District Courts are Article III judges: That is, they are appointed by the president with the advice and consent of the Senate. In general, when a vacancy occurs, the attorney general's staff begins making lists of potential candidates for the position.[14] With recommendations from state and federal officials, interest groups, bar associations, and the president, a list is compiled. Those on the list receive a preliminary questionnaire pertaining to their personal life that they return to the Department of Justice and, sometimes, to the American Bar Association's (ABA's) Committee on the Federal Judiciary, which rates the candidates as "very qualified," "qualified," or "not qualified." Presidents have differed in the degree to which they rely on these ratings, but even without heavy reliance by the president, the ABA is certainly the most involved and influential interest group in this process. Once candidates survive initial screening, the FBI does a background check and then either the president or presidential advisers make the decision whom to nominate.

However, at this level, presidents also concern themselves with making appointments acceptable to the senators from the state in which the judge resides if the senators are members of the president's party. Presidents differ in the degree to which they follow this norm but rarely nominate someone to whom the home-state senator is opposed because the norm of senatorial courtesy basically decrees that if a home-state senator of the president's party opposes the nomination, the senate will reject it. Senatorial courtesy is not without controversy because it injects individual senators into a process that the Constitution primarily delegates to the president.

Once the nomination is made, it is referred to the Senate Judiciary Committee. That committee holds hearings and votes on whether or not to send the nominee's name to the Senate floor for a confirmation vote. Confirmation requires a majority vote. Historically, nominations have sailed through the Senate. However, when threshold competence is wanting or when the

---

[12] See http://www.census.gov for details.

[13] Barrow et al., *Federal Judiciary*, pp. 17–18, 41–42, 62–63, 92.

[14] See Sheldon Goldman, *Picking Federal Judges* (New Haven, CT: Yale University Press, 1997), for detailed information on this process.

Table 8.1. *Authorized Judgeships in the District Courts*

State	District	Authorized Judgeships	Circuit
Alabama	Northern District	7	11th
	Middle District	3	
	Southern District	3	
Alaska		3	9th
Arizona		8	9th
Arkansas	Eastern District	5	8th
	Western District	3	
California	Northern District	14	9th
	Eastern District	6	
	Central District	27	
	Southern District	8	
Colorado		7	10th
Connecticut		8	2nd
Delaware		4	3rd
District of Columbia		15	DC
Florida	Northern District	4	11th
	Middle District	11	
	Southern District	16	
Georgia	Northern District	11	11th
	Middle District	4	
	Southern District	3	
Guam		1	9th
Hawaii		3	9th
Idaho		2	9th
Illinois	Northern District	22	7th
	Southern District	3	
	Central District	3	
Indiana	Northern District	5	7th
	Southern District	5	
Iowa	Northern District	2	8th
	Southern District	3	
Kansas		5	10th
Kentucky	Eastern District	4	6th
	Western District	4	
	Eastern and Western	1	
Louisiana	Eastern District	13	5th
	Middle District	2	
	Western District	7	
Maine		3	1st
Maryland		10	4th
Massachusetts		13	1st
Michigan	Eastern District	15	6th
	Western District	4	
Minnesota		7	8th
Mississippi	Northern District	3	5th
	Southern District	6	
Missouri	Eastern District	6	8th
	Western District	5	
	Eastern and Western	2	

State	District	Authorized Judgeships	Circuit
Montana		3	9th
Nebraska		3	8th
Nevada		4	9th
New Hampshire		3	1st
New Jersey		17	3rd
New Mexico		5	10th
New York	Northern District	4	2nd
	Eastern District	15	
	Southern District	28	
	Western District	4	
North Carolina	Eastern District	4	4th
	Middle District	4	
	Western District	3	
North Dakota		2	8th
Northern Mariana Islands		1	9th
Ohio	Northern District	11	6th
	Southern District	8	
Oklahoma	Northern District	3	10th
	Eastern District	1	
	Western District	6	
	Northern, Eastern, Western Districts	1	
Oregon		6	9th
Pennsylvania	Eastern District	22	3rd
	Middle District	6	
	Western District	10	
Puerto Rico		7	1st
Rhode Island		3	1st
South Carolina		9	4th
South Dakota		3	8th
Tennessee	Eastern District	5	6th
	Middle District	4	
	Western District	5	
Texas	Northern District	12	5th
	Southern District	18	
	Eastern District	7	
	Western District	10	
Utah		5	10th
Vermont		2	2nd
Virgin Islands		2	3rd
Virginia	Eastern District	9	4th
	Western District	4	
Washington	Eastern District	4	9th
	Western District	7	
West Virginia	Northern District	3	4th
	Southern District	5	
Wisconsin	Eastern District	4	7th
	Western District	2	
Wyoming		3	10th

ideological distance between the Senate and the nominee is too great, confirmation may not occur. This is especially true during periods of divided government.

Presidents are most likely to nominate like-minded judges to the district courts, just as they do to the Supreme Court. One study reports a same-party appointment rate for both Democratic (93.5 percent) and Republican (93.0 percent) presidents.[15]

Most presidents make a substantial mark on the lower federal bench. Of twenty-three presidents evaluated, only two failed to leave office with the judiciary in his party's hands, and one of those, Nixon, nearly did so. (Cleveland was the other president.) Some presidents left office after having appointed more than 50 percent of all federal judges (Grant and the two Roosevelts), and Eisenhower left with exactly 50 percent.

Of course, the president cannot appoint a judge unless a vacancy occurs or Congress authorizes additional judgeships. In 1801, there were 20 district court judgeships; by 1933, there were 136. Near the end of the twentieth century, 634 judgeships were authorized. The number of judgeships is driven not only by the increase in caseload documented previously, but by politics, as presidents with sympathetic congresses tend to get additional judgeships. Even when the president is not blessed with a like-minded Senate, retirements may allow presidents to leave their mark on the judiciary.

Judges themselves play a role in the appointment process through use of strategically timed departures. During periods of unified government, the largest single source of vacancies results from same-party resignations and retirements. The attractiveness of retirement helps this process. Congress passed legislation in 1869 and 1919 that initially allowed for retirement at age seventy with full pay, and then for senior status in which a judge could retain his or her salary but carry less than a full caseload. Sixty-three percent of Democrats engaged in "political leaving," as did 52.4 percent of Republicans. Indeed, replacements are the most important source of appointment opportunities.

Arguably, these departures and the ever increasing number of judges cause concern for the independence, autonomy, and expertise of the district courts. "The true crisis is ... [the] serious undermining of their institution through enormous increases in new members, often of very different political/ideological persuasions, coupled with record-shattering annual departures and declining length of service."[16]

JURISDICTION

As trial courts, the U.S. District Courts have original jurisdiction. As federal courts, they can hear only cases that pertain to a provision of the U.S. Constitution, an act of Congress, or a treaty of the United States. The Framers also authorized these courts to hear cases involving diversity of citizenship (i.e., cases in which a resident of one state sues one from another state). Given that

---

[15] The rest of this section is based on Barrow et al., *Federal Judiciary*.
[16] *Id.*, p. 101.

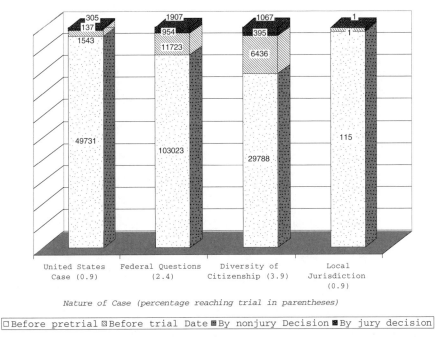

Nature of Case (percentage reaching trial in parentheses)

☐ Before pretrial ☒ Before trial Date ▨ By nonjury Decision ▪ By jury decision

Figure 8.1. Types of Civil Cases and Their Resolution in the U.S. District Courts, 2002. *Source:* Administrative Office of the U.S. Courts, "Judicial Business of the U.S. Courts, 2002," Table C-4.

Americans defined themselves as citizens of their state of residence rather than as citizens of the United States, the Framers feared judicial bias toward the home-state resident. However, when district courts hear such cases, they must apply the law of the state in which they sit. In order to lessen the burden of hearing these cases, Congress requires that they involve at least $75,000 in injuries or damages. However, as Figure 8.1 shows, they still hear plenty of them. Finally, the district courts have jurisdiction over petitions from state and federal prisoners, most often in the form of a writ of habeas corpus. These prisoner petitions make up almost half of the courts' federal question docket, asking the district courts to review the prisoner's imprisonment to determine whether s/he is incarcerated lawfully. Most of these cases, as one can imagine, are frivolous, last-ditch attempts to get out of prison. The court, therefore, often resolves these cases before they reach trial (only 1.3 percent do so).

Nevertheless, before any case is heard, claimants must satisfy various jurisdictional requirements. These courts, as for all federal courts, can only hear cases in which (1) the district court has jurisdiction (i.e., it is the "correct" district court geographically, and the case either contains a federal question or involves diversity jurisdiction); (2) a real controversy exists (i.e., the parties are not collusive and do not seek an advisory opinion; the plaintiff has standing to sue; and the controversy is live, not moot); (3) all other remedies (state and federal) are exhausted (e.g., if the claim relates to an administrative

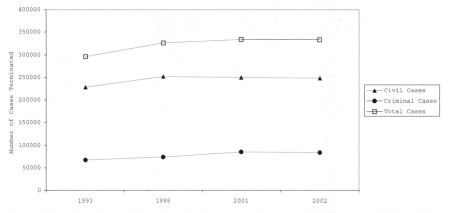

Figure 8.2a. Caseload of the U.S. District Courts. *Source:* Administrative Office of the U.S. Courts, "Judicial Business of the U.S. Courts."

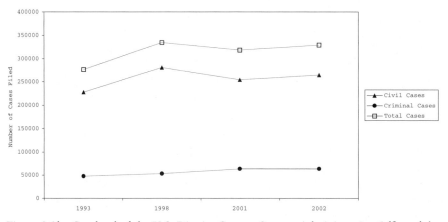

Figure 8.2b. Caseload of the U.S. District Courts. *Source:* Administrative Office of the U.S. Courts, "Judicial Business of the U.S. Courts."

agency's jurisdiction, the plaintiff must have first completed the administrative procedure); (4) the issue is not a so-called political question, one whose resolution is left for a coordinate branch of government. Failure to meet any of these jurisdictional or standing requirements necessitates dismissal of the case.

CASELOAD

As mentioned earlier, the district courts collectively make hundreds of thousands of decisions each year. According to the Administrative Office of the U.S. Courts, the district courts terminated 265,321 civil cases and 58,844 criminal cases in 2002 for a total of 324,165. (See Figure 8.2a for the number of cases terminated in the years 1993, 1998, 2001, and 2002; Figure 8.2b, for the number of filings.) This means each judge on the district courts in 2002 averaged 494 cases filed in his or her court. In addition, the U.S. Bankruptcy Courts, a legislatively created adjunct of the district courts, terminated 1,395,967 cases in 2002. The median civil case in 2002 took 8.1 months; of those that went to trial (only 2.4 percent of all civil cases in 2002), the median time taken from filing to termination was 20.4 months.[17]

These data establish the district courts' characterization as workhorses. In this section, we take a closer look at the types of cases they hear, the procedures used to decide them, and the considerations affecting the district court judge's decision making.

Types of Cases

As the raw numbers of terminations in 2002 show, the district courts hear far more civil than criminal cases. Indeed, in every year for which data are available (see Figures 8.2a and 8.2b), civil filings exceed criminal filings by more than 77 percent. So how do these courts deal with these large numbers of filings?

First, pretrial settlement disposes of the vast majority of civil cases, as Figure 8.1 indicates. Indeed, 182,657 cases were settled even before the pretrial conference, an additional 19,703 settled sometime before the scheduled trial date. Pretrial settlement, then, accounts for almost 98 percent of the dispositions of all civil cases. Within specific categories of civil cases, the largest trial rate occurs in diversity of citizenship cases and the smallest in cases in which the United States is a party and those that arise in U.S. territories. Federal questions constitute the largest category, with the most numerous subset those involving federal statutes. This illustrates the control Congress has over the workload of the courts: It can increase their caseload by legislation that engenders legal action, or decrease their caseload by limiting legal remedies for certain situations. Congress did the former when it passed the Americans with Disabilities Act, opening the courtroom doors to claims of discrimination on the basis of disability to millions of disabled persons; it did the latter when it passed the Prison Litigation Reform Act, which limited the conditions under which prisoners might sue for unconstitutional prison conditions. The statutes litigated most often involve prisoner petitions (especially motions to vacate sentences and habeas corpus) and disability insurance cases.

Table 8.2, which presents the disposition of criminal cases, shows that few cases actually go to trial. However, a higher percentage of criminal cases than civil cases do end up as either a bench or a jury trial; overall, 5 percent are such. Drug offenses are the largest category by far. Indeed, in 2002, the district courts disposed of 28,411 cases involving federal drug charges, of which 26,199, or 92 percent, resulted in convictions, most by guilty pleas. Homicides had the

[17] Administrative Office of the U.S. Courts, http://www.uscourts.gov. Unfortunately, the AOC does not keep track of the time until termination for criminal cases.

Table 8.2. *Types of Criminal Cases and Court Action in the U.S. District Courts, 2002*

Offense	Not Convicted			Convicted and Sentenced				
	Dismissed	Court Decision	Jury Decision	Plea of Guilty	Nolo Contendere	Court Decision	Jury Decision	% Reaching Trial
Homicide	42	3	8	219	0	2	30	14.1
Robbery	54	1	7	1,454	0	4	58	4.4
Assault	126	6	8	427	3	7	31	8.6
Burglary	9	0	0	66	0	1	2	3.8
Larceny and theft	729	10	15	2,486	33	20	65	3.3
Embezzlement	104	0	4	907	2	2	18	2.3
Fraud	675	20	51	9,105	6	15	355	4.3
Auto theft	30	1	2	168	0	0	19	10
Forgery and counterfeiting	135	1	4	1,294	0	2	31	2.6
Sex offenses	78	0	9	858	1	5	42	5.6
Drugs	1,993	57	162	25,215	18	56	910	4.2
Miscellaneous general	2,062	259	87	9,666	202	203	462	7.8
Immigration laws	565	3	11	10,708	4	32	110	1.4
Liquor, Internal Revenue	0	0	0	8	0	0	3	27
Federal statutes	363	29	41	2,444	12	442	103	17.9
Grand Total	**6,965**	**390**	**409**	**65,025**	**281**	**791**	**2,239**	**5.0**

Source: Administrative Office of the U.S. Courts, "Judicial Business of the U.S. Courts."

highest trial rate: 14 percent that went to trial. Again, many more homicide cases ended in convictions than acquittals, and most followed from a guilty plea. This result may be due to the high incidence of plea bargaining in these cases, which we discuss later.

According to the Administrative Office of the Courts, among the fastest growing areas of civil litigation between 1993 and 2002 were personal injury/ product liability cases related to breast implants and asbestos claims, recovery of defaulted student loans (although these decreased dramatically, by 57 percent, in 2002), and prisoner petitions. The asbestos claims were particularly prevalent in the Eastern District of Virginia, the Northern District of Ohio, and the Southern District of New York. In criminal cases, the district courts had increases for seven consecutive years due to growth in immigration, drug, and firearm filings. Bankruptcy filings, heard by the special Bankruptcy Courts, rose 60 percent from 1993 with filings per judge growing from 2,883 in 1993 to 4,644 in 2002.[18]

PROCEDURES

As noted, the district courts are the federal system's trial courts. Judges preside over civil and criminal trials, often accompanied by a jury. The U.S. Constitution gives every person the right to a jury trial in both criminal and civil cases.[19] Over time, the Supreme Court has specified the accoutrements of jury trials in criminal cases: a public trial that occurs shortly after commission of the alleged offense, confrontation of opposing witnesses and compulsory process for obtaining favorable ones, and assistance of counsel. State criminal cases do not require a twelve-person jury[20] or unanimous verdicts.[21] However, the Federal Rules of Criminal Procedure (discussed in Chapter 5) do require a twelve-person jury and a unanimous verdict in federal criminal cases.[22] Generally, six-person juries are used in civil cases.

Justice Byron White, in his opinion in *Duncan v. Louisiana*, suggested that the need for juries stemmed from a need to protect citizens from prosecutorial abuse. Others suggest that juries temper the application of "bad" laws by refusing to enforce them. Jury opponents, however, argue that they are not qualified to find facts and reach verdicts; that they are not really

---

[18] "Federal Judicial Caseload Statistics, March 31, 2002." Office of Human Resources and Statistics, Statistics Division, Administrative Office of the United States Courts.

[19] The Seventh Amendment's right to a jury trial in civil cases does not apply to the states.

[20] *Williams v. Florida*, 399 U.S. 78 (1970).

[21] *Johnson v. Louisiana*, 406 U.S. 356 (1972), and *Apodaca v. Oregon*, 406 U.S. 404 (1972). *Apodaca* does require unanimity in federal cases, however.

[22] The rule requires twelve jurors unless otherwise agreed by the parties and allows for an eleven-member jury should the need to remove a juror occur. Federal Rules of Criminal Procedure, 23(b).

composed of one's peers; and that peremptory challenges and those for cause produce stacked juries, especially by the exclusion of minorities.[23] Yet, although "the jury system is far from being perfect, it acts as a great democratizing principle that brings the people of our country directly into the government system."[24]

Not all federal cases are tried by jury, however, as the defendant (or civil plaintiff) can waive a jury trial, opting instead for a bench trial. Most of the time, a jury is empanelled, but in 2002, in 35 percent of civil cases and 31 percent of criminal cases that were terminated at trial, the judge determined the outcome.

Much of the work of the district courts takes place outside the courtroom. Indeed, in 2002, only 2.3 percent of all civil cases went to trial. Likewise, only 5 percent of defendants' cases went to either the court or the jury for resolution. What happened in the other filings? In a criminal case, the defendant may have pled guilty, obviating the need for trial. Indeed, as mentioned, this happens often; in 2002, 85 percent of all criminal cases were so terminated. In such a situation the judge merely makes certain that the defendant made the guilty plea voluntarily. The judge then sentences the defendant. The same is true of a plea of nolo contendere or "no contest." Here, the defendant neither admits nor denies guilt but does agree to accept the sentence of the judge. The benefit to the defendant is that his or her plea cannot be used in any future proceedings related to the case (e.g., a civil suit for wrongful death that follows a manslaughter conviction).

Out of court settlements do not formally involve the district court in the negotiation of the plea bargain or settlement. They are left to the parties and their attorneys. The judge, however, may informally suggest terms of settlement and encourage an agreement. In sum, trial, though often the focus of commentators, scholars, and the public, is the exception, not the rule.

DECISION MAKING

In addition to their resolution of trials, district court judges rule on various motions and decide whether to set bail in a criminal case before it begins. During the trial, the judge must make decisions sustaining or overruling attorney objections to questioning, witnesses, and evidence. And, in a jury trial, the trial judge must give instructions before the jury retires to deliberate. All of these are consequential matters, but few result in a written opinion.

In this section we focus on what influences the judges to make their decisions both on the merits and in sentencing.

[23] Walter F. Murphy, C. Herman Pritchett, and Lee Epstein, *Courts, Judges, and Politics: An Introduction to the Judicial Process* (New York: McGraw-Hill, 2002), pp. 365–368.

[24] Tracy Gilstrap Weiss, "The Great Democratizing Principle: The Effect on South Africa of Planning a Democracy without a Jury System," *Temple International and Comparative Law Journal*, Volume 11, 1997, 404–408, 407 (1997).

Dispute Resolution

What drives a district court judge to determine that a given defendant is either guilty or innocent or that a respondent is liable for some injury? At the Supreme Court level policy preferences play a very large role, and one is able to predict large percentages of decisional outcomes solely on that basis.[25] However, because of differences in the institutional position of the district courts (and the courts of appeals, to be discussed in the next chapter), attitudes are not as strong a predictor. Rather, precedent and the facts of the case loom much larger, along with other external influences, although we still expect judges of different parties to behave differently. Indeed, as discussed earlier, presidents purposefully appoint like-minded judges to the federal bench in order to exert a lasting impact on U.S. policy. Surely they would not work so hard to obtain like-minded judges on these lower benches if they thought partisan affiliation, or ideology, did not matter.

Figure 8.3 presents the percentage of all decisions made in a liberal direction by both Democratic and Republican judges for a variety of issue areas. In the first seven issue areas (right to privacy, local economic regulation, race discrimination, rights of the handicapped, women's rights, freedom of religion, and freedom of expression) a substantial difference in voting by Democratic and Republican judges exists. In other areas, the differences between the two are not large. This finding suggests, as noted, that although party does influence judicial votes at this level, it does not fully account for the voting behavior of the district court judges. But the differences suggest that policy-oriented presidents do well to nominate like-minded judges to these lower courts.

At least two reasons explain why ideology does not substantially drive decision making at this level: (1) Precedent governs many of these cases and (2) case facts clearly favor one party rather than the other. Only when a judge finds herself in an unprecedented situation or relevant precedents support both parties does she rely on her personal attitudes. Additionally, law schools, bar associations, and other law-related institutions socialize would-be judges into a belief that precedent and law matter. Of course, no more than partisanship does this focus explain all the judges' decisions. But how the judge perceives his or her role may affect decision making, at least on the margins.

Influences other than partisanship and the legal subculture also affect judicial behavior. Some argue that regionalism may play a role: Judges in different parts of the country may decide cases differently. However, Figure 8.4 shows that substantial differences do not exist.

Some scholars also suggest that the "courtroom workgroup" influences trial court decision making.[26] Because these judges interact daily with prosecutors

---

[25] See Chapter 12.

[26] James Eisenstein, Roy B. Flemming, and Peter Nardulli, *The Contours of Justice* (Boston: Little, Brown, 1988).

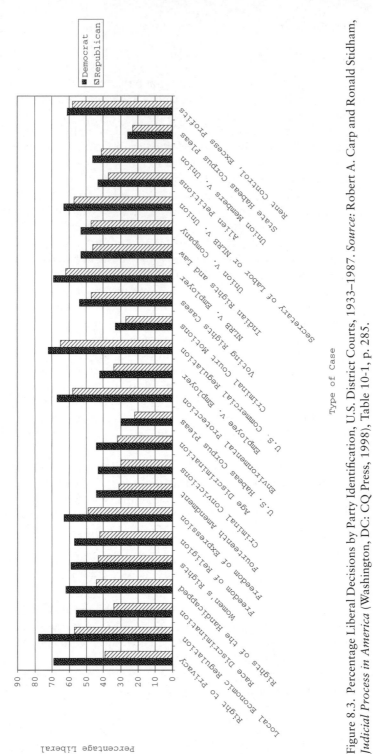

Figure 8.3. Percentage Liberal Decisions by Party Identification, U.S. District Courts, 1933–1987. *Source:* Robert A. Carp and Ronald Stidham, *Judicial Process in America* (Washington, DC: CQ Press, 1998), Table 10-1, p. 285.

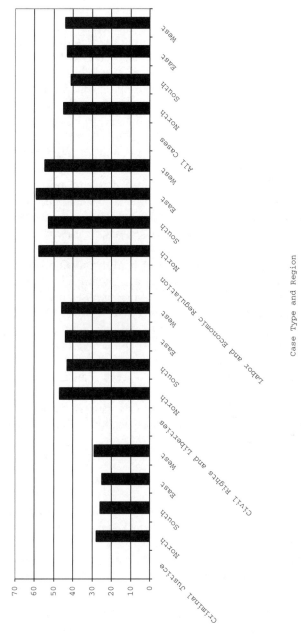

Figure 8.4. Percentage Liberal Decisions by Region, U.S. District Courts, 1933–1987. *Source:* Robert A. Carp and Ronald Stidham, *Judicial Process in America* (Washington, DC: CQ Press, 1998), Table 10-2, p. 293.

and defense attorneys, they surmise, these relationships can affect group behavior and hence decisional outcomes.

Scholars have also attempted to discern whether public opinion influences judicial decision making, especially at this most local federal court level.[27] They posit that we might expect such influence, even on these insulated judges, because they are subject to the same influences as everyone else. But if trial court judges become more or less conservative on the basis of the same crime rates, inflation rates, and so on, that move public opinion, this would mean a *correspondence* with public opinion, not a direct *influence* of it.

Alternatively, in certain kinds of cases (obscenity, for example) local public opinion is alleged to be an explicit factor in the trial courts' decision making. Finally, federal judges are aware that without voluntary compliance and strong public esteem, their decisions may lack implementation. But though these reasons support such influence, scholars have been unable to show a definitive link between public opinion and federal judicial decision making even in areas in which it should matter most, such as Southern school desegregation.[28]

Overall, the picture of district court decision making is that of a court subject to multiple influences and constraints. First, it is a trial court, and so its judges make many intermediate decisions short of final disposition. Those decisions are made as the trial progresses and are not accompanied by written opinions. What influences the judge to rule in favor of one party rather than the other in these decisions is not entirely clear; nor is it as simple as it is at the Supreme Court level, where ideology drives decision making. Here, we expect the facts of the case and precedent to play a major role but also find that partisanship matters. Indeed, in cases in which legal evidence is contradictory or precedent is nonexistent (as in a new issue), ideology has a greater impact. In addition, some judges may be more comfortable making policy than others, with the result that ideological impact might vary across judges as well. But overall, Democrats do behave differently from Republicans, especially in more salient areas of the law.

Sentencing

District judges also control the important matter of criminal case sentencing. In this section, we discuss sentencing, the federal sentencing guidelines, and the factors that influence judicial sentencing decisions.

Sentencing receives much attention from Congress, the public, and scholars. Indeed, the extent of the discretion district court judges should exercise

---

[27] Beverly B. Cook, "Public Opinion and Federal Judicial Policy," 21 *American Journal of Political Science* 567 (1977). But see Herbert M. Kritzer, "Federal Judges and Their Political Environments: The Influence of Public Opinion," 23 *American Journal of Political Science* 194 (1979).

[28] E.g., Micheal Giles and Thomas G. Walker, "Judicial Policy Making and Southern School Segregation," 37 *Journal of Politics* 917 (1975).

has been a hot topic of debate. George W. Bush's attorney general, John Ashcroft, concerned about the frequency of "downward departures" of sentences from those prescribed by the Federal Sentencing Guidelines, engaged in two strategies: First, the Justice Department crafted, Congress passed, and the president signed into law the Feeney Amendment to the Amber Alert bill. That amendment sets minimum mandatory sentences for sex offenses and child kidnapping charges, thereby decreasing district court discretion in these areas.

In addition, the amendment makes it easier for the prosecution to appeal downward departures and for appellate judges to increase sentences that are shorter than the guidelines prescribe. Chief Justice Rehnquist, not one known to be soft on crime, reacted to the passage of this amendment by writing in a letter to Senator Patrick Leahy (Democrat – Vermont) that the measure "would seriously impair the ability of the courts to impose just and reasonable sentences."[29] District Court Judge John S. Martin, Jr., of Manhattan resigned in 2003, citing increasingly limited discretion over sentencing decisions. He argued, "The Justice Department is telling us that every defendant should be treated in the same way, that there should be no flexibility to deal with individuals."[30]

Ashcroft has furthered his goal of promoting harsher sentencing by circulating an internal memo that directs government prosecutors to report judges who give sentences less than those prescribed in the guidelines so that the Justice Department can pursue appeals of these lighter sentences. In 2001, federal district court judges lessened sentences in 10,026 cases and the Justice Department appealed only 50.[31] Ashcroft says that too many are overlooked, whereas Judge Martin asserts that most sentences are not appealed because the U.S. attorneys involved understand that they are reasonable, given the particular situation. The Supreme Court has also ordered deference to district court sentencing decisions,[32] which would be an additional reason not to appeal them. The Feeney Amendment may change this. The heart of the debate seems to be a question of who is better qualified to make sentencing decisions. Ashcroft and Congress view the federal government as better positioned, and critics argue that those closest to the individual cases should decide. William Young, the chief judge of the U.S. District Court for Massachusetts, asks, "Why does Congress hold the courts in such a low regard that they were uninterested in obtaining the views of those whose duty it is to fashion fair and just sentences in every case?"[33]

---

[29] Edward Walsh and Dan Eggen, "Ashcroft Orders Tally of Lighter Sentences: Critics Say He Wants 'Blacklist' of Judges," *Washington Post*, 7 August 2003, p. A1.

[30] Laurie P. Cohen and Gary Fields, "Ashcroft Intensifies Campaign against Judges' Soft Sentences," *Wall Street Journal*, 6 August 2003, p. A1.

[31] *Id.*

[32] *Koon v. United States*, 518 U.S. 81 (1996).

[33] Seth Stern, "Federal Judges Rebel over Limits to Sentencing Power," *Christian Science Monitor*, 8 July 2003, p. 2.

Associate Supreme Court Justice Anthony Kennedy would go even further in sentencing discretion. In a speech to the American Bar Association in August 2003, Kennedy suggested that Congress should end the practice of mandatory minimum sentences altogether and reduce the sentencing guidelines. Citing several notable cases, Kennedy said, "I can accept neither the necessity nor the wisdom of federal mandatory minimum sentences. In too many cases mandatory minimum sentences are unwise and unjust."[34] Kennedy noted that there are 2.1 million people in prison in the United States, 1 of every 143. That rate is only 1 of 1,000 in England, Italy, France, and Germany. Because of harsh sentencing guidelines, according to Kennedy, too many people are in jail. He also called for greater use of the president's pardon power to correct these disparities, saying that we ought not be afraid to show mercy. In 2005, the Supreme Court decided for itself that district court judges should treat the guidelines as advisory, not mandatory, for sentencing enhancement factors that were not proved beyond a reasonable doubt by the jury.

The Federal Sentencing Guidelines. The Sentencing Reform Act of 1984, intended to "further the basic purposes of criminal punishment: deterrence, incapacitation, just punishment, and rehabilitation,"[35] created the U.S. Sentencing Commission to develop sentencing guidelines. The act carefully delineated instructions on how these sentencing guidelines should be formulated and how categories of offenses should be arranged. The U.S. Sentencing Commission based the guidelines on the congressional statutory language and extensive quantitative analysis of current sentencing processes. The act, while mandating specific sentencing ranges, does allow judges to vary from them when a case presents atypical features. The commission views this process, according to its manual, as ever-changing and is empowered to submit amendments to Congress regularly.

The guidelines work by taking into account both characteristics of the offense and characteristics of the offender. Specifically, they base sentence lengths on the seriousness of the crime and the criminal history of the perpetrator. There are forty-three levels of seriousness of crimes, and each type of crime is first assigned a base level. For example, homicide has a base level of 43, and the failure of a material witness to appear in a misdemeanor case has a base level of 4. Between these extremes are theft (base = 6), statutory rape (base = 18), robbery (base = 20), and selling or buying of children for use in the production of pornography (base = 38), among many others. Specific offense characteristics (SOCs) can increase the base. For example, if during the course of a robbery (base = 20), a firearm is displayed, the level is increased to 25; if the firearm is actually discharged, the level is increased to 27.[36] After the base level and the SOCs are taken into consideration, the court can also make adjustments to

---

[34] Gail Appleson, "Justice Kennedy Attacks U.S. Sentencing Mandates," *FindLaw Legal News and Commentary*, 9 August 2003.

[35] United States Sentencing Commission, *Guidelines Manual*, §3El.1 November 2002.

[36] *Id.*

the sentence for the offender's role in the crime, for the characteristics of the victim, or for the defendant's obstruction of justice.

As noted, in addition to offense severity, the guidelines take into account the criminal history of the offender, by using one of six criminal history categories. Criminal history I is for first-time offenders; criminal history VI is for offenders with lengthy records. Using a table in which one axis is the severity of the crime and the other is the criminal history category, the judge can locate the range of the sentence, found in the body of the table and expressed in months (see Table 8.3). If the judge has reason to do so, she can adjust either upward or downward. An upward departure is grounds for the offender to appeal the sentence; a downward departure, as mentioned, gives the government grounds for an appeal.

What Drives Sentencing Decisions. As federal judges do not fully abide by the sentencing guidelines, extralegal factors such as race, sex, and age of the defendant may influence decisions of judges; early research suggests that racial minorities and older defendants receive harsher sentences and women receive lighter sentences.[37] Guilty pleas are appropriately accompanied by decreased sentences,[38] and poor defendants who have public defenders inappropriately receive higher sentences.

Although we cannot look at all of these influences, it seems prudent to examine data from the sentencing of the district judges in 2001 in order to see whether any of these influences on length of sentence holds today.

A Model of Sentencing. Using data provided by the Administrative Office of the U.S. Courts, we explore the correlates of sentencing in this section. Because of the need to control for several factors simultaneously, we construct a multivariate regression model of sentence length.

In a nutshell, regression models allow us to determine what effect a set of independent variables (crime severity, prior record, race, gender, etc.) have on our dependent variable of interest (sentencing decision in months), while controlling for the effects of each of the other independent variables (see the discussion of sentencing in Chapter 6).

We begin with legal factors specifically provided by the U.S. Sentencing Commission: the defendant's criminal history and the severity of his or her crime as combined in the sentencing guidelines table. We operationalize this by using the maximum sentence allowable for any offense/offender category.[39]

---

[37] James L. Croyle, "Measuring and Explaining Disparities in Felony Sentences: Courtroom Work Group Factors and Race, Sex, and Socioeconomic Influences on Sentence Severity," 5 *Political Behavior* 135 (1983). In this study, however, race does not reach statistical significance overall (but does for some individual judges). Walter Markham does find race to be a significant factor in Walter Gray Markham, "Draft Offenders in the Federal Courts: A Search for the Social Correlates of Justice" (Ph.D. Diss., University of Pennsylvania, 1971).

[38] Jeffrey A. Schafer, "Prosecutions for Selective Service Offenses: A Field Study," 22 *Stanford Law Review* 356 (1970).

[39] We exclude cases in which the maximum includes life imprisonment, 0.8 percent of the data, as that cannot be formulated into months.

Table 8.3. *U.S. Sentencing Commission Sentencing Table*

	Offense Level	Criminal History Category (Criminal History Points)					
		I (0 or 1)	II (2 or 3)	III (4, 5, 6)	IV (7, 8, 9)	V (10, 11, 12)	VI (13 or more)
	1	0–6	0–6	0–6	0–6	0–6	0–6
	2	0–6	0–6	0–6	0–6	0–6	1–7
	3	0–6	0–6	0–6	0–6	2–8	3–9
	4	0–6	0–6	0–6	2–8	4–10	6–12
Zone A	5	0–6	0–6	1–7	4–10	6–12	9–15
	6	0–6	1–7	2–8	6–12	9–15	12–18
	7	0–6	2–8	4–10	8–14	12–18	15–21
	8	0–6	4–10	6–12	10–16	15–21	18–24
Zone B	9	4–10	6–12	8–14	12–18	18–24	21–27
	10	6–12	8–14	10–16	15–21	21–27	24–30
Zone C	11	8–14	10–16	12–18	18–24	24–30	27–33
	12	10–16	12–18	15–21	21–27	27–33	30–37
Zone D	13	12–18	15–21	18–24	24–30	30–37	33–41
	14	15–21	18–24	21–27	27–33	33–41	37–46
	15	18–24	21–27	24–30	30–37	37–46	41–51
	16	21–27	24–30	27–33	33–41	41–51	46–57
	17	24–30	27–33	30–37	37–46	46–57	51–63
	18	27–33	30–37	33–41	41–51	51–63	57–71
	19	30–37	33–41	37–46	46–57	57–71	63–78
	20	33–41	37–46	41–51	51–63	63–78	70–87
	21	37–46	41–51	46–57	57–71	70–87	77–96
	22	41–51	46–57	51–63	63–78	77–96	84–105
	23	46–57	51–63	57–71	70–87	84–105	92–115
	24	51–63	57–71	63–78	77–96	92–115	100–125
	25	57–71	63–78	70–87	84–105	100–125	110–137
	26	63–78	70–87	78–97	92–115	110–137	120–150
	27	70–87	78–97	87–108	100–125	120–150	130–162
	28	78–97	87–108	97–121	110–137	130–162	140–175
	29	87–108	97–121	108–135	121–151	140–175	151–188
	30	97–121	108–135	121–151	135–168	151–188	168–210
	31	108–135	121–151	135–168	151–188	168–210	188–235
	32	121–151	135–168	151–188	168–210	188–235	210–262
	33	135–168	151–188	168–210	188–235	210–262	235–293
	34	151–188	168–210	188–235	210–262	235–293	262–327
	35	168–210	188–235	210–262	235–293	262–327	292–365
	36	188–235	210–262	235–293	262–327	292–365	324–405
	37	210–262	235–293	262–327	292–365	324–405	360–life
	38	235–293	262–327	292–365	324–405	360–life	360–life
	39	262–327	292–365	324–405	360–life	360–life	360–life
	40	292–365	324–405	360–life	360–life	360–life	360–life
	41	324–405	360–life	360–life	360–life	360–life	360–life
	42	360–life	360–life	360–life	360–life	360–life	360–life
	43	Life	life	Life	Life	life	life

Table 8.4. *Determinants of Sentencing in U.S. District Courts, 2001 (in months)*

Variables	B	Std. Error	Sig. Level
U.S. Sentencing Guidelines Variable			
Max guideline range for imprisonment	0.680	0.004	0.000
Judicial Characteristics			
Proportion Democrat in district	−1.524	1.518	0.315
Defendant Characteristics			
Disposition of defendant's case (1 = trial, 0 = other)	27.063	1.452	0.000
Defendant's gender (1 = female)	−7.145	0.693	0.000
Defendant's race (1 = minority)	4.622	0.596	0.000
Citizenship of defendant (1 = noncitizen)	−1.751	0.550	0.001
Education of defendant (1 = less than high school, 4 = college graduate)	−0.949	0.290	0.001
Type of counsel used (1 = public defender or court appointed, 0 = other)	2.424	0.594	0.000
Marital status of defendant (1 = married, 0 = other)	−3.315	3.154	0.293
Dependents whom defendant supports (actual number)	−0.574	0.141	0.000
Defendant's age at time of offense	0.004	0.023	0.877
Circuit 1	−1.167	1.492	0.434
Circuit 2	−9.567	0.988	0.000
Circuit 3	−3.716	1.450	0.010
Circuit 4	2.131	1.272	0.094
Circuit 6	−3.779	1.214	0.002
Circuit 7	6.090	1.592	0.000
Circuit 8	−5.040	1.218	0.000
Circuit 9	−6.933	0.732	0.000
Circuit 10	−2.183	1.034	0.035
Circuit 11	3.357	0.912	0.000
(Constant)	3.943	1.437	0.006

Note: $N = 27{,}726$; $R^2 = 0.607$; Adj $R^2 = 0.606$; $F = 1815.431$, significant at 0.000; standard error of the estimate = 36.68.

We then add a series of extralegal factors that ought not affect sentencing: a proxy for the judge's ideology,[40] plus the defendant's characteristics: race, age, marital status, education, family status, and immigration status. Additionally, we consider whether the accused was tried by a jury and whether the accused was represented by a public defender or court-appointed attorney. Finally, we include variables indicating the circuit in which the defendant was sentenced to determine whether there are differences in sentencing across circuits not captured by our model, using the busiest sentencing circuit, the Fifth Circuit Court, as the baseline. Table 8.4 presents the results.

[40] The proportion of the district's judges appointed by a Democratic president. Obviously, we would rather have the specific judge's ideology, or even partisanship, but the commission's data

As can be seen, even after controlling for the strong effects of the U.S. Sentencing Guidelines, some characteristics of the defendant that should not be relevant indeed are. We discuss how each variable is coded and how to interpret the regression output for each in the discussion that follows.

The first variable listed, "Max guideline range for imprisonment," is our measure of the influence of the Federal Sentencing Guidelines. This refers to the maximum sentence provided for under the guidelines for a particular offense given the criminal history of the defendant, as presented in Table 8.3. This variable should positively relate to sentence length. As expected, we find that as the guideline maximum increases, so, too, does the defendant's sentence. The slope coefficient (under column B in the table) of 0.68 suggests that federal judges sentence defendants at 68 percent of the maximum sentence, plus or minus other variables in the model. Clearly, the judges pay heed to the federal sentencing guidelines.

Nevertheless, the story does not end here as defendant characteristics also matter to the sentencing decision even after controlling for the sentencing guidelines. Indeed, whether the defendant has a trial is significantly related to the sentence imposed. It is positive, meaning, as expected, that cases that involve trials beget longer sentences – more than twenty-seven months longer – than similar cases that involve pleas of guilty or settlements. Outside the sentencing guideline range, this variable exerts the strongest influence on sentences in the model. Clearly, the right to a trial has a steep price for defendants found guilty.

Next, a set of extralegal characteristics matter. For example, the gender of the defendant influences sentencing. As earlier studies have suggested, our results show that female defendants receive substantially lighter sentences, by almost seven months, than similarly situated males.

Also posited by the literature and confirmed by our results is the influence of race. When the defendant is a minority (either black or Hispanic), he or she is sentenced more harshly, by nearly five months, even after controlling for the severity of the crime and the record of the defendant. But given the endemic racism of American society, this hardly surprises any but the most jejune.

Related to race is citizenship. Here we find a counterintuitive result. Aliens receive lighter sentences (two months) than those who are U.S. citizens.

The education of the defendant also matters. Higher levels of education beget lower sentences. This probably results from any number of factors that correlate with education (affluence, type of crime committed), but even after controlling for some of the potential correlated variables, we see that the better educated the defendant, the lighter the sentence. To wit, each level of education, from a high school diploma, to some college, to a college diploma, drops one's sentence by almost a month.

The type of defense counsel also significantly relates to sentence length, and, as expected, defendants represented by either public defenders or

do not identify the specific judges. We obtained the proxy data from the Federal Judicial Center: http://www.fjc.gov/history/home.nsf.

court-appointed attorneys receive harsher sentences. Conventional wisdom supports this finding, suggesting that these attorneys are inferior or less motivated than their paid counterparts and, hence, less successful. Defendants who have a public defender or court-appointed counsel receive a sentence more than two months longer than that of those who hire an attorney.

The number of dependents the defendant has also matters to sentence length. One might expect a judge to be more sympathetic to a defendant with mouths to feed, hence keeping that defendant behind bars for a shorter time. Indeed, judges sentence those with more children more leniently, easing their sentence by about a half-month per dependent.

Neither marital status nor age at the time of offense affects sentence length.

Quite notably, the proportion of Democratic judges in the district also has no influence on the length of sentence. This is, of course, contrary to what many Republicans see as the leniency of Democratic judges. Although the coefficient is correctly signed plus or minus (the higher the proportion of Democrats, the lower the sentence), it is not statistically significant, and so we can conclude that, once we control for severity of the sentence (coupled with the accused's record), legal representation, trial or lack of trial, and the various characteristics of the defendant mentioned, there is no difference between liberal and conservative judges in their sentencing decisions, at least as operationalized here.

Finally, we find considerable variation across the circuits. Compared with the Fifth Circuit (which is used as the baseline because it is the busiest), the Seventh and Eleventh impose significantly longer sentences and the Second, Third, Eighth, Ninth, and Tenth impose shorter sentences. This suggests the existence of circuit variation not accounted for by the guidelines and defendant characteristics. Overall, the harshest sentencing circuit is the Fourth Circuit, with a mean sentence of seventy-four months, and the most lenient the Ninth, with a mean sentence of only thirty-three months. These two circuits have a reputation as being, respectively, the most conservative and the most liberal. Nevertheless, as discussed, our aggregate proxy of judicial ideology – percentage Democratic judges in district – does not significantly explain individual sentencing decisions. Because the sentencing data do not contain judge-level information, we cannot determine whether this result is due to the lack of impact of ideology on sentencing, or rather, on our indirect measure of ideology. Nevertheless, the negotiated context of plea bargain deals plus the restrictions created by the guidelines suggest that we should not expect more than a relatively weak link between judicial ideology and sentencing.

CONCLUSION

The U.S. District Courts are a busy and understudied institution. They are, indeed, the workhorses of the federal judiciary, hearing hundreds of thousands of cases yearly. The district court judges largely work alone; they mainly decide civil matters, and much of their activity occurs in their chambers, not the courtroom. There is much to debate about these district courts: Do we need more judges? How should they best be appointed? Do they use too much discretion in sentencing? Should we use juries so often? In general, though, the system works and substantial caseloads are adequately – though not optimally – handled. If we can obtain more data about their decisions, we will know better how these courts work and how these judges make decisions. For now, we see these courts as largely constrained, but not without an extralegal bent.

9

The U.S. Courts of Appeals

District Court Judge Middlebrooks, as discussed in Chapter 8, denied the preliminary injunctive relief sought by Bush and Cheney and some voters after the 2000 Florida election votes. Those parties, as is their right, appealed the decision to the Eleventh Circuit of the U.S. Court of Appeals. As the courts of appeals have mandatory jurisdiction – that is, they must rule on the cases brought to them – and the case was properly before them, they heard and decided it. Nevertheless, the appeals court apparently thought this question particularly important and scheduled it for hearing *en banc*, meaning all twelve judges of the Eleventh Circuit participated, rather than the three-judge panel that usually hears cases. Although the judges did not fully agree, the majority agreed with Judge Middlebrooks, affirming his decision denying the injunction.

The facts of the case are familiar: Bush and Cheney (and some voters) alleged First and Fourteenth Amendment violations stemming from the manual recounts being conducted in some Florida counties, and they asked that those recounts be enjoined. Middlebrooks found no injury, and the appeals court, in an 8–4 decision, agreed.

In its *per curiam* – that is, unsigned – opinion, the court noted first that it did have jurisdiction over the matter because (1) it was not reviewing a state court decision; (2) the case was not moot; (3) it did not warrant federal court abstention; and (4) it did not depend wholly on a question of state law. The court then spent some time discussing its role with respect to the decision made by the district court. The judges noted, "We may reverse the district court's order only if there was a clear abuse of discretion."[1] They went on to recite the standards to which they adhere in cases requesting injunctive relief, which include the following: (1) the plaintiff is likely to succeed on the merits; (2) the plaintiffs will be irreparably injured without the injunction; (3) such injury outweighs any damages to the defendant; and (4) the injunction would not run afoul of the

---

[1] *Siegel v. Lepore*, 234 F. 3d 1163 (2000), at 1175.

public interest.[2] Using the deferential "abuse of discretion" standard of review, as well as the criteria for granting an injunction, the appeals court rejected the plaintiffs' claim.

First, the court asserted that the plaintiffs would suffer no irreparable injury merely because ballots were manually counted. Bush and Cheney were suffering no harm because they were in fact ahead in the balloting and had, by that time, been certified as the winners of Florida's electoral votes even with some of the manual recounts included in the vote totals. Even if all recounts were to proceed, a change in the winner of the state's electoral votes was only speculative, and, given state court rulings thus far denying the resumption of the manual recounts, neither the plaintiffs nor the voters were in danger of irreparable harm. Their votes were counted; they did not allege discrimination in registration; and they were not prevented from voting. Even if they could show that some sort of injury might result from the recounts, its lack of immediacy did not warrant injunctive relief. Additionally, any injury suffered by the voters could be remedied later. Damage to the legitimacy of the presidency caused by these problems in Florida also did not rise to the level of a "cognizable injury,"[3] said the court.

In accordance with the high level of deference accorded to the district courts in matters of injunctive relief, the court of appeals concluded that

we cannot say that the district court abused its broad discretion in finding that Plaintiffs did not meet their burden of showing at least a substantial likelihood of irreparable injury. Because proof of irreparable injury is an indispensable prerequisite to a preliminary injunction, Plaintiffs are not entitled to a preliminary injunction at this time and the district court's order must be affirmed.[4]

The four dissenters, on the other hand, gave several reasons why the court should have granted the injunction. Judge Birch argued that because of the lack of legislative standards guiding the recounts, the scheme did not pass constitutional muster as it disenfranchised some in the state. Judge Dubina argued that the court ought to have considered the case on the merits and not focused primarily on injunctive relief. Judge Carnes opined that irreparable injury was shown by the selective manual recounts: "If manual recounting had been conducted in all the counties using the punch card voting system so that all voters who were at risk of having their intended votes disregarded were protected . . . there would be no federal constitutional violation."[5] The Supreme Court's decision on December 12, 2000, agreed with the dissenters' decision.

---

[2] *Id.* at 1176.
[3] *Id.* at 1177.
[4] *Id.* at 1179.
[5] *Id.* at 1198.

Table 9.1. *Circuit Judgeships*

Circuit	Number of Authorized Judgeships
First (ME, MA, NH, RI, PR)	6
Second (CT, NY, VT)	13
Third (DE, NJ, PA, VI)	14
Fourth (MD, NC, SC, VA, WV)	15
Fifth (LA, MS, TX)	17
Sixth (KY, MI, OH, TN)	16
Seventh (IL, IN, WI)	11
Eighth (AR, IA, MN, MO, NE, ND, SD)	11
Ninth (AK, AZ, CA, HI, ID, MT, NV, OR, WA, GU, MP)	28
Tenth (CO, KS, NM, OK, UT, WY)	12
Eleventh (AL, FL, GA)	12
District of Columbia	12
Federal	12

Note: State postal abbreviations in parentheses; PR = Puerto Rico; VI = Virgin Islands; GU = Guam; MP = Northern Mariana Islands.

THE U.S. COURTS OF APPEALS

From *Siegel v. Lepore* we learn a few things about the U.S. Courts of Appeals. First, they are not trial courts; rather they review decisions of the district courts and administrative agencies to determine whether either applied the law incorrectly. They do not find facts; nor do they dispute the facts as established by a district court.

In addition, although the courts of appeals vary in size, the judges usually sit in panels of three, and sometimes the entire court sits (*en banc*). (Table 9.1 shows how many judges each circuit is authorized to have.) This means they are a collegial decision-making body, more akin to the Supreme Court. In fully argued cases, they receive briefs, hear oral arguments, and then decide the case. They do not use juries or hear the testimony of witnesses; they rely on the lower court record for that sort of information. Their decisions result in some type of written disposition, and the judges are free to write separate opinions. In *Siegel v. Lepore*, there were one concurring opinion and four dissenting opinions. Dissent is unusual in three-judge decisions; it typically occurs when they decide *en banc*.

Courts of appeals often defer to the judgment of the district court, as seen in our sample case. Reversals occur far less frequently than in the Supreme Court. We discuss this form of deference later.

In this chapter, we examine the U.S. Circuit Court of Appeals, its origins, its caseload, its processes, its judges, and its decision making. We also pay attention to its relationship with its judicial superior – the United States Supreme Court.

ORIGINS

The Judiciary Act of 1789 created three circuit courts along with the fifteen district courts. The circuit courts were staffed by two Supreme Court justices, who "rode circuit" to hear cases along with one district court judge. Believing that the Supreme Court did not have enough work to do, Congress required the justices to ride circuit. In addition, riding circuit would keep the High Court "in touch with the country."[6]

Judges on the three circuits – Eastern, Middle, and Southern Circuits – sat semiannually in each district within their circuit. Though superior to the district courts, they had limited appellate jurisdiction, as most appeals went directly to the Supreme Court. For major federal criminal cases and cases involving residents of different states, the circuit courts were the court of first instance. An odd situation resulted: Sometimes the same district or Supreme Court judge would hear the trial and the appeal.

District court judges had difficulty keeping up with their work in their district when they also had to participate on circuit panels. It was hard on the Supreme Court justices as well, as they often had to leave home for long stretches to ride circuit. Some justices traveled more than two thousand miles in a year, a substantial rate of travel for that time. This activity took its toll on the health of the justices; Justice James Wilson died of malaria while riding circuit, and the circuit riding probably caused the retirement of Justice John Blair.[7]

The first congressional change to the system occurred in 1793, when Congress decided that only one Supreme Court justice need sit on each circuit court. And, after some controversy, in 1869, Congress created the position of circuit judge and appointed nine such judges, thereby removing some circuit riding from the Supreme Court justices.

In 1891, the Evarts Court Reform Bill created a separate court of appeals to hear most appeals from the district courts. One court of appeals located in each circuit and consisted of three judges: the circuit judge created by the 1869 act, the new circuit judge created by the Evarts Act, and one district court judge. The Supreme Court justice assigned to the circuit could still sit but no longer had to do so. The creation of this court eased the caseload burden on the Supreme Court; indeed, the Federal Judicial Center reports that the number of Supreme Court cases declined from 623 in 1890 to 379 in 1891 and to 275 in 1892.[8]

---

[6] William F. Swindler, "The Numbers Game," *Supreme Court Historical Society 1977 Yearbook*, http://www.supremecourthistory.org.

[7] http://www.ushistory.org/tour/tour_cityhal.htm.

[8] Available online at http://www.fjc.gov/history/home.nsf/page/12a_bdy.

In 1948 Congress renamed the circuit courts the *circuit courts of appeals.* They are now staffed exclusively by their own judges.

GROWTH

As noted, Congress originally established three circuits. That number grew to six in 1802 and seven in 1807. Because circuit riding still occurred, Congress added a seventh justice to the Supreme Court. In 1837, the addition of new states to the Union occasioned two new circuits. The number of circuits remained at nine until 1893, when the District of Columbia circuit was added. In 1929, the Eighth Circuit was split to create a new Tenth Circuit, and in 1981, the Fifth Circuit was split to create the Eleventh. Congress, however, has taken no action to split the huge Ninth Circuit. Finally, in 1982, Congress established the U.S. Court of Appeals for the Federal Circuit.[9] It is the only circuit defined by its subject matter jurisdiction. It replaced the Court of Customs and Patent Appeals and the Court of Claims. This court hears appeals from the U.S. Court of International Trade, the Merit Services Protection Board, the Board of Contract Appeals, and certain administrative decisions of the secretaries of agriculture and commerce, as well as all patent appeals.[10]

Obviously, expansion of the circuits also meant expansion of the number of authorized judgeships for these courts. Indeed, in 1869, only 9 judgeships existed; in 1933, there were 45; and by the end of the G. H. W. Bush presidency (1992), there were 167, an 85 percent increase in judgeships since 1968.[11] By 2003, there were 179 authorized judgeships, of which 25 were vacant.[12]

Interestingly, the Supreme Court retains a personal relationship with the courts of appeals. At the beginning of each term the chief justice assigns himself and the associate justices to the circuits, traditionally assigning to circuits with which each has some connection or to those for which a departing justice had responsibility.[13]

Table 9.2 contains recent assignments. Circuit duties are certainly not as taxing as they once were:

The individual Supreme Court justice is presently empowered to grant bail both before and after conviction, to grant stays and injunctions in both criminal and civil cases, to grant extensions of time, to permit other procedural variances, to issue writs of habeas corpus and writs to show cause, and to take any other action necessary to protect the jurisdiction of the Court and the rights of parties.[14]

---

[9] http://www.fjc.gov/history/home.nsf/page/22a_bdy.

[10] *Id.*

[11] Deborah J. Barrow, Gary Zuk, and Gerard S. Gryski, *The Federal Judiciary and Institutional Change* (Ann Arbor: University of Michigan Press, 1996).

[12] Patrick Leahy, "Judicial Nominations Update," 23 January 2003. Available online at http://leahy.senate.gov.

[13] Frank Felleman and John C. Wright, Jr., "Notes: The Powers of the Supreme Court Justice Acting in an Individual Capacity," *University of Pennsylvania Law Review* 112 (1964): 981–1024.

[14] *Id.* at 981.

Table 9.2. *Circuit Assignments of the Supreme Court Justices*
Effective September 30, 1994

Justice	Circuit(s)
William H. Rehnquist, chief	District of Columbia, Fourth, Federal Circuit
David H. Souter	First, Third
Ruth Bader Ginsburg	Second
Antonin Scalia	Fifth
John Paul Stevens	Sixth, Seventh
Clarence Thomas	Eighth
Sandra Day O'Connor	Ninth
Stephen Breyer	Tenth
Anthony M. Kennedy	Eleventh

Such applications are screened through the clerk's office and can be reviewed by the entire Court, should the justices so choose. Most of these petitions are simple applications for time extensions for filing various papers with the Court and are granted automatically. Justices generally also grant stays of execution pending a petition to the Supreme Court, regardless of whether the Court is likely to hear the case.

APPOINTMENT PROCESS

As are district court and Supreme Court judges, the judges of the courts of appeals are Article III judges: That is, they are appointed by the president and confirmed by the Senate and serve "during good behavior," effectively for life. Because the policy-making stakes are higher at this intermediate court level than at the district court level, confirmation battles are more likely. Battles occur both over ideology and over "turf"; for example, nominees should reside in the state of their predecessor.

As part of increasing controversy over judicial nominations, both Presidents Clinton and G. W. Bush have had difficulty securing confirmation of their nominees because of intense party conflict. A Senate rule allows for filibusters, which prevent the Senate from taking action unless it can muster the supermajority (sixty votes) needed to stop the filibuster (called *cloture*). Majority party partisans argue that a 60–40 vote on nominations is unconstitutional, as the Constitution does not require a supermajority for judicial confirmation. Some favor a "nuclear option" that would change Senate rules to prohibit the filibustering of judicial nominees.

Nevertheless, minority partisans defend their right to prevent confirmations of extreme ideologues. They argue that though the Constitution does not require a supermajority for judicial confirmation, neither does it require a simple majority – it just does not say. Additionally, they assert that they are protecting minority rights, a matter of major importance given the life term served by federal judges.[15]

Republicans have claimed that Democrats are being uncooperative, denying President Bush the opportunity to make appointments to the lower federal courts. Nevertheless, according to a report by Senator Leahy, who chaired the Senate Judiciary Committee during Democratic control, the Senate held hearings on 103 of 114 Bush nominees during the 107th Congress (2001–2002).[16] The committee approved and the Senate confirmed 100 of those nominations.

Senator Leahy also presents average time from nomination to confirmation, showing that during Democratic control, nominees waited 150 days on average from nomination to confirmation, compared with 375 days on average during Republican control immediately before the Democratic takeover. He also shows that Democrats confirmed more judges than did Republicans when they were in control: 245 judges in five Grand Old Party (GOP) years, as compared with 100 in a year and a half. The confirmation of 72 judges in 2002 was more than in any other year of Republican control.

Democrats complain about Republicans and Republicans about Democrats in this regard. Indeed, some notable Democrats opposed filibusters of Democratic nominations. To wit, during the Clinton administration, Senator Tom Daschle: "An up or down vote, that is all we ask";[17] "I find it simply baffling that a Senator would vote against even voting on a judicial nomination";[18] Senator Patrick Leahy said, "I would object to and fight against any filibuster on a judge, whether it was somebody I opposed or supported,"[19] and "It is the responsibility of the U.S. Senate to at least bring them to a vote."[20] Both, of course, support and defend filibusters against GOP nominees. And Republicans now label Democrats anti-Hispanic, anti-Catholic, anti-Baptist, and antiwoman because of these filibusters. Jorge C. Rangel, a Hispanic Clinton nominee who received neither a committee hearing nor a vote by the Republican-controlled Senate, asked in September 2003, "Where was the outrage from your Republican colleagues when Enrique Moreno and I were denied the courtesy of a hearing on our nominations? Where was their disappointment and cry for diversity on the bench when I was compelled to [withdraw]?"[21]

Of course, nomination disputes revolve about the ideology of nominees. A 2003 *New York Times* editorial got it right when it pointed out that "Republican and Democratic senators know what they are fighting over: legitimate disagreements over how to interpret the Constitution and define the role of a

---

[15] National Women's Law Center, "A Response to Arguments That a Filibuster on the Estrada Nomination Is Unprecedented or Inappropriate." Available online at http://www.nwlc.org.

[16] Leahy, "Nominations."

[17] *Congressional Record*, 5 October 1999.

[18] *Id.*

[19] *Congressional Record*, 18 June 1998.

[20] *Congressional Record*, 22 October 1997.

[21] David Espo, "Dems Unmoved by Notion of Estrada Payback," *Associated Press*, 5 September 2003.

federal judge. They owe it to the American people to be honest about their differences."[22]

As mentioned in Chapter 8, same-party appointment rates to the federal courts run very high. Overall, presidents nominate members of their party 93.2 percent of the time.[23] At least nine of ten appointees to the court of appeals were members of the president's political party during the Roosevelt, Truman, Eisenhower, Kennedy, Johnson, Nixon, Ford, and Reagan administrations. Only Carter appointed fewer partisans – his rate was 82 percent.[24]

The objects of these nomination battles look a lot like the judges at the district court level: They are male, white, around fifty years old, and wealthy, although the Clinton cohort was notably less male and less white – 45 percent of his nominees were white males compared with 70 percent of Bush's, 92 percent of Reagan's, and 61 percent of Carter's.[25] The one notable difference between district court and court of appeals nominees is that the latter tend to have had prior judicial experience: 69 percent of Clinton's nominees, 62 percent of Bush's, 60 percent of Reagan's, and 54 percent of Carter's.[26]

JURISDICTION

Geography bounds the jurisdiction of the court of appeals, as states are placed in circuits (see Table 8.1 for a listing of states and territories in each circuit) and jurisdiction is, as mentioned, both appellate and mandatory. Courts of appeals receive frivolous as well as important cases and have little power to curb the former or encourage the latter. The courts do not treat all such cases equally, however, granting oral argument and producing a published opinion in only a small portion of their cases.

The cases usually originate in the district courts (see Figure 9.1); most of the others are decisions of administrative agencies. Because of its geographical location, the District of Columbia circuit hears most of the administrative agency appeals. Whereas they constitute only 7 percent of the total caseload of the circuit courts, 33 percent of the D.C. court's docket is devoted to these cases.[27]

The subject matter jurisdiction of the district courts also applies here: a federal question or diversity of citizenship. They cannot render advisory opinions, can hear only real controversies, cannot resolve so-called political questions, and can hear a case only after all other remedies are exhausted. If these conditions are not met, or if the appeal was not properly made, the court disposes of the case procedurally, not on its merits.

[22] *New York Times*, Editorial, "Straight Talk on Judicial Nominees," 10 September 2003.

[23] Barrow et al., *Federal Judiciary*.

[24] Sheldon Goldman, *Picking Federal Judges: Lower Court Selection from Roosevelt through Reagan* (New Haven, CT: Yale University Press, 1997).

[25] Robert A. Carp and Ronald Stidham, *Judicial Process in America*, 4th ed. (Washington, DC: Congressional Quarterly Press, 1998), pp. 214–216.

[26] *Id.*

[27] Administrative Office of the U.S. Courts, Table B-3.

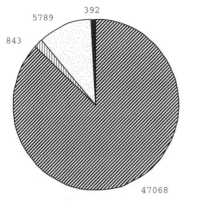

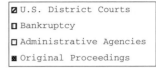

Figure 9.1. Sources of Appeals in the Circuit Courts, September 2002. *Source:* Administrative Office of the U.S. Courts, "Judicial Business of U.S. Courts, 2002," Table B-3.

CASELOAD

As noted, the original courts of appeals sat as both trial and appellate courts. In 1892, they heard a total of 840 cases.[28] By 1925, when they became full appellate courts, 2,525 cases were appealed to them; by 1975, the number had exploded to 16,571; and by 1988, to 37,524.[29]

Nevertheless, district court dockets have increased much more than those of the courts of appeals, although the latter also set a new caseload record each year.[30] In 2002, appeals from administrative agencies showed the highest increase, surging 75 percent over 2001 largely as a result of immigration cases. On average, 25.9 months elapsed from initial filing in the lower court (usually the district court) to final appellate disposition in 2002.[31]

Numbers

Figure 9.2 represents the total caseload of the circuit courts for the years 1992–2003. The raw numbers show that these courts are busy, but not nearly as busy as the district courts (compare Figures 8.2a and 8.2b.); second, appeals increased each year except 1994, 2000, and 2002, but they are small; finally (not shown on the figure), the Ninth Circuit is consistently the busiest, not surprisingly given its size, but the Fifth Circuit is not far behind, especially in recent years. The First and D.C. Circuits and the Federal Circuit receive the smallest number of appeals each year.

[28] Barrow et al., *Federal Judiciary*, p. 30.
[29] Donald R. Songer, Reginald S. Sheehan, Susan B. Haire, *Continuity and Change on the United States Courts of Appeals* (Ann Arbor: University of Michigan Press, 2000).
[30] Administrative Office of the United States Courts, *2002 Annual Report of the Director: Judicial Business of the United States Courts* (Washington, DC: U.S. Government Printing Office, 2003).
[31] *Id.*

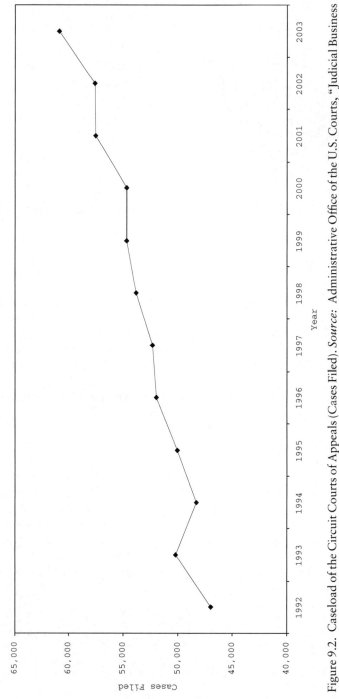

Figure 9.2. Caseload of the Circuit Courts of Appeals (Cases Filed). *Source:* Administrative Office of the U.S. Courts, "Judicial Business of U.S. Courts, 2002," Table B.

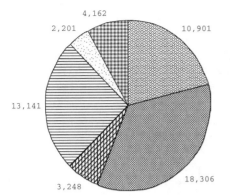

Figure 9.3. Types of Cases Terminated in the Courts of Appeals, September 2001–September 2002. *Source:* Administrative Office of the U.S. Courts, "Judicial Business of U.S. Courts, 2002," Table B-7.

Types of Cases

The types of cases the courts hear reflect those heard in the district courts, where most of them begin. Civil cases far outnumber criminal cases and, as are cases ended before trial, quite a few are disposed of procedurally, either because the court lacks jurisdiction or because the appeal was not perfected. Note also that the D.C. Circuit, as mentioned earlier, receives the largest percentage of administrative appeals (35 percent in September 2001–September 2002). Over time, the courts of appeals have attracted more policy-laden cases, hearing a larger proportion of civil rights cases than earlier in their history.[32] See Figure 9.3.

In addition to procedural grounds for termination, the circuits lessen their workload by disposing of cases either without written opinion or by order and without publication. Figure 9.4a shows the type of opinion issued in all cases decided between September 2001 and September 2002, and Figure 9.4b specifies the published proportion. A large majority (80.5 percent) are unpublished decisions; for instance, the Fourth Circuit publishes a mere 8 percent of its decisions!

What exactly does nonpublication mean? When a panel finds that a case resolves no new point of law, makes no circuit precedent, and does not conflict with another decision of another circuit or panel, it can opt to leave the decision unpublished. If the decision locates in a new or evolving area of law, has substantial political importance, has ramifications for parties not before the court, or is accompanied by a dissent or if the lower court published its decision, publication usually results. This system allows judges to focus their

---

[32] Songer et al., *Continuity*, Table 1.2, p. 15.

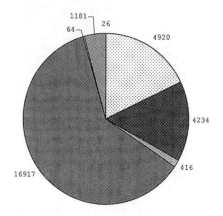

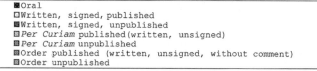

Figure 9.4a. Types of Opinions or Orders Filed, September 2001–September 2002. *Source:* Administrative Office of the U.S. Courts, "Judicial Business of U.S. Courts, 2002," Table S-3.

attention on more important cases and lessens attention to cases superfluous to the circuit's case law.[33]

The decision to designate a disposition as *not for publication* once meant that only the parties would receive the opinion, although one could purchase these opinions at the circuit's courthouse. Today, however, it has a fuzzier meaning. Because judicial decisions are now published electronically, and because a publisher now publishes these unpublished decisions,[34] we face the odd phenomenon of "published unpublished" decisions. This leaves lawyers arguing before the circuits in a quandary: Do they consider unpublished decisions, or do they pretend these do not exist?

For the most part, unpublished decisions are not to be cited as precedent. Yet violations occur as lawyers do refer to them during argument.[35] Judges sometimes cite unpublished decisions in published opinions. In *Valdez v. McPheeters,*[36] for example, the judges wrote, "This court has recently agreed in

---

[33] Jonathan Matthew Cohen, *Inside Appellate Courts: The Impact of Court Organization on Judicial Decision Making in the U.S. Court of Appeals* (Ann Arbor: University of Michigan Press, 2002).

[34] West Publishing now publishes *The Federal Supplement*, which contains all unpublished decisions.

[35] Sara C. Benesh, "Nonpublication and the Hierarchy of Justice: Supreme Court Review of Circuit Court Decisions," Presented at the Annual Meeting of the Midwest Political Science Association, 2002.

[36] 172 F. 3d 1220 (1999), at 1224.

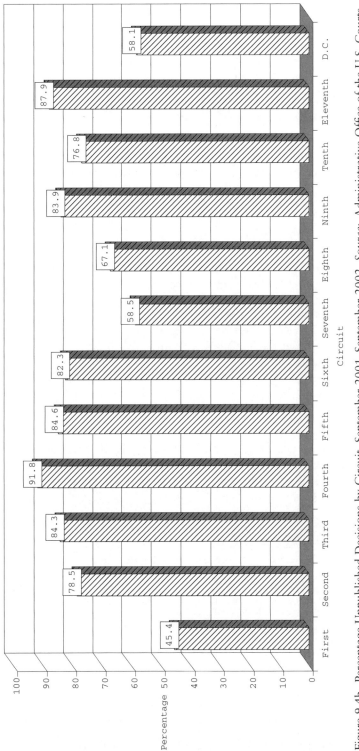

Figure 9.4b. Percentage Unpublished Decisions by Circuit, September 2001–September 2002. *Source:* Administrative Office of the U.S. Courts, "Judicial Business of U.S. Courts, 2002," Table S-3.

an unpublished decision, *Anderson v. Campbell*, 1996 WL 731244 (10th Circ. 1996)." An advisory committee of the U.S. Judicial Conference is considering a new rule mandating that such opinions be citable.[37] This might affect the stated reason for the no-citation rule: that of saving time. According to some, if attorneys freely cited these decisions and if judges also did so, they might as well make them published opinions.

Much controversy surrounds this process, besides their citability. Indeed, some call it "a harmful practice that undermines the legitimacy of the judicial process as well as the ability of lawyers and the public to know and apply the law."[38] In addition, scholars differ about whether or not the circuits actually leave only "unimportant" and "nonprecedential" cases unpublished. Some say that the circuits do well determining which decisions should be precedential and which should not.[39] Others argue that these decisions are not made in an informed manner.[40] Still others suggest that perhaps the circuits hide decisions that are noncompliant with Supreme Court precedent in unpublished opinions.

Nevertheless, the Supreme Court has done nothing to dissuade the circuits (or the districts, for that matter) from nonpublication.[41] Litigants do receive unpublished dispositions even if the rest of the world does not. If the appeals court were misbehaving in these cases, losing litigants would probably appeal, and no evidence indicates that the appeal rate of unpublished decisions approximates that of published decisions.

PROCEDURES

The courts of appeals are collegial courts. Indeed, in each circuit, panels of three judges are assigned usually randomly and usually by the central support staff to hear a set of cases each month. This means that they have a much different institutional makeup than the Supreme Court, as colleagues change each time

---

[37] Tony Mauro, "Toward Citing the Uncitable," *National Law Journal*, 26 May 2003.

[38] Cohen, *Appellate Court*, p. 74.

[39] See, e.g., Stephen L. Wasby, "Unpublished Dispositions: Are the Criteria Followed?" Presented at the 99th Annual Meeting of the American Political Science Association, Philadelphia, August 2003.

[40] See, e.g., William L. Reynolds and William M. Richman, "The Non-Precedential Precedent – Limited Publication No-Citation Rules in the United States Courts of Appeals," 78(6) *Columbia Law Review* (1978): 1167–1208, and Pamela Foa, "A Snake in the Path of Law: The Seventh Circuits' Non-Publication Rule," 39 *University of Pittsburgh Law Review* (1977): 309–40.

[41] In 1972, the Supreme Court, while remanding to the court of appeals for further explanation, failed to comment on the practice of nonpublication (*Taylor v. McKeithen*, 407 U.S. 191). In 1976, *Do-Right Auto Sales v. U.S. Court of Appeals for the Seventh Circuit* (429 U.S. 917) mounted a direct attack on the no-citation rule for unpublished decisions, and again, the Supreme Court declined comment. In 1977, the Supreme Court denied an application for an order to issue a printed opinion (*Chin v. U.S.*, 434 U.S. 937), and in *Browder v. Director, Department of Corrections of Illinois* (434 U.S. 257 (1978)) the Court said they would leave questions of the validity of the Seventh Circuit's nonpublication rule "to another day" (at 258, 1).

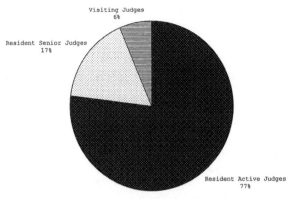

Figure 9.5. Total Case Participations on the Circuit Courts by Judge Type. *Source:* Administrative Office of the U.S. Courts, "Judicial Business of U.S. Courts, 2002," Table S-3.

they hear a new set of cases. In addition, the circuits use senior, district court, and visiting judges from other circuits to help with their caseload. Therefore, a judge's colleague on the bench may be an old friend or someone he or she has only just met, and that situation may affect decision making.

Although circuit court judges generally seem to appreciate the extra help from their retired and district court brethren, they also complain about it, because, in their view, it causes more work for the full-time judges on that particular panel. The visitors are less predictable; they disrupt the culture; they tend to defer to the circuit judges; they decrease collegiality; and they do not pull their weight, according to some judges. Obviously, visitors who are district court judges have plenty of their own work to do. However, in addition to providing a third body, the presence of a visiting judge may encourage circuit judges to be more prepared and more congenial, and one judge described the visitors from neighboring circuits as "somebody coming off the bench from your own baseball team."[42]

Regardless of the circuit judges' views, visitors are employed quite often. As Figure 9.5 indicates, a senior or visiting judge participated in 23 percent of all cases (again, numbers are for September 2001–September 2002). Indeed, in the Sixth Circuit 49 percent of all cases contained a senior or visiting judge.

Agenda Setting

The first step in agenda setting is the screening process. The central staff, composed of attorneys, screen all of the appeals that go to the circuit court, deciding which should receive "full dress treatment" and which should not. For those that do not merit full treatment, they draft memorandum dispositions and present them to the panel for discussion. These cases become summary

---

[42] Cohen, *Appellate Courts*, p. 193.

dispositions (e.g., a disposition accompanied only by a memorandum and without oral argument), and the memorandum drafted by the staff attorney is usually endorsed by the panel as dispositive.

Once cases are deemed meritorious enough for full-dress treatment, they are randomly assigned to panels whose membership varies. Only a few exceptions apply: A set of similar cases are usually all assigned to one panel, and especially complex cases are distributed as evenly as possible across panels. Politics may also intervene. In the early 1960s, the chief judge of the Fifth Circuit overassigned civil rights cases to the minority of judges in the circuit who supported civil rights. This favoritism lasted until one of the conservative judges objected. No bias occurred thereafter, but by then, the circuit had a pro–civil rights majority.[43]

In preparation for oral argument, bench memoranda are prepared, in some circuits by each judge's chambers individually and in others via use of a pool of chambers. These bench memoranda, which are "road maps" to the case, are usually written by clerks, as judges rarely have time to review the entire record.[44] These road maps, which vary in their length, also vary in importance to the judges. Some judges use them as their sole preparation for oral argument; others regard them as a reminder of key aspects of the case; still others do not use them at all. Judges differentially rely on case briefs, clerical research, and oral argument.

Oral Argument

The number of appeals decided without oral argument is increasing rapidly and is, as is publication, a means for dealing more efficiently with circuit workload. For example, in 1981, 63 percent of cases were orally argued; in 1987, 51 percent; in 1995, 40 percent; and in 2000, only 35 percent. Although this saves time, it may also preclude judges from receiving pertinent information.

Nevertheless, many cases in each circuit continue to be argued orally. All judges sit on a three-judge panel one week during most months, and the panels hear oral argument in roughly twenty to thirty cases. Several panels sit at once on some circuits; in others, where all argument is heard in one location, they occur almost weekly. They vary in length, as the judges' discretion determines the time allotted. Most common is twenty to thirty minutes per side.[45]

Opinion Writing

After argument, the judges convene to determine who will write the opinion in all cases, argued or not. The chief judge of the circuit, when on the panel and in

[43] Burt Atkins and William Zavoina, "Judicial Leadership on the Courts of Appeals," 18 *American Journal of Political Science* 701 (1974).

[44] Cohen, *Appellate Courts*. Much of what follows is from Cohen.

[45] Songer et al., *Continuity*.

the majority, assigns the majority opinion to one of the judges; on other panels, the most senior active judge on the panel assigns. If shared bench memoranda are used, usually the author of the bench memo in the case is given the task of writing the opinion, because that judge's chambers are most familiar with the case. Some circuits allow judges to request cases of particular interest, others employ random opinion distribution, but care is taken to spread the workload evenly.

Each judge is authorized to hire three clerks, and the chief of the circuit has the option of having either four clerks or an additional administrative assistant. The judges directly select their clerks, employing personal criteria (law school pedigree, grades, law review editorship, ideological congruence, interview, etc.) as they see fit. Most judges rely on their law clerks for a first draft of a decision. Generally, the judge indicates to the clerk the result preferred and what the general argument ought to be. Some judges supervise the initial draft, and others do not. Most judges interviewed in one study asserted that, through editing, the resulting opinion was most certainly their own.[46]

The opinion author makes the decision to publish, taking into account the preferences of the other judges on the panel. Some judges who disagree with the decision but would otherwise quietly assent threaten to dissent if publication occurs.[47]

Circuit court judges do not verbally communicate much with one another over drafts of opinions, preferring written communication. According to interviews with judges and clerks, very little communication occurs before oral argument or with those not on the panel.[48] They do have a postargument conference, at which they express their preferences and assign the opinion, but other than that work continues independently, and communication is largely limited to e-mail because the judges return to their home offices, which are not necessarily near the place where they hear cases.

En bancs

Once a panel makes a decision, any judge in the circuit or any party to the case may request that the case be reviewed *en banc*. *En banc* review means that all active judges on the circuit review the decision of the panel, although in the large Ninth Circuit, mini–*en bancs*, in which ten randomly chosen judges, plus the chief judge, review the appealed decision, are used. Once an *en banc* is requested, the judge calling for *en banc* review, as well as the panel judges, circulates memos whether to review the decision.[49] All active judges on the circuit then vote whether to rehear the case. If a majority of the judges believe the

[46] Cohen, *Appellate Courts*, p. 116.
[47] Wasby, "Unpublished Dispositions."
[48] Cohen, *Appellate Courts*, p. 91.
[49] Stephen L. Wasby, "The Supreme Court and Courts of Appeals En Banc," 33 *McGeorge Law Review* (2001), pp. 20, 23.

case to be "exceptionally important," or necessary to ensure circuit uniformity, or to correct an error in the application of Supreme Court precedent, an *en banc* is scheduled.[50] Most often, the judges so vote because they do not agree with the decision reached by the panel.[51]

Circuits rarely decide *en banc*, resolving fewer than 1 percent of cases in that manner.[52] The *en banc* is both a signal to the Supreme Court of an important decision and another way to keep circuit panels in line with circuit and Supreme Court precedent.[53]

DECISION MAKING

As noted, the courts of appeals have mandatory jurisdiction. Nevertheless, they receive plenty of noteworthy appeals and make plenty of noteworthy decisions. Indeed, over time, they have had increased opportunities to make policy. In the 1925–1936 decade, they mainly heard private economic disputes that had little effect on public policy; in 1970–1988, they mainly heard criminal cases, and, more importantly, 18.5 percent of their docket dealt with civil rights and civil liberties. In 1925–1936, only 1.7 percent of their docket was so composed.[54]

So these courts clearly have the capability to make policy. They have been the final arbiter in many controversial policies, one example of which is the ability of homosexuals to serve in the military.

Recall the Clinton administration's "Don't Ask, Don't Tell" policy. That policy, codified both in congressional legislation and in Department of Defense directives, amended the military's old policy, that homosexuality was incompatible with military service, to the policy that "persons who demonstrate a propensity or intent to engage in homosexual acts would create an unacceptable risk."[55] In other words, *being* a homosexual is no longer prohibited; however, engaging in or intending to engage in homosexual acts is. No longer does the military ask recruits about their sexual orientation. However, if it is called to the attention of the military that a service person "engages in or intends to engage in homosexual acts";[56] "makes a statement that he is homosexual and fails to rebut the presumption, raised by that statement, that he has a propensity to

---

[50] Songer et al., *Continuity*, p. 12. These reasons derive from Rule 35 of the Federal Rules of Appellate Procedure.

[51] Wasby, "The Supreme Court," pp. 20–23.

[52] Tracey E. George, "The Dynamics and Determinants of the Decision to Grant En Banc Review," 74 *Washington Law Review* 213–274 (1999).

[53] See, e.g., Virginia Hettinger, Stefanie Lindquist, and Wendy L. Martinek, "Comparing Attitudinal and Strategic Accounts of Dissenting Behavior on the U.S. Courts of Appeals," 48 *American Journal of Political Science* 123 (2004).

[54] Songer et al., *Continuity*, p. 54.

[55] 10 U.S.C. S 654(a) (15).

[56] *Id*. at S 654(b) (1).

engage in homosexual acts";[57] or "has married or attempted to marry a person of the same biological sex,"[58] that service member is discharged.

Neither that policy nor the exclusionary policy that preceded it (which completely banned gays from military service) has ever been reviewed by the Supreme Court. Rather, the policy has been tested in the circuit courts,[59] and, because those circuits all deemed the policy constitutional, service in the military remains open only to those who are not likely to engage in homosexual activity.

Take, for example, the Ninth Circuit's decision in *Holmes v. California National Guard.*[60] At issue in that case was the discharge of two servicemen, both of whom had an excellent service record. In one case, Watson, a navy lieutenant, disclosed his homosexual orientation in the interest of honesty and a desire to preclude fodder for blackmail. In so doing, he did not rebut the assumption made by the "Don't Ask, Don't Tell" legislation that admitting homosexual orientation presumes one is likely to engage in homosexual activity. If that presumption is not rebutted, that assumed propensity to engage in homosexual activity is grounds for discharge. Hence, he was honorably discharged "by reason of homosexual conduct."[61] Watson appealed the discharge, making a statement in which he denied engaging in or intending to engage in any type of homosexual conduct with any military student or service member or on any military base. However, because he failed to deny intent or actual activity outside the base and because this regulation against homosexual conduct reaches to off-base, off-duty activity as well, the discharge was upheld. Watson appealed this action to the district court, alleging that "the 'don't ask/don't tell' policy, on its face or as applied, violates Watson's right to equal protection and substantive due process under the Fifth Amendment and to free speech under the First Amendment."[62] The district court rejected his claim because Watson's discharge, according to the court, was based on a likelihood of homosexual conduct as inferred from his statements.

The other service member involved in this appeal is Holmes, a first lieutenant in the California and United States National Guards. Holmes, as did Watson, voluntarily disclosed his homosexual orientation "as a matter of conscience, honesty, and pride."[63] On the basis of this statement, which again triggered the section of the policy that presumes that a statement regarding homosexual orientation is also an admission of homosexual conduct or intent to engage in such conduct, the commanding officer began the process of withdrawing

[57] *Id.* at S 654(b) (2).
[58] *Id.* at S 654(b) (3).
[59] *Holmes v. California National Guard,* 124 F. 3d 1126 (1997); *Richenberg v. Perry,* 97 F. 3d 256 (1996); *Able v. United States,* 88 F. 3d 1280 (1996); *Thomasson v. Perry,* 80 F. 3d 915 (1996).
[60] The circuit combined two claims in this case, both Andrew Holmes's and Richard P. Watson's. 124 F. 3d 1126 (1997).
[61] *Id.* at 1130.
[62] *Id.*
[63] *Id.* at 1131.

Holmes's membership in the Guard. Holmes did not rebut that presumption and so was discharged. Holmes appealed this decision to the district court and won. That court determined that "the presumption in S 654(b) (2), which is triggered by a statement of homosexual orientation, unconstitutionally punishes Holmes for speech and for status as a homosexual, rather than for conduct."[64]

The Ninth Circuit upheld the Watson court, which found that "Don't Ask, Don't Tell" is not violative of the First and Fifth Amendments, and overturned the Holmes court, which did find such a violation. Relying on precedents in the Second, Fourth, and Eighth Circuits[65] and the Supreme Court's denial of certiorari in *Thomasson v. Perry*,[66] Judge Wiggins's opinion declared that the policy is constitutional both on its face and as applied.

Using a "rational basis" level of review, the court found that the regulations against homosexual conduct are rationally related to the legitimate governmental purpose of "discipline and combat readiness in the military by preventing risks to unit cohesion posed by the presence of . . . homosexuals."[67] Additionally, the government may rationally presume from statements admitting homosexual orientation that a person will engage in homosexual activity. Quoting an Eighth Circuit decision, Wiggins ruled that "it is rational to assume that both homosexuals and heterosexuals are likely to act in accordance with their sexual drives."[68] Because neither Watson nor Holmes rebutted that link between orientation and action, they tacitly accepted that linkage. Therefore, because the court found that the servicemen were discharged not for their statement or their sexual orientation but for an inference of homosexual conduct, their discharges were constitutional. This was not speech, according to the court, but conduct.

This decision, unlike most at the courts of appeals level, was accompanied by a strong dissent, connoting the strong policy ramifications of this decision. Judge Reinhardt took issue with the court's finding that the discharges were not based on speech. Although he categorized the "Don't Ask, Don't Tell" policy as "somewhat schizoid,"[69] he relied on its distinction between being a homosexual and engaging in homosexual conduct to reach his decision. According to Judge Reinhardt, because homosexual status is acceptable and is not a ground for discharge,

admitting to that status – the statement that "I am a homosexual" – cannot itself be a cause for discharge. There can be nothing wrong about admitting to a status that is proper. . . . Clearly, therefore, it is not the status that is being punished; it is the speech. Punishing speech that does no more than acknowledge a permissible status violates the First Amendment. There is no legitimate, let alone compelling, governmental interest in

---

[64] *Id.* at 1131.
[65] *Holmes v. California, Richenberg v. Perry, Able v. United States, Thomasson v. Perry.*
[66] 117 519 U.S. 548 358 (1996).
[67] 124 F. 3d 1126 (1997), 1133.
[68] *Id.* at 1135.
[69] *Id.* at 1137.

punishing a serviceman's acknowledgment that he is a member of a group that is eligible for military service.[70]

He continues,

There can be no doubt that the "Don't Ask, Don't Tell" policy severely burdens speech. It unquestionably has the effect of chilling speech by homosexual service members – speech that is of tremendous importance to the individuals involved, speech that goes to the right to communicate the core of their emotions and identity to others. Given the regulation's provisions that permit homosexuals to serve in the armed forces, and that punish only homosexual conduct, there is no reasonable basis for prohibiting a service member from engaging in speech that serves only to declare his or her homosexual status. Lieutenants Holmes and Watson will be discharged not because they have engaged in prohibited conduct and not because they are homosexual. Rather the military seeks to exclude them because they spoke openly of their homosexual status.[71]

A couple of votes on a couple of panels could, presumably, change the face of the military. The decision to uphold "Don't Ask, Don't Tell" has had a profound effect on the membership of the military, on the deference given Congress and the president on matters military, and on the rights of a large group of American servicemen and servicewomen. And the Supreme Court has had nothing to say about it.

As with the set of cases discussed, the Supreme Court rarely concerns itself with the rulings of the courts of appeals: It reviews less than one-half of 1 percent of their cases.[72] And of those, it reverses only two-thirds, leaving the court of appeals decision intact in 99.7 percent of all cases.[73] Scholars have struggled, therefore, to determine what drives the high rates of compliance the appeals courts exhibit toward Supreme Court precedent. (These studies are discussed in detail in Chapter 14.) One might assume, and judges have told us, that the desire to prevent reversal is great and that this desire drives compliance.[74] Though reversal rates are low, the most aberrant decisions might be prime targets for Supreme Court review (see Chapter 11). Think of the few nails that stick out as being most likely to get the hammer. Because no one wants to be hammered, this puts pressure on individual panels generally to comply with the Supreme Court.

Nevertheless, given the rarity of that review, perhaps that interpretation does not wholly explain the propensity of the lower court to heed its principal. It is certainly true that when someone claims she will take her case all the way to the Supreme Court, the sentiment is heartfelt. Nevertheless, it would be more realistic to say she will take it all the way to the U.S. Courts of Appeals.

---

[70] *Id.* at 1138.

[71] *Id.* at 1140.

[72] Songer et al., *Continuity*, p. 17.

[73] *Id.*

[74] Lawrence Baum, "Lower-Court Response to Supreme Court Decisions: Reconsidering a Negative Picture," 3 *Justice System Journal* 208 (1978).

Perhaps legal socialization helps drive compliance: That is, "The impetus to comply comes from what the Supreme Court *is* rather than what it *does*."[75] Indeed, interviews with judges report that they are dedicated to achieving the "right" result in each case, usually defined as the one that comports most closely with Supreme Court and circuit court precedent.[76]

That said, it becomes increasingly important to understand the decision making of these courts. Because we have established that they can and do make policy, and that the Supreme Court does not often interfere, these courts become highly interesting and significant from a behavioral standpoint. How do they make decisions? How do the correlates of their decisions differ from those of trial courts and the Supreme Court? Scholars have only begun to answer these questions.

Institutional Constraints

The court of appeals is unusually positioned institutionally. Located in the middle of the federal judicial hierarchy, it must concern itself both with the Supreme Court, in terms of complying with its rulings, and with the district courts, in terms of gaining their compliance. Many scholars have noted decision-making differences between the circuits and the Supreme Court. "Members of the Supreme Court further their policy goals because they lack electoral or political accountability, ambition for higher office, and comprise a court of last resort that controls its own jurisdiction."[77] But judges on the appeals court may have ambition for higher office, and perhaps that ambition affects their decision making. Judges deny being motivated by the possibility of elevation given the small number of vacancies that occur. Some would rather avoid the harsh confirmation battles that a High Court nomination can trigger, as did that of Clarence Thomas.[78] It is possible, however, that these judges may, at times, temper their decisions with an eye toward how they might be received in the Supreme Court confirmation process.

Second, these courts do not constitute a court of last resort, at least not in theory. The Supreme Court does not often review and overturn their decisions; in practice, they are the court of last resort for most federal litigation. Nevertheless, the fact of possible Supreme Court review may indeed affect their decision making. Interviews provide mixed evidence, as some judges admit to keeping track of their reversal records and others say that it matters not at all to them whether they are reversed or not. Nevertheless, the formal constraint that theirs is not the last word almost certainly affects their behavior. Indeed,

---

[75] Sara C. Benesh, *The U.S. Court of Appeals and the Law of Confessions: Perspectives on the Hierarchy of Justice* (New York: LFB Scholarly Publishing, 2002), p. 129.

[76] Cohen, *Appellate Courts*, p. 44, and David E. Klein, *Making Law in the United States Courts of Appeals* (Cambridge: Cambridge University Press, 2002).

[77] Jeffrey A. Segal and Harold J. Spaeth, *The Supreme Court and the Attitudinal Model* (Cambridge: Cambridge University Press, 1993), p. 69.

[78] Cohen, *Appellate Courts*, p. 45.

as the studies in Chapter 14 show, the Supreme Court matters heavily to the decision making of the court of appeals, whether measured by the influence of Supreme Court precedent or Supreme Court ideology.

Finally, as mentioned, these courts do not control their own dockets; they have mandatory jurisdiction. Unlike the Supreme Court, they receive many cases in which "the law" clearly points in one direction, leaving them little decisional discretion. Moreover, mandatory jurisdiction means that these courts spend most of their time deciding cases of little consequence. Though these courts do make policy and occasionally draw national attention, in general, they deal with more mundane cases, and, hence, their caseload likely affects the determinants of their behavior.

Other constraints also affect decision making at this level, such as legal socialization. As one judge stated:

Judges are constrained to follow the formal doctrinal rules by both formal means (the threat of being overturned either by the Supreme Court or by an en banc panel of the circuit court) and by a cultural, institutional force. Moreover, the cultural imperative carries more force than the formal imperative because . . . justices recognize how unlikely it is that they will be reversed.[79]

Additionally, when the Supreme Court is silent or not particularly helpful on a given point of law, these judges may pursue a variety of goals.[80] These include promoting policies consistent with a judge's policy preferences; seeking legally sound decisions; maintaining legal coherence and consistency; and limiting time spent deciding any one particular case. Several considerations influence acceptance of a new rule promulgated by one of their colleagues: Ideological distance between a rule and the judge considering adoption reduces the likelihood that adoption will occur; more prestigious rule authors (especially in difficult cases) and those with greater expertise in the area are more likely to be followed; rules garnering more circuit support are advantaged; rules accompanied by dissents are less likely to be adopted.[81] These considerations point to some ideological as well as legal influences.

Norms may affect decision making as well. For example, a norm of consensus seems manifest.[82] (See Figure 9.6 for the percentage of cases over time with at least one dissent.) Perhaps it results because judges believe that "court culture teaches that a court that presents a unified face, has fewer fragmented opinions, has a higher degree of civility among its judges, speaks with a higher degree of moral authority and enjoys a higher degree of legitimacy."[83] Or maybe it is just that they do not have enough time to engage in the luxury of dissenting.

All of the preceding analysis suggests that court of appeals decision making involves much more than the judges' policy preferences. Ideology matters, but it

[79] *Id.* at 180.
[80] Klein, *Making Law*, pp. 11, 133–134.
[81] *Id.*
[82] Hettinger et al., *Dissenting Behavior*, p. 130.
[83] Cohen, *Appellate Courts*, p. 173.

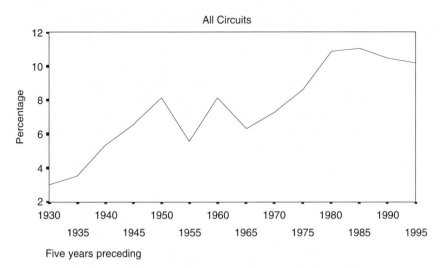

Figure 9.6. Dissensus in the Appeals Courts: Percentage of Cases with Dissenting Votes. *Source:* Donald R. Songer, "The United States Courts of Appeals Database, Phase I," available at http://www.as.uky.edu/polisci/ulmerproject.htm.

is not ideology alone that explains this decision making.[84] Because of differences from the Supreme Court and resulting institutional constraints, we expect these judges to behave in a less ideologically charged manner.

Testing for Ideology in Decision Making

In order to determine the extent to which ideology matters in the court of appeals, we employ a series of simple cross-tabulations designed to measure the differences in behavior of Democrats and Republicans and then of men and women and of minorities and whites. The results of our analyses can be found in Tables 9.3–9.10.[85] We start with Figure 9.7, which shows the percentage liberal (pro–rights of the accused) votes over time in criminal cases, and Figure 9.8, which shows the same percentage in civil rights cases (prowomen or prominorities). Most striking is the low percentage decided liberally. Given

---

[84] See, e.g., Benesh, *Law of Confessions*, p. 18; Hettinger et al., "Dissenting Behavior," p. 134; Donald R. Songer and Susan Haire, "Integrating Alternative Approaches to the Study of Judicial Voting: Obscenity Cases in the U.S. Court of Appeals," 36 *American Journal of Political Science* 963 (1992); Donald R. Songer, Jeffrey A. Segal, and Charles M. Cameron, "The Hierarchy of Justice: Testing a Principal–Agent Model of Surpeme Court–Circuit Court Interactions," 38 *American Journal of Political Science* 673 (1994); Steven Van Winkle, "Three-Judge Panels and Strategic Behavior on the U.S. Courts of Appeals," paper presented at the Annual Meeting of the Southern Political Science Association, Atlanta, 1996.

[85] Donald R. Songer, "The United States Courts of Appeals Database, Phase I," and Gary Zuk, Deborah J. Barrow, and Gerard S. Gryski, "Attributes of the United States Courts of Appeals Judges, 1801–1994." Both available online at http://www.as.uky.edu/polisci/ulmerproject.htm.

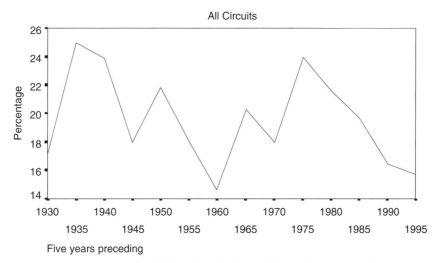

Figure 9.7. Percentage Liberal Decisions in Criminal Procedure Cases. *Source:* Donald R. Songer, "The United States Courts of Appeals Database, Phase I," available at http://www.as.uky.edu/polisci/ulmerproject.htm.

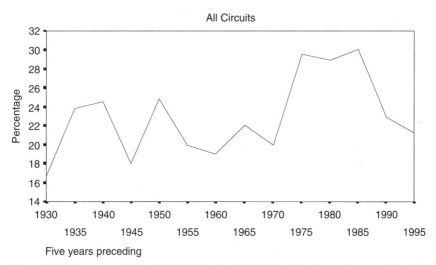

Figure 9.8. Percentage Liberal Decisions in Civil Liberties Cases. *Source:* Donald R. Songer, "The United States Courts of Appeals Database, Phase I," available at http://www.as.uky.edu/polisci/ulmerproject.htm.

that Democratic judges dominated the court of appeals bench at least some of the time, this shows, we think, the lack of meritorious appeals; ideology simply does not always explain all decision making.

Tables 9.3 and 9.4 show that although statistically significant differences exist between Democrats and Republicans in criminal and civil rights cases, they are not nearly as stark as one would expect at, say, the Supreme Court

Table 9.3. *Voting in Criminal Cases Sample, 1960–1996*

Direction of Vote	Party Identification of Judge		
	Republican	Democrat	Independent
Conservative	81.5%	76.2%	83.5%
Liberal	18.5%	23.8%	16.5%

Note: Chi-square = 45.252, significant at 0.000; N = 9,776.
Source: Donald R. Songer, "The United States Courts of Appeals Database, Phase I," and Gary Zuk, Deborah J. Barrow, and Gerald S. Gryski, "Attributes of the United States Courts of Appeals Judges, 1801–1994." Both available online at http://www.as.uky.edu/polisci/ulmerproject.htm.

Table 9.4. *Voting in Civil Rights Cases Sample, 1960–1996*

Direction of Vote	Party Identification of Judge		
	Republican	Democrat	Independent
Conservative	63.7%	53.9%	60.5%
Liberal	36.3%	46.1%	39.5%

Note: Chi-square = 28.942, significant at 0.000; N = 3,203.
Source: Donald R. Songer, "The United States Courts of Appeals Database, Phase I," and Gary Zuk, Deborah J. Barrow, and Gerald S. Gryski, "Attributes of the United States Courts of Appeals Judges, 1801–1994." Both available online at http://www.as.uky.edu/polisci/ulmerproject.htm.

Table 9.5. *Voting in Criminal Cases Accompanied by Dissent Sample, 1960–1996*

Direction of Vote	Party Identification of Judge		
	Republican	Democrat	Independent
Conservative	66.8%	42.7%	67.4%
Liberal	33.2%	57.3%	32.6%

Note: Chi-square = 49.200, significant at 0.000; N = 834.
Source: Donald R. Songer, "The United States Courts of Appeals Database, Phase I," and Gary Zuk, Deborah J. Barrow, and Gerald S. Gryski, "Attributes of the United States Courts of Appeals Judges, 1801–1994." Both available online at http://www.as.uky.edu/polisci/ulmerproject.htm.

level. We find, as expected, that Republicans vote more conservatively, but the differences are not large.

Perhaps significant or salient cases may produce a larger difference in partisan affiliation. As a proxy for salience, we use cases containing at least one dissent. We expect that judges will behave more ideologically in cases involving a dissent, the thinking being that these cases are more ideologically charged. Tables 9.5 and 9.6 test our expectations in this regard, and we do see a

Table 9.6. *Voting in Civil Rights Cases Accompanied by Dissent Sample, 1960–1996*

Direction of Vote	Party Identification of Judge		
	Republican	Democrat	Independent
Conservative	69.8%	35.6%	60%
Liberal	30.2%	64.4%	40%

Note: Chi-square = 39.937, significant at 0.000; $N = 354$.

Source: Donald R. Songer, "The United States Courts of Appeals Database, Phase I," and Gary Zuk, Deborah J. Barrow, and Gerald S. Gryski, "Attributes of the United States Courts of Appeals Judges, 1801–1994." Both available online at http://www.as.uky.edu/polisci/ulmerproject.htm.

Table 9.7. *Voting in Criminal Cases by Gender and Party Sample, 1960–1996*

Direction of Vote	Gender of Judge	
	Male	Female
	Republican	
Conservative	81.6%	76.0%
Liberal	18.4%	24.0%

Chi-square = 2.559, not significant
$N = 4,731$

	Democratic	
Conservative	76.2%	75.7%
Liberal	23.8%	24.3%

Chi-square = 0.017, not significant
$N = 4,493$

	Independent	
Conservative	82.5%	78.3%
Liberal	17.5%	21.7%

Chi-square = 0.204, not significant
$N = 86$

Source: Donald R. Songer, "The United States Courts of Appeals Database, Phase I," and Gary Zuk, Deborah J. Barrow, and Gerald S. Gryski, "Attributes of the United States Courts of Appeals Judges, 1801–1994." Both available online at http://www.as.uky.edu/polisci/ulmerproject.htm.

substantial ideological difference between the parties. In the criminal case subset (Table 9.5) Democrats vote liberally in a majority of their cases and Republicans vote conservatively in a majority of theirs. Likewise with civil rights cases, in which Democrats vote liberally even more often (see Table 9.6). It appears to be the case, then, that ideology matters in general, but it matters even more when the stakes are high.

Finally, we test the notion that party identification alone does not adequately capture ideology. Therefore, we examine judicial attributes, especially sex and race. We find (results not reported in tables) that in civil rights cases, women are more liberal (significant at 0.058), and in criminal cases, minorities are more liberal (significant at 0.000). (Sex does not produce a significant difference in criminal cases; minorities do not behave statistically differently in civil rights cases.) But what if we control for partisanship? Do these apparent differences between men and women and between minorities and whites disappear? To test for ideological differences across sex and race controlling for party, we present Tables 9.7–9.10. Now we see something a little different. Differences

Table 9.8. *Voting in Civil Rights Cases by Gender and Party Sample, 1960–1996*

Direction of Vote	Gender of Judge	
	Male	Female
Republican		
Conservative	63.6%	64.5%
Liberal	36.4%	35.5%
Chi-square = 0.020, not significant N = 1,563		
Democratic		
Conservative	54.7%	39.1%
Liberal	45.3%	60.9%
Chi-square = 6.386, significant at 0.012 N = 1,369		
Independent		
Conservative	61.3%	55.6%
Liberal	38.7%	44.4%
Chi-square = 0.096, not significant N = 40		

Source: Donald R. Songer, "The United States Courts of Appeals Database, Phase I," and Gary Zuk, Deborah J. Barrow, and Gerald S. Gryski, "Attributes of the United States Courts of Appeals Judges, 1801–1994." Both available online at http://www.as.uky.edu/polisci/ulmerproject.htm.

Table 9.9. *Voting in Criminal Cases by Race and Party Sample, 1960–1996*

Direction of Vote	Race of Judge	
	Minority[a]	White
Republican		
Conservative	77.1%	81.6%
Liberal	22.9%	18.4%
Chi-square = 1.258, not significant		
N = 4,731		
Democratic		
Conservative	67.7%	76.8%
Liberal	32.3%	23.2%
Chi-square = 12.163, significant at 0.000		
N = 4,493		
Independent		
Conservative	78.6%	83.6%
Liberal	21.4%	16.4%
Chi-square = 0.255, not significant		
N = 552		

[a] Included in minority are African American, Hispanic, Asian American, and Native American.

Source: Donald R. Songer, "The United States Courts of Appeals Database, Phase I," and Gary Zuk, Deborah J. Barrow, and Gerald S. Gryski, "Attributes of the United States Courts of Appeals Judges, 1801–1994." Both available online at http://www.as.uky.edu/polisci/ulmerproject.htm.

between women and men and between minorities and whites appear to locate exclusively within the Democratic Party. Table 9.8 shows that among Democrats, women are significantly more liberal than men in civil rights cases. In Table 9.9 we again find that only among Democrats are minorities significantly more liberal in criminal cases. No differences appear between women and men in criminal cases, nor between minorities and whites in civil rights cases. Notably, Republicans (and Independents) do not differ from one another in criminal or civil rights cases regardless of their race or sex.

CONCLUSION

The importance of the courts of appeals seems to be increasing as a result of the cases they hear and the infrequency of Supreme Court review. Clearly, they are on the radar screen of national politicians, as evidenced by reactions to their salient decisions and by the raucous fighting over who will staff this

Table 9.10. *Voting in Civil Rights Cases by Race and Party Sample, 1960–1996*

Direction of Vote	Race of Judge	
	Minority[a]	White
Republican		
Conservative	63.0%	63.7%
Liberal	37.0%	36.3%
Chi-square = 0.008, not significant		
N = 1,563		
Democratic		
Conservative	50.0%	54.3%
Liberal	50.0%	45.7%
Chi-square = 0.823, not significant		
N = 1,369		
Independent		
Conservative	62.5%	60.5%
Liberal	37.5%	39.5%
Chi-square = 0.014, not significant		
N = 271		

[a] Included in minority are African American, Hispanic, Asian American, and Native American.

Source: Donald R. Songer, "The United States Courts of Appeals Database, Phase I," and Gary Zuk, Deborah J. Barrow, and Gerald S. Gryski, "Attributes of the United States Courts of Appeals Judges, 1801–1994." Both available online at http://www.as.uky.edu/polisci/ulmerproject.htm.

bench. Looking more closely, we find an institution constrained both by its institutional rules (including a mandatory docket and norms of consensus) and by its institutional position (as inferior to the U.S. Supreme Court), but that remains concerned with and capable of making policy. As scholarly study of this court is in its infancy, we still have much to learn. But what we do know counsels against underestimating its importance.

PART IV

THE SUPREME COURT

10

Staffing the Court

I plead with you that, whatever you do, don't try to apply the rules of the political world to this institution; they do not apply. The last political act we engage in is confirmation.

– Justice Clarence Thomas (C-SPAN), on the day after *Bush v. Gore*

At the end of the Supreme Court's 1990 term, Thurgood Marshall announced his retirement. Marshall, a towering figure as a litigator for the National Association for the Advancement of Colored People (NAACP) Legal Defense Fund, Inc., successfully argued *Brown v. Board of Education* and dozens of other cases before the Court. He made history as a member of the Court, though more for what he was – the first African American to sit on the tribunal – than for anything he did. Faced with replacing him, President George H. W. Bush quickly nominated Clarence Thomas to the Court. In reply to charges that Bush nominated Thomas because he was black, Bush responded that Thomas was "the best man for the job on the merits. And the fact that he's a minority, so much the better."[1]

Clarence Thomas was an outspoken conservative who curried favor in the Reagan and the elder Bush administrations by speaking forcefully against affirmative action. Under Reagan he served as director of the Civil Rights Office in the Department of Education and then as chairman of the Equal Employment Opportunity Commission (EEOC). President Bush nominated him to the United States Circuit Court for the District of Columbia, the same court on which Warren Burger, Antonin Scalia, Robert Bork, and Daniel Ginsburg served before their Supreme Court nominations.

Liberal interest groups immediately expressed concern about his Supreme Court nomination. His long opposition to affirmative action alarmed civil rights groups. Indeed, the NAACP executive board voted unanimously, with

---

[1] John E. Yang and Sharon LaFraniere, "Bush Picks Thomas for Supreme Court," *Washington Post*, 2 July 1991, p. A6.

one abstention, to oppose the nominee. A speech in which Thomas seemingly endorsed using the Constitution to outlaw abortion outraged women's groups. Senior citizens complained that Thomas let more than one thousand age discrimination suits lapse during his tenure at EEOC.

Moreover, Thomas's qualifications were increasingly under question. Though Thomas had graduated from Yale Law School, university officials admitted that he was only admitted because of the school's affirmative action program,[2] the same sort of program Thomas now condemned.[3] Thomas's career on the federal bench was short (one and a half years) and undistinguished. An American Bar Association (ABA) committee, which formally evaluates the qualifications of nominees, could give him no better than a rating of "qualified." And he received this barely acceptable ranking from twelve of the committee's fifteen members; two thought him unqualified, and one did not vote. Of twenty-five ABA-rated Supreme Court nominees, Thomas is the only one who failed to receive at least a unanimous "qualified" rating or a majority "superior" rating.[4]

At the first round of confirmation hearings, Thomas refused to state his position on abortion and even tried to suggest that he had never really thought about the issue. Yet at the same time he tried to disown his previous statements on fetal rights. He also, for the first time in his career, managed to praise affirmative action programs. This led to Democratic charges of a confirmation conversion.

Neither his conservative ideology, nor the interest group opposition, nor the questions of qualifications were enough to bring Thomas down. Four days before the scheduled October 8, 1991, vote only about forty senators opposed the nominee. Then on October 6, Timothy Phelps of *Newsday*[5] and Nina Totenberg of National Public Radio reported that a law school professor in Oklahoma, Anita Hill, had told Senate Judiciary Committee staffers that Thomas sexually harassed her in the early 1980s while she worked for him at the Department of Education and later at the EEOC. Hill, who had spoken to the committee on conditions of confidentiality, was drawn out by the media after someone on or working for the committee leaked the story.

The Senate delayed the vote for a week in order to give the Judiciary Committee time to consider the charges. It would take a book-length manuscript to recount the charges and countercharges leveled at the hearings. Most persuasive from Hill's side was the fact that she told several people of the alleged harassment at the time it occurred. Most persuasive from Thomas's side was the fact that Hill never filed a complaint against Thomas at the time and actually

[2] "Judge Thomas Takes the Stand," *New York Times*, 8 September 1991, sec. 4, p. 18.

[3] Especially see his dissenting opinion in *Grutter v. Bollinger*, 539 U.S. 306 (2003).

[4] "Thomas: The Least Qualified Nominee So Far?" *National Law Journal*, 16 September 1991, p. 5. Also see Neil A. Lewis, "A.B.A. Is Split on Fitness of Thomas for High Court," *New York Times*, 28 August 1991, p. A1.

[5] Timothy Phelps, "The Thomas Charge: Law Professor Told FBI That He Sexually Harassed Her at EEOC," *Newsday*, 6 October 1991, p. 7.

followed him from the Department of Education to the EEOC. Nevertheless, one of the strongest journalistic critics of Anita Hill's credibility now admits that he fabricated information against her in order to ingratiate himself with the Republican Party.[6]

Democrats and Republicans treated the hearings quite differently. "The Democrats made a pass at figuring out what had happened in the case. The Republicans tried to win. While the Democrats were pronouncing themselves flummoxed by two diametrically opposing stories, the Republicans had already launched a scorched-earth strategy against Professor Hill."[7] Thus Arlen Specter (Republican – Pennsylvania) charged Hill with committing perjury; Orrin Hatch (Republican – Utah) accused her of concocting her story in coordination with liberal interest groups; and Alan Simpson (Republican – Wyoming) even questioned her sexual proclivities.[8] The Democrats, either not understanding that the Republicans were playing hardball or unable to compete in the game, never asked Thomas about his alleged penchant for watching pornographic movies, which would have corroborated part of Hill's testimony; did not call other witnesses who claimed that Thomas had harassed them; and did not introduce into evidence the positive results of Hill's lie detector test.

The final vote for Thomas was 52–48. Charges relating to the qualifications of the nominee were acted on only by those ideologically opposed to the nominee: Conservative senators overwhelmingly supported Thomas, and liberal senators overwhelmingly opposed him.[9] Partisanship was similarly in evidence: Forty-one of forty-three Republicans supported Thomas; forty-six of fifty-seven Democrats opposed him.

To the extent that the legal aspects of judicial decision making require justices to find the "correct" answer to legal questions, it should not matter much whom the president nominates or whether the Senate confirms, given a requisite modicum of legal training and intelligence. Differences might result, say, from followers of intent versus followers of text, but there would be overwhelming agreement on the basic principles of government. But if, as Thomas's decision to join his four most conservative colleagues in preventing a recount of Florida's ballots suggests, the Court largely bases its decisions on the attitudes and values of the justices, then clearly, as President Nixon noted, "The most important appointments a President makes are those to the Supreme Court of the United States."[10]

---

[6] David Brock, *Blinded by the Right: The Conscience of an Ex-Conservative* (New York: Crown, 1992).

[7] Maureen Dowd, "Going Nasty Early Helps G.O.P. Gain Edge on Thomas," *New York Times*, 15 October 1991, p. A1.

[8] Anthony Lewis, "Time of the Assassins," *New York Times*, 14 October 1991, p. A19; William Safire, "The Plot to Savage Thomas," *New York Times*, 14 October 1991, p. A19.

[9] The correlation between ADA scores, which measure how liberal senators are, and the vote on the Thomas nomination was −.81.

[10] Richard Nixon, "Transcript of President's Announcements," *New York Times*, 22 October 1971, p. 24.

Following Nixon's contention, a case can be made that among the most important *decisions* a president makes are his nominations to the Supreme Court. It is certainly one of the longest-term policy-affecting choices a president makes. What, for example, among Eisenhower's decisions compares to his appointment of Earl Warren? What among John Adams's compares to his nomination of John Marshall? In this chapter, we examine the process by which presidents nominate and senators confirm or reject appointees to the Supreme Court.

PRESIDENTIAL SELECTION

Article II, Section 2, clause 2, of the United States Constitution gives the president the power, "by and with the Advice and Consent of the Senate," to appoint "Judges of the supreme Court." Despite the wording of this clause, the role of the Senate in Supreme Court nominations has been limited to consent; presidents have sought advice only in the naming of lower court judges, especially those to the district courts, particularly when there is a senator of the president's party from the state in which the court is located. If the senator disapproves of the president's nominee, he or she can invoke "senatorial courtesy" and block the nomination. This process has not applied to the Supreme Court for nearly a century, nor was it ever intended to. According to Alexander Hamilton in Number 66 of *The Federalist Papers*:

There will, of course, be no exertion of *choice* on the part of the Senate. They may defeat one choice of the Executive and oblige him to make another; but they cannot themselves *choose* – they can only ratify or reject the choice he may have made. They might even entertain a preference to some other person at the very moment they were assenting to the one proposed, because there might be no positive ground of opposition to him; and they could not be sure, if they withheld their assent, that the subsequent nomination would fall upon their own favorite.[11]

Modern presidents usually delegate the initial phases of the selection process to the attorney general, chief of staff, or other top advisers. Recommendations from politicians, legal professionals, and interest groups are filtered through the Justice Department's Office of Legal Policy. The president's advisers then pass the names of one or more top candidates to the FBI for exhaustive investigative checks. The final choice is the president's, but the influence of others can be felt. The Reagan attorney general, Edwin Meese, lobbied hard, first for Robert Bork and next for Daniel Ginsburg, against a more moderate position urged by the chief of staff, Howard Baker. Chief Justice Warren Burger obviously influenced Nixon's choice of Harry Blackmun, Burger's childhood friend. The former president William Howard Taft lobbied successfully for his own appointment to the chief justiceship.[12]

---

[11] Alexander Hamilton, James Madison, and John Jay, *The Federalist* (New York: Mentor, 1961), p. 405.

[12] See Henry F. Pringle, *The Life and Times of William Howard Taft*, vol. 2 (New York: Farrar & Rinehart, 1939), chap. 50.

Factors Affecting Nomination

Presidential selection undoubtedly involves complex choices. We can, nevertheless, examine some of the factors that influence presidential selection.

Partisanship and Ideology. Given the Supreme Court's role as a national policymaker, it would boggle the mind of Court watchers and suggest that the president had lost his if he did not pay careful attention to the ideology and partisanship of potential nominees. This factor has been crucial from the Republic's beginning, when President Washington nominated eleven consecutive Federalists to the Court. Overall, 128 of 147 nominees (87 percent) have been members of the president's party.[13] Simple partisanship paints an incomplete picture. In his discussions with Senator Henry Cabot Lodge about a Democrat, Horace Lurton, President Theodore Roosevelt observed that "the nominal politics of the man have nothing to do with his actions on the bench. His *real* politics are all important." Roosevelt had earlier sought assurances from Lodge that Oliver Wendell Holmes was "in entire sympathy with our views" before nominating him to the Supreme Court.[14]

In more recent times, the presidential candidate Richard Nixon campaigned in 1968 on the promise to appoint justices who would support the "peace forces" of society instead of those who favored the rights of accused criminals. His appointees were indeed consistently conservative on criminal procedure. Ronald Reagan's 1980 campaign platform included support for judicial nominees who were harsh on crime, opposed abortion, and favored school prayer. In 1986, Reagan argued that

the proliferation of drugs has been part of a crime epidemic that can be traced to, among other things, liberal judges who are unwilling to get tough with the criminal element in this society.... We don't need a bunch of sociology majors on the bench. What we need are strong judges who will aggressively use their authority to protect our families, communities and way of life; judges who understand that punishing wrongdoers is our way of protecting the innocent; judges who do not hesitate to put criminals where they belong, behind bars.[15]

Political Environment. Although a rational president will wish to nominate someone with views as close to his or her as possible, political reality may make such a choice difficult. A president who chooses an unconfirmable nominee will lose more than she or he will gain.

---

[13] We compiled the data here and later, which are current through the end of the 2003 term. We exclude from consideration two nominations: William Paterson, whose first nomination in 1793 was temporarily withdrawn so that he could officially resign from the Senate, and Homer Thornberry, whose nomination in 1968 was conditional on Fortas's promotion to chief justice. This leaves us with 147 nominations, the number we use throughout this chapter.

[14] Henry Cabot Lodge, *Selections from the Correspondence of Theodore Roosevelt and Henry Cabot Lodge, 1894–1918* (New York: Scribner's, 1925), vol. 2, p. 228; vol. 1, p. 519.

[15] "Reagan Aims Fire at Liberal Judges," *New York Times*, 9 October 1986, p. A32.

A classic example of a president's "trimming his sails" to prevent a battle with the Senate was Ford's nomination of John Paul Stevens. Ford, who became president after Nixon's resignation, entered office with the lowest initial approval ratings of any president since George Gallup began polling. That low level of popularity fell even further when Ford pardoned Nixon for any crimes he may have committed during his administration. When Justice Douglas resigned, Ford faced a Senate that consisted of sixty-two Democrats and thirty-eight Republicans. Further, Ford was replacing the Court's most liberal justice, whom Ford himself had tried to impeach while he was House minority leader. Under these circumstances, the conservative Ford pragmatically chose the moderate Stevens rather than a conservative such as Robert Bork.

Prior Experience. All 147 individuals nominated to the High Bench have been attorneys, though the Constitution does not require that they be. Virtually all have had experience in public affairs of one sort or another, including several as senators, governors, and one as a former president. Most commonly, they have previously served as jurists. Four of the five justices on the first Supreme Court had prior judicial experience. Overall, 93 of the 147 nominees (63 percent) have occupied judicial positions. This overall rate masks strong partisan differences: Seventy-three percent of Republican nominees have had prior experience, versus only 50 percent of Democratic nominees.

Region. The Judiciary Act of 1789 divided the nation into six circuits, then corresponding to the number of seats on the Supreme Court. As the number of circuits increased, so also did the number of justices. Until the end of the nineteenth century, each justice served in a dual capacity: as a circuit court judge and as a member of the Supreme Court. The assumption from the beginning was that the justice would reside within the circuit he served: The Judiciary Act of 1802 explicitly refers to "the justice of the supreme court residing within the said circuit."[16] Thus began the tradition of regional representation.

When circuit riding ended in 1891, the need for regional representation lessened. In fact, Lincoln ignored regional representation "rules" during the Civil War, and, though such practices were revived after the war, "by the late 1880's presidents disregarded it with increasing frequency."[17] In 1930, however, Hoover declined to nominate Judge Benjamin Cardozo on the ground that two New Yorkers were sitting on the Court, one of whom, as was Cardozo, was Jewish. When another vacancy occurred, Justice Stone, one of the New Yorkers, offered to resign if his doing so would secure Cardozo's nomination.[18] Hoover then selected Cardozo without calling Stone's bluff.

---

[16] Act of April 29, 1802, 2 Stat. 156–157.

[17] Richard Friedman, "The Transformation in Senate Response to Supreme Court Nominations," 5 *Cardozo Law Review* 1 (1983) at 50.

[18] Walter F. Murphy, *Elements of Judicial Strategy* (Chicago: University of Chicago Press, 1964), p. 76.

The most recent use of regionalism was Nixon's attempt to nominate a Southerner to replace Justice Black in 1971. Nixon hoped that doing so would win him electoral support from conservative Southerners, who traditionally voted Democratic. The "Southern strategy" resulted in the failed nominations of Clement Haynsworth (South Carolina) and G. Harrold Carswell (Florida) and the successful nomination of Lewis Powell (Virginia).

Religion, Race, and Sex. Of the 147 people nominated to the Supreme Court, 145 have been white, 145 have been male, and 126 have been Protestant. The only African Americans to date have been Thurgood Marshall and Clarence Thomas; the sole females are Sandra Day O'Connor and Ruth Bader Ginsburg. Though it is often claimed that no Hispanics have served on the Court,[19] why Benjamin Cardozo, a Sephardic Jew of Spanish heritage, should not count is not clear. Ethnically, virtually all of the white Protestant nominees have been Anglo-Saxon. Antonin Scalia was the first Italian American. Of the twenty-one non-Protestants named to date, nine were Jewish, twelve Roman Catholic.

The first Catholic named to the Court was Roger Taney, who was nominated, defeated, renominated in 1835, and finally confirmed in 1836. A second Catholic, Edward White, was not named until 1894. Since then, for all but eight years, at least one Catholic has sat on the Court. After Murphy's death in 1949, no Catholic sat until Brennan's appointment in 1956, which resulted in part from direct lobbying by Cardinal Spellman for a Catholic on the Court.[20] Three Catholics served simultaneously during the 1988 and 1989 terms: Brennan, Scalia, and Kennedy. A so-called Jewish seat existed from 1916, when Louis Brandeis was confirmed, until 1969, when Abe Fortas resigned. Douglas Ginsburg, who is Jewish, was nominated by Reagan in 1987 but withdrew after allegations that he smoked marijuana while on the faculty of Harvard Law School. Both of President Clinton's nominees, Ruth Bader Ginsburg and Stephen Breyer, are Jewish. The first President Bush's choice of Clarence Thomas as Thurgood Marshall's successor did not surprise us; indeed, we predicted as much at the time of Marshall's statement at the end of the 1990 term that he would retire when a successor was confirmed.[21]

Friendship and Patronage. Sometimes it's not what you know; it's whom you know. About three-fifths of those named to the Supreme Court personally knew the president who nominated them.[22] Most of Washington's appointees, for instance, had personal ties to him. Harry Truman nominated four close friends: Harold Burton, Fred Vinson, Tom Clark, and Sherman Minton.

---

[19] E.g., Stephen Wasby, *The Supreme Court in the Federal Judicial System* (Chicago: Nelson-Hall, 1988), p. 117.

[20] David Alistair Yalof, *Pursuit of Justices* (Chicago: University of Chicago Press, 1999), chap. 3.

[21] On News 12, a local Long Island television station, June 29, 1991.

[22] Updated from Robert Scigliano, *The Supreme Court and the Presidency* (New York: Free Press, 1971), p. 95.

Lyndon Johnson named his longtime crony Abe Fortas as associate justice and failed in his attempt to have him elevated to chief justice. Had Fortas been confirmed to the latter position, another friend of Johnson's, Homer Thornberry, would have been selected to fill Fortas's seat.

A position on the Supreme Court may also be used to pay political debts. In 1952, Earl Warren, seeing his chances for obtaining the Republican presidential nomination falter, threw his support and that of the California delegation to General Eisenhower rather than Eisenhower's rival, Senator Robert Taft of Ohio. One year later, Eisenhower nominated Governor Warren to replace Chief Justice Fred Vinson. Similarly, Kennedy's friend Byron White, best known as an All-American football player, received a seat on the Supreme Court in 1962, two years after he organized Citizens for Kennedy–Johnson.

SENATE CONFIRMATION

After nomination by the president, the American Bar Association (ABA) conducts its own inquiry about the nominee, rating him or her along a qualified/not qualified dimension, as noted earlier.

The bar's involvement in Supreme Court nominations has been controversial. In 1969, it initially and unanimously ranked Haynsworth "highly qualified," then reconsidered and reaffirmed its judgment by a divided vote. In 1970, it labeled Carswell "qualified," though even his Senate supporters thought him mediocre. For a short period after the Haynsworth debacle, the Nixon administration gave the ABA the right to prescreen potential nominees. This practice ended when ABA votes against the potential nominees Mildred Lillie and Herschel Friday were leaked to the press. When Nixon nominated Lewis Powell and William Rehnquist in 1971, he did not apprise the ABA until after he had sent their names to the Senate Judiciary Committee. In 1975, President Ford gave the ABA a list of names that included John Paul Stevens, who received the committee's top ranking. Reagan discontinued the prescreening practice and gave the ABA no advance word on Sandra Day O'Connor. The committee found O'Connor "qualified" and Scalia and Rehnquist "highly qualified." Robert Bork received ten "highly qualified" votes, one vote "not opposed," and four votes "not qualified."

After the submission of a nominee's name to the Senate, the Judiciary Committee holds hearings. The committee hears testimony from the legal community, interest groups, and the nominee. Nominees did not appear before the committee before 1925, and the practice did not become established until the mid-1950s. Often nominees refuse to answer substantive legal questions because to do so would compromise their presumed open-mindedness when such cases are before the Court. This practice prevents an appearance of partiality, not partiality itself, for why the communication of a prior view biases one less than a flat refusal to communicate one's position is not clear. Such silence, however, does serve to keep nominees out of political trouble. For instance, had nominee Souter stated his views on abortion, he would have instantly alienated

Figure 10.1. DILBERT reprinted by permission of United Feature Syndicate, Inc.

half of the Senate. Nevertheless, the Judiciary Committee has generally recommended nominees who have refused to talk substance. Thus, Clarence Thomas refused to admit that he had ever discussed the merits of *Roe v. Wade* with anyone at any time, and that, of course, is most difficult to believe.

The great exception to strategic silence is the Bork nomination. Bork had criticized certain Supreme Court decisions so outspokenly that he could not avoid telling senators under oath what he had repeatedly told the rest of the world in articles and speeches. Though Bork attempted to assume a moderate stance at the hearings, his previous writings and speeches, some of which he had made only weeks before his nomination, led many to believe that his moderation was part of a "confirmation conversion" that would not last once he joined the Court. Of course, Bork also failed to receive confirmation.

If the Judiciary Committee does not table a nomination, it goes to the full Senate for consideration. The nomination is debated on the floor, and unless it is filibustered, as was the second Fortas nomination, the full chamber votes on it. Confirmation requires a simple majority of those present and voting.

Of the 147 nominees whom the Senate considered through the end of the millennium, 120 (82 percent) have been confirmed. Not all of the 122 have served; 7 declined their seat. Robert Harrison, for instance, declined Washington's appointment in order to become chancellor of Maryland, and John Jay declined reappointment because of the Court's low prestige.[23]

Of the twenty-seven rejections, the Senate formally repudiated twelve, failed to act on five, indefinitely postponed four, and forced the president to withdraw six.[24] We list the rejected nominees in Table 10.1.

In order to gain insight into the factors that lead to rejection, we take three approaches: First, we examine the five nominations that failed since 1968. Then, we conduct a systematic analysis of the factors affecting rejection since 1789. Finally, we examine the roll call votes of senators between the nomination of Earl Warren in 1953 and that of Stephen Breyer in 1994.

[23] Elder Witt, ed., *The Supreme Court and Its Work* (Washington, DC: Congressional Quarterly Press, 1981), pp. 4, 74.

[24] The six withdrawn candidates include Daniel Ginsburg, who withdrew as much because of misgivings within the Reagan administration as within the Senate.

Table 10.1. *Rejected Supreme Court Nominees*

Name	President	Year[a]	Vote
John Rutledge	Washington	1795	10–14
Alexander Wolcott	Madison	1811	9–24
John Crittenden	J. Q. Adams	1828	Postponed
Roger Taney	Jackson	1835	Postponed
John Spencer	Tyler	1844	21–26
Reuben Walworth	Tyler	1844	Withdrawn
Edward King	Tyler	1844	Postponed
Edward King	Tyler	1844	Withdrawn
John Read	Tyler	1845	No action
George Woodward	Polk	1845	20–29
Edward Bradford	Fillmore	1852	No action
George Badger	Fillmore	1853	Postponed
William Micou	Fillmore	1853	No action
Jeremiah Black	Buchanan	1861	25–26
Henry Stanbery	Johnson	1866	No action
Ebenezer Hoar	Grant	1869	24–33
George Williams	Grant	1873	Withdrawn
Caleb Cushing	Grant	1874	Withdrawn
Stanley Matthews	Hayes	1881	No Action
William Hornblower	Cleveland	1893	24–30
Wheeler Peckham	Cleveland	1894	32–41
John Parker	Hoover	1930	39–41
Abe Fortas[b]	Johnson	1968	45–43[c]
Clement Haynsworth	Nixon	1969	45–55
G. Harrold Carswell	Nixon	1970	45–51
Robert Bork	Reagan	1987	42–58
Douglas Ginsburg	Reagan	1987	Withdrawn

[a] Year nominated.

[b] Fortas's rejection led to the withdrawal of the nomination of Homer Thornberry, who was to take Fortas's place as associate justice.

[c] Vote on cloture failed to reach two-thirds majority. Nomination was subsequently withdrawn.

The Case Studies

Between 1930 and 1967, presidents nominated twenty-four consecutive persons to the Supreme Court without a single rejection. Thereafter, the Senate rejected five of the next fifteen nominees. We examine the five rejections in sequence.

Abe Fortas. After Lyndon Johnson's theft of the Democratic Senate nomination in the Texas primary in 1948,[25] he called on the attorney Abe Fortas to prevent

[25] Robert A. Caro, *The Years of Lyndon Johnson: Means of Ascent* (New York: Knopf, 1990), chaps. 13–16.

a legal maneuver by his opponent, the former governor, Coke Stevenson, to keep Johnson off the November ballot. Fortas's successful efforts resulted in a close personal and professional relationship that culminated in Johnson's naming Fortas to the Supreme Court in 1965. Fortas remained a close adviser of Johnson's while he was on the Court. According to one report, "Few important Presidential problems are settled without an opinion from Mr. Justice Fortas."[26]

In June 1968, Chief Justice Warren announced his retirement from the Court, effective at Johnson's pleasure. Johnson declared that the retirement would not take effect until "such time as a successor is qualified."[27] This in essence told the Senate that if they did not approve Warren's successor, Warren would simply stay on as chief justice, but it also allowed Senate opponents to claim that no actual vacancy existed. Ironically, Fortas may have suggested the contingent retirement scenario to Johnson.[28]

Johnson named Fortas to replace Warren, and another Johnson crony, Homer Thornberry, to occupy Fortas's place as associate justice.

The timing of the vacancy worked against Fortas. By the summer of 1968, a presidential election was only months away. In and out of Washington, Johnson's popularity was plummeting. Republicans and conservative Southern Democrats had every reason to believe that if they defeated the Fortas nomination, Richard Nixon would make the new appointment. Historically, Supreme Court nominees have fared poorly during the fourth year of a president's term in office. Johnson was particularly weak during his fourth year because he had already announced his decision not to seek a second term: Presidential threats would not be effective; presidential promises could not be kept.

The second factor to work against the nomination was Fortas's and the Warren Court's liberal ideology. In his four terms, Fortas had supported the liberal position in civil liberties cases more than 80 percent of the time, aligning himself with a bloc that included Warren, Douglas, Marshall, and Brennan. Members of the Judiciary Committee during the hearings grilled Fortas about liberal decisions he had rendered,[29] and even about some that antedated his tenure.[30]

The third factor to work against the promotion of Fortas concerned a matter of ethics. The hearings disclosed that he had accepted a fifteen-thousand-dollar fee for teaching a nine-week seminar at American University. The money was raised by Fortas's former law partner, Paul Porter, from wealthy businessmen

---

[26] *Newsweek*, 8 July 1968, p. 18.

[27] "Warren–Johnson Letters," *New York Times*, 27 June 1968, p. A30.

[28] John Massaro, *Supremely Political* (New York: State University of New York, 1990), p. 41.

[29] E.g., *Brown v. Louisiana*, 383 U.S. 131 (1966), which vacated the breach of peace conviction of blacks engaged in a stand-in at a segregated library.

[30] *Mallory v. United States*, 354 U.S. 449 (1957), which overturned the conviction and death sentence of an alleged rapist who confessed after a seven-hour unarraigned interrogation. Mallory was subsequently convicted of another rape in 1960 and died in a shootout with police after yet another rape in 1972.

involved in litigation that could go to the Supreme Court. Additionally, some senators questioned the propriety of Fortas's close relationship with Johnson. These considerations enabled conservative senators to oppose Fortas without appearing partisan.

The motion to confirm Fortas never had a direct vote because of a filibuster on the Senate floor. The vote to invoke cloture (i.e., end debate and vote on the nomination) shows the influence that ideology had on the nomination. We rely here and in the subsequent case studies on the simple correlation coefficient, which ranges from −1.0 (a perfect relationship between conservatism and support for the nomination) to 0.0 (no relationship between ideology and support for the nomination) to +1.0 (a perfect relationship between liberalism and support for the nomination). We measure senators' ideology with support scores compiled by Americans for Democratic Action (ADA). The correlation between the vote to invoke cloture and the Senator's ADA score is .79, showing that liberals were *much* more likely to vote to invoke cloture than conservatives. Though there were forty-five votes to invoke cloture and only forty-three opposed, this was far less than the two-thirds then needed to end Senate debate. With a direct vote on Fortas precluded, Johnson withdrew the nomination.

Clement Haynsworth. After Richard Nixon's election, Warren announced his unconditional resignation at the end of the 1968 term. On May 21, 1969, Nixon named Warren Burger to replace him. Burger was confirmed on June 9 with little controversy. Meanwhile, a *Life* magazine story in May 1969 disclosed that in 1966 Fortas had accepted twenty-thousand dollars as part of an annual "consulting" fee from Louis Wolfson, a millionaire businessman later convicted of stock manipulations. Though Fortas returned the money and accepted no future handouts from Wolfson, the ensuing controversy forced him to resign.

On August 18, 1969, Nixon chose the circuit court of appeals judge Clement Haynsworth, a Democrat from South Carolina, to replace Fortas. The selection of Haynsworth was part of Nixon's "Southern strategy," by which he hoped to win the votes of white conservative Southern Democrats in 1972.

Haynsworth at first appeared certain of confirmation. Though the Democrats controlled the Senate, a working majority of Republicans and conservative Southern Democrats existed. Confidence in Haynsworth began to erode when Judiciary Committee hearings focused on cases decided by Haynsworth in which he had a direct financial interest. One case concerned parties who had direct business dealings with a company in which he had a substantial stake. In another, Haynsworth bought stock in a company after deciding a case involving the company but before the decision was announced. Although Haynsworth gained but few dollars from these transactions, his behavior made him an easy target as a person who was nominated to restore high ethical standards that were lacking in Fortas.

Similarly to the Fortas case, Haynsworth's ideological opponents viewed the ethics charges as most serious. Liberals alleged that Haynsworth had compiled an antiunion, anti–civil rights record as an appellate judge. On the union front, Haynsworth had ruled that businesses could shut down specific factories solely for the purpose of punishing union activity.[31] As for civil rights, Haynsworth had allowed private hospitals receiving federal funds to discriminate racially.[32] He also upheld "freedom of choice" school plans, in which students were allowed to choose the schools they would attend, with the inevitable result that the schools remained segregated.[33]

Liberal opposition to Haynsworth produced vigorous lobbying. On November 21, 1969, the Senate rejected Haynsworth by a vote of 55 to 45. According to the Nixon aide John Ehrlichman, Haynsworth "was not confirmed because of a highly expert, expensive and intensive lobbying campaign by organized labor and civil rights groups."[34] The correlation between ADA scores and the votes supporting Haynsworth was −.79, demonstrating the strong opposition to Haynsworth by liberal senators.

G. Harrold Carswell. In angry reaction to Haynsworth's defeat, Nixon nominated G. Harrold Carswell, a little-known Florida federal judge who had graduated from a local Southern law school. So poorly qualified was he that the dean of the Yale Law School was moved to declare that he "presents more slender credentials than any nominee put forth this century."[35] Carswell was reversed significantly more frequently – 40 percent – than the average district court judge in the Fifth Circuit, the circuit in which he served.[36] So deficient were Carswell's qualifications that his Senate floor leader, Roman Hruska (Republican – Nebraska), declared, "Even if he were mediocre, there are a lot of mediocre judges, and people and lawyers. They are entitled to a little representation, aren't they, and a little chance."[37] Even Nixon administration insiders considered him a "boob" and a "dummy."[38]

Carswell's record as a federal judge and as a private citizen made him far more suspect on civil rights than Haynsworth. One of his opinions delaying implementation of desegregation explicitly deviated from higher court rulings; another made challenging segregation in public reform schools virtually impossible.[39] In 1956, Carswell, then a United States attorney, had helped transform

---

[31] *Darlington Manufacturing Company v. NLRB*, 325 F. 2d 682 (1963).

[32] *Simkins v. Moses H. Cone Memorial Hospital*, 323 F. 2d 959 (1964).

[33] *Green v. County School Board*, 372 F. 2d 338 (1967).

[34] Quoted in Massaro, *Supremely Political*, p. 22.

[35] U.S. Senate, Hearings on the Nomination of G. Harrold Carswell, of Florida, to be Associate Justice of the Supreme Court of the United States, 91st Congress, 2d Session, 1970, p. 242.

[36] Massaro, *Supremely Political*, p. 6.

[37] Warren Weaver, Jr., "Carswell Nomination Attacked and Defended as Senate Opens Debate on Nomination," *New York Times*, 17 March 1970, p. A21.

[38] Massaro, *Supremely Political*, p. 116.

[39] *Id.*, pp. 3–4.

a public golf club built with federal funds into a private club in order to prevent desegregation. While a U.S. attorney, he also helped charter a Florida State University booster club with membership limited to "any white person." But the most damaging blow to Carswell's candidacy occurred when a Florida television station found film of a 1948 speech in which he declared, "I yield to no man as a fellow candidate or as a fellow citizen in the firm vigorous belief in the principles of White Supremacy, and I shall always be so governed."[40] Yet to William Rehnquist, then an assistant attorney general, the allegations presented no more than "some rather thin evidence of personal hostility toward blacks."[41]

Given the case against Carswell, the vote against him was surprisingly close, 51–45. More than two-thirds of the Republicans supported Carswell, as did fewer than a third of the Democrats. The correlation between ADA scores and pro-Carswell voting was −.84. If Nixon had had a Republican Senate majority, Carswell, amazingly, would have been confirmed.

Robert Bork. President Reagan nominated Robert Bork to the seat vacated by the retirement of Justice Powell in 1987. Bork first gained public attention on October 20, 1973, when as solicitor general he fired the Watergate special prosecutor Archibald Cox at President Nixon's request after Attorney General Elliott Richardson and Deputy Attorney General William Ruckleshaus had refused to do so. Richardson resigned in protest of Nixon's order; Ruckleshaus was fired for refusing to obey. Bork executed Nixon's order, which later became known as the "Saturday Night Massacre."

The turning point in Bork's confirmation occurred not in 1987, when he was nominated, but in 1986, when partisan control of the Senate switched from the Republicans to the Democrats. Reagan had worked feverishly to retain Republican control of the Senate. At campaign stops in Missouri and Alabama, he echoed concerns he first raised in North Carolina:

Today, Senators Strom Thurmond and Jim Broyhill are in a majority on the Senate Judiciary Committee, overseeing judicial appointments. Without Jim Broyhill and a Republican Senate majority, that job will be turned over to Teddy Kennedy and Joe Biden. . . . You can strike a blow against drugs, thugs and hoodlums by casting your vote for Jim and keeping him as a force for law and order in the United States Senate. The future of our country, its safety and security, is in our hands.[42]

On November 4, 1986, the Democratic Party won twenty of thirty-four open Senate seats, taking a decisive 55–45 majority. Behind a huge black vote, Democrats won Republican seats in Alabama, Florida, Georgia, and North Carolina.[43]

[40] "Excerpts from Carswell Talk," *New York Times*, 22 January 1970, p. A22.
[41] Massaro, *Supremely Political*, p. 109.
[42] "Reagan Aims Fire at Liberal Judges," *New York Times*, 9 October 1986, p. A32.
[43] Lena Williams, "Blacks Cast Pivotal Ballots in Four Key Senate Races, Data Show," *New York Times*, 6 November 1986, p. A33.

On the day of Bork's nomination, Ted Kennedy set the negative tone for the campaign to follow:

Robert Bork's America is a land in which women would be forced into back alley abortions, blacks would sit at segregated lunch counters, rogue police could break down citizens' doors in midnight raids, writers and artists could be censored at the whim of the government, and the doors of the federal courts would be shut on the fingers of millions of citizens.[44]

Liberal interest groups opposed to Bork joined the fray. The People for the American Way, the Women's Legal Defense Fund, the Alliance for Justice, and the National Abortion Rights Action League immediately went on the attack. The American Federation of Labor – Congress of Industrial Organizations (AFL-CIO) joined the anti-Bork forces in August 1987 along with the American Civil Liberties Union, which dropped its fifty-one-year-old policy of noninvolvement in Supreme Court nominations. Planned Parenthood ran advertisements that read: "State controlled pregnancy? It's not as far fetched as it sounds. Carrying Bork's position to its logical end, states could ban or require any method of birth control, impose family quotas for population purposes, make abortion a crime, or sterilize anyone they choose."[45]

Opponents' allegations stemmed from Bork's published writings on and off the bench. In 1963, Bork declared that the proposed Civil Rights Act, which prohibited race discrimination in places of public accommodations, invoked a "principle of unsurpassed ugliness."[46] Most of the fodder, however, originated in a 1971 article in which Bork criticized Supreme Court rulings that created a right to privacy, struck down prohibitions on the use of birth control *by married people*, voided state court enforcement of racial covenants, and declared unconstitutional malapportioned state legislative districts.[47] He also argued that the equal protection clause of the Fourteenth Amendment should be limited to racial discrimination, to the exclusion, for instance, of sexual discrimination; and that the First Amendment is entirely inapplicable to scientific, literary, or artistic speech.[48]

During the Judiciary Committee hearings Bork repudiated many of his previous views. He did not, however, recant his statements about the right to privacy. Moreover, his newly found moderation was seen as part of a "confirmation conversion," which impeached his credibility without softening his right-wing image.

Public pressure on the Senate to vote against Bork was enormous. Senator John Breaux (Democrat – Louisiana), who was first elected in 1986, told the *New York Times* that "many Southern Democrats were elected by black votes

---

[44] James Reston, "Kennedy and Bork," *New York Times*, 5 July 1987, Sec. 4, p. 15.

[45] "Robert Bork's Position on Reproductive Rights," *New York Times*, 13 September 1987, p. B9.

[46] Robert Bork, "Civil Rights – a Challenge," *New Republic*, 31 August 1963, p. 22.

[47] Robert Bork, "Neutral Principles and Some First Amendment Problems," 47 *Indiana Law Journal* 1 (1971): 8–11, 15–17, 18–19.

[48] *Id.* at 11–12, 20–35.

and that his black supporters were making the Bork vote a 'litmus test' issue. 'You can't vote maybe.'"[49] Constituent pressure was so great that even John Stennis of Mississippi, onetime leader of Southern segregationists, voted against Bork.

Bork was defeated by a 58 to 42 vote. Ideology played a huge role – the correlation between ADA scores and the confirmation vote was −.83 – but so did partisanship and interest group pressure.[50] Because of constituent pressure, the anti-Bork coalition included moderate and conservative Southern Democrats who otherwise might have supported him. Ninety-six percent of the Democrats opposed Bork, whereas 87 percent of the Republicans supported him.

Douglas Ginsburg. During the floundering Bork campaign President Reagan threatened to nominate someone liberals would abhor just as much as they did Bork if Bork were rejected.[51] He attempted to accomplish that with the nomination of Douglas Ginsburg, a former Harvard Law School professor, who had served for fourteen months on the District of Columbia Circuit Court of Appeals. Unfortunately for Ginsburg's opponents, he had left no paper trail that tied him to unpopular views, unlike Bork. A potential scandal inhered in a Ginsburg vote on a cable television contract decided while Ginsburg held $140,000 in another cable company that directly benefited by the ruling. That story soon became secondary when Nina Totenberg of National Public Radio reported that Ginsburg smoked marijuana with some of his students while he was at Harvard. The antidrug, anticrime, "just say 'no'" administration quickly dropped its support of the nominee, who then asked Reagan not to forward his nomination to the Senate.

These five rejections, plus the tenuous case of Clarence Thomas, lead to the following tentative conclusions: First, the probability of rejection is greatest when the president is in a weak institutional position. Every rejection occurred when either the nominating president was in the fourth year of his term of office or when his party did not control the Senate. Second, qualifications play a crucial role in confirmation politics. Every rejected nominee, with the possible exception of Bork, confronted a serious question of ethics or competence. Third, the role of qualifications is largely interactive. Lack of qualifications only leads ideologically opposed senators to vote against the nominee. Fourth, electoral politics influence confirmation voting: Interest groups and constituents have an impact.

These conclusions are tentative as they are based only on case studies of rejected nominees. To assess the impact of these and other variables on

---

[49] Steven Roberts, "White House Says Bork Lacks Votes for Confirmation," *New York Times*, 26 September 1987, p. 1.

[50] On interest group influence, see Gregory A. Caldeira and John R. Wright, "Lobbying for Justice: Organized Interests, Supreme Court Nominations, and the United States Senate," 42 *American Journal of Political Science* 499 (1998).

[51] *New York Times*, 14 October 1987, p. A1.

confirmation voting, we turn to more systematic analyses. We start with an aggregate analysis that examines confirmation decisions since 1789. Because we lack reliable information about relevant variables for many eighteenth- and nineteenth-century nominees, we supplement the aggregate analysis with an individual-level focus on the votes of senators, starting with the nomination of Earl Warren.

An Aggregate Analysis

As noted, from 1789 through 2001, 147 people have been nominated to the Supreme Court, of whom the Senate has confirmed 122 (83 percent). Published research suggests that the Senate's decision to confirm particular nominees can be explained by partisan and institutional politics between the Senate, on the one hand, and the president or the Court, on the other.[52]

From this framework we test several hypotheses about the confirmation process. First is a pro-Senate bias that manifests itself rather simply: namely, that the Senate should be more likely to confirm those nominees who are U.S. senators than those who are not. Second, a weak-president effect should most likely surface under divided government, which for our purposes occurs when the president's party does not control the Senate (e.g., Reagan and Bork, Nixon and Haynsworth/Carswell) and during the fourth year of the president's term of office (e.g., Johnson and Fortas), except the period between reelection and the start of a new term. Presidents in the fourth year are likely to have minimal influence over senators of either party.

A president's strength may also depend on his or her electoral base. Thus, we hypothesize that the larger the president's previous electoral victory, the more likely his nominees are to be confirmed. Although the president and vice president are elected as a team, the electoral coalition may not remain loyal if the vice president succeeds to office through the death or resignation of the president. Thus, elected presidents should more readily secure confirmation of their nominees than succession presidents. John Tyler, for instance, the successor to William Henry Harrison, failed in four consecutive attempts to secure confirmation of his nominees.

Whereas the Senate may add to its prestige by confirming one of its own, it may particularly damage the president by rejecting those closest to him, such as members of the cabinet. Similarly, an anti-Court motivation can manifest itself in a refusal to promote an associate justice to chief justice (e.g., Fortas).

Our examination of these hypotheses suggests the following: First, we find little support for a pro-Senate bias in confirmation voting. The Senate has confirmed eight of nine of its own (89 percent), but this proportion is virtually indistinguishable from the 81 percent of nonsenators whom the Senate has confirmed.

---

[52] Jeffrey A. Segal, "Senate Confirmation of Supreme Court Justices: Partisan and Institutional Politics," 49 *Journal of Politics* 998 (1987).

We do find substantial support for weak-president effects, however. Only 56 percent of nominees (fourteen of twenty-five) have been confirmed in the fourth year of a president's term, versus 87 percent in the first three years (106 of 122). Similarly, the Senate has confirmed only 59 percent of nominees under divided government (twenty-three of thirty-nine), as compared with 90 percent when the president's party controlled the Senate (97 of 108). Additionally, elected presidents appear to fare substantially better (86 percent) than succession presidents (53 percent). Nevertheless, such success does not depend on the size of the president's electoral coalition. The correlation between the percentage of the president's electoral college vote and Senate approval or disapproval is slightly negative −.15. Nominees politically close to the president fare especially poorly: Twenty-nine percent of current cabinet members have been rejected versus only 17 percent of noncabinet nominees.

Finally, the simple relationship between promotion from associate justice to chief justice lacks strength. Eighty-two percent of nonjustices have been confirmed as compared with only 71 percent of promoted associate justices.

These results, of course, distort reality to some extent. We treat Senate confirmation votes as single units when in fact they consist of as many as one hundred individual voters, each of whom faces a distinct decision calculus. Additionally, we exclude crucial factors that may influence confirmation votes, such as the ideology or qualifications of the nominee. Because of data limitations, we cannot measure such factors for all confirmation votes. Nevertheless, we can measure most of the factors that influence confirmation from the nomination of Earl Warren in 1953 to that of Stephen Breyer in 1994.

An Individual-Level Analysis

We next examine the 2,451 votes cast by individual senators in twenty-six confirmation roll calls from the nomination of Earl Warren (1953) through the nomination of Stephen Breyer (1994).

Any examination of the individual votes of senators must begin with an explanation of their motivations. First and foremost, senators should be concerned with reelection. Though it may be too much to claim that senators are "single-minded seekers of reelection,"[53] one cannot long enjoy the perquisites of Senate life if one's roll-call behavior systematically antagonizes one's constituents.

Public concern about nominees turns on the nominees' perceived judicial ideology and perceived qualifications. Ideologically proximate nominees should be perceived as attractive; poorly qualified nominees, unattractive; and ideologically distant and poorly qualified nominees, very unattractive.

Beyond these factors, the president may take an active role in the confirmation process, particularly if the confirmation becomes controversial. The

---

[53] David Mayhew, *Congress: The Electoral Connection* (New Haven, CT: Yale University Press, 1974), p. 17.

president generally has more political resources to deploy and can use them more effectively when his party controls the Senate and when he is not in the final year of his term. In addition, presidential resources are likely to impact members of his own party more than those of the other party. We also include the president's popularity, which has been extensively linked to executive success in the legislative arena.[54]

Finally, we account for organized interest groups, representing as they do more active citizens and potential campaign contributions. Historical evidence clearly indicates that lobbying has influenced the confirmation process. For example, the rejection of Judge Parker in 1930 may have been due in large part to the activity of organized labor and the NAACP.[55] The nomination of Haynsworth summoned a torrent of interest group activity, which in turn was exceeded by the almost frenetic mobilization of groups during the Bork nomination.

We measure the variables by the criteria discussed in the sections that follow.

Nominee Qualifications. To determine perceptions of nominees' qualifications and judicial philosophy, we use a content analysis from statements in newspaper editorials from the time of the nomination until the Senate vote on the nominee's capabilities and ethics. The analysis used four of the nation's leading papers, two with a liberal stance, the *New York Times* and the *Washington Post*, and two with a more conservative outlook, the *Chicago Tribune* and the *Los Angeles Times*. Each paragraph in every relevant editorial was coded as positive (1.0), negative (0.0), or neutral (0.5).[56] Thus for Qualifications, 1.0 represents the highest score (every paragraph dealing with the qualifications of the nominee is positive), 0.0 the lowest (every paragraph dealing with qualifications of the nominee is negative) (see Table 10.2). To aid in the presentation of the results we then aggregated these scores, coding Qualifications as high, medium, or low.[57]

Nominee Ideology. Similarly to the method for nominee qualifications, we derived Nominee Ideology from a content analysis of newspaper editorials from the time of the nomination until the Senate vote, using the same newspapers. For Nominee Ideology, 1.0 represents the most liberal score, 0.0 the most

---

[54] George C. Edwards, *At the Margins: Presidential Leadership of Congress* (New Haven, CT: Yale University Press, 1989).

[55] "Spite Nominations to the United States Supreme Court: Herbert Hoover, Owen J. Roberts, and the Politics of Presidential Vengeance in Retrospect," 77 *Kentucky Law Journal* 545 (1989).

[56] Charles M. Cameron, Albert D. Cover, and Jeffrey A. Segal, "Senate Voting on Supreme Court Nominees: A Neoinstitutional Model," 84 *American Political Science Review* 525 (1990).

[57] As the qualifications variable is skewed toward the high end, we classify nominees as highly qualified if their qualifications score from the content analysis is greater than .90, moderately qualified if their score is greater than or equal to .50 and less than .90, and unqualified if their score is less than .50.

Table 10.2. *Nominee Margin, Vote Status, Ideology, and Qualifications*

Nominee	Year	Pres's Status[a]	Margin	Qual[b]	Ideol[c]
Warren	1954	Strong	96–0[d]	74	.75
Harlan	1955	Weak	71–11	.86	.88
Brennan	1957	Weak	95–0[d]	1.00	1.00
Whittaker	1957	Weak	96–0	1.00	.50
Stewart	1959	Weak	70–17	1.00	.75
White	1962	Strong	100–0[d]	.50	.50
Goldberg	1962	Strong	100–0[d]	.92	.75
Fortas	1965	Strong	100–0[d]	1.00	1.00
Marshall	1967	Strong	69–11	.84	1.00
Fortas2	1968	Weak	45–43[e]	.64	.85
Burger	1969	Weak	74–3	.96	.12
Haynsworth	1969	Weak	45–55	.34	.16
Carswell	1970	Weak	45–51	.11	.04
Blackmun	1970	Weak	94–0	.97	.12
Powell	1971	Weak	89–1	1.00	.17
Rehnquist	1971	Weak	68–26	.89	.05
Stevens	1975	Weak	98–0	.96	.25
O'Connor	1981	Strong	99–0	1.00	.48
Rehnquist2	1986	Strong	65–33	.40	.05
Scalia	1986	Strong	98–0	1.00	.00
Bork	1987	Weak	42–58	.79	.10
Kennedy	1988	Weak	97–0	.89	.37
Souter	1990	Weak	90–9	.77	.33
Thomas	1991	Weak	52–48	.41	.16
Ginsburg	1993	Strong	96–3	1.00	.68
Breyer	1994	Strong	87–9	.55	.48

[a] The president is labeled "Strong" in a nonelection year in which the president's party controls the Senate, and "Weak" otherwise.
[b] Qualifications [Qual] are measured from 0.00 (least qualified) to 1.00 (most qualified).
[c] Ideology [Ideol] is measured from 0.00 (most conservative) to 1.00 (most liberal).
[d] Voice vote.
[e] Vote on cloture – failed to receive necessary two-thirds majority.
Source: Updated from Cameron, Cover, and Segal, "Senate Voting on Supreme Court Nominees: A Neoinstitutional Model," 84 *American Political Science Review* 526 (1990).

conservative. We then aggregated these scores, coding Nominee Ideology as liberal, moderate, or conservative. The ideology ratings are not perfect, but they do a fairly good job of capturing the perceived ideology of the nominees. For example, Harlan and Stewart were perceived as fairly liberal, but the main issue concerning their nomination was civil rights, an area in which they were in fact relatively liberal; indeed, the opposition that existed to their nominations was from Southern segregationists. Table 10.2 reports the results for Nominee Qualifications and Nominee Ideology.

We then measured the ideological closeness of each nominee to each senator voting on his or her nomination, using the senators' ADA scores.[58] On the basis of this distance, we then categorized each nominee–senator pair (e.g., Bork–Kennedy, Fortas–McGovern) as ideologically close (liberals to liberals, moderates to moderates, or conservatives to conservatives), moderate (moderates to either conservatives or liberals), or distant (liberals to conservatives, or vice versa).[59]

Presidential Strength and Same-Party Status. We measure Presidential Strength as "strong" when the president's party controls the Senate and the president is not in the fourth year of a term, and as "weak" otherwise. "Same-Party" simply categorizes senators as members of the president's party or not.

Presidential Popularity. We measure presidential Popularity as the percentage of people who approve of the job the incumbent is doing as measured by the findings of the Gallup survey that preceded the Senate vote. We code Presidential Popularity as high if the approval rating is greater than 70 percent, as moderate if the rating is between 50 percent and 70 percent, and as low if the rating is less than 50 percent.

Interest Group Opposition. We counted the number of organized interests presenting testimony against the nominee at the Senate Judiciary Committee hearings. We coded the amount of opposition as none, moderate (one to six groups testifying against), or high (seven or more groups testifying against).

Results. We begin our examination with the influence of qualifications. Although we expect that ideology should strongly affect votes, other nominee characteristics also influence senators. If they did not, explaining how certain strong liberals (e.g., Brennan) and conservatives (e.g., Scalia) breezed through the Senate would be impossible. Senators may find it difficult, for instance, to justify opposition to highly qualified nominees. We see in Table 10.3 a strong positive relationship between qualifications and votes. Senators voted for highly qualified nominees 98 percent of the time, for moderately qualified nominees 82 percent of the time, and for lesser-qualified nominees but 53 percent of the time. In other words, if one hundred votes are cast, a poorly qualified nominee will receive forty-five fewer votes on average than a highly qualified nominee. We can measure the strength of the bivariate relationship by gamma (γ),

---

[58] We first divided ADA scores by 100 to put them on a 0.0 to 1.0 scale, similar to the Nominee Ideology scores. We then took the absolute value of the distance between the two scores. In previous work we then undertook scaling procedures to find the best relationship between the Nominee Ideology scores and the senators' ADA scores. See Cameron et al., *Senate Voting*. We find, however, that the unscaled scores work essentially as well and that the results are overwhelmingly similar.

[59] Distance scores of 0 to .33 are "Close," .33 to .66 are "Moderate," and .67 to 1.0 are "Far."

Table 10.3. _Confirmation Voting by_
Nominee Qualifications

	Qualifications		
Vote	Low	Medium	High
No	187	167	24
	47.5%	17.9%	2.1%
Yes	207	765	1,109
	52.5%	82.1%	97.9%

Note: γ = .81.

Table 10.4. _Confirmation Voting by_
Ideological Distance

	Ideological Distance		
Vote	Close	Moderate	Far
No	29	121	228
	2.4%	17.0%	42.8%
Yes	1,176	589	305
	97.6%	83.0%	57.2%

Note: γ = −.79.

a measure of association that runs from −1.0 (perfect negative relationship) through 0.0 (no relationship) to 1.0 (perfect positive relationship). The gamma of 0.81 indicates that senators are much more likely to vote for nominees who are perceived as well qualified.

We next examine ideology, or more explicitly, the ideological distance between a senator and the nominee. Senators should be most likely to vote for nominees who are ideologically close to them (e.g., liberals and liberals) and least likely to vote for nominees who are ideologically distant from them (e.g., liberals and conservatives). This is exactly what we find. We see in Table 10.4 the percentage of senators voting for ideologically proximate, ideologically moderate, and ideologically distant nominees. Overall, senators voted almost 98 percent of the time for nominees who were ideologically close to them, 83 percent of the time for nominees who were of moderate distance, and but 57 percent of the time for nominees who were ideologically distant. The gamma of −0.79 indicates that senators are much less likely to vote for nominees who are ideologically distant from them.

What is perhaps most interesting about ideology is the manner in which it interacts with qualifications. Table 10.5 examines the percentage of yes votes senators cast by both constituent ideological distance and qualifications. The results could not be clearer. Reading across the top row of data, we see that senators are willing to vote for highly qualified candidates regardless of ideological distance. Reading down the first column of data, we see that they

Table 10.5. *Confirmation Voting by Qualifications and Distance: Percentage Pro*

Qualifications	Ideological Distance		
	Near	Medium	Distant
High	99.3 (601)	97.3 (297)	94.8 (231)
Medium	97.6 (422)	83.0 (317)	44.9 (187)
Low	91.8 (182)	38.5 (96)	1.7 (115)

Note: Number in parentheses is total votes in that category. Thus, 99.3% of the 602 votes for ideologically close, highly qualified nominees were positive.

Table 10.6. *Confirmation Voting by Presidential Status*

Vote	Status	
	Weak	Strong
No	322	56
	21.6%	5.8%
Yes	1,171	910
	78.4%	94.2%

Note: The President is "weak" under divided government and/or in the fourth year of the term of office. $\gamma = .63$.

are also willing to vote for ideologically close nominees regardless of qualifications. Charges against Fortas no more influenced liberals than charges against Thomas did conservatives. But as we move to the bottom, right cells, in which nominees are both distant and poorly qualified, opposition is virtually certain.

Confirmation votes occur in the political world, not in a vacuum. The most important player in this political world is the president, who is expected to use his influence to secure a successful nomination. The president's resources are lower, and thus he will have less influence, when he is in the final year of his term and when his party does not control the Senate. In fact, presidents have secured more than 94 percent of the votes on the average when they are in a strong position vis-à-vis the Senate as compared with only 78 percent of the votes when in a weak position (gamma = 0.63) (see Table 10.6). Thus, a weakly positioned president can cost his nominee an average of fourteen votes. Additionally, the president's influence is likely to be lower on members of the opposition party. Senators of the president's party support his nominees with 94 percent of their votes, whereas senators of the opposition party do so only 76 percent of the time (gamma = 0.66) (see Table 10.7).[60]

[60] More extensive analysis shows that these relationships, as do all the others we present here, hold up under multivariate testing, i.e., after controlling for the other variables that we look at. See Cameron et al., *Senate Voting*.

Table 10.7. *Confirmation Voting by Presidential Partisanship*

	Partisanship	
Vote	Opposing	Same
No	302	76
	24.5%	6.2%
Yes	932	1,148
	75.6%	93.8%

Note: $\gamma = .66$.

Table 10.8. *Confirmation Voting by Presidential Approval*

	Approval		
Vote	Low	Moderate	High
No	151	216	11
	17.9%	18.8%	2.4%
Yes	691	932	458
	82.1%	81.2%	97.7%

Note: $\gamma = .30$.

Unquestionably, no one-to-one relationship between presidential popularity and confirmation approvals exists. President Nixon, for instance, was at the height of his popularity when Haynsworth and Carswell were rejected (65 and 63 percent approval, respectively). President Johnson's approval rating was only at 39 percent when Thurgood Marshall was confirmed. Yet, it is also true that Johnson's approval ratings were almost as low when Fortas was rejected as chief justice (42 percent), and President Reagan was near his second-term low when Bork was defeated (50 percent). Overall, though, presidents who have high approval ratings (greater than 70 percent) average 98 percent of the votes, and unpopular presidents (approval ratings less than 50) average about 82 percent (gamma = 0.30). This indicates that an unpopular president costs a nominee an average of about fifteen votes (see Table 10.8).

Finally, we expect interest groups to influence the votes of senators. When nominees face fierce opposition by organized interests at confirmation hearings – for example, Haynsworth and Bork – they receive on average 71 percent of the votes, but when they have no opposition, they average 97 percent of the votes (gamma = −0.64) (see Table 10.9). Because supportive interest group mobilization arises largely in reaction to interest group mobilization against nominees, there is no relationship between votes and positive group support.

Table 10.9. *Confirmation Voting by Interest Group Opposition*

| Vote | Opposition | | |
	None	Moderate	High
No	20	129	229
	2.7%	14.0%	29.1%
Yes	729	795	557
	97.3%	86.0%	70.9%

Note: $\gamma = -.64$.

In sum, although a variety of factors influence senators' votes, the most important findings are that ideologically close senators vote to confirm a nominee regardless of the nominee's qualifications; that highly qualified nominees receive yes votes from even the most distant senators; but that ideologically distant senators refuse to support nominees as soon as substantial questions about the nominees' qualifications arise.

Presidential Influence

Few presidents had as much opportunity to influence the Supreme Court as Ronald Reagan did. The conservative Republican reached out again and again to social conservatives, calling for the return of school prayer and the overruling of *Roe v. Wade*.[61] Fate smiled upon the fortieth president, granting him four appointees to the High Court and hundreds of appointees to the lower federal courts. Yet the Supreme Court he left was no more conservative than the one he inherited. Moreover, despite his appointees, the twentieth century ended with organized school prayer still unconstitutional and *Roe v. Wade* the law of the land.

In contrast, the more moderate Richard Nixon had a much greater impact in pulling the Court to the right. The Warren Court, he declared in his 1968 campaign, had gone too far in protecting the criminal forces in society, as opposed to the peace forces. He wanted "strict constructionists" who would not read their preferred views of public policy into law. Nixon won the election, earning the opportunity, as did Reagan, to name four new justices to the Supreme Court.[62]

Nixon, however, was successful in ways that Reagan was not. Though the Burger Court placed limits on the death penalty, it upheld its constitutionality provided procedural safeguards were followed;[63] limited the reach of the

[61] "Reagan Aims Fire at Liberal Judges," *New York Times*, 9 October 1986.

[62] This section is based in part on Jeffrey A. Segal and Robert Howard, "Justices and Presidents," in Steven A. Shull (ed.), *Presidential Policymaking* (New York: M. E. Sharpe, 1999).

[63] *Gregg v. Georgia*, 428 U.S. 153 (1976).

Mapp[64] and *Miranda* decisions;[65] increased the ability of states to ban obscene materials;[66] refused to equalize state spending among school districts;[67] refused to extend the right to privacy to homosexual conduct;[68] and allowed sexually discriminating colleges and universities to lose funds for the specific programs that do so, but not for the entire institution.[69]

Nevertheless, a variety of factors limited the conservative thrust of the Burger Court. First, outside criminal justice, Nixon was not exceptionally conservative on social issues, and we would not necessarily expect his justices to be universally conservative either. Moreover, we could not have expected him to have paid attention to issues such as privacy and abortion before they became salient issues for the Court.

Second, like most presidents, Nixon was not able to place a majority of justices on the Court. William Rehnquist has voted liberally in civil liberties cases just 20.9 percent of the time, far less often than any other justice sitting on the Court at the time of Rehnquist's appointment.[70] This helped make for a more conservative Court, but even four nominees did not give President Nixon a guaranteed winning coalition on the Court. In fact, power devolved to the moderate swing justices.

Third, justices who fit ideologically on one end of the spectrum may change over time, a situation exemplified by the career of the Nixon appointee Harry Blackmun. Similarly, David Souter's liberalism scores jumped from 41.5 under Bush to above 60 under Clinton. Justice Stevens has become increasingly liberal with each administration, while Byron White has become increasingly conservative.

Fourth, no justice, however ideologically concordant with his or her appointing president, supports the president on every issue. Warren Burger wrote the majority opinion in support of racial busing in unconstitutionally segregated districts,[71] opposing the view of President Nixon. The Reagan appointees Sandra Day O'Connor and Anthony Kennedy (along with David Souter) coauthored an opinion of the Court upholding the right of a woman to have an abortion.[72] Thus, though the Burger Court clearly reversed the trend

---

[64] *Stone v. Powell*, 428 U.S. 465 (1976) and *United States v. Leon* 468 U.S. 897 (1984).

[65] *New York v. Quarles*, 467 U.S. 649 (1984).

[66] *Miller v. California*, 413 U.S. 15 (1973).

[67] *San Antonio v. Rodriguez*, 411 U.S. 1 (1973).

[68] *Bowers v. Hardwick*, 478 U.S. 186 (1986). But cf. *Lawrence v. Texas*, 539 U.S. 558 (2003).

[69] *Grove City College v. Bell*, 465 U.S. 555 (1984).

[70] Here and later we take civil liberties scores from the Supreme Court Database, using orally argued citation plus split votes as the unit of analysis. http://www.as.uky.edu/polisci/ulmerproject.htm.

[71] *Swann v. Charlotte-Mecklenburg County Board of Education*, 402 U.S. 1 (1971).

[72] *Planned Parenthood of Southeastern Pennsylvania v. Casey*, 505 U.S. 833 (1992). Reagan nominated O'Connor despite her previous support for abortion rights. The Reagan administration also knew of Kennedy's support for the right to privacy before his nomination (Yalof, *Pursuit*, p. L2) but desperately needed a confirmable nominee after the Senate rejection of Robert Bork and the administration's withdrawal of Douglas Ginsburg.

of increasingly liberal Warren Court decisions, it was the Burger Court that first created abortion rights,[73] protected women under the Fourteenth Amendment,[74] permitted school busing,[75] and accepted race-based affirmative action plans.[76] But as Nixon supported the Equal Rights Amendment (ERA) and introduced some early affirmative action programs into the executive branch, at least some of these liberal decisions were consistent with Nixon's preferences.

Beyond the cases of Nixon and Reagan, we can more generally examine the success of presidents in their Supreme Court appointments. Using expert judges to assess presidential Ideology,[77] we find fairly strong correlations between presidential preferences and the justices' behavior: .45 in civil liberties cases and .58 in economic cases. But as was the case with Blackmun, this association is not constant across time. During the first four years of the justices' tenure, their voting behavior correlates at .55 with their appointing president's preferences in civil liberties cases and at .58 with their appointing president's preferences in economic cases. But for years 11–20 of the justices' tenure, those figures drop to .10 and .28, respectively.[78]

We examine the impact of presidential regimes on the Court's behavior in Figure 10.2. We begin with a moderate Eisenhower Court, which decided 57.5 percent of its civil liberties cases in the liberal direction. As expected, the average liberalism score rose during the presidencies of Kennedy and Johnson and decreased during Nixon's and Ford's tenures. With no appointees, Carter had no impact on the Court. Yet Ronald Reagan, perhaps the most conservative president of the twentieth century, oversaw a Court that had only a marginally lower average score than Ford and Carter despite four appointees.

Influence depends not just on whom the president places on the Court, but on whom that justice replaces. For example, Reagan placed the extremely conservative Antonin Scalia on the Court, but Scalia took the associate justice seat of William Rehnquist, another strong conservative. Appointments such as that may have little impact on the Court's decisions.

Thus, explanations of presidential impact become clear when we examine Figure 10.3, which displays the average annual voting scores of each president's appointees and the justices they replaced.

At the time Richard Nixon took office in 1969, the Supreme Court consisted of Chief Justice Earl Warren and Associate Justices Black, Harlan II, Brennan, Stewart, Fortas, White, Marshall, and Douglas. The average civil liberties score for these nine justices was 68.9. The four justices whom President

---

[73] *Roe v. Wade*, 410 U.S. 113 (1973).

[74] *Reed v. Reed*, 404 U.S. 71 (1971).

[75] *Swann v. Charlotte-Mecklenburg Board of Education* (1971).

[76] *Regents v. Bakke*, 438 U.S. 265 (1978).

[77] Jeffrey A. Segal, Richard Timpone, and Robert Howard, "Buyer Beware: Presidential Success in Supreme Court Appointments," 53 *Political Research Quarterly* 557 (2000). The expert judges were a random sample of scholars in the Presidency section of the American Political Science Association.

[78] *Id.*

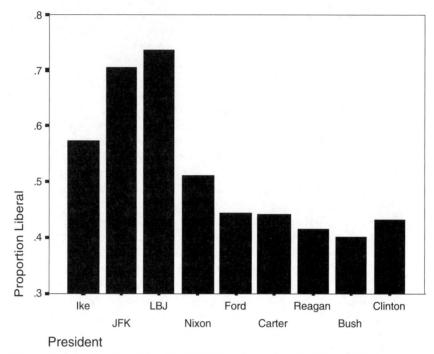

Figure 10.2. Proportion Liberal in Civil Liberties during Presidential Regimes.

Nixon replaced (Warren, Black, Fortas, and Harlan II) averaged 69.3, almost exactly the same as the Court average. The four justices Nixon appointed in their place averaged 35.2, lowering the Court's average to 52.9, almost directly in the middle of the civil liberties score. But although Reagan's nominees were as conservative as Nixon's, Reagan's appointees replaced other conservatives, leaving his short-run impact on the High Court fairly negligible.

Given the discretion that justices have, and the impact of ideology in shaping that discretion, Chief Justice Rehnquist finds it "normal and desirable for Presidents to attempt to pack the Court."[79] As he explains:

Surely we would not want it any other way. We want our federal courts, and particularly the Supreme Court, to be independent of public opinion when deciding the particular cases or controversies that come before them. The provision for tenure during good behavior and the prohibition against diminution of compensation have proved more than adequate to secure that sort of independence. The result is that judges are responsible to no electorate or constituency. But the manifold provisions of the Constitution with which judges must deal are by no means crystal clear in their import, and reasonable minds may differ as to which interpretation is proper. When a vacancy occurs on the

[79] William Rehnquist, *The Supreme Court: How It Was, How It Is* (New York: Morrow, 1987), p. 236.

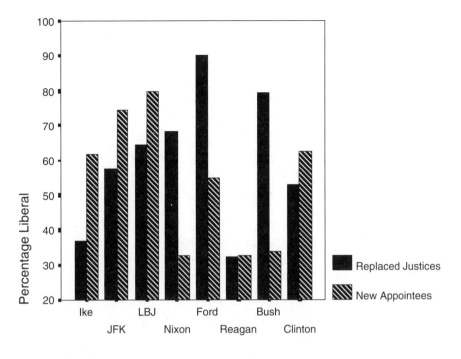

President

Figure 10.3. Liberalism of Outgoing and Incoming Justices, by Presidential Regime.

Court, it is entirely appropriate that the vacancy be filled by the President, responsible to a national constituency, as advised by the Senate.[80]

Whether packing the Court is a laudable goal or not, a variety of factors can conspire against presidents. Presidents may have goals beyond policy when naming Supreme Court justices, as in Eisenhower's preelection selection of the Catholic Democrat William Brennan or Reagan's redemption of a campaign promise by naming a woman to the Court. And changing attitudes can rob a president of the long-lasting influence he may have wished from one of his justices. But the public that elected Richard Nixon in 1968 desired and received a more conservative Supreme Court. Though the Reagan revolution did not make the Court *more* conservative, it did guarantee another generation of conservative domination and provided four of the five votes (all but Thomas's) needed to select George W. Bush as the forty-third president.

SUMMARY AND CONCLUSION

Presidents nominate individuals to the Court in order to satisfy certain goals. For some presidents policy concerns are paramount; others are more concerned

[80] *Id.*

with garnering future electoral support or paying off past political debts. Although the Senate routinely confirms most nominations, it rejects a substantial number. Five nominees were not confirmed between 1968 and 1987. We find that senators' votes greatly depend on the ideological distance between senators and the nominee, the perceived qualifications of the nominee, and crucially, the interaction between the two. In short, a nominee's reception hinges on the characteristics of the nominee and the composition of the Senate.

So, too, the context of a nomination strongly influences the outcome. The strength and popularity of the president emerge as important determinants of individual votes. In addition, the relative mobilization of interest groups around a nominee has pronounced effects.

The appointment process, in which presidents typically nominate justices ideologically close to them and the Senate closely evaluates the nominees' ideology, ensures that even if the justices follow their own preferences, those preferences are usually shared by the dominant political coalition.[81]

Thus although Justice Thomas was undoubtedly correct that confirmation is a political process, it remains for us to ascertain whether, as he also suggests, politics evaporates once justices are seated on the Court.

---

[81] Robert Dahl, "Decision-Making in a Democracy: The Supreme Court as National Policy Maker," 6 *Journal of Public Law* 179 (1957).

11

Getting into Court

Assertions by persons about to initiate a lawsuit, as well as by those who have already lost, that they will take their case all the way to the United States Supreme Court undoubtedly bespeak their deeply felt intentions, but in most cases their avowals lack credibility. Individuals who wish to file a lawsuit must be proper parties; that is, they must have standing to sue. If they do have such credentials, they must also take their case to the proper forum: The court in question must have jurisdiction – the capability to resolve their dispute. Assuming that the plaintiff is a proper party and is in the proper forum, a third hurdle to Supreme Court resolution remains: The justices themselves must deem the matter worthy of their consideration. The last is by far the most difficult to surmount.

Decisions about access, whether they concern proper parties or the proper forum, may appear to be purely legalistic and to have no policy effects. Not so. "'Jurisdiction,' the Court has aptly observed, 'is a word of many, too many meanings.'"[1] And although its definition does not resolve the merits of cases, it does determine which litigants will obtain a meritorious resolution of their disputes. In this chapter, we present the procedure whereby cases reach the Supreme Court and the factors that affect the justices' decision to accept a case for consideration. We conclude with a discussion of the Court's caseload.

CASE SELECTION

The procedure that the Court employs to select the cases that it wishes to decide is formally uncomplicated. But because the justices provide very little information about this stage of their decision making, we do not know whether its operation is comparably simple. However, we can infer that the procedure the Court uses to choose its cases does work efficiently. The justices manage to stay abreast of their docket, unlike judges in the vast majority of courts, state and federal.

[1] *Kontrick v. Ryan*, 157 L. Ed. 2d 867 (2004), at 879.

Little time elapses between receipt of a case and its disposition: A decision not to hear a case may be made within a week or two, but not for several months if the case reaches the Court during the summer, when it is not in session. Cases that the Court agrees to review are almost always heard and decided within a year. Finally, lay and professional criticism is notable by its absence, whereas assuredly if an affected or interested public considered the Court dilatory or thought it was ducking important issues, criticism would be swift.

The Court has authority to adopt rules governing its own operations, and a goodly number of these rules lay out the processes whereby losing litigants call cases to the Court's attention and the criteria that govern the justices' decision to review a lower court's judgment.[2]

For all practical purposes, the justices are free to accept or reject cases called to their attention as they see fit. That is to say, the Court has full control over its docket.[3] But that is not to say that the Court has no obligation to decide certain sorts of cases. The justices would not likely refuse to review a decision by a lower federal court that voided a major act of Congress; nor would it decline to consider a state court's decision that substantially redefined the scope of the First Amendment, absent extenuating circumstances.

Procedure

Because the Court had far less control over its docket in the nineteenth and early twentieth centuries than it has now, a remnant of this situation still persists in the technical distinction between the two major methods for accessing the Court: the writ of certiorari and the writ of appeal. Within one to three months of the date the highest state or federal court with authority to hear the matter has entered its judgment or refused to decide the case, the losing litigant may petition the Supreme Court for a writ of certiorari if the case is one that Congress has not required the Court to review. If Congress has mandated review, which the Court may nonetheless refuse to provide, the losing litigant files a writ of appeal. Although the effect of a denial differs from the one writ to the other, the Court uses the same procedure to grant either writ: the vote of four of the nine justices, three if only six or seven participate.

Statutes and court rules specify the time within which losing litigants must petition the Court to review their case. In all but the most exceptional circumstances, petitioning parties must have exhausted the remedies provided by the lower courts. Most often, this means a final judgment of either a state supreme court or a federal court of appeals. Many states, however, permit their supreme courts to deny a litigant leave to appeal, in which case the loser may

---

[2] *The Rules of the Supreme Court of the United States* are published at periodic intervals in the *United States Reports*. The most recent compilation appears at 515 U.S. 1197 (1995).

[3] Especially since 1988, when Congress eliminated virtually all of what remained of the Court's mandatory jurisdiction. See Lynn Weisberg, "New law eliminates Supreme Court's mandatory jurisdiction," 72 *Judicature* 138 (1988).

petition the Supreme Court once the inferior court of appeals or the trial court has issued a final judgment or decree, as the case may be.

The Supreme Court's Rules specify the format that petitions for writs of certiorari and appeal must take, the information they shall include, and the number of copies to be filed. Other parties to the litigation are notified and provided an opportunity to submit briefs in opposition to Supreme Court review. Additionally, interested third parties or interest groups have the opportunity to file amicus curiae (friend of the court) briefs supporting or opposing a petition for review. Nongovernmental entities may do so with the consent of both parties or, failing that, with the consent of the Court. National, state, and local governmental units are automatically granted the right to file briefs. The Court occasionally asks third parties, usually the United States or a state, to file amicus briefs.

On receipt of a petition and the winning party's brief in opposition, plus an optional reply by the petitioner, the clerk of the Supreme Court compiles and reviews the documents, along with the lower court's record of the case. If the clerk deems the petition frivolous – undeserving of review – he or she so informs the chief justice, who, in turn, has his or her clerks prepare a digest of the case. If the chief justice and clerks agree that the case does not merit review, it is deadlisted. The material and recommendations pertaining to the case are sent to the other justices, who, assisted by their clerks, review the file. If all the justices agree with deadlisting, the case is not discussed in conference and is automatically denied review. This fate apparently befalls well over half the petitions. But if any justice objects to deadlisting, the case is discussed in conference.

Cases not deadlisted are further considered in each justice's chambers, where memos are prepared by the clerks. To cut down on the work of the clerks, all but Justice Stevens have instructed their clerks to form a "cert pool," whereby the participating clerks divide the petitions among themselves. Other justices have their clerks write memos on each case or those considered important. In conference, the justices discuss the cases and vote on the basis of seniority. If, after discussion, at least four justices support review (three if seven or fewer participate), the petition is granted and the case is scheduled for oral argument. This is called the *Rule of Four*.

Not all the justices agree with the Rule of Four. In a short article in a nonlegal publication, Justice Stevens has said: "I am convinced that a careful study of all cases that have been granted on the basis of only four votes would indicate that in a surprisingly large number the law would have fared just as well if the decision of the Court of Appeals or the state court had been allowed to stand."[4] Stevens has not lobbied for the elimination of the Rule of Four in any of his judicial opinions, however.

---

[4] John Paul Stevens, "Deciding What to Decide: The Docket and the Rule of Four," in David M. O'Brien (ed.), *Judges on Judging: Views from the Bench* (Chatham, NJ: Chatham House, 1997), p. 94.

Of the eight thousand or so petitions the Court receives per term, approximately one hundred are granted and become candidates for formal decision.[5] One-third of the petitions for review are cases in which the Court's filing fee is paid and the requisite number of copies are filed, and better than two-thirds are *in forma pauperis* petitions in which the filing fee and the requirement of multiple copies are waived.[6] The vast majority of these are filed by incarcerated indigents. The justices accept and decide only a handful of these cases per term, well under 1 percent of the total submitted.

Criteria for Selection

In stating the criteria for granting a writ of certiorari, the justices give heaviest emphasis to decisions "in conflict" with another court of appeals, with a state court of last resort, or with "relevant decisions" of this Court.[7] The other two stipulated criteria are decisions that have "departed from the accepted and usual course of judicial proceedings, or sanctioned such a departure" and those that have "decided an important question of federal law that has not been, but should be, settled by this Court." Although conflict may be amenable to objective determination, the Court does not limit itself to the enumerated considerations, which, according to Rule 10, are "neither controlling nor fully measuring the Court's discretion."[8]

Although no comparable rule addresses the granting of writs of appeal, the rules provide indirect guidance by instructing appellants and appellees about the kind of arguments and considerations their briefs should contain. The fact that the Court uses the same procedure – the Rule of Four, described earlier – to dispose of petitions for certiorari as well as writs of appeal suggests that their criteria for selection may be fungible.

That four or more justices agree to review a case does not necessarily ensure a decision on the merits of the controversy. After oral argument, a majority may rule that the writ was improvidently granted or dismiss an appeal for lack of jurisdiction, for want of a substantial federal question, or for some other nonmeritorious reason.

But that does not end the story. Consider the following: An attorney tells his client who has been convicted of a capital offense and who has petitioned the Supreme Court for review that he has good news and bad news. The good news is that four justices voted to grant certiorari. The bad is that five have not voted to stay his execution pending review of his case. The upshot: He is executed (by Texas, not surprisingly). Justice Brennan explains: "Four Members of this Court have voted to grant certiorari in this case, but because a stay cannot be

---

[5] Granting of a petition does not necessarily preclude a summary decision on the merits without the benefit of oral argument and a formal opinion of the Court. Rule 16.1 specifically so provides.

[6] 518 U.S. 1059 (1995).

[7] Rule 10, 515 U.S. (1995), at 1204.

[8] *Id.*

Table 11.1. *Nonmeritorious Resolution of Orally Argued Cases,*
1953–2003 Terms

	Court			
Nonmeritorious Action	Warren	Burger	Rehnquist	Total
Writ improvidently granted	34	35	26	95
Want of adequate federal question	13	3	2	18
Want of jurisdiction	3	3	1	7
Adequate nonfederal grounds	7	10	2	19
To determine basis of state decision	4	5	2	11
Miscellaneous	2	6	2	10
Nonmeritorious total	63	62	35	160

entered without five votes, the execution cannot be halted."[9] Normally in such cases, "one of the five justices who does not believe the case certworthy will nonetheless vote to stay; this is so that the 'Rule of Four' will not be rendered meaningless by an execution that occurs before the Court considers the case on the merits."[10] In earlier terms, Justice Powell was willing to provide the fifth vote to stay executions when cert had been granted. But in the *Hamilton* case neither Rehnquist nor White nor O'Connor nor Scalia nor Kennedy was willing to issue the stay.

From the beginning of the Warren Court through the end of the 2003 term, the justices addressed the advisability of a nonmeritorious decision after oral argument in 160 cases (see Table 11.1). In almost 90 percent, the justices did deny the plaintiffs access notwithstanding their initial decision to the contrary (143 of 160). In only fifteen cases did the justices reconfirm the grant of access. Ten denied the states' contentions that their decisions rested on adequate non-federal grounds (of a total of twenty cases). Three reconsidered cases requested the state supreme court to answer certain questions of law; the other two sought determination of the basis for the state court's decision.

Reconsideration that follows a grant of access does not necessarily undermine the integrity of the Rule of Four. But, as Justice Douglas pointed out: "If four can grant and the opposing five dismiss, then the four cannot get a decision of the case on the merits. The integrity of the four-man vote rule ... would then be impaired."[11] The justice who most assiduously subverted the rule was Frankfurter. In workers' compensation cases, he regularly refused to address the merits after he had voted to deny cert. He self-righteously rationalized his position as follows:

The right of a Justice to dissent from an action of the Court is historic. ... Not four, not eight, Justices can require another to decide a case that he regards as not properly before

[9] *Hamilton v. Texas*, 497 U.S. 1016 (1990), at 1016–1017.
[10] *Straight v. Wainwright*, 476 U.S. 1132 (1986), at 1135 (Brennan, dissenting).
[11] *United States v. Shannon*, 342 U.S. 288 (1952), at 298.

the Court. The failure of a Justice to persuade his colleagues does not require him to yield to their views, if he has a deep conviction that the issue is sufficiently important.... Even though a minority may bring a case here for oral argument, that does not mean that the majority has given up its right to vote on the ultimate disposition of the case as conscience directs. This is not a novel doctrine. As a matter of practice, members of the Court have at various times exercised the right of refusing to pass on the merits of cases that in their view should not have been granted review.[12]

If, however, one or more of the those voting to dismiss originally voted to grant, no impairment of the Rule of Four results.

Effects of Denial or Dismissal

The Court's refusal to decide a case arising on certiorari has no precedential effect. It means nothing more than that the case did not acquire the necessary votes to warrant review under the Rule of Four. Denial of cert does not legally indicate that the Supreme Court approves of the decision of the lower court. With regard to appeals, however, unqualified assertions that "dismissal and affirmance are treated legally [the same] as decisions on the merits of cases, and they have some weight as precedents for future cases" are "not quite correct."[13] Affirmation, with or without opinion, whether on certiorari or appeal, clearly has precedential value. So also when an appeal is dismissed for want of a substantial federal question as distinct from lack of jurisdiction. When the Court rules a question insubstantial, it says something about the merits of the case. But when it dismisses for want of jurisdiction, it has "no occasion to address the merits of the constitutional questions presented in the jurisdictional statements."[14]

Although peripheral to the denial and dismissal of petitions, the justices' practice of "holding" one or more of a number of cases that raise similar issues until the one that has been granted review has been decided warrants attention. The justices' docket books, which contain the votes and other actions taken before final disposition, are rife with references to cases being held. Once the Court makes its decision in the case selected for full review, the justices decide the disposition to be made of the held case(s). Although we lack systematic data on these cases, we may safely conclude that most of them are either conjoined with the formally decided case or otherwise subjected to grant–vacate–remand (GVR) treatment; that is, certiorari is granted; the decision of the lower court is vacated; and the case is remanded for further consideration in light of the

---

[12] *Rogers v. Missouri Pacific R. Co.*, 352 U.S. 500 (1957), and *Ferguson v. Moore-McCormick Lines*, 352 U.S. 521 (1957), at 528. Also see Glendon Schubert, *Quantitative Analysis of Judicial Behavior* (Glencoe, IL: Free Press, 1959), pp. 210–267, and Glendon Schubert, "Policy without Law: An Extension of the Certiorari Game," 14 *Stanford Law Review* 284 (1962). Since the beginning of the Warren Court in 1953, other than Frankfurter, in only five other cases did a justice dissenting from the grant of certiorari when four justices voted to grant refuse to address the merits and instead vote to dismiss the case.

[13] Lawrence Baum, *The Supreme Court*, 2d ed. (Washington, DC: Congressional Quarterly Press, 1985), p. 89.

[14] *Hopfmann v. Connolly*, 471 U.S. 459 (1985), at 460–461.

Court's decision in the formally decided case. Cases receiving GVR treatment are neither briefed nor orally argued but rather are "an appropriate exercise of our discretionary certiorari jurisdiction."[15] They are treated in the same way as cases in which certiorari is denied, except that the decision of the court that last decided them is not final. Further proceedings will occur.

Distinct from held cases are those that are relisted. This practice apparently began in the early 1970s and has the effect of postponing – that is, delaying – action on petitions to review decisions of lower courts. References to relisting are found in the docket sheets of both Brennan and Powell. Brennan makes no mention of it prior to the 1971 term, which was Powell's first term on the Court. According to H. W. Perry, the only source who makes more than passing reference to relisting,[16] any justice may request that a case be held over until the next conference (usually one week later). The reasons for relisting vary: Sometimes a justice wishes to persuade colleagues to grant cert; other times a justice wants more time to consider the case. Not uncommonly, one justice's request may be followed by another's. Although most such requests do not extend beyond a week, some run on for months. Thus, for example, Powell requested that *Snepp v. United States* be relisted five times between October 26, 1979, and January 11, 1980, and that its companion, *United States v. Snepp*, be relisted six times between October 5, 1979, and January 11, 1980. Thereafter, Stevens had both cases relisted on January 18, 1980.[17]

Although Perry quotes a justice in support of his assertion that with a couple of exceptions "relisting is not a favored practice,"[18] Brennan's and Powell's docket sheets identify well over two thousand relisted cases during the last fifteen terms of the Burger Court. Though many relisted cases end with certiorari's being denied, a substantial number do receive full treatment. The effect of this obviously delays the Court's productive process, with what cost we will not know, absent a systematic analysis of these cases and the behavior of the individual justices.[19]

THE SUPREME COURT'S CASELOAD

Tremendous growth has occurred in the Supreme Court's caseload over time. As shown in Figure 11.1, little change occurred in the number of cases filed

---

[15] *Lawrence v. Chater*, 516 U.S. 163 (1996), at 166.

[16] H. W. Perry, *Deciding to Decide* (Cambridge, MA: Harvard University Press, 1991), pp. 49–51.

[17] 444 U.S. 507 (1980). The cases were decided *per curiam* without oral argument on February 19, Stevens, Brennan, and Marshall dissenting. The cases concerned a Central Intelligence Agency (CIA) employee who breached a government agreement that he would publish nothing about the CIA without submitting it to the agency for prepublication review. His profits were validly subjected to governmental safekeeping. The dissenters noted that the government conceded the book contained no classified material and that, as a result, the restraint violated the First Amendment.

[18] Perry, *Deciding to Decide*, p. 51.

[19] For a preliminary analysis of relisting, see Harold J. Spaeth, "Relisting: An Unexamined Feature of Supreme Court Decision Making," 25 *Justice System Journal* 143 (2004).

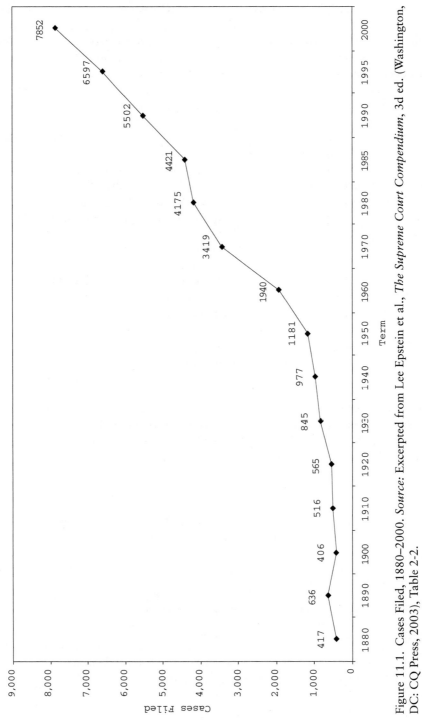

Figure 11.1. Cases Filed, 1880–2000. *Source:* Excerpted from Lee Epstein et al., *The Supreme Court Compendium*, 3d ed. (Washington, DC: CQ Press, 2003), Table 2-2.

between 1880 and 1920. Small increases occurred between the 1930s and 1950s, with explosive growth since. Between 1789 and 1950 the number of cases filed climbed from fewer than ten per term to slightly more than one thousand. By 1961 the Court faced two thousand filings. It took only six years after that to reach three thousand and but another six to reach four thousand. Between 1950 and 1995 the total number of filings almost sextupled.

Case filing fees are either paid to the Court or unpaid. The latter are placed on the *in forma pauperis* docket, which was known as the miscellaneous docket until the 1977 term. Through 1958 the paid cases annually exceeded the unpaid cases. During the Warren Court, the number of unpaid cases grew substantially and exceeded that of the paid cases every year from 1959 until 1978. They then held steady through the early 1980s but began to grow dramatically at the end of the decade, reaching more than forty-five hundred by the mid-1990s.[20]

The Supreme Court can review only a small percentage of the cases filed. Indeed, the Court reviews only about 5 percent of the paid cases and well below 1 percent of the *in forma pauperis* cases. Moreover, not all of these cases receive full treatment (oral argument and written opinions) by the Court; the remainder result in summary dispositions.

The early Warren Court decided fewer than 100 cases per year, whereas the later Burger Court heard and disposed of 185 cases in the 1982 term.[21] That appears to be close to the Court's institutional limit, for since then the Court has never decided more than 175 cases in a single term. The 1989 term of the Court, which made headlines for the rate at which it rejected petitions for review,[22] decided but 130 cases, the lowest total since 1980. Since then the number has dropped precipitously. In the 1998 and 1999 terms, counting case citations, it formally decided only eighty-one cases in each term, eighty-seven in 2000, and eighty-nine in 2001.[23]

We present the broad issues contained in the Warren, Burger, and Rehnquist Court's cases through the 2003 term in Table 11.2. As can be seen, continuity characterizes the issues decided. Criminal procedure was most frequently litigated in the Burger and Rehnquist Courts and was second only to economic cases in the Warren Court. Economic activity, civil rights, judicial power, and the First Amendment have received substantial attention from all three Courts. Yet, although economic activity is second overall in type of case heard, it occupies a decreasing share of the Court's agenda. A full quarter of the Warren Court's cases dealt with economic activity as compared with less than a fifth of the Burger and Rehnquist totals. Also showing a substantial decrease are cases dealing with unions and federal taxation, now with less than half the proportion they had in the Warren Court. Alternatively, issues of federalism are

[20] 518 U.S. 1059 (1996).

[21] Lee Epstein et al., *The Supreme Court Compendium*, 3d ed. (Washington, DC: Congressional Quarterly Press, 2003), Table 3-6.

[22] Linda Greenhouse, "As Its Workload Decreases, High Court Shuns New Cases," *New York Times*, 28 November 1989, p. A1.

[23] *Id.*

Table 11.2. *Case Selection by Issue Area Controlled for Court*

Terms	Warren 1953–1968	Burger 1968–1985	Rehnquist 1986–2003	Row Total
Criminal procedure	351	516	432	1299
	(19.6%)	(21.5%)	(24.2%)	(21.7%)
Economic activity	443	429	321	1193
	(24.7%)	(17.9%)	(18.0%)	(20.0%)
Civil rights	225	494	267	986
	(12.6%)	(20.6%)	(15.0%)	(16.5%)
Judicial power	232	271	250	753
	(13.0%)	(11.3%)	(14.0%)	(12.6%)
First Amendment	155	208	132	495
	(8.7%)	(8.7%)	(7.4%)	(8.3%)
Unions	127	108	50	285
	(7.1%)	(4.5%)	(2.8%)	(4.8%)
Federalism	82	86	111	279
	(4.6%)	(3.6%)	(6.2%)	(4.7%)
Federal taxation	114	68	54	236
	(6.4%)	(2.8%)	(3.0%)	(3.9%)
Due process	37	128	76	241
	(2.1%)	(5.3%)	(4.3%)	(4.0%)
Attorneys	10	32	28	70
	(0.6%)	(1.3%)	(1.6%)	(1.2%)
Privacy	3	40	37	80
	(0.2%)	(1.7%)	(2.1%)	(1.3%)
Interstate relations	9	17	13	39
	(0.5%)	(0.7%)	(0.7%)	(0.7%)
Miscellaneous	3	6	12	21
	(0.2%)	(0.2%)	(0.7%)	(0.4%)
Column total	1,791	2,403	1,783	5,977

Source: U.S. Supreme Court Judicial Database, using formally decided citation as the unit of analysis. http://www.as.uky.edu/polisci/ulmerproject.htm.

substantially more frequently litigated by the Rehnquist Court than its two predecessor Courts. A likely explanation for these trends may be the justices' perception that business, labor, and tax matters have relatively little salience, as compared with increased autonomy for the state and local governments. If we combine the six areas commonly lumped together as civil rights and liberties – criminal procedure, civil rights, First Amendment, due process, attorneys, and privacy – we find that more than half the Court's formal output concerns these matters. Finally, although the content of the cases heard might give some guide to the type of questions the Court deems important, it is not a foolproof indicator. Criminal procedure covers a wide array of constitutional issues, including Fourth, Fifth, Sixth, and Eighth Amendment rights. Privacy, on the other hand, has largely dealt with contraception and abortion. This does not necessarily make privacy a less important issue to the Court.

WHICH CASES FOR DECISION?

What leads the Court to grant cert? We take two approaches to answering this question. We first examine those factors linked with justice-level decisions to grant cert and then consider the aggregate decisions of the Court itself.

Individual-Level Models

No consensus exists among scholars as to what factors influence justices to vote to grant certiorari. Some view the process as essentially legalistic; others see it as essentially extralegal or policy based. Furthermore, among the extralegal school, dissensus exists as to whether the justices are forward thinking in their certiorari votes, that is, whether they consider the likelihood that they will win on the merits when voting to grant review.

We use data from the extended Burger Court Judicial Database to examine the factors motivating the justices' certiorari voting.[24]

Reversal Strategies. A major premise of most prior work on certiorari is the assumption that the justices prefer to hear cases they wish to reverse. Given a finite number of cases that can be reviewed in a given term, the Court must decide how to utilize its time, the Court's most scarce resource. Certainly, overturning unfavorable lower court decisions has more of an impact – if only to the parties to the litigation – than affirming favorable ones. Moreover, reversal of erroneous or malfeasant lower courts can help keep those courts in line. Thus, the justices should hear more decisions with which they disagree, other considerations being equal.

Tests using Burger Court data show that the relationship between the vote on the merits and the vote on cert is quite strong (see Table 11.3). We assume that when voting on cert the justices have a pretty good idea as to whether they would prefer to see the lower court's decision reversed or affirmed. Using whether they *actually* voted to reverse or affirm as an indicator of their *intention* to reverse or affirm, we see that every justice on the Burger Court was substantially more likely to vote to grant when she or he wished to reverse than when she or he wished to affirm. For cases decided on the merits, Justice Black voted to grant 82.2 percent of the time in cases when he wished to reverse, but only 48.6 percent of the time when he wanted to affirm.[25] Similar results can be found for the other justices.

---

[24] This database, along with others funded by the National Science Foundation (NSF) that pertain to the Supreme Court, is freely available, along with its documentation, at http://www.as.uky.edu/polisci/ulmerproject.htm.

[25] Statistically astute readers will notice a selection bias in this model. That is, we only observe this relationship for cases in which the Court granted cert, not for the population of cases. Correcting for this bias shows an even stronger relationship between the justices' preferences on the merits and their votes on cert. See Scott Graves and Jeffrey A. Segal, "Strategic Decision-Making on the Supreme Court: Aggressive Grants and Defensive Denials on the Vinson and Warren Courts," paper presented at the 2002 Annual Meeting of the American Political Science Association.

Table 11.3. *Grant Rate Percentage by Desire to Affirm or Reverse in the Burger Court, 1969–1986*

Justice	Reverse	Affirm	Gamma
Black	82.2 (118)	48.6 (111)	.66
Blackmun	81.9 (1,229)	61.3 (966)	.45
Brennan	74.9 (1,203)	42.4 (1,194)	.60
Burger	73.6 (1,275)	48.8 (797)	.49
Douglas	80.7 (415)	39.2 (339)	.73
Harlan	78.6 (117)	71.9 (114)	.18
Marshall	69.0 (1,212)	43.6 (1,155)	.48
O'Connor	85.9 (377)	72.4 (225)	.40
Powell	81.6 (1,225)	71.3 (722)	.28
Rehnquist	87.4 (1,274)	50.6 (757)	.74
Stevens	75.8 (718)	42.4 (655)	.62
Stewart	73.6 (991)	58.8 (631)	.32
White	89.4 (1,513)	78.7 (958)	.39

Note: Numbers in parentheses are total number of votes to affirm or reverse. Thus O'Connor voted to grant in 85.9% of the 377 cases in which she later voted to reverse and 72.4% of the 225 cases in which she later voted to affirm.

Source: Burger Court Database, using formally decided cases with docket plus split votes as the unit of analysis. Votes are from cases in which cert was actually granted. http://www.as.uky.edu/polisci/ulmerproject.htm.

The overall relationship between wishing to reverse and voting to grant can be measured by gamma, a measure of association that ranges from $+1.0$ (a perfect positive association) through 0.0 (no relationship) to -1.0 (a perfect negative relationship). All of the gammas for the simple reversal relationship are positive and, typically, fairly strong. This suggests, again, that justices wishing to reverse are more likely to vote to grant than are justices wishing to affirm.

Prediction Strategies. Although reversal is a major premise determining which cases to review, one ought not consider it the only extralegal factor guiding the cert votes of policy-minded justices. First, with approximately eight thousand cases confronting the Court annually, justices who voted to review every case with which they disagreed would generate institutional paralysis. Salience obviously matters. Moreover, even if the Court could hear all cases with which a justice disagreed, it is not necessarily in that justice's best policy interest to have all such cases reviewed. If the justice will likely lose on the merits, it is preferable that the case not be heard at all.

A series of obscenity cases during the 1970s exemplifies. By a 5–4 vote in *Miller v. California*,[26] the majority decided that states and local governments could ban sexually explicit, patently offensive work that lacked serious literary,

[26] 413 U.S. 15 (1973).

artistic, political, or social value and that violated contemporary local community standards. The four dissenters preferred constitutional standards more protective of freedom of communication. When lower courts upheld convictions based on *Miller*, three of the dissenters – Brennan, Stewart, and Marshall – voted to grant certiorari. Justice Stevens, who replaced Justice Douglas, also opposed *Miller* but nevertheless voted to deny cert:

Nothing in Mr. Justice Brennan's opinion dissenting from the denial of certiorari in this case persuades me that any purpose would be served by such argument. For there is no reason to believe that the majority of the Court which decided *Miller v. California* . . . is any less adamant than the minority. Accordingly, regardless of how I might vote on the merits after full argument, it would be pointless to grant certiorari in case after case of this character only to have *Miller* reaffirmed time after time.[27]

Alternatively, justices who favored a particular lower court decision might vote to grant cert if they were confident of affirmation. Thus, although reversal clearly is a part of the justices' policy-based strategy, so also prediction may be.

We thus examine the extent to which justices' cert behavior depends upon their prediction of the ultimate outcome. A basic strategic calculus suggests that those who will win on the merits should be more likely to vote for certiorari than those who will lose on the merits. This assumes, of course, that the justices should have some indicator of how their colleagues are likely to vote. Our best defense of this assumption is that this book's senior author has been able to predict the justices' votes with almost 90 percent accuracy.[28] We assume that the justices are even better able to assess each other's behavior than this outsider is.

Our findings, though, find a rather weak relationship between the likelihood of winning on the merits and voting to grant (see Table 11.4). Whereas Black is substantially more likely to vote to grant when he is going to win (72.8 percent) than when he is going to lose (60.9 percent), four justices – Harlan, O'Connor, Powell, and Stewart – show the opposite relationship. The gammas, which ran from .73 to .28 in the reversal model, run only from .27 to −.28 in the prediction model.[29]

Before we close the book on the prediction strategy, we note that justices may engage in different strategies when they are reversal minded than when they are affirmation minded.[30] Consider a lower court decision that a justice likes. Granting the case could prove beneficial because the Court could take a case that applies to the lower court's jurisdiction, affirm it, and thus have it

---

[27] *Liles v. Oregon*, 425 U.S 963 (1976), at 963–964.

[28] Harold J. Spaeth, *Supreme Court Policy Making* (San Francisco: W. H. Freeman, 1979).

[29] Correcting for the selection bias yields comparably weak results. See Graves and Segal, "Stategic."

[30] Saul Brenner and John F. Krol, "Strategies in Certiorari Voting on the United States Supreme Court," 51 *Journal of Politics* 828 (1989); John F. Krol and Saul Brenner, "Strategies in Certiorari Voting on the United States Supreme Court: A Reevaluation," 43 *Political Research Quarterly* 335 (1990); and Robert L. Boucher, Jr., and Jeffrey A. Segal, "Supreme Court Justices as Strategic Decision Makers," 57 *Journal of Politics* 824 (1995).

Table 11.4. *Grant Rate Percentage by Winning or Losing on the Merits in the Burger Court, 1969–1986*

Justice	Lose	Win	Gamma
Black	60.9 (69)	72.8 (184)	.27
Blackmun	69.8 (334)	74.3 (2053)	.11
Brennan	51.9 (774)	61.6 (1856)	.20
Burger	63.6 (346)	65.8 (2124)	.05
Douglas	60.8 (344)	62.9 (493)	.05
Harlan	78.6 (117)	71.9 (114)	−.18
Marshall	49.9 (723)	59.0 (1835)	.18
O'Connor	84.2 (95)	80.4 (612)	−.13
Powell	80.4 (224)	78.1 (1835)	−.07
Rehnquist	66.4 (458)	75.8 (1775)	.23
Stevens	54.7 (369)	61.3 (1173)	.13
Stewart	68.7 (278)	68.0 (1467)	−.02
White	84.0 (356)	85.7 (2320)	.07

Note: Numbers in parentheses are total number of votes to affirm or reverse. Thus O'Connor voted to grant in 84.2% of the 95 cases in which she later lost on the merits and 80.4% of the 612 cases in which she later won on the merits.

Source: Burger Court Database using formally decided cases with docket plus split votes as the unit of analysis. Votes are from cases in which cert was actually granted. http://www.as.uky.edu/polisci/ulmerproject.htm.

apply to the entire country. Of course, this strategy could be very risky because the Court could take that favorable lower court decision and *reverse* it, thus taking a favorable decision from one circuit and having the opposite result applied to the entire nation. Thus, a justice wishing to affirm must be very careful when voting to grant!

Alternatively, a justice wishing to reverse has somewhat less to lose: An affirmance of the lower court outcome may nationalize the decision but does not change the result for the parties at hand. Moreover, a justice who wishes to reverse knows that reversal on the merits is more likely than affirmance on the merits. Since voting to grant and wishing to affirm is a riskier strategy than voting to grant and wishing to reverse, and since reversal is the more likely outcome, affirmance-minded justices need to pay much more attention to probable outcomes than do reversal-minded justices. In other words, we should be more likely to find a positive relationship between winning on the merits and voting to grant for those justices who desire to affirm than for those justices who wish to reverse.

We compare the relationship between winning on the merits and voting to grant for affirmance- and reversal-minded justices (see Table 11.5). In order to avoid overwhelming readers with numbers, we simply provide the gammas, which measure the degree of association. Note that we find no positive

Table 11.5. *Effect of Predicted Success on the Merits on Granting Certiorari (gamma coefficients) Contingent on Affirming or Reversing in the Burger Court, 1969–1986*

Justice	Reverse	Affirm
Black	−.37	.34
Blackmun	−.16	.08
Brennan	−.18	.19
Burger	−.16	.11
Douglas	−.31	.03
Harlan	−.17	.09
Marshall	−.02	.19
O'Connor	−.62	.08
Powell	−.42	.13
Rehnquist	−.23	.37
Stevens	−.18	.03
Stewart	.01	−.10
White	−.28	.24

Note: Gamma coefficients are from the relationship between winning on the merits and voting to grant cert, contingent on the justice's vote to affirm or reverse.

Source: Burger Court Database using formally decided cases with docket plus split votes as the unit of analysis. Votes are from cases in which cert was actually granted. http://www.as.uky.edu/polisci/ulmerproject.htm.

relationship between winning on the merits and voting to grant for reversal-minded justices.[31] There is generally a positive relationship between winning on the merits and voting to grant for affirmance-minded justices, but this would have to be labeled *weak* for everyone except Black, Rehnquist, and White.

Thus, we conclude that at the individual level, justices are strongly influenced by their own preferences on the case, uninfluenced by what their colleagues may do on the merits when the justice wishes to reverse, and weakly influenced by what their colleagues may do when they wish to affirm.

Aggregate-Level Models

If the members of the Supreme Court are motivated by their policy preferences, then they would presumably want justice done as they perceive it and not just

---

[31] We are hesitant about drawing firmer conclusions about defensive denials, cases in which a justice wants to reverse on the merits but votes to deny at cert out of fear that the majority would affirm on the merits, because cases in which defensive denials successfully prevented the Court from hearing the case do not show up in our data set.

Table 11.6. *Affirmation and Reversal by Court*

Terms	Warren 1953–1968	Burger 1969–1985	Rehnquist 1986–2003	Row Total
Affirm	748 (35.2%)	956 (34.7%)	811 (40.4%)	2,515 (36.5%)
Reverse	1,378 (64.8%)	1,798 (65.3%)	1,195 (59.6%)	4,371 (63.5%)
Column total	2,126	2,754	2,006	6,886

Source: U.S. Supreme Court Judicial Database using formally decided cases with docket plus split votes as the unit of analysis. http://www.as.uky.edu/polisci/ulmerproject.htm.

to the litigants before it, but to the hundreds of thousands of litigants whose decisions the Court cannot review. It would do the Court little good to require the exclusion of evidence illegally obtained against Dollree Mapp, the petitioner in the case that established the exclusionary rule, only to have lower courts flout this decision.

Unfortunately, the Supreme Court has few of the traditional mechanisms available to hierarchical superiors for controlling judicial subordinates.[32] It can neither hire nor fire lower court judges, promote nor demote them, raise their salary nor dock their pay.

There is one tool available to it, though: It can reverse lower court decisions. This act, we believe, is costly to lower court judges in terms of their professional status and policy preferences. Thus it is crucial for a policy-based Court to use the primary hierarchical tool at its disposal, reversal, as a mechanism for controlling lower court behavior.

We report the extent to which the Supreme Court reverses lower court decisions for the Warren, Burger, and Rehnquist Courts in Table 11.6.[33] As can be seen, the Warren, Burger, and Rehnquist Courts all reversed more cases than they affirmed, though the proportion is a bit smaller for the Rehnquist

[32] Charles M. Cameron, Jeffrey A. Segal, and Donald R. Songer, "Strategic Auditing in a Political Hierarchy: An Informational Model of the Supreme Court's Certiorari Decisions," 94 *American Political Science Review* 101 (2000), at 102.

[33] Our data consist of all orally argued cases decided from the 1953 through 2003 terms except those that arose on original jurisdiction. This period includes the Warren and Burger Courts and the 1986–2003 terms of the Rehnquist Court. We use docket number as our unit of analysis because the Court does not necessarily dispose of all cases decided by a single opinion in the same fashion. We also count as separate cases the handful that contain split votes, in the sense that one or more of the justices voted with the majority on one aspect or issue of the case and dissented on another. We include these to preclude making an arbitrary judgment of whether the Court affirmed or reversed the lower court's decision. Because the Court's formal disposition of the cases it decides does not unerringly indicate affirmation or reversal, we focus instead on whether the petitioning party prevailed in whole or in substantial part or not. If the petitioning party prevailed, we count the case as a reversal of the lower court. If the petitioning party did not prevail, we count the case as affirmed.

Table 11.7. *Reversal Rate Percentage by Term*

Term	Rate	Term	Rate	Term	Rate	Term	Rate	Term	Rate
53	48.2	62	74.7	71	61.2	81	65.0	91	64.5
54	66.7	63	76.2	72	68.2	82	62.6	92	61.7
55	53.3	64	72.5	73	67.5	83	72.1	93	44.0
56	66.0	65	71.1	74	68.1	84	63.6	94	59.6
57	56.6	66	69.9	75	65.5	85	58.3	95	59.6
58	57.1	67	68.0	76	64.6	86	60.8	96	65.2
59	60.3	68	72.1	77	68.7	87	48.2	97	51.6
60	53.1	69	64.5	78	66.9	88	49.4	98	63.1
61	68.9	70	60.1	79	61.5	89	55.2	99	55.3
				80	66.7	90	60.8	00	54.8

Source: Jeffrey A. Segal and Harold J. Spaeth, *The Supreme Court and the Attitudinal Model Revisited* (Cambridge: Cambridge University Press, 2002), p. 264.

Court (57 versus 64 percent). When we break down the data by term (see Table 11.7), we find that except in the first term of the Warren Court and the 1987, 1988, and 1993 terms of the Rehnquist Court, reversals invariably outnumber affirmances. Reversals peaked in the 1962, 1963, and 2003 terms at 74.7, 76.2, and 80.4 percent, respectively. The reversal rates for the post-2000 terms are 70.0 (01), 65.1 (02), and 80.4 (03).

Conflict with Supreme Court Preferences. A focus on reversal rates allows us to make inferences about the cases the Court chooses to hear, but it does not allow for inferences about cases the Court chooses not to hear. For instance, the preceding data are consistent with a Supreme Court that consciously seeks hierarchical control through reversal, but they are also consistent with a Court oblivious to such concerns facing lower courts whose preferences and behavior diverge from those of the Court. Without any certiorari strategy a majority of cases would be reversed under such conditions. But if the Court's certiorari behavior is consciously policy based, those cases that are granted should be more likely to be reversed than those cases that are denied. Of course, this requires us to know what would have happened to cases in which cert was denied.

One solution is to make judgment calls as to whether lower court decisions appealed to the Supreme Court conflict with Supreme Court preferences. Using this strategy, Sidney Ulmer shows that conflict between lower court decisions and (his assessment of) Supreme Court preferences is the most important factor affecting the grant of certiorari. The Court granted cert in 44 percent of the conflict cases, but only 7 percent of those without.[34]

---

[34] S. Sidney Ulmer, "The Supreme Court's Certiorari Decisions: Conflict as a Predictive Variable," 78 *American Political Science Review* 901 (1984).

Our own work has found similar results. Using a model of the Supreme Court's search and seizure decisions,[35] we calculated the probability that any lower court search and seizure decision would be reversed if heard by the Supreme Court.[36] We found that the likelihood of reversal has an enormous impact on the probability of granting cert. For example, when the likelihood of reversal is below 10 percent, the probability of granting certiorari is near zero, even when other factors such as the presence of the United States as petitioner or dissent on the lower court is present. But when the likelihood of reversal is above 80 percent, the probability of granting cert can jump to .5 or greater. This is a remarkable increase in a population in which the mean probability of a grant is .05 or less. Thus, a substantial increase in the likelihood of reversal can increase by a factor of 10 or more the probability that cert is granted.

Information and Lower Court Ideology. Although these studies support the notion that a policy-minded Court uses its certiorari jurisdiction to control the lower court, they do not suggest how the Court might most efficiently go about doing so.[37]

One useful piece of information available to a Supreme Court seeking doctrinal compliance is the ideology of the lower court. Consider a conservative Supreme Court reviewing lower court decisions in search and seizure cases. If the lower court is liberal and it issues a conservative decision (i.e., one upholding the admission of seized evidence), there is little reason for the Supreme Court to grant review, for if a conservative decision is acceptable to a more liberal court, it would certainly be acceptable to the more conservative Supreme Court. Similarly, the Supreme Court would have little reason to second-guess a liberal decision by a lower court more conservative than it is.

Alternatively, if a liberal lower court facing a conservative Supreme Court renders a liberal decision, it may be inherently suspect, and thus regardless of the apparent facts (presence of a warrant, probable cause, etc.), petitions in those cases will face the strictest scrutiny.

Models similar to this help explain a wide variety of political events. For example, many conservatives accepted Nixon's opening to China, believing that if a staunch anti-Communist such as Nixon thought it was in the national

[35] See Jeffrey A. Segal, "Deciding Supreme Court Decisions Probabilistically: The Search and Seizure Cases, 1962–1981," 78 *American Political Science Review* 891 (1984).

[36] To do this, we began with Segal's search and seizure model, which uses the facts of each case, such as a warrant, or probable cause, to calculate the probability p that the Supreme Court would uphold any given search. See Segal, "Deciding." If the lower court rejected the search, the probability that the Supreme Court would reverse is $1 - p$. If the lower court upheld the search, the probability that the Supreme Court would reverse is p. See Jeffrey A. Segal, Charles M. Cameron, and Donald R. Songer, "A Rational Actor Model of Supreme Court Decisions to Accept Cases for Review," paper presented at the Annual Meeting of the American Political Science Association, Washington, DC, 1993.

[37] This section is based on Cameron, Segal, and Songer, "Model."

interest to do so, then perhaps it was okay. Of course, had a moderate Democrat attempted such a move, cries of treason would have been heard.

More relevant to our concerns, an informational model along these lines does an extremely good job of explaining certiorari decisions in search and seizure cases during the conservative Burger Court. For example, the Court almost never reviewed conservative decisions from liberal, moderate, or conservative courts of appeals. It did, however, generally review liberal decisions from moderate to conservative lower courts except when the apparent facts showed an extremely intrusive search. In such cases, the Court was willing to deny cert. But when liberal courts reached liberal decisions, the Court frequently granted cert and did so regardless of the apparent intrusiveness of the search. The Court viewed such decisions to be inherently untrustworthy. Thus the data support the model's hypothesis that the Court uses certiorari grants and merits reversals to keep control of the lower courts, and most efficiently does so by considering the interactions of case facts, decisions, and lower court ideology.

Cue Theory. Beyond hierarchical control, the major theoretical focus of studies examining aggregate cert decisions is cue theory, first applied to judicial behavior by Tanenhaus and associates.[38] Arguing that the justices can give petitions no more than cursory consideration, they hypothesize that certain cues will merit further consideration while those without any cues will be dropped. The cues they examined were the parties involved, the subject area of the case, and conflict in the court below.

Parties and Groups as Cues for Review. Various parties may have an effect on the grant of review. One party who might particularly be advantaged is the United States, whose cases are usually briefed and argued by the office of the solicitor general. The solicitor general appears before the Court more than any other attorney and appears to benefit from this repeat experience.[39] As Chief Justice Rehnquist observed: "We depend heavily on the Solicitor General in deciding whether to grant certiorari in cases in which the government is a party."[40] According to one justice, "The ablest advocates in the U.S. are the advocates in the Solicitor General's Office."[41] The office has been considerate of the Court's caseload, appealing only one-tenth or so of the

[38] Joseph Tanenhaus, Marvin Schick, Matthew Muraskin, and Daniel Rosen, "The Supreme Court's Certiorari Jurisdiction: Cue Theory," in Glendon Schubert (ed.), *Judicial Decision-Making* (New York: Free Press, 1963), pp. 111–132.

[39] See, generally, Marc Galanter, "Why the 'Haves' Come Out Ahead: Speculations on the Limits of Legal Change," 9 *Law and Society Review* 95 (1974), and, specifically, Doris Marie Provine, *Case Selection in the United States Supreme Court* (Chicago: University of Chicago Press, 1980).

[40] *Alvarado v. United States,* 497 U.S. 543 (1990), at 546.

[41] Karen O'Connor and Lee Epstein, "States Rights or Criminal Rights: An Analysis of State Performance in U.S. Supreme Court Litigation," paper presented at the Annual Meeting of the Northeastern Political Science Association, Philadelphia, 1983.

cases that the government loses.[42] These are presumably the most meritorious ones.

Study after study has found that the United States is a vastly privileged party in relation to cert.[43] For example, between 1947 and 1958, when the United States sought review, cert was granted 47 percent of the time, but when the United States did not seek review and no other cues were present, cert was granted only 6 percent of the time.[44] Overall, the evidence is overwhelming: Solicitor general requests for review enormously increase the probability of acceptance.

Additionally, the existence of a repeat player can signal the Court as to the importance of a case.[45] One-shot attorneys representing clients who lost below have little to lose by insisting to the Court that their case is of the utmost importance. Even if the Court grants cert and eventually discovers that the case is not earth-shaking, the attorney has lost little. Not so for the repeat player, whose credibility in future cert briefs is decidedly at stake.

Influences on cert decisions are not limited to the parties. As noted, interest groups and various organizations can file amicus curiae briefs. These briefs, in addition to providing legal arguments that the parties themselves may not make, may enable the Court to judge the importance of the litigation. Indeed in one case, Justice Stevens in dissent buttressed his view that the case was an unimportant one that never should have been reviewed, noting that "not a single brief *amicus curiae* was filed."[46] If briefs amicus curiae signal a case's importance, then briefs both in favor and in opposition should further enhance review, and they do. One study found that cert was granted in 36 percent of the cases they examined that had at least one brief, but in only 5 percent of those without any. Although briefs favoring review produced stronger effects, briefs opposed also increased the probability of review.[47]

---

[42] Robert Scigliano, *The Supreme Court and the Presidency* (New York: Free Press, 1971), p. 169.

[43] Provine, *Case Selection*, p. 87; S. Sidney Ulmer, William Hintze, and Louise Kirklosky, "The Decision to Grant or Deny Certiorari: Further Consideration of Cue Theory," 6 *Law and Society Review* 637 (1972); Stuart H. Teger and Douglas Kosinski, "The Cue Theory of Supreme Court Certiorari Jurisdiction: A Reconsideration," 42 *Journal of Politics* 834 (1980); Virginia Armstrong and Charles Johnson, "Certiorari Decision Making by the Warren and Burger Courts: Is Cue Theory Time Bound," 15 *Polity* 141 (1982); Gregory A. Caldeira and John Wright, "Organized Interests and Agenda Setting in the U.S. Supreme Court," 82 *American Political Science Review* 1109 (1988).

[44] Joseph Tanenhaus, Marvin Schick, Matthew Muraskin, and Daniel Rosen, "The Supreme Court's Certiorari Jurisdiction: Cue Theory," in Glendon Schubert (ed.), *Judicial Decision-Making* (New York: Free Press, 1963), pp. 111–132.

[45] Kevin T. McGuire and Gregory A. Caldeira, "Lawyers, Organized Interests, and the Law of Obscenity: Agenda Setting in the Supreme Court," 87 *American Political Science Review* 717 (1993).

[46] *United States v. Dalm*, 494 U.S. 596 (1990), at 612.

[47] Caldeira and Wright, "Organized Interests," p. 1119.

Lower Court Conflict. When circuits conflict with one another, or when state supreme courts conflict with one another on national questions, "federal law is being administered in different ways in different parts of the country; citizens in some circuits are subject to liabilities or entitlements that citizens in other circuits are not burdened with or otherwise entitled to."[48] Thus the Court should grant review to such cases even though they otherwise would not merit review. Indeed, Rule 10 of the Supreme Court specifically lists conflicts between or among lower courts as a reason for granting cert.

Not all justices agree that sufficient credence is paid to lower court conflicts. In a dissent to a denial of review on the final day of the 1989 term, Justice White pointed out that he had dissented from denial of certiorari sixty-seven times during the term:

My notes on these dissents indicate that on 48 occasions I dissented because in my view there were conflicts among courts of appeals sufficiently crystallized to warrant certiorari if the federal law is to be maintained in any satisfactory uniform condition. In 7 other cases, there were differences on the same federal issue between courts of appeals and state courts; in another case state courts of last resort differed with each other. Finally, there were 11 cases that did not involve a conflict but in my view presented important issues that had not been settled but should be settled by this Court.[49]

White admitted that though some of these conflicts may not have been "real" or "square," in most cases the court of appeals "expressly differs" with another court, "yet certiorari is denied because the conflict is 'tolerable' or 'narrow,' or because other courts of appeals should have the opportunity to weigh in on one side or another of the unsettled issue, or for some other unstated reason."[50]

At the other extreme, the Court sometimes manufactures a conflict in order to justify review. Thus, in a suit for equitable recoupment of a time-barred tax refund, the majority asserted that the "approach taken" by two courts of appeals conflicted with that "adopted" by another.[51] The dissenters, however, persuasively documented the absence of conflict.[52] Significantly, the majority made no effort to refute the dissenters' assertions.

Systematic analyses find White's concerns somewhat overstated. Ulmer's extensive treatment of the issue indicates the cruciality of intercircuit conflict to cert decisions of the Vinson and Warren Courts, but less to Burger Court decisions, after controlling for other factors.[53] Caldeira and Wright also show conflict to have significant effects, but unfortunately they do not distinguish between conflict among lower courts and conflict with the prevailing direction

[48] *Beaulieu v. United States*, 497 U.S. 1038 (1990), at 1039.
[49] *Id.*
[50] *Id.*
[51] *United States v. Dalm*, 494 U.S. 596 (1990), at 601.
[52] *Id.* at 614, note 2, 620–621, 623.
[53] Ulmer, "Certiorari Decisions."

of the Supreme Court's decisions on the issue that the case concerns.[54] The importance of intercircuit conflict suggests some level of rule-bound (i.e., Rule 10) behavior at cert.

Tanenhaus and associates studied a variant of the conflict hypothesis: whether disagreement within the court below or disagreement between different courts in the same case affected the likelihood of review. Neither of these is what Rule 10 means by "conflict," but both may signal the Court that something may be amiss. The authors found that the Court granted review 13 percent of the time when there were dissension between or within lower courts and no other cues present, versus 6 percent of the time when these cues were absent.[55]

Petition Type. We note again that the Court is more likely to grant review to paid petitions than to unpaid ones. Less than 5 percent of the former gain review in a given year, as opposed to only a fraction of 1 percent of the latter. Although this difference may suggest a bias against indigent petitioners, the lack of filing fees no doubt produces a large number of completely frivolous claims.[56]

Entirely apart from the factors we have addressed are questions of standing and jurisdiction. Perry argues that the clerks who review the thousands of petitions the Court receives each year need some quick way of discarding as many petitions as possible.[57] Procedural defects such as standing, jurisdiction, or the like provide the clerks with a valid justification for recommending denial, one that only a handful of petitions survive. Though all but unexamined by other political scientists, these factors obviously affect the Court's decisions concerning review.

FUTURE CHANGES?

The system that the first Congress created in 1789 exists today with only a few significant structural changes. The most important occurred in 1891, when Congress created nine circuit courts of appeals and in 1925 when the Judges' Bill of that year drastically reduced the Court's obligation to decide certain cases. Many factors seem to mitigate reformist inclinations.

First, the justices do not sit from late June or early July until the first Monday in October.[58] Because they may visit their offices, hire staff, and evaluate petitions for certiorari and writs of appeal during this time, they are not totally

---

[54] Caldeira and Wright, "Organized Interests."

[55] Tanenhaus, Schick, Muraskin, and Rosen, "Certiorari Jurisdiction."

[56] E.g., *In re Demos* 500 U.S. 16 (1991).

[57] Perry, *Deciding to Decide*, pp. 218–219.

[58] Special sessions in 1958 and 1972 cut into this hiatus. The justices issued a half-dozen orders between August 28 and September 17, 1958, in addition to hearing arguments and deciding the school desegregation ruckus in Little Rock, Arkansas: *Cooper v. Aaron*, 358 U.S. 1. In 1972, they reconvened on July 7, a week after adjournment, to stay three judgments of the D.C. Circuit concerning the seating of delegates to the Democratic National Convention. *O'Brien v. Brown*, 409 U.S. 1.

duty free.[59] But though it may not be accurate to view the interterm recess as a three-month vacation, it is markedly lengthier than that of the average full-time worker.

Second, the burdens of office do not preclude the justices from speaking at bar and other associational meetings, granting interviews, and writing books and articles. The same year he became chief justice, Rehnquist published a book on the Court,[60] and throughout his tenure, Chief Justice Burger heavily involved himself in matters of judicial administration. Frankfurter and Fortas closely advised Presidents Roosevelt and Johnson. Warren served as head of the commission that investigated the assassination of President Kennedy, and Justice Jackson left the country for more than a year to preside at the Nuremberg Trials of Nazi war criminals.

Third, notwithstanding generous retirement benefits, recent Courts have been among the most aged in history. The presence of sitting justices who are in their eighties belies the characterization of an overburdened bench.

Fourth, the most time-consuming portion of the justices' work consists of writing opinions. The justices equally divide the task of writing opinions of the Court among themselves, thereby requiring each to write an average of ten or twelve per term. At their own volition, the Warren Court justices also wrote an average of 1.24 special opinions (concurrences and dissents) per orally argued case; the Burger Court justices averaged 1.59.[61] On the Rehnquist Court, except the chief justice and Blackmun, the justices write approximately twice the minimum (one-ninth), Stevens more than three times the minimum, and Brennan slightly less (see Chapter 12). Overworked justices would hardly display such behavior.

Finally, Congress effectively eliminated the last vestiges of the Court's obligatory jurisdiction in 1988. The justices, of course, may voluntarily view certain cases as obligatory, for instance, a declaration that an important federal law is unconstitutional or a decision clearly counter to a very recent Supreme Court decision. But no longer must the Court hear appeals in which a state court voided an act of Congress or upheld a state law against a challenge to its constitutionality. Although these cases composed less than 5 percent of the Court's docket, the justices had complained that they usurped too much of their time and resources.

SUMMARY AND CONCLUSIONS

Unlike in the vast majority of American courts, state and federal, the justices remain abreast of their docket. Notwithstanding a substantial increase in the

---

[59] Their clerks are certainly busy. See Stuart Taylor, Jr., "When High Court's Away, Clerks' Work Begins," *New York Times*, 23 September 1988, p. A12.

[60] William H. Rehnquist, *The Supreme Court: How It Was, How It Is* (New York: Morrow, 1987).

[61] Harold J. Spaeth and Michael F. Altfeld, "Influence Relationships within the Supreme Court: A Comparison of the Warren and Burger Courts," 38 *Political Research Quarterly* 70 (1985).

number of cases the Court has been petitioned to review over the past half-century, the justices make their decisions to grant or deny review within a few weeks of their receipt with the notable exception of "relisted" cases, which may remain in limbo for months. If accepted during the first four months of the Court's term, a case will likely be decided before adjournment, otherwise the following term. Because of the currency of its docket, the luxury of a three-month summer vacation, and the justices' failure to speak with a single un-equivocal voice, the likelihood of appreciable change in the Court's jurisdiction or procedures is slight.

The link that connects the various factors that determine whose case is considered by the Supreme Court are the individual justices' personal policy goals. Given the freedom to select for review such cases as they wish, the factors that govern selection and the strategies that the various justices employ in voting to review a case are matters of individual determination.[62]

Although analyses of case selection have primarily focused on petitions for certiorari rather than writs of appeal, a fairly detailed picture of the considerations that enter into the justices' choice has emerged.

The two legal requirements for being heard by the Court – jurisdiction and standing to sue (fully discussed in Chapter 4) – are subject to the justices' control, although Congress, compatibly with the provisions of Article III of the Constitution, determines the Court's jurisdiction.[63] As with other congressional legislation, the Court interprets the language and intentions of Congress. So also here. And though some of the elements of standing to sue are constitutionally grounded, and decisional law has produced others, the precedents governing both kinds are no less subject to judicial manipulation than are those governing other areas of the law, as we documented in Chapter 2.

As for the policy-based factors that govern case selection, we know that the justices are primarily concerned with a desire to reverse errant lower court decision and, to a lesser extent, the likelihood of winning on the merits (at least for affirmance-minded justices). Aggregate analyses confirm the Court's role in exercising hierarchical control over lower courts.

---

[62] Lee Epstein, who has examined the justices' papers as extensively as anyone we know, has found absolutely no examples of logrolling (personal communication, February 11, 2000). Moreover, no systematic evidence exists that junior justices cue on signals from senior justices during conference votes on cert. See, e.g., Perry, *Deciding to Decide*, p. 48. But Burger did pass at conference and merits votes – especially the latter – far more than any of his colleagues. We assume he did so to control the assignment of the Court's opinion.

[63] We no longer vouch for the accuracy of the statement that Congress determines the Court's jurisdiction, given the Court's current penchant for indiscriminately declaring acts of Congress unconstitutional.

12

Supreme Court Decision Making

It isn't ideology and it isn't politics.
> – Justice Stephen Breyer, on the explanation for the Court's decision in *Bush v. Gore*

The Supreme Court reached one noteworthy and one colossal decision during the 2000 election campaign. First, on December 4, it remanded the Florida Supreme Court decision in *Palm Beach County Canvassing Board v. Harris*[1] back to the Florida high court. That court, as we noted in Chapter 7, took the contradictory phrases about late returns, "may be ignored" and "shall be ignored," and melded them to mean "may not be ignored." In doing so, the Florida Supreme Court relied, as courts often do, on both statutory and constitutional commands.

The problem with this, according to the U.S. Supreme Court, is that Article II of the Constitution requires that each state's presidential electors be appointed "in such Manner as the Legislature thereof may direct." If the Florida Supreme Court, under the guise of statutory interpretation, replaced the legislature's formula ("may" or "shall" ignore) with an alternative formula ("may not ignore") from an alternative authority, such as their interpretation of the state's constitution, then arguably an Article II violation occurred. The U.S. Supreme Court's unanimous remand in this case asked the Florida Supreme Court to clarify whether its decision in the *Palm Beach County* case was based entirely on statutory law as set by the Florida legislature, or whether the court inappropriately incorporated state constitutional law in purported violation of Article II.

In one sense, the Supreme Court's decision in this case was largely moot, for it involved only the Florida secretary of state's ruling in the initial *protest* period. The parties had since moved beyond the preliminary protest phase and into the *contest* phase, in which the election would be decided. Nevertheless,

---

[1] *Bush v. Palm Beach County Canvassing Board*, 531 U.S. 70 (2000).

the Supreme Court's ruling in the *Palm Beach County Canvassing Board* case was not without political significance. When the U.S. Supreme Court ruled on the *Palm Beach* case, the Florida Supreme Court was considering Gore's request for a recount of all undervotes in *Gore v. Harris*, the case that would become *Bush v. Gore*.[2] By deciding the *Palm Beach County* case as it did, the U.S. Supreme Court was signaling the Florida Supreme Court that it would carefully scrutinize any decision in *Gore v. Harris* that went beyond Florida's statutory scheme for contesting elections.

As for *Gore v. Harris*, Florida law allows broad power to provide relief any time there exists "receipt of a number of illegal votes or rejection of a number of legal votes sufficient to change or place in doubt the result of the election."[3] Thus the Florida Supreme Court voted 4–3 on December 8 to allow a recount of all undervotes.

Deciding to recount undervotes does not answer the criteria by which to count undervotes. Many of the undervotes were from International Business Machine (IBM)-style punch cards that were only partially indented or perforated, the so-called dimpled, hanging, and pregnant chads. Because the U.S. Supreme Court had just warned the Florida Supreme Court not to exceed Florida's statutory scheme in any of its presidential election cases, and because Florida election law makes no mention of the criteria for counting undervotes, the Florida court ordered a recount with no guidance other than a determination of "the intent of the voter." This vague standard meant that identical ballots, say, with a pregnant chad, might be counted differently in one county and another and might also be counted differently by different officials in the same county. The Florida Supreme Court potentially could have prevented this problem by establishing a statewide standard, but had it done so, it had every reason to believe it would have been walking into an Article II trap by going beyond the language established by "the legislature thereof."

The Bush campaign immediately appealed *Gore v. Harris* (now labeled *Bush v. Gore*) to the U.S. Supreme Court. On December 9, the Supreme Court not only granted certiorari, but took the extraordinary step of issuing an emergency stay halting the recount. The vote was 5–4, with the Court split along ideological lines, as the five most conservative members (Thomas, Scalia, Rehnquist, Kennedy, and O'Connor) supported the stay.[4]

The heavy burden required to sustain a stay rests on the party seeking it and is based on the concept of irreparable harm. The harm to Governor Bush, explained Justice Scalia, was that a recount of votes that might later be deemed improper might put Gore in the lead, and that any subsequent Bush presidency would be burdened by claims of illegitimacy. Alternatively, although Gore did not have the burden of showing irreparable harm by a stopped count, we note what the harm done to him by granting the stay might be: that time for the

---

[2] 531 U.S. 98 (2000).
[3] §102.168.
[4] 531 U.S. 1046 (2000).

recount would run out (as it did) and that he would lose the election despite possibly having obtained more votes in Florida than Governor Bush. Whatever the merits of the case, Gore was in greater danger of suffering irreparable harm by the Supreme Court's stopping the recount (losing the presidency) than Bush was by having it continue (some loss in legitimacy).

The Supreme Court handed down its decision at 10:00 P.M. on December 12. The justices wrote six different opinions expressing four different positions. The *per curiam* opinion (without a signed author) of the Court represented the views of the same five who granted the injunction. It stated that the standardless recount ordered by the Florida Supreme Court violated the equal protection clause of the Fourteenth Amendment. Moreover, rather than remand for a recount based on appropriate standards, the majority ruled that the deadline for recounting votes was midnight on December 12. With only two hours left, no proper recount could possibly take place.

Of the five justices who joined the *per curiam* opinion, the three most conservative members also found an Article II violation in the very notion of a recount. According to Rehnquist's concurrence, which was joined by Scalia and Thomas, recounts could only be granted under Florida law for mistakes in the vote tabulation, and hanging, dimpled, and pregnant chads did not constitute tabulation errors.

Two more justices, Souter and Breyer, agreed with the Court's equal protection analysis but rejected the December 12 deadline, voting to remand so that Florida officials could conduct a proper recount.

Finally, the Court's most liberal members, Stevens and Ginsburg, rejected the Court's equal protection arguments and the December 12 deadline. They would allow the recount to continue as ordered by the Florida Supreme Court.

To what extent might this decision, and Supreme Court decisions in general, be explained by legal rather than extralegal (e.g., policy-based) factors? This is the question we will answer in this chapter. We begin with the process by which the Court decides cases.

PROCESS

Oral Argument

Oral argument is the only publicly visible stage of the Court's decision-making process. The extent to which it affects the justices' votes is problematic. The justices aver that it is a valuable source of information about the cases they have agreed to decide,[5] but that does not mean that oral argument regularly, or even infrequently, determines who wins and who loses. Justice Powell's docket sheets, which systematically summarize the position taken by each justice in

[5] Robert L. Stern and Eugene Gressman, *Supreme Court Practice*, 5th ed. (Washington, DC: Bureau of National Affairs, 1978), pp. 730–735; William H. Rehnquist, *The Supreme Court: How It Was, How It Is* (New York: Morrow, 1987), pp. 271–285.

conference, make virtually no reference to oral argument. Presumably, if oral argument proved pertinent, Powell would have reported it.[6] The conference vote on the merits, the Court's preliminary vote as to which party wins the case, occurs within seventy-two hours of oral argument; hence, it is likely to be fresh in the justices' minds. On the other hand, the Court rigorously limits the time for argument to thirty minutes for each side, with a few exceptions when an hour is allotted.

The Court devotes fourteen weeks per term to oral argument, two weeks each during the months of October through April. During this time, it sits in public session on Mondays, Tuesdays, and Wednesdays, from 10:00 A.M. to noon, and from 1:00 to 3:00 P.M. This schedule provides an upper bound for the number of orally argued cases that the Court will consider during a term: four per day for three days over each of fourteen weeks, for a normal maximum of 168 cases. The clerk of the Court schedules oral argument; it typically occurs between four and six months after the justices have agreed to review the case. Several weeks before the date of argument, the justices receive the briefs filed by the parties to the litigation along with those that interested nonparties (amici curiae) may have submitted. Such nonparties receive permission from the litigants themselves or may motion the justices for permission to file a brief stating their view of the proper resolution of the controversy. The parties' consent need not be had for the solicitor general to file a brief on behalf of the United States or for the authorized official of a federal agency, state, territory, or political subdivision of a state or territory to file on its behalf. Nongovernmental interests generally have little trouble gaining permission from the Court to file briefs. Between 1969 and 1981, the Court denied only 11 percent of motions for leave to file amicus briefs.[7] Most frequent amici participants are states, followed by corporations and business groups, and citizen organizations. Individuals rarely file.[8]

Lawyers who file amicus briefs on behalf of organized interests may not present oral argument except "in the most extraordinary circumstances."[9] Nevertheless, interest groups are often direct parties, in which case their lawyers may engage in the oral argument. For instance, the NAACP Legal Defense Fund (LDF) sponsored the historic case of *Brown v. Board of Education*[10] with the plaintiff represented by the LDF's chief counsel, Thurgood Marshall. For public interest lawyers representing groups such as the NAACP or the American Civil Liberties Union (ACLU), the Supreme Court serves as a forum not

---

[6] Justice Powell's docket sheets are housed in the law library of the Washington and Lee Law School in Lexington, Virginia. We greatly appreciate the unstinting assistance – far beyond the call of duty – provided by John N. Jacob, the Law School's archivist, in making these documents available to us and to Lee Epstein.

[7] Karen O'Connor and Lee Epstein, "Court Rules and Workload: A Case Study of Rules Governing Amicus Curiae Participation," 8 *Justice System Journal* 35 (1983).

[8] Gregory Caldeira and John Wright, "Amici Curiae Participation before the Supreme Court: Who Participates, When, and How Much," 52 *Journal of Politics* 782 (1990).

[9] Supreme Court Rule 38.7.

[10] 347 U.S. 483 (1954).

just for winning clients' cases, but for promoting the cause that the group espouses.[11]

Although we know of no systematic information indicating the influence of oral argument on the justices' decisions, we do know what interests the justices most about oral argument: the policy implications of potential decisions. More than 40 percent of the justices' questions at oral argument involve policy, whereas less than 10 percent involve either precedential or constitutional issues.[12]

The Conference

Only the justices themselves may attend the justices' conferences. At these meetings, they decide whether to hear the cases they have been asked to review; they discuss and vote on whether to affirm or reverse the cases orally argued earlier in the week; and assignments to write the opinion of the Court are made. What transpires in the conference is often described as Washington's best-kept secret. Apart from an occasional statement in an opinion, what little we know we learn long after the fact from the justices' private papers and their off-the-bench communications.

According to Chief Justice Rehnquist, conferences convene on Wednesday afternoons after oral argument and on Friday mornings. The Wednesday conference votes on the cases at which oral argument was heard the preceding Monday; the Friday conference disposes of the orally argued cases from Tuesday and Wednesday. The second part of the conferences that dispose of orally argued cases is devoted to the consideration of cases the Court has been asked to review.[13]

The Court follows basically the same procedure with regard to whether to decide a case, except that the discussion on the merits is much more detailed than the discussion of petitions for certiorari.[14] Chief Justice Rehnquist reports that "with occasional exceptions, each justice begins and ends his part of the discussion without interruption from his colleagues." He further states:

When I first went on the Court, I was both surprised and disappointed at how little interplay there was between the various justices during the process of conferring on a case. Each would state his views, and a junior justice could express agreement or disagreement with views expressed by a justice senior to him earlier in the discussion, but the converse did not apply; a junior justice's views were seldom commented upon, because votes had been already cast up the line. Like most junior justices before me must have felt, I thought I had some very significant contributions to make, and was disappointed that they hardly ever seemed to influence anyone because people did not

[11] Jonathan Casper, *Lawyers before the Warren Court* (Urbana: University of Illinois Press, 1972).
[12] Timothy Johnson, "Information, Oral Arguments, and Supreme Court Decision Making," 29 *American Politics Research* 331 (2001). Oral arguments from thousands of the Court's cases are available at http://www.oyez.org.
[13] Rehnquist, *Supreme Court*, pp. 287–288, 289.
[14] *Id.*, p. 289.

change their votes in response to my contrary views. I thought it would be desirable to have more of a round-table discussion of the matter after each of us had expressed our views. Having now sat in conferences for fifteen years [as of 1987], and risen from ninth to seventh to first in seniority, I now realize – with newfound clarity – that while my idea is fine in the abstract it probably would not contribute much in practice, and at any rate is doomed by the seniority system to which the senior justices naturally adhere.[15]

Justice Scalia has echoed Rehnquist's sentiments, but without endorsing Rehnquist's approval of the lack of interchange among the justices. In response to questions that followed a 1988 speech at the George Washington University Law School, Scalia said that "not very much conferencing goes on" in conference. He used *conferencing* in the sense of efforts to persuade others to change their mind by debating matters of disagreement. "In fact," he said, "to call our discussion of a case a conference is really something of a misnomer. It's much more a statement of the views of each of the nine Justices, after which the totals are added and the case is assigned." He went on to say that he does not like this system: "Maybe it's just because I'm new. Maybe it's because I'm an ex-academic. Maybe it's because I'm right." He concurred with Rehnquist's observation that his own remarks "hardly ever seemed to influence anyone because people did not change their votes in response to my contrary views."[16] However, Powell's annotated docket sheets report many instances of a justice's acceding to or being persuaded by the views of another justice. Not uncommonly, vote changes did result. Admittedly, most such instances resulted when the changing justice was initially ambivalent: "not at rest," to use Powell's phrase.

On the other hand, according to a former clerk for Justice Blackmun, the give and take of conference is so unimportant to the justices that Justice Stevens would sometimes phone in his votes from his winter home in Florida.[17] Justices absent from the conference do commonly cast a vote, usually via a written memo.

Although the other branches of government have opened their proceedings to a degree of public scrutiny, the Supreme Court has adamantly refused to do so. On the other hand, unlike Congress and the executive branch, the Court provides the public with all relevant materials pertaining to its decisions: briefs, transcripts of oral argument, the record of lower court proceedings, as well as the opinions of the justices themselves. The Court justifies its refusal to open its conferences to public examination on the ground that doing so would jeopardize its effectiveness as an authoritative policy-making body. While still an associate justice, Rehnquist provided what appears to have been the first full-blown defense of the practice. He gave four reasons for the secrecy:

First, "A remarkably candid exchange of views" occurs. "No one feels at all inhibited" about being quoted out of context or thinks that "half-formed

---

[15] *Id.*, pp. 290–291.

[16] "Ruing Fixed Opinions," *New York Times*, 22 February 1988, p. 20.

[17] Edward Lazarus, *Closed Chambers: The First Eyewitness Account of the Epic Struggles inside the Supreme Court* (New York: Times Books, 1998), p. 279.

or ill conceived ideas" might subsequently be "held up to public ridicule." Second, each justice is required to do his or her own work. Unlike members of the president's cabinet, who are "generally flanked by aides," the justices are forced to prepare themselves personally for the conference. Third, public scrutiny or press coverage could subject the Court to "lobbying pressures" intended to affect the outcome of decisions. Fourth, "occasionally short-tempered remarks or bits of rancorous rhetoric" are uttered that might transcend the cordiality that exists among the justices if they became part of a public record.[18]

The Majority Opinion

After the conference vote, the chief justice, if he or she is in the majority, or the senior associate justice in the majority if the chief dissents, assigns the writing of the Court's opinion to one of the justices in the majority vote coalition. If that justice persuades a majority of the Court to agree to her opinion, it becomes a majority opinion and has full precedential force. If less than a majority join the opinion, then it becomes a judgment, which may have lessened precedential force on lower court judges.[19] During this time and until the decision is publicly announced, justices can and occasionally do switch the side they support, behavior known as *fluidity*. Eventually, however, each justice must make a final determination as to which party to support on the merits, whether to join the majority opinion, and whether to write or join any concurring or dissenting opinions. We fully discuss opinion assignment and opinion coalitions in Chapter 13. For the rest of this chapter we focus on the final vote on the merits, with a particular look at legal and extralegal approaches to such decisions.

THE (FINAL) VOTE ON THE MERITS: LEGAL APPROACHES

To what extent may the Supreme Court's decisions be appropriately explained by legal approaches? We begin with an analysis of *Bush v. Gore* and find legal factors of little influence here. Because this is no surprise, we then shift our analysis to *Planned Parenthood v. Casey*,[20] the 1992 abortion decision that reaffirmed a woman's right to an abortion, for this decision is frequently cited as a prime example of principled, precedent-based decision making. We conclude our analysis of the legal approach with a more systematic analysis of the role of precedent in Supreme Court decision making.

---

[18] Mort Mintz, "Rehnquist Strongly Defends Secrecy in Supreme Court," *Washington Post*, 28 January 1977, p. A2.

[19] The *may* depends on whether the judgment includes the median justice. See *Marks v. United States*, 430 U.S. 188 (1977).

[20] 505 U.S. 833.

Bush v. Gore: Legal Considerations

As we noted in Chapter 2, legal justifications almost always support both sides of the dispute in the type of cases that go to the Supreme Court. That makes it difficult to conclude that legal factors such as the language of the statute or the Constitution, intent, or precedent significantly influence a particular decision. Nevertheless, the decision in *Bush v. Gore* so completely deviated from the majority's previously stated legal views that accepting even the most basic legal consideration – that the majority sincerely believed its own arguments – strains credulity. We consider the Court's equal protection argument, the December 12 deadline, and the decision to stop the recount.

Equal Protection. Unequal outcomes abound in life, some through intentional actions, others through inadvertence. The Fourteenth Amendment, which guarantees that no state shall deny any person the equal protection of the law, cannot prevent all inequalities, or even all state-sponsored inequalities. States may make restaurants abide by hygiene laws that are inapplicable to banks, and banks must abide by financial rules inapplicable to restaurants. States can give tax breaks to senior citizens, people who have children, or almost any group it chooses without running afoul of equal protection. As Justice Kennedy wrote, "Non-uniformity cannot be equated with constitutional infirmity."[21]

The most clear-cut violations of equal protection occur when government purposefully discriminates against so-called discrete and insular minorities, such as racial, religious, or ethnic groups. According to Justice Thomas (joined in pertinent part by Scalia), "The Equal Protection Clause shields only against purposeful discrimination. A disparate impact, even upon members of a racial minority, the classification of which we have been most suspect, does not violate equal protection."[22]

The fact that *Bush v. Gore* occasioned no purposeful discrimination or violation of an identifiable group's rights – to say nothing of a discrete and insular one – makes it extraordinarily difficult to believe that the Court majority would have ruled for Gore if he had brought the challenge. As the noted Supreme Court scholar Howard Gillman remarked, "Before this presidential election, not one justice on the majority ever expressed a view about equal protection that would lead someone to think that they would have constitutional problems with hand recounts of ballots governed by a general 'intent of the voter' standard."[23]

So inconsistent was the majority's stated position on equal protection with its true beliefs that the justices needed to make sure that this expansion of equal protection would not stand as precedent for future cases. Thus, with unconscionable cynicism and analphabetic legality, they sanctimoniously stated:

[21] *Pacific Mutual Life Insurance Co. V. Haslip*, 499 U.S. 1 (1991), at 41.
[22] *M.L.J. v. S.L.U.*, 519 U.S. 102 (1996), at 135.
[23] Howard Gillman, *The Votes That Counted: How the Court Decided the 2000 Election* (Chicago: University of Chicago Press, 2001), p. 161.

"Our consideration is limited to the present circumstances, for the problem of equal protection in election processes generally presents many complexities."[24]

The December 12 Deadline. The ipsedixitist majority also behaved with unconscionable temerity beyond its equal protection argument. Consider the December 12 recount deadline established in the Supreme Court's 10:00 P.M. December 12 decision. This deadline prevented the Florida Supreme Court from creating guidelines that could have resolved equal protection concerns. (Recall, however, that the Supreme Court had indicated a willingness to use the Article II argument to strike down any plan that transcended the plain meaning of Florida statutory law. Thus if the Florida Supreme Court had originally created statewide standards for counting undervotes, the Supreme Court might well have struck that decision. Therefore, the justices created for Bush an unbeatable situation: Heads I win; tails you lose.)

Where did this December 12 deadline originate? Congress had established it as a safe harbor: If states chose their electoral slates by that date, Congress would not challenge them. Congress did not set a deadline, but rather an incentive to complete the vote count. Neither was it a deadline under Florida law.

Markedly more plausible was December 18, the congressionally established date of the electoral college vote. Given the Constitution's command that the electoral college shall vote on the same day, delay beyond December 18 might have meant that Florida's electoral votes would not have counted.

How then did the U.S. Supreme Court justify the December 12 deadline? In the Florida Supreme Court's repudiated *Palm Beach County* decision, the Florida court decided how long an extension to give Gore by calculating backward from December 12, the safe harbor date. But Florida statutory law, the only legitimate source of Florida's laws governing presidential elections according to the *Palm Beach County* decision, nowhere mentions this date. The fact that the December 12 deadline guaranteed Bush victory was obvious.

Stopping the Recount. Irreparable harm, like any legal criterion, is a judgment call, but, as we have noted, the potential harm to Gore of stopping the recount – and thereby losing a presidential election he might actually have won – far exceeded the potential harm to Bush – winning the election but having people question his legitimacy if undervote recounts showed that Gore might have received more votes. For those who think the Court truly believed its unprecedented language, consider the alternate scenario: Would the Court have issued a stay to stop the recount if Gore had been ahead and Bush wanted the undervotes counted? Hardly.

The majority in *Bush v. Gore* stopped a recount that might have given Gore the lead in order to prevent "casting a cloud upon what (Bush) claims to be the

---

[24] *Bush v. Gore*, 531 U.S. 98 (2000), at 109.

legitimacy of his election";[25] formulated an equal protection argument flatly and completely contradictory to its consistently adhered to century-old rule that a violation of the equal protection clause requires purposeful governmental discrimination; decided that this novel and expanded view of equal protection applied only to this case; and created a mocking deadline that guaranteed victory to Bush. The Court's use of legal factors was an unconscionable charade: Not only does this decision not begin to clothe the majority's nakedness, it does not even begin to meet the far more lenient standard of plausible sincerity.[26] In short, *Bush v. Gore* is a decision that in its unparalleled cynicism surpasses the most disgusting in its history: *Dred Scott v. Sandford*. At least *Scott* had some precedent to support it.

Planned Parenthood v. Casey: The Case for Precedent

Given the implausibility of *Bush v. Gore* as a case for legal influence, we should not be very surprised that we found none.[27] Alternatively, the Supreme Court's plurality opinion in *Planned Parenthood v. Casey*[28] has frequently been cited as a quintessential example of principled, precedential decision making. Thus, it should be easy to find legal influence here, assuming it exists anywhere.

Certainly, the plurality's explanation of why it voted as it did focused heavily on the doctrine of *stare decisis* (precedent). Opening with the stirring claim "Liberty finds no refuge in a jurisprudence of doubt,"[29] the Court declared, "After considering the fundamental constitutional questions resolved by *Roe*, principles of institutional integrity, and the rule of *stare decisis*, we are led to conclude this: the essential holding of *Roe v. Wade* should be retained and once again reaffirmed."[30] Noting that *stare decisis* in constitutional questions is far from an inexorable command,[31] the Court explained why *Roe* differed:

Where, in the performance of its judicial duties, the Court decides a case in such a way as to resolve the sort of intensely divisive controversy reflected in Roe and those rare, comparable cases, its decision has a dimension that the resolution of the normal case does not carry. It is the dimension present whenever the Court's interpretation of the Constitution calls the contending sides of a national controversy to end their national division by accepting a common mandate rooted in the Constitution.

The Court is not asked to do this very often, having thus addressed the Nation only twice in our lifetime, in the decisions of *Brown* and *Roe*. But, when the Court does act in this way, its decision requires an equally rare precedential force to counter the

---

[25] *Bush v. Gore*, 531 U.S. 1046 (2000), at 1047.

[26] Gillman, *Votes*, pp. 187–189.

[27] Parts of this section derive from Harold J. Spaeth and Jeffrey A. Segal, *Majority Rule or Minority Will: Adherence to Precedent on the U.S. Supreme Court* (Cambridge: Cambridge University Press, 1999).

[28] 505 U.S. 833.

[29] *Id*. at 843.

[30] *Id*. at 845–846.

[31] *Id*. at 854.

inevitable efforts to overturn it and to thwart its implementation. Some of these efforts may be mere unprincipled emotional reactions; others may proceed from principles worthy of profound respect. But whatever the premises of opposition may be, only the most convincing justification under accepted standards of precedent could suffice to demonstrate that a later decision overruling the first was anything but a surrender to political pressure, and an unjustified repudiation of the principle on which the Court staked its authority in the first place. So to overrule under fire in the absence of the most compelling reason to reexamine a watershed decision would subvert the Court's legitimacy beyond any serious question.[32]

Thus, one scholar declares that "the joint opinion in Casey emphasizes that a continuing commitment to *stare decisis* requires a reaffirmation of *Roe*."[33]

This is not a solipsistic view. Journalists and scholars alike quickly accepted the triumvirate's explanation that *stare decisis* influenced its decision. Linda Greenhouse's analysis of the decision accepts at face value the claim that adherence to *Roe v. Wade* was necessary even for justices who continued to have doubts about the decision.[34] The *Chicago Tribune* declared that the "decision relied on the time-honored doctrine of respecting legal precedent."[35]

We could not disagree more.[36]

We begin with the basic notion that those wishing to assess systematically the influence of precedent must recognize that in many cases Supreme Court decision making would appear exactly the same whether precedent influenced the justices or not. Consider the Court's decision in *Roe v. Wade*. The majority "found" a constitutional right to abortion that could not be abridged without a compelling state interest.[37] The dissenters found no such right. In subsequent cases, Justices Blackmun, Brennan, Marshall, and others continued to support abortion rights. Although we could say that choices in these cases were based on the precedent set in *Roe*, it is equally reasonable – arguably more so – to say that those justices would have supported abortion rights in subsequent

---

[32] *Id.* at 866–867.

[33] Ronald Kahn, "Interpretive Norms and Supreme Court Decision Making: The Rehnquist Court on Privacy and Religion," in Cornell W. Clayton and Howard Gillman (eds.), *Supreme Court Decision Making: New Institutionalist Approaches* (Chicago: University of Chicago Press, 1999), p. 180.

[34] Linda Greenhouse, "A Telling Court Opinion," *New York Times*, 1 July 1992, p. A1.

[35] William Neikirk and Glen Elsasser, "Top Court May Face Backlash," *Chicago Tribune*, 1 July 1992, p. 1. Also see Erin Daly, "Reconsidering Abortion Law: Liberty, Equality and the Rhetoric of *Planned Parenthood v. Casey*," 45 *American University Law Review* 77 (1995); C. Elaine Howard, "The Roe'd to Confusion: *Planned Parenthood v. Casey*," 30 *Houston Law Review* 1457 (1993); and Earl M. Maltz, "Abortion, Precedent and the Constitution: A Comment on *Planned Parenthood v. Casey*," 68 *Notre Dame Law Review* 11 (1992).

[36] Evidenced in part by our prediction of the outcome of *Planned Parenthood* on the day before the decision was announced, interview with Gene Healy, WJR Radio, Detroit, June 28, 1992. The prediction correctly specified how each of the justices would vote, largely for the reasons specified in the remainder of this section.

[37] Judges, along with lawyers and laypersons, continue to use the verb *find* to rationalize – albeit unconsciously – their decisions, policies, and preferences. The process apparently approximates that of finding a valuable diamond in a malodorous pile of offal.

cases even without the *Roe* precedent. Thus, even in a system without a rule of precedent Justice Scalia would continue to support the death penalty, nonracial drawing of congressional districts, limited privacy rights, and so forth. When preferences and precedents do not differ, speaking of decisions as being influenced by precedent is not meaningful. For precedent to matter as an *influence* on decisions, it must achieve results that would not otherwise have obtained. As Judge Jerome Frank stated: "*Stare decisis* has no bite when it means merely that a court adheres to a precedent that it considers correct. It is significant only when a court feels constrained to stick to a former ruling although the court has come to regard it as unwise or unjust."[38]

Did the plurality opinion in *Casey* give any indication that its authors considered the ruling in *Roe* to be unwise or unjust? For the most part, the answer is no. Although the authors pointed out that "time has overtaken some of *Roe*'s factual assumptions,"[39] and that some parts of *Roe* were unduly restrictive, the decision "has in no sense proven unworkable,"[40] has facilitated "the ability of women to participate equally in the economic and social life of the nation,"[41] and fits comfortably with doctrinal developments before and after 1973.[42] Indeed, the Court refers to *Roe* as an "exemplar of *Griswold* liberty."[43]

Although the Court does fault *Roe* somewhat, every time it does it substitutes its own personal judgment for that of *Roe*! Thus the Court supplants the trimester framework with viability[44] and exchanges the compelling interest standard for an undue burden standard.[45] Additionally, the Court reversed holdings in *Akron v. Akron Center for Reproductive Health*[46] and *Thornburgh v. American College of Obstetricians and Gynecologists*.[47] In sum, nowhere in the plurality opinion does the Court clearly substitute *Roe*'s judgment, or that of any other case, for its own contemporary and solipsistic preference.

Our answer about the influence of *Roe* changes a bit if we look to the past for the views of the justices. Undoubtedly, an arguable case for precedential impact can be made for Justice Kennedy. In 1989, Kennedy joined Rehnquist's opinion in *Webster v. Reproductive Health Services*, which, among other things, questioned why the "State's interest in protecting human life should come into existence only at the point of viability."[48] But as a federal court of appeals judge, Kennedy "only grudgingly upheld the validity of naval regulations prohibiting homosexual conduct," citing *Roe v. Wade* and other privacy cases very

---

[38] *United States ex rel. Fong Foo v. Shaughnessy*, 234 F. 2d 715 (1955), at 719.
[39] 505 U.S. 833, at 860.
[40] *Id.* at 855.
[41] *Id.* at 856.
[42] *Id.* at 857–858.
[43] *Id.* at 857.
[44] *Id.* at 870.
[45] *Id.* at 876.
[46] 462 U.S. 416 (1983).
[47] 476 U.S. 747 (1986).
[48] 492 U.S. 490, at 519. As we note, however, the *Casey* plurality adopted precisely that position.

favorably.[49] According to the dossier prepared on Kennedy for the Reagan Justice Department, "This easy acceptance of privacy rights as something guaranteed by the Constitution is really very distressing."[50] Thus it is difficult to categorize Kennedy as an opponent of *Roe*.

Even more ambiguous is the position of Justice Souter. Though appointed by a purportedly pro-life president,[51] Souter had sat on the board of directors of a New Hampshire hospital that performed voluntary abortions, with no known objections from Souter. Without any clear indications of his prior beliefs about *Roe*, it is nearly impossible to determine the extent to which *Roe* influenced his position in *Casey*.

Alternatively, no ambiguity surrounded Justice O'Connor's preferences. O'Connor supported abortion rights while a legislator in Arizona[52] and, once on the Court, frequently found problems with the trimester format of *Roe* but never doubted that a fundamental right to abortion existed.[53] Indeed, *Casey*'s attacks on *Roe*'s trimester framework and its adoption of the undue burden standard are taken directly from O'Connor's dissent in *Akron v. Akron Center for Reproductive Services*.[54] So, too, *Casey*'s overruling of *Akron* and *Thornburgh* comports perfectly with her dissents in those cases.

We summarize these points in Table 12.1, which, for each issue in *Casey*, presents the established doctrine or precedent of the Court, O'Connor's prior position on the issue, and the result in *Casey*. It is extraordinarily difficult to argue that *stare decisis* influenced O'Connor in any manner in this purported paragon of precedent. Where precedent and her previously expressed preferences met, she followed precedent. But where any majority opinion in any abortion case differed from her previously expressed views, she stuck to her previously expressed views. Justice O'Connor "followed" precedent to the extent that she used precedent to justify results she agreed with, but there is no evidence whatsoever that these precedents influenced her positions.

The Influence of Precedent

Although we believe our position on the justices' votes to be reasonable, we are struck by a lack of hard evidence as to how, for example, Justice Souter might have felt about *Roe* as an original matter. Thus, the best evidence about whether a precedent influences a justice would not be obtained from justices who joined the Court after the decision in question, for we usually cannot be certain what their position on the case would have been as an original matter. Nor can we

---

[49] David Yalof, *Pursuit of Justices* (Chicago: University of Chicago Press, 1999), p. 211.

[50] *Id.*

[51] Bush supported abortion rights until Ronald Reagan nominated him to be vice president in 1980. He had even been an active supporter of Planned Parenthood.

[52] "It's about Time," *Los Angeles Times*, 13 September 1981.

[53] E.g., *Webster v. Reproductive Health Services*, 492 U.S. 490 (1989), and *Thornburgh v. American College of Obstetricians and Gynecologists*, 476 U.S. 747 (1986).

[54] 462 U.S. 416 (1983).

Table 12.1. *The Impact of Precedent versus Preferences on the O'Connor, Kennedy, and Souter Opinion in* Casey

Issue	Court's Prior Ruling (Precedent)	O'Connor's Prior View	Casey Result
Framework	Trimester (*Roe*)	"Neither sound constitutional theory nor our need to decide cases based on the application of neutral principles can accommodate an analytic framework according to the 'stages' of pregnancy" (*Akron I*, O'Connor dissent, at 452)	"We reject the trimester framework" (at 872)
Standard	Compelling interest (*Roe*)	"A lawful abortion is not unconstitutional unless it unduly burdens the right" (*Akron I*, O'Connor dissent, at 453)	"The right protects the woman from unduly burdensome interference" (at 874)
Spousal notice	Unconstitutional (*Danforth*)	None	Unconstitutional
Informed consent	Unconstitutional (*Akron I*)	Informed consent provisions "impose no undue burden" (*Akron I*, O'Connor dissent, at 472)	"To the extent that *Akron I* and *Thornburgh* find a constitutional violation when the government requires, as it does here, the giving of truthful and nonmisleading information . . . , those decisions are overruled" (at 882)
24-hour waiting	Unconstitutional (*Akron I*)	"Although the waiting period may impose an additional cost on the abortion decision, this increased cost does not unduly burden the availability of abortions" (*Akron I*, O'Connor dissent, at 473)	"We consider [*Akron*'s decision striking the waiting period] to be wrong" (at 885)
Parental consent	Valid (*Akron II*)	O'Connor joined the *Akron II* majority opinion	Valid (at 899)
Record keeping	Valid (*Danforth*)	None	No "substantial obstacle" (at 900)

gather such evidence from those on the Court who voted with the majority, for the precedent established in that case coincides with their revealed preferences (whatever their cause). Rather, the best evidence for the influence of precedent must be obtained from those who dissented from the majority opinion in the case under question, for we know that these justices disagree with the precedent. If the precedent established in the case influences them, that influence should be felt in that case's progeny, through their votes and opinion writing. Thus, determining the influence of precedent requires examining the extent to which justices who disagree with a precedent move toward that position in subsequent cases.

This is not an unobtainable standard. For example, in *Griswold v. Connecticut* (1965),[55] Stewart rejected the creation of a right to privacy and its application to married individuals. Yet in *Eisenstadt v. Baird* (1972)[56] he accepted *Griswold*'s right to privacy and even willingly applied it to unmarried persons. And although Justice Rehnquist dissented in the jury exclusion cases, *Batson v. Kentucky* (1986)[57] *and Edmonson v. Leesville Concrete Co.* (1991),[58] he concurred in *Georgia v. McCollum* (1992), providing an explicit and quintessential example of what it means to be constrained by precedent: "I was in dissent in *Edmonson v. Leesville Concrete Co.* and continue to believe that case to have been wrongly decided. But so long as it remains the law, I believe it controls the disposition of this case. . . . I therefore join the opinion of the Court."[59]

Using this standard for the influence of precedent, we systematically examined thousands of Supreme Court decisions to determine the extent to which precedent, or alternatively, the justices' prior preferences, can best be considered an influence on the justices' behavior.[60]

Our sample resulted in 2,418 votes and opinions, of which 285, or 11.8 percent, appear to be influenced by precedent, whereas 2,133, or 88.2 percent, appear to be influenced by the justices' prior preferences. Though there may be some subset of justices or some types of issues or some periods within our sample in which precedential behavior might be greater, we can state our overall conclusion straightforwardly: The justices are rarely influenced by *stare decisis*.

The Justices' Behavior. Table 12.2 presents the summary voting scores for each justice who served during the Rehnquist Court era for whom we have at least one vote to consider in either a landmark or an ordinary case.[61] We will label justices *preferential* if their preferential scores are above 66.7 percent,

[55] 381 U.S. 479.
[56] 405 U.S. 438.
[57] 476 U.S. 79.
[58] 500 U.S. 614.
[59] 505 U.S. 42, at 52.
[60] For further details on our methodology, see Spaeth and Segal, *Majority Rule*, pp. 23–44.
[61] To allow time for progeny to develop, we ended our sampling of precedents in 1989. Thus we do not have votes for Souter, Thomas, Ginsburg, or Breyer.

Table 12.2. *Justices' Precedential Behavior by Case Type*

| Justice | | Type | | Total |
		Landmark	Ordinary	
Blackmun	Precedential	13	3	16
		20.0%	21.4%	20.3%
	Preferential	52	11	63
		80.0%	78.6%	79.7%
	Total	65	14	79
		100.0%	100.0%	100.0%
Brennan	Precedential	2		2
		1.4%		1.2%
	Preferential	146	25	171
		98.6%	100.0%	98.8%
	Total	148	25	173
		100.0%	100.0%	100.0%
Kennedy	Preferential	4		4
		100.0%		100.0%
	Total	4		4
		100.0%		100.0%
Marshall	Precedential	2		2
		1.3%		1.1%
	Preferential	154	28	182
		98.7%	100.0%	98.9%
	Total	156	28	184
		100.0%	100.0%	100.0%
O'Connor	Precedential		3	3
			60.0%	9.4%
	Preferential	27	2	29
		100.0%	40.0%	90.6%
	Total	27	5	32
		100.0%	100.0%	100.0%
Powell	Precedential	8	1	9
		34.8%	10.0%	27.3%
	Preferential	15	9	24
		65.2%	90.0%	72.7%
	Total	23	10	33
		100.0%	100.0%	100.0%
Rehnquist	Precedential	5	3	8
		3.9%	11.5%	5.2%
	Preferential	122	23	145
		96.1%	88.5%	94.8%
	Total	127	26	153
		100.0%	100.0%	100.0%

Justice		Type		
		Landmark	Ordinary	Total
Scalia	Precedential		1	1
			100.0%	16.7%
	Preferential	5		5
		100.0%		83.3%
	Total	5	1	6
		100.0%	100.0%	100.0%
Stevens	Precedential	4	8	12
		9.8%	38.1%	19.4%
	Preferential	37	13	50
		90.2%	61.9%	80.6%
	Total	41	21	62
		100.0%	100.0%	100.0%
White	Precedential	22		22
		13.5%		13.3%
	Preferential	141	3	144
		86.5%	100.0%	86.7%
	Total	163	3	166
		100.0%	100.0%	100.0%

moderately preferential if their scores are between 33.3 percent and 66.7 percent, and *precedential* if their scores are below 33.3 percent. In landmark cases, for justices deciding ten or more cases, no justice can be labeled a precedentialist, but Lewis Powell (65.2 percent preferential) can be labeled a moderate. Alternatively, Brennan (98.6 percent), Marshall (98.7 percent), O'Connor (100.0 percent), and Rehnquist (96.1 percent) each voted preferentially more than 95 percent of the time.

In ordinary cases, no justice with ten or more votes can be labeled a precedentialist, but John Paul Stevens (61.9 percent preferential) can be labeled a moderate. At the other end of the spectrum, Brennan and Marshall are 100 percent preferential, and Powell, surprisingly, reaches 90 percent preferential.

In *Dickerson v. United States*, the Supreme Court upheld *Miranda v. Arizona*,[62] striking a congressional attempt to overturn it. In response to the majority opinion, Justice Scalia declared, "I dissent from today's decision, and, until [the congressional law] is repealed, will continue to apply it in all cases where there has been a sustainable finding that the defendant's confession was voluntary."[63] This explicit refusal to abide by the Court's precedent distinguishes Scalia in words, but not deeds, from what the justices do day in and day out.

[62] 384 U.S. 486 (1966).
[63] 530 U.S. 428 (2000), at 465. Dissenters almost always "respectfully" dissent. Scalia did not so state.

Crisis *Stare Decisis*

Dickerson aside, perhaps *stare decisis* does not constrain justices in their everyday decisions, in which fact freedom abounds. Maybe its constraint is only felt in crisis, in the most extreme of circumstances, when justices must confront overruling a previous decision. As Chief Justice Rehnquist noted in 2000, "While *stare decisis* is not an inexorable command, particularly when we are interpreting the Constitution, even in constitutional cases, the doctrine carries such persuasive force that we have always required a departure from precedent to be supported by some 'special justification.'"[64]

Certainly, the Court rather infrequently overrules its prior decisions. According to the leading authorities on such overruling, the Supreme Court overturns merely 2.5 cases per year or so.[65] In any given decade, the Court overturns less than 0.002 percent of its previous decisions![66]

Thus, unlike in the everyday *stare decisis* examined, in which deference to precedent was found only at minimal levels, the gravitational force of *stare decisis* should be relatively greatest when the doctrine is pushed to its outermost limit: that is, when justices must confront overturning previous decisions. Arguably, if justices do not defer to precedent here, they never will.

We test this by using the research strategy first used to test for judicial restraint in the mid-1960s.[67] Spaeth first noted that although justices frequently cast votes that could be classified as "restrained" (e.g., supporting state economic regulations or upholding the decisions of federal regulatory commissions), such support was conditional on the ideological direction of the agency decision. For example, Justice Frankfurter, the purported paragon of judicial restraint, voted to uphold 60 percent of National Labor Relations Board decisions during the first seven terms of the Warren Court. But breaking down the data by ideological direction of the agency's decision reveals that although Frankfurter upheld 88 percent of the agency's antiunion decisions, he upheld only 29 percent of the agency's pro-union decisions. Frankfurter's voting behavior was consistent with economic conservatism, not judicial restraint.

Similarly, one can conclude that a justice generally upholds precedent in the face of a decision to overturn if she generally defers both when that precedent works a liberal result and when that precedent produces a conservative outcome.

We test this by examining the votes of the justices overturning precedent during the Rehnquist Court (see Table 12.3). A preliminary version of Benesh and

---

[64] *Id.* at 419. Internal citations omitted.

[65] Saul Brenner and Harold J. Spaeth, *Stare Indecisis: The Alteration of Precedent on the U.S. Supreme Court, 1946–92* (Cambridge: Cambridge University Press, 1995).

[66] Jack Knight and Lee Epstein, "The Norm of *Stare Decisis*," 40 *American Journal of Political Science* 1018 (1996).

[67] Harold J. Spaeth, "The Judicial Restraint of Mr. Justice Frankfurter – Myth or Reality," 8 *American Journal of Political Science* 22 (1964).

Table 12.3. *Justices' Votes on Overturning Precedents*

	Liberal Precedents			Conservative Precedents		
	Uphold	Overturn	% Overturn	Uphold	Overturn	% Overturn
Marshall	14	4	22.2	0	5	100.0
Brennan	10	5	33.3	0	4	100.0
White	4	18	81.0	2	4	66.7
Blackmun	15	9	37.5	1	5	83.3
Powell	2	3	60.0	1	1	50.0
Rehnquist	7	25	78.1	9	4	30.8
Stevens	25	7	21.9	2	10	83.3
O'Connor	9	23	71.9	9	4	30.8
Scalia	3	29	90.6	4	9	69.2
Kennedy	7	18	72.0	1	9	90.0
Souter	10	7	41.2	3	6	66.7
Thomas	1	13	92.9	3	5	62.5
Ginsburg	8	2	20.0	1	6	85.7
Breyer	7	1	12.5	2	5	71.4

Spaeth's "flipped" database[68] contains these data, defined as any case in which one or more justices say in so many words that one or more of the Court's own precedents should be overruled or are "disapproved," "no longer good law," or equivalent language. Note that cases that the justices "distinguish" alter no precedents. In no way does such language alter the scope of a precedent. However, a subsequent decision may state that an earlier one overruled a precedent, even though the earlier one nowhere says so. For example, the majority in *Patterson v. McLean Credit Union* said that a 1973 decision overruled a 1948 precedent.[69]

The results could not be more clear. When the Court votes to overturn liberal precedents, liberals such as Brennan and Marshall insist that the precedents be upheld. But when conservative precedents are attacked, those liberal justices show no inclination to uphold them. Marshall's statement that "*Stare decisis* . . . 'is essential if case-by-case judicial decision-making is to be reconciled with the principle of the rule of law'"[70] obviously applies only to liberal precedents.

The situation for conservatives, however, is not so clear-cut. Rehnquist, for example, rarely votes to overturn conservative precedents (30.8 percent) but is quite willing to overturn liberal precedents (78.1 percent). But Scalia, Kennedy, and Thomas defer to neither conservative nor liberal precedents. Overall, not

[68] NSF grant SES-9910535.

[69] 485 U.S. 617 (1988), at 618.

[70] *Payne v. Tennessee*, 501 U.S. 808 (1991), at 849. Of course, as an attorney, Marshall may have been (properly) responsible for more precedents' being overturned than any other litigator in the twentieth century.

one justice on the Rehnquist Court exercised deference to precedent by voting to uphold both liberal and conservative precedents.

Text and Intent

Although the systematic study of *stare decisis* has resulted in far greater understanding of this mainstay of legal approaches, text and intent have received far less consideration. Nevertheless, Rehnquist era justices tend to support legal arguments based on text or intent when those arguments are posed by ideologically consonant parties.[71] That is, liberal justices accept arguments based on the intent of the framers when made by liberal parties, but not when made by conservative parties. Similarly, conservative justices accept intent-based arguments when made by conservative parties, but not liberal ones. The partial exception to this rule is that the Court's most conservative justices, Scalia and Thomas, show a tendency to be more supportive of liberal claimants when those claimants make arguments based on textual plain meaning.

Although the evidence presented here does not exhaust the case against legal factors as an influence on Supreme Court decisions, little systematic evidence supports such an effect.

THE DECISION ON THE MERITS: EXTRALEGAL APPROACHES

With little evidence for legal factors in Supreme Court decisions, we next examine extralegal or policy-based factors, with a special emphasis on the justices' attitudes.

Bush v. Gore: An Attitudinal Perspective

It does not take a rocket scientist, or even a political scientist, to make the following observations about *Bush v. Gore*: The most anti-Gore position was taken by the Court's three most conservative justices: Rehnquist, Thomas, and Scalia. These justices voted to grant the stay, set aside the recount on equal protection grounds, establish the December 12 deadline, and void Florida's recount decision on Article II grounds. The Court's more moderate conservatives, Kennedy and O'Connor, did not go quite as far. They voted to grant the stay, set aside the recount on equal protection grounds, and establish the December 12 deadline. Two moderates, Souter and Breyer, took positions that were, overall, supportive of Gore's position. They voted against the stay but voted to set aside the recount on equal protection grounds. Nevertheless, they rejected the December 12 deadline and would have allowed a recount to go forward under guidelines to be established by the Florida Supreme Court. Finally,

---

[71] Robert M. Howard and Jeffrey A. Segal, "An Original Look at Originalism," 36 *Law and Society Review* 113 (2002).

the Court's most liberal justices, Ginsburg and Stevens, voted the Gore line across the board: They voted against the stay, rejected the equal protection challenge, and rejected the December 12 deadline.

Attitudes

Although the preceding analysis helps demonstrate the compatibility of the justices' decisions in this case with their ideological preferences, we do not wish to rest our results on a single case; nor do we wish to rely on subjective measures of the justices' ideology. Using the U.S. Supreme Court database, we can examine the Court's decisions across hundreds or thousands of cases. But we still need an independent and reliable measure of the justices' ideology.

Our solution to this problem focuses on the judgments in newspaper editorials that characterize nominees before confirmation as liberal or conservative insofar as civil rights and liberties are concerned.[72] The scores range from $+1$ (most liberal) to -1 (most conservative), with scores around 0 representing moderate positions. The scores of the justices are reprinted in Table 12.4.

We believe that the scores accurately measure the perceptions of the justices' values at the time of their nomination. Although not everyone would agree that every score precisely measures the perceived ideology of each nominee, Fortas, Marshall, and Brennan are expectedly the most liberal, and Scalia and Rehnquist the most conservative. Harlan and Stewart are liberal because the debate about them centered around their support for the overriding issue of the day: segregation. Goldberg is not perceived to be as liberal as Fortas or Marshall because of an evenhandedness at the Department of Labor that even the conservative *Chicago Tribune* could support. O'Connor emerges as a moderate, given her previous support for women's rights and abortion. Indeed, the only hint of opposition to her nomination arose from right-wing interest groups and the archconservative Senator Jesse Helms (Republican – North Carolina).

Consistently with criminal justice analyses in earlier chapters, we use as our initial dependent variable the votes of all justices appointed since the beginning of the Warren Court in all formally decided criminal cases from the beginning of the 1953 term through the end of the 2001 term, as derived from the Original U.S. Supreme Court Judicial Database. Liberal decisions are pro–person accused or convicted of a crime; conservative decisions are progovernment. The data are presented in Table 12.4.

Figure 12.1 presents the relationship between the justices' ideology and their votes in criminal cases. As can readily be seen, justices who are more liberal have substantially higher rates of support for accused criminals than do justices who are more conservative. Indeed, the fit of the model is extremely high, with a correlation between ideology and votes of .78 (corresponding to an r^2 of .61).

---

[72] Jeffrey A. Segal and Albert D. Cover, "Ideological Values and the Votes of U.S. Supreme Court Justices," 83 *American Political Science Review* 557 (1989). See Chapter 10 for details.

Table 12.4. *Justices' Ideology, Liberalism in Criminal Cases, and Liberalism in All Cases, 1953–2001 Terms*

Name	Ideol[a]	Crim[b]	All[c]
Warren	.50	75.1	76.7
Harlan	.75	42.0	46.5
Brennan	1.00	76.4	73.2
Whittaker	.00	44.8	42.4
Stewart	.50	46.5	50.2
White	.00	33.3	49.4
Goldberg	.50	80.0	73.5
Fortas	1.00	80.0	72.1
Marshall	1.00	80.3	74.0
Burger	−.77	19.8	35.6
Blackmun	−.77	42.3	54.3
Powell	−.67	28.7	39.9
Rehnquist	−.91	16.6	30.7
Stevens	−.50	64.9	60.7
O'Connor	−.17	25.5	39.7
Scalia	−1.00	25.3	35.7
Kennedy	−.27	28.7	42.2
Souter	−.34	51.0	57.1
Thomas	−.68	20.3	32.5
Ginsburg	.36	58.3	59.6
Breyer	−.05	52.6	57.3

[a] Ideol: Justices' ideology from Jeffrey A. Segal and Harold J. Spaeth, *The Supreme Court and the Attitudinal Model Revisited* (Cambridge: Cambridge University Press, 2002), p. 322.
[b] Crim: percentage liberal in criminal cases.
[c] All: percentage liberal of justices' votes in all cases except interstate relations and miscellaneous. Crim and All derived from U.S. Supreme Court Judicial Database. http://www.as.uky.edu/polisci/ulmerproject.htm.

If we rank order the justices' liberalism scores with the score derived for each of them from the content analysis of the editorials in four newspapers (two liberally oriented, two conservative), the probability that the similarity in the two rankings occurred by chance is .0001.[73] Thus, notwithstanding the discrepancy between the rankings of Harlan (fourth most liberal according to the editorials, twelfth in criminal case voting), Stevens (fourteenth and sixth), and Souter (thirteenth and eighth), the rankings of the other seventeen justices differ little between editorial judgment and subsequent criminal voting behavior.

Of course, it is not just in criminal cases that this relationship exists. When we examine the population of Supreme Court cases, excluding only a small number

[73] Sidney Siegel, *Nonparametric Statistics* (New York: McGraw-Hill, 1956), pp. 213–223.

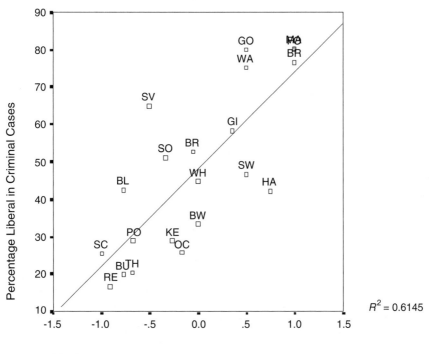

Figure 12.1. Scatterplot of Justices' Ideology and Voting Liberalism in Criminal Cases.

of miscellaneous cases plus interstate disputes,[74] we find essentially the same results. These are presented in Figure 12.2. Again, justices who are more liberal ideologically are much more liberal in their voting behavior. The correlation between the justices' ideology and their voting in all cases drops a bit from before: from .78 all the way to .76, while the rank order probability remains at .0001. Given the fact that no study, to our knowledge, has ever found this relationship to be spurious (e.g., by finding other variables that explain away this relationship), the most obvious conclusion is that the justices' ideology has an enormous impact on their votes.

In reality, relating newly nominated justices' attitudes to their subsequent behavior requires only knowledge of the public policies the Court addresses and the putative attitudes of the nominee. Our senior author had no trouble ideologically positioning the Reagan, Bush, and Clinton nominees relative to their

---

[74] Certainly, however, the attitudinal model is not going to accomplish much in areas that typically have no ideological content, such as boundary disputes between states. Nevertheless, we were distressed to see Justice Ginsburg of Brooklyn vote with the Court majority that much of Ellis Island belongs to New Jersey. Segal's grandparents, along with Breyer's, did not leave the old country for Ellis Island, New Jersey. See *New Jersey v. New York*, 523 U.S. 767 (1998), Breyer concurring, at 812.

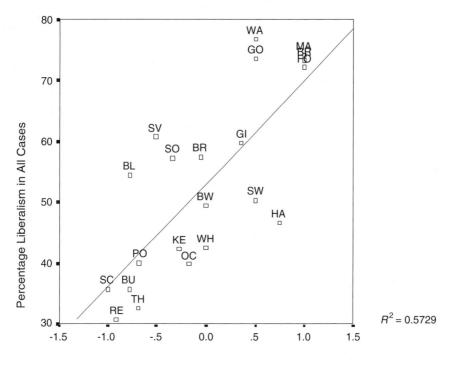

Figure 12.2. Scatterplot of Justices' Ideology and Voting Liberalism in All Cases.

incumbent colleagues when asked by the media to do so. Given O'Connor's legislative record, she was likely to locate in the middle of the Court that she joined in 1981, occupying the same ideological position as Potter Stewart, the justice she replaced. With Rehnquist's ascension to the chief justiceship after Burger's retirement, it required no crystal ball to judge that Scalia would be at least as staunchly conservative as Rehnquist, given his outspoken court of appeals opinions and his previous academic record. Kennedy, Powell's replacement, would prove to vary little from him, proving to be somewhat less conservative than Rehnquist and Scalia, but more so than O'Connor. Souter's moderation may have surprised some people, but as our senior author happened to be vacationing at an inn a few miles up the road from Souter's lifelong home when his nomination was announced, neighbors and acquaintances convincingly described him as middle of the road: hence, his placement slightly left of the moderately conservative O'Connor. If it were not clear before his televised hearings, Clarence Thomas, the elder Bush's final nominee, made it pellucid that he would give Scalia a run for his money as the Court's most conservative member. Given Clinton's moderation, he chose two justices who were moderate or moderately liberal, selecting Ruth Bader Ginsburg, the Court's second woman, followed by Stephen Breyer. Absent any liberals among the incumbent justices, they would occupy the Court's left wing and provide the Court's sole moderate, Stevens, a bit of company. On the basis of their respective court of appeals records, Ginsburg was projected to be a tad more liberal than Stevens; Breyer, a bit more conservative.

The effect of these predictions is a Court that since Breyer's appointment in 1994 has been one of tripartite division: Ginsburg, Stevens, and Breyer on the left; Rehnquist, Scalia, and Thomas on the right; and Souter, O'Connor, and Kennedy in the middle. O'Connor and Kennedy combine most often with the three conservatives to form majorities. These predictions required no special insight. Any Court watcher who realizes that the justices are wedded to their individual policy preferences – and are not nanocerebral nonentities slavishly adhering to the diaphanous fabric of ethereal legal principles and doctrine – could have done as well.

Alternative Influences

Although the justices' ideologies certainly influence the Court's behavior, other extralegal influences may too. We examine sequentially the influences of the solicitor general, Congress, public opinion, and interest groups.

Before we begin this investigation, a brief methodological note is in order. One cannot demonstrate that the Supreme Court is influenced by the solicitor general, Congress, public opinion, interest groups, or any other external factor, by the simple expedient of correlating the Court's decisions with the preferences of any of these actors. For instance, it may be possible to show that the Warren Court supported the position taken by the NAACP Legal Defense Fund, Inc. (LDF), in every desegregation case before it. But this does not necessarily mean that the Court was influenced by the LDF. The liberal Warren Court most likely would have supported desegregation with or without the support of the LDF. Before influence can be inferred, we must show that an actor in the Court's environment had an independent impact after controlling for other factors.

The Solicitor General. As discussed in Chapter 11, the solicitor general represents the executive branch of the United States before the Supreme Court and is quite successful in having cases heard by the Court. The favorable treatment accorded the United States at access continues when the case is decided on the merits: It won about 62 percent of its cases in the nineteenth century and 64 percent in the twentieth.[75]

Many times the United States is not a direct party but nevertheless has a substantial interest in the outcome of the litigation. For instance, in *Brown v. Board of Education*,[76] the famous racial desegregation case, the solicitor

---

[75] Robert Scigliano, *The Supreme Court and the Presidency* (New York: Free Press, 1971).
[76] 347 U.S. 483 (1954).

general filed only an *amicus* brief. It was in the government's brief in the second *Brown* case that the Court found the "all deliberate speed" proposal.[77] When looking at the amicus cases more generally, it becomes clear that despite the government's success as a litigant, it "has an even better record as amicus curiae."[78] For the years 1943, 1944, 1963, and 1965, the party supported by the solicitor general won 87 percent of the time.[79] Such results are consistent with more recent findings.[80]

Evidence suggests that these results hold after controlling for the facts of the case. One tested area is the sex discrimination cases heard by the Supreme Court between 1971 and 1984.[81] The Court supported the solicitor general 64 percent of the time when it favored a conservative (antiequality) decision and 90 percent of the time when it favored a liberal (proequality) decision. After controlling for several case facts, changes in the Court's membership, and the Court's tendency to reverse, the position taken by the solicitor general still had a large influence, affecting the probability of a liberal or conservative decision by as much as .28. So, too, has evidence of solicitor general influence been found in death penalty cases.[82]

Recent evidence suggests that the justices' ideologies leaven this influence. Liberal justices tend to defer to positions endorsed by Democratic administrations, whether those positions are liberal or conservative. Alternatively, conservative justices tend to defer to positions endorsed by Republican administrations, again whether the positions are liberal or conservative. But liberal justices do not defer to Republican solicitors, and conservative justices do not defer to Democratic solicitors.[83]

Congress. Unlike the president, who has no control over sitting members of the Supreme Court, Congress possesses explicit constitutional power to check and balance judicial and Supreme Court decision making. Structurally, it can impeach and remove judges; it can increase or decrease the size of any federal court; and it can limit – or even terminate – the Court's appellate jurisdiction,

---

[77] Lincoln Caplan, *The Tenth Justice* (New York: Knopf, 1987), p. 31.

[78] Scigliano, *Presidency*, p. 179.

[79] *Id.*

[80] Karen O'Connor, "The Amicus Curiae Role of the U.S. Solicitor General in Supreme Court Litigation," 66 *Judicature* 256 (1983); Steven Puro, "The United States as Amicus Curiae," in S. Sidney Ulmer (ed.), *Courts, Law and Judicial Processes* (New York: Free Press, 1983); Jeffrey A. Segal, "Amicus Curiae Briefs by the Solicitor General during the Warren and Burger Courts," 41 *Western Political Quarterly* 135 (1988); Rebecca Salokar, *The Solicitor General: The Politics of Law* (Philadephia: Temple University Press, 1992).

[81] Jeffrey Segal and Cheryl Reedy, "The Supreme Court and Sex Discrimination: The Role of the Solicitor General," 41 *Western Political Quarterly* 553 (1988).

[82] Tracey George and Lee Epstein, "On the Nature of Supreme Court Decision Making," 86 *American Political Science Review* 323 (1992).

[83] Michael E. Bailey, Brian Kamoie, and Forrest Maltzman, "Signals from the Tenth Justice: The Political Role of the Solicitor General in Supreme Court Decision-Making," 49 *American Journal of Political Science* (2005).

along with all the jurisdiction of the lower federal courts. Thus, Congress has the power, for example, to eliminate the Court's ability to hear abortion or flag burning or reapportionment cases. These structural factors potentially give Congress some sway over the Court's constitutional decisions. And at a more mundane level, Congress can overturn the Court's statutory decisions. Thus, more so than the executive branch, one might expect, and policy-based rational-choice scholars do expect, Congress to impact the Court's decisions.

Nevertheless, at the structural/constitutional level, Congress has rarely exercised its powers to sanction the Supreme Court. Only one justice, Samuel Chase, was impeached, and that was a blatant partisan attempt by the Jeffersonians to gouge the Federalists. The Senate's attempt to remove Chase fell short of the requisite two-thirds majority. Congress has similarly been circumspect in limiting the Court's appellate jurisdiction. It has on occasion played with the number of justices – during Reconstruction, for example, it shrank the size of the Court – but that was due to Congress's battles with President Andrew Johnson rather than efforts to curb the Court. When Ulysses Grant was elected president, Congress quickly restored the seats. Recall our discussion in Chapter 3 of Franklin Roosevelt's inability to secure passage of his Court-packing plan, notwithstanding his landslide reelection in 1936 and the overwhelming Democratic control of Congress.

Perhaps this structural deference by Congress results from the fact that the Court typically defers to congressional preferences in constitutional cases. But given the Court's willingness and ability to strike at actions overwhelmingly supported by Congress – school prayer, flag burning, gun-free schools, and malapportioned districts, to name a few – this hypothesis cannot be maintained.

This is not to say that the Court never considers congressional preferences in its constitutional decisions. On those rare occasions that Congress has mounted a clear and imminent threat to the Court's institutional policy-making powers, as in the Court-packing plan of 1937, the Court would be foolish not to back down, and in such situations the Court has in fact done so.[84]

On the other hand, Congress can and does override Supreme Court statutory decisions with some regularity, about six times per year.[85] Does the Supreme Court act in anticipation of such reversals by deferring to Congress as an initial matter? This question has been asked in a number of different ways, but most scholars who have systematically examined the question have found that the Court's statutory decisions change as its own preferences change, but not as congressional preferences change.[86] Consider the conclusions of one of the most

---

[84] See *Ex Parte McCardle*, 7 Wallace 506 (1869), and *Barenblatt v. United States*, 360 U.S. 109 (1959).

[85] William N. Eskridge, "Overriding Supreme Court Statutory Interpretation Decision," 101 *Yale Law Journal* 331 (1991).

[86] See Jeffrey A. Segal and Harold J. Spaeth, *The Supreme Court and the Attitudinal Model Revisited* (Cambridge: Cambridge University Press, 2002), chap. 8, for an extended discussion of these works.

prominent *supporters* of congressional influence on Supreme Court statutory decisions:

The Court that decided *Patterson* and the other 1989 decisions was producing results that did not reflect current legislative preferences. However, this was also true of the Warren Court (which thrived on such independence and never got overruled) and was often true of the Burger Court (which in almost every instance was promptly overruled). Therefore, again, ignoring legislative preferences is nothing new. Finally, the Rehnquist Court approached *Patterson* and the other 1989 decisions from a perspective substantially more conservative than that of Congress. But that has been true of the Court since 1972, when Justices Rehnquist and Powell started voting.[87]

Public Opinion. Supreme Court decisions by and large correspond with public opinion.[88] This should not be surprising, as Supreme Court justices are chosen by the president, who in turn is selected by vote of the people. Thus, the public mood became more conservative around 1967, helping Richard Nixon be elected president in 1968. Nixon then appointed four conservative justices to the Supreme Court, substantially moving the Court to the right. The question of concern is whether public opinion – however defined – directly influences the Court.

Theoretically, there is little reason to think so. Institutionally, the justices are immune from majoritarian pressures. The public neither elects nor removes them from office. Moreover, from a normative perspective, the Constitution's Framers did not intend the Court to represent majoritarian concerns. As Justice Jackson so eloquently stated in *West Virginia Board of Education v. Barnette*:

The very purpose of a Bill of Rights was to withdraw certain subjects from the vicissitudes of political controversy, to place them beyond the reach of majorities and officials and to establish them as legal principles to be applied by the courts. One's right to life, liberty, and property, to free speech, a free press, freedom of worship and assembly, and other fundamental rights may not be submitted to vote; they depend on the outcome of no elections.[89]

In interpreting certain clauses – cruel and unusual punishments" is a noted example – the Court claims to look to public opinion for guidance. But if, as we have shown in Chapter 2, the watchword of the plain meaning rule is that words mean what the Court says they mean and not the way *Webster*'s or *Black*'s define them, the watchword of the Court's use of public opinion data is that there are three types of lies: lies, damn lies, and statistics. In originally

---

[87] William N. Eskridge "Reneging on History? Playing the Court/Congress/President Civil Rights Game," 79 *California Law Review* 613 (1991), p. 683.

[88] David Barnum, "The Supreme Court and Public Opinion: Judicial Decision Making in the Post–New Deal Period," 47 *Journal of Politics* 652 (1985); Thomas Marshall, *Public Opinion and the Supreme Court* (New York: Longman, 1989).

[89] 319 U.S. 624 (1943), at 638.

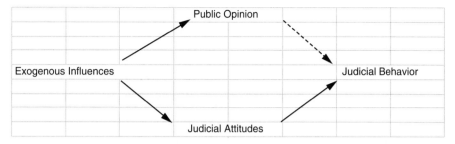

Figure 12.3. A Conceptual Model of the Influence of Public Opinion on Supreme Court Decisions.

determining whether the Constitution prohibited the death penalty for retarded individuals, the Court noted that in Texas, Florida, and Georgia, three states with overwhelming support for the death penalty, opinion opposed execution of the retarded by 73 percent, 71 percent, and 66 percent, respectively. Yet the Court then declared that "there is insufficient evidence of a national consensus against executing retarded people."[90] So, too, Justice Thurgood Marshall, defeated in his quest for a nation opposed to the death penalty, justified his continued antagonism with the belief that an "informed public" would agree with him if they knew all the facts.[91]

Conceptually, the question of whether public opinion directly influences the Court poses more difficulty than questions whether Congress or the solicitor general does. This is because the justices are members of the public and the same factors that might influence the public may influence the justices, even if the public itself has no influence on the Court.[92] An example of this relationship is depicted in Figure 12.3.

Briefly, real world factors such as unemployment, the crime rate, war, recession, inflation, and government spending, influence the attitudes of the public at large, who presumably include judges. Additionally, public opinion may directly influence judges' behavior. But by merely assessing the correlation between public opinion and judges' behavior, scholars fail to control for the potentially spurious nature of that relationship.

Consider as an example district court sentencing decisions in draft-dodging cases during the Vietnam War. As public opinion turned against the war, sentencing by federal judges became more lenient.[93] But needless to say, it is hard to imagine that the same events that turned the public at large against the war did not also by and large turn federal judges against it. Thus, "while there is some evidence that judicial behavior in the area of sentencing of draft offenders

[90] *Penry v. Lynaugh*, 492 U.S. 302 (1989), at 335.

[91] *Gregg v. Georgia*, 428 U.S. 153 (1976), at 232.

[92] William Mishler and Reginald S. Sheehan, "Public Opinion, the Attitudinal Model, and Supreme Court Decision Making: A Micro-Analytic Perspective," 58 *Journal of Politics* 169 (1996).

[93] Beverly B. Cook, "Public Opinion and Federal Judicial Policy," 21 *American Journal of Political Science* 567 (1977).

during the Vietnam War moved in a direction consistent with public opinion, there is no evidence that the movement reflected a response to the opinion."[94] Rather, the changes were due to changes in "the judges' own doubts about the war."[95]

Similarly, more recent studies that claim public opinion directly influences the Supreme Court fail to account for the factors that move public opinion. This sort of design makes it impossible to determine whether the Court is reacting to public opinion itself or whether the purported relationship, for example, that involving draft dodgers, is spuriously influenced by real world factors that influence both the public's and the justices' preferences.[96] Thus, the most appropriate characterization of the relationship found in most studies between public opinion and judicial behavior is an "association."

Among recent works, one study found no direct, significant association between public opinion and Court decisions.[97] Another does find a significant association between Court behavior and public opinion, but the study's best model finds that a 29 percent change in public opinion is associated with but a 1 percent change in the Court's decisions.[98] By any reasonable interpretation, this is substantively meaningless.

Interest Groups. Interest groups are among the prime shapers of public policy in the United States. They contribute vast amounts of money and personnel to political campaigns. Additionally, they can organize and support grassroots lobbying of representatives, as the frenetic campaign for and against Judge Bork exemplified. Interest groups also lobby the judiciary through direct sponsorship of cases and through the filing of briefs amicus curiae. They certainly play a crucial part in getting cases and issues on the Court's agenda.[99] The question this section considers, however, is once the case is on the docket, do interest groups have an ability to influence the Court's decisions?

As in the case of public opinion, it is not clear why they should. Unlike legislators and elected judges, interest groups have little to offer the justices,

---

[94] Herbert M. Kritzer, "Federal Judges and Their Political Environment: The Influence of Public Opinion," 23 *American Journal of Political Science* 194 (1979), at 204.

[95] *Id.*, p. 198.

[96] See Mishler and Sheehan, "Public Opinion," p. 174. They note that it is "virtually impossible" to distinguish a causal impact of public opinion from a spurious one.

[97] James A. Stimson, Michael B. MacKuen, and Robert S. Erikson, "Dynamic Representation," 89 *American Political Science Review* 543 (1995).

[98] Roy Flemming and B. Dan Wood, "The Public and the Supreme Court: A Pooled Time Series Analysis of Individual Justice Responsiveness to American Policy Moods," 41 *American Journal of Political Science* 468 (1997). The 1 percent change is based on their Generalized Least Squares (GLS) model. Their "first stage" Ordinary Least Squares (OLS) model, which shows significant autocorrelation, differs only by rounding error (p. 484), from the more appropriate GLS model.

[99] See, e.g., Gregory Caldeira and John Wright, "Interest Groups and Agenda-Setting in the Supreme Court of the United States," 82 *American Political Science Review* 1109 (1988); and Karen O'Connor, *Women's Organizations' Use of the Courts* (Lexington, MA: Lexington Books, 1980).

apart from some information – occasionally not otherwise available – that may marginally ease their reaching a decision. Nor do normative reasons support interest group influence on the judiciary. Although pluralist theory suggests that some public good might emerge from a battle of competing interest groups in the legislative arena, no definition of the public good includes buying and selling judicial decisions.

Nevertheless, journals of political science are awash with "evidence" that interest groups are invincible litigators,[100] most of which consists of case studies of particular groups, such as the NAACP Legal Defense Fund, who are examined precisely because of their success. Few people want to spend a year or two studying losing litigators. Systematic analysis, however, shows them to have relatively little impact. The best Supreme Court study used precision matching to compare cases with interest group *amicus* briefs with similar cases without such briefs. The analysis found that 48.5 percent of litigants supported by amicus briefs won, while 47.7 percent of similarly situated litigants who were not supported by amicus briefs won. The study uncovered "no evidence that support from amici substantially increases the chance of success of the supported litigants."[101] Overall, we have virtually no evidence to date that interest groups have an independent impact on the merits of Supreme Court decisions.

CONCLUSION

Whereas lower courts may be influenced by precedents established by higher courts, the preferences of the citizens who elect them, and a variety of other legal and extralegal variables, Supreme Court justices are overwhelmingly influenced by only one salient extralegal characteristic: their own attitudes.

Why is the Supreme Court so different? The answer lies with the Supreme Court's rules and structures, along with those of the American political system in general, which give our life-tenured justices enormous latitude to reach decisions based on their personal policy preferences. Members of the Supreme Court can further their policy goals because they lack electoral or political accountability, have no ambition for higher office, and compose a court of last resort that controls its own caseload.

We start our elaboration of these issues with the fact that unlike most other appellate courts, the Supreme Court controls its own docket. Although this does not guarantee that the justices will vote their policy preferences, it is requisite for their doing so. Many meritless cases that no self-respecting judge would decide solely on the basis of his or her policy preferences undoubtedly exist. If a citizen sought to have the younger Bush's tax cuts declared unconstitutional, and if the Supreme Court had to decide the case, we would not expect the votes

---

[100] For refutation of this "evidence," see Lee Epstein and C. K. Rowland, "Debunking the Myth of Interest Group Invincibility in the Courts," 85 *American Political Science Review* 205 (1991).

[101] Donald R. Songer and Reginald S. Sheehan, "Interest Group Success in the Courts: Amicus Participation in the Supreme Court," 46 *Political Research Quarterly* 339 (1993).

in the case to depend on whether the justices favored the cuts. But because the Supreme Court does have control over its docket, the justices may refuse to decide such a meritless case. With but a few exceptions, those that the Supreme Court does decide tender plausible legal arguments on both sides.

With regard to electoral accountability, many state court judges are subject to electoral sanctions. Such judges react to factors such as public opinion, at least in some highly salient areas.[102] But in low-visibility areas and especially in cases that contain a federal question, state supreme courts do not appear to follow public wants.[103] The evidence on life-tenured federal court judges also suggests no such influence, including for those who sit on the Supreme Court.[104]

Relatedly, justices are virtually immune from political accountability. Congress can impeach Supreme Court justices, but this has only happened once and the vote to remove failed.[105] The Court's appellate jurisdiction totally depends on Congress, and Congress may alter it as it sees fit. Rarely, however, has Congress used this power to check the justices.[106] Overall, the negative political consequences, electoral or otherwise, of limiting judicial independence far outweigh whatever short-run policy gains Congress might achieve by reining in the Court.

Moreover, although the president nominates the justices, he has no authority over them once they are confirmed. *United States v. Nixon* forcefully illustrates this point, as three Nixon appointees joined a unanimous Court requiring the president to relinquish the Watergate tapes and thus delivered the coup de grâce that forced Nixon to resign.[107]

This is not to say that a lack of political finality necessarily characterizes all Supreme Court decisions. Congress can overturn judicial interpretations of statutory language, and amendments can undo constitutional interpretation. Nevertheless, the fact that the president and the Senate choose the justices means that the justices' preferences will rarely be out of line with that of the dominant political coalition.

With regard to ambition, lower court judges may desire higher office and thus be influenced by significant political others. Lobbying for a Supreme Court

---

[102] James Kuklinski and John Stanga, "Political Participation and Governmental Responsiveness," 73 *American Political Science Review* 1090 (1979); James Gibson, "Environmental Constraints on the Behavior of Judges," 14 *Law and Society Review* 343 (1980); Paul Brace and Melinda Gann Hall, "Neo-Institutionalism and Dissent in State Supreme Courts," 52 *Journal of Politics* 54 (1990).

[103] Sara C. Benesh and Wendy L. Martinek, "The Applicability of Various Models of State Court Decision Making to Confession Cases," 23 *Justice System Journal* 109 (2002).

[104] E.g., Micheal Giles and Thomas G. Walker, "Judicial Policy Making and Southern School Segregation," 37 *Journal of Politics* 917 (1975).

[105] The justice was Samuel Chase, a Federalist, whom the Jeffersonians impeached in 1804.

[106] One such instance occurred after the Civil War, when Congress denied the Court authority to hear appeals of persons detained by the military authorities. The Supreme Court complied with Congress's decision in *Ex parte McCardle*, 7 Wallace 506 (1869).

[107] 418 U.S. 683 (1974).

seat from the lower court, through speeches or through written opinions, is not uncommon. One interested in reaching the High Court could hardly vote his or her personal policy preferences on abortion during the Bush administrations if those preferences were prochoice. Lower court judges may also be interested in other political positions besides the Supreme Court. Howell Heflin (Democrat – Alabama) went from the Supreme Court of Alabama to the United States Senate. Thus we cannot assume that those interested in higher office necessarily vote their personal policy preferences.

Efforts to seek higher office – assuming that such exist – are most improbable for today's justices. During the first decade of the Court's existence, members used the office as a steppingstone to run for positions such as governor,[108] but today few if any positions have more power, prestige, and security than that of Supreme Court justice. Three times in the twentieth century members resigned for alternative (or at least the potential of alternative) political positions, but in only one case was the move for a potentially higher office. That occurred in 1916, when Charles Evans Hughes resigned in order to seek the presidency. The other two cases occurred in 1942, when the exigencies of World War II led President Roosevelt to ask James Byrnes to become director of economic stabilization, and 1965, when President Johnson convinced Arthur Goldberg to become United Nations ambassador in order, Goldberg believed, to negotiate an end to the Vietnam War.

Finally, the Supreme Court is the court of last resort. Other judges are subject to courts superior to their own. Unless they wish to be reversed, they must follow the legal and policy pronouncements of higher courts. Examination of appellate court decisions in several different issue areas shows little overtly noncompliant behavior.[109]

Unlike all other courts, the Supreme Court sits at the pinnacle of both the federal and state judicial systems, freeing it to "do justice" as it sees fit.

---

[108] The first chief justice, John Jay, twice ran for governor of New York while on the Supreme Court and left the bench when he finally won.

[109] See Donald R. Songer, "An Overview of Judicial Policymaking in the United States Courts of Appeals," in John B. Gates and Charles A. Johnson (eds.), *The American Courts: A Critical Assessment* (Washington, DC: Congressional Quarterly Press, 1990); and Sara C. Benesh, *The U.S. Court of Appeals and the Law of Confessions: Perspectives on the Hierarchy of Justice* (New York: LFB Scholarly Publishing, 2002).

13

Opinions and Assignments

The Supreme Court's role as a national policymaker depends in most cases substantially less on its decision on the merits – who wins or loses – than on the opinion of the Court, which establishes the policy guidelines that affected actors (e.g., lower court judges, executive branch officials, and private citizens) must follow. It matters less that Jane Roe won her famous suit against Texas's abortion statute than that the Supreme Court's opinion in that case essentially established abortion on demand as national policy.[1] Nor does it matter to many that Barbara Grutter lost her bid to be admitted to the University of Michigan Law School. The case made national headlines because the Court's opinion declared that race could legally be used as a factor in university admissions.[2]

Not so with *Bush v. Gore*. So irrelevant was the Court's opinion that the unconscionably cynical Court did not even accept it as a precedent worthy of future adherence. "Our consideration is limited to the present circumstances, for the problem of equal protection in election processes generally presents many complexities."[3] As much or more "complexity" exists in other aspects of equal protection, such as affirmative action, voting, employment, juvenile justice, indigency, and immigration policy. What mattered in *Bush v. Gore* was that the recount was over: Bush won, period.

Hypocritical as this aspect of the case is, *Bush v. Gore* still exemplifies certain common aspects of the opinion-writing process: attempts at persuasion, concurring opinions, and vehement dissents. We examine these and other aspects of the opinion-writing process in this chapter.

VOTING AND OPINION OPTIONS

As noted, a court's decision only indicates who won and who lost the case. The Court's opinion details the putative reasons why the Court decided the matter

---

[1] *Roe v. Wade*, 410 U.S. 113 (1973).
[2] *Grutter v. Bollinger*, 156 L. Ed. 2d 304 (2003).
[3] *Bush v. Gore*, 531 U.S. 98, 109 (2000).

as it did. If more than one judge decides the case, the Court's opinion must have the approval of a majority of those participating – assuming, of course, that a quorum of the judges take part in the decision. In the U.S. Supreme Court, six justices constitute a quorum.

Judges, however, are free agents, in the sense that they are not required to join the Court's opinion. Instead, they may dissent, thereby indicating their disagreement with the result reached by the majority; alternatively, they may write or join a special concurrence, which agrees with the result the majority reaches (i.e., who wins or loses), but not with its opinion; they may write or join a regular concurrence, which agrees with the decision and opinion of the Court but nevertheless makes additional points. They may fail to participate in the case because of illness or some other reason that absents them from the proceedings, or they may believe that their participation may appear to produce a conflict of interest either personally or financially. Thus, it behooves conscientious judges to recuse themselves (not participate) in cases in which they own substantial stock in a business that is party to the case at hand, or in one in which an attorney representing one of the parties is a member of the judge's former law firm. But apparently it is perfectly OK to go on a duck-hunting trip with a litigant whose case is before the judge's Court and whose vote put the litigant into the vice presidency.[4]

Whether judges recuse themselves is left to their own discretion. As we noted in Chapter 10, Judge Haynsworth's failure to do so in a couple of cases in which he supported the litigant with whom he shared a financial interest led to the rejection of his nomination to the Supreme Court.

Another voting option is the so-called jurisdictional dissent, of which there are two kinds: (1) a dissent from the majority's refusal to address the merits of a case and (2) disagreement with the majority's assertion of jurisdiction without providing the parties an opportunity to argue the case orally.

Finally, a judge may agree with the majority's disposition of the case and silently join its opinion. In all multimember American courts, this is the most frequently exercised voting option by far. Early in our history, however, before John Marshall became chief justice in 1803, the Supreme Court decided its cases seriatim, an arrangement in which each justice wrote his own opinion. Apart from time-consuming opinion writing, the rendering of decisions seriatim made it very difficult – indeed, impossible – to determine the basis for the Court's decision. The outcome was determinable, because the various opinions indicated who won and who lost, but the reasons why were not. Nonetheless, some courts of British origin still use this method, notably the Australian High Court.

Associated with these voting options is the opportunity to write an opinion explaining the reasons for the Court's action. The most important of these

---

[4] Ian Ayres and Barry Nalebuff, "The Wrong Ticket to Ride," *New York Times*, 24 March 2004, p. A23; David Von Drehle, "Scalia Rejects Pleas for Recusal in Cheney Case," *Washington Post*, 12 February 2004, p. A35; Michael Janofsky, "Scalia's Trip with Cheney Raises Questions of Impartiality," *New York Times*, 6 February 2006, p. A14.

options, of course, is the opinion of the Court in which a majority of the participating judges agree with the opinion writer. This opinion constitutes the core of the Court's policy-making process. It specifies the constitutional and legal principles on which the majority rests its decision; it guides the lower courts in deciding future cases; and it establishes precedents for the Court's own subsequent rulings – even if such decisions and their supporting opinions can be overturned by the court in question or the one that is supreme over it.

Justice Dooley of the Vermont Supreme Court, concurring in the first state supreme court decision to void state marriage laws because they exclude single-sex partnerships, states the matter very well:

> I recognize that to most observers the significance of this decision lies in its result and remedy. In the cases that come before us in the future, however, the significance of this case will lie in its rationale – that is, how we interpret and apply . . . the Vermont Constitution. Moreover, in this, the most closely-watched opinion in this Court's history, its acceptability will be based on whether its reasoning and result are clearly commanded . . . and whether it is a careful . . . exercise of the Court's . . . powers. I do not believe that the majority's rationale meets this . . . standard, and I fear how it may be applied – or ignored – in the future.[5]

Dissenting Opinions

Though opinions other than that of the Court have no binding authority, they are not exercises in futility. Charles Evans Hughes, before becoming chief justice in 1930, probably most euphuistically stated the rationale of the dissenting opinion: "an appeal to the brooding spirit of the law, to the intelligence of a future day, when a later decision may possibly correct the error into which the dissenting judge believes the court to have been betrayed."[6] In support of Hughes's statement, one may reference the first Justice Harlan's dissent in *Plessy v. Ferguson*, which formed the basis for its overruling in *Brown v. Board of Education*.[7] Opinions dissenting from the Court's refusal to apply portions of the Bill of Rights to state criminal procedure during the 1940s and 1950s laid the groundwork for the liberal Warren Court majority to do so during the 1960s.

Concurring Opinions

Concurring opinions, though far fewer than dissents, also serve a purpose. Concurrences take two forms: regular and special. Both, of course, support the result reached by the majority. The former effectively agrees with all the language in the majority opinion. Judges typically write a regular concurrence for two reasons: to express their understanding of the Court's reasoning, which may

---

[5] *Baker v. State*, 170 Vt. 194 (2000), at 229.

[6] Charles Evans Hughes, *The Supreme Court of the United States* (New York: Columbia University Press, 1928), p. 68.

[7] *Brown v. Board of Education*, 163 U.S. 537 (1896), at 552; 347 U.S. 483 (1954).

highlight more or less subtle differences from the majority's position, which, in turn, may lead to subsequent litigation, the effect of which may qualify the original majority's opinion. The second reason for a regular concurrence attacks the contents of the dissenting opinion(s). This allows the concurring judge to critique the dissent more harshly or at greater length than would be appropriate if included in the majority opinion.

The other type of concurrence – the special concurrence – indicates agreement with the majority's disposition of the case but *disagrees* with the reasoning by which the majority reached its conclusion. In all other respects except its agreement with the majority's disposition, the special concurrence amounts to a dissent. Indeed, if the majority *vote* coalition is minimum winning by the smallest possible plurality – such as 5–4 or 4–3 – a special concurrence precludes the formation of a majority *opinion* coalition. Fewer than a majority of the participants agree on common language. As a result, the case is decided by a *judgment of the Court*. Its authority as a precedent, as a guide to the decisions of other courts, is severely compromised. Only the decision is authoritative, not necessarily the reasoning whereby the Court reached its conclusion.[8]

Judgments of the Court infrequently manifest themselves on the U.S. Supreme Court. From the beginning of the Warren Court in 1953 until the end of the 2003 term, the Court handed down only 213 of them. These amounted to but 3.1 percent of the 6,911 orally argued docketed cases. However, this 3 percent disproportionately fell into the three most salient of the thirteen "values" into which we divide the Court's decisions: criminal procedure, 70; civil rights, 45; and First Amendment, 40 – a total of 155 of the 213 judgments, 72.8 percent.

Frequency of Behavioral Options Exercised by the Justices

The frequency with which the justices engaged in these options during the first eighteen terms of the Rehnquist Court (1986–2003) is displayed in Table 13.1 The unit of analysis in this table is orally argued docketed cases excluding decrees.[9] The rare single docket that required more than one vote to decide are included.[10]

The table shows that silent membership in the vote coalition is by far the most common action of each of the justices. As the only bona fide liberals on the conservative Rehnquist Court, Marshall and Brennan so behaved least, 57.7 and 57.1 percent, respectively. Powell and Rehnquist did so most. As the justices voting least frequently with the majority, Marshall and Brennan obviously also lead in proportion of dissents, with 33.5 and 31.5 percent, followed by

---

[8] See *Marks v. United States*, 430 U.S. 188 (1977).

[9] Decrees typically ratify, automatically and without any named justice's authoring an opinion, the report of the special master whom the justices chose to hear a dispute that arose under the Court's original jurisdiction.

[10] E.g., *Denver Area Educational Television v. FCC*, 518 U.S. 727 (1996); *Allentown Mack Sales v. FCC*, 522 U.S. 359 (1998).

Table 13.1. *Behavioral Options Exercised by the Rehnquist Court Justices, 1986–2003 Terms*

	Behavior					
Justice	1	2	3	4	5	6
Marshall	57.7	33.5	2.2	6.0	0.3	0.3
Brennan	57.1	31.5	3.4	6.9	0.9	0.2
Blackmun	60.9	26.2	4.0	8.2	0.5	0.3
Stevens	61.0	26.8	4.5	6.9	0.5	0.2
Ginsburg	70.4	19.5	6.4	3.6	0.1	0.0
Breyer	65.8	20.7	8.0	4.3	1.1	0.0
Souter	73.2	15.9	5.7	4.2	0.9	0.1
White	79.4	13.2	2.5	4.5	0.3	0.1
O'Connor	73.5	13.5	6.1	5.0	1.8	0.1
Powell	80.3	10.5	6.4	1.7	1.2	0.0
Kennedy	77.1	9.3	5.3	4.3	4.0	0.0
Rehnquist	80.2	16.6	1.3	1.9	0.2	0.0
Scalia	65.6	18.5	6.0	9.0	0.7	0.1
Thomas	62.8	21.3	6.5	7.4	1.9	0.1

Note: 1, Voted with majority or plurality without concurring; 2, dissent; 3, regular concurrence; 4, special concurrence; 5, nonparticipation; 6, jurisdictional dissent.

Stevens (26.8) and Blackmun (26.2). Kennedy locates at the other extreme, with 9.3 percent, more than a point lower than the next justice, Powell.

Although commentators now accept the propriety of judicial dissent,[11] many disapprove of concurrences as unnecessary nit-picking.[12] Most culpable in this regard is Scalia, 9 percent of whose votes are special concurrences. Blackmun follows with 8.2 percent. The Clinton justice Breyer leads in proportion of regular concurrences at 8.0 percent, followed by Thomas at 6.5. The chief justice set the best example by far among the justices, casting only 1.3 and 1.9 percent of his votes as regular and special concurrences, respectively. These percentages are also markedly lower than Rehnquist's percentage during his tenure as an associate justice, suggesting that chief justices display a special level of institutional concern.[13]

Note should be made of how infrequently the justices recuse themselves. The Rehnquist Court presumably has an appreciably better record in this regard than any of its predecessors. Kennedy alone accounts for 36.5 percent of the total (72 of 197). This largely results because he took his seat midway through the 1987 term after many cases had been argued, thus requiring his recusal.

---

[11] Thomas G. Walker, Lee Epstein, and William Dixon, "On the Mysterious Demise of Consensual Norms in the United States Supreme Court," 50 *Journal of Politics* 361 (1988).

[12] E.g., Robert W. Bennett, "A dissent on dissent," 74 *Judicature* 225 (1991).

[13] Ellen R. Baik, "Distinguishing Chief: An Analysis of Justice Rehnquist, 1971–1997 Terms," paper presented at the 2000 Meeting of the Midwest Political Science Association.

By comparison nine of the other thirteen justices recused themselves less than 1 percent of the time.

The remaining behavior accounts for markedly less than 1 percent of the justices' votes (the two types of jurisdictional dissent). Indeed, five of the justices never cast one such vote, and another five only 0.1 percent of their votes.

Not surprisingly, the coalition behavior of the justices depends in substantial part on their policy preferences compared to those in the majority decision coalition (affirmation or reversal of the lower court decision). Those who join the majority opinion are ideologically closer to the median of the majority decision coalition than those who write regular concurrences; regular concurrers, in turn, are ideologically closer to the median of the majority decision coalition than special concurrers; and to complete the picture, special concurrers are ideologically closer to the median of the majority decision coalition than are justices who dissent.[14] We further examine the extent to which the justices agree with one another, but we first consider opinion assignment.

OPINION ASSIGNMENT

Although the individual justices are free to write dissenting and concurring opinions, they do not have that freedom where the Court's opinion is concerned. These are controlled by the senior justice in length of service who votes with the majority decision coalition. Seniority, however, is not solely a matter of the number of years a justice has sat on the Court. By reason of his position, the chief justice is defined as the most senior even though, like Warren and Burger, he was the junior justice when he became chief.

Even though the Court's *Reports* identify who wrote the opinion of the Court, we do not know who assigned that opinion except by reference to the assignment sheets compiled by the chief justice and the memoranda that supplement this document. It would appear that one could infer the assigner of the Court's opinion from membership in the decision coalition. If the chief justice is a member of this coalition, he should have assigned it; if not, the senior associate justice in length of service.

But this is not necessarily the case because of shifts in the membership of the decision and opinion coalitions. The opinion assignment typically occurs later in the week in which oral argument occurred, after the justices have voted whether to affirm, modify, or reverse the lower court's decision. Between that date and the day on which the decision is publicly announced – a few weeks to several months later – any justice is free to change his or her vote. Hence, the members in the publicly announced decision coalition may differ from those who were in the majority at the conference in which the opinion was assigned. If the justice who appears to have assigned the opinion joined the prevailing

---

[14] Chad Westerland, "Who Owns the Majority Opinion? An Examination of Policy Making on the U.S. Supreme Court," paper presented at the 2003 Annual Meeting of the American Political Science Association.

coalition after the conference vote, he would not have made the assignment. On the other hand, a justice who dissented at the final vote may have been the senior member of the conference majority and done the assigning.

And although such shifting does not occur very often,[15] one nonetheless should rely on the chief's assignment sheets for this information rather than infer it from the membership of the final opinion coalition. Use of these documents informs us that if a coalition breaks up and the writer of a dissenting or specially concurring opinion now finds himself in the majority he automatically becomes author of the Court's opinion. And if the chief justice joins the majority after the assignment was made, he may reassign the opinion. Thus: "You will recall that when we discussed No. 24 – *Halliburton Oil Well Cementing Co. v. Reily* – I did not vote because I was uncertain as to what my decision would be, and Justice Black assigned the case further. I have decided to vote to reverse. I am, therefore, reassigning the case to myself."[16]

The assignment sheets indicate that assigners sometimes make mistakes. Justice White, for example, had occasion to inform Burger that he "appreciate[d] the opportunity to see the light, but my notes show that I was in the minority. . . . Someone else should take this one."[17] Deviations from the seniority rule also occur for reasons that the docket books unfortunately do not specify. Thus, Justice O'Connor self-assigned a case though only Scalia had less seniority.[18] With only Scalia and Kennedy junior, she self-assigned *Penry v. Lynaugh*, involving execution of the mentally retarded.[19] Justice Stevens, sixth in seniority, assigned *Tompkins v. Texas;*[20] Justice Blackmun, fifth in seniority, assigned the famous Christmas display case, *Allegheny County v. ACLU;*[21] and Justices Brennan and White jointly assigned *Missouri v. Jenkins.*[22]

As indicated, the chief justice, because he is defined as most senior, assigns the Court's opinion when he is a member of the majority vote coalition. A few exceptions have occurred, none of significance. For example, Warren's assignment sheets indicate that Black, the senior associate justice, assigned the opinion in six cases in which he and Black were in the majority on the first assignment day, October 19, 1953, after Warren became chief justice.

This assignment rule effectively guarantees that the chief justice will make the overwhelming majority of assignments, as the totals in Tables 13.2 through 13.5 show. The percentages range from 87 percent for Burger, to 81 percent

---

[15] Saul Brenner, "Fluidity on the United States Supreme Court: A Reexamination," 24 *American Journal of Political Science* 526 (1980).

[16] Quoted in David M. O'Brien, *Storm Center*, 2d ed. (New York: Norton, 1990), p. 287.

[17] Memorandum to the chief justice, William J. Brennan's Docket Books, Library of Congress, Washington, DC, November 16, 1976. The case in question was *Ingraham v. Wright*, 430 U.S. 651 (1977).

[18] *Boos v. Barry*, 485 U.S. 312 (1988).

[19] 492 U.S. 302 (1989).

[20] 490 U.S. 784 (1990). No opinion resulted because of a tied vote.

[21] 492 U.S. 573 (1989).

[22] 495 U.S. 33 (1990).

Table 13.2. *Opinion Assignment in the Vinson Court*

Majority Opinion Writer	Majority Opinion Assigner					Total
	Vinson	Black	Reed	Frankfurter	Douglas	
Vinson	78					78
Black	84	28				112
Reed	61	8	11			80
Frankfurter	47	13	6	5		71
Douglas	81	17	6	2		106
Jackson	69	11	2	1		83
Burton	38	12	2	1	1	54
Minton	32	7	2	1		42
Clark	37	5	1	1		44
Murphy	24	11		1		36
Rutledge	22	6	1			19
Total	573	118	31	12	1	760[a]

[a] Includes 25 per curiam assignments.

Table 13.3. *Opinion Assignment in the Warren Court*

Majority Opinion Writer	Majority Opinion Assigner							Total
	Warren	Black	Reed	Frankfurter	Douglas	Clark	Harlan	
Warren	171	2						173
Black	153	24						177
Reed	11	3	15					29
Frankfurter	48	4	8	29				89
Douglas	171	10		2	2			185
Jackson	2	1	4					7
Burton	25	3	4	4				36
Minton	18	5						23
Clark	130	12	5	22	2	6		177
Harlan	101	20	4	25	2	3	2	157
Brennan	137	6	2	8	4	5	2	164
Whittaker	35	3		5				43
Stewart	107	12		14	2	2		137
White	71	9			1	1	1	84[a]
Goldberg	39	3			1	1		44
Fortas	40	1			2		1	44
Marshall	22	1					1	24
Total	1,281	119	42	109	16	18	7	1,771[b]

[a] Includes one assignment from Brennan.
[b] Includes 178 per curiam assignments.

Table 13.4. *Opinion Assignment in the Burger Court*

Majority Opinion Writer	Majority Opinion Assigner								
	Burger	Black	Douglas	Brennan	Stewart	White	Marshall	Harlan	Total
Burger	283[a]								283
Black	17	10							27
Douglas	65	4	14						84[b]
Harlan	18	4	1					1	24
Brennan	148	1	21	79					249
Stewart	164	1	13	10	10			1	199
White	258	2	7	15	2	6			290
Marshall	213	1	3	17	2		1		237
Blackmun	190		3	26	1				220
Powell	219		7	14	1	1			242
Rehnquist	245		3	6	2		1		257
Stevens	142			12	3	1	1		159
O'Connor	78			2		4			84
Total	2,040	23	72	181	21	12	3	2	2,355[c]

[a] Includes five assignments to a "write team" in a set of death penalty cases.
[b] Includes a "conference" assignment.
[c] Includes an assignment jointly made by Burger and Brennan; 35 per curiam assignments; 13 unknown assignments; and 3 miscellaneous assignments.

Table 13.5. *Opinion Assignment in the Rehnquist Court, 1986–1990 Terms*

Majority Opinion Writer	Majority Opinion Assigner							
	Rehnquist	Brennan	White	O'Connor	Stevens	Marshall	Blackmun	Total
Rehnquist	85							85
Brennan	26	39						65
White	75	7	8					90
Marshall	57	13						70
Blackmun	48	15			1		2	66
Powell	18	2						20
Stevens	63	10	2		1			76
O'Connor	73	3	2	3				81
Scalia	58	7	2					67
Kennedy	37	6	4					47
Souter	7							7
Total	547	102	18	3	1	1	2	676[a]

[a] Includes two joint assignments: Brennan–White and Rehnquist–Marshall.

for Rehnquist, 80 percent for Warren, and 75 for Vinson. Because we lack assignment sheet data for any but the first five terms of the Rehnquist Court, 1986–1990, his percentage is limited to them. In Burger's case, the data are a bit misleading. His higher percentage results because his assignment sheets identify the assigner and the justice assigned to write the brief *per curiam* opinion in orally argued cases that the justices found easy to resolve. Most of these were decided unanimously. The Court's official *Reports* do not indicate the author of *per curiam* opinions.

Assignment Patterns

Tables 13.2 through 13.5 list the assigners and the assignees of all the Court's opinions between 1946 and 1990. We count these cases by assignment and include *per curiam* decisions even though more than one docketed case may be included in a single assignment. Judgments of the Court are taken into account because, at the time assignment was made, it was expected that a regular opinion of the Court would result. Multiple assignments in the same case are included except when a second assignment was made to the original justice. Multiple assignments rarely occurred, more frequently in the Warren and Vinson Courts than in the latter two. The Warren Court required 107 assignments to resolve 100 percent of their orally argued citations; the Vinson Court, 103. But the Burger and Rehnquist Courts required only 101 assignments to resolve all their orally argued cases. We deem the Rehnquist Court the more efficient, however, because the Burger Court data include the nondivisive *per curiam* cases, whereas the assignment sheets of the Rehnquist Court do not list such cases.

The data in the tables show that the senior associate justice makes most of the assignments when the chief justice is not a member of the majority decision coalition. This was especially true in the Vinson and Rehnquist Courts. The senior associates, Black and Brennan, made 73.8 and 80.3 percent, respectively, of the assignments that Vinson and Rehnquist did not. But a different result obtained in the Warren and Burger Courts: Whereas Black assigned 118 opinions on the Vinson Court, he assigned 120 on the Warren Court, notwithstanding that (1) he served for the duration of both Courts and (2) the Warren Court existed more than twice as long as the Vinson Court: sixteen years versus seven years. Why this discrepancy?

The answer is clear. Vinson was ideologically conservative, Black a quasi liberal. Hence, when Vinson dissented, Black was virtually always in the majority. But on the Warren Court, when the liberal Warren dissented, Black also tended to do so. As a result, the next senior justices, Reed and Frankfurter, both conservative, made the assignments. Reed did so until early 1957, when he retired; Frankfurter did thereafter, until his retirement in 1962. Ideological divergence also explains the frequency with which Frankfurter assigned the opinion. He was fourth in seniority throughout the Vinson Court and for all but his last four terms on the Warren Court. Because of his ideological affinity with the conservative Vinson, but not the liberal Warren, he assigned more than nine times as many opinions on the latter Court (117) as on the former (12).

Ideological dissimilarity also explains the assignment patterns on the Burger and Rehnquist Courts. Brennan, fourth in seniority at the start of the Burger Court, became senior associate with the retirement of the liberal Douglas in 1975 and remained such until he left the Court in 1990. When either chief dissented, the liberal Brennan rarely did so.

Note also that the associate justices disproportionately self-assign, whereas the chiefs do not deviate much from an equitable one-ninth of their assignments. Of the associates who made more than a dozen assignments on a given Court, White self-assigned 50 percent on the Burger Court and Frankfurter self-assigned 41.7 percent of his cases on the Vinson Court. White on the Rehnquist Court, and Black, Brennan, and Stewart on the Burger Court, exceeded 40 percent, reaching 44.4, 43.5, 43.6, and 47.6 percent, respectively. At the other extreme, only Douglas among the associate justices placed himself in the vicinity of the chiefs, at 12.5 percent on the Warren Court and 19.4 on the Burger Court.

A couple of factors explain these findings: First, self-assignment increases congruence – at least a better fit – between the writer's policy preferences and those contained in the Court's official opinion. Second, because the opportunity to assign the Court's opinion does not arise frequently, associate justices can afford the luxury of paying no heed to the unwritten rule that over the course of a term the Court's opinions should be divided equally among the justices. Their attitude seems to be that because the chief assigns 75 to 80 percent of the Court's opinions, we will let him worry about equal distribution.

Equal Distribution of the Court's Opinions

Deviation from the Court's unwritten rule that each justice should write one-ninth of the opinions of the Court handed down during the course of a term apparently produces discord. According to Chief Justice Warren:

> I do believe that if [assigning opinions] wasn't done . . . with fairness, it could well lead to gross disruption in the Court. . . . During all the years I was there . . . I did try very hard to see that we had an equal work load.[23]

The rule refers to absolute equality, not that which is based on the frequency with which a given justice is in the majority vote coalition. If 99 opinions are to be assigned, each justice should receive 11, even though Justice A voted with the majority in half the cases, and Justice B in only a quarter of them.

Efforts to apportion opinions equally among the justices are more complicated than facially apparent. Although, as we have noted, the chief justice assigns the vast majority of the opinions, equal distribution obviously depends on the behavior of the senior associate justices also. As Burger pointed out late in one term:

> With respect to the assignments, it is a particularly difficult matter at this time of the year, since it is the last opportunity to strike a balance for all the Brethren. For that reason, in those cases in which I am in the majority, I will not undertake to make the assignments until after all the other cases are decided in Conference.[24]

[23] Anthony Lewis, "A Talk with Warren on Crime, the Court, the Country," *New York Times Magazine*, 19 October 1969, p. 130.

[24] Memorandum of Burger to W. O. Douglas, William J. Brennan's Assignment Books (Library of Congress, Washington, DC, April 25, 1974).

A petulant Burger memo further documents the matter: "Just as I was about to send the current assignments out, I received Bill Brennan's assignment of cases. This requires me to do a total and complete revision, and it will not be out today."[25]

Vote changes in the aftermath of the conference also make equitable assignment difficult. In reference to several cases in which crucial justices had not cast votes, Burger wrote: "I am not in a position to make these final assignments until all votes are firmly in hand. Even one change has a 'domino' impact on all other assignments – especially at this time of the Term."[26]

Notwithstanding these complications, the Court has achieved remarkably equal distribution during the forty-one terms for which we have complete data, 1950–1990. We rest our findings on the periodic assignment days – usually eight per term – at which the chief justice compiles an "assignment sheet" that lists the docket number of the case and the names of the assigning and the assigned justice. Scattered assignments – usually a day or two later – are combined with those of the proximate assignment day. Use of assignment day as our measure of equality in the distribution of opinions has one shortcoming: the two or three opinions per term that are assigned weeks removed from a regular assignment day. We exclude such cases from our analysis simply because they are not part of our unit of analysis. Consider *Lefkowitz v. Newsome*,[27] which Douglas assigned to Stewart on December 30, 1974. The next assignment day did not occur until January 27, 1975. Omission of such cases from analysis slightly lessens the degree of distributional equality that would otherwise obtain. Thus, in the *Lefkowitz* situation, Stewart was the only underassigned justice on the assignment day that followed his receipt of *Lefkowitz*.

The number of assignments made per assignment day typically ranges from ten to twenty and includes those made by associate justices as well as the chief. Apart from assignments made by associate justices, nothing limits the chief's discretion. Retention of an opinion does, of course, obviously depend on the assignee's continued membership in the majority vote coalition. If the assignee loses his or her majority, a new assignment is made to one of the members of the new coalition. However, analysis of the Warren Court has shown that the original assignee retained the opinion almost 60 percent of the time if the conference vote coalition broke up and was minimum winning.[28] What happened in these cases was that the assignee simply changed sides and the original four dissenters joined him. But if the original assignee did lose his majority and reassignment occurred within three days of the original assignment, we disregard the first one; however, we do count separately the 116 reassignments made

---

[25] Memorandum to the conference, William J. Brennan's Assignment Books, Library of Congress, Washington, DC, April 4, 1977.

[26] *Id.*, April 28, 1978.

[27] 420 U.S. 283 (1975).

[28] Saul Brenner and Harold J. Spaeth, "Majority Opinion Assignments and the Maintenance of the Original Coalition on the Warren Court," 32 *American Journal of Political Science* 72 (1988).

Table 13.6. *Deviation of Assignments per Assignment Day from Distributional Equality (by Term)*

Term	Deviation from Mode				% 0	N
	0	1	2	3		
Vinson Court						
1950	48	12	3		76.2	63
1951	59	11	1	1	81.9	72
1952	60	11	1	–	83.3	72
Total	167	34	5	1	80.7	207
Warren Court						
1953	74	6	1		91.4	81
1954	41	11	6		70.7	58
1955	62	18	1		76.5	81
1956	61	19	2		74.4	82
1957	68	19	3		75.6	90
1958	67	11	3		82.7	81
1959	64	12	5		79.0	81
1960	46	28	7		56.8	81
1961	47	8	3		81.0	58
1962	55	13	4		76.4	72
1963	81	6	2	1	90.0	90
1964	51	18	2	1	70.8	72
1965	45	22	5		62.5	72
1966	39	19	5		61.9	63
1967	43	16	4		68.3	63
1968	47	12	4	–	74.6	63
Total	891	238	57	2	75.2	1,188
Burger Court						
1969	67	14	7		76.1	88
1970	45	18	9		62.5	72
1971	47	17	7	2	64.4	73
1972	46	15	2		73.0	63
1973	64	8			88.9	72
1974	51	7	1		86.4	59
1975	47	12		1	78.3	60
1976	49	11	3		77.8	63
1977	58	11	3		80.6	72
1978	60	2			96.8	62
1979	48	14	1		76.2	63
1980	64	6	2		88.9	72
1981	66	5	1		91.7	72
1982	57	13	2		79.2	72
1983	49	11	3		77.8	63
1984	57	10	3		81.4	70
1985	51	15	6	–	70.8	72
Total	926	189	50	3	79.3	1,168

Term	Deviation from Mode				% 0	N
	0	1	2	3		
Rehnquist Court						
1986	59	2	2		93.7	63
1987	67				100.0	67
1988	72				100.0	72
1989	61	2			96.8	63
1990	57	5	1		90.5	63
Total	316	9	3		96.3	328
Grand total	2,300	470	115	6	79.6	2,891

Source: Sara Benesh, Reginald S. Sheehan, and Harold J. Spaeth, "Equity in Supreme Court Opinion Assignment," 39 *Jurimetrics* 377 (1999), pp. 382–384.

more than three days later. These 116 reassignments constitute 4 percent of all assignments in the forty-one terms we analyze.

Assignments are made during the week in which oral argument occurs. We measure equality of opinion distribution by dividing the total number of assignments (A), excluding those assigned as *per curiam* opinions, by the number of participating justices (J). Only one apportionment achieves equal distribution regardless of the number of participating justices:

$$A/J = Er\,X$$

where X is the remainder resulting from the division of A by J. If $X=0$, each justice received the same number of assignments. A justice whose assignments do not fit perfectly into this pattern is scored as deviating by that number. Thus, assume 13 opinions are distributed among 9 justices as follows: $A = 4$; B, C, and $D = 2$; E, F, and $G = 1$; and H and $I = 0$. A, H, and I are deviant; A is overassigned by 2 cases, H and I underassigned by 1, since the most equitable division of 13 among 9 recipients is for 5 to receive 1 and 4 to receive 2.

Table 13.6 lists by term the deviation from perfect equality that each assignment day during that term produced. Thus, the 1950 term shows that of the sixty-three assignments made, forty-eight were equally apportioned on the relevant assignment day, twelve assignments deviated from equality by one assignment (six on the first assignment day, and four on the fifth), and three assignments deviated from equality by two assignments (all on the second assignment day, along with the other two single-deviation assignments). Accordingly, 76.2 percent of the term's assignments were equally distributed.

Table 13.6 clearly confirms adherence to the equality norm. Eighty percent of the assignments deviated not a whit from perfect equality. Sixteen percent (470) deviated by only a single assignment, and less than 5 percent by more than one assignment. Surprisingly perhaps, the Rehnquist Court achieved the most equitable distribution (96.3 percent), notwithstanding the reputed contentiousness that afflicted it during these five terms.[29] But the other Courts did not fare especially poorly, except when compared to the Rehnquist Court: Vinson 81, Warren 75, and Burger 79 percent.

The Effect of Equal Distribution on Ideology

Does the equal distribution of the Court's opinions adversely impact ideological behavior? In other words, do conservative justices receive favorable treatment on a conservative Court when the number of assignments on an assignment day is not divisible by 9, and vice versa if the Court is liberal? Given equal distribution overall, one would think not. And that appears to be the situation on the Vinson and Warren Courts, although not on the conservative Burger and Rehnquist Courts, on which conservative justices were overassigned (see Table 13.7).

Only four of the nine Vinson Court justices deviate by more than a single assignment per term, along with five of the seventeen Warren Court justices. Black and Douglas, the Court's only two liberals, were favored, although Black's imbalance largely resulted from self-assignment. But Vinson favored neither himself nor his fellow conservatives. Faring worst was Burton, probably because he was a sluggish writer.[30] No justice, other than Black, Douglas, and Burton, deviated by an average of more than 1.33 assignments per term. On the Warren Court, the briefly serving Burton, Minton, and Whittaker – conservatives all – were disfavored, Burton, again, probably because he wrote so slowly. Minton's underassignments all occurred in his final term when he was seriously ill.[31] And Whittaker was never well during his five terms and finally retired on his physician's advice. Warren, as did Vinson, underassigned himself and most favored Clark and Douglas.

Clark, though distant from Warren on criminal procedure, shared Warren's attitudes on economic matters. This was the area in which Warren overassigned him. But as a group the liberals were not advantaged. Warren underassigned himself, and Black, the senior associate throughout the Warren Court, advantaged himself by only a quarter of an assignment per term. Other liberals did not fare well: Brennan 0.0, Fortas −0.75, and Goldberg −1.00. Nonliberals, such as Frankfurter (−0.22), White (−0.42), and Harlan (−0.46), fared slightly better.

These essentially equal assignment patterns preclude an ideological cast to the assignments of the Vinson and Warren Courts. Not so, however, for the Burger and Rehnquist Courts, whose patterning evidences a definite ideological orientation: Conservatives were favored, liberals disfavored. Thus,

---

[29] William Lazarus, *Closed Chambers* (New York: Times Books, 1998).

[30] William O. Douglas, *The Court Years* (New York: Vintage Books, 1980), pp. 247–248.

[31] N. E. H. Hull, "Minton, Sherman," in K. L. Hall (ed.), *The Oxford Companion to the Supreme Court of the United States* (New York: Oxford University Press, 1992), p. 552.

Table 13.7. *Cumulative Number of Deviations from the Most Equal Distribution of Assignments per Assignment Day per Justice per Term*

	Court			
Justice	Vinson	Warren	Burger	Rehnquist
Black	3.33[10/3]	0.25[4/16]	3.50[7/2]	
Blackmun			−0.75[−12/16]	−1.00[−5/5]
Brennan		0.00[0/13]	−0.35[−6/17]	1.20[5/4]
Burger			0.76[13/17]	
Burton	−2.33[−7/3]	−2.60[−13/5]		
Clark	−0.33[−1/3]	1.43[20/14]		
Douglas	1.67[5/3]	1.13[18/16]	−1.29[−7/5.43]	
Fortas		−0.75[−3/4]		
Frankfurter	−1.33[−4/3]	−0.22[−2/9]		
Goldberg		−1.00[−3/3]		
Harlan		−0.46[−7/15]	−0.50[10/2]	
Jackson	−1.00[−3/3]	1.00[1/1]		
Kennedy				−0.59[−2/3.4]
Marshall		0.50[1/2]	−0.59[−10/17]	0.00[0/5]
Minton	−1.00[−3/3]	−2.33[−7/3]		
O'Connor			0.20[1/5]	1.80[9/5]
Powell			0.76[11/14.5]	4.00[4/1]
Reed	0.67[2/3]	−0.86[−3/3.5]		
Rehnquist			1.72[25/14.5]	0.80[4/5]
Scalia				0.00[0/5]
Souter				−3.00[−3/1]
Stevens			−0.48[−5/10.5]	0.80[4/5]
Stewart		−0.18[−2/11]	0.83[10/12]	
Vinson	−0.67[−2/3]			
Warren		−0.69[−11/16]		
White		−0.42[−3/7.14]	1.53[26/17]	3.40[17/5]
Whittaker		−1.60[−8/5]		

Source: Sara C. Benesh, Reginald S. Sheehan, and Harold J. Spaeth, "Equity in Supreme Court Opinion Assignment," 39 *Jurimetrics* 377 (1999), p. 387.

the five reputed liberals on the Burger Court all received negative scores, notwithstanding that two of them functioned as the senior associate: Douglas (1970–1974 terms) −1.29 and Brennan (1975–1985 terms) −0.35. Joining them were Marshall at −0.59, who was underassigned four opinions in the 1971 and 1983 terms and three in 1984; Stevens −0.48; and Blackmun −0.75. Blackmun fell into disfavor once he separated himself from Burger, his "Minnesota twin." He was underassigned two opinions in the 1982 and 1983 terms and four in 1985. By contrast, the conservatives all received more than their share except Harlan, who served only two years on the Burger Court, during which he received one less opinion than equity decreed. Burger preferred himself, +0.76; Stewart and Powell were similarly favored: +0.83 and +0.76, respectively. Most advantaged – other than Black, who served only two years – were White (+1.53) and Rehnquist (+1.72).[32]

As did his conservative predecessor, Rehnquist preferred his ideological allies but did so while achieving almost perfect equity during his first five terms: a deviation of only 0.3, with two terms perfectly equitable. He most advantaged White (+3.40), providing him with four extra assignments in three successive terms (1986–1988), two in 1989, and three in 1990. Rehnquist's behavior reciprocated that of Burger, who favored Rehnquist most, followed by White. Rehnquist also overassigned to O'Connor (+1.80) and himself (+0.80). Surprisingly, perhaps, he did not overassign to either Scalia (0.0) or Kennedy (−0.59). On the other hand, Stevens did better than expected (+0.80), and Marshall could have anticipated less than his share rather than perfect equity. Brennan received a decidedly positive score (+1.20), but only because of self-assignment.

OPINION ASSIGNMENTS AND OPINION COALITIONS

We have already noted that the tendency of associate justices to self-assign when the chief justice dissents complicates efforts to equalize the distribution of the Court's opinions among the justices. If the norm of equal distribution did not exist, we would expect the chief justice hugely to favor himself and those justices ideologically closest to him. As the vehicle whereby the majority expresses its policy preferences and provides guidance to the lower courts in deciding similar disputes, authorship of the Court's opinion provides a product more or less congruent with the author's policy preferences.

We say more or less because the authors of the Court's opinions are not free to do as they please. They must take into account the views of at least four other justices. Failure to do so means loss of the opinion. Balancing the preferences of several justices is not an easy task, but the most effective way to do so is to play to the preferences of the median member of the majority decision coalition. Thus, although the name of the authorship game is accommodating the views of other justices, not all other justices are in an equal bargaining position.[33] Needless to say, the author may consider the views of more than four colleagues, but they are not crucial to his or her majority.

When an issue generates a great deal of controversy and the Court is closely divided, the "swing" justice – the one who holds the balance of power between the four on each side of the controversy – tends to receive the Court's opinion.[34] This so-called marginal justice is hugely advantaged for several reasons: First, the probability that the majority opinion will have to be reassigned

[32] These findings withstand multivariate scrutiny. After one controls for a host of other factors, Burger was more likely to assign to those ideologically closest to him. Sara C. Benesh, Reginald S. Sheehan, and Harold J. Spaeth, "Equity in Supreme Court Opinion Assignment," 39 *Jurimetrics* 377 (1999), at 388–389.

[33] Westerland, "Who Owns."

[34] Brenner and Spaeth, *Assignments*.

to another justice because the conference vote coalition breaks up is lessened. Breakups occur when the vote coalition shifts from affirm to reverse, or the converse. The reassignment of the opinion obviously takes time and slows the Court's productive process.[35] Moreover, once assigned the Court's opinion, the marginal member of the vote coalition retains it, regardless of whether or not the coalition breaks up. But when nonmarginal members receive the assignment, they are much less likely to retain it when the coalition breaks up.[36]

Other considerations that may cause assigners to favor the marginal justice include an opinion of moderate content that should help retain support for the Court's position in future cases. Tension may also be reduced between the majority and minority.[37] And because the marginal justice is ideologically closer to the minority than any other member of the majority, assigning the opinion to this justice may keep the original coalition intact.

THE POLITICS OF COALITION FORMATION

Substantively, among the most important decisions a justice makes is whether or not to join the majority opinion coalition. If fewer than a majority of the justices so join, judgments of the Court result, precluding an authoritative resolution of the controversy at issue.

To a markedly greater extent than in earlier Courts, the Burger and Rehnquist justices have failed to produce opinions of the Court to explain their decisions and guide affected publics and lower courts in the resolution of all similar cases. Typically, the number of judgments is not large – 4.2 percent of the Burger Court's signed opinions and 2.9 percent of those of the Rehnquist Court during its first seventeen terms (1986–2002) – as opinion writers often attempt to accommodate conference coalition members.[38] Nevertheless, these figures compare unfavorably with the Warren Court's 2.3 percent.[39]

---

[35] Saul Brenner, "Reassigning the Majority Opinion on the United States Supreme Court," 11 *Justice System Journal* 186 (1986).

[36] Brenner and Spaeth, *Assignments*, p. 78.

[37] William P. McLauchlan, "Ideology and Conflict in Supreme Court Opinion Assignment, 1946–1962," 25 *Political Research Quarterly* 16 (1972): 26.

[38] Lee Epstein and Jack Knight, *The Choices Justices Make* (Washington, DC: Congressional Quarterly Press, 1998), chap. 3.

[39] For analytical purposes we consider all orally argued signed opinion cases by using docket number, rather than case citation, as the unit of analysis. We scrupulously define a judgment according to the Court's own language. Though only a small part of the prevailing opinion may constitute the "opinion of the Court," we exclude the case from consideration. Thus, the convoluted statement in *Arizona v. Fulminante*, 499 U.S. 279 (1991), at 281, constitutes an opinion, not a judgment: "WHITE, J., delivered an opinion, Parts I, II, and IV of which are for the Court, and filed a dissenting opinion in Part III. MARSHALL, BLACKMUN AND STEVENS, JJ. joined Parts I, II, III, and IV of that opinion; SCALIA, J., joined Parts I and II; and KENNEDY, J., joined parts I and IV. REHNQUIST, C. J., delivered an opinion, Part II of which is for the Court, and filed a dissenting opinion in Parts I and III, *post*, p. 302. O'CONNOR, J.,

   The vast majority of these cases concern civil rights and liberties – 85 percent
of the Burger Court's and 83 percent of the Rehnquist Court's (as compared
with 57.1 and 54.4 percent, respectively, of the cases decided by an opinion of
the Court). Almost 41 percent of the Burger Court's judgments concern criminal procedure, and an additional 16 percent pertain to the First Amendment,
whereas 30 percent of the Rehnquist Court's concern civil rights and an additional 21 percent the First Amendment. Both of these proportions approximately double the percentage of cases decided by an opinion of the Court. On
the Rehnquist Court, the proportion of the judgments accounted for by First
Amendment and due process cases each constituted two and a half times the
proportion decided by an opinion of the Court. This rather clearly indicates that
judgments occur in cases the justices deem highly salient. Supporting their importance is the inordinate number of opinions they contain, an average of 4.47
in the Burger Court and 4.02 in the Rehnquist Court. The Rehnquist Court,
unlike its predecessors, labels even a small portion of its controlling opinion as
the *opinion of the Court* rather than a judgment so long as five justices join any
given portion of it.
   The justices' behavior indicates that they vote their attitudes – their personal
policy preferences – in cases decided by a judgment with at least as much regularity as they do overall. What characterizes these cases is the unusual amount
of overt conflict they engender – an inability to compromise and resolve differences. Thus, failure to form a majority opinion coalition may result because the
policy preferences of one or more of the members of the majority vote coalition
are insufficiently satisfied, resulting in a special concurrence. Conversely, the
fault may lie with the opinion assignee who fails to bargain effectively because
he or she gives primacy to his or her own policy preferences; alternatively, the
opinion assigner may have selected an assignee unable to effect the necessary
compromises.

Patterns of Interagreement in Special Opinions

We noted at the beginning of this chapter that the justices are free agents in the
sense that they cannot be forced to agree with one another. The only compulsion
rests on the justice who has been assigned to write the opinion of the Court.
Retention of this responsibility requires that she obtain the agreement of a majority of the justices who participated in the assigned case. The question then
becomes which justices agree with whom. We could simply ascertain the overall frequency with which each justice agrees with the others. But this frequency
would be badly skewed and greatly wash out the differences between the justices
because by far the most common action of each justice is to agree silently with

joined Parts I, II and III of that opinion; KENNEDY and SOUTER, JJ., joined Parts I and II; and
SCALIA, J., joined Parts II and III. KENNEDY, J., filed an opinion concurring in the judgment,
post, p. 313." Although this is an extremely cumbrous example, by no means is it sui generis
for either opinions or judgments of the Court.

the author of the opinion of the Court. As Table 13.1 shows, even Brennan and Marshall, the most disaffected of the Rehnquist Court justices, silently agreed with the Court's opinion markedly more than half the time, and the others did so as frequently as four-fifths of the time. As a result, we focus on interagreement in special opinions (dissents and concurrences), a much richer source of information, because any justice who dissents or concurs may do so just as readily alone as in conjunction with others. To the extent that justices choose the latter option, we have an informative indicator of interagreement.

Table 13.8 presents the interagreement of each Rehnquist Court justice with the others over the Court's first sixteen terms (1986–2001). The rows indicate the number of times the named justice joined special opinions written by the justice named at the head of the column. Thus, whereas Rehnquist joined Scalia seventy-one times, he joined Ginsberg, Breyer, and Souter only seven, five, and five times, respectively. Scalia reciprocated by joining Rehnquist thirty-seven times and joining Ginsberg, Breyer, and Souter even less frequently than Rehnquist did: two, seven, and six times, respectively.

The numbers at the foot of the table represent the average number of joiners the columnar justice obtained for his or her special opinions. It can range from 0 to 4. The former indicates nobody ever joined the author. If more than four joined, the special opinion becomes the opinion of the Court.

The table presents a couple of interesting findings. First, very little interagreement occurs. Brennan gained the most joiners per special opinion, 1.55, followed by Rehnquist at 1.46, Marshall at 1.37, and Powell, who served only during the first term of the Rehnquist Court, at 1.32. But note that Brennan accounts for 44 percent of Marshall's joinees (50 of 114), and Marshall produces a whopping 53 percent (109 of 205) of Brennan's, and O'Connor 41 percent of Powell's (12 of 29). By comparison, Rehnquist's most frequent joiner, Scalia, accounts for only 23 percent of his total (37 of 161).

At the other extreme, six of the fourteen Rehnquist Court justices garnered an average of less than one joiner per special opinion: Thomas and Scalia the fewest with 0.88, followed by Stevens at 0.91, and Kennedy and O'Connor at 0.94. We may parenthetically note that four of these five justices (all but Stevens) are conservatives, suggesting that these conservatives may have a tendency to split ideological hairs even with fellow conservatives.

Second, like-minded justices agree with one another, infrequently with those attitudinally distant. Thus, the justices positioned at the upper left and lower right corners of Table 13.8 associate closely, and those at the lower left and upper right rarely do so. Thus, for example, the liberal Marshall joined his fellow liberal, Brennan, and the next two justices closest to him – Blackmun and Stevens – 225 times but joined the other six with whom he served a grand total of only 30 times. The Court's conservatives behaved reciprocally. Thus, Scalia joined Thomas, Rehnquist, Kennedy, and O'Connor 182 times, but Marshall, Brennan, Blackmun, and Ginsberg only 5 times. Thomas joined Scalia 110 times, the rest of the other nine justices with whom he served a grand total of

Table 13.8. *Interagreement in Special Opinions, 1986–2001 Terms*

	Marshall	Brennan	Blackmun	Stevens	Ginsburg	Breyer	Souter	White	O'Connor	Powell	Kennedy	Rehnquist	Scalia	Thomas
Marshall	**83**	109	55	61	–	–	–	11	5	2	3	0	9	–
Brennan	50	**132**	46	40	–	–	–	7	6	3	1	0	6	–
Blackmun	34	51	**185**	81	6	–	16	27	15	1	10	10	11	2
Stevens	26	37	35	**489**	33	40	48	22	21	1	10	6	11	7
Ginsburg	–	–	2	67	**100**	39	49	–	7	–	9	2	7	3
Breyer	–	–	–	54	28	**131**	39	–	19	–	5	1	2	3
Souter	–	–	10	51	35	34	**148**	3	21	–	12	5	13	6
White	1	5	2	21	–	–	5	**121**	7	1	10	20	15	0
O'Connor	2	2	16	329	6	16	9	19	**251**	12	23	29	51	9
Powell	0	0	2	0	–	–	–	3	5	**22**	–	1	1	–
Kennedy	0	1	2	8	3	2	6	7	20	–	**178**	16	45	15
Rehnquist	0	0	2	15	7	5	5	29	42	6	35	**110**	71	35
Scalia	1	0	2	10	2	7	6	11	44	3	36	37	**398**	65
Thomas	–	–	1	8	0	1	7	2	25	–	13	34	110	**165**
Joiners/Opinion	1.37	1.55	0.95	0.91	1.20	1.10	1.28	1.17	0.94	1.32	.94	1.46	0.880	0.88

Note: Rows represent the frequency with which the named justice functioned as a joiner: a joiner of the opinions of another justice; columns represent the frequency with which the various justices joined the opinions of the named justice; boldface entries specify the number of special opinions identified justice wrote; –, not on the Court together.

Table 13.9. *Frequency of Special Opinions as a Proportion of Votes Cast*

Justice	Special Opinions	Number of Participations	Special Opinions/ Participation
Marshall	83	762	10.9
Brennan	132	635	20.8
Blackmun	185	1,095	16.9
Stevens	489	1,796	27.2
Ginsburg	100	802	12.5
Breyer	131	695	18.9
Souter	148	1,151	12.9
White	121	999	12.1
O'Connor	251	1,777	14.1
Powell	22	170	12.9
Kennedy	178	1,538	11.6
Rehnquist	110	1,802	6.1
Scalia	398	1,791	22.2
Thomas	165	1,019	16.2
Totals	2,513	16,032	15.7

91 times. Reciprocity also tends to obtain. Marshall and Brennan never joined Rehnquist, and Rehnquist returned the favor.

Overall, it is clear that the justices exert little influence on one another, except those of like mind. Accordingly, bloc voting results. And bloc voting arguably results from like-mindedness, not influence. Our earlier research indicates that the patterns displayed in Table 13.8 also manifested themselves on the Warren and Burger Courts.[40]

Although Table 13.8 indicates that the justices do not do much joining in the other justices' special opinions, it is not because they rarely write such opinions. They do so with a vengeance as Table 13.9 clearly shows. The data in this table, along with Table 13.8 and Table 13.10, include all orally argued docketed decisions.[41] Stevens leads the pack, writing more than a special opinion for every four votes he casts. Scalia and Brennan follow with proportions of 22.2 and 20.8 percent, respectively. Do keep in mind that each justice is expected to write one-ninth of the Court's majority opinions per term. That amounts to 11 percent. If we add that proportion to those in Table 13.9, we find that Stevens

[40] Jeffrey A. Segal and Harold J. Spaeth, *The Supreme Court and the Attitudinal Model* (Cambridge: Cambridge University Press, 1993), pp. 281–282 and the references cited therein.

[41] A docketed decision differs from a case citation in that more than a single case may be combined with another or others under a single controlling opinion. Each such case will contain a separate docket number. We count by docket number rather than citation because a justice may vote with the majority in one such docket but dissent or concur in the second docket that is combined with the first in a single controlling opinion.

writes in almost 40 percent of the cases in which he participates, Scalia in a third of his. Except Rehnquist, the others wrote in 20 to 30 percent of the cases in which they cast a vote.

Inasmuch as special opinions have no binding or controlling legal effect, an institutionally minded justice rarely writes them, preferring instead that the Court show as united a front as possible: That is, a unanimous decision or one with only a single dissent or special concurrence is preferable to a minimum winning 5-to-4 decision. In this regard, Rehnquist shows himself to be the Court's institutional loyalist, writing special opinions at less than half the frequency of most of his colleagues (6.1 percent). Note, however, that Rehnquist was not so restrained during his tenure as associate justice.[42]

Viewed somewhat differently, the Court decided 1,805 orally argued docketed cases between the beginning of the Rehnquist Court in 1986 and the end of its 2001 term. In these 1,805 cases, the justices wrote 2,513 special opinions, an average of 1.39 such opinions for every docketed case. As every one of these 2,513 opinions has no legally controlling effect, the authors of these opinions were attempting to influence either one another, lower court judges, the legal community generally, or elements of the public. Or perhaps they sought only to burnish and amplify their own egos. Whatever the motivation(s), one conclusion appears inescapable: The justices clearly are not overworked. Overworked judges simply do not have the luxury of the preening self-indulgence that special opinion writing requires.

WHO INFLUENCES WHOM?

The preceding section, focusing on the extent to which each justice agreed with the others (or, more likely, failed to do so), tells us nothing about the character of these relationships. But to the extent that Justice A agrees more with B than B does with A, we may be able to detect a degree of "influence" for some pairs of justices. So, do the relationships in Table 13.8 manifest a mutual or one-sided relationship? If the former, A and B will interagree at about the same frequency: A with B and B with A. Or is the relationship one-sided: A agrees much more frequently with B, than B with A?

Our procedure for measuring this relationship is straightforward. We count the number of special opinions a justice wrote – again multiply counting the number of orally argued docketed cases to which the opinion applies – and the number of times a given justice joined them. The fraction, presented as a decimal, becomes our measure of influence. We have no a priori sense of what an "influential" proportion might be. We base such a judgment on the contents of Table 13.10. Even though a justice may have served only for a term or two, that does not preclude her being influential. Thus Powell, who served only in the 1986 term, had O'Connor agree with 54.5 percent of his special opinions and Rehnquist with 27.3 percent of them. Both percentages are far above any justice's average, as the bottom row of Table 13.10 indicates.

---

[42] Baik, *Chief*.

Table 13.10. *Dyadic Influence Matrix, 1986–2001 Terms*

Special Opinion Joiner	Special Opinion Writer													
	Marshall	Brennan	Blackmun	Stevens	Ginsburg	Breyer	Souter	White	O'Connor	Powell	Kennedy	Rehnquist	Scalia	Thomas
Marshall	82.5	29.7	12.5	–	–	–	9.1	2.0	9.1	1.7	0.0	2.3	–	–
Brennan	60.2	–	24.9	8.2	–	–	–	5.8	2.4	13.6	0.6	0.0	1.5	1.2
Blackmun	41.0	38.6	–	16.6	6.0	–	10.8	22.3	6.0	4.5	5.6	9.1	2.8	4.2
Stevens	31.3	28.0	18.9	–	33.0	30.5	32.4	18.2	8.4	4.5	5.6	5.5	2.8	1.8
Ginsburg	–	–	1.1	13.7	–	29.8	33.1	–	2.8	–	5.1	1.8	1.8	1.8
Breyer	–	–	–	11.0	28.0	–	26.4	–	7.6	–	2.8	0.9	0.5	1.8
Souter	–	–	5.4	10.4	35.0	26.0	–	2.5	8.4	–	6.7	4.5	3.3	3.6
White	1.2	3.8	1.1	4.3	–	–	3.4	–	2.8	4.5	5.6	18.2	3.8	0.0
O'Connor	2.4	1.5	8.6	5.9	6.0	12.2	6.1	15.7	–	54.5	12.9	26.4	12.8	5.5
Powell	0.0	0.0	1.1	0.0	–	–	–	2.5	2.0	–	–	0.9	0.3	–
Kennedy	0.0	0.8	1.1	1.6	3.0	1.5	4.1	5.8	8.0	–	–	14.5	11.3	9.1
Rehnquist	0.0	0.0	1.1	3.1	7.0	3.8	3.4	24.0	16.7	27.3	19.7	–	17.8	21.2
Scalia	1.2	0.0	1.1	2.0	2.0	5.3	4.1	9.1	17.5	13.6	20.2	33.6	–	39.4
Thomas	–	–	0.5	1.6	0.0	0.8	4.7	1.7	10.0	–	7.3	30.9	27.6	–
Average	15.3	17.2	7.9	7.0	13.3	13.7	12.9	10.6	7.3	16.5	7.8	11.3	6.8	8.8

Note: Entries are the proportion of the time the row justice joined the columnar justice's special opinions; –, not on the Court together.

Thus, with only a few exceptions (e.g., Ginsburg and Blackmun, and vice versa, and Kennedy and Thomas, also vice versa) the percentages of the justices on the upper left and lower right are high enough to indicate influence on one another.

By and large, influence – whether high or low – appears reciprocal: A influences B to the extent that B influences A. Thus Stevens joined 18.9 percent of Blackmun's special opinions, Blackmun 16.6 of Stevens's, Ginsburg 29.8 percent of Breyer's, Breyer 28.0 of hers. Thomas joined 7.3 percent of Kennedy's, Kennedy 9.1 percent of his. Clearly, the conservatives interact among themselves, as do the others. A close reading of Table 13.10 indicates that the top seven justices interact well together, as do the bottom six. Although it is a stretch, we may characterize the former group as *liberals*, though, except for Marshall and Brennan, a more accurate label is *moderate*. The bottom six clearly warrant a *conservative* label. This leaves Byron White as neither fish nor fowl, but rather as the balance of power between the two wings of the Court. Not until he left the Court at the end of the 1992 term did O'Connor become the swing vote, and, as Table 13.10 shows, she disproportionately swung in a conservative direction.

A more precise method of illustrating the presence of influential relationships relies on the standard deviation of the justices' scores in Table 13.10.[43] We employ a modest criterion of one standard deviation (3.7) above the mean (11.2) as our measure of influence (= 14.9). Pair interagreements exceeding this level are boldface in Table 13.10. By this criterion, every justice influenced at least one colleague (the columns of Table 13.10), and White and Rehnquist influenced most, four each. Conversely, no justice influenced Powell or Kennedy (the rows of Table 13.10), and only one influenced White (Rehnquist). Stevens and Rehnquist were most influenced by their colleagues, Stevens by seven, Rehnquist six. Interestingly, Stevens influenced only one justice (Blackmun). No other justice was influenced by as many as four justices except Blackmun and Scalia.

Figure 13.1 presents the influential relationships on the Rehnquist Court graphically. Three distinct clusters emerge, two liberal–moderate and one conservative, each with three reciprocally interacting members. The two liberal–moderate clusters exist independently because the Souter–Ginsburg–Breyer coalition sat after Brennan and Marshall left the Court. The only linkage between these two clusters – an extremely tenuous one – joined Blackmun with Stevens in a mutual relationship, with the Souter–Ginsburg–Breyer cluster influencing Stevens, but not being influenced by him. The figure also shows that at the end of the period under analysis (the 2001 term) the liberal–moderate

---

[43] *Standard deviation* measures the dispersion in a set of scores and is calculated as follows: Each justice's average score (the bottom row of Table 13.10) is added to the others and the mean calculated (11.2). From each justice's average score this mean is subtracted. The result is a deviation score for each justice. These scores are then squared and added together (175.4). This number is divided by the 14 justices, less one (175.4/13). The result, 13.5, is the variance, the square root of which, 3.7, is the standard deviation of the justices' average scores.

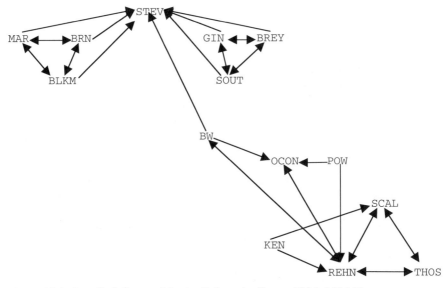

Figure 13.1. Dyadic Influence Matrix, Rehnquist Court, 1986–2001 Terms.

blocs lacked a majority as all members of the Marshall–Brennan–Blackmun cluster had left the Court. Although the remaining trio could count on Stevens as a fourth vote, to gain a majority they had to obtain one of the conservatives, either O'Connor or Kennedy.

The conservatives are much better positioned, as Figure 13.1 shows. The only linkage among the three clusters, White, left the Court at the end of the 1992 term. The remaining five justices (excluding the long-departed Powell) form a tight cluster, however. Rehnquist, Scalia, and Thomas form its heart. O'Connor has a mutual relationship with Rehnquist, and Kennedy influences both Rehnquist and Scalia.

The patterns these tables and figure reveal indicate that the breakdown in consensual norms continues apace.[44] Recent research indicates that the lack of consensus may result from either legal or extralegal factors or both. Analysis of the contents of the Rehnquist Court's special opinions shows that these opinions do not disagree with the majority over what the case is all about. That is, the justices do not disagree about the legal provision, issue, or basis for decision (e.g., constitutional, statutory, common law, or administrative regulation). Rather, disagreement revolves about the disposition to be made of the case, not what the case involves. Hence, disagreement appears to be extralegal, rather than legal, notwithstanding the many opportunities for the latter to manifest itself.[45]

---

[44] Thomas G. Walker, Lee Epstein, and William Dixon, "On the Demise."
[45] Sara C. Benesh and Harold J. Spaeth, "Disagreement on the Court: Have All Consensual Norms Collapsed?" paper presented at the 2001 meeting of the Southern Political Science Association.

SUMMARY AND CONCLUSIONS

Insofar as opinion assignment is concerned, the four Courts we have considered have achieved aggregate equality, in spite of the ideologically based opinion assignments by the chief justices and, even more pronouncedly, by the senior associate justices. Leftward preferences counterbalance those from the right. The various chief justices have further enhanced their ideological goals by retaining a disproportionate segment of important cases for themselves.

A modicum of what may loosely be termed "specialization" manifests itself, as justices closest to the chief write the Court's opinions in cases in issue areas of interest or salience. The Court's opinions in cases with less attractive issues are written by the justices least often in majority opinion coalitions. This makes them "specialists" also, but not in matters of much importance or interest to their authors (e.g., Native American cases, internal revenue, and matters involving the jurisdiction or authority of the lower courts). Thus, although the Court divides its required workload remarkably equally, though certain justices write much more frequently on certain issues rather than others, neither of these constraints impedes ideologically based opinion assignments by opinion assigners.

Although coalition formation occurs in an inherently interactive environment, the justices' policy preferences go a long way toward explaining their decisions, whereas interactive factors such as bargaining and negotiation do not. Indeed, when we consider the formation of special opinion coalitions, analysis has demonstrated that such interactive considerations as bargaining and negotiation are notably absent. Epstein and Knight, for example, in their examination of the justices' interoffice communications for the 1983 term, find absolutely no bargaining statements between the opinion writer and any other justice in a majority of the cases.[46] The frequency with which the justices write special opinions – almost one and a half per orally argued docketed case with an average of barely one joining justice – further bespeaks a lack of persuasive interaction. Influence seems a function of like-mindedness: the Marshalls and Brennans, the Frankfurters and Harlans, and the Scalias and Thomases.

However, the Court's ability to arrive at majority decisions with an efficiency and dispatch that put other courts to shame does evidence robust institutional health. Nevertheless, as Justice Powell pointed out, the Court "is perhaps one of the last citadels of jealously preserved individualism. To be sure, we sit together for the arguments and during the long Friday conferences when votes are taken. But for the most part, perhaps as much as 90 percent of our total time, we function as nine small, independent law firms."[47] Perhaps it is the Court's behavior as nine independent law firms that lessens the justices' willingness to

---

[46] Lee Epstein and Jack Knight, *The Choices Justices Make* (Washington, DC: Congressional Quarterly Press, 1998), p. 74.

[47] Lewis Powell, Jr., "Report to the Labor Law Section of the American Bar Association," Atlanta, August 11, 1976.

compromise their differences and adhere instead to their personal policy preferences. And though attitudinal rigidity appears markedly less pronounced in less salient issue areas, such as those dealing with federal taxation, administrative agency action, and the exercise of judicial power, it dominates behavior in salient issues and cases (i.e., criminal procedure, civil rights, due process, and First Amendment), as we have seen.

PART V

IMPACT

14

The Impact of Judicial Decisions

> Let there be no doubt, while I strongly disagree with the court's decision, I accept it. I accept the finality of this outcome which will be ratified next Monday in the Electoral College.... Tonight, for the sake of the unity of the people and the strength of our democracy, I offer my concession.[1]
>
> – Al Gore, vice president and candidate for president

Only one court in the history of our nation has decided a presidential election – the U.S. Supreme Court on December 12, 2000, at 10:00 P.M. The impact of the decision was something never before seen. The Supreme Court, not the voters, "decided the outcome of the 2000 presidential election."[2] How much more impact, how much more power, can one judicial institution have than that? And Vice President Al Gore's statement introducing this chapter is telling as well. He accepts the decision of the Supreme Court although he emphatically disagrees with it.

Nevertheless, many, including the dissenters in *Bush v. Gore*, predicted that the Court's reputation would suffer considerably after the decision. Indeed, Justice Stevens wrote in dissent, "Although we may never know with complete certainty the identity of the winner of this year's Presidential election, the identity of the loser is perfectly clear. It is the Nation's confidence in the judge as an impartial guardian of the rule of law."[3] But by all accounts, the decision did no such thing.[4] One analysis shows that although there is an impact depending on party (Democrats became less trusting of the Court, Republicans more

---

[1] Al Gore's concession speech as quoted at CNN.com, December 13, 2000.

[2] Howard Gillman, *The Votes That Counted: How the Court Decided the 2000 Presidential Election* (Chicago: University of Chicago Press, 2001).

[3] Justice Stevens, dissenting, *Bush v. Gore*, 531 U.S. 98 (2000), at 128–129.

[4] See, e.g., James L. Gibson, Gregory A. Caldeira, and Lester Kenyetta Spence, "The Supreme Court and the U.S. Presidential Election of 2000: Wounds, Self-Inflicted or Otherwise?" 33 *The British Journal of Political Science* 535 (2003), and Herbert M. Kritzer, "The Impact of *Bush v. Gore* on Public Perceptions and Knowledge of the Supreme Court," 85 *Judicature* 32 (2001).

so), that impact was not very large. Similarly, another study concludes that the Court's legitimacy itself actually lessened opposition to the decision. Indeed, that study argues that "institutional loyalty inoculates against an unwelcome policy decision" and that "the Court may well have diminished its legitimacy by its ruling in *Bush v. Gore*, but only by a trivial amount."[5] And so the Court remains a legitimate institution with a stunning capacity for political impact. In this chapter, we look more carefully at the notion of the impact of courts and their decisions both in general and with respect to our nation's highest court. It seems an apt way to conclude our look at the American legal system.

THE IMPACT OF COURTS IN AMERICA

Alexis de Tocqueville, more than a century before the activism of the Warren Court, stated, "There is hardly a political question in the United States which does not sooner or later turn into a judicial one." Thus, "the judge is one of the most important political powers in the United States."[6] Broadly speaking, this chapter concerns the impact of court decisions, a somewhat nebulous concept.

Consider the Supreme Court's 1973 decision striking down state antiabortion laws.[7] On the most concrete level, the ruling impacted the parties to the suit. The pseudonymous "Jane Roe" won an injunction barring Henry Wade, the district attorney of Dallas County, from enforcing the state's antiabortion statute. Roe, however, was unable to obtain the abortion she desired as nearly four years passed from filing of the original suit until the Supreme Court disposed of the case. Because the Constitution and the Court's interpretation of it are the supreme law of the land,[8] *Roe* impacted the abortion laws in the forty-nine states that were not in complete compliance with its holding.[9] Thus, under the broad wording of Justice Blackmun's majority opinion, state and local governments could neither ban abortions during the first six months of pregnancy nor regulate them in the first trimester. Prosecutors and law enforcement officials could not enforce unconstitutional laws.

Which laws are such is debatable because no single decision provides a completely definitive answer to all questions about a subject area, so lower court judges would need to determine whether local regulations complied with *Roe*. Impact would also extend to the millions of women who obtained legal abortions since 1973, to medical professionals, hospital administrators, potential fathers, and of course, the unwanted fetuses.

Roe also impacted the political arena. Public attitudes toward abortion polarized. Partisans on both sides claimed that the public supported them. Thus,

---

[5] Gibson et al., "Election of 2000," pp. 554 and 553, respectively.

[6] Alexis de Tocqueville, *Democracy in America* (Garden City, NY: Anchor, 1969), p. 270.

[7] *Roe v. Wade*, 410 U.S. 113 (1973).

[8] *Cooper v. Aaron*, 358 U.S. 1 (1958).

[9] Although four states allowed abortion on demand in 1973, only New York allowed it through the end of the second trimester with no hospitalization required during the first trimester.

a survey paid for by Planned Parenthood indicated that the public opposed a decision banning abortion counseling in federally subsidized family planning clinics,[10] 65 percent to 33 percent. Not to be outdone, the National Right to Life Committee conducted its own poll two weeks later and reported supportive results of 69 percent to 27 percent.[11] So much for the objectivity of public opinion polls. As in other respects, the piper's payer calls the tune.

The legalization of abortion occasioned the creation of the pro-life movement, contributed to the rise of the "New Right," and substantially demobilized prochoice forces. As a prime example of the law of unintended consequences, one may plausibly claim that *Roe* helped nominate and elect Ronald Reagan in 1980. And if evidence from the winner of the John Bates Clark Medal in economics is to be believed, *Roe* also led to a significant decrease in the crime rate years later by limiting the number of unwanted children who would grow up to prey on society.[12] So if *Roe* is overruled in the future, the prime beneficiary may be the Democratic Party, or perhaps, a generation later, defense attorneys.

A FRAMEWORK FOR UNDERSTANDING IMPACT

As the preceding discussion makes obvious, "impact" is a multifaceted concept, subject to examination at three different levels at least: the result of the decision on the parties; the implementation of and compliance with the decision by judges, public officials, and citizens (the interpreting and implementing populations); and the impact of the decision on society at large.[13]

Result on the Parties

A decision most narrowly influences the parties to the suit. In *Roe*, the result little impacted the parties. The plaintiff already had had her unwanted child, so the result of the decision affected her no more than it did any other woman of childbearing age. We do not know whether she availed herself of her newly

---

[10] *Rust v. Sullivan*, 114 L. Ed. 2d 233 (1991).

[11] The Planned Parenthood question, in a Louis Harris poll, asked: "A few weeks ago, the U.S. Supreme Court, by a 5–4 vote, upheld the Government's rule prohibiting any discussion about abortion in family-planning clinics that receive federal funds. The only exception would be if a pregnant woman's life was in danger. Do you favor or oppose that Supreme Court decision preventing clinic doctors and medical personnel from discussing abortion in family planning clinics that receive federal funds?" The Right to Life question as posed by the Withlin Group asked: "If you knew that any government funds not used for family-planning programs that provide abortion will be given to other family-planning programs that provide contraception and other preventive methods of family planning, would you then favor or oppose the Supreme Court's ruling?" See Adam Clymer, "Abortion Foes Say Poll Backs Curbs on Counseling at Clinics," *New York Times*, 25 June 1991, p. A7.

[12] John Donohue and Steven Levitt, "The Impact of Legalized Abortion on Crime," 116 *Quarterly Journal of Economics* 379 (2001). Levitt is the award winner.

[13] See Stephen Wasby, *The Impact of the United States Supreme Court* (Homewood, IL: Dorsey, 1970), chap. 2, for a similar typology.

won rights since then, but we doubt it, given that she now styles herself as staunchly pro-life.[14] The result of the case probably had even less effect on Henry Wade. He would no longer be prosecuting women who sought or doctors who performed abortions, but no evidence indicates that he spent much time before *Roe* doing that anyway.

By contrast, decisions on other issues may be far more consequential to the parties. In capital punishment cases, for example, life or death literally results. In other lawsuits, victory may be entirely Pyrrhic. Some of the winning litigants in *Brown v. Board of Education*,[15] for example, never attended a desegregated public school.

Implementation and Compliance

Beyond the effect of a decision on the parties, we can examine impact on those charged with interpreting and implementing it.[16] As stated, few Supreme Court decisions (or the decisions of other courts, for that matter) definitively answer all questions about an issue. The interpreting population must, then, as its name implies, interpret the decision in order to apply it rightly. *Roe*, for instance, said nothing about spousal consent, parental consent, or Medicaid funding. Until such time as the Supreme Court authoritatively speaks to such issues, the lower courts are responsible for interpreting *Roe* and filling in the gaps. In the second *Brown* desegregation decision,[17] the Supreme Court expressly mandated Southern federal district court judges to determine the pace at which desegregation was to proceed within their states.

When the Supreme Court or lower courts declare that abortion rights must be protected, or that schools must be desegregated, usually public officials or private persons are required to implement those decisions. In *Roe*, prosecutorial implementation was quite simple: No longer could women who obtained or doctors who performed first- and second-trimester abortions be prosecuted. For public and private health care administrators, implementation was a bit more complex, for they had to decide whether to use their facilities for abortions. In *Brown*, the implementing population consisted largely of local school boards, who in conjunction with federal district courts had to develop plans that would produce desegregation "with all deliberate speed," a standard that gave them wide-ranging discretion.

Thus, implementation of a decision can be problematic. At one end of the spectrum, automatic compliance results: That is, all charged with the implementation of the policy do so perfectly. That fairly well described the situation

---

[14] Lee Epstein and Thomas G. Walker, *Constitutional Law for a Changing America: Rights, Liberties and Justice*, 4th ed. (Washington, DC: Congressional Quarterly Press, 2001).

[15] 347 U.S. 483 (1954).

[16] Bradley C. Canon and Charles A. Johnson, *Judicial Policies: Implementation and Impact*, 2d ed. (Washington, DC: Congressional Quarterly Press, 1999).

[17] 349 U.S. 294 (1955).

in *Roe*. At the other end of the spectrum is obstruction, which consists of attempts to prevent enforcement of court decisions. Take, for example, Judge Moore, former chief judge of the Alabama State Supreme Court. Judge Moore, the so-called Ten Commandments Judge, openly defied a U.S. District Court and the Eleventh Circuit of the U.S. Court of Appeals when they told him that he could no longer display a 5,280-pound four-foot-high granite monument to the Ten Commandments in the lobby of the state supreme court. He defiantly declared: "I have no intention of removing the monument. This I cannot and will not do."[18] He tried to gain support from the U.S. Supreme Court, but that Court also denied him relief, most likely because all of its rulings were consistent with the decisions of the two lower federal courts.[19] Finally, because the associate justices of the state supreme court unanimously ordered the removal of the monument, the Alabama court complied with the federal courts.[20] Of course, an out-of-state contractor had to be hired to do the removal as no in-state contractor would risk the ire of the public, many of whom held vigils to try to prevent the monument's removal.

Although this story is quite interesting, obstruction by the interpreting population does not often occur; lower courts seldom overtly defy higher courts' decisions. Indeed, one study examines the odd situation that occurs when the Supreme Court overrules its own precedent, affirming a court of appeals decision in doing so.[21] This indicates, of course, that the court of appeals did not follow the relevant precedent but actually anticipated a change by the High Court (perhaps because of a line of decisions consistently chipping away at the precedent or a large membership change since the time the precedent was established). Therefore, even behavior that appears to be systematic "obstruction" by the lower court may actually be a response to the Supreme Court's own signals that the relevant precedent no longer holds. Indeed, according to this study, lower courts rarely explicitly defy Supreme Court precedent when such precedent is clearly relevant to a case under consideration.

Obstruction can also manifest itself in the implementing population, and perhaps does so more often. A classic example occurred when Governor Faubus of Arkansas mobilized the U.S. National Guard to prevent court-ordered desegregation in Little Rock in 1957. Less dramatic but more pervasive is the action of Bible Belt public school teachers who continue to lead their students in prayer in violation of *Engel v. Vitale* and *School District of Abington Township v. Schempp*.[22] "Secondary populations,"[23] those not directly affected by a Court

---

[18] Julia Duin, "Judge Keeps Ten Commandments," *Washington Times*, 15 August 2003. Available at http://www.washtimes.com/national/200308141104073224r.htm.

[19] *In re Roy S. Moore*, 157 L. Ed. 2d 405 (2003).

[20] Bryan A. Keogh and Jan Crawford Greenburg, "Alabama High Court Defies Boss; 10 Commandments Must Go, They Rule," *Chicago Tribune*, 22 August 2003, p. 1.

[21] Malia Reddick and Sara C. Benesh, "Norm Violation by the Lower Courts in the Treatment of Supreme Court Precedent: A Research Framework," 21 *Justice System Journal* 117 (1999).

[22] 370 U.S. 421 (1962), and 374 U.S. 203 (1963).

[23] Canon and Johnson, *Judicial Politics*, chap. 5.

decision, can engage in obstruction as well. These include racists who stand in schoolhouse doors, Operation Rescue workers who mob abortion clinics, and public library workers who continue to display a crèche in front of the public library every year (despite the Court's decision in *County of Allegheny v. ACLU*)[24] in a small Wisconsin city.

A large gray area called *evasion* occupies the space between compliance and obstruction.[25] Evasion can be said to exist when interpreting and implementing populations comport with the letter but not the spirit of a ruling. For instance, the Court's reliance on the special character of education in *Brown* led some lower courts to exclude other public facilities from its compass, such as public transportation and swimming pools.[26] Yet such decisions conflicted with the basic notion of *Brown*: the inherent inequality of racially separate institutions. Indeed, many of the complaints against Judge Carswell's nomination to the Supreme Court (discussed in Chapter 10) centered on his stingy application of *Brown* to related litigation.

Strictly speaking, however, a court's decision binds only the parties thereto. Its extension either to other litigants or to those situated similarly to the original parties may not be warranted. The Court itself commonly limits the scope and applicability of its precedents. Thus, in *Miranda v. Arizona*, the Court mandated that suspects, once taken into custody and before questioning, be advised of their rights: to remain silent; anything they said could be used against them in a court of law; to have an attorney; to have an attorney appointed for them if they could not afford one. The decision was eroded subsequently, as various exceptions to the rule that *Miranda* rights be read to all accused gained favor with the Supreme Court.

In *New York v. Quarles*,[27] the Court created a public safety exception to *Miranda*, after a case in which police chased down a suspect in a supermarket after a rape complaint. The officer, after seeing the suspect's empty shoulder harness, asked the accused where his gun was. The accused answered and the gun was used as evidence against him. According to Justice Rehnquist, for the majority, "Under the circumstances involved in this case, overriding considerations of public safety justify the officer's failure to provide *Miranda* warnings before he asked questions devoted to locating the abandoned weapon."[28]

Illinois v. Perkins provides another exception to *Miranda*; in it the Court considered an "interrogation" by an officer posing as a fellow inmate of a prisoner suspected of other crimes. The Court explained, "Conversations between suspects and undercover agents do not implicate the concerns underlying *Miranda*.

---

[24] 492 U.S. 573 (1989). The small town in question is Oconto, Wisconsin, population approximately 5,000. The display can be seen every Christmas season on Main Street in front of the Farnsworth Public Library.

[25] Wasby, *Impact*, pp. 30–32.

[26] See Walter F. Murphy, "Lower Court Checks on Supreme Court Power," 53 *American Political Science Review* 1017 (1959).

[27] 467 U.S. 649 (1984).

[28] *Id.* at 651.

The essential ingredients of a 'police-dominated atmosphere' and compulsion are not present when an incarcerated person speaks freely to someone that he believes to be a fellow inmate."[29] The Supreme Court has also ruled that *Miranda* does not apply to roadside stops[30] and that statements received without *Miranda* warnings can be used in court in order to impeach the defendant's testimony, should he or she choose to testify.[31]

As a result of the Court's seeming retreat from its *Miranda* decision, the Fourth Circuit directly challenged the precedent, relying on an obscure congressional amendment that the Justice Department refused to enforce. On appeal, the Supreme Court reversed, specifying a constitutional basis for the *Miranda* decision that barred Congress from statutorily overturning it.[32] But despite this reaffirmation of *Miranda*, previous narrowing of its scope surely affected compliance and impact.

Impact on Society

Although compliance and impact greatly overlap, impact is generally considered to be broader in scope than compliance because it includes consequences directly attributable to a given decision. Alternatively, impact is narrower than the "aftermath," which includes everything that happens after a decision, whether directly caused by it or not. The trick, of course, is to determine which consequences are directly attributable to a decision and which are not. For instance, *Brown* presumably caused the end of Southern school segregation, but districts did not actually desegregate until Congress enacted the 1964 Civil Rights Act denying funds to segregated schools. And although *Roe* undoubtedly increased the number of abortions, the number of legal abortions was in fact climbing before *Roe* and might have continued upward without it, as we discuss later.

A final aspect of impact, which is frequently overlooked or disregarded, merits attention. Private persons and public officials not party to litigation are substantially free to adapt their conduct to accord with court decisions as they individually see fit. Thus, for example, in reaction to the possibility that the justices might overrule *Roe v. Wade*, the Connecticut legislature approved legislation that made abortion a statutory right under state law.[33] Because the Constitution provides a floor for individual rights, not a ceiling, any state is free to provide individuals with more freedom than the Constitution mandates.

With this framework in mind, we undertake a more systematic examination of compliance and impact.

---

[29] 496 U.S. 292 (1990), at 296.

[30] *Berkemer v. McCarty*, 468 U.S. 420 (1984).

[31] *Harris v. New York*, 401 U.S. 222 (1971).

[32] *Dickerson v. United States*, 530 U.S. 428 (2000).

[33] Kirk Johnson, "Connecticut Acts to Make Abortion a Statutory Right," *New York Times*, 28 April 1990, pp. 1, 7.

COMPLIANCE

Normative models of judicial decision making, that is, those that attempt to explain how courts should act, hold that lower courts ought to adhere to the decisions of their judicial superiors. Nevertheless, lower court judges, as do Supreme Court justices, have their own policy preferences about the issues in a particular case, which they might seek to follow to the extent possible. Because in the overwhelming majority of trial court cases the decision is final and because the Court grants review to markedly less than 1 percent of petitioned cases (to say nothing of the fact that most decisions are never even appealed to the Supreme Court), the potential exists for less than full compliance by lower courts, that is, the interpreting population.

Interpreting Population

Many early studies of lower courts found striking examples of lower courts' ignoring or misinterpreting Supreme Court decisions.[34] One noted that by and large federal judges applied the law adversely to the claims of African Americans in the first six years of litigation after *Brown*. Some judges were so opposed to desegregation that they believed the safety of the nation depended on their minimizing *Brown*'s scope.[35]

Other scholars have noted dramatic examples of noncompliance with juvenile justice,[36] search and seizure,[37] and a variety of other areas.[38] One concluded that these studies evidenced "a judicial system in which judges reach decisions with little regard for the rulings of the highest court – in effect a system in near anarchy."[39]

Nevertheless, this work arguably focused on an unrepresentative sample of trees in the forest of compliance by investigating only state court implementation of controversial Warren Court civil liberties decisions. Systematic analyses in 1987 and 1990 found that the federal courts overwhelmingly comply with express commands of the Supreme Court.[40] Thus, in the field of libel, only a

---

[34] This section is based in part on Jeffrey A. Segal, Donald Songer, and Charles M. Cameron, "The Hierarchy of Justice: Testing a Principal–Agent Model of Supreme Court–Circuit Court Interactions," 38 *American Journal of Political Science* 673 (1994).

[35] J. W. Peltason, *Fifty-Eight Lonely Men: Southern Federal Judges and School Desegregation* (New York: Harcourt, Brace & World, 1961), p. 93.

[36] Bradley Canon and K. Kolson, "Compliance with *Gault* in Rural America: The Case of Kentucky," 10 *Journal of Family Law* 300 (1971).

[37] D. R. Manwaring, "The Impact of *Mapp v. Ohio*," in D. H. Everson (ed.), *The Supreme Court as Policy-Maker: Three Studies on the Impact of Judicial Decisions* (Carbondale: Southern Illinois University Press, 1968).

[38] Jerry K. Beatty, "State Court Evasion of United States Supreme Court Mandates during the Last Decade of the Warren Court," 6 *Valparaiso Law Review* 260 (1972).

[39] Lawrence Baum, "Lower Court Response to Supreme Court Decisions: Reconsidering a Negative Picture," 3 *Justice System Journal* 208 (1978): 208.

[40] Donald Songer, "The Impact of the Supreme Court on Trends in Economic Policy Making in the United States Courts of Appeals," 49 *Journal of Politics* 830 (1987); Donald Songer and

handful of district court decisions failed to comply during a ten-year period.[41] In confession cases, "we find a highly compliant lower court."[42] Rather than outright defiance, lower courts are more likely to avoid or mitigate Supreme Court rulings.[43] Indeed, in one study, disregard of Supreme Court precedent was nowhere to be found; "distinguishings," sometimes legitimate and sometimes not, occurred much more frequently.[44] But those authors also found substantial and rapid compliance by the courts of appeals with the Supreme Court, even when the Supreme Court altered precedent, a situation in which we might expect lower compliance levels.

One interesting study showed that the courts of appeals actually chose to comply with the Court rather than Congress when the two were at odds.[45] This report attempted to discern the level of support for religious exercise claimants, first after *Employment Division v. Smith*,[46] then after enactment of the Religious Freedom Restoration Act (RFRA), and subsequently after the Court's response to the RFRA in *City of Boerne v. Flores*.[47] The author discovered that the lower courts heeded the Court's decision in *Employment Division* limiting the rights of free exercise claimants. The Court had held that "the right of free exercise does not relieve an individual of the obligation to comply with a 'valid and neutral law of general applicability on the ground that the law proscribes (or prescribes) conduct that his religion prescribes (or proscribes),'"[48] thereby abandoning the compelling interest test first established in *Sherbert v. Verner*.[49] The lower courts subsequently heeded Congress when it nullified *Employment Division* by passing the RFRA, which restored the compelling interest test from *Sherbert*. However, when the Court struck back and ruled Congress's actions inconsistent with the judiciary's power to interpret the Constitution, the lower courts heeded that, too, and again became less supportive of free exercise claimants. The Supreme Court, then, won compliance from the courts of appeals even in the face of a congressional mandate to the contrary: "[T]he Supreme Court, by providing an unequivocal repudiation of Congress's attempts to subvert its will, succeeded in reestablishing the loyalty of its agents."[50]

Reginald Sheehan, "Supreme Court Impact on Compliance and Outcomes: *Miranda* and *New York Times* in the United States Courts of Appeals," 43 *Western Political Quarterly* 297 (1990).

[41] John Gruhl, "The Supreme Court's Impact on the Law of Libel: Compliance by Lower Federal Courts," 33 *Western Political Quarterly* 502 (1980).

[42] Sara C. Benesh, *The U.S. Court of Appeals and the Law of Confessions: Perspectives on the Hierarchy of Justice* (New York: LFB Scholarly Publishing, 2002).

[43] Beatty, "State Court Evasion."

[44] Sara C. Benesh and Malia Reddick, "Overruled: An Event History Analysis of Lower Court Reaction to Supreme Court Alteration of Precedent," 64 *Journal of Politics* 534 (2002).

[45] James Brent, "Research Note: A Principal–Agent Analysis of U.S. Courts of Appeals Responses to *Boerne v. Flores*," 31 *American Politics Research* 557 (2003).

[46] 494 U.S. 872 (1990).

[47] 521 U.S. 507 (1997).

[48] *Employment Division v. Smith*, 494 U.S. 872 (1990), at 879.

[49] 374 U.S. 398 (1963).

[50] Brent, "Research Note," p. 565.

Table 14.1. *Confessions Upheld in the Courts of Appeals before and after* Miranda

Decision on Confession	Time Frame	
	Pre-*Miranda*	Post-*Miranda*
Uphold	118 (70%)	374 (80%)
Overturn	50 (30%)	95 (20%)

Note: Chi-square = 6.358, significant at 0.012.

Table 14.2. *Confessions Upheld in the Courts of Appeals during and after the Warren Court*

Decision on Confession	Supreme Court	
	Warren Court	Burger Court
Uphold	199 (71%)	293 (82%)
Overturn	81 (29%)	64 (18%)

Note: Chi-square = 10.803, significant at 0.001.

Of course, lower courts differ, especially state courts. Nevertheless, several studies demonstrate that state supreme courts behave much as do the courts of appeals in search and seizure cases, substantially complying with the policy prescriptions of the Supreme Court,[51] and another found adherence in cases involving confessions.[52] Not even the state courts, then, thwart the will of the High Court. Compliance is the rule and not the exception.

To illustrate the compliance of the courts of appeals in the area of confession, we assess the percentage of confessions overturned before (1953–1965) and after (1966–1981) *Miranda v. Arizona*. We expect more confessions to be invalidated after *Miranda* than before, but perhaps, because of the Court's erosion of the precedent, the lower courts would not completely change their behavior. Table 14.1 contains the results.

As can be seen, the courts of appeals did not invalidate confessions at a greater rate after *Miranda*; in fact, the rate of confession acceptance actually increased. This may result from a number of factors, as Tables 14.2–14.4 show. Table 14.2 indicates that it matters who sits on the Supreme Court. As expected, when the judicial boss is more liberal, so, too, are the courts of appeals: They upheld 71 percent of confessions during Warren's tenure. But when the Supreme

---

[51] Wendy L. Martinek, "Judicial Impact: The Relationship between the United States Supreme Court and State Courts of Last Resort in Search and Seizure Decision Making" (unpublished Ph.D. diss., Michigan State University, 2000).

[52] Sara C. Benesh and Wendy L. Martinek, "State Court Decision Making in Confession Cases," 23 *Justice System Journal* 109 (2002).

Table 14.3. *Confessions Upheld in the Courts of Appeals by Partisanship of Panel Majority*

| | Panel Majority | |
Decision on Confession	Democratic	Republican
Uphold	245 (71%)	247 (84%)
Overturn	99 (29%)	46 (16%)

Note: Chi-square = 15.396, significant at 0.000.

Table 14.4. *Confessions Upheld in the Courts of Appeals by Lower Court Disposition*

| | Lower Court Disposition | |
Decision on Confession	Uphold	Overturn
Uphold	454 (89%)	38 (30%)
Overturn	56 (11%)	89 (70%)

Note: Chi-square = 201.990, significant at 0.000.

Court was more conservative, the lower courts began behaving that way as well: upholding 82 percent of all challenged confessions during Burger's tenure.

We expect ideology to condition this behavior as well. Table 14.3 shows the percentage of confessions upheld or overturned by majority Democratic (and thus relatively more liberal) and majority Republican (and thus relatively more conservative) panels. Democratic panels overturned more confessions (29 percent) than Republican panels (16 percent).

But conditioning court of appeals' behavior more than ideology or the Supreme Court's policy preferences is the fact that the courts of appeals hear "easier" cases; in other words, cases that are less likely to contain a meritorious claim than those that achieve Supreme Court review. Table 14.4 gives some evidence of this: Eighty-nine percent of the courts of appeals' confession cases affirmed the lower court decision. Additional evidence of a difference between courts of appeals cases and those heard by the Supreme Court is the average number of relevant case facts present in a case. Those heard by the latter contained five, whereas the courts of appeals had two.[53] This suggests that the Supreme Court cases are more complicated, and hence, possibly more meritorious.

Implementing Population

The implementing population consists of those public and occasionally private officials charged with carrying out the Court's commands. To an appreciable

[53] Benesh, *U.S. Court of Appeals*, p. 60.

extent, the implementing population's compliance with Supreme Court decisions is also unclear. A major deficiency of compliance studies is their inability to measure compliance validly and reliably. Typical methods include querying whether respondents have complied with particular Supreme Court decisions and following them around to see whether they do so. Needless to say, such studies substantially overestimate compliance. People generally do not admit to breaking the law and are less likely in fact to do so when they are being monitored. As one critic noted:

Asking movie censors...or district attorneys...whether they conform to Supreme Court guidelines on obscenity and inquiring of school teachers whether they lead prayers in school is not much more revealing than it would be to ask taxpayers whether they declare all their income or fabricate any deductions. It is naive to expect people to incriminate themselves, and it can be assumed that those implicated in unlawful actions will generally take steps to conceal or whitewash them.[54]

Alternatively, compliance is dramatically underestimated if, for example, one asks criminal defendants whether the police read them their rights.[55]

Findings of noncompliance are thus particularly dramatic when substantial numbers of people admit they disobey the law. Robert Birkby, for instance, wrote to Tennessee school superintendents inquiring whether they were adhering to the decision in *Abington School District v. Schempp*,[56] which prohibited devotional Bible readings. Although such inquiries should overestimate compliance, only 1 of 122 reporting districts admitted to the elimination of all Bible reading and devotional exercises. Fifty-one districts altered their policies somewhat, and seventy made no changes whatsoever.[57] And despite the fact that surveilled police should more likely abide by the *Miranda* requirements, only 25 of 118 suspects in a New Haven study received the full warnings required by the Supreme Court ruling in a study conducted shortly after the ruling was made.[58] Noncompliance also occurs in other settings as well. The University of California, under state legislative prodding, set racial quotas on admissions that severely limited the number of Asian students despite the express prohibition on quotas in *Regents v. Bakke*.[59] Never mind difficulties in gaining compliance from a small Wisconsin town during the Christmas season.

[54] James Levine, "Methodological Concerns in Studying Supreme Court Efficacy," 4 *Law and Society Review* 583 (1970).

[55] Richard Medalie, Leonard Zeitz, and Paul Alexander, "Custodial Police Interrogation in Our Nation's Capital: The Attempt to Implement *Miranda*," 66 *Michigan Law Review* 1347 (1968).

[56] 374 U.S. 203 (1963).

[57] Robert Birkby, "The Supreme Court in the Bible Belt: Tennessee Reaction to the *Schempp* Decision," 10 *American Journal of Political Science* 304 (1966).

[58] Michael Wald, Richard Ayres, David W. Hess, Mark Schantz, and Charles H. Whitebread II, "Interrogations in New Haven: The Impact of *Miranda*," 76 *Yale Law Journal* 1519 (1967).

[59] 438 U.S. 265 (1978). See Dinesh D'Souza, *Illiberal Education: The Politics of Race and Sex on Campus* (New York: Free Press, 1991), chap. 2.

One study of compliance at the implementing population level considers the reaction of federal administrative agencies to specific Supreme Court rulings.[60] By looking at all Supreme Court decisions reversing and/or remanding agency decisions from 1953 to 1990, the author finds that characteristics of the Supreme Court's decision (e.g., how specific it is), the policy preferences of the agency (measured as whether or not the Court is making a programmatic change, which the agency would oppose), the age of the agency (whether the agency has been in existence ten years or longer), and outside interest group support (difference between the number of amicus briefs supporting and opposing the agency) all influence the decision by the agency over whether and how much to comply with the Supreme Court decision. Compliance is seemingly the rule, although the extent of compliance (e.g., how much the agency changes in accordance with the Supreme Court decision) depends on the factors noted.

As is true in the interpreting population, noncompliance in the implementing population is easy to overestimate. Prosecutions against women who obtained, or doctors who performed, first- and second-trimester abortions stopped immediately when *Roe* was decided. Readings of the *Miranda* requirements did increase after the police began to understand the rule better.[61] No executions took place in the United States between the striking of the death penalty in *Furman v. Georgia*[62] and its reimposition in *Gregg v. Georgia*.[63] And the Court's infamous decision in *Plessy v. Ferguson*[64] ushered in full-scale segregation. Twenty-two states passed more than 250 statutes compelling or permitting segregation in schools, colleges, libraries, trains, waiting rooms, buses, streetcars, steamboats, ferries, circuses, theaters, public halls, parks, playgrounds, beaches, racetracks, poolrooms, hospitals, orphanages, and homes for the aged. Six states prohibited prisoners of different races from being chained together, one required separate phone books, and another prohibited interracial boxing.[65]

Congressional Compliance

Examples of congressional and presidential compliance also have their drama. In 1962, the Supreme Court decided the first in a short series of cases that, in the words of one observer, "involved the most remarkable and far reaching

---

[60] James F. Spriggs II, "The Supreme Court and Federal Administrative Agencies: A Resource-Based Theory and Analysis of Judicial Impact," 40 *American Journal of Political Science* 1122 (1996); see also James F. Spriggs II, "Explaining Federal Bureaucratic Compliance with Supreme Court Opinions," 50 *Political Research Quarterly* 567 (1997).

[61] Wald et al., "Interrogations."

[62] 408 U.S. 238 (1972).

[63] 428 U.S. 153 (1976).

[64] 163 U.S. 537 (1896)

[65] Epstein and Walker, *Constitutional Law*, p. 633; "Jim Crow Laws," National Park Service ParkNet, http://www.nps.gov/malu/documents/jim_crow_laws.htm; "Jim Crow Laws," Remembering Jim Crow, presented by American Radioworks, http://www.americanradioworks.org/features/remembering/laws.html.

exercise of judicial power in our history."[66] The issue was the reapportionment of Congress and the legislatures of each and every one of the fifty states.

The Court initially asserted that legislative apportionment was properly a matter for judicial resolution,[67] thereby overruling a precedent in which Justice Frankfurter had held such controversies to be political questions inappropriate for judicial resolution.[68] In his dissent in *Baker v. Carr*, Frankfurter had asserted that the idea that courts "could effectively fashion" a remedy for "the abstract constitutional right" of electoral districting to be mere "judicial rhetoric ... not only a euphoric hope. It implies a sorry confession of judicial impotence in place of a frank acknowledgment that there is not under our Constitution a judicial remedy for every political mischief, for every undesirable exercise of legislative power." Appeal for relief, he said, "does not belong here," but belongs rather "to an informed, civically militant electorate." He then predicted: "There is nothing judicially more unseemly nor more self-defeating than for this Court to make *in terrorem* pronouncements, to indulge in merely empty rhetoric, sounding a word or promise to the ear, sure to be disappointing to the hope."[69]

The majority paid him no heed and, in the process, proved him a false prophet. In its next decision, the Court stipulated that within a single legislative constituency the operative districting principle must be one person, one vote.[70] This was followed by a ruling that in congressional elections, one person's vote "as nearly as practicable ... is to be worth as much as another's."[71] The Court topped off its policy making four months later, when it made its one-person, one-vote standard binding on *both* houses of the state legislatures.[72] Lest it appear that the Court rode herd only on Congress and the state legislatures, note also that the justices subsequently penned all popularly elected local government officials in the same barnyard as the legislators.[73]

Thus in the twenty-seven-month period from March 1962 to June 1964, the Court utterly abolished the stranglehold that farm and rural interests had had on the nation's legislatures since the time of Thomas Jefferson. This was no small accomplishment for the governmental branch that possesses neither purse nor sword – especially since it concerned a matter that is not exactly of minor moment to legislators. The name of the legislative game is reelection, and reelection depends on the boundaries and characteristics of constituencies. Nonetheless, within one year of the decision in *Reynolds v. Sims*, forty-five of the fifty states took action to comply with the one-person, one-vote principle. It ought to be kept in mind that this occurred at a time when substantial segments of the population were more than a little riled at the Court's

---

[66] Richard C. Cortner, *The Apportionment Cases* (New York: Norton, 1970), p. 253.
[67] *Baker v. Carr*, 369 U.S. 186 (1962).
[68] *Colegrove v. Green*, 328 U.S. 549 (1946).
[69] 369 U.S. 186, at 269–270.
[70] *Gray v. Sanders*, 372 U.S. 368 (1963).
[71] *Wesberry v. Sanders*, 376 U.S. 1 (1964), at 7–8 (footnote omitted).
[72] *Reynolds v. Sims*, 377 U.S. 533 (1964).
[73] *Avery v. Midland County*, 390 U.S. 474 (1968); and *Hadley v. Junior College District*, 397 U.S. 50 (1970).

policies: God-fearing citizens outraged about the ascediastic ban on organized prayer and Bible reading in the public schools; police, prosecutors, and law-and-order elements nattering about the "crippling" of law enforcement;[74] and prudes and bluenoses dismayed and distraught over the demise of Victorian morality.[75]

Presidential Compliance

The Court has also successfully imposed its will on the executive branch, and, again, a theoretically coequal branch has acceded to judicial supremacy at the cost of its own status. The prime example is the Watergate tapes case.[76] Unprecedented circumstances gave rise to the litigation: President Nixon threw down the gauntlet and dared the Court to force him to turn over his confidential papers. Federal District Court Judge John Sirica had ordered Nixon to hand over sixty-four specified tapes and documents that related to private conversations between Nixon and his closest and most trusted advisers. The defendants requested the tapes for evidence in their pending Watergate trials. On several occasions, including oral arguments before the Supreme Court, Nixon and his henchmen hinted that they might not comply with a decision ordering the surrender of the tapes.

The justices, however, were not intimidated, rejecting Nixon's challenge to their authority. With a lapse of only sixteen days between oral argument and the announcement of their decision, the justices delivered a unanimous opinion (written, ironically, by the man whom Nixon himself had nominated as chief justice) that unequivocally subjected the president to the rule of law. The opinion stated that the aphorism "The King can do no wrong" has no place in the American constitutional system; that when a president claims the privilege of confidentiality in his communications, that claim "cannot prevail over the fundamental demands of due process of law in the fair administration of criminal justice. The generalized assertion of privilege must yield to the demonstrated specific need for evidence in a pending criminal trial."[77]

Nixon promptly released the tapes, which included specific conversations ordering aides to cover up the Watergate break-in. Six weeks later, Nixon resigned under threat of impeachment and removal from office. That a president would resign his office in disgrace rather than disobey the Court speaks volumes about the Court's authority.

Potential Reasons for Noncompliance

Several explanations exist for the potential lack of compliance. More often than not these reasons, though limiting the Court in theory, do not limit it in practice.

---

[74] E.g., *Mapp v. Ohio*, 367 U.S. 643 (1961); *Escobedo v. Illinois*, 378 U.S. 478 (1964).
[75] E.g., *Manual Enterprises v. Day*, 370 U.S. 478 (1962); *Jacobellis v. Ohio*, 378 U.S. 184 (1964); and *A Quantity of Books v. Kansas*, 378 U.S. 205 (1964).
[76] *United States v. Nixon*, 418 U.S. 683 (1974).
[77] *Id.*, at 713.

The Lack of Coercive Capacity. The justices possess neither the power of the purse nor that of the sword.[78] Hence they must rely on the executive branch to give force and effect to their decisions when resistance occurs. In 1958, for example, an order by a reluctant President Eisenhower to nationalize the Arkansas National Guard was required to enforce desegregation in Little Rock. The sole weapon the Court has at its disposal is its moral authority, and though moral authority may appear to be a fragile weapon when compared with dollars, nightsticks, nuclear weapons, and other elements of realpolitik, the Court's policy-making capacity – based on the respect and reverence accorded justices, the perceived legitimacy of the Court's decisions even when they are disapproved of by substantial segments of society, and the factors described in Chapter 1[79] – compares favorably with these tangible forms of persuasion, whether they are gently or roughly applied.

Decisions Bind Only the Parties to Litigation. The decision of a court, at all levels of the judicial system, technically binds only the parties to the litigation. Other persons, though similarly situated, have no legal duty to comply. Even so, the Supreme Court virtually never finds it necessary to spend time applying a decision to other persons simply because they were not formally parties to the litigation. School desegregation and obscenity have constituted important exceptions, however. Other exceptions are cases on their way to the Court at the time the Court announces its decision. These merely receive summary treatment: That is, the Court simply cites its controlling decision as authority for the action to be taken. Thus, four days after its July 1976 death penalty decisions, in which the majority declared that a mandatory death sentence for premeditated murder constituted cruel and unusual punishment,[80] the Court took summary action in the cases of sixty-three other persons who were under sentence of death: thirty-eight in North Carolina, nine in Georgia, seven in Oklahoma, six in Florida, and three in Louisiana. In each instance, the summary action rested on the formal decisions announced four days earlier.

The Court's 1976 decisions were not its first encounter with the death penalty. Four years earlier, in *Furman v. Georgia*,[81] the justices, with one fell swoop, had voided the capital punishment laws of thirty-nine states, plus the District of Columbia. Thereupon, thirty-five states and Congress enacted new legislation to comply with what they perceived to be the Court's mandate, even though the laws of only two states – Georgia and Texas – were at issue in *Furman*. But more than half of the reenacting states found that their new laws still failed to pass muster when the Court handed down its 1976 decisions, which held the

---

[78] See *Missouri v. Jenkins*, 495 U.S. 33 (1990), however, in which the Court upheld the authority of lower courts to order elected officials to raise taxes.

[79] See Walter F. Murphy and Joseph Tanenhaus, *The Study of Public Law* (New York: Random House, 1972), pp. 40–44.

[80] *Gregg v. Georgia*, 428 U.S. 153; and *Woodson v. North Carolina*, 428 U.S. 280.

[81] 408 U.S. 238.

death penalty constitutionally permissible, at least for murder, only if the judge and jury had been given adequate information and guidance to enable them to take account of aggravating and mitigating circumstances and the character of the defendant before passing sentence.

As evidence of compliance, the states' response to the Court's capital punishment decisions is instructive. From the time the Court grappled with the constitutionality of the death penalty in a 1968 decision[82] until Utah's execution of Gary Gilmore in January 1977, not a single one of the several hundred occupants of death row was executed – notwithstanding American society's overwhelming endorsement of capital punishment and the rapidity with which all but fifteen of the fifty states successfully managed to crank up their creaky legislative machinery in order to comply with the Court's 1972 decision declaring existing capital punishment constitutionally defective.

The Court's Opinion Lacks Clarity. We observed in Chapter 13 that a majority of the justices must agree on an opinion for it to become the opinion of the Court. When the Court is closely divided, bargaining, negotiation, and compromise among the majority coalition are especially costly and difficult to come by. Sometimes the majority justices cannot accommodate their differences, and in such cases only a "judgment of the Court" results. These judgments provide little guidance to the lower courts or to those affected by the Court's decision. Even those who desire to comply with the Court's mandate find determination of the Court's position difficult. Nonetheless, compliance typically occurs. Consider again the Court's 1972 death penalty decision. Although the opinion of the Court was announced *per curiam* rather than as a judgment of the Court, it approximated the latter more than the former. In pertinent part it read as follows: "The Court holds that the imposition and carrying out of the death penalty in these cases constitute cruel and unusual punishment in violation of the Eighth and Fourteenth Amendments. The judgment in each case is therefore reversed insofar as it leaves undisturbed the death sentence imposed, and the cases are remanded for further proceedings."[83]

Each of the five justices who constituted the majority wrote his own separate opinion. Nonetheless, as previously mentioned, fully 70 percent of the states and the Congress promptly rewrote their capital punishment laws, hoping they had accurately fathomed the Court's inscrutable position. More than half of these states guessed wrong when the Court handed down its five 1976 death penalty decisions, every one of which was announced via a judgment of the Court to which only Justices Stewart, Powell, and Stevens subscribed. Again, compliance was complete.

Moreover, a systematic analysis of lower court decision making found that neither the size of the voting majority, the size of the opinion majority, the number of dissenting justices, the number of dissenting opinions, or the author of the

---

[82] *Witherspoon v. Illinois*, 391 U.S. 510 (1968).
[83] *Furman v. Georgia*, 408 U.S. 238 (1972), at 239–240.

majority opinion affected compliance,[84] although another study did find that some of these factors affected the speed with which the lower court complied.[85]

But even when every justice joins the opinion of the Court, its position may still lack more clarity than mud. The decisions in *Brown v. Board of Education* aptly illustrate. The Court first said that "separate educational facilities are inherently unequal"[86] and that the segregation the plaintiffs complained of deprived them of the equal protection of the laws guaranteed by the Fourteenth Amendment. This was a perfectly clear and comprehensible statement. The Court then addressed the matter of implementation, ruling one year later that public schools must desegregate "with all deliberate speed," and that the task of eradicating this racist legacy belonged to the federal district courts "because of their proximity to local conditions."[87] Needless to say, the formula "with all deliberate speed" hardly lent itself to consensual application. No wonder that a decade elapsed before any appreciable changes occurred in the Deep South – especially since the Court itself chose to say virtually nothing more on the subject until 1965, when it tersely asserted that "delays in desegregation of school systems are no longer tolerable."[88] Not until the Burger Court was the matter of implementation clarified. And then clarity resulted only because the Court discarded the "all deliberate speed" formula: "Continued operation of segregated schools under a standard of 'all deliberate speed' for desegregation is no longer constitutionally permissible. . . . The obligation of every school district is to terminate dual school systems at once and to operate now and hereafter only unitary schools."[89]

Thus did desegregation finally occur in the South, the border states, and parts of the North, aided and abetted by provisions in the Civil Rights Act of 1964 that permitted a cutoff of federal funds from school districts that failed to desegregate. If the fifteen-year interval between 1954 and 1969 constitutes noncompliance with the Court's mandate in *Brown v. Board of Education*, the blame should at least partially fall on the occupants of the Marble Palace.

IMPACT

The impact of a Supreme Court decision includes those societal consequences that directly or indirectly result from its decision. As noted, the basic difficulty in determining impact is separating all that which occurs after a decision from that which the decision *caused*, that is, its impact.

---

[84] Charles A. Johnson, "Lower Court Reactions to Supreme Court Decisions: A Quantitative Examination," 23 *American Journal of Political Science* 792 (1979).

[85] Benesh and Reddick, "Overruled," pp. 534–550.

[86] 347 U.S. 484, at 495.

[87] 349 U.S. 294, at 301, 299.

[88] *Bradley v. Richmond School Board*, 382 U.S. 103 (1965), at 105; and *Rogers v. Paul*, 382 U.S. 198 (1965), at 199.

[89] *Alexander v. Holmes County Board of Education*, 396 U.S. 19 (1969), at 20.

Methodological Problems

One of the least effective methods of determining impact is that which is called a post-test design or "one-shot case study."[90] Here the researcher waits for the Court's decision and at some later point measures one or more types of responses to that decision. For instance, after the decision in *In re Gault*[91] one might measure the number of juveniles granted procedural rights.[92] Without knowing the extent of pre-*Gault* rights, one cannot even begin to assess the impact of the decision. "Such studies have such a total absence of control as to be of almost no value."[93]

Another typical but flawed method of assessing impact measures a certain activity at one time point before and one time point after the decision in question. This is called a *one-group pretest–post-test design*. Thus, to measure the impact of *Roe* one could count the number of legal abortions in 1972 and the number of legal abortions in 1973. Indeed, if one did so, one would find a 27 percent increase from about 587,000 to approximately 745,000.[94] On the basis of these numbers, one might then assume that *Roe* had a substantial impact on abortion rates. Yet such a jump could be consistent with any of the trends pictured in Figure 14.1 *D*, where O_4 represents the number of 1972 abortions and O_5 represents the number of 1973 abortions. Yet only *A* provides justification for inferring impact, whereas almost nothing justifies inferring impact in *E*, *F*, *G*, or *H*. The one-group pretest–post-test design is simply a bad example of how to do research.[95]

The difficulty of assessing impact increases when the Court focuses on fundamental principles rather than on the specific controversy before it – that is, on the larger question or issue, of which the case before it represents only a part. The opinion of the Court is, after all, the core of the justices' policy-making power. The opinion lays down the broad constitutional and legal principles that bind the lower courts, other governmental instrumentalities, and affected private persons; establishes precedents for the Court's future decisions; and, least importantly, resolves the litigation at hand.

Thus, in *M'Culloch v. Maryland*,[96] Chief Justice Marshall upheld the power of Congress to establish a national bank and concomitantly prohibited the states from taxing or regulating it. If the outcome of the controversy had been analyzed twenty years after the decision was announced, the conclusion would

---

[90] Donald Campbell and Julian Stanley, *Experimental and Quasi-Experimental Designs for Research* (Chicago: Rand McNally, 1963), p. 7.

[91] 387 U.S. 1 (1967). The *Gault* decision extended due process protections to juvenile court proceedings.

[92] E.g., Norman Lefstein, Vaughn Stapleton, and Lee Tietelbaum, "In Search of Juvenile Justice: *Gault* and Its Implementation," 3 *Law and Society Review* 491 (1969).

[93] Campbell and Stanley, "Experimental," p. 6.

[94] Gerald Rosenberg, *The Hollow Hope: Can Courts Bring About Social Change* (Chicago: University of Chicago Press, 1991), p. 180.

[95] Campbell and Stanley, "Experimental," p. 7.

[96] 4 Wheaton 316 (1819).

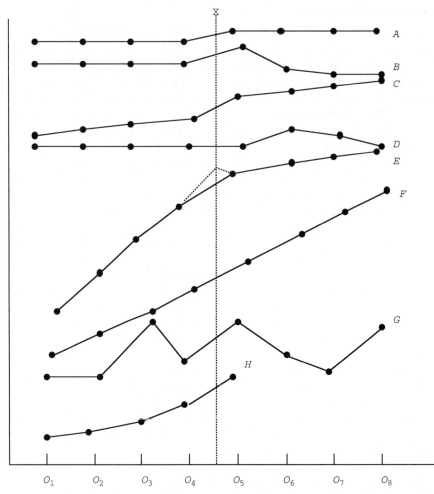

Figure 14.1. Pretest–Post-test Possibilities. *Source:* Donald Campbell and Julian Stanley, *Experimental and Quasi-Experimental Designs for Research* (Chicago: Rand McNally, 1963), p. 38.

be inescapable: The "case was more interesting as a monument to judicial impotence than as an example of judicial power."[97] In 1832, President Jackson vetoed a bill to extend the charter of the Bank of the United States. One year later, he withdrew federal funds from the bank's vaults, and in 1837 its charter expired. The bank, a shell of its former self, lingered for a few more years until bankruptcy put it out of business in 1841.

But the significance of *M'Culloch* is not that it affected the eventual fate of the bank, but rather that in that decision, Marshall formulated the doctrine

[97] Murphy and Tanenhaus, *Public Law*, p. 56.

of implied powers. His assertion of this principle provided the basis for the expansion of federal power and the rise of the welfare state that began during the depression of the 1930s. Though these developments did not occur until more than a century after *M'Culloch*, the decision in that case doomed the strict constructionists of federal power to defeat; thereafter, to the extent that *M'Culloch* was relevant (and it was not always so considered) assertions that that government is best that governs least would have an unmistakably hollow ring.

Other studies have examined the impact of the courts on public policy. We examine analyses in four such areas: the Fourth Amendment's exclusionary rule, reapportionment, desegregation, and abortion.

The Exclusionary Rule. The Fourth Amendment's exclusionary rule holds that evidence obtained in violation thereof typically cannot be used in criminal trials. The Supreme Court imposed the rule on the federal government in 1914,[98] and on the states in 1961.[99] Critics of the exclusionary rule, such as Chief Justice Burger, have claimed that the rule does not deter the police.[100] The truth is quite the contrary, for police compliance with the warrant requirement of the Fourth Amendment surged from the pre-*Mapp* to the post-*Mapp* period.[101] For example, the Cincinnati police obtained only three search warrants in 1958 and not a single one in 1959. In the five months before the 1962 decision, they obtained three. Yet, by 1963, the Cincinnati police obtained 100 warrants, and the number increased thereafter. A less dramatic but similar situation existed in Boston. The deterrent effect of the exclusionary rule is the only plausible explanation for these data.

Alternatively, supporters of the exclusionary rule claim that the rule does not hamper the police. According to one journalist, "The myth has spread that streams of criminals are going free because the exclusionary rule prevents the evidence from being used in court."[102] He cites statistics that only a minuscule number of cases – less than 1 percent – are dropped because of flaws in obtaining evidence. But by failing to consider cases in which the police make no arrest because the rule deters them from making a questionable search in the first place, his findings lack validity.

These two views are internally inconsistent: One argues that the rule hampers police but does not deter; the other, that the rule deters but does not hamper. Clearly, the rule deters. Just as clearly, arrests are not made but for the presence of the rule. The latter, though, is true of any rule, exclusionary or not, that

---

[98] *Weeks v. United States*, 232 U.S. 383 (1914).

[99] *Mapp v. Ohio*, 367 U.S. 643 (1961).

[100] *Bivens v. Six Unknown Federal Agents*, 403 U.S. 388 (1971), at 416.

[101] Bradley C. Canon, "Is the Exclusionary Rule in Failing Health? Some New Data and a Plea against a Precipitous Conclusion," 62 *Kentucky Law Journal* 681 (1974). Of course, the absence of a warrant is not per se unreasonable, so there is no absolute proof that the police were acting in outright disregard of the Fourth Amendment before *Mapp*.

[102] Tom Wicker, "Exploding a Myth," *New York Times*, 10 May 1983, p. A25.

enforces the Fourth Amendment. But such a trade-off was made when the Fourth Amendment was adopted.

Reapportionment. As discussed earlier in this chapter, Supreme Court rulings in the early 1960s required the apportionment of the House of Representatives and both houses of state legislatures on a one-person, one-vote basis. The rulings, though hostile to the well-being of incumbents, received almost immediate compliance.

The question here, though, is not compliance, but impact. Chief Justice Warren, for one, thought the impact of these decisions was enormous. Reflecting on his tenure, he viewed the reapportionment decisions as the most important,[103] for they freed the cities – and especially suburbia – from the stranglehold of rural rule.

The reapportionment decisions clearly affected the number of urban and rural representatives, increasing the former at the expense of the latter. But if the reapportionment decisions were more than just a jobs program for big-city and suburban politicians, the influx of such legislators should have had an impact on the budget priorities set by states after reapportionment.[104] Comparing reapportioned to malapportioned states, and states before reapportionment to states after reapportionment, studies showed that state aid to cities increased significantly in 31 percent of the reapportioned states but in only 23 percent of the nonreapportioned states. Superficially surprising was a finding that reapportionment benefited suburbia more than central cities.[105] But because central cities antedated suburban sprawl, states commonly malapportioned the former to a lesser extent than the latter.

School Desegregation. A more pessimistic view about the Court's impact on American life is presented in a book by Gerald Rosenberg, which contains a series of case studies that challenge the conventional wisdom about the efficacy of Supreme Court decisions.[106] Two of the more interesting accounts concern school desegregation and abortion.

It has been said of *Brown v. Board of Education*[107] that probably no case ever to go before the nation's highest tribunal affected more directly the minds, hearts, and daily lives of so many Americans. Citizens, politicians, and scholars have assigned the case a high place in the literature of liberty. The decision marked the turning point in America's willingness to face the consequences of centuries of racial discrimination.[108]

---

[103] David W. Rohde and Harold J. Spaeth, *Supreme Court Decision Making* (San Francisco: Freeman, 1976), p. 178.

[104] Roger Hanson and Robert Crew, "The Effects of Reapportionment on State Public Policy Outputs," in Theodore Becker and Malcom Feeley (eds.), *The Impact of Supreme Court Decisions* (New York: Oxford University Press, 1973), pp. 155–174.

[105] *Id.*, p. 172.

[106] Rosenberg, *Hollow Hope.*

[107] 347 U.S. 483 (1954).

[108] Richard Kluger, *Simple Justice* (New York: Vintage, 1977), p. x.

Nevertheless, in 1955, the year after the *Brown* decision, only twenty-three black children in the entire South attended desegregated schools.[109] And in 1956, the year after the *Brown* implementation decision,[110] only 0.11 percent of black children did so. In 1959, a year after *Cooper v. Aaron*[111] held that threats of violence could not delay desegregation, the proportion had increased to only 0.16 percent. By the end of the 1963–1964 school year, ten years after *Brown* I, only 1.2 percent of black children were enrolled in desegregated schools.

A phenomenal increase occurred thereafter: The rate grew to 2.3 percent in 1964, 6.1 percent in 1965, 16.9 percent in 1966, 32.0 percent in 1968, 85.9 percent in 1970, and 91.3 percent in 1972. A crucial intervening factor – in Rosenberg's analysis *the* crucial intervening factor – was the passage of the Civil Rights Act of 1964. Title VI of the act declared, "No person in the United States shall, on the ground of race, color, or national origin, be excluded from participation in, be denied the benefits of, or be subjected to discrimination under any program or activity receiving Federal financial assistance." This became significant when, in 1965, Congress began pouring billions of dollars into education as part of President Lyndon Johnson's Great Society. After the 1964 act, the Department of Health, Education, and Welfare (HEW) set increasingly rigid standards for compliance with Title VI, culminating in regulations in 1968 that required complete desegregation by the fall of 1969.

The Supreme Court, however, had not completely abandoned the field of school desegregation. A 1965 decision declared that "delays in desegregation of school systems are no longer tolerable."[112] And in 1969 the Supreme Court ended the era of "all deliberate speed," declaring that "the obligation of every school district is to terminate dual school systems at once."[113]

Apportioning credit for desegregation is no simple task. Rosenberg relies on a survey conducted by the U.S. Commission on Civil Rights. The commission found that between 1954 and 1975, federal district courts desegregated 207 southern districts, while HEW desegregated 152.[114] We need not accept Rosenberg's conclusion that "*Brown* and its progeny stand for the proposition that courts are impotent to produce significant social change"[115] to realize that the courts' acting alone did not produce much desegregation. On the other hand, nothing prevented Congress and its administrative agency from desegregating schools before 1954, or even in the immediate aftermath of *Brown*. Congress did not do so. Suffice it to say that the Court's leadership was a necessary but insufficient cause of Southern school desegregation.

---

[109] All data are from Rosenberg, *Hollow Hope*, p. 50.

[110] 349 U.S. 294 (1954).

[111] 358 U.S. 1 (1958).

[112] *Bradley v. Richmond School Board*, 382 U.S. 103 (1965), at 105.

[113] *Alexander v. Holmes County Board of Education*, 396 U.S. 19 (1969), at 20.

[114] Rosenberg, *Hollow Hope*, p. 53. The survey probably underestimated HEW's effectiveness by giving only the courts credit for responses that listed both the courts and HEW as the primary source of desegregation pressure.

[115] Rosenberg, *Hollow Hope*, p. 71.

Yet the impact of *Brown* cannot be measured simply in terms of desegregated schools:

The mass movement sparked by *Brown* was unmistakenly thriving as soon as six months after the Court handed down its implementation decree. It began in the Deep South, in Montgomery, Alabama, when a forty-three-year-old seamstress and active NAACP member named Rosa Parks refused to move to the back of a city bus to make room for a white passenger. Within days, and thanks to the leadership of Mrs. Parks's pastor, the Reverend Martin Luther King, Jr., all blacks were staying off the buses of Montgomery in a massive show of resentment over the continuing humiliation of Jim Crow.... Lunch counter sit-ins started in North Carolina in 1960, and soon in hundreds of communities blacks were making personal statements of protest – and risking their necks – to demonstrate the depth of their demand for equal treatment as human beings.[116]

Abortion. Many believe that absent the decision in *Roe v. Wade*[117] legal abortions would be oxymoronic. Senator Edward Kennedy expressed the fears of millions of prochoice women when he declared in 1987 that Robert Bork's America, one in which *Roe* would be overturned, would be one in which "women would be forced into back alley abortions."[118]

Roe undoubtedly had a substantial impact on the number of abortions in the United States. As one text declares, the response to *Roe* was "immediate from women who sought abortions. In the first three months of 1973, 180,000 abortions were performed in the United States; during the first year following the Supreme Court's decision a total of 742,460 abortions were performed nationwide."[119] The upward trend continued, exceeding 1 million in 1975.[120] The number plateaued in 1979 at approximately 1.5 million.

The conventional wisdom, which gives the Supreme Court full and total credit and blame for abortion rates in the United States, is not completely correct. Although the number of legal abortions climbed strikingly after *Roe*, the number of legal abortions actually escalated dramatically before *Roe*, as shown in Figure 14.2. In 1969, 22,000 legal abortions were performed in the United States. In 1970, three years before *Roe*, the number was 194,000, a 752 percent increase. The following year saw the number jump to 486,000, a 151 percent increase. The largest increase since *Roe*, 27 percent, occurred in the year of the decision. From a purely statistical viewpoint, the year of *Roe* did not produce a substantial change in the incidence of abortion.

What impact, then, did the Court have? Clearly, it did not instigate abortions. That responsibility locates elsewhere. First, from the mid-1960s through the early 1970s, public opinion increasingly liberalized. One study found approval at 41 percent in 1965, and 63 percent in 1972. According to the National

---

[116] Kluger, *Simple Justice*, pp. 749–750.
[117] 410 U.S. 113 (1973).
[118] James Reston, "Kennedy and Bork," *New York Times*, 5 July 1987, Sec. 4, p. 15.
[119] Canon and Johnson, *Judicial Politics*, p. 6.
[120] All data are from Rosenberg, *Hollow Hope*, p. 180.

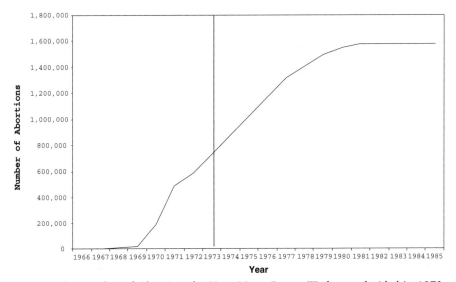

Figure 14.2. Number of Abortions by Year. *Note: Roe v. Wade* was decided in 1973. *Source:* Gerald Rosenberg, *The Hollow Hope: Can Courts Bring About Social Change* (Chicago: University of Chicago Press, 1991), p. 180.

Opinion Research Center, by 1972, 40 percent endorsed the broadest abortion alternative, abortion on demand.[121] These increases can be traced to several factors, including the burgeoning women's movement, dramatic changes in attitudes toward sexual relations, and fetal deformities caused by the drug thalidomide and the rubella virus.

Second, state legislatures began to react to these changes in public opinion. In 1967, with 73 percent of Californians supporting abortion reform,[122] Governor Ronald Reagan signed a liberalization bill into law. The first state virtually to legalize abortion on demand was Hawaii, which acted in 1970. Three more states did so that year: New York, which acted despite a large Catholic population; Alaska, whose legislature overturned a gubernatorial veto; and Washington, whose liberalization provisions were duly enacted after a referendum that passed by a margin of 12 percent.

After the prochoice victories of 1970, the legislative movement stalled somewhat. Though substantial liberalization of abortion laws took place, no state completely legalized abortion in 1971 or 1972. After the January 1973 *Roe* decision, repeal became superfluous. Though it cannot be proved, it seems likely that several other states would have repealed their laws in part or in whole during the remainder of the 1970s had *Roe* not been decided. But it is just as probable that many states would never have eliminated their antiabortion laws without *Roe*, and others would have adopted a position between no choice

[121] Rosenberg, *Hollow Hope*, pp. 260–261.
[122] *Id.*, p. 261.

and *Roe*. Thus the Supreme Court dramatically boosted abortion rights, but as in school desegregation, the Court did not act alone. Public opinion (and legislative) changes preceded the Court's action.

THE COURTS AND PUBLIC OPINION

Related to impact is the question of whether the courts directly affect not only public policies as discussed previously, but also public opinion. The ignorance of the mass public about the workings and decisions of the Court arguably precludes it from having much of an impact, much less a legitimizing one, even though experimental research has shown that a policy statement said to be emerging from the Court is more readily accepted than one from one of several other institutions, hence showing the capacity of the Court to legitimate policies.[123]

Public ignorance about the Court is substantial, though perhaps no more so than other areas of politics. A 1964–1966 national study, during the height of Warren Court activism, found that less than half of all respondents could name a single recent Court decision that they liked or disliked.[124] Moreover, having an opinion does not guarantee its rationality. The minority of people who mentioned a specific like or dislike included one person who opposed the Court for "getting us mixed up in this war," and another who supported the Court because "they gave us Medicare."[125] Perhaps the best example of the public's ignorance of the Court was a 1989 *Washington Post* survey.[126] Nine percent correctly named William Rehnquist as chief justice of the United States. Among associate justices, recall ranged from 23 percent for Sandra Day O'Connor, to 0.6 percent for John Paul Stevens. All this pales in comparison to the 54 percent who correctly named Joseph Wapner as the judge on the TV show *The People's Court*.

It should occasion no surprise then that the Court's decisions largely do not affect public support for various issues, at least in the aggregate. Examination of national surveys taken on eighteen issues before and after Supreme Court decisions between 1937 and 1983 supports this judgment.[127] The issues, typically controversial, received significant media play. They included the death penalty, abortion, miscegenation, and affirmative action. "Overall, the average poll shift was virtually zero – a bare +0.06, or six one-hundredths of one percent. These

---

[123] Rosalee A. Clawson, Elizabeth Kegler, and Eric N. Waltenberg, "The Legitimacy-Conferring Authority of the U.S. Supreme Court: An Experimental Design," 29 *American Politics Research* 566 (2001).

[124] Murphy and Tanenhaus, *Public Law*, p. 41.

[125] *Id.* at 42.

[126] Richard Morin, "What Americans Think: The Case for TV in the Highest Court," *Washington Post National Weekly Edition*, 26 June–2 July 1989, p. 37.

[127] Thomas R. Marshall, *Public Opinion and the Supreme Court* (Boston: Unwin Hyman, 1989), chap. 6.

results provide little evidence that Court rulings influence mass public opinion. The polls shifted away from the Court's position more often than toward it."[128]

One partial explanation for these nonfindings, particularly among highly salient issues, is that rather than producing an increase or decrease in support, they polarize public opinion. After *Roe*, for example, white Protestants showed increased support for abortion rights while white Catholics decreased theirs.[129] Polarization resulted from the Court's initial death penalty case as well, but in subsequent death penalty and abortion cases, the Court did not influence public opinion.[130]

Another author suggests another reason for these nonfindings: She argues that although aggregate public opinion may not be influenced by Court behavior, public opinion in the areas from which the controversies arise may well be.[131] Indeed, she demonstrates that the people living in and around localities from which Supreme Court cases derive are much more informed about those decisions than the usually ignorant public and that, when the issue is particularly salient to them or the community, the Supreme Court's decision affects their evaluation of the High Court as an institution. In terms of the question being litigated, those in the immediate community typically have well-crystallized views and thus are largely immune to Court influence. But those who live in outlying communities usually absorb the saturation press coverage that attends a locally generated Supreme Court decision and do show significant shifts in the direction of the Court's decision. This creates an odd condition for impact: Citizens must learn of a Court decision, usually through some form of saturated news coverage, but not have strong initial opinions about the issue.

All of these studies, however, comport with the judgment that the Court's decisions have little or no aggregate impact on public opinion. The cumulative effect of court decisions on public opinion, both about the issue under study and about the courts, then, depends on how widespread these interested publics are.

SUMMARY AND CONCLUSIONS

We have noted throughout the courts' role as some of the predominant shapers of American public policy. Abortion, busing, affirmative action, and flag burning are but a few of the highly salient issues that courts have addressed. In Chapter 12 on the Supreme Court and in Chapters 7, 8, and 9 on the lower courts, we demonstrate how judges, to varying degrees tied to varying institutional circumstances, base their decisions on their ideological attitudes and

[128] *Id.* at 146.
[129] Charles Franklin and Liane Kosaki, "Republican Schoolmaster: The U.S. Supreme Court, Public Opinion, and Abortion," 83 *American Political Science Review* 751 (1989).
[130] Timothy R. Johnson and Andrew D. Martin, "The Public's Conditional Response to Supreme Court Decisions," 92 *American Political Science Review* 299 (1998).
[131] Valerie J. Hoekstra, "The Supreme Court and Local Public Opinion," 94 *American Political Science Review* 89 (2000).

values. In this chapter, we have altered our focus to consider what happens to issues after the courts have articulated a policy. In doing so, we distinguish between compliance and impact. *Compliance* refers to the extent that those charged with interpreting and implementing court rulings obey them; *impact* refers to the effect of such rulings on society.

Despite a few contrary instances, compliance with Supreme Court decisions occurs. Lower court judges do not like to be overruled and generally want to "get it right" – that is, they perceive their role to be that of implementers of Supreme Court policy – and thus outright defiance rarely happens. Nevertheless, lower court judges, no less than Supreme Court justices, have tools that enable them to mitigate the full import of High Court rulings. Precedents can be found on both sides of cases; unfavorable precedents can be distinguished; facts can be obfuscated. Even while complying, these courts also vote in accordance with their attitudes, at least to some extent. Given the small percentage of appealed cases, and the even smaller percentage of cases that the Court reviews, lower court judges have substantial leeway to do as they wish.

Compliance with Supreme Court rulings by those in the implementing population may also be problematic. If a teacher in a small, homogeneous Bible belt community leads a class in prayer and no one complains, there is little the Supreme Court or the American Civil Liberties Union can do about it. So, too, is there little that the Court can do to sanction police officers who falsely claim to have read defendants their rights or who routinely assert that incriminating evidence came into their possession not because they made an unreasonable search or seizure, but because the defendant suffered from "dropsy." In sum, full compliance with the Court's decisions is no more likely than full compliance by motorists with speed limits. Even so, compliance is the rule rather than the exception, even among those who disagree with the law.[132]

Decisional impact is much more difficult to assess than compliance. Apportionment of credit and blame bedevils all impact analyses. The Civil War is blamed on the Court's most despicable decision;[133] the end of Southern apartheid is a claimed result of its most respected decision;[134] and tens of millions of abortions are both claimed for and blamed on what may be its most controversial decision.[135] Yet in none of these decisions did the Supreme Court or the lower courts charged with implementation of the Supreme Court's decisions solely shape public policy. With or without *Scott v. Sandford*, a nation divided between slavery and freedom could not endure. Though Congress may never have acted without the Court's lead in civil rights, acting alone the courts accomplished precious little in the fight against school segregation. The increased incidence in abortion was initially spurred by public opinion and state

---

[132] Tom R. Tyler, *Why People Follow the Law: Procedural Justice, Legitimacy, and Compliance* (New Haven, CT: Yale University Press, 1990).

[133] *Scott v. Sandford*, 19 Howard 393 (1857).

[134] *Brown v. Board of Education*, 347 U.S. 483 (1954).

[135] *Roe v. Wade*, 410 U.S. 113 (1973).

legislatures, which are where the fight will return if *Roe* is ever overturned. And although the Supreme Court guaranteed George W. Bush's presidential selection in 2000, it could not have done so for George McGovern in 1972 or anyone else in any other year who had categorically lost. On the other hand, reapportionment, the exclusionary rule, and First Amendment protections are almost exclusively judicial creations. The U.S. courts are but one set of actors, albeit a highly significant one, impacting public policy.

Case Index

Able v. United States, 231, 232
Abney v. United States, 141
AFL-CIO v. Eu, 169
Aguilar v. Texas, 126, 127
Akron v. Akron Center for Reproductive
    Health, 310, 311
Alden v. Maine, 70
Alexander v. Holmes County Board of
    Education, 380, 385
Allegheny County v. ACLU, 338, 368
Allgeyer v. Louisiana, 52
Alvarado v. United States, 293
Anderson v. Campbell, 226
Apodaca v. Oregon, 91, 135, 199
Argersinger v. Hamlin, 59, 130
Arizona v. Fulminante, 349
Asgrow Seed Co. v. Winterboer, 24
Avery v. Georgia, 181
Avery v. Midland County, 376

Bailey v. Drexel Furniture Co., 53
Baker v. Carr, 37, 376
Baker v. State, 334
Bakke v. California, 61
Batson v. Kentucky, 134, 313
Beaulieu v. United States, 295
Bell v. United States, 122
Berkemer v. McCarty, 369
Betts v. Brady, 130
Bivens v. Six Unknown Federal Agents,
    383
BMW of North America v. Gore, 93

Board of Trustees v. Garrett, 34, 178
Boerne v. Flores, 37
Boos v. Barry, 338
Bordenkircher v. Hayes, 133
Bouie v. City of Columbia, 141
Bowers v. Hardwick, 63–64, 167, 270
Boy Scouts of America v. Dale, 64
Bradley v. Richmond School Board, 380,
    385
Brand Name Prescription Drugs
    Antitrust Litigation, In re, 115
Brandenburg v. Ohio, 57
Browder v. Director, 226
Brown v. Board of Education, 60, 245,
    302, 323, 334, 366, 368, 369, 370,
    380, 384–386, 390
Brown v. Louisiana, 255
Burnham v. Superior Court, 81
Bush v. Gore, 4, 5, 19, 34, 35, 57, 62,
    69–70, 71, 148, 156, 184, 299, 300,
    305, 306–308, 318–319, 322, 363,
    364
Bush v. Palm Beach Canvassing Board,
    299–330

Calder v. Bull, 44
California Department of Corrections v.
    Morales, 122
California Legislature v. Deukmejian,
    169
Chavez v. Martinez, 143
Chin v. United States, 226

Chisholm v. Georgia, 44, 177
Civil Rights cases, 50–51
Cleveland v. United States, 123
Clinton v. New York City, 68
Colegrove v. Green, 376
Colgrove v. Battin, 91
College Savings v. Florida Board,
    70
Concord Boat v. Brunswick, 115
Cooper v. Aaron, 296, 364, 385
*Cooper Industries v. Leatherman Tool
    Group*, 93
Costa v. Desert Palace, 105
Cruzan v. Missouri Health Department,
    31, 64

Darlington Manufacturing Co., v. NLRB,
    257
Daubert v. Merrell Dow, 34, 113,
    114–115, 116, 117
*Denver Area Educational Television v.
    FCC*, 335
Dickerson v. United States, 129, 315,
    316, 369
Dimick v. Schiedt, 92
*Do-Right Auto Sales v. U.S. Court of
    Appeals*, 226
Douglas v. California, 141
Duncan v. Louisiana, 133, 199

Edmond v. United States, 68–69
Edmonson v. Leesville Concrete Co., 92,
    313
Edwards V. Aguillard, 27
Eichman v. United States, 37
Eisenstadt v. Baird, 313
Employment Division v. Smith, 371
Engel v. Vitale, 367
Erie Railroad Co. v. Tompkins, 185
Escobedo v. Illinois, 130, 377
Ewing v. California, 143

Ferguson v. Moore-McCormick Lines,
    280
Fletcher v. Peck, 46
Florida Board v. College Bank, 70
Frye v. United States, 117
Furman v. Georgia, 139–140, 375,
    378–379

Gault, In re, 381
Georgia v. McCollum, 313
Gerstein v. Pugh, 131
Gibbons v. Ogden, 45
Gideon v. Wainwright, 130
Gomillion v. Lightfoot, 20
Gore v. Harris, 148, 300
Gratz v. Bollinger, 61
Gray v. Sanders, 37, 376
Gregg v. Georgia, 140, 269, 327, 375,
    378
Griswold v. Connecticut, 25, 31, 62–63,
    123, 310, 313
Grove City College v. Bell, 270
Grutter v. Bollinger, 61, 246, 332

Hadley v. Junior College District, 376
*Halliburton Oil Well Cementing Co. v.
    Reily*, 338
Hamdi v. Rumsfeld, 66
Hamilton v. Texas, 279
Hammer v. Dagenhart, 53
Harris v. New York, 129, 369
*Harris County Commissioners Court v.
    Moore*, 183
Holmes v. California National Guard,
    231, 232
Hopfmann v. Connolly, 280
Hoyt v. Florida, 62
Humphrey's Executor v. United States,
    32

Idaho v. Coeur d'Alene Tribe, 70
Illinois v. Gates, 126–127
Illinois v. Perkins, 368
*Immigration and Naturalization Service
    v. Lopez-Mendoza*, 125
International Shoe Co. v. Washington,
    80

Jacobelis v. Ohio, 377
Jaffee v. Redmond, 111
Johnson v. Louisiana, 199

Kansas v. Hendricks, 122
Katz v. United States, 127
Kimel v. Florida Board of Regents, 70
Kirby v. Illinois, 130
Kolender v. Lawson, 123

Kontrick v. Ryan, 275
Koon v. United States, 205
Korematsu v. United States, 65–66, 67
Kumbo Tire Co. v. Carmichael, 114–115

L. C. & C. R. Co. v. Letson, 25
Labine v. Vincent, 32
Lawrence v. Chater, 281
Lawrence v. Texas, 64, 123, 167, 270
Lefkowitz v. Newsome, 343
Lekkas v. Mitsubishi Motors Corp., 105
Levy v. Louisiana, 32
Liles v. Oregon, 287
Lochner v. New York, 25, 34
Locke v. Davey, 59
Lockyer v. Andrade, 139, 143
Longden v. Philip Morris USA, 105
Loving v. Virginia, 61, 123, 179
Lucas v. Forty-Fourth Colorado
    Assembly, 37

M. L. J. v. S. L. U., 306
Maher v. Roe, 33
Mallory v. United States, 255
Manual Enterprises v. Day, 377
Mapp v. Ohio, 125, 270, 377, 383
Marbury v. Madison, 13–16, 38, 44, 45,
    48, 58, 67
Marks v. United States, 305, 335
Martin v. Hunter's Lessee, 174–175,
    179
Maryland v. Craig, 107–108, 135
McBoyle v. United States, 122
McCardle, Ex parte, 325, 330
McCloskey v. Kemp, 140
M'Culloch v. Maryland, 46, 381,
    382–383
Memphis Light, Gas, and Water Division
    v. Craft, 84
Michigan v. Long, 183–184
Miller v. California, 270, 286–287
Miller v. Florida, 122
Miller-El v. Cockrell, 105, 134
Mincey v. Arizona, 176
Miranda v. Arizona, 124, 270, 315,
    368–369, 372, 374, 375; see also
    self-incrimination (General Index)
Missouri v. Jenkins, 338, 378
Morrison v. Olson, 68–69

Moseley v. Secret Catalogue Inc., 105
Mullane v. Central Hanover Co., 83
Myers v. United States, 32

New Jersey v. New York, 321
New York v. Quarles, 129, 270

O'Brien v. Brown, 296
Oregon v. Hess, 129

Pacific Mutual Life Insurance Co. v.
    Haslip, 93, 306
Palko v. Connecticut, 120
Palm Beach County Canvassing Board v.
    Harris, 148, 299, 307
Papachristou v. City of Jacksonville,
    123
Parker v. North Carolina, 133
Patterson v. McLean Credit Union, 317
Payne v. Tennessee, 317
Pennoyer v. Neff, 80
Penry v. Lynaugh, 327, 338
People v. Bierenbaum, 105
People v. Defore, 125
People v. Lee, 117
Permoli v. New Orleans, 119–120
Planned Parenthood v. Casey, 63, 270,
    305, 308–311
Plessy v. Ferguson, 51, 334, 375
Powell v. Alabama, 129–130
Printz v. United States, 70

A Quantity of Books v. Kansas, 377

Railroad Commission of Texas v.
    Pullman Co., 180
Rasul v. Bush, 66
Reed v. Reed, 271
Regents v. Bakke, 271, 374
Republican Party of Minnesota v. White,
    151, 153, 155–156
Reynolds v. Sims, 37, 376
Richenberg v. Perry, 231, 232
Roe v. Alabama, 188
Roe v. Wade, 33, 63, 253, 269, 271,
    308–309, 310, 332, 364, 366, 369,
    375, 381, 386–387, 389, 390
Rogers v. Lodge, 27
Rogers v. Missouri Pacific R. Co., 280

Rogers v. Paul, 380
Romer v. Evans, 64
Roudebush v. Hartke, 188
Roy C. Moore, In re, 367
Rummel v. Estelle, 139
Rumsfeld v. Padilla, 66
Rust v. Sullivan, 365

San Antonio v. Rodriguez, 270
Santa Clara County v. Southern Pacific R. Co., 25, 52
Santobello v. New York, 133
School District of Abington Township v. Schempp, 367, 374
Scott v. Sandford, 14, 34, 48, 49–50, 308, 390
See v. Seattle, 127
Seminole Tribe v. Florida, 70
Shaffer v. Heitner, 82–83
Sherbert v. Verner, 371
Siegel v. Lepore, 213–214, 215
Silverman v. United States, 127
Simkins v. Moses H. Cone Memorial Hospital, 257
Smith v. Doe, 122
Snepp v. United States, 281
South Carolina v. Gathers, 31
Southern Pacific Terminal Co. v. Interstate Commerce Commission, 167
Spinelli v. United States, 126, 127
Stack v. Boyle, 131
Stanton v. Stanton, 62
State Farm Mutual Automobile Insurance Co. v. Campbell, 93
Steelworkers v. Weber, 28, 34
Stenberg v. Carhart, 94, 123
Stogner v. California, 122
Stone v. Powell, 125, 175–176, 270
Straight v. Wainwright, 279
Sullivan v. Stroop, 24
Swann v. Charlotte-Mecklenburg County Board of Education, 270, 271
Swift v. Tyson, 184–185
Swift and Co. v. United States, 53

Tarasoff v. Regents, 111–112
Taylor v. McKeithen, 226
Texas v. Johnson, 37

Thapar v. Zezulka, 112
Thomasson v. Perry, 23, 232
Thompson v. Utah, 134
Thornburgh v. American College of Obstetricians and Gynecologists, 310, 311
Tompkins v. Texas, 338
Trammel v. United States, 110
Turner v. Williams, 117

United States v. Butler, 16
United States v. Calandra, 125
United States v. Cruikshank, 50
United States v. Dalm, 294, 295
United States v. E.C. Knight, 53
United States v. Janis, 125
United States v. Johnson, 113
United States v. Leon, 125, 270
United States v. Lopez, 70, 124
United States v. Morrison, 62
United States v. Nixon, 67, 135, 330, 377
United States v. Reese, 50
United States v. Salerno, 131
United States v. Shannon, 279
United States v. Snepp, 281
United States v. Wade, 130
United States v. Williams, 132
United States v. Yoshida, 105
United States ex rel. Fong Foo v. Shaughnessy, 310

Vacco v. Quill, 64
Valdez v. McPheeters, 224–225

Washington v. Glucksberg, 64
Washington v. Texas, 108
Weaver v. Graham, 122
Webster v. Reproductive Health Service, 33, 310
Weeks v. United States, 125, 383
Wesberry v. Sanders, 376
West Coast Hotel v. Parrish, 55
West Virginia Board of Education v. Barnette, 326
Westside Community Schools v. Mergens, 24
Williams v. Florida, 134, 199
Williams v. Georgia, 181, 183

Williams v. State, 181
Winship, In re, 135
Wisconsin Public Intervenor v. Mortier, 27
Witherspoon v. Illinois, 379
WMCA v. Lomenzo, 37
Wolf v. Colorado, 125

Woodson v. North Carolina, 140, 378
Worldwide Volkswagen Corp. v. Woodson, 81
Wynehamer v. People, 52

Youngstown Sheet and Tube Co. v. Sawyer, 66–67

General Index

abortion, 5, 33, 63, 94, 246, 252, 259, 270, 271, 284, 309, 331, 364, 381, 386–388
abstention doctrine, 56, 171, 179–183
access, 275–298; case selection, 275–276; caseload, 281–284; conflict with Supreme Court preferences, 291–292, 295–296; denial or dismissal, effects of, 280–281; future changes in, 296–297; procedure, 276–278; appeal, writ of, 276, 277; certiorari, writ of, 286–281; sought by United States, 293–294
Adams, John, 13, 248
additur, 92
adequate and independent state grounds for decision, 183–184
adversary system, 76–78, 96, 99, 117
affirmative action, 61, 246
Agriculture Department, 97
Al Qaeda, 107
Alexander, Paul, 374
Alien and Sedition Acts, 59
Altfeld, Michael F., 297
Alzheimer's Disease, 63
American Bar Association, 120, 191, 206, 246, 252
American Civil Liberties Union, 259, 302, 390
American Judicature Society, 157
American University, 255
Americans with Disabilities Act, 178, 197

amicus curiae brief, 277, 294, 302, 324, 328, 329, 375
appeals, 140–141
Appleson, Gail, 206
Armstrong, Virginia, 294
arraignment, 132–133
Articles of Confederation, 8, 42, 43, 52
Ashcroft, John, 106, 205
Atkins, Burt, 228
attainder, bill of, 119
attitudinal model, 19, 21, 34–35, 38–39, 40, 48, 201, 318–319, 319–323, 329
Ayres, Ian, 333
Ayres, Richard, 374

Baer, Judith, 26
Baik, Ellen R., 336
Bail Reform Act, 131
Bailey, Michael E., 324
Baker, Howard, 248
bankruptcy courts, 197, 199
Barnum, David, 326
Barrow, Deborah J., 190, 191, 194, 215, 220, 221, 236, 239, 240, 241, 242
Baum, Lawrence, 19, 151, 233, 280, 370
Baumeister, Roy, 34
Beatty, Jerry K., 370, 371
bench memoranda, 228
Benesh, Sara C., 159, 166, 172, 173, 224, 234, 236, 316–317, 330, 331, 345, 348, 357, 367, 371, 372, 373, 380

Bennett, Robert W., 336
beyond a reasonable doubt, 94
Bill of Rights, 42, 43, 55, 56–57, 62, 119, 120; selective incorporation of, 121, 132, 175, 334
Bird, Rose, 152
Birkby, Robert, 374
Black, Hugo, 26, 251, 271, 272, 285, 287, 289; opinions and assignments of, 338, 341, 342, 346, 348
Blackmun, Harry, 32, 135, 248, 270, 271, 297; opinions and assignments of, 336, 347, 356, 357, 364; voting behavior of, 304, 309
Blair, John, 216
Bodine, Lawrence, 39
Bok, Derek, 155, 186
Bork, Robert, 245, 248, 250, 252, 253, 270; nomination of, 258–260
Boucher, Robert L., Jr., 35, 287
Brace, Paul, 159, 330
Brandeis, Louis, 54, 251
Brazill, Timothy, 70
Breaux, John, 259–260
Brennan, William J., 83, 107, 135, 140, 251, 255, 265, 271, 273, 278–279, 281, 287, 297; opinions and assignments of, 335, 338, 341, 342, 343, 347, 348, 351, 353, 356, 357, 358; voting behavior of, 309, 315, 317, 319
Brenner, Saul, 287, 316, 338, 343, 348, 349
Brent, James, 371
Breyer, Stephen, 114, 218, 251, 253, 262; opinions and assignments of, 351, 356; voting behavior of, 299, 301, 313, 318, 321, 323
Brock, David, 247
Buchanan, Pat, 3
Buckley, William F., 78
Burch, Gregory S., 183
burden of proof, 93–94
Burger, Warren, 28, 32, 135, 248, 256, 270, 297, 298, 373, 384; opinions and assignments of, 337, 342–343; voting behavior of, 322
Burger Court, 57, 59, 60, 61–62, 125, 127, 128–129, 130, 176, 183, 184,

269–271, 281, 283, 285, 290, 293, 297, 380; opinions and assignments, 341, 343, 346, 349, 350
Burton, Harold H., 251, 346
Bush, George H. W., 245, 251, 322
Bush, George W., 4, 66, 69–70, 147, 158, 187, 205, 213, 218, 219, 220, 273, 300–301, 307–308, 329, 391
Bush administration, 66, 106, 245, 321, 331
Butler, Pierce, 54
Byrnes, James F., 39, 55, 331

Caldeira, Gregory A., 260, 294, 295, 296, 302, 328, 363
Calhoun, John C., 70, 178
Cameron, Charles, M., 35, 236, 263, 265, 267, 290, 292, 370
Campbell, Donald, 381, 382
Canon, Bradley C., 366, 367, 370, 383, 386
capital punishment, 139–140
Caplan, Lincoln, 324
Cardozo, Benjamin, 54, 125, 250, 251
Caro, Robert A., 254
Carp, Robert A., 189, 202, 203, 220
Carroll, Lewis, 96
Carswell, G. Harrold, 251, 252, 268, 368; nomination of, 257–258
Carter, Jimmie, 220, 271
Carter, Lief, 28
case of controversy requirement, 46
Casper, Jonathan, 303
Catron, John, 119
Cavanagh, Michael, 152
cert pool, 277
Chambers, Marcia, 118
Chapin, Bradley, 42
Chase, Samuel, 325, 330
Cheney, Dick, 187, 213
Chicago Tribune, 309, 319
child labor, 53
choice of law, 184–185
civil procedure, 75–96
Civil Rights Act of 1964, 28, 259, 369, 380, 385
Civil Service Reform Act, 169
Civil War, 47–49, 70, 175, 250, 390
Clark, Tom, 125, 251, 346

class action, 168
Clawson, Rosalee A., 388
clear and convincing evidence, 94
clear and present danger doctrine, 57
Cleveland, Grover, 194
Clinton, Robert Lowry, 38
Clinton, Bill, 67, 68, 218, 220, 251, 322
Clinton administration, 219, 230, 321
Clymer, Adam, 365
Cochran, Johnnie, 79
Coffin, Frank M., 31
Cohen, Jonathan Matthew, 224, 226, 227, 228, 229, 234, 235
Cohen, Laurie P., 205
Cole, George F., 124, 128, 130, 142
comity, 56, 171, 179–183
common law, 41, 42, 43, 85, 88, 91, 94, 95, 97, 108, 111, 117, 118, 120, 177
Congressional Record, 28
Constitutional Convention, 7, 8, 15, 43–44
constitutionalism, 9
contemporaneous objection rule, 181, 183
Continental Congress, 8
contract clause, 46, 47; freedom of, 52, 53, 55
Conwell, Russell, 51
Cook, Beverly B., 204, 327
correlation coefficient, 256
Cortner, Richard C., 376
Corwin, Edward A., 7
Cotton, Ronald, 116
counsel, right to, 129–130
counterclaim, 95
Court-packing plan, 55
Courts of Appeals, U.S., 213–242; agenda setting, 227–228; appointment process, 218–220; caseload, 221–223; decision making, 230–234, 235; growth, 217–218; ideology in, 236–241; institutional constraints, 234–236; jurisdiction, 220–221; opinion writing, 228–229; origins, 216–217; procedures, 226–227; types of cases, 223–226; unpublished, 223–226; visiting judge, 226–227
Cover, Albert D., 263, 264, 319

Cox, Archibald, 258
Crew, Robert, 384
criminal procedure, 59–60, 119–143
Croyle, James L., 207
cue theory, 293

Dahl, Robert, 274
Daly, Erin, 309
Daschle, Tom, 219
Davey, Monica, 91
de Tocqueville, Alexis, 364
deadlisting, 277
death penalty, 59–60, 327, 378–379
Declaration of Independence, 42, 49–50
Defense Department, 66, 67, 230
Defense of Marriage Act, 179
demurrer, 88
Department of Justice, 191
deposition, 89
desegregation, 5, 609–661, 179; school, 384–386
Dickerson, Brian, 155
Dickson, Del, 183
die, right to, 64–65
directed verdict, 92
discovery, 78–80, 84–85, 86, 88–89, 90, 109, 133
discrimination; de facto, 61; de jure, 61
district courts, federal, 43–44, 187–212, 214; appointment process, 191–194; senatorial courtesy, 191; caseload, 196–199; decision making, 200–204, 207; growth, 190–191; jurisdiction, 194–196; origins, 190; procedures, 199–200; sentencing, 204–211
Dixon, William, 336, 357
Donohue, John, 365
Donovan, Brian, 127
double jeopardy, 94, 136–137
Douglas, William O., 30, 135, 140, 183, 250, 255, 271, 279, 287; voting behavior, 341, 342, 346, 347
Dowd, Maureen, 247
Dropkin, Drew D., 106
D'Souza, Dinesh, 374
Ducat, Craig R., 176
due process, 52, 56, 80, 82, 83–84, 108; *see also* substantive due process

Duin, Julia, 367
Dworkin, Ronald, 19, 22
Dwyer, Jim, 116

Easterbrook, Frank H., 31
Edwards, George C., 263
Eggen, Dan, 205
Ehrlichman, John, 257
Eighth Amendment, 59, 119, 131, 139
Eisenhower, Dwight D., 194, 248, 252, 273, 378
Eisenstein, James, 201
Eleventh Amendment, 24, 34, 44, 70, 177
Elliott, Martha, 59
Ellsworth, Oliver, 13, 15, 44
Elsasser, Glen, 309
Emanuel, Steven L., 104, 117
Emmert, Craig, 159
en banc, 165, 166, 213, 229–230
Epstein, Lee, 35, 38, 151, 200, 282, 283, 293, 298, 302, 316, 324, 329, 336, 349, 357, 358, 366, 375
Equal Employment Opportunity Commission, 245, 247
equal protection clause, 60–62, 123, 181, 259, 301, 306–308
Equal Rights Amendment, 271
Erikson, Robert S., 328
Eskridge, William N., 325, 326
Espo, David, 219
estoppel, 170–171
Evart Court Reform Act, 216
Everson, D. H., 370
evidence, 97–118; admissibility of, 99–101; character evidence, 102–103; circumstantial, 105–106; cross examination, 104, 108; expert testimony, 112–115; eyewitness testimony, 115–117; habit, 102–103; hearsay, 103–104, 108, 112, 113; privileges, 108–112; attorney–client, 109; physician–patient, 111–112; priest–penitent, 110; spousal, 109–110; relevance, 98–99, 101–103, 105; remedial measures, 101; settlement offers, 101–102; spoliation, 106

ex post facto clause, 44, 119, 121–122
exclusionary rules, 23, 383–384; good faith exception to, 125; *see also* Fourth Amendment

facts, 23, 38–39
falsifiability, 21, 34, 36, 113
Farrand, Max, 7, 28
Faubus, Orville, 367
Federal Bureau of Investigation, 106, 191
Federal Circuit, Court of Appeals for, 117
Federal Communications Commission, 158
Federal Energy Regulatory Commission, 158
Federal Judicial Center, 210, 216
federal questions, 160–161, 173, 183, 184
Federal Rules of Civil Procedure, 78–79, 83, 85, 88
Federal Rules of Criminal Procedure, 199
Federal Rules of Evidence, 97, 99, 101, 102, 104, 108, 109, 111, 113, 114
federalism, 10–11, 12, 13, 173, 178, 183
Federalist Papers, 248
Feeley, Malcolm, 79
Feeney, Amendment, 205
Felleman, Frank, 217
Fields, Gary, 205
Fifth Amendment, 26, 59, 107, 119, 124, 132, 136
filibuster, 218–219, 256
First Amendment, 43, 56, 57–59, 62, 70, 120, 156, 259, 284
Fleming, Roy B., 201, 328
Florida State University, 258
fluidity, voting, 305
Foa, Pamela, 226
Ford, Gerald R., 250, 252, 271
Fortas, Abe, 249, 251, 252, 253, 267, 268, 271, 272, 297, 319, 346; nomination of, 254–256
forum non conveniens, 85
Fourteenth Amendment, 24, 26, 34, 42, 50–51, 61, 64, 92, 120

Fourth Amendment, 59, 107, 119, 126, 127, 175; exclusionary rule, 124–125; preliminary hearing, 132; probable cause, 126, 127, 128, 131; unreasonable search and seizure, 125–128; warrant requirement, 126, 128; *see also* search and seizure
Frank, Jerome, 17, 69, 77, 78, 310
Frankfurter, Felix, 181, 183, 279–280, 297, 316, 341, 346, 358, 376
Franklin, Charles, 389
French and Indian War, 8
Friday, Herschel, 252
Friedman, Lawrence M., 42
Friedman, Richard, 250
Friendly, Fred, 59
full faith and credit clause, 178–179
fundamental law, 5–7, 8, 12

Galanter, Marc, 293
Gallup, George, 250, 265
gamma, 265–266, 289
Gates, John B., 331
George, Tracey E., 230, 324
Gibson, James, 330, 363, 364
Giles, Micheal, 204, 330
Gillman, Howard, 33, 306, 308, 363
Gilmore, Gary, 379
Ginsburg, Douglas, 245, 248, 251, 253, 270; nomination of, 260–261
Ginsburg, Ruth Bader, 218, 251; opinions and assignments, 351, 356; voting behavior, 301, 313, 319, 321, 322–323
Glick, Henry R., 159
Goldberg, Arthur, 39, 319, 331, 346
Goldman, Ronald, 136
Goldman, Sheldon, 191, 220
Gore, Albert, Jr., 4, 70, 147, 148, 300–301, 306, 318, 319, 363
governmental power, distrust of, 7–10, 12
grand jury, 132
Grant, Ulysses S., 194, 325
Graves, Scott, 285
Greenawald, Kent, 22
Greenburg, Jan Crawford, 367
Greenhouse, Linda, 31, 33, 105, 283, 309

Gressman, Eugene, 301
Grofman, Bernard, 70
Gruhl, John, 371
Grutter, Barbara, 332
Gryski, Gerald S., 190, 217, 236, 239, 240, 241, 242
Gun Free School Zone Act, 124

habeas corpus, 119, 141, 175–176
Hagle, Timothy M., 70
Haire, Susan B., 221, 236
Hall, Kermit L., 5, 168
Hall, Melinda G., 6, 157, 159, 330
Hamilton, Alexander, 43, 46, 48, 248
Hamiltonianism, 47, 48–49
Hanson, Roger, 384
Hardwick, Michael, 167
Harlan, John Marshall, 51
Harlan, John Marshall II, 264, 271, 272, 287; opinions and assignments, 346, 347, 358; voting behavior, 319, 320
harmless error, 92
Harris, Amanda, 127
Harris, Katherine, 3, 148
Harrison, Robert, 253
Harrison, William Henry, 261
Hatch, Orrin, 247
Hayes, Rutherford, 4
Haynsworth, Clement, 251, 252, 268, 333; nomination of, 256–257
Healy, Gene, 309
Hechler, David, 115
Heflin, Howell, 331
Helms, Jesse, 319
Henry II, 41
Hess, David W., 374
Hettinger, Virginia, 230, 235
Hill, Anita, 246–247
Hintze, William, 294
Hoekstra, Valerie J., 389
Holmes, Andrew, 231, 232
Holmes, Oliver Wendell, 122, 249
homicide rate, 124
homosexuality, 63–64, 123, 230–233, 270
Hoover, Herbert, 250
Howard, C. Elaine, 309

Howard, Robert M., 22, 269, 271, 318
Hruska, Roman, 257
Huber, Gregory A., 139
Hughes, Charles Evans, 39, 54, 331, 334
Hull, N. E. H., 346
Hunter, Marjorie, 28

ideology, lower court, 292–293
immunity, transactional, 109
impact of decisions, 363–391; compliance, 370–380; congressional, 375–377; presidential, 377; implementation and compliance, 366–369, 390; implementing population, 373–375; interpreting population, 370–373; noncompliance, reasons for, 377–380; on society, 369–370; understanding of, 365–366
implied powers, doctrine of, 382–383
in forma pauperis docket, 283
Independent Counsel Act, 68, 69
interest groups, 328–329
intergovernmental tax immunity, 46
Interior Department, 97
interpretivism, 26, 29
interrogatory, 89
interstate commerce clause, 45, 52–53, 60
irrebutable presumption, 82–83
Israel, Jerold H., 124

Jackson, Andrew, 47, 48, 67, 149, 382
Jackson, Robert H., 297, 326
Jacob, John N., 302
Janofsky, Michael, 333
Janoski, Robert J., 79
Japanese American internment, 65–66
Jaworski, Leon, 67
Jay, John, 44, 248, 253, 331
Jefferson, Thomas, 13, 38, 57, 58, 376
Jeffersonianism, 48
Jim Crow, 51, 61, 91
Johnson, Andrew, 325
Johnson, Charles A., 294, 331, 366, 367, 380, 386
Johnson, Kirk, 369
Johnson, Lyndon B., 39, 255, 256, 268, 271, 297, 331, 385

Johnson, Timothy R., 303, 389
Johnson, William, 46
joinder, 95–96
Judges' Bill of 1801, 13
Judges' Bill of 1925, 296
judgment notwithstanding the verdict, 92
judgment of the Court, 305
judicial review, 11, 12–16, 45–46
Judiciary Act of 1789, 13–14, 15, 43, 45, 174, 190, 216, 250
Judiciary Act of 1802, 250
jurisdiction, 80–83, 85, 160–166, 275; diversity, 96, 108, 173, 184; *in personam*, 80–82, 83, 85; *in rem*, 82–83; *quasi in rem*, 82–83; *see also* standing to sue
jury selection, 134
jury trial, 91–92, 97–98, 117, 118, 199–200

Kahn, Ronald, 309
Kalven, Harry, 136
Kamisar, Yale, 124, 132, 141
Kamoie, Brian, 324
Kauder, Neal B., 171, 172
Kaufman, Ira, 152
Kaufman, Nathan, 152
Kavanagh, Thomas G., 152
Kavanagh, Thomas M., 152
Kegler, Elizabeth, 388
Kennedy, Anthony M., 68, 69, 105, 178, 206, 218, 251, 270, 279; opinions and assignments, 336, 338, 348, 351, 356, 357; voting behavior, 300, 306, 310–311, 317, 318, 322, 323
Kennedy, John F., 252, 271, 297
Kennedy, Ted, 259, 386
Keogh, Bryan A., 367
King, Don, 125
King, Nancy J., 124
King, Rodney, 137
Kirklosky, Louise, 294
Klein, David E., 234, 235
Kluger, Richard, 384, 386
Knight, Jack, 38, 316, 349, 358
Kolson, K., 370
Koppel, Nathan, 112
Korean War, 66
Kosaki, Liane, 389

Kosinski, Douglas, 294
Kozinski, Alex, 28
Kritzer, Herbert M., 204, 328, 363
Krol, John F., 287
Kuklinski, James, 330

LaFave, Wayne R., 124
LaFountain, Robert C., 171, 172
LaFraniere, Sharon, 245
laissez-faire economics, 51, 54, 55
Lazarus, Edward, 304, 346
Leahy, Patrick, 205, 217, 219
Lefstein, Norman, 381
legal model, 18, 19, 22–34, 38, 40, 70;
  Bush v. Gore as exemplification of,
  305–308
legislative intent, 24, 25–30, 31,
  70
Lerner, Max, 10
Levine, James, 374
Levinson, Laurie L., 143
Levitt, Steven, 365
Lewinsky, Monica, 68
Lewis, Anthony, 66, 247, 342
Lewis, Neil A., 107, 246
Lewis, Terry, 148
Life, 256
Lillie, Mildred, 252
Lincoln, Abraham, 50, 67, 250
Lind, Michael, 79
Lindquist, Stefanie, 230
Line Item Veto Act, 68
Lippman, Arthur, 17
Liptak, Adam, 106, 179
Lodge, Henry Cabot, 249
long-arm statutes, 84, 96
Lurton, Horace, 249

MacKuen, Michael B., 328
Madison, James, 13, 27–28, 248
Magrath, C. Peter, 168
Maltz, Earl M., 309
Maltzman, Forrest, 324
Mann Act, 122, 123
Manwaring, D. R., 370
Marbury, William, 13
Margolick, David, 132
Markham, Walter Gray, 207
Markovits, Richard S., 22

marriage: interracial, 61, 64, 179; same
  sex, 5, 6, 109, 179
Marshall, John, 13–16, 38, 44, 45–46,
  67, 69, 248, 333, 381, 382
Marshall, Thomas R., 140, 326, 388
Marshall, Thurgood, 107, 135, 140, 176,
  245, 251, 255, 271, 281; opinions and
  assignments, 335, 347, 351, 353, 356,
  357, 358; voting behavior, 302, 309,
  315, 317, 319, 327
Marshall Court, 44–47, 48, 55–56
Martin, Andrew D., 70, 389
Martin, John S., Jr., 205
Martinek, 159, 166, 172, 173, 230, 330,
  372
Mason, A. T., 51
Massachusetts Body of Liberties, 41
Massaro, John, 255, 257, 258
Matasar, Richard A., 183
Mauro, Tony, 226
Mayhew, David, 262
McGovern, George, 391
McGrath, C. Peter, 46
McGuire, Kevin T., 294
McIlwain, Charles H., 9
McKinley, James C., Jr., 117
McLauchlan, William P., 349
McNollgast, 26, 30
McReynolds, James, 54
mechanical jurisprudence, 22, 40
Medalie, Richard, 374
Meese, Edwin, 248
Michigan Bar Association, 78
Microsoft Windows, 178
Middlebrook, Donald M., 187–188, 189,
  213
minimum contacts test, 80, 82, 83, 95
Minton, Sherman, 251
Mintz, Mort, 305
Miranda warnings, 59, 143
Mishler, William, 327
models, 20–21; aggregate level, 289–291;
  generalized least squares, 328;
  individual, 285–289
Moore, Ray S., 367
Moreno, Enrique, 219
Morin, Richard, 388
Morris, Richard, 42
Moss, Michael, 107

multiple regression analysis, 137–138
Muraskin, Matthew, 293, 294, 295
Murphy, Frank, 251
Murphy, Walter F., 69, 200, 250, 368, 378, 382, 388
Murray, Peter, 100

Nalehuff, Barry, 333
Nardulli, Peter, 201
National Association for the Advancement of Colored People (NAACP), 245, 263, 302, 323, 329
National Labor Relations Act, 55
National Labor Relations Board, 316
National Motor Vehicle Theft Act of 1919, 122
National Opinion Research Center, 386–387
National Public Radio, 260
National Right to Life Committee, 311
National Science Foundation, 285
national supremacy, 44, 45, 174–175
necessary and proper clause, 46
Neikirk, William, 309
Nelson, Lemrick, 137
Nelson, William E., 42
Neufeld, Peter, 116
New Deal, 54–55
New York Times, 219–220, 259–260
Newman, Leonard, 34
Nixon, Richard M., 67, 125, 135, 194, 247, 248, 249, 250, 251, 252, 255, 256, 257, 258, 268, 269, 270, 271–272, 273, 292, 326, 377
nolo contendere, 200
Norris, Clarence, 129
notice, 83–84, 85
Nuremberg Trials, 297

obiter dicta, 32
O'Brien, David M., 277, 338
obscenity, 57
O'Connor, Karen, 293, 302, 324, 328
O'Connor, Sandra Day, 39, 69, 107, 178, 218, 251, 252, 270, 279, 286, 287, 288, 388; opinions and assignments, 338, 348, 354, 357; voting behavior, 300, 311, 315, 318, 319, 322, 323

opinions, 332–337, 358–359; assignment, 337–359; equal distribution of, 342–346; effect of equal distribution of, 346–348; coalitions, 348–350; politics of, 349–350; interagreement in special opinions, 350–354; options, 332–334; concurring, 333, 334–335, 336; Court's opinion, 333–334, 337; dissenting, 333, 334, 335, 337; judgment of the Court, 335, 341, 349, 350, 379; seriatim, 333
originalism, 26, 29
Ostrom, Brian J., 171, 172

Parental Kidnapping Prevention Act, 169
parties, necessary and indispensable, 96
Paterson, William, 249
Patterson, Hayward, 129
Pear, Robert, 28
Peltason, J. W., 60, 370
per curiam decision, 213, 281, 340–341, 379
peremptory challenges, 134
Perrotta, Tom, 105
Perry, H. W., 281, 296, 298
Phelps, Tomothy, 246
plain meaning, 23–24, 25, 28, 30, 31, 70, 326
Planned Parenthood, 311, 365
plea bargain, 132–133, 139, 141, 200
pleadings, 85–88; answer, 87; challenges to, 87–88; complaint, 86–87
police powers, 60
policy making, judicial, 4–18, 34–39, 55, 378
policy preferences, personal, 32, 35, 38, 39, 201, 235, 298, 318–323, 329, 346–348
Poole, Bobby, 116
Poole, Keith, 70
Porter, Paul, 255
Posner, Richard, 33
post-positivism, 22, 33–34, 40
Powell, Lewis, 135, 184, 251, 252, 258, 279, 281, 287, 379; opinions and assignments, 335, 336, 347, 351, 354, 358; voting behavior, 301–302, 304, 315, 322

precedent, 25, 30–33, 40, 52, 70, 79, 201, 390; alteration of, 316–318; *Planned Parenthood v. Casey* and, 308–311
preponderance of evidence, 94
presentment clause, 68
presidential selection, of Supreme Court justices, 248–252; friendship and patronage, 251–252; nominee ideology, 263–265; nominee qualifications, 263; partisanship and ideology, 249; political environment, 249–250; prior experience, 250; region, 250–251; religion, race, and sex, 251; senate confirmation, 252–261; staffing the Court, 251
pretrial conference, 86, 89–90
Pringle, Henry F., 248
Pritchett, C. Herman, 69, 200
privacy, right to, 62–63, 70, 123, 259, 281
Provine, Doris Marie, 293
public opinion, 204, 326–328; courts and, 388–389; polls, 365
punitive damages, 92–93
Puro, Steven, 324

Quinn, Kevin M., 70

Randazzo, Kirk A., 107
Rangel, Jorge L., 219
Rappeport, Mike, 115
Rastafarians, 123
ratio decidendi, 32
rational choice model, 35, 36–37, 40
Reagan, Ronald, 220, 245, 249, 258, 268, 269, 271, 272, 273, 311, 321, 365, 387
reapportionment, 376–377, 384
recusal, 14
Reddick, Malia, 367, 371, 380
redeeming social value, 57
Reed, Stanley, 341
Reedy, Cheryl, 324
regression models, 207–209
Rehnquist, William, 28, 31, 62, 64, 69, 108, 111, 131, 135, 178, 184, 185, 205, 218, 252, 258, 270, 271, 272–273, 279, 289, 293, 297, 388;

opinions and assignments, 335, 340, 341, 348, 351, 353, 354, 357; voting behavior, 300, 301, 303–304, 304–305, 310, 315, 316, 317, 318, 319, 322, 323
Rehnquist Court, 11, 24, 44, 57, 58, 59, 61–62, 68, 71, 124, 125, 130, 140, 177–178, 179, 185, 283–284, 290–291, 297; opinions and assignments, 335–336, 340, 341, 342, 345–346, 349, 350, 351, 357; voting behavior, 313, 316, 318
reliability, 114
religious freedom, 58–59
Religious Freedom Restoration Act, 58, 371
relisting, 281, 298
remittitur, 92
res judicata, 87, 170–171
Reston, James, 259, 386
Revolutionary War, 6, 8
Reynolds, William L., 226
Richardson, Elliott, 258
Richman, William M., 226
Roberts, Owen, 16, 54
Roberts, Steven, 260
Roe, Jane, 332
Rohde, David W., 384
Rokeach, Milton, 38
Roman Catholic Church, 76
Roosevelt, Franklin D., 39, 54, 55, 65, 194, 297, 325, 331
Roosevelt, Theodore, 53, 194, 249
Rosen, Daniel, 293, 294, 295
Rosenbaum, Yankel, 137
Rosenberg, Gerald, 60, 381, 384, 385, 387
Ross, David F., 117
Rowland, C. K., 329
Ruckleshaus, William, 258
Rule of Four, 277, 278, 279, 280
Rules of the Supreme Court of the United States, 276, 277, 278, 295–296
Rummel, William James, 139
Ryder, Winona, 137

Safire, William, 247
Salerno, Tony, 131
Salokar, Rebecca, 324

Saul, N. Sanders, 4
Scalia, Antonin, 27, 30–31, 64, 68, 69, 107, 111, 178, 218, 251, 252, 265, 271, 279; opinions and assignments, 338, 348, 351, 353, 354, 357, 358; voting behavior, 300, 301, 304, 306, 315, 317, 318, 319, 322, 323
Schaefer, Jeffrey A., 207
Schantz, Mark, 374
Scheck, Barry, 116
Schick, Marvin, 293, 294, 295
Schubert, Glendon A., 35, 280, 294
Scigliano, Robert, 251, 294, 323, 324
search and seizure, 59, 62, 124, 131; *see also* Fourth Amendment
Securities and Exchange Commission, 157
Segal, Jeffrey A., 9, 10, 19, 22, 35, 39, 99, 234, 236, 261, 263, 264, 269, 271, 285, 287, 290, 291, 292, 308, 313, 318, 319, 320, 321, 324, 325, 353, 370
self-incrimination, 62, 109, 128–129; Miranda warnings, 128–129
senatorial courtesy, 248
sentencing, 137–140, 204–211
Sentencing Commission, U.S., 206, 207–209
Sentencing Reform Act of 1984, 206
separate but equal doctrine, 51, 60
separation of powers, 11–12, 13
separation of powers model, 36, 37
Seventh Amendment, 76, 91, 92, 199
sex abuse, 135
sex discrimination, 61–62
Shay, Daniel, 43
Sheehan, Reginald S., 221, 327, 329, 345, 348, 371
Sheldon, John, 100
Shepsle, Kenneth, 30
Sherman Antitrust Act, 53, 189
Shull, Steven A., 269
Siegel, Sidney, 320
Simpson, Alan, 247
Simpson, Nicole, 136
Simpson, O. J., 79, 136
Sirica, John, 377

Sixteenth Amendment, 9
Sixth Amendment, 26, 29, 59, 91, 119, 133–135; confrontation clause, 107–108, 134–135; compulsory process clause, 107, 108, 135; cross-examination, 134
Smith, Christopher E., 124, 128, 130, 142
Social Security Act, 55
solicitor general, 293–294, 323–324
Songer, Donald R., 35, 221, 223, 228, 230, 233, 236, 237, 239, 240, 241, 242, 290, 292, 329, 331, 370
Souter, David A., 218, 252, 270; opinions and assignments, 351, 356; voting behavior, 301, 311, 313, 318, 320
sovereign immunity, 177–178
Spaeth, Harold J., 9, 10, 19, 22, 28, 70, 99, 234, 281, 287, 291, 297, 308, 313, 316, 316–317, 320, 325, 343, 345, 348, 349, 353, 357, 384
Specter, Arlen, 247
Spellman, Cardinal, 251
Spence, Lester K., 363
Spriggs, James F., II, 375
standard deviation, 356
standing to sue, 166–171, 298; advisory opinions, 167; case or controversy requirement, 167–168; collusive disputes, 167; exhaustion of administrative remedies, 171; finality of decision, 169–170; legal injury, 168; personal injury, 168–169; political question, 169; taxpayers' suits, 168–169; *see also res judicata*
Stanga, John, 330
Stanley, Julian, 381, 382
Stapleton, Vaughn, 381
state courts, 47, 53–54, 55–56, 147–186; caseload, 171–172; decision making, 172–173; federal–state relationships, 173–185; selection of judges, 149–160; appointment, 149; election, 149–155; Missouri Plan, 149, 157–160, 186; structure of, 148–149
Staudt, Nancy C., 168
Stennis, John, 260
Stern, Robert L., 301
Stern, Seth, 205

Stevens, John Paul, 24, 27, 69, 107, 218, 250, 252, 270, 277, 281, 287, 294, 363, 379, 388; opinions and assignments, 335–336, 338, 347, 353–354, 356, 357; voting behavior, 301, 315, 319, 320, 323

Stewart, Potter, 62, 135, 140, 264, 271, 287, 379; opinions and assignments, 342, 343, 347; voting behavior, 319, 322

Stidham, Ronald, 189, 202, 203, 220

Stimson, James A., 328

Stone, Harlan, F., 54, 55, 250

strict scrutiny, 57, 58

Strier, Franklin, 77, 78

Struve, Catherine T., 183

substantive due process, 51, 52, 53, 56, 63, 231

summary judgment, 90

supremacy clause, 10, 44–45, 46, 55, 169, 174

Supreme Court decision making, 299–331; conference, 303–305; extralegal influences, 323–329; final vote, 305–311; the justices' behavior, 313–316, 346–348; majority opinion, 305; precedent, influence of, 311–313, 316–318; policy-based factors, 318–323; text and intent, influence of, 318

Sutherland, George, 54

Swindler, William F., 216

Taft, Robert A., 252

Taft, William Howard, 17, 248

Taliban, 66

Tanenhaus, Joseph, 293, 294, 295, 378, 382, 388

Taney, Roger, 47, 49, 50, 251

Taney Court, 48–49

Taper, Bernard, 20

Taylor, Stuart, Jr., 297

Teger, Stuart H., 294

Ten Commandments, 367

Tenth Amendment, 179

Texans for Public Justice, 155, 156

Thomas, Clarence, 64, 69, 105, 134, 178, 218, 234, 251, 253, 260, 267, 273,

274; confirmation hearing, 245–246; opinions and assignments, 351, 356, 357, 358; voting behavior, 300, 301, 306, 313, 317, 318, 322, 323

Thompson, Jennifer, 116, 117

Thornberry, Homer, 249, 252, 255

three-judge district court, 189

Tietelbaum, Lee, 381

Tilden, Samuel, 4

Timpone, Richard, 271

Totenberg, Nina, 246, 260

treason, 7, 119

trial by battle, 76

trial by jury, 76–77, 133–134

trial procedure, 90–91

Truman, Harry S, 66, 251

Twelve Angry Men, 135

Twentieth Amendment, 13

Twenty-First Amendment, 169

Tyler, John, 261

Tyler, Tom R., 390

Ulmer, S. Sidney, 291, 294, 295, 324

United Nations, 45

United Steelworkers Union, 66

University of Michigan Law School, 332

validity, 114

Van Alstyne, William, 15

Van Devanter, Willis, 54, 55

Van Winkle, Steven, 236

venue, 84–85

verdict, 135–136

Vietnam War, 39, 327, 328, 331

Vinson, Fred, 251, 340, 341, 346

Vinson Court, 295, 341, 346

Violence against Women Act, 62

voir dire, 92–93, 134

Von Drehle, David, 333

Wachtler, Sol, 132

Wade, Henry, 364, 366

Wald, Michael, 374, 375

Walker, Thomas G., 35, 204, 330, 336, 351, 366, 375

Walsh, Edward, 205

Waltenberg, Eric N., 388

Wapner, Joseph, 388

Warren, Charles, 15

Warren, Earl, 65, 248, 252, 253, 255, 261, 262, 271, 272, 372, 384; opinions and assignments, 337, 338, 340, 342
Warren Court, 33, 56, 57, 58, 59, 62, 120, 125, 126, 127, 130, 141, 142, 255, 269, 271, 283–284, 290, 291, 295, 297, 364, 370, 388; opinions and assignments, 334, 335, 341, 346, 349; voting behavior, 316, 319, 323
Wasby, Stephen L., 226, 229, 230, 251, 365
Washington, George, 68, 249
Watson, Richard P., 231
Weaver, Warren, Jr., 257
Weems, Charlie, 129
Weisberg, Lynn, 276
Weiss, Tracy Gilstrap, 200
Westerland, Chad, 337, 348
White, Byron, 135, 140, 199, 252, 270, 271, 279, 289, 295; opinions and assignments, 338, 342, 346, 348, 356, 357
White, Edward, 251
Whitebread, Charles H., II, 374

Whittaker, Charles E., 346
Wicker, Tom, 130, 383
Williams, Aubrey, 180–181, 182
Williams, Lena, 258
Wilson, James, 7, 216
Witt, Elder, 253
Wolfson, Louis, 256
Wood, B. Dan, 328
World War I, 53, 56, 57
World War II, 55, 56, 157
Wright, Andrew, 129
Wright, John C., Jr., 217
Wright, John R., 260, 294, 295, 302, 328

Yalof, David A., 251, 270, 311
Yang, John E., 245
Young, William, 205

Zavoina, William, 228
Zeisel, Hans, 136
Zeitz, Leonard, 374
Zuk, Gary, 190, 217, 236, 238, 239, 240, 241, 242